HAILE SELASSIE I
SILVER JUBILEE

HAILE SELASSIE I

SILVER JUBILEE

BY

DAVID ABNER TALBOT

W. P. VAN STOCKUM & ZOON, PUBLISHERS
THE HAGUE

TWENTY-FIVE YEARS OF REIGN
TWENTY-FIVE YEARS OF BUILDING!

✱

For the structure that we raise,
Time is with materials filled;
Our todays and yesterdays
Are the blocks with which we build.
LONGFELLOW

✱

ROYAL PRINTING OFFICES LANKHOUT-IMMIG LTD.
ROYAL DUTCH PRINTING OFFICE LATE J. VÜRTHEIM & SON LTD.
THE HAGUE — ROTTERDAM

CONTENTS

APPENDIX

INTRODUCTION

Jubilees are non-recurrent events so far as an individual or a particular event is concerned. The dictum "three score years and ten" moves only in one direction. Time passed can never be retraced. This book, a humble contribution of the author, has been inspired by his years of service in Ethiopia, by the compelling evidence of the general progress seen and by his desire to add, in his limited capacity, to the occasion of the Silver Jubilee of the reign of His Majesty the Emperor. The work is intended to serve as a marker on the highway of the beneficent regime of the Emperor, Haile Selassie I. At best it is an inconclusive report which, even at the time of its publication, is being revised by the unchecked course of Ethiopian history, marked by events, articulate and inarticulate.

The staccato of happenings which results from and is constantly called forth in the day to day march of the country's progress, charts a course of history which, inspite of ourselves, not only forms an essential part of the drama; it provides the background and looms visibly in the foreground of the piece. Thus, certain scenes and episodes connected with His Imperial Majesty's life mission have been recalled. The objective of the author has been to illustrate and portray the main lines which have gone into producing this historical picture. The incidents related, however, must be considered in a dispassionate vein; they are so intended. Government and people are not always synonymous, even if they bear the same name. Ethiopia and Haile Selassie I can count on a number of important beneficial contacts with foreign countries; so also have some of these international contacts brought them grief. Incidentally, this is true, without exception, in the life of every country from the earliest times. Historical events, no matter how unorthodox, need no apologies. As creatures of statesmen, they represent the stark realities of human and international relations. More than not they are controlled by the prevailing circumstances and very often weighted by the stakes involved. Taking into consideration the exigencies of time and occasion, the author has relied, in parts of the text, on the opinions and judgments of other writers, some of them more intimately associated with specific issues.

The opportunity is here seized then to express thanks to those authors and publishers who so readily consented to permit me to quote from their publications to illustrate the theme of this book. I should like to mention them all in this introduction, but find this impracticable. Among them I should likte to mention three particularly from whose works I have quoted copiously: His Majesty's Stationery Office, the *Abyssinian Campaigns*, Miss Sylvia Pankhurst, well known for her first line defence of the Ethiopian and other causes, whose book *Ethiopia and Eritrea*, is co-authored by Dr. Richard K. Pankhurst and His Excellency Balambaras Mehteme Selassie Wolde Maskal, *Zekre Negar*. They stand among the others found in the bibliography, from some of whom I have quoted and from others have gained valuable information on the subject.

Mr. Stephen Wright of the Ethiopian National Library, who has contributed the section on Literature and Fine Arts in Chapter 28, gave me valuable hints in developing the story and Mr. Thomas Michael Downes of the University College of Addis Ababa helped in reading the manuscript and also with suggestions. In writing about the specific progress made during these twenty-five years of His Majesty the Emperor's reign, I enjoyed the co-operation of the Ministries, departments and special agencies of the Imperial Ethiopian Government for which I am also extremely grateful. Last, but by no means least, a good deal of the credit goes to my wife who kept the home fires burning so that I could devote the long hours entailed in getting this work out in time for this historic occasion of the Silver Jubilee celebrations.

DAVID ABNER TALBOT

The Hague, September 22nd, 1955

PREFACE

There are evident difficulties in writing a book on a living and continuing system or era; even more, on a living person. This is so because there is constant change. Should the historical approach prevail in the writing of this book, which has to deal with the twenty-five years of His Imperial Majesty's Reign, the writer is liable to fall into the error of leaving out the accumulative effects and the implications of the subject on the present and the future. Most of the changes brought about during the period in question have their greatest significance on Ethiopia as a growing organism.

It would seem, therefore, that the subject should be approached as an ethos. For it is natural that His Imperial Majesty, as the guiding spirit of this 25 years, inherited certain tangible and intangible assets from his predecessors. He could not have existed at all, nor have the opportunity to serve, except as head of a community which preceded him, which produced him, and which bestowed on him the privilege and honour of this high leadership.

A fact recognised by the Emperor so many times in his speeches, this is what he said on the occasion of the opening of the new Parliament House on November 2nd, 1934:

The means whereby Ethiopia's liberty was protected, her fame enhanced, and her borders respected, was that her ancient heroes planted their bones about her frontiers, imbuing it with their blood: indeed by their blood they fixed a border-mark which they have passed down to the generation of the present-day. Their deeds of heroism and the renown of their names will remain recorded in the world and Ethiopian history. As intelligence grows with a man's increasing age, so now the sons of Ethiopia are hastening along the pathway cleared for them by their fathers: as everyone knows, they are bound together in unity and burning with love of their country, and this is to their credit.

Certainly, the characteristic spirit of the Ethiopian people — their customs, traditions, history, culture and the general way of life — constitute the cosmos of the Emperor's being. They shaped the course of events more than can probably be easily recognised. His Imperial Majesty Haile Selassie I is reigning over Ethiopia and the Ethiopians. That he has been able, therefore, as head of this state to do so remarkably well is a credit to himself and to the community which he heads.

In this approach to the subject, then, the concrete reports of events which took place during the 25 years of His Imperial Majesty's reign cannot alone suffice. It will be necessary to bring into focus the interplay of those internal and external forces which had the effect of moulding the character of His Majesty the Emperor. Also pertinent are the challenges which the situation offered; how he met them; and what the results have thus far been because of his approach to them.

It should be at once clear that even if the name of His Majesty the Emperor is not mentioned, admitting his position, the scope of the work, the political framework of the country, the stage of civilised development and the nation's background, the guiding hand of the Emperor is everywhere evident.

The stress is, of necessity, laid on political, economic and cultural affairs since, as Head of State, even the family life and the humanitarinism of the Emperor fall within the scope of his publics acts.

By and large, this book, a souvenir, is intended to enable the reader to see what has been accomplished during these 25 years, even if it does not provide a complete basis for its evaluation. What is contained in these pages can be considered as part of an unfinished symphony. The majority of reforms introduced by His Majesty the Emperor (25 years is a very short time in the life of a nation) are just taking root. Any thorough appraisal of them must, inevitably, await the end of his reign or of his era.

In the earlier part of the book it has been found necessary to give a portrait of His Majesty the Emperor and to broadly delineate what part he has primarily played in shaping the destiny of his country for these 25 years. This is so for two reasons: first, the book is intended for the Silver Jubilee of the Emperor's reign now being celebrated. Secondly, and springing from the first, the Jubilee of the Emperor's reign marks a notable stage in his biography.

CHAPTER 1

Honouring Menelik II

Appropriately on the eve of the coronation, on November 1st, 1930, His Majesty the Emperor unveiled the Menelik II statue in Addis Ababa, located in the center of the capital in a square facing the St. George Cathedral. As is recognised, it was Menelik II who completed the task undertaken by his predecessors — Yohannes and Theodore — of unifying the country. More concretely, His Majesty the Emperor was taking over, as it were, from the former Emperor Menelik. Because, except for the brief period when Lij Iyasu reigned under a regency — 1913-1916 — the reins of government lay in his hands for 14 years while Her Majesty Empress Zauditu, Menelik's daughter, ruled.

It was in September, 1916, when Lij Iyasu was dethroned and Princess Zauditu was proclaimed Empress, that His Majesty the Emperor, then Dejazmach Tafari, became Regent of the Realm and Heir-Apparent of the throne with the title of Ras. He was then invested with the insignia of the Grand Cordon of the Order of Solomon.

Not much had been so far accomplished to change appreciably the Menelik II legacy. What the Emperor had to work with then, in the fields of modern statecraft, bore the stamp and merit of Menelik, often known in Ethiopia as *Danyo*, ' the Unifier''.

Besides sealing off the era of internal struggle of the Ethiopian chieftains and princes for personal power, which was very pronounced from the middle of the eighteenth century to his coming, Menelik had the good fortune by force of arms, to bring the warring kingdoms together under one central rule. If he had done no more than this, his name would still have been revered among his countrymen. Menelik II, however, appreciated the signs of the times. He sought to safeguard the integrity of his country. He endeavoured to strengthen Ethiopia internally by introducing reforms, and consolidated the hard-won national unity.

The former was hedged about with problems. In the early period of this reunification, he pressed his purpose by bringing together the peoples of the areas south, south-east and east of the province of Shoa. His predecessor, the Emperor Yohannes, had fought to repel invasion from the north. This was the time that foreign governments were showing keen interest in the Ethiopian coast. Despite the resistance of Yohannes, in 1896, Assab and in 1885, Massawa and Sahati were taken by Italy; the Dervishes were pressing from the north-west, the repelling of whom cost Yohannes his life at Matemma in 1889.

The situation created by the death of Emperor Yohannes and Menelik's preoccupation with national unity was favourable to further Italian expansion. Menelik, who was a shrewd negotiator, had to work fast to check this expansion and at the same time prevent a relapse into disunity.

Asmara was taken by Italy. In order to stem the continued encroachment into the territory of his country, which had by this time been cut off completely from her foot-hold on the Red Sea, Menelik signed in 1889 the treaty of Ucciali, as a means to guarantee the integrity of the rest of his country and to advance and expand his interests with the European powers.

A conflict in the interpretation of the terms of this treaty concerning Ethiopia's independence brought war between Italy and Ethiopia. Menelik's victory over the Italians at Adwa on March 1st, 1896, put a temporary end to Italian expansion into Ethiopian territory. He must be given the credit for stabilising the Ethiopian frontiers at what they were in 1930 when Haile Selassie I became Monarch.

In the period following the famous battle of Adwa, Menelik II strengthened friendly relations with the Great Powers and sought vigorously to follow up his plan for national unity and reorganisation. His authority was recognised throughout the empire; he opened the first public school, bearing his name, in 1905; and he encouraged the establishment of schools in the country. His reforms touched such vital fields as telegraph and telephones, the army, the church and the capital, which was removed from Entoto to Finfini, now Addis Ababa, in 1889. The Franco-Ethiopian railway, the main artery of Ethiopian commerce, was conceived and partially executed in Menelik's reign. He did not, however, have the fortune to see his plans for modern Ethiopia unfold. He died on December 12th, 1913.

That His Majesty the Emperor thought fit to erect a monument to the honour of Menelik II then, seems to form part of one piece with the Emperor's coronation. It was very appropriate, therefore, that the statue was unveiled on the eve of his coronation, a most fitting prelude to his accession to the throne, the aura of which has been preserved by this worthy predecessor.

The unveiling ceremony, which was attended by the high foreign representatives who had come from many parts of the world to take part in the coronation ceremonies, was as well most appropriate. It was Menelik who had done most in the preceding period to establish and solidify Ethiopia's foreign relations — the commendable foundation on which His Majesty the Emperor has built the present structure.

Complete recognition of Menelik's contribution was expressed by His Majesty the Emperor in his speech unveiling the statue in Addis Ababa:

All of you, veterans and heroes of Ethiopia, know that the Emperor Menelik was Emperor of Ethiopia by imperial descent and ancient lineage, but that apart from that he was fortunate in being able, through various campaigns, to follow up the task initiated and put under way by the Emperors Theodore and Yohannes — that of reuniting the provinces of Ethiopia which had been divided and split up by the wars of Ahmed Gran in the time of our ancestor, the Emperor Lebna-Dengel. In all this effort of his, God aided him, and since he united Ethiopia his name became known in the world.

After he had consolidated and strenghtened Ethiopian unity, he began

The mausoleum where lies the remains of Menelik II

to effect friendly relations with foreign governments, thus bringing
Ethiopia into association with the states of the world; and he caused his
people to take strides towards civilisation. His good fortune also made
his reign a reign of peace, so that the farmer by his husbandry, and the
merchant by his trade, acquired great wealth.
I have no time to tell the whole story of the benefits that the Emperor
Menelik brought to his people; history will recount them. But in this
world there lives no man, however prudent and zealous, who can escape
death: after labouring to the utmost of his power for Ethiopia's expansion
and for his people's prosperity, on Tahsas 3, (12 December, 1913) he
passed from this temporal world to the heavenly.
When we measure all the benefits that the Emperor Menelik bestowed
upon his country and his people, this monument is indeed an insufficient
reward: but man is but a creature, and more than this he cannot do.
It is due to the establishment by the Emperor Menelik of friendly relations

11

with foreign states that treaties of friendship have been concluded, and the princes and representatives of these and various other states have come for our coronation; and since it happens that they are present here with us at the inauguration of this monument to the Emperor Menelik, to participate in our happiness — this demonstrates more than anything else the good fortune of the Emperor Menelik.

Thus a fitting prelude to the coronation of His Imperial Majesty Haile Selassie I was performed on the eve of the birth of a new era.

CHAPTER 2

His Majesty the Emperor

On this Silver Jubilee of His Imperial Majesty's reign, of necessity, a brief biographical sketch seems appropriate. Not that within the pages of this book the full picture of the Emperor's many and varied activities can be ventured. Such a work is one quite apart, which is sure to have its deserved attention in due course. Something should be known about the events and forces which have influenced the Emperor's mission — the Emperor who has been the prime actor in the drama of the evolution of modern Ethiopia. How he met the various currents of these events and forces and was able to channel them into the stream of peace and progress which characterises his reign must here at least be mentioned. For the emergence of Haile Selassie I poses the unanswered question asked by Lord Macaulay, as to whether the age makes the man or the man his age.

Now sixty-three years old, the Ethiopian Monarch was born close to the end of the nineteenth century and blossomed forth during the first quarter of the twentieth. Far reaching events, which have shaped and are destined to continue to shape the destiny of Africa, took place during this period. At this time the major part of Africa had fallen as prey to European expansion. Why and how Ethiopia has remained independent partially explains the unique position of this ancient kingdom; it also provides the framework for the rise of Haile Selassie I.

The legendary setting of Ethiopia's history is a very fascinating aspect of the background of His Majesty the Emperor. It is, besides, a contributing factor, lending strength to the Ethiopian Monarchy. "The Lion of the Tribe of Judah hath Conquered", part of the imposing motto of the Crown, identifies him with a dynasty of hoary ancestry. Menelik the First, the son of Queen Makeda (Sheba) and King Solomon of Old Testament record, reigned over Ethiopia from 975 to 950 B.C. Makeda herself descended from a powerful line of kings, who ruled over the African kingdom. Consciously and unconsciously, from this ancient historic foundation of unbroken continuity, spring certain social and cultural drives which exert a strong stabilising influence on the Monarchy. During the 3,000 years of Ethiopia's civilisation many of the Emperor's forebears exemplified the sagacity and courage which he reflects.

Equally pertinent to his appearing are the circumstances of the birth and the personal qualities of Haile Selassie I. He was favoured with being born under a fortunate star. His illustrious father, His Highness Ras Makonnen, cousin of Menelik II, was a man cast in a heroic mould. Besides, he was a man of affairs — diplomat, General, and confidant of Menelik. During Haile Selassie's boyhood, H.H. Ras Makonnen kept him close to his side. There was between father and son an intimate

13

relationship, the counsel of which was the Emperor's immediate heritage. No wonder, as a young prince, he was regarded as a prodigy, not only by those close to him, but by others who could be presumed to be his critics. As a result, at the tender age of fourteen he was governor of a district and was given the title of Dejazmach, which nowadays normally means governor of a fairly large area. When his father, H.H. Ras Makonnen, died in 1906, Dejazmach Tafari, as he was called, was already recognised for his keenness of mind and his quick understanding. By 1908, then only sixteen years old, Haile Selassie I had already proved his mettle as an able administrator with a flair for reorganising the important offices to which he was assigned. He had good tutors and benefited immensely from the instruction received.

But there were other contributing factors which brought Haile Selassie I forward as a staunch leader of his people and later as a recognised world statesman. And the most telling of these were in the international sphere. The scramble for Africa, which was most active between 1885 and 1920, supplied one of the challenges of his life mission; it dictated to a great extent his line of action. A close scrutiny of Emperor Haile Selassie's philosophy on both domestic and foreign affairs would show that it was forged by the heat of events which took place with reference to the continent, with both direct and indirect consequences to his country. Within the period stated above the British empire in Africa had increased to over 3,700,000 square miles, with over 57,000,000 inhabitants. France had garnered 3,500,000 square miles with 38,000,000 people. The German colonial empire was built up to 1,000,000 square miles with approximately 20,000,000 inhabitants.

The era of "manifest destiny" saw, among other European contenders, the appearance of Italy. Partly as a result of the Franco-Prussian war of 1870, that country had become a united nation. Her dream then was to join the vogue of European expansion into Africa. Italy tried to annex Tunisia, the position of which was favourable for her defence. In 1881, however, France got the prize by occupying Tunisia. The raising of the Italian flag over the coaling station of the Rubattino Company thereafter placed Italy on the Red Sea in the Assab Bay. Ethiopia was thus brought most vividly and in a physical sense within the caravan of European expansion. The seed was then sown for future events that greatly influenced the mission of His Imperial Majesty Haile Selassie I.

Ethiopia, because of her geographic features and the characteristics of her people, was up to that time by-passed, so far as actual physical seizure is concerned. Freedom for these people was historic. Their terrain was a formidable ally to their ability as warriors.

But there was another side to the picture. Great Britain and France, Ethiopia's interested neighbours, while not wishing to share their colonial spoils in Africa with Italy, showed little qualm of conscience when Italy tried to annex Ethiopia. The only condition required was that she should not tread on their rights. They were willing, if need be, not to oppose Italy in her venture to conquer Ethiopia.

From the building of the Suez Canal in 1869, all the countries interested

14

in the west-east trade route to India sought to entrench themselves on the Red Sea route. Since Ethiopia, favourable in many respects, was the only unconquered spot, they all vied either to possess or control her. Disappointed Italy looked toward the Red Sea area where Ethiopia was considered the desirable part of the continent not as yet partitioned.

Haile Selassie's country became the question mark to the many dreams of expansion held by the contending powers. For one thing, her water potential, so important to Egypt and eastern Sudan, which flowed from the Ethiopian mountains through the Blue Nile and the river Atbara, determined to a great extent the attitude of Great Britain to Ethiopia's future. The rivalry of the European powers placed France, Germany, Italy, and Great Britain particularly, in different rôles, all of which had something to do with the future course of events in Ethiopia.

The results of this interplay and counterplay of events provided a legacy which was inherited by the Emperor. Within a mere twenty years before his birth the Italians were entrenched in Assab, Massawa, Somaliland and Asmara. The entire Red Sea and Indian Ocean coast which provided normal access and egres for his country were in the hands of the European powers. Their diplomacy, so far as it dealt with Ethiopia, was secret with the complete exclusion of the latter.

The Haile Selassie I era began with evident preparation of plans by Ethiopia's powerful neighbours to partition or dismember his country. By 1890, two years before his birth, the European powers interested in northeast Africa had the stage set to include Ethiopa in their colonial spheres or possessions. Along the Red Sea, Great Britain, France and Italy all held positions which resulted in making her completely landlocked. By this time Italy was in Somaliland and in Eritrea; France, with French Congo, stakes in West Africa and stations on the Somali Coast, had begun to extend towards Bahr-el-Ghazal; England held Egypt, had penetrated south in the Sudan to the Ethiopian border and was stationed in British Somaliland and East Africa. Italy, however, had in mind to take the whole of Ethiopia by conquest. Amidst all these entanglements Ethiopia held her independence; and the preservation of this age-old status was an imperative summons to Haile Selassie I when he entered public life. He knew the strategic position of his country and as well its uneasy relations with the European neigbours.

It boiled down to these facts: 1) the Nile and Red Sea, apart from their geographical importance, became sources of political interest to the expansionists in the second half of the 19th century; 2) the legendary fabulousness of Africa, then to a great extent unexplored, excited their desire and whetted their appetites to include Ethiopia in the scramble. The rivals also looked upon each other's colonial possession as a threat to the European balance of power.

Ethiopia then lay in the direct line of conquest. The episode of Adwa in 1896, which sprang directly from Italy's pretensions to make the African kingdom a protectorate, and the intricate pattern of intrigues and shady diplomacy which surrounded as well as preceded it was an ever-present warning sign to the Emperor.

15

He had a chance to view the landscape of the continent from an independent vantage. His father, His Highness Ras Makonnen, had played a big part in the making of the history of the period that immediately preceded his emergence. He was tutored in the methods used to keep his country free. Not only did he find Ethiopia the only bastion in free Africa: she was, as well, the only island of Christianity in a sea of Islam in which fate had placed her.

Haile Selassie I needed no terms of reference. During the 3,000 years, while civilisations had waxed and waned, Ethiopia remained intact. The world had changed considerably, however, and the older ways that were applied to maintain this independence could no longer suffice. Herein lay his absorbing challenge. He knew his country and its deficiencies. They had to be remedied, for the Emperor realised, even in his youth, that the first step was to keep his country in line with modern progress. In international relations, among his first major acts was to destroy isolation and to bind the fate and future of Ethiopia with the fate and future of the progressive nations of the world.

On the international scene through which Haile Selassie I entered firmly into world stature, the membership of his country into the League of Nations in 1923, completely opened the way for the nation's world participation. It was really a sweeping blow to Ethiopia's centuries old isolation. That this move was achieved over the objections of the diehards within the country and the protests of some League members indicates clearly the trend of his thinking. Haile Selassie I was resolute in his position. Even though this League membership called for strong internal measures to meet the attendant obligations, he followed his conviction.

Menelik II placed Ethiopia on the road to participate in the blessing of western civilisation. As Regent of the Realm, it was His Imperial Majesty who, not only carried forward Menelik's ideas; he destroyed the walls of isolation completely by several moves credited to his initiative. It was during this period that he secured the admission of Ethiopia to the League of Nations. This move, more than any other in his very fruitful reign, opened the screen on the most dramatic episode in the history of modern Ethiopia — the Italo-Ethiopian conflict.

In 1923, Emperor Haile Selassie I, then Crown Prince and Regent of the Empire, addressed to the Secretary General of the League of Nations a formal request for admission. The request met with some difficulties in the Sixth Commission, which was charged to study it. Among the objections raised figured the importation of arms and munitions, of slavery and of the extension of the power of the central authority.

In spite of much opposition, the Commission, upon the happy intervention of the French delegate, decided to recommend to the General Assembly the admission of Ethiopia, under the reservation that Ethiopia should sign a declaration accepting the following points:

"The Empire of Ethiopia, inspired by the examples of other sovereign states which have undertaken the special engagements at the moment of their admission into the League of Nations, declare that:

16

Their Imperial Majesties at Coronation ceremony, November 2nd, 1930

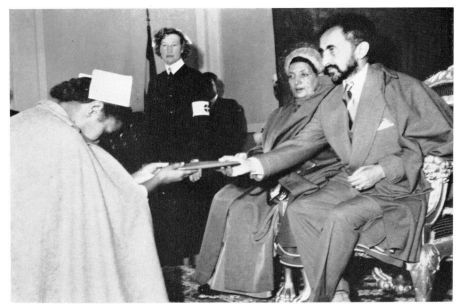

Emperor hands diploma to trained nurse at graduation

Imperial Chancellor awards first degrees at Commencement
Exercises of University College of Addis Ababa

"1. The Empire adheres to the engagements formulated in Article II paragraph 1, of the Convention dealing with the revision of the general Act of Berlin of February 1885 and of the General Act and the Declaration of Brussels of July 2nd, 1890, signed at Saint-Germain-en-Laye on September 19th, 1919.

"2. Ethiopia, respecting the regime already established in what concerns the importation of arms and ammunitions, engages herself to conform to the principles elaborated in the convention relative to the control of the commerce in arms and munitions, and the Protocol signed at Saint-Germain-en-Laye on the 10th September, 1919, and particularly to the stipulations of Article 6 of the said Convention.

"3. Ethiopia agrees to be ready to furnish the Council all information and to take into consideration all recommendations which the Council would make to her on the subject of the execution of these engagements which she recognises as of interest to the League of Nations."

Ethiopia subscribed to the above declaration and, on 28th September, 1923, at 11 o'clock in the morning, the General Assembly pronounced the admission of the Empire of Ethiopia into the League of Nations. By this move, Ethiopia became a full-fledged and recognised member of the community of nations.

A significant period in the life of His Imperial Majesty was when he was Regent of the Realm and later *Negus* (King). Since called to public office as Regent of the Realm in 1916, His Imperial Majesty has spent a life completely dedicated to the progress of his country. Immediately upon the assumption of that great authority the Emperor, then His Highness Ras Tafari began his programme of reorganisation of the country. He established schools and hospitals in the capital and in the chief towns of the country to fight against illiteracy and disease. He launched the successful programme of sending the most promising students to study in colleges and universities in England, France, America, Egypt and Libanon, Beirut, and cadets were sent to the French Military Academy at St. Cyr. He travelled through the Middle East and Europe and there saw with his own eyes what the pattern for the future of his country should be.

The successive moves made by the Emperor, ever since his Regency, both internally and externally, were designed to bring Ethiopia within the pale of modernisation. By instituting the necessary reforms to build his country — politically, economically and culturally — he sought to lift Ethiopia up by her own boot straps to meet the challenge, within and without. He built roads, in an effort to expand and strengthen the nation's communications as a means of finishing the programme of unification started by Emperors Yohannes IV and Menelik II. He supported the church because he has always believed that the material and moral advance of a people must go hand in hand.

The Regent felt the need for starting a military school in Ethiopia along modern lines. He secured military instructors to train the Imperial Guard. Many difficulties were encountered in trying to get a supply of arms and it was not until 1930, that an agreement was signed between Britain, France, Italy and Ethiopia and a quantity of arms was secured.

The progress of Ethiopia during the Regency was due to the infinite patience and tact with which His Majesty the Emperor dealt with the problems of modernising his country.

To assist his ministers in technical matters he engaged as advisers foreign experts from England, France, United States, Belgium, Switzerland and Sweden. The activities of His Imperial Majesty were not always to the liking of the old guard. As is customary, they thought of change not as growth but as endangering the ancient customs and traditions which they held dear. They were, in addition, very suspicious of western ways and even more so of western nations with whom the Regent was bent to align Ethiopia. As Regent and Heir-Apparent the responsibility for strengthening the political, economic and cultural life of the country lay completely in his hands. He took a personal hand in encouraging the people to embrace newer ways of life.

Up to 1925, apart from the Menelik II school and a few others, education was very limited. The Regent opened the Tafari Makonnen school and called on the leading Ethiopians to follow his example of founding schools in various parts of the country. As a result in 1928 the Waizaro Sehin school in Dessie, and the Waizaro Menen school in Addis Ababa, were opened in answer to this request. Dejazmach Birru pledged to build a hospital and to engage teachers to open another school.

A significant statement of the Regent at a prize giving ceremony at the Tafari Makonnen School on July 7th, 1928 is illustrative:

It was my expectation, having the confidence I did in the great nobles, that after I had created this school, following up the intensions of the Emperor Menelik II, many schools would be built in succession in our land of Ethiopia. Therefore three years ago, when we were celebrating the first opening of this school, I said in my speech that love of Ethiopia was to be expressed not only in words but with the addition of deeds. I then took up the theme that in course of time this small beginning of education would grow and expand, and schools would be built in each of the main provinces of Ethiopia: for I could see all this revealed as it were in a mirror. Much of what I said is now, by the mercy of God, well on the way to fulfilment.

First: You know that Waizaro Sehin was a very clever and intelligent woman; and here is a proof of her serious preoccupations. On making her will at the time of her death, she made a bequest in these terms: "I charge you to have a school built at Dessie with my money, for the education of poor children." For premises I have renovated the house of her son Ras Haila-Maryam, and in the coming Maskaram (September-October) the school will be opened and lessons will begin.

Second: Waizaro Menen, coming to the conclusion that when Ethiopian boys have completed their education they will want educated wives, and moreover that it will be to the country's advantage, has founded a school for girls at her own expense. You must have heard that the foundation of the building has already been laid.

Third: Dejazmach Birru informed me that he was proposing to build a school and a hospital, and engage a teacher and a doctor, at his own expense, to help the people living in the province which he governs; he asked for my assistance, and I gladly welcomed his proposal. It has been decided that I shall send him a teacher and a doctor, despatching them in time for the opening in the coming Maskaram (September-October).

As it my mission to watch over and assist without reserve all the schools which have been or will be established for the benefit of the children of Ethiopia, if there is anybody, whether of the nobility or of the people, who has decided or who may decide in the future to establish a school, I shall not grudge him my help to the full extent of my ability.

The Regent never ceased in his endeavours to bring his wisdom and ability to bear on the direction of his country. Such efforts as modernising the Municipal Police, encouraging the development of modern customs administration, opening of the Bible Society building in Addis Ababa, organising the national finance, seeing to the establishment of the Franco-Ethiopian railway station in Addis Ababa and opening the new post office premises engaged his attention.

The institution of slavery which was known to practically all civilisations existed here in Ethiopia up to the second decade of the century. Menelik II, in the last decade of the nineteenth century, resolutely occupied himself in ameliorating the treatment of slaves in the Empire. Long before subscribing to the Brussels Act of 1890, he had taken energetic measures for the suppression of this odious traffic.

Animated by the same sentiments and at the same time as one of the requirements for League membership, Emperor Haile Selassie I, proclaimed a series of edicts intended to bring about in the minimum of time the freedom of the last slave in Ethiopia.

Faithful to the League of Nations engagement, the Regent published, six months afterwards, in 1924, a law for the liberation of slaves which was designed not only to free them, but to provide methods of their absorption into the normal social and economic life of the country. The law also provided severe penalties for its infringement.

Violation of the Law carried harsh penalties. Any person found guilty of buying or selling a person into slavery after the proclamation was liable to a fine of 500 Thalers, or ten years imprisonment, if unable to pay the fine. Frequent violation was punishable by life imprisonment. Any one who deceived a slave into returning to servitude was liable to pay 500 Thalers and to serve five years imprisonment; frequent offenders were subject to life imprisonment.

Heavy responsibilities also rested on the provincial governors, the tribal chiefs and the sub-chiefs of the villages. If they were found neglecting their duty in enforcing the Abolition Proclamation, severe fines were provided. Their third violation would relieve the Governor of his functions, the tribal chief would have his property confiscated, and the sub-chief of the village would lose the privileges attached to his office.

Slavery had to be abolished. There was no vacillation. The abolition was proclaimed and the eradication of the institution vigorously followed up.

Although the type of slavery practised was not altogether of the chattel variety, it was deeply set into the framework of the society. Even after it became statutorily taboo, some of those so held, pleaded to remain attached to the homes to which their families had been bound, probably for generations. Both from an economic and social angle this reform created opposition. But Haile Selassie I was an astute leader. He knew how to overcome opposition and how to convert it to fellowship which was achieved with the minimum of social or political dislocation.

Pursuing his efforts to complete the abolition of slavery in Ethiopia, His Imperial Majesty, in the second year of his reign, published another proclamation amending the 1924 law on slavery. This amendment was intended to plug the loopholes of the former law and to provide other measures to aid the children of the freedmen.

His wise, able and beneficent rôle at the helm of administration of the country for twelve years as Regent bore fruits that could not go unnoticed by the people. This occasioned a spontaneous request in the form of a petition by chieftains to Empress Zauditu, who gladly welcomed this popular move. The happy result — His Highness Prince Tafari was nominated *Negus* (King) and crowned as such on Maskaram 27, 1921 (October 7th, 1928).

The new royal status was a boon to the country; to him, it was a widening of the scope to carry forward with redoubled zeal and effect, the mission — the mission of service to his people and country — that he had initiated as Ras.

This trend of evolution in his national leadership was soon accelarated by the hand of destiny. The passing away of Empress Zauditu on April 2nd, 1930, brought a call to enhanced duties and reponsibilities, from which he did not shrink. For the shouldering of this heavy burden, the years past had well prepared him — as the only man equal to the situation.

Thereafter the programme for modernisation was continued in various directions. Haile Selassie I was working fast. He wished to introduce a rule of law and to share responsibility with his people. Thus, in July, 1931, he gave his people, of his own free will, a written constitution. That document, suited to its time and the prevailing circumstance, established a parliament of two chambers and delegated to the ministers of the Crown the responsibilities and duties of their various offices. Vested rights and civil liberties were guaranteed and protected. This step was unique in both Ethiopian and world political history.

With Ethiopia a member of the League of Nations, a new phase of diplomacy began. We witness an extension of diplomatic missions abroad and a multiplication of special emissaries and envoys taking care of the country's interests in other capitals of the world. There was an Ethiopian mission sent to Geneva in 1923, to attend the ceremony of admission of the country as member of the League of Nations. Another commercial mission visited Geneva in 1925. In 1931 a diplomatic mission was dispatched to Japan; one was sent to Greece in 1933. Ethiopia was represented at the economic conference in London, there was a special mission sent to Washington, D.C., both in 1933. A special mission was sent to Yemen in 1935 just as special envoys were dispatched to foreign countries, like the one to Paris in 1932.

By 1935 when the Italian aggression broke out against Ethiopia, the country had treaties with Britain, Germany, France, Italy, Greece, Egypt, Japan, Switzerland, Yemen, Sweden, Austria, Belgium, Hungary, Turkey and the United States of America. She had also adhered to non-aggression, conciliation and arbitration pacts, and of particular interest had signed the Italo-Ethiopian Treaty of Friendship in 1928.

These acts showed the enlightened thinking of the Emperor. But greater opportunities for service were yet to come to prove him a world figure and a moving spirit. While the modern reforms were taking root, Italy struck. The blow was weighted with the vehemence of years of preparation and of many more years of psychological momentum. The Italian battery of conquest was being charged since their flag was hoisted in the Assab Bay in 1882. Moreover, this was the day that Italy was waiting for to avenge the defeat at Adwa by Menelik's patriots in 1896.

The battle was joined on October 2nd, 1935, when, without a declaration of war, and in violation of the Covenant of the League of Nations, Italy invaded Ethiopia. The Emperor personally took part in the fray by the side of his Imperial Body Guard at Maichaw. He had, however, to redeploy his troops to other defence positions in the unfair military struggle and to fight for the survival of his country on the diplomatic front. In his absence his valiant patriots took to resistance and so harassed the Italians that their fleeting occupation was extremely uneasy.

That was an ill wind, but it did the Emperor a great deal of good; Haile Selassie I had arrived. His impassioned plea before the fifty-two member nations assembled at Geneva was a plea and a challenge. The plea was unsuccessfully considered by that world body. Italy triumphed for a while. The challenge, however, was side-tracked; but its echoes continue even now to reverberate throughout the civilised world.

Most people remember him from his appearance at Geneva. The moral force of the Emperor's declarations and their prophetic nature made friends for Ethiopia in all parts of the world. Last year on a series of State visits, dealt with in chapter 32, His Imperial Majesty's League declarations were recalled by many in high places.

Haile Selassie's position in world politics is unequivocal. He has always kept the faith with the free world. It is problematic as to what would have been the turn of events in Europe, Africa and the world, had it not been for his faith in the principles which have been so battered in the course of the rise of materialism. The Emperor has battled against heavy odds but stuck to his faith in the ultimate triumph of justice. He applies a deep Christian conviction in his approach to world problems and exemplifies an astuteness in weighing world events born from experience.

Had His Majesty the Emperor accepted the offers made by Mussolini to put his personal advantage and ease above his sacred trust to his people and humanity, the entire current of world events from 1936 to the present might have changed its course. Addressing the League Assembly in June, 1936, these were his words:

In December, 1935, the Council made it quite clear that its findings were in harmony with those of hundreds of millions of people who, in all parts of the world, had protested against the proposal to dismember Ethiopia... And that is why I personally refused all proposals to my personal advantage made by the Italian Government if only I would betray my people and the Covenant of the League of Nations. I was defending the cause of all small peoples who are threatened with aggression.

When, in 1931, the question was debated in the Italian Press whether the railway line Dessie-Assab, indicated in the Treaty of Friendship between Ethiopia and Italy (2nd August, 1928) should be substituted for by another, Mussolini wrote in his organ, the "Popolo d'Italia", in an article dealing with that question:

"The blame (for the delay in building that railway) rests on those who should have studied the question of economic penetration more deeply before signing the treaty, and who after signing it, should have executed it rapidly in order not to lag behind the initiative of the YOUNG, RESOLUTE AND INTELLIGENT MAN who has the supreme power in his hand in Ethiopia now." This intelligent man was His Majesty, the Emperor Haile Selassie I.

By defending his trust as leader of the people and his position as an exemplar of the head of a small state, at a most critical stage of his life, the Emperor played a unique rôle. A man of high principle, he has defied conquest of his country, subdued the greater physical force of the enemy, retained his crown and kept his moral equilibrium in the face of dire stress. When His Majesty the Emperor speaks his words gain their eloquence from the truth of a situation born from the negation of principles which he has never ceased to recall to the attention of world leaders.

Haile Selassie I weathered the storm. He came out victorious; for in World War II, which he predicted, and in which Italy joined ranks with Hitler, he returned to his throne and his people supported by friendly allies. Since then he has been back at the mission of raising the standards of his people and country and cementing Ethiopia's ties with friendly nations.

Since His Majesty the Emperor's return to his throne and the end of the Second World War, tempered by experience, he has shown himself a stickler for the principle of collective security. His ardour has not been the least bit damped by the vicissitudes of aggression of which his country was the victim. Haile Selassie I entertained no bitterness towards fis former foe. Significant of this attitude is his Proclamation to the Ethiopian people after the Italian surrender, in which the Emperor said:

I charge you to protect and to receive with love the Italians who surrender to Ethiopian patriots, whether with their arms or unarmed. (Nevertheless you should take care lest some of them may practise deceit upon you.) Do not repay them with the violence they committed upon our

22

people; show them that you are soldiers who have a sense of honour and a humane heart.

In 1954 His Majesty the Emperor as guest of President Eisenhower, Queen Elizabeth II and other heads of States was cordially received by their peoples, of all classes. The enthusiasm, spontaneity and warmth of his reception is another testimony to the high esteem in which the Emperor is held. President Eisenhower, in moving a toast to the honour of the Emperor when he was his official guest at the White House, said: "I read once that no individual can really be known to have greatness until he has been tested by adversity. By this test, our guest of honour has established new standards in the world. In five years of adversity, with his country over-run but never conquered, he never lost for one single second his dignity, he never lost his faith in himself, in his people and in his God."

In a toast to the Emperor at Buckingham Palace, Queen Elizabeth II said: "Through Your Majesty's inspiring leadership, the Ethiopian people have made clearly remarkable progress in the years that have followed the war. I am very proud of the part that my country played in the liberation of Ethiopia, together with your own patriotic forces. In those war-time days, close bonds of friendship were made between our two countries, and between the men of our armies who fought together side by side. It is my sincere wish, as I know it is Your Majesty's, that this friendship should be preserved and strengthened in the days of peace."

The Emperor kept his faith in international co-operation high. Ethiopia staked her life on the League Covenant. Haile Selassie I made her a charter member of the United Nations. His belief in the principles of the Charter is concrete and convincing. He relied on the United Nations to settle the Eritrean problem. This was accomplished peacefully, a fact which strengthens that world body as an instrument for the settling of international disputes. Moreover, when the Security Council appealed for assistance from members of the United Nations to resist aggression in Korea, Ethiopia was among those who responded financially and militarily. The Ethiopian soldiers sent to Korea have fought bravely side by side with the soldiers of other member states to uphold the principle of collective securety, since 1923 the cornerstone of the Emperor's foreign policy. (See chapter 21).

When His Majesty the Emperor visited the United Nations Headquarters in New York in June 1954, he restated this position, when he declared: *It is a significant moment for me when, after eighteen years, I again find myself in a centre where are concentrated the passionate hopes of thousands of millions of human beings who desperately long for the assurance of peace.*

The years of that interval, somber as they were and sacred as they remain to the memory of millions of innocent victims, hold forth for us bright hope for the future. The League of Nations failed basically because of its inability to prevent aggression against my country. But, neither the depth of that failure nor the intervening catastrophes could dull the perception of the need and the search for peace.

CHAPTER 3

The Coronation

It was Sunday, November 2nd, 1930. Nature seemed to have agreed that the weather should be appropriately fine. The circumstances were so auspicious that every aspect seemed designed to serve one purpose, to meet one end — the coronation of His Imperial Majesty, Haile Selassie I. The four-month-long rainy season had ended. The sky above the city was clear and serene. The air, invigorating and free from dust, carried the aroma of the tall, elegant eucalyptus, imported into the country by Menelik II. Vegetation was luxurious throughout the whole countryside, and Addis Ababa was, in truth, a garden city, bedecked as never before in its brief 40-year history.

Ethiopia had never seen so grandiose a ceremony except probably in mediaeval times. The occasion was crowned with pomp, grandeur and solemnity. Her Imperial Majesty, Empress Zauditu was the only monarch crowned in this city before and Ras Tafari, as regent, was crowned Negus (King) on October 7th, 1928, about two years before. But this occasion was distinctly different!

The capital city whose monuments and statues today testify to Ethiopia's history, was, prior to its foundation in 1889 by Emperor Menelik II, no more than hills of pasture and of forest. It was in 1830 that King Sahla Selassie, who came from Ankober on a visit to his subjects, and while camping at the very spot now known as Addis Ababa, pronounced these prophetic words, "In this place my children and my great grandchildren will be crowned and will rule." As if in testimony to the words pronounced by King Sahla Selassie, the town was festooned with flowers and other tokens of joy; dressed completely with the tri-colour and embossed with festal decorations, ready in mind and spirit for the grand occasion — a day rich in pageantry!

The month which preceded November 2nd, 1930 was devoted to feverish activities. Engineers, architects and labourers worked day and night to embellish the capital which had assumed a new aspect with its imposing triumphal arches to the glory of the new Emperor. Villas and the palace, under the supervision of the Emperor-elect himself, were made ready for the accommodation of the numerous foreign guests.

It was the dawn of a new era, the awakening of the old soul which, as history records, animated Ethiopia in olden times; it was the Renaissance of an ancient empire. Indeed, the day was in the making 14 years before, for the Emperor-elect had worked and merited the acclaim and the right to this supreme honour and privelege, as well as to the splendid manifestations which characterized the historic coronation event.

The population of the city had been swollen by the heavy influx of people from all parts of the country. They had come, from far and near,

24

by train, on horseback, mule-back, and on foot. They had travelled days and nights, many of them for several weeks, to be there in time to take part in these unique festivities. Not even the lack of modern communications prevented people in every nook and corner of the Empire, those who were physically able, to come, after hearing about the coronation, to be present to lend their voice and acclaim to the occasion! It should not surprise one who knew the country-wide popularity of the Emperor-elect, dating back to the days of his Regency. From man to man, village to village, by the ancient method of whisper and drums, news of the event had been relayed. As it were every man, woman and child, moved by enthusiasm, was a courier on this particular mission. Preparations were afoot for weeks in advance.

Just as Menelik II had done, the Emperor-elect and his government had invited representatives from friendly powers to take part in this international event. Among the many distinguished foreign guests were: His Royal Highness the Duke of Gloucester, representing Britain; His Excellency Marshal Franchet d'Espery, one of the heroes of World War I, representing France; His Excellency Baron von Waldthausen of Germany; His Royal Highness Principe di Udine for Italy; Mr. Maxim Gerard of Belgium; Baron Bildt of Sweden; Jonkheer Hendrik Maurits van Haersma de With of the Netherlands; Special Ambassador, Mr. Murray Jacob of the United States of America; Mr. Isaburo Yoshida of Japan; Mr. Mohammed Tawfiq Nasib Pasha of Egypt; Count P. Metaxas of Greece and many others.

His Majesty himself received the official personalities of Britain, France and Italy at the Railway Station. Other foreign guests were met by His Imperial Highness the Crown Prince.

Every one was busy in his own sphere. So was the church of Ethiopia which had to play the important religious rôle of the coronation. In fact, the pomp and splendour of the event were enhanced by the rich religious rites that rendered the ceremony solemn and sublime. The five-hour long ceremony with scores of clergy taking part with its numerous and meticulous details, highlighted the whole function — fittingly so in a country which embraced Christianity as early as 330 A.D., and whose dynasty reaches even further back to the Old Testament days.

The paraphernalia of the Ethiopian Coronation are many and splendid. There were the Emperor's sword of gold, studded with precious stones; the Imperial sceptre of ivory and gold; the golden globe of the earth; the diamond crusted ring; the two traditional lances, filigreed in gold; the Imperial garments; the crown; the gilded Holy Bible; as well as a diamond ring; the Imperial robes and crown of the Empress — all had been gathered and stored in the church in the Palace grounds two weeks before.

In the prolonged ceremony which began two weeks before, 49 devout priests and monks, specially selected from the different parts of the Empire, gathered at the church in the palace compound and prayed over the royal ceremonial garments. In groups of seven they chanted continu-

25

ously by turn for seven days the Psalms of David and sang praises to God.

On the coronation day at 7 a.m., the Emperor and Empress-elect, followed by the members of the Imperial Family, dignitaries and others, arrived at the Church of St. George. This followed a night of prayer and thanksgiving. His Imperial Majesty took his seat on the twin throne, Her Imperial Majesty to his right. As part of the solemn and majestic ceremony the Emperor read Psalm 101 aloud. Arrayed before him were the sceptre, the crown and other symbolic appurtenances of the coronation. He was now ready for the venerated service of anointing and to take the supreme vow as Head of State in continuation of a dynasty which is hoary with age.

His Holiness Abuna Kyrillos, the Archbishop, exhorted the people to be loyal and obedient to the Emperor, the Elect of God. A part of the exhortation read:

"Ye Princes and Ministers; ye nobles and chiefs of the army; ye soldiers and people of Ethiopia; ye doctors and chiefs of the clergy; ye professors and priests; look ye upon the Emperor, Haile Selassie I, descended from the dynasty of Menelik I, who was born of Solomon and of the Queen of Sheba, a dynasty perpetuated without interruption from that time to King Sahla Selassie and to our time."

St. George's Church, built during the reign of Menelik II and associated with the recent history of the country, was the scene of the crowning of Empress Zauditu in 1916. It was full with the personages from various nations and with distinguished Ethiopians in varied walks of life: venerable chieftains, wearing the ancient style of the lion's mane regalia were there among those who had won their station as members of the Ethiopian aristocracy. They were representing every part of the Empire. There were several bishops and priests in their colourful ceremonial robes, bearing crosses and censers. All these added conspicuously to the pageantry of the picturesque ceremony.

Outside the Church were groups of hardy Ethiopian warriors with their impressive head dress and collar of the lion's mane and shields of rhinoceros skin, some with rifles and others with spears.

One's attention must return now to the interior of the Church where the impressive service is going on. His Holiness the Archbishop reads some verses from the 80th Psalm and perfumes the royal vestments and insignia with holy incense, assisted by priests and deacons. Thereupon a gold thankoffering from the Emperor to the church is placed on the sacred table, followed by readings from the Holy Scriptures, His Holiness the Archbishop recites the prayer of the Covenant, at the end of which the choir, with the usual musical accompaniment chants the 48th Psalm. Abbots from various monasteries in this interval bring the royal vestments one by one, hand them to the bishops who, in their turn, pass them to Abuna Kyrillos to be blessed. The garments are thereafter returned to the respective bishops who then present them to His Imperial Majesty, reciting appropriate lines.

After the presentation of the royal regalia His Majesty the Emperor is

26

anointed with the holy oil during which ceremony the 20th Psalm is read. Archbishop Kyrillos, with his hand upon the Holy Bible, poses a series of questions to the Emperor to which the latter replies in the affirmative, swearing that he will fulfil his duties as ruler.

"Are you willing to defend the permanent laws established by the Orthodox Church of Alexandria which, from the time of the Holy Kings, Abraha and Asbaha, have been in existence and in force? Do you pledge that during your reign you will handle the populace with justice, kindness and integrity? Will Your Majesty be under the obligations of the laws that Your Majesty has establisheid, and will you protect your Empire and people in accordance with the codes of law you will have established?"

With his hand on the Holy Bible, His Imperial Majesty pledges his word of honour that he will be the righteous monarch demanded of himself, kisses the Bible with a strikingly obvious gesture of sincerity and solemnity, and then affixes his signature to a book in which is recorded all the words of the oath. Then the Emperor sits back on his throne.

After the course of prayers, chanting and benediction, the Archbishop passes the Imperial vestments and the sword, with this exhortation: "May you be enabled with this sword to punish the wicked and protect the righteous." The bestowal of the sceptre, the orb of gold and ring, the two spears, and finally the crown, followed. Then, the Crown Prince, on bended knee before his father, pledged his service and support.

Her Imperial Majesty, accompanied by her ladies of honour had entered from the right side of the sanctuary and had taken her throne to the right of His Imperial Majesty for her coronation. She is then handed a diamond-encrusted ring, His Imperial Majesty addressing His Holiness the Archbishop:

"As I have received from you the crown granted me by God, I am willing to share my honour with her." The Archbishop then places the crown on the Empress's head who then bows to His Imperial Majesty and takes her seat.

Then the Archbishop, standing before the Emperor, gave the pledge of loyalty on his own behalf and on behalf of the church. Afterwards he kissed the shoulders of the Emperor and sat down. He was followed by other Bishops who individually offered their felicitation to His Imperial Majesty. The nobility, thereafter, came and bowed before the Emperor. These were followed by other dignitaries, including the Ministers of the Crown and the leading men of the Empire, who had all come to wish the Emperor a happy, long and peaceful reign. The playing of the National Anthem concluded the historic and impressive ceremony.

The coronation now having been consummated, His Holiness the Archbishop, in a lengthy prayer, invoked God's blessings upon Their Imperial Majesties and members of the Imperial Family.

Their Imperial Majesties and train then led the grand procession around the church before retiring to the Imperial palace. Driven in a luxurious landau pulled by eight white horses, the Imperial train passed through detachments of guards of honour and throngs of people who flanked the roadside shouting their felicitations and best wishes. At the Palace they received foreign residents and other distinguished guests who tendered their greetings.

Commemorative medals were given to each delegate and to Members of foreign Missions.

Thus, on November 2nd, 1930, Haile Selassie I, in whom the Ethiopian dynasty has continued unbroken, became head of State. In recognition of the high responsibility in the eyes of the Ethiopian people and the world, thousands of loyal subjects joined the procession and many distinguished representatives from foreign lands, representing as they did their Governments and people, witnessed the accession of Haile Selassie I as Emperor of Ethiopia.

The following days were devoted to banquets offered by His Imperial Majesty to the invited officials, to dignitaries, high functionaries, officers, soldiers and the clergy.

The newly crowned Heads visited all the churches of the City the day after to thank the Almighty. They passed through the main streets of the Capital in the midst of a people delirious and enthusiastic.

The correspondents of the big papers of London, Paris, Rome and New York had come to attend and to describe the magnificent coronation celebration which was portrayed on the screens in the major cities of the world. A grand dinner was given in honour of the representatives of the Press and cinema, during which the Minister of Foreign Affairs gave them commemorative medals of the memorable occasion.

Europe had largely shown its sympathy to the Emperor Haile Selassie I, who had already given proof of his intelligence and of his eminent qualities of government and administration.

Haile Selassie I, who had been directing the administrative life of Ethiopia for the past fourteen years, now assumed the mantle of head of state — of Emperor. It was a happy augury, for the plans and problems of the nation were fully known to him — an experience which fitted him more than any other man in the Empire to direct the interesting drama which has unfolded itself during these 25 years.

It was not long after the coronation that the Emperor's daring and progressive talents began to be felt. In the 9th month after the Coronation a written constitution, the first in the country's long history, became the fundamental law of the land. This came about not by the usually known method of revolution and its attendant bloodshed. His Majesty the Emperor, as a mark of his ability to read the signs of the times, and desiring to democratise the legal and constitutional bases of his country, gave the constitution voluntarily to the Ethiopian people. It is undoubtedly true that the Emperor, peacefully settling all internal opposition, had stirred the people from their lethargy, given them a new self-confidence and responsibility, united them in their resolve to keep their freedom and to co-operate for the general progress of the community.

In sharing the Imperial authority with his people, the Emperor has set machinery afoot to safeguard their political rights, to afford the Government the liberal opportunity to exercise responsibility and to keep the machinery of justice and the law functioning without arbitrary restraint. At the time of the coronation little did His Majesty the Emperor know that within five years the tragedy of war and occupation would have befallen his country and people. It so happened, however, that he remained true to his trust and in the thick of adversity did not falter. The story, briefly described in succeeeding chapters, of this near-tragedy in the life of the ancient kingdom of which he became Emperor on November 2nd, 1930, is not very cheerful. It forms part of the historical evolution of modern Ethiopia, however, in which His Majesty the Emperor has been and continues to be the centrifugal force.

CHAPTER 4

The Italo-Ethiopan War

By the average reader the Walwal incident is usually considered the beginning of the Italo-Ethiopian war. While this pretext was created by Mussolini to give some moral justification to the long-designed plan of aggression and conquest, the facts, even before his undeclared war against Ethiopia on October 2nd, 1935, had completely discarded the validity of Walwal as a *casus belli*.

One must look further back and even farther afield for the contributing factors and the compelling issues which lay at the bottom of this conflict. Even scant knowledge of the European spheres of influence in North Africa since the turn of the century will convince the reader that Mussolini would not have dared to open his campain of aggression against Ethiopia adverse to the wishes of those colonial powers then already entrenched on the continent. The two greatest of these were, Great Britain and France. This fact came out most vividly in the League of Nations' discussions on the Italian aggression and on the imposing of League sanctions, when, after fruitless debates, the Covenant was robbed of its power to stop aggression.

Complementary to this African interest, the state of the political balance in Europe, following Germany's revival after the First World War, left no doubt that Mussolini was also aided by the circumstances to a free hand in his war objectives against Ethiopia.

The background of this Italo-Ethiopian episode is a very interesting chapter in the history of European expansion into the continent of Africa. A section of that chapter, in a sense, ended with the tripartite treaty of 1906. This Franco-Anglo-Italian Treaty opened a new page of bargaining between three European powers for spheres of interest in Ethiopia. Thereafter through the form of "peaceful penetration" and military threats, the diplomatic struggle continued.

Two years after Emperor Haile Selassie I (then Regent Ras Tafari) had succeeded in putting his signature to the League of Nations Covenant in September 1923, that is, in December 1925, the British and the Italian Governments entered into an agreement by which it was agreed that the British Government would support the Italian Government in obtaining a concession from Ethiopia to build a railway linking Eritrea with Italian Somaliland; in return the Italian Government pledged its support to the British Government in obtaining a concession from Ethiopia for building a dam over Lake Tana and a motor road extending from the Sudan to the Lake.

This agreement was apparently of an economic nature and did not explicitly allow Mussolini to wage war against Ethiopia. However, Sir Austen Chamberlain, the British Foreign Secretary, was not oblivious of the fact that a railway system across Ethiopia could not have been built by Italy without the support of a strong military force; in actual fact, what Sir Austen was doing in December 1925, was to pledge the British Foreign Office not to interfere with Mussolini even if he landed himself in a war with Ethiopia, on condition that British "special interests" in the Tana region remained unchallenged. ([1])

Both England and France sought Italy's support in European matters, and although the English people were sympathetic toward Ethiopia, England's official attitude, when the controversy began between Italy and Ethiopia, indicated that she wished to maintain a friendly neutrality toward Italy. Moreover, in a very real sense, England had bound herself by the Anglo-Italian agreement of 1925, to work for Italian interests in western Ethiopia. Along with this agreement they recognised Ethiopia as within their respective spheres of influence.

When the two governments had matters all arranged, they, through their respective representatives in Addis Ababa, presented simultaneously the finished product to the Ethiopian Government.

When this arrangement was presented, June 9, 1926, to Haile Selassie I, then Regent of Ethiopia, he strenuously objected to it upon the grounds that these two foreign countries were making plans to secure concessions in Ethiopia, without even informing the Ethiopian government of the transactions. It seemed to him an infringement of Ethiopia's sovereignty and he appealed to the League of Nations. He recited to the League the actions of these two nations in respect to Ethiopia and called attention to the fact that within the League of Nations all member states had entered upon the same basis as sovereign states and here, it seemed to him, was a direct thrust at the independence of Ethiopia. He wrote: *The people of Ethiopia are anxious to do right...but throughout their history they had seldom met with foreigners who did not desire to possess themselves of Ethiopian territory and to destroy their independence. With God's help, and thanks to the courage of our soldiers, we have always, come what might, stood proud and free upon our native mountains.*

France, too, objected, not because she wished to defend Ethiopia but because England and Italy had not included France in their partition of Ethiopia as they should have done according to the treaty of 1906. In the face of this opposition England and Italy dropped the matter but they did not withdraw their mutual support. Evidently there was then an understanding among them to permit Italy *carte blanche* in dealing with Ethiopia. ([2])

If matters of such complexity can be summarised briefly, it may be said that for the Ethiopian war the guilt lies squarely on the shoulders of Mussolini, but that he was aided and abetted by two accessories before the fact. The first of these was the British Foreign Office under Sir Austen Chamberlain and his successors. By the agreement of 1925, Sir Austen had pledged Britain to support Mussolini in Ethiopia. He had done this

([1])   Gaetano Salvemini, *Prelude to World War II;* E. Work, *Ethiopia A Pawn in European Diplomacy.*
([2])   Work, Op. Cit.

in pursuance of the traditional British policy of friendship with Italy, directed now, not against France as had been the case between 1887 and 1904, but to guard against the possibility that France, with Italian support, might pursue a line independent of, or even hostile to Britain. Sir Austen Chamberlain's successors in 1935, as far as can be judged on the documentation available, must plead guilty to having made a show of opposing Mussolini while being pledged since 1925 to support him. The second accessory who abetted Mussolini was Laval, whose collusion was direct, his motive for throwing Ethiopia to Mussolini in 1935 being to balance a re-emergent Germany by creating a Franco-Italian group which might turn into a Franco-Italian-German bloc independent of, or even hostile to, Britain. (3)

With this background Mussolini knew the cards and the game, and when he began the campaign of forceful penetration into Ethiopia, the League of Nations notwithstanding, he was cocksure that Ethiopia's claims to justice would fall on deaf ears. As His Imperial Mejesty said in his speech before the Assembly:

The Treaty of Friendship it (Italy) signed with me was not sincere; their only object was to hide the real intention from me. The Italian Government asserts that for 14 years it has been preparing for the present conquest. It therefore recognises today that when it supported the admission of Ethiopia to the League of Nations in 1923, when it concluded the Treaty of Friendship in 1928, when it signed the Pact of Paris outlawing war, it was deceiving the whole world.

Because of this background the League of Nations, in which Britain and France were alternately leaders at the time that Ethiopia's case came before that body, could not act. The mesh of national interests and prejudices, and the need to maintain a certain favourable balance of power in Europe rendered the Covenant of the League ineffective. The United States was not a member of the League; and, despite her adherence to the Kellogg-Briand Pact, was not in a position to, and, primarily because of the isolationist policy of the then American Administration, did not care actively to intervene.

Whilst, in July, 1935, France, the close friend of Italy was the leading nation in the League, in November she was playing second fiddle to England, and in spite of the fact that throughout these months England had consistently opposed the Italian adventure. What was the reason for this remarkable change? The answer is that, as she saw it, her balance of power was threatened.

Now the crux in this problem was not Italy, but Germany. By 1929 it was found impossible to crush that virile country, in spite of the fact that during the preceding ten years every effort had been made to do so. And what was the result? France, unsupported by Great Britain, turned to Russia and to Italy; one a Communist and the other a Fascist State, not a very agreeable pair of partners.

Then, once the Italo-Abyssinian War was launched, France, considering

(3)   G. Salvemini, *Op. Cit.*

His Majesty the Emperor making Throne Speech at opening of Parliament

Emperor lays cornerstone of new Great Palace in Addis Ababa

His Imperial Majesty attends Timkat (Epiphany) ceremony

Italy temporarily useless as a military ally, surrendered her League leadership to Great Britain and opened a violent flirtation with the U.S.S.R. Once in command of this formidable organisation, the policy of the British Government was neither normal, crank nor altruistic; though shifty, it was pre-eminently common sense, namely, to compel Italy to abandon the war as soon as possible, because Italian weakness meant German strength, and if German strength grew above a certain point the balance would be totally upset.

Thus we arrive at the following conclusions: France wanted an ally and turned from Italy to the U.S.S.R., Germany welcomed a weak Italy so that she might gain control over Austria and central Europe; Great Britain wanted a strong Italy in order to balance German military expansion, and Russia wanted an Italian collapse in order to spread Bolshevism in western Europe. [4]

The tragedy of it all was that the League of Nations was not what it was put up to be. In practice, Mussolini knew that the League was a ramshackle conglomeration of self-interested states. Therefore, when the infamous Walwal incident took place and His Majesty the Emperor tried by all means to avoid a conflict, he was working against a preordained Italian plan.

The story of the Walwal incident is well known. His Majesty the Emperor in a speech closing the Ethiopian Parliament on April 11th, 1935, told the members of the Italian provocations at Walwal and of Mussolini's clear intent. He said:

As you have already heard and will be aware, the Ethiopian and British experts who had gone as boundary commissioners with instructions to delimit the grazing grounds under the terms of the treaty, were accompanied by some of our troops, to protect them from any danger; when they had arrived at Walwal in our territory of Ogaden, although they had provoked no quarrel, they were suddenly subjected to a surprise attack by Italian soldiers, who caused them serious casualties.

Although it is known that Walwal is within Ethiopian jurisdiction, and we proposed to demand compensation for the losses suffered by our soldiers through an unexpected attack, the Italians, in vast hurry, addressed to us a demand that we should pay compensation, and other such things.

We had no intention of making war on account of this clash; it is indeed our primary wish to dwell on terms of peace and understanding with the states neighbouring Ethiopia; therefore we made every effort we could to get the matter settled in a friendly way. But when we became convinced that this was not to be achieved, we finally brought it before the League of Nations for settlement.

Since then, we have not failed to try to get it settled through direct talks with the Italian Government; but although we have shown, on various occasions, that our entire purpose is to deal with the matter in the correct way, and though our intentions to seek peace was quite definitely known,

[4]   Major General J. G. C. Fuller, *The First of the League's Wars.*

yet we hear reports that the Italian Government are mobilising troops in the metropolitan territory of Italy, and are uninterruptedly sending troops, with much equipment, to their colonies of Eritrea and Somalia. We have therefore again addressed the League of Nations: and we are awaiting the decision of this League which is the guardian of world peace. The number of soldiers, officers and equipment is clearly revealed in the telegrammes transmitted daily from Rome to recipients all over the world.

Italy had designs on Ethiopia at that time that dated back over 40 years. The signs were most evident, and the Great Battle of Adwa, fought and won by Emperor Menelik II, 1896, is part of the historic evidence of these persistent designs. When Mussolini became the Roman Dictator, he resusciated the dream of "Africa Orientale" and sought international backing for its fulfilment. As quoted above from Professor Salvemini, as early as 1925 he secured the Anglo-Italian Treaty which was covertly intended to free his hand when the time came for Italy's onslaught against Ethiopia. In addressing the Italian Parliament on May 25th, 1935, Il Duce said:

"The Italo-Ethiopian problem dates back to 1925, as is found in documents which can be published when the time comes."

Fascist Italy, using Eritrea and Italian Somaliland, planted spies within Ethiopia. They used their diplomatic and consular missions to strengthen this network and even tried the old game of "divide and rule", by attemping unsuccessfully to sow dissension among the Ethiopian chiefs.

One might be inclined to believe that the Italian people, at the outset, as many newspapers have reported, were not in agreement with Mussolini's Ethiopian exploits. He, however, had the power in his hands and convinced the people of Italy, especially the youth, that to attack Ethiopia was the heroic call of destiny. According to Mr. Ward Price, one of Il Duce's admirers, and quoted by Professor Salvemini:

"This Abyssinian campaign was a personal undertaking of Mussolini's. The people of Italy felt no desire for such an enterprise until he infused them with it. The defeat of Adwa forty years before, had filled Italian hearts with detestation for the very name of Abyssinia. The Italian General Staff believed that the conquest of that country would be a long, costly process... In April, five months before the war began, I found many Italians full of anxiety about the risks and cost of the approaching campaign." (5)

Between June and September 1934, confirmation of which came from Rome, the Italian Government began to assemble war material on a large scale in Eritrea and Italian Somaliland. Ethiopia's diplomatic enquirers in the Italian capital were informed that this was a defensive measure against Ethiopia's intention of attacking Eritrea and Somalia. When Italy started her unprovoked aggression against Ethiopia, however, the country had not the barest means of self-defence. Italy had, through

(5) Salvemini, *Op. Cit.*

34

connivance with certain European powers, thwarted all Ethiopia's efforts to obtain arms to meet the Fascist thrust. Italy had, on the other hand, an up-to-date mechanised land army and modern navy and airforce.

With their colony of Eritrea to the north and Somaliland on the south, the Roman "civilisers" were able to press into Ethiopia from two directions simultaneously. Although poorly armed, Ethiopia had to try to defend herself on two fronts against an incomparably better prepared adversary. His Majesty the Emperor, who was bent on advancing the peaceful progress of his country, did not want war. In fact, there was the Italo-Ethiopian 1928 Treaty of Friendship, the provisions of which were for perpetual peace between the two countries. The treaty provided also that if a quarrel arose between the two countries, such a dispute should be settled peacefully by arbitrators. Ethiopia immediately invoked this latter provision.

Italy categorically refused the arbitration. She submitted fictitious demands which Mussolini claimed should be settled without investigation and without any formulated judgment.

Italy's refusal to adopt the procedure provided for in the Treaty of Friendship forced Ethiopia to take the matter to the Council of the League of Nations. Both the King of Italy and Mussolini were notified in writing of the detailed reason why this latter procedure was adopted. The Council, after examining the affair, decided in January, 1935, that the case should be the subject of arbitration. Italy accepted in bad grace. She used delaying tactics in the diplomatic search for arbitrators to give effect to the League Council's recommendation.

Animated by the desire to have the problem settled by lawful and peaceful means, and knowing by the evident signs what Fascist Italy had up her sleeves, on March 17th, Ethiopia again submitted the matter to the Council of the League of Nations. Apart from discarding the Treaty of Friendship and Arbitration which was concluded on August 2nd, 1928, flouting the offers of Britain to mediate and disregarding the decision of the League Council to arbitrate, Italy continued to mobilise a huge army on Ethiopia's northern and southern borders. It was publicly made known through the radio and newspapers that troops, war-material and ammunition were daily sent without interruption to Eritrea and Somaliland.

The die seemed already cast. Mussolini used diplomatic pressure on Ethiopia and on those European nations whom she knew were committed to permit her a free hand against this country. The impact of the Franco-Anglo-Italian treaty of July 6th to December 13th, 1906 was easily felt in the attitude taken by Il Duce against the attempt of the League of Nations to interfere in the Italo-Ethiopian conflict. In that treaty, France, England and Italy had not bound themselves, in case of trouble within Ethiopia, to lend aid to the Ethiopian Government. While they were not obliged to maintain the *status quo*, they might, if they wished to do so, consult together as to measures that should be adopted to maintain it, and if it appeared impossible to maintain this status then they were to decide among themselves what was to be done. ([6]) No wonder the League dallied and dickered, but took no effective action to stop Italy.

As a result of Ethiopia's second submission of the case to the League of Nations, the decision to arbitrate was confirmed. The League declared that arbitrators should definitely be chosen to examine the matter. Ethiopia wished ardently that any judgement reached should be based entirely on law and free from partiality.

For arbitrators she chose two well-known experts on international law: one French and the other American. Italy selected two of her own nationals a fact, by its very nature, inimical to impartiality, without which arbitration could be nothing but a sham.

Britain, suspecting Italy's choice of arbitrators could hardly lead to any respectable settlement, took the initiative of mediating in the matter. The British proposed that Ethiopia should cede part of the Ogaden to Italy, while in exchange for this the British would cede to Ethopia the Port of Zeila and part of the adjacent territory in British Somaliland. Ethiopia, despite the fact that the Ogaden was a legitimate part of her sovereign territory, indicated her readiness to examine the British peace proposal. Mussolini bluntly refused even to accord the proposal any examination. All through Italy's uncompromising attitude, Emperor Haile Selassie continued to appeal to the League of Nations Council for quick and firm action against Il Duce's most obvious aggression. Apprehensive of the impending conflict, in addressing the Parliament on July 8th, 1935, the Emperor said:

At the moment, it has not been possible for the arbitrators to complete the business for which they were chosen. The peace proposal put forward by the British Government was cut short by the head of the Italian Government. The Italians have not interrupted their preparations. The high officials of the Italian Government openly declare that the chief thought of their hearts is to take our country. Therefore from now onwards the time of war steadily approaches.

On Sane last (8 June) the head of the Italian Government, standing in front of five thousand soldiers who had been ordered to Eritrea and Somalia, newly named "East Africa", but addressing as is his wont the Italian people, said in order to arouse their minds to warlike desires. "You who are departing are going to inscribe in our history a most sublime tale of valour."

According to Signor Mussolini, what Italy desires is to "civilise" our people. Italy has decided from henceforth to ensure that the matter be not settled by peaceful means. Her intention is to shed much blood so as to exact revenge for the former affair of Adwa.

Again on August 12th, when the Italians were busily beating the war drums and preparing feverishly for aggression, in a speech to the Princes, Lords and Army commanders, His Majesty the Emperor declared:

Nevertheless, Ethiopia does not abandon hope that the regrettable inci-

([6]) Work, *Op. Cit.*

36

dent that has arisen between Ethiopia and Italy will be ended in a peaceful way. We are confident that the State Members of the League of Nations, and all those States of the world, whether great or small, who have not joined the League of Nations, will observe the fearful situation in which Ethiopia now stands, and will not fail to award her righteous justice and sincere consideration.

At a time when the world, after its trial in the Great War, is beginning and planning firmly to establish peace, and to secure the factors necessary to a good life for mankind, there is seen approaching the outbreak of war which will bring great harm, felt across the world. In the prayers we address to God, we declare our faith that He will send down His grace, to the end that all those who have received the trust from God to improve the lot and the life of peoples, will fulfil His holy will by confirming peace among the nations of the world.

During the Italo-Ethiopian war, the fact that until then had lacked definite proof, became evident to all — namely that the two most power-ful European countries belonging to the League — Britain and France, lacked the determination to enforce the Covenant of the League.

Both Governments had announced their willingness to curb any agressor who disturbed the peace. But the British were interested in the Mediter-ranean, and were therefore concerned with Italy; while the French were interested in the Rhine, and were therefore concerned with Germany. The French considered it unreasonable to let an affair in Africa stand in the way of Franco-Italian understanding, and urged moderation on the English in dealing with Italy. The English considered the French to be moderate in dealing with Germany. (⁷)

In addition collective security, which the League was designed to guaran-tee and uphold, had been hit a severe blow in 1931 in the Far East by the Manchukuo fracas. In the autumn of that year, President Hoover and the British Government struck the first blow. With Italy's aggression against Ethiopia, the system had collapsed in Africa. When Germany reoccupied the Rhineland, which strengthened Mussolini's hand in pressing his unprovoked war against this country, the system died in Europe.

While the League of Nations because of the picture drawn above became helpless in protecting the independence of Ethiopia, one of its members, His Mjesty the Emperor had to do it alone. This was a most uneven struggle. Italy was armed to the teeth, had the means for pro-producing her own weapons and armament, and had, by diplomatic chicanery, blocked the doors for any arms and ammunition reaching this country. Although the League of Nations, by an overwhelming majority, condemned Italy's agression, she went ahead with her plans and thrust war on Ethiopia on October 2nd, 1935. The Italians told the League of Nations that Ethiopia should be a protectorate of the Fascists in order that they might "civilise" the people. In the meantime the Covenant of the League of Nations, which had guaranteed the integrity of its mem-

(⁷)   Salvemini, *Op. Cit.*

bers, was the centre of the Emperor's hope that the war would be averted. Because of this Ethiopia failed to mobilise her patriot army in time to meet the Fascist onslaught.

Ethiopians had always defended their country. The Adwa episode of 1896 was proof of this. The 1935 Italian aggression could be considered the second major attempt in no less than 40 years to conquer the country by force of arms. In informing the Ethiopian people of war conditions, on October 12th, 1935 the Emperor brought this out most vividly when he said:

The enemy who has now come against us is no new, unexpected enemy, but one with whom from long ago we have been engaged in bloodshed. Since we trusted in the League of Nations, which seeks peace, we did not send our armies to the front beforehand to meet the enemy; and now, as well as cruelly killing all he meets, we can be sure that he shows mercy neither to the soldiers nor to the old men, the women and the children. We have heard from the start that he is merciless towards the women and children.

Two days after the treacherous blow against Ethiopia was struck, in contravention of the Italo-Ethiopian Treaty of Friendship of 1928, and as well against the League Covenant and its decision that Mussolini was the aggressor, His Majesty the Emperor issued the Mobilization Proclamation, calling on the people to rise in defence of their liberty. The Proclamation read:

The Lion of the Tribe of Judah hath conquered
Haile Selassie the First by the Grace of God
King of the Kings of Ethiopia.

People of my land of Ethiopia! You know that Ethiopia has moved on her way continuously from the time of Menelik the First, and has endured, recognised and respected in her liberty.

Previously — forty years ago — Italy, proud in her skill and in her strength, desired to destroy the liberty of Ethiopia, and to enslave her people and to rule over them: she came into the midst of our land and fought against us. Our God, Who loves not violence, aided us and gave us the victory; but we did not seek to recover that part of our land which had gone from us. Pushing forward on the frontiers by Hamasien and Somalia they took our territory: and you can see with your eyes and hear with your ears how our brothers, in that land they took, have borne the yoke of slavery.

While we grieve at the violence perpetrated against them, we do not seek the territory which has gone from us. But now once again they are planning to cast the yoke of slavery upon the people dwelling in the whole of our country. They brought troops by stealth into Ogaden and killed our men who were seeking no quarrel: they have broken the treaty we concluded with them. We had already entered the League of Nations, which was established to maintain the peace of the world, therefore we gave notice to the League of Nations, so that the quarrel at Walwal might be looked into by arbitrators according to law, and the guilty party might be recognised.

Thereafter the Emperor summoned his armies to Addis Ababa for instructions. Italy's armies had reached Adwa without much opposition at that time. The Minister of War was instructed by His Imperial Majesty to advise the leaders of Ethiopia's Defence Forces and to deploy them into the battlefield against the ruthless enemy. Among the words of advice His Majesty said:

It is heroic to die for one's country, and moreover the enemy being one which had previously made an unsuccessful attack on the Empire, the army as a whole should never retreat nor surrender. I would not advise you to brave the enemy without protecting yourself as was done by your forefathers. You should use present day military tactics.

The Emperor also gave advice about the pitching of tents; what should be done when an aeroplane is detected and to maintain order and to take all necessary precautions in the struggle so as to avoid unnecessarily heavy losses.

After the armies were advised, they were despatched to the north and south to meet the enemy. His Majesty the Emperor, accompanied by Prince Makonnen, Fituarari Birrou, Dejazmach Haile Selassie Abayneh, Dejazmach Wandirad, Dejazmach Adafrisau left for Dessie on November 25th, reaching there two days later. During the Emperor's march to join his armies in the north, reports reached him of a number of Italians taken prisoner along with their arms.

Italy's efforts within Ethiopia to cause deflection among the chiefs, bore some little fruit. For shortly after, one of the army officers of Ras Hailu's army, named Dejazmach Gassasa Balau with six of his sub-officers, abandoning the army, left the ranks and returned to their home in Gojjam.

The Ethiopian armies were ill-equipped to meet Italy's modern, mechanised troops and air-force. They, however, because of their traditional valour and fighting spirit, plastered the enemy so, using their difficult terrain as an effective ally, that the Fascist High Command was forced to use unorthodox methods to gain an advantage. Without any scruple and openly against the Geneva Convention of 1907, the enemy resorted to indiscriminate aerial bombardment. But, following the instructions of His Majesty the Emperor, their Supreme Commander, the Italian air-attack proved ineffective on the Ethiopian warriors. Many Italian prisoners with their arms were taken by the defenders in many of the encounters in the battle.

At Maichew, March 31st, 1936, the Emperor personally led his troops on the battlefield.

Poison gas bombs were tried on the wholesale basis. These were at first dropped on the army and in populous districts. The Ethiopian soldiers found their way, however, to reduce the effect of these tactics to the minimum. It was then, as a last and desperate resort, in order to subdue the Emperor's fighting men, that the Italians began to spray the whole country promiscuously with mustard gas on men, women, children and animals. Even the water was polluted by this deadly, inhuman device. The people had to try the best way they knew to save themselves from the untold agony of poison gas which burnt and blistered their skins, tore their lungs, blinded their eyes and caused psychologic panic. As Dr. John Melly said in his book:

This isn't war, it isn't even a slaughter — it is the torture of tens of thousands of defenceless men, women and children with bombs and poison gas. They are using it incessantly and we have treated hundreds of cases, including infants in arms — and the world looks on — and passes on the other side. ([8])

Against such fearful odds were the Ethiopians forced back. Realising that further resistance meant the slaughter of defenceless people, the Emperor resolved to go to Geneva and personally make his appeal for help to the assembled conscience of the world. The Emperor believed implicitly in the moral claims of the world body. He never thought for one moment that the Covenant would be set aside by "spoliation by procedure." His advisers were doubtful of the efficacy of the League because of the painful experiences thus far in checking Italy's unprovoked aggression. Dr. Warqneh Martin, then Ethiopia's Minister to Britain, in a public statement said:

"The position would have been much better for Ethiopia had we not trusted to the League, had we not relied on the pledge that if we should refrain from hostilities, the collective power of the League States would protect us. But for that promise we should have tackled the Italians when first preparations began; we should have marched into Eritrea before they were able to accumulate war material and troops there and we should have secured a victory. The Governments which stood by urging us not to fight promising us help which they never gave, are accessories to the crime. Had they said to us: 'We cannot help you; help yourselves', our position would have been altogether different today. When a man knows that the police are not going to assist him, he takes the best chance of defending himself when attacked.

"The long tragedy of the Ethiopian invasion has not been like a sudden accident. It is not as if a man's house had suddenly caught fire and there was no time for the fire brigade to arrive. No, it is as though the fire had been slowly and steadily built up, and all around men had been pouring oil on it. All the time we were told by the League Governments of Europe: 'We will help you.'

"If this breach of faith results from private understandings between the Governments or the Foreign Offices, one can only say of them: 'If they are dishonest they have no right to blame the Italians for being the same.'

"The resolution adopted by the Assembly of the League makes no mention of the use by Italy of poison gas or of bombing the Red Cross. Even these things, which are universally recognised as horrible crimes in defiance of international agreements and are the greatest possible

([8])   Dr. John Melly, *Ethiopia and the War.*

40

disgrace to the Italian Government, go without mention. If the League representatives connive at crime in this shameless fashion, what hope is there for the League?

"The Italian Government is still to be permitted to retain its membership of the League, and even to help in reforming the League. It is like putting the robber and murderer on the Municipal Council to help in making laws for the good of the community." (9)

The League failed and Mussolini enjoyed a temporary victory.

His Majesty the Emperor returned from the northern front to Addis Ababa, April 30th, 1936, his heart sad with grief for the prospects of his people, open to Fascist poison gas. It was also heavy with doubt because of the previous experiences with the League; but, and what is most unusual, he was also fortified with the hope that the last gun had not been fired in the fray. The Emperor believed firmly that the League would somehow vindicate his cause and save the independence of his country, the liberty of his people. He ordered the Italian prisoners be turned over to the French Legation for safe keeping. By proclamation of May 1st, the Emperor appointed Ras Imru to lead the armies in the west, Ras Desta in the south; Dejazmach Hailu Kabbada and others in the north; while Dejazmach Fiqra Mariam was ordered to take charge of the army in the Debra Berhan section to hold the Italian advance. Orders were also given to move the Government from Addis Ababa and establish it at Goré in western Ethiopia. After giving final instructions to the officials who remained behind, His Imperial Majesty left the capital en route to Geneva in the early hours of the morning of May 2nd, 1936.

As a result of their rapid advance with the help of aeroplanes and poison gas, the Italians took Addis Ababa on May 5th, 1936, but the Ethiopians were never conquered. The resistance continued unabated, His Majesty while in exile submitted evidence to the League time and again to indicate the incompleteness of Mussolini's boast of the conquest of the country. Indeed, the civil administration of the Emperor's Government was actively maintained in a substantial part of the Empire. That this fact was recognised could be gleaned from Lord Cecil's words in the Lords when British recognition of Mussolini's loot raised high protest in both Houses of the British Parliament. He said:

"When you come to recognise a new Government over territory which it did not have before, two things have usually been thought essential, in the first place that the conquest of that territory has been complete; and, secondly, that it has lasted a sufficient time to make tolerably certain that the conquest is going to be permanent. I see no evidence that either one or other of these conditions have been fulfilled in this case."

Count Ciano in a conversation with the French Ambassador at Rome on July, 1936 gave a plausible hint of the unsettled occupation of the Fascists in Ethiopia. In reporting on an interview with the French Ambassador, he said:

(9) *New Times and Ethiopian News.*

"I had, however, to draw his attention to the gravity of the situation which is developing in Addis Ababa owing to the presence of foreign legations there. It is true that the country is completely "calm" and that only a few marauding formations maintain a state of guerrilla warfare, but it is equally true — and this we have on irrefutable grounds — that it would all come to an end if the foreign Ministers and the armed legation guards left Addis Ababa. The continued presence of foreign diplomatic representatives in the former capital of the Negus gives rise in the native mind to the illusion that a return to the past is not completely impossible. That, obviously, cannot be tolerated by us. For the time being there is no question of an official request but I drew the French Ambassador's attention to the advisability of bearing in mind our desire to see this problem resolved as soon as possible. Germany had given a good example. The sooner the others followed it, the more we would appreciate the gesture." ([10])

([10]) *Ciano's Diplomatic Papers*, Editor, M. Muggeridge.

CHAPTER 5

Resistance and Ordeal

When the Emperor, on May 2nd, left Addis Ababa to continue the struggle for Ethiopia's liberty on the political and diplomatic fronts in Europe, he made sure to provide for keeping the flame of resistance to the enemy burning.

After the fall of Dessie His Majesty the Emperor summoned the elders to a meeting over which he presided. Four points of view emerged from this conference: (1) that the seat of government be transferred from Addis Ababa to some other spot and that the fight should continue; (2) that His Majesty the Emperor take the cause to the League of Nations at Geneva; (3) that, despite Italian superiority in modern arms and equipment, the Ethiopian army be regrouped and continue fighting the enemy; and (4) that in face of the overwhelming odds, terms of surrender from the Italians be accepted. (This last proposal was supported by very few of the elders.) The conclave finally agreed upon His Majesty's personal appeal to the League of Nations as the most effective measure, under the circumstances, for the recovery of the country's freedom.

His Majesty the Emperor, reluctant and sad to leave his beloved country and people, recommended that the patriots should keep the enemy busy fighting in his absence, while he put the case of Ethiopia before the assembled world conscience. His Majesty's departure, therefore marked the beginning of the sustained resistance against the enemy.

General Badoglio, after entering Addis Ababa on May 5th, 1936, sent a telegram to Il Duce announcing his arrival in the Ethiopian capital. Before he arrived there the patriot cadres had already become effective. The majority of the able-bodied men and youths abandoned the city to begin their new life in defence of their country in the hills and in the uninhabited areas. Badoglio was soon relieved from his post and General Graziani was ordered by Mussolini to take over the command. The "empire" lay within the Fascist grasp, but it had to be pacified. This is exactly what the patriots had sworn to prevent, and which called forth several methods of ruthlessness and brutality from the occupiers. Historic buildings, shrines, and monuments were pulled down. Force was the weapon wantonly used; as if force could ever crush the human spirit!

Dejazmach Fiqra Mariam, Dejazmach Aberra Kassa, Dejazmach Balcha, Grazmach Zaude Asfau and Major Mesfin, however, had the intention of recapturing the capital. It was besieged from the south-west on the Jimma road, from Bitcho; from Salulta to the North; the doughty Dejazmach Fiqra Mariam came as far as the old palace and killed numerous Italians. In the outer regions, for instance, at Goré, Ras Imru with his men, fought gallantly until he was betrayed into the hands of the enemy. Graziani was hard pressed. He found it extremely difficult to subdue the forces of Ras Desta, Dejazmach Gabra Mariam and Dejazmach Bayene in southern Ethiopia. He himself had visited that area and when he returned to Addis Ababa, irritated by the extent and the force of the resistance, he decided to torture the nobles and to decimate the educated among those who had surrendered.

But the fire of the resistance grew with every act of brutal reprisal by the Fascists. In fact, plans were discussed to carry on the fight, come what might. The indomitable fighting spirit of the Ethiopians, as attested at the famous battle of Adwa in 1896, despite hardships, was a flaming sword searing the enemy at every turn.

Graziani was frantic. Rome had broadcast to the world the complete conquest of Ethiopia. Yet the soldiers were only safe when in their garrisons. The Ethiopian guerillas harassed the occupiers unceasingly. Italian nerves were given no respite. The country was partially occupied but never pacified.

On February 19th, 1937, Graziani summoned the Ethiopian residents of Addis Ababa to the palace, where he promised to give alms to the poor. Two young men, Abraha Deboch and Mogas Asgadom, typical of the patriots who felt the heel of the oppressor and had the itch to do something about it, threw hand grenades at Graziani and his air-commander. Both of them were seriously wounded. As a reprisal the Fascist butcher ordered his troops to open fire on the Ethiopians — Moslem and Christian alike. Blood flowed everywhere; countless bodies of innocent people lay for days where they first fell. Homes were burnt with their inmates. People were hauled out of the town in trucks and shot in cold blood and at close range — a really black deed on the escutcheon of the Roman "civiliser".

Why did the Italians maintain concentration camps in Ethiopia during the uneasy occupation? Because the prisons were full of resisters, because the people fought back against their tyranny! They made the people suffer, but the rebellion, instead of lessening, grew until it blossomed into the army of liberation which the Emperor led to triumph on May 5th, 1941. Balambaras Mehtama Selassie, now Minister of Agriculture, who was one of the victims of the Fascist concentration camps, gives this eye-witness report:

"On March 20th, 1937, we were taken from the big stable and sent to Akaki radio station area where, under heavy armed guard, we remained under the open sky all night, drenched by rain. Next morning about 100 trucks were brought up and we were loaded in batches of 40 and started on our fateful journey. Where, we did not know!

"Our only ration was flour, and that once a day. To prepare the flour into a meal was made difficult by the mode of travel; therefore, many often went hungry. Of all the prisoners the mothers were the most to be pitied. Many of their children died each day from the desert heat and the hot air and dust from the trucks. Many a mother had to carry her dead child for long distances and long hours before the vehicle stopped. We were hungry, tired and thirsty, to such an extent that we wished we had died in Addis Ababa at the start.

44

"On May 8th, 1937, we reached the small town called Denane. Without accusation nor trial we were handed over to the Chief of the concentration camp to serve a term of hard labour. Life was so rough and treatment so severe that many died from contagious diseases. The death toll of the Ethiopian prisoners in this camp was more than one thousand.

"After a year and a half at Denane the enemy decided to move us to another place called Jenalle where there were 117 plantations. We were ordered to work for our ration which was really insufficient although the labour was very tough. The scourge of the Israelites in Egypt seemed to have befallen us; while the Ethiopians were working, the Roman "civilisers" whipped them from behind. The death roll continued to rise daily. In their propaganda to whip us into submission, whenever Ethiopian patriots were captured the Fascists took pains to report to the prisoners in detail how they were tortured to death."

This eye-witness report highlights the resistance of the people to the boasted conquest of Ethiopia by Mussolini's forces. Italy had gained the military decision because of her superiority of arms and munition. She failed miserably, however, in winning the Ethiopians over to her side. Since pure brute force failed to win submission, other tactics were used. In fact, the unconquered patriots forced the Italians to alter their policy of subjugation by force time and again.

At one period they used the old "divide and rule" formula. They tried to set Ethiopian against Ethiopian, tribe against tribe, religion against religion.

The Fascist occupiers were of the opinion that the people of Tigré, Gojjam, Shoa and Begemder, generally known as Amharas, were descendants of Shem. The people of the south and west in Wallaga, Jimma, Sidamo, Arusi and the neighbouring territories, were considered as the descendants of Ham. They tried by a concentrated method of propaganda and alternate favouritism to set these two large segments of the population against each other. This scheme failed. Most of the people, not only remaind united under their original banner; they joined and supported the patriots and kept the claws and teeth of the Roman wolf continually pruned.

The resistance continued without any visible signs of change. The patriots threatened the enemy and gave him no rest. In many of the clashes the defenders were victorious — they killed many Italians and took their arms. This unceasing war caused the Fascists to change their attitude to the Ethiopians in some measure. They abandoned their tribal favouritism and decided that all Ethiopians, who resisted their "benign" rule, should be exterminated. This was the view of the Duke of Aosta and General Nasi. General Franca disagreed, and suggested to use the sword of "peaceful diplomacy." This ruse, which was agreed to by Rome, was to seek ways and means of reconciling the patriots to the Italians. The principal cause of this temporary measure sprang from the European political situation. War was raging throughout Europe, and the Fascist government in Rome was planning to share in the spoils of a possible Axis victory.

45

Suddenly the Ethiopian prisoners in Nakurra and Denane were released though thousands had died earlier. Confiscated land and property were returned to their former owners, even compensation was made for unpaid rents. Many Ethiopian titles were given as a mark of bribery even to those who did not deserve them. Increased salaries were offered to those who served; compensations were given in tens of thousands of lire. The Italians began to fraternise with the Ethiopian people, paid visits to their homes and in many other ways tried to create an atmosphere of friendship. Even the patriots, those who were brought to the Italians through their friends and relatives, were given excellent accomodation, cars and money. Several of these patriots were even taken to Rome on sight-seeing trips.

The Italians tried by subtlety to become friends with the Ethiopians whom they had abused, and whose country they had overrun by unprovoked aggression. In fact, the Fascists went so far as to send representatives to negotiate with the heroes in the hills and received their representatives with great courtesy. The enemy continued to bestow gifts and treasures on the patriots in order to turn them from their set purpose. Through the continuous encouragement and admonition of His Majesty the Emperor to these warriors, however, through letters and other methods of contact, Italy's wiles did not bear fruit.

As early as 1938 and published in the "New Times and Ethiopian News", May 14th, 1938, the patriot situation in Ethiopia read:

"During last autumn, and throughout recent months, there has been energetic opposition to the Italian operations, which sometimes has developed into fighting on a considerable scale. There have been revolts in the provinces of Tembien and Sokota under Dejazmach Hailu Kabbada and further to the North-East in Tigré under the daring Dejazmach Gabra Heywat. In the provinces of Begemder and Lasta there has been almost continuous fighting, resulting in the destruction of Italian posts and the capture of supply columns."

The list of a number of dispatches received from Ethiopia was published in a statement issued by the Ethiopian Legation in London on January 25th, 1938; and this may be quoted in a somewhat condensed form.

"Flying and motorised columns of the Italian army have tried to recapture the posts evacuated or lost some months before. Despite the ceaseless activity of the Italian Air Force, which continues to make use of bombs and poison gas, these attempts have never had more than ephemeral success. A position which they might have been able to occupy on the previous day often proved to be their grave on the following day.

"The desertion of three battalions of Eritrean troops has reinforced the resisting forces in the Northern regions with arms and ammunition, and has completed the disorder of the Italian Staff Officers who, in the words of the Italians themselves, "manifest evident signs of despair". A group of Italian soldiers who deserted is now in the ranks of the Ethiopian warriors. The soldiers declare that there is general discontent among the Italians compelled to stay in Ethiopia, but that the least manifestation of it is suppressed with unheard of brutality. Spies, highly paid by the regime, scatter terror and hatred among the Italians themselves. Barbarous acts on the Ethiopians are considered as inherent in the 'civilising mission'. Suicides among the Italians have become, for some months past, a frightful epidemic. 'That is why', declared the Italian deserters, 'we have preferred to offer our lives to serve a just cause rather than die as beasts'. These Italian soldiers swore on the cross to help the Ethiopians to regain their complete independence.

"The following is the list of losses sustained by the invading forces of the enemy in the above mentioned Northern and North-Western regions of Ethiopia: —

"Killed: Eleven Senior Officers (Maggiori); Five Officers, of whom one was a Lieutenant (Tenente) and the remaining four Junior Officers of the Transport and Radio Departments;

"Five thousand nine hundred and ninety-three men, Italians and Askaris, were also killed.

"One Senior Officer (Maggiore) was made prisioner and eighty-three wounded men were picked-up. Forty-three lorries were destroyed.

"The number of the Ethiopian warriors killed during the engagements was equally large.

"A considerable amount of arms — machine guns, rifles and field artillery — and ammunition have been captured from the enemy".

Reports have also been received that fierce engagements are taking place at different points of the Ethiopian territory. Even in Tigré, the province bordering Eritrea, Italian troops control only the towns and the villages where they have posted garrisons. In the rest of the province of Begemder there are only two Italian garrisons, at Debra Tabor and Gondar, and these are isolated and have to be supplied by air.

"Gojjam Province has violently broken its benevolent neutrality toward the invading army by massacring eighteen officers, whose presence in Debra Markos (capital of the province) had been tolerated under certain conditions, which the Italians felt they were no longer obliged to observe. By way of reprisals, from thirty to forty aeroplanes leave Addis Ababa every day to go and bombard the towns and villages of the vast province, which had been completely freed from Italian troops.

"In the Wallaga region and more particularly in the districts of Chelleag, Gaido, Guder and up to the neighbourhood af Ambo, to the West of the capital, the Ethiopians remain masters of the situation" (Statement of 25th January, 1938).

The two garrisons in the province of Wallaga (which has gold and platinum mines) cannot control the extensive hills and fertile country beyond their immediate neighbourhood.

In the province of Shoa there have been revolts under Dejazmach Fiqra Mariam. The railway to Jibuti has been frequently attacked. Ethiopian armed troops are frequently raiding the main roads leading from Addis Ababa to the North and West.

Early in March about 5,000 Italian troops were sent out to guard the road between Dessie and Addis Ababa (the north road mentioned above which is being continually harassed by the Ethiopians). The Italians were surrounded and great difficulty was being found in relieving the force. The Ethiopians are gaining ground and there is a marked hardening in their resistance. Great aerial activity continues but is not having much effect.

South and South-West:

In the whole of this vast area of about 100,000 square kilometres, there are Italian garrisons only at five towns, namely: Jiren, Yirga-Alem, Mega, Goba and Ginir. All other parts of the territory had to be evacuated owing to the pressure of numerous guerrilla bands. Quite recently there have been revolts in the district of Bako on the River Omo led by Dejazmach Bayen Marid.

In the provinces of Gurafarda, Gimira and Kaffa many Italian garrisons have been forced to withdraw and the roads are unsafe.

South-East:

Reports received in recent months show that there have been numerous concentrations of armed Ethiopians which have attacked Italian convoys on the road through Harar to Mogadishu. Between Harar and Jijiga more than 9,000 Italian native troops have deserted with arms.

East:

The Italians exercise no control whatever over the provinces of Danakil and Aussa.

The resistance of the population of different races and religions is more intensive, united and effective than at any time since the Italian Army extended its invasion in the autumn of 1936. There is every reason to believe that armed resistance will be intensified on a greater scale than heretofore during the coming rainy season, when the Italian Air Force cannot be effectively employed.

The reasons for the growth of resistance should be understood. The Italians have attempted by costly and malicious propaganda, carried on for years before and during the progress of the war, to set the Mohamedans against the Christians. After the occupation of Addis Ababa the Italian military authorities continued and intensified this propaganda.

The Mohamedans have waited in vain for those blessings of civilisation so lavishly promised them in Italian leaflets distributed from the air. They have also been horrified, as have all sections of the population, by the mass execution of hundreds of men, women and children in various towns and villages as reprisals for raids on Italian troops in which the victims could have played no part; by the indiscriminate bombing of villages; by the ghastly slaughter of over 6,000 of the inhabitants of Addis Ababa on February 19th-21st, 1937; by the gross and immoral treatment of their women; and by many horrible acts of cruelty, such as burning people alive in their huts when they were supposed to have

48

been guilty of firing upon Italian troops. They have also been incensed by the laws and coercive measures which the Italian authorities are trying to enforce and which are entirely contrary to the traditions and customs of the people of the country; such, for example, as refusing to regard the Maria Theresa dollar as legal tender and forcing the people to accept paper currency in lire; the fixing of arbitrarily low prices; restrictions and compulsions in regard to trade and the bringing in of supplies; the displacement of cultivators without compensation from land acquired by Italians, or with very small compensation in paper lire, practically valueless to the recipient.

As a result of these cruelties and injustices, the Mohamedans began to make up their minds twelve months ago to unite with the Christians and to rid the country of the Italian invader. Thus the local chieftains, many of whom are fired with military ambition and inflexible determination to drive the Italians out of the country, are able to raise levies of Mohamedans, as well as Christians. The two sects have worked well in unison, the religious differences between them being sunk in a growing feeling of common nationality and longing for freedom and peace.

It has been frequently asserted that the resistance with which the Italian authorities are trying to cope is that of a few isolated bands. In the period of confusion which followed the capture of some of the Chiefs at the end of 1936, it may have been possible that the armed bands which continued resistance worked independently with no co-ordination. Experience proved the weakness of these attempts, and during the past six months a movement for securing co-ordination between the armed forces, in widely separated parts of the country, has made great headway. There are numerous reports of this and the following letter, written by a leader in the Lasta district to the Commander at Semien in the West will serve as an example.

"To Kanyazmach A.S.

"How are you for your health? I, by the Grace of God, am well. I have received your letter, from which I learned with great pleasure all you have done for the liberation of your country, Ethiopia. You have shown by your deeds that you are a truly great and Christian man.

"I for my part, being convinced that the Italians have invaded our country for the sole purpose of destroying the great men of Ethiopia and their children, to dishonour and expropriate us from our properties; to destroy the Christianity of our ancestors and supplant it with their own; being convinced of all these things, have up to now succesfully fought against them.

"I was therefore glad to learn of your successes also. I will help you with arms and ammunition, so persevere. I have sent to you Fitaurari F.L. and Grazmach R.B. to discuss with you future action and they will give you all information. They are men whom I trust as I trust myself, and I commend their words to you."

Magabit 9th, 1930   (Seal)
(March 16th, 1938)   Dejazmach H.M.

The present situation in Ethiopia will be appreciated if it is realised that over at least three-quarters of the country the Italian authorities have no military control beyond an area varying from roughly 10 to about 30 miles radius around the larger towns. In fact, over at least half the country there is no military control, the military posts only maintaining their existence through fortifications, and the troops being unable to venture to a distance or to penetrate the hilly and mountainous regions. Thus, throughout most of the North, West and South-West, the greater part of the country is still under the authority of Ethiopian Chiefs, who, if they once submitted to the Italians have now revolted because the Italians have broken their word.

It follows from the above: (1) that the country is in a continuous state of opposition to the invader over large areas; (2) that the Italian forces have not occupied the country completely; (3) that their military posts which have not been destroyed or withdrawn are, in many cases, on the defensive, and survive only because they receive their supplies by aeroplane; (4) that the growing ascendency of the Ethiopian troops over the larger part of the country is due to the coordination of plans between widely separated commanders.

These facts are corroborated by the indepedent evidence of the news and articles published in the Press; but if any doubts are felt about the above statements, an opportunity for establishing them will present itself shortly when the Ethiopian representatives will place all their information and documents before the League of Nations, whether it be at meetings of the Council or of the Assembly. In any case an international investigation of the real facts of the existing situation in Ethiopia would be welcomed by the Ethiopian Government. (1)

(1) *New Times and Ethiopian News.*

CHAPTER 6

Ethiopia and the League

When Italy let loose her aggression against Ethiopia on October 3rd, 1935, collective security and the world stood at one of the great turning points of history. As we reflect on what transpired since, it could be truthfully said that all the foibles of civilised contacts among states were pressed together. The whole range of international life embracing the Ancient, the Mediaeval and the Modern worlds was set into motion. The whole range of amity or conflict — the interplay of friendship and hostility, of peace or war was brought out.

Ethiopia was the victim and Italy the aggressor. In a broader sense, however, as gathered from even those who were principals in the drama, not only had the conflict sprung from endemic causes in the world body politic but the result brought out many facets of the imperfect structure of international life, and set off a chain reaction, the end of which will encompass many generations yet unborn.

The crux of the matter is that Europe was chained to its past sins. Her statesmen were tethered to the old dogmas of forceful expansion into less articulate areas, and even the presence of the League of Nations which necessity had forced upon them, did not open their eyes to the fact that these dogmas could not forever hold valid. When Mussolini took the Walwal incident as a pretext for realising Italy's old dream, he set aside the terms of the 1928 Treaty of Friendship under which any Italo-Ethiopian dispute was to be the subject of arbitration. He flouted the League Covenant. Why? Because he believed in the old dogma of Europe's forceful penetration; in fact he had well prepared the ground for the encounter. According to Viscount Templewood, in his book *Nine Troubled Years:*

"In support of the punitive action that he clearly intended, Mussolini could point to many precedents from the past. Had not the British Fleet bombarded Alexandria, and the British Army pursued the Mahdi to the Frontier of Abyssinia? Had not the French and the Spanish made their wars of conquest in Morocco? Had not a British General occupied Magdala, at the time the capital of Abyssinia? All this was perfectly true, but Mussolini, who always lived in the past, ignored the change that had come over the world since the First World War. It was of no account to him that his own Government, together with the French Government, had insisted in 1923 upon the admission of Abyssinia into the League of Nations." ([1])

And the author could have added the position of the Japanese policeman in the Far East — the first aggression which paved the way for the

([1]) Viscount Templewood, *Nine Troubled Years.*

debility of the League. The Japanese militarists' attack on Manchukuo in 1931 was done contrary to treaty provisions; they created an incident as a pretext and marched on China. The Lytton Commission branded Japanese military action in Manchukuo as naked aggression and violation of existing covenants. The Japanese did not like this, they walked out of the League Assembly and threatened to withdraw from the League.

The Chinese proposed punitive sanctions. Sir John Simon, the British Foreign Secretary, bluntly opposed the demand as unjustified. The unprovoked assault of Japan on the Chinese was not dealt with on its merits. There were ulterior and extraneous matters which were of interest to the leading League powers. So, "the opposition of Great Britain to any embroilment with Japan made action impossible and left the League declaration a mere piece of harmless palaver, allowing the Japs to continue their course of conquest on the Asiatic mainland uninterrupted." (2)

On March 11th, 1932, the Assembly of the League of Nations voted the following resolution:

"The Assembly declares that it is the duty of the members of the League of Nations not to recognise any situation, treaty or accord which may be made by means contrary to the Pact of the League of Nations or the Paris Pact."

Ethiopia's case against Italy before the League of Nations, therefore, struck a familiar note. Several phases of it, with the exception of its specific background, are similar to the League's abdication in the Sino-Japanese issue four years before. His Imperial Majesty Haile Selassie I, a firm believer in the possibility of international law, morality and justice, and moreso representing a small state, denied arms for its elemental defence, pinned his faith in the possible efficacy of this world body. It failed him and his country as it did the Chinese. But he was able to predict the future failures of the League and to live to see them come true to the detriment both of the member States which doomed Ethiopia's case and the world in general.

As explained in Chapter 4, the failure of the League of Nations rested primarily on the fact that its leaders were not certain what policy to adopt in the face of the shifting balance of power in Europe. "This failure was not due to some blunder or fiasco in reference to the material details of the organisation. It was due more to the fact that the very organising principles of the League itself, condemned it to impotence and sterility. The League was a thin façade, not a vital expression of the living authority of the times grounded in intimate decisions of day to day existence. Hence, it possessed no true force and no powers of normal self-adjustment to shifting conditions." (3)

A creation of the first world war, the League was embraced with enthusiasm and given the aura of a power for peace. One of its greatest misfortunes, however, as is agreed by many, was the aloofness of the

(2) William B. Ziff, *The Gentlemen Talk of Peace.*
(3) *Ibid.*

52

United States whose own President, Woodrow, Wilson, with his "14 points", did so much to initiate the world body. The leading States Members kept on toying with treaties, pacts, coalitions, and secret diplomacy, on the one hand, and with the League idea of collective security on the other, which Sir Samuel Hoare said was, "neither collective nor secure". This contradiction lay at the root of the delays and inaction that killed Ethiopia's cause and brought the League down.

And these treaties, pacts, coalitions, and secret diplomacy, even more, lay at the bottom of the whole Italo-Ethiopian problem. The triple agreement of 1906, for instance, had partitioned Ethiopia *in absentia;* the Anglo-Italian Treaty of 1925, concluded even during the lifetime of the League, when Ethiopia was a full-fledged member, was aimed at exploiting Ethiopian territory to the advantage of the signatories without consulting Ethiopia. The Franco-Italian Treaty of 1935 overtly laid the basis for high-handed trading between the two signatories at Ethiopia's expense. Strangely enough, the Ethiopian case before the League of Nations was sealed and doomed in April 1938 by the Anglo-Italian Agreement which "normalised" the relations between the two great powers leaving Ethiopia completely at the mercy of Mussolini.

Mr. William B. Ziff, in *The Gentlemen Talk of Peace,* illustrated the weakness of these alliances in which the Leviathans among the world states lay such store when he wrote: "We examine all of these treaties in vain for a single sign that such instruments can survive beyond the period of usefulness to the stronger powers. A long list of alliances and inalienable promises were made and smashed in relation to the Balkan problem alone. As often as not the treaty which concluded one phase of the conflict bred new and more destructive struggles.

"Today the very names of these solemn conventions are practically unknown. The treaties of Tilsit, of Berlin, of Paris, of Bucharest, of Utrecht, of Aix-La-Chapelle, of Vienna, of Fontainebleau, of Westphalia and the Hague, of Sevris, of Lausanne and Versailles, all have disappeared together with the alliances, groupings and coalitions by which they were formed and guaranteed. In practically every case their stipulations proved to be, at the best, a pious fraud in which the power element entered as nakedly as if the treaty had never been concluded." (4)

From the beginning of the Italo-Ethiopian conflict, when Mussolini refused to accept arbitration as was previously shown, His Imperial Majesty exercised the right as a Member of the League to seek redress therefrom. As a logical sequel to the pressure of Italy's modern might against his ill-organised armies of defence, in a struggle well-known to all to have been severely uneven, and to spare his people the dangers of bombing and poison gas, His Majesty took the struggle personally to Geneva and to the world public. On His way to Europe, the Emperor, on His arrival at Jerusalem despatched the following message to the League on the 9th May, 1936:

To the Secretary-General of the League of Nations, Geneva

---

(4)   Ziff, *Op. Cit.*

We beg that you will be good enough to communicate the following to States Members of the League of Nations.

Since there has been waged against us an illegal and outrageous war, of a brutality such as is not perpetrated against mankind in modern civilised times, we decided to go abroad, so that we should not bring a vain anni-hilation upon the people of Ethiopia; so that the independence of Ethiopia — who has existed for many thousands of years guarding her freedom — should now be preserved; so that those fundamental ideas might be fulfilled which have been established that there should be guarantees of mutual help to prevent the violation of the independence of states and of international obligations such as Italy has transgressed; and so that we might work in peace and freedom.

When the matter which arose between Ethiopia and Italy started, we made all the efforts we could that peace might not be disturbed. Until Italy poured down on us, as it were, a rain of poisonous gas, we fought for our country in a proper manner. But when upon our army and upon our peaceful folk poison came down like rain, we felt that we must recognise the impossibility of any strong defence against poison. If we had put up a strong defence, the result would have been a vain annihilation by poison of the Ethiopian people. Therefore we request that the League of Nations may now continue for the future the support and the efforts it has previously made to secure respect for the Covenant of the League; and that, in view of Italy's transgression of many and various obligations which have been accepted by the countries of the world, the League of Nations neither recognise as pertaining to Italy the territory she has seized by improper and outlawed force of arms, nor accept Italian claims to sovereignty over any such territory.

9th May, 1936   *Haile Selassie I*
                                                   Emperor of Ethiopia

This could be considered the first event during His Imperial Majesty's exile in the diplomatic battle which was to end so tragically, both for the Ethiopian cause and the League of Nations. After spending a few days in the Holy City, where He prayed to God to help him in the unpre-dictable struggle for the liberation of his people, the Emperor left for the United Kingdom. At the end of this eventful trip, on the 4th June 1936, His Imperial Majesty was greeted at London by those friends who knew the story and expected him. Many Londoners prophesied his return in full grasp of the independence of his country and his crown. But the going was rough!

In His Imperial Majesty's entourage were: Her Imperial Majesty Itegue Menen, Their Imperial Highnesses the Crown Prince Asfa Wossen, the Duke of Harar, Princess Tanagne Work, Princess Tsehai, and Prince Sahle Selassie, His Highness Ras Kassa, His Excellency Fitaurari Birru, Ras Getachew, Dejazmach Yignezu, Dejazmach Adafresau, Dejazmach Nasibu Zamanuel, Dejazmach Makonen Endelkatchew, Dejaz-mach Abebe Damtew, Dejazmach Amde, Dejazmach Wolde Emanuel,

54

Tsehafi Taezaz Haile, Blatten Gueta Herouy, Fitaurari Tafasse, Ato Wolde Giorguis Wolde Yohannes, Ato Lorenzo Taezaz and others. His Majesty the Emperor sailed in the famous H.M.S. "Enterprise" from the port of Jibuti after having been protected there by the Governor of French Somaliland.

He had left behind a people terrorised by poison gas and facing a future of harassment through the ruthless desire of the Italian conquerors to subdue them. So also had he before him the confusion which had gripped the League of Nations since he had placed the case of Italy's unprovoked aggression against his country before that body in December of the previous year.

Mussolini flouted the Covenant and had pressed his ill-equipped and ill-trained warriors in a corner. His Majesty had changed the venue of the defence so as to save his defenceless people from complete annihilation. The principles of the League had become his faith, however. He knew that the Covenant pledged Member States to settle disputes by conciliation and arbitration. According to the Covenant, any one of the Member States which disregarded its provisions and resorted to war should be deemed as to have committed an act of war against all other Members, who would take all necessary economic and military sanctions to enforce the Covenant. This was in line with post-war world public opinion which abhorred war and which, in 1919, influenced the formation of a world moral movement aimed at supplanting the rule of force.

With these principles in mind, immediately on his arrival in London, His Imperial Majesty began to prepare his appeal, which he decided to make personally to the League Assembly and the world, that took place twenty-four days after his arrival.

The Emperor's reception at Geneva had exceeded in magnitude anything previously witnessed when a head of a foreign state visited Switzerland. Accompanied by Ras Kassa, Blatten Gueta Hirouy, Ato Wolde Giorguis Wolde Yohannes (His Private Secretary), Ato Lorenzo Taezaz, Dejazmach Nasibu, and His Foreign Advisers, Auberson, Spencer and Colson, and by Professor Jeze who was to present Ethiopia's case after it had been formally opened by the Emperor who bore the heavy mantle on his frail shoulders of a cause which had a tremendous impact on the world.

The opening of the Assembly, called at the request of Argentine, was fixed for 5 o'clock, Tuesday, June 28th, 1936. The General Committee of the Assembly, which had decided to accept the Emperor as head of the Ethiopian Delegation, with the opportunity to present the Ethiopian case, had earlier notified His Majesty's delegation. M. van Zeeland, Prime Minister of Belgium, was President of the session. Mr. Anthony Eden, (now Sir) was Chairman.

His Majesty Haile Selassie I was then called on by the President to speak on behalf of his country. When the Emperor reached the tribune and turned to face the Assembly, there broke out a noise of whistling and catcalls from the Italian newspapermen from the press gallery. A few shouts, and Swiss police, assisted by other press correspondents, had the interrupters expelled. His Majesty the Emperor remained in silent dignity facing the scene, and a great and prolonged wave of applause soon drowned the whistling and the noise of ejection. Italy, who brazenly rebuffed the Covenant by her aggression, remained true to her colours. Representatives of her press had now insulted the dignity of the Assembly in an attempt to still the voice of the Emperor — the voice of truth.

The convocation of this Sixteenth Assembly of the League of Nations was branded the League Session of the "Great Betrayal at Geneva". Mr. Cantilo of Argentine, who had requested this session, was the first speaker, after the President, M. van Zeeland, who in calling the Assembly, succinctly said: "The destinies of a large portion of mankind are now in the balance." How true!

The Argentine delegate declared that the "request for the session was an expression of faith in the absolute equality of States of democratic spirit." Further: "If American ideas cannot be harmonised with the manner of applying the Covenant, if we cannot secure the practical universality of a principle of justice, and if the attempt to do so might create a danger to peace, or might prove incompatible with the forms devised to secure it, the Argentine Republic would be obliged to reconsider the possibility of continuing its collaboration."

The famous speech of His Majesty the Emperor followed. He gave a brief recapitulation of preceding events in the case. Many commentators believed this declaration one of the most historic of the 20th Century. The Emperor charged those League Members who had connived with Italy to tear up the Covenant, clearly detailed their responsibility, and predicted that they were digging their own graves. Subsequent events have adequately demonstrated those predictions. He declared:

I, Haile Selassie I, Emperor of Ethiopia, am here today to claim that justice which is due to my people, and the assistance promised to it eight months ago, when fifty nations asserted that an aggression had been committed in violation of international treaties.

None other than the Emperor can address the appeal of the Ethiopian people to these fifty nations.

There is no precedent for a head of a State himself speaking in this Assembly. But there is also no precedent for a people being victim of such injustice and being at present threatened by abandonment to its aggressor. Also, there has never before been an example of any Government proceeding to the systematic extermination of a nation by barbarous means, in violation of the most solemn promises made to all the nations of the earth that there should not be used against innocent human beings the terrible poison of harmful gases. It is to defend a people struggling for its age-old independence that the head of the Ethiopian Empire has come to Geneva to fulfil this supreme duty, after having himself fought at the head of his armies.

I pray Almighty God that he may spare nations the terrible sufferings that have just been inflicted on my people, and of which the chiefs who accompany me here have been the horrified witnesses.

It is my duty to inform the Governments assembled in Geneva, responsible

56

as they are for the lives of millions of men, women and children, of the deadly peril which threatens them, by describing to them the fate which has been suffered by Europe.

It is not only upon warriors that the Italian Government has made war. It has above all attacked populations far removed from hostilities, in order to terrorise and exterminate them.

At the beginning, towards the end of 1935, Italian aircraft hurled upon my armies bombs of tear-gas. Their effects were but slight. The soldiers learned to scatter, waiting until the wind had rapidly dispersed the poisonous gases.

The Italian aircraft then resorted to mustard gas. Barrels of liquid were hurled upon armed groups. But this means also was not effective; the liquid affected only a few soldiers, and barrels upon the ground were themselves a warning to troops and to the population of the danger.

It was at the time when the operations for the encircling of Makale were taking place that the Italian command, fearing a rout, followed the procedure which it is now my duty to denounce to the world. Special sprayers were installed on board aircraft so that they could vaporise, over vast areas of territory, a fine, death-dealing rain. Groups of nine, fifteen, eighteen aircraft followed one another so that the fog issuing from them formed a continuous sheet. It was thus that, as from the end of January, 1936, soldiers, women, children, cattle, rivers, lakes, and pastures were drenched continually with this deadly rain. In order to kill off systematically all living creatures, in order the more surely to poison waters and pastures, the Italian command made its aircraft pass over and over again. That was its chief method of warfare.

The very refinement of barbarism consisted in carrying ravage and terror into the most densely populated parts of the territory — the points farthest removed from the scene of hostilities. The object was to scatte, fear and death over a great part of the Ethiopian territory.

These fearful tactics succeeded. Men and animals succumbed. The deadly rain that fell from the aircraft made all those whom it touched fly shrieking with pain. All those who drank the poisoned water or ate the infected food also succumbed in dreadful suffering. In tens of thousands, the victims of the Italian mustard gas fell. It is in order to denounce to the civilised world the tortures inflicted upon the Ethiopian people that I resolved to come to Geneva.

None other than myself and my brave companions in arms could bring the League of Nations the undeniable proof. The appeals of my delegates addressed to the League of Nations had remained without any answer; my delegates had not been witnesses. That is why I decided to come myself to bear witness against the crime perpetrated against my people and give Europe a warning of the doom that awaits it, if it should bow before the accomplished fact.

Is it necessary to remind the Assembly of the various stages of the Ethiopian drama. For 20 years past, either as Heir Apparent, Regent of the Empire, or as Emperor, I have been directing the destinies of my people. I have never ceased to use all my efforts to bring my country the *benefits of civilisation, and in particular to establish relations of good neighbourliness with adjacent Powers. In particular I succeeded in concluding with Italy the Treaty of Friendship of 1928, which absolutely prohibited the resort, under any pretext whatsoever, to force of arms, substituting for force and pressure the conciliation and arbitration on which civilised nations have based international order.*

In its report of October 5th, 1935, the Committee of Thirteen recognised my effort and the results that I had achieved. The Governments thought that the entry of Ethiopia into the League, whilst giving that country a new guarantee for the maintenance of her territorial integrity and independence, would help her to reach a higher level of civilisation. It does not seem that in Ethiopia today there is more disorder and insecurity than in 1923. On the contrary the country is more united and the central power is better obeyed.

I should have procured still greater results for my people if obstacles of every kind had not been put in the way by the Italian Government, the Government which stirred up revolt and armed the rebels. Indeed the Rome Government, as it has today openly proclaimed, has never ceased to prepare for the conquest of Ethiopia. The Treaty of Friendship it signed with me was not sincere; their only object was to hide its real intention from me. The Italian Government asserts that for fourteen years it has been preparing for its present conquest. It therefore recognises today that when it supported the admission of Ethiopia to the League of Nations in 1923, when it concluded the Treaty of Friendship in 1928, when it signed the Pact of Paris outlawing war, it was deceiving the whole world.

The Ethiopian Government was, in these solemn treaties, given additional guarantees of security which would enable it to achieve further progress along the pacific path of reform on which it had set its feet, and to which it was devoting all its strength and all its heart.

The Walwal incident, in December, 1934, came as a thunderbolt to me. The Italian provocation was obvious and I did not hesitate to appeal to the League of Nations. I invoked the provisions of the treaty of 1928, the principles of the Covenant! I urged the procedure of conciliation and arbitration.

Unhappily for Ethiopia this was the time when a certain Government considered that the European situation made it imperative at all costs to obtain the friendship of Italy. The price paid was the abandonment of Ethiopian independence to the greed of the Italian Government. This secret agreement, contrary to the obligations of the Covenant has exerted a great influence over the course of events. Ethiopia, and the whole world have suffered and are still suffering today its disastrous consequences.

This first violation of the Covenant was followed by many others. Feeling itself encouraged in its policy against Ethiopia, the Rome Government feverishly made war preparations, thinking that the concerted pressure which was beginning to be exerted on the Ethiopian Government might perhaps overcome the resistance of my people to Italian domination.

The time had to come; thus all sorts of difficulties were placed in the way with a view to breaking up the procedure of conciliation and arbitration.

58

All kinds of obstacles were placed in the way of that procedure; Governments tried to prevent the Ethiopian Government from finding arbitrators amongst their nations; when once the arbitral tribunal was set up pressure was exercised so that an award favourable to Italy should be given.

All this was in vain; the arbitrators — two of whom were Italian officials — were forced to recognise unanimously that in the Walwal incident, as in the subsequent incidents, no international responsibility was to be attributed to Ethiopia.

Following on this award, the Ethiopian Government sincerely thought that an era of friendly relations might be opened with Italy. I loyally offered my hand to the Rome Government.

The Assembly was informed by the report of the Committee of Thirteen, dated October 5th, 1935, of the details of the events which occurred after the month of December, 1934, and up to October 3rd, 1935. It will be sufficient if I quote a few of the conclusions of that report. (Nos. 24, 25 and 26):

'The Italian memorandum (containing the complaints made by Italy) was laid on the Council table on September 4th, 1935, whereas Ethiopia's first appeal to the Council had been made on December 14th, 1934. In the interval between these two dates, the Italian Government opposed the consideration of the question by the Council on the ground that the only appropriate procedure was that provided for in the Italo-Ethiopian Treaty of 1928. Throughout the whole of that period, moreover, the despatch of Italian troops to East Africa was proceeding. These shipments of troops were represented to the Council by the Italian Government as necessary for the defence of its colonies menaced by Ethiopia's military preparations. Ethiopia, on the contrary, drew attention to the official pronouncements made in Italy which, in its opinion, left no doubt as to the hostile intentions of the Italian Government.'

From the outset of the dispute, the Ethiopian Government has sought a settlement by peaceful means. It has appealed to the procedures of the Covenant. The Italian Government desiring to keep strictly to the procedure of the Italo-Ethiopian Treaty of 1928, the Ethiopian Government assented; it invariably stated that it would faithfully carry out the arbitral award, even if the decision went against it. It agreed that the question of the ownership of Walwal should not be dealt with by the arbitrators, because the Italian Government would not agree to such a course. It asked the Council to despatch neutral observers and offered to lend itself to any enquiries upon which the Council might decide.

Once the Walwal dispute had been settled by arbitration, however, the Italian Government submitted its detailed memorandum to the Council in support of its claim to liberty of action. It asserted that a case like that of Ethiopia could not be settled by the means provided by the Covenant.

It stated that, 'since this question affects vital interests and is of primary importance to Italian security and civilisation, it would be failing in its most elementary duty, did it not cease once and for all to place any confidence in Ethiopia, reserving full liberty to adopt any measures that may become necessary to ensure the safety of its colonies and to safeguard its own interests.'

Those are the terms of the report of the Committee of Thirteen. The Council and the Assembly unanimously adopted the conclusions of that report and solemnly proclaimed that the Italian Government had violated the Covenant and was in a state of aggression.

I did not hesitate to declare that I did not wish for war; that it was imposed upon me, and that I should struggle solely for the independence and integrity of my people and that in that struggle I was defender of the cause of all small States exposed to the greed of a powerful neighbour.

In October, 1935, the fifty-two nations who are listening to me today, gave me an assurance that the aggressor would not triumph, that the resources of the Covenant would be employed in order to ensure the reign of right and the failure of violence.

I ask the fifty-two nations not to forget today the policy upon which they embarked eight months ago, and on faith of which I directed the resistance of my people against the aggressor whom they had denounced to the world. Despite the inferiority of my weapons, the complete lack of aircraft, artillery, munitions, hospital services, my confidence in the League was absolute. I thought it to be impossible that fifty-two nations, including the most powerful in the world, should be successfully opposed by a single aggressor. Counting on the faith due to treaties, I had made no preparation for war, and that is the case with certain small countries in Europe.

When the danger became more urgent, being aware of my responsibilities towards my people, during the first six months of 1935 I tried to acquire armaments. Many Governments proclaimed an embargo to prevent my doing so, whereas the Italian Government, through the Suez Canal, was given all facilities for transporting without cessation and without protest, troops, arms and munitions.

On October 3rd, 1935, the Italian troops invaded my territory. A few hours later only, I decreed general mobilisation. In my desire to maintain peace I had, following the example of a great country in Europe on the eve of the Great War, caused my troops to withdraw thirty kilometres so as to remove any pretext of provocation.

War then took place in the atrocious conditions which I have laid before the Assembly. In that unequal struggle between a Government commanding more than forty-two million inhabitants, having at its disposal financial, industrial and technical means which enabled it to create unlimited quantities of the most death-dealing weapons, and, on the other hand, a small people of twelve million inhabitants, without arms, without resources, having on its side only the justice of its own cause and the promise of the League of Nations. What real assistance was given to Ethiopia by the fifty-two nations who had declared the Rome Government guilty of a breach of the Covenant and had undertaken to prevent the triumph of the aggressor? Has each of the States Members, as it was its duty to do in view of its signature appended to Article 16 of the Covenant, considered the aggressor as having committed an act of war

60

personally directed against itself? I had placed all my hopes in the execution of these undertakings. My confidence had been confirmed by the repeated declarations made in the Council to the effect that aggression must not be rewarded, and that force would end by being compelled to bow before right.

In December, 1935, the Council made it quite clear that its feelings were in harmony with those of hundreds of millions of people who, in all parts of the world, had protested against the proposal to dismember Ethiopia. It was constantly repeated that there was not merely a conflict between the Italian Government and the League of Nations, and that is why I personally refused all proposals to my personal advantage made to me by the Italian Government if only I would betray my people and the Covenant of the League of Nations. I was defending the cause of all small peoples who are threatened with aggression.

What has become of the promises made to me? As long ago as October, 1935, I noted with grief, but without surprise, that three Powers considered their undertakings under the Covenant as absolutely of no value. Their connections with Italy impelled them to refuse to take any measures whatsoever in order to stop Italian aggression. On the contrary, it was a profound disappointment to me to learn the attitude of a certain Government which, whilst ever protesting its scrupulous attachment to the Covenant, has tirelessly used all its efforts to prevent its observance. As soon as any measure which was likely to be rapidly effective was proposed, various pretexts were devised in order to postpone even consideration of that measure. Did the secret agreements of January, 1935, provide for this tireless obstruction?

The Ethiopian Government never expected other Governments to shed their soldiers' blood to defend the Covenant when their own immediate personal interests were not at stake. Ethiopian warriors asked only for means to defend themselves. On many occasions I have asked for financial assistance for the purchase of arms. That assistance has been constantly refused me. What, then, in practice, is the meaning of Article 16 of the Covenant and of collective security?

The Ethiopian Government's use of the railway from Jibuti to Addis Ababa was in practice hampered as regards transport of arms intended for the Ethiopian forces. At the present moment this is the chief, if not the only, means of supply of the Italian armies of occupation. The rules of neutrality should have prohibited transports intended for Italian forces, but there is not even neutrality, since Article 16 lays upon every State Member of the League the duty not to remain a neutral and to come to the aid not of the aggressor but of the victim of aggression. Has the Covenant been respected? Is it today being respected?

Finally, a statement has just been made in their Parliaments by the Governments of certain Powers, amongst them the most influential Members of the League of Nations, that since the aggressor has succeeded in occupying a large part of Ethiopian territory they propose not to continue the application of any economic and financial measures that may have been decided upon against the Italian Government.

61

These are the circumstances in which, at the request of the Argentine Government, the Assembly of the League of Nations meets to consider the situation created by Italian aggression.

I assert that the problem submitted to the Assembly today is a much wider one. It is not merely a question of the settlement of Italian agression. It is collective security; it is the very existence of the League of Nations. It is the confidence that each State is to place in international treaties. It is the value of promises made to small States that their integrity and their independence shall be respected and insured. It is the principle of the equality of States on the one hand, or otherwise the obligation laid upon small Powers to accept the bonds of vassalship. In a word, it is international morality that is at stake. Have the signatures appended to a Treaty value only in so far as the signatory Powers have a personal, direct and immediate interest involved?

No subtlety can change the problem or shift the grounds of the discussion. It is in all sincerity that I submit these considerations to the Assembly. At a time when my people is threatened with extermination, when the support of the League may ward off the final blow, may I be allowed to speak with complete frankness, without reticence in all directness, such as is demanded by the rule of equality as between all States Members of the League? Apart from the Kingdom of the Lord there is not on this earth any nation that is superior to any other. Should it happen that a strong Government finds it may, with impunity, destroy a weak people, then the hour strikes for that weak people to appeal to the League of Nations to give its judgment in all freedom. God and history will remember your judgment.

I have heard it asserted that the inadequate sanctions already applied have not achieved their object. At no time, in no circumstances, could sanctions that were intentionally inadequate, intentionally badly applied, stop an aggressor. This is not a case of the impossibility of stopping an aggressor, but of the refusal to stop an aggressor. When Ethiopia' requested and requests that she should be given financial assistance, was that a measure which it was impossible to apply, whereas financial assistance of the League has been granted, even in times of peace, to two countries, and exactly to two countries who have refused to apply sanctions against the aggressor?

Faced by numerous violations by the Italian Government of all international treaties that prohibit resort to arms, and the use of barbarous methods of warfare, it is my painful duty to note that the initiative has today been taken with a view to raising sanctions. Does this initiative not mean in practice the abandonment of Ethiopia to its agressor? On the very eve of the day when I was about to attempt a supreme effort in the defence of my people before this Assembly, does not this initiative deprive Ethiopia of one of her last chances to succeed in obtaining the support and guarantee of State Members? Is that the guidance the League of Nations and each of the States Members are entitled to expect from the great Powers when they assert their right and their duty to guide the action of the League?

62

*Placed by the aggressor face to face with the accomplished fact, are
States going to set up the terrible precedent of bowing before force?*

*Your Assembly will doubtless have laid before it proposals for the reform
of the Covenant and for rendering more effective the guarantee of
collective security. Is it the Covenant that needs reform? What
undertakings can have any value if the will to keep them is lacking? It is
international morality which is at stake and not the Articles of
the Covenant.*

*On behalf of the Ethiopian people, a Member of the League of Nations,
I request the Assembly to take all measures proper to ensure respect for
the Covenant. I renew my protest against the violations of treaties of
which the Ethiopian people has been the victim. I declare in the face of
the whole world that the Emperor, the Government and the people of
Ethiopia will not bow before force, that they maintain their claims, that
they will use all means in their power to ensure the triumph of right and
the respect of the Covenant.*

*I ask the fifty-two nations who have given the Ethiopian people a pro-
mise to help them in their resistance to the aggressor, what are they
willing to do for Ethiopia? And the great Powers who have promised the
guarantee of collective security to small States on whom weighs the
threat that they may one day suffer the fate of Ethiopia, I ask, what
measures do you intend to take?*

*Representatives of the world, I have come to Geneva to discharge in
your midst the most painful of the duties of the head of a State. What
reply shall I have to take back to my people?*

We give hereunder significant excerpts from some of the speeches which
followed His Imperial Majesty's declaration before the Sixteenth Session
of the Assembly, as reported by the "New Times and Ethiopian News",
for what they are worth.

The new "Popular Front" Premier of France, M. Blum, led the great
retreat from the Covenant, the great betrayal of Ethiopia:

"Our plans for adaptation limit it to the Powers which are nearest, geographically or politically, to the Power that is attacked.

"We are glad to note that the memorandum communicated by the
Italian Government does make a contribution."

Then spoke Mr. Te Water of South Africa. He made an impassioned
appeal in which he strongly condemned the Governments of the great
Powers for their declared intention to stop sanctions and abandon
Ethiopia to her fate. In his long speech he said:

"There must inevitably come a time in the affairs of nations when
resignation in the face of calamity is not enough. Events so inexorably
shape themselves that to control them decisions must be supported by
courage and action by determination and sacrifice.

"My Government, whom I have the honour to represent, desires me to
say here that this renunciation by the most powerful Members of the
League of the collective decision most solemnly taken by us all, under
the obligation by which we declared ourselves bound, can alone be

63

interpreted as surrender by them of the authority of the League — a surrender of the high trust, and ideals of world peace entrusted to each member nation of this institution.

"And if there is to be no loyalty to that pledge, if fear, like a wedge, is to be driven into the ranks of the Covenanters, or if the nations are to be cut into separate groups, cowering into their separate pens, what must be their inevitable fate, what black despair must settle upon the face of Europe."

The Honourable Vincent Massey of Canada then led the appalling retreat from sanctions. He indicated that his Government had from the first been reluctant to join the sanctions front.

The apology of Anthony Eden for his own retreat and that of the National Government was a lame performance:

"It is not that the measures in themselves have been without effect, but that the condition in which they were expected to operate have not been realised .... The sanctions at present in force are incapable of reversing the order of events in that country .... In existing conditions the continuation of the sanctions at present in force can serve no useful purpose. At the same time, it is the view of His Majesty's Government that this Assembly should not in any way recognise Italy's conquest over Abyssinia .... Our endeavour must be centred upon the task of reconstruction."

Soviet Russia was the third great government which agreed to abandon sanctions:

"However, sooner than might have been expected, the moment came when the necessity for reconsidering the measures taken at Geneva, from the angle of their serving any useful purpose, became absolutely clear .... By economic sanctions alone it would be impossible to drive the Italian army out of Ethiopia and restore the independence of that country. Such an objective could only be attained by more serious sanctions, including those of a military nature. Such measures could only be considered if one or several States could be found which, in virtue of their geographical position and special interests, would agree to bear the main brunt of a military encounter. Such States were not to be found among us; ....

"The people of the Soviet Union cherish nothing but the greatest respect and sympathy for the Italian people. They are interested in the uninterrupted development and consolidation of their existing political, economic and cultural relations with Italy. Nevertheless, the Soviet Government expressed its readiness to take part in general international action against Italy in defence of a country with which the Soviet Union has no relations whatsoever either *de jure* or *de facto*."

The delegate of Chile declared that on signing the Covenant of the League, his Government had renounced its neutrality in return, as is thought, for collective security. Public opinion in his country was losing confidence in the League:

"If we do not secure peace or collective security, we must resume our neutrality."

64

Next spoke the representative of Sweden:

"Sweden by following a strict policy of neutrality, has enjoyed more than one hundred years of peace. At the present day we must ask ourselves whether, as has been the case with sanctions, we shall subsequently be confronted by a further series of *fait accompli* bearing upon the situation in Ethiopia."

Next spoke Mr. De Valera for the Irish Free State and expressed a sense of bitter humiliation that fifty nations had abandoned the victim of aggression to her fate. Yet he acquiesced in the decision:

"For the sake of a Nation in Africa, apparently, no one is ready to risk war that would be transferred to Europe. If we want to be realists we will concentrate upon Europe without delay... and leave aside for the moment such questions as how the Covenant should be altered to make it as a world organisation effective and universal."

Sir James Parr expressed New Zealand's disappointment and distress. New Zealand favoured intensified sanctions and would go that road if a majority would agree.

M. Pflugal of Austria spoke as a slavish servant of the Fascist Government of Italy "inspired by the spirit of the Covenant" and that she had "assumed the sacred mission of civilisation" in Ethiopia.

Dr. Wellington Koo for China reminded the League that the League had failed to protect China against armed aggression in 1931, and declared the present tragedy was the result.

M. de Velico of Hungary displayed the known friendship of his Government for Fascist Italy.

Mr. Sepahbodi for Iran declared the failure to save Ethiopia was not due to any imperfection in the Covenant, but to lack of sincerity in those who undertook to implement it. So long as sincerity failed to reign in that Assembly no Covenant would prove effective.

Mr. Monteiro of Portugal lamented that the Covenant, which was intended, above all "to guarantee the independence and integrity of nations even by war" had failed.

Mr. Barcia Trelles spoke for Spain. He said that the failure to protect Ethiopia was not due to defects in the Covenant.

"The law is good; what is bad is the way it has been enforced. Members of the League cannot recognise political or administrative changes brought about by force or contrary to the principles of the Covenant or the Pact of Paris."

The stage seemed now set for the final act of abdication of the League in the Ethiopian cause. The sanctions which were in sufficient and grudgingly applied, through pressure, were now finally thrown overboard. Studies had shown, however, that the economic sanctions did have some effect on the aggressor.

"Prospects of the future cumulative effects, of League sanctions, applied or likely to be applied, drove Mussolini to have recourse to poison gas in order to finish his victims before these sanctions should take greater effect", as Ato Lorenzo Taezaz told the Seventeenth League Assembly.

By 1937 Ethiopia's case had completely dropped from the agenda of the

League Council. His Majesty the Emperor, most oddly, still believed that the League could do something. His thinking was based on the principle that it was not his country alone which faced the lawlessness of aggression — it was all small states which comprised the majority of the States Members of the League. He knew that the restistance by his patriots was continuing and, even more so, he believed in 'the promises made two years before by Britain and France; he had faith in the triumph of international justice.

On the 18th September, 1937, the Emperor, in a letter to the Secretary General of the League wrote:

In this month of September, which marks the anniversary of the greatest effort which has ever been made in the history of the world for the triumph of international justice, the Ethiopian Government cannot but recall the declarations made to Ethiopia two years ago with almost complete unanimity of members of the League of Nations, which gave to the Ethiopian people in their feebleness without arms, having nothing but right on its side, the promise that it could rely with faith upon the support of the civilised world.

'The ideas enshrined in the Covenant', said the representative of the United Kingdom in the Assembly on the 11th September 1935, 'and in particular the aspiration to establish the rule of law in international affairs, have appealed as I have already said, with growing force to the strain of idealism which has its place in our national character, and they have become a part of our national conscience......... Following this same line of thought, we believe that small nations are entitled to a life of their own and to such protection as can collectively be afforded them in the mainten- ance of their national existence......... In conformity with its precise and explicit obligations, the League stands, and my country stands with it, for the collective maintenance of the Covenant in its entirety, and particularly for steady and collective resistance to all acts of unprovoked aggression. The attitude of the British nation in the last few weeks has clearly demon- strated the fact that this is no variable and unreliable sentiment, but a principle of international conduct to which they and their government hold firm with enduring and universal persistence.'

The delegate of France declared from his side: 'France is faithful to the Covenant......... The Covenant remains our international law......... All our Agreements with our friends and with our allies are now concluded through Geneva, or culminate at Geneva......... Every attack against the institution of Geneva is an attack against our own security......... Our obligations are inscribed in the Covenant. France will not shirk them.'

The delegate of Portugal, who was President of the Committee of Thir- teen and enjoyed a great and recognised authority, declared in his turn: 'Collective security would be worth little if it did not safeguard the inte- grity of each national territory and the political independence of all nations; and that against conquest, of course, but also against any decisions not freely accepted. For my part, I must say that there is one thing I loathe even more than war, and that is spoliation by procedure.'

These comforting promises sustained the Ethiopian people during their ordeals. They never believed that day would come when those promises would be disowned. There could not be "spoliation by procedure." Such was their conviction and their confidence. The independence of a people, however weak they might be, would never be the medium of exchange of a bargain with the aggressor.

Our faith in the League of Nations remains unalterable. In spite of our weakness in material things, the moral force of our case sustains us and we are convinced that a day will come when the League of Nations will succeed in obtaining the liberation of our country and in aiding its reconstruction. Thus will be re-established the reign of law which is the essential basis of peace.

With sanctions now discarded, the League was now readied to complete the betrayal by recognition of Italy's illegal conquest. This, in face of the fact that it was unanimously agreed by fifty of the League Members, and in a resolution similair to the one on Manchukuo, that the Members of the League would not recognise territory obtained by a violation of the Covenant.

Fascist propaganda was still hard at work to convince the world and the League Powers that Ethiopia was Italian. The British and the French Governments, under the guise of "stabilising" peace, dealt secretly with Mussolini. The Anglo-Italian Treaty, referred to above, was concluded in April 1938. A British delegate in the League Council of 1938 informed the States Members of this Agreement which destroyed at a fell swoop the League's claim to a collective security system; it cleared the way for promiscuous recognition of Italy as sovereign over Ethiopia. At this time a few States Members, over the protest of His Majesty the Emperor, had recognised *de facto* and *de jure* such a sovereignty.

The famous League Council met on May 12th, 1938, and the 18th item on its agenda, suggested by His Britannic Majesty's Delegation, concerned Ethiopia. His Imperial Majesty Haile Selassie I took occasion to be present to address that body. Before the item was taken up, Mr. Munters of Latvia, presiding, said:

"It is the desire of the Council to assure the participation of delegates of the Emperor Haile Selassie in the discussions of the Council on Item 18 of this agenda, without prejudice to question of principle, and irrespective of the precise character of their full powers. I have been informed that His Majesty Haile Selassie has expressed the wish himself to participate in the discussion and, in accordance with the desire of the Council, I invite him to come to the Council table."

After the Emperor took His seat at the Council table, Lord Halifax, Mr. Chamberlain's spokesman, delivered his speech in which he took the responsibility of placing the item on the agenda concerning "the consequences arising out of the existing situation in Ethiopia." In a masterpiece of circumlocution, Lord Halifax made it more than clear that collective action by the League States was not meant. He said: "Having regard to the action taken by so many States who are perfectly loyal to the League, His Majesty's Government do not think that the various steps which the League has taken in the course of the Italo-Ethiopian dispute can be held to constitute any binding obligation upon Member States to withhold recognition until a unanimous decision has been taken.

"Accordingly, I think it right plainly to state the view of His Majesty's Government that the situation is one in which Members of the League may, without disloyalty, take such action at such time as may seem to them appropiate." He continued, "In raising this question at this meeting, His Majesty's Government have in view a strictly limited objective. It is far from their purpose to suggest that the Council or any member of the League should condone the action by which the Italian Government have acquired their present position in Ethiopia, and which the League in corporate action thought it right to condemn. Nor do they propose that any organ of the League should modify the resolutions and decisions which they took in the earlier stages of the dispute. On this issue we have declared our judgment in plain terms, and we cannot go back upon it. His Majesty's Government hope, however, that other members of the Council will share their opinion that the question of the recognition of Italy's position is one which every member of the League must be held entitled to decide for itself in the light of its own situation and obligations.

"I do not overlook the fact that there are many in my own country, as perhaps in others, who feel that none the less any action designed to facilitate recognition of the Italian conquest does impinge on principle, and who would therefore deplore the adoption of such a course. I respect, but I cannot share, their view.

"Anxiety arises in great part from the resolution adopted by the League in 1932 in the case of Manchukuo upon the subject of non-recognition of the results of aggressive action. In that resolution it was agreed by all members of the League that they would not recognise any situation, treaty, or agreement, which was brought about by means contrary to the Covenant, and if we desire to be honest with ourselves and with our fellow-members of the League, we must not be afraid squarely to face the facts in the light of that expression of opinion.

"Those who seek to establish a better world upon the basis of universal acknowledgment of League principles are clearly right to feel reluctance to countenance action, however desirable on other grounds, by which these may appear to be infringed. But when, as here, two ideals are in conflict, on the one hand, the ideal of devotion, unflinching but unpractical, to some high purpose; on the other, the ideal of a practical victory for peace — I cannot doubt that the stronger claim is that of peace.

".....................It is necessary to reconcile that which may be ideally right with what is practically possible. That is, in truth, one of the hardest laws which operate in a world so strangely composite of good and evil.....................

"Thus in an imperfect world, the indefinite maintenance of a principle, envolved to safeguard international order, without regard to the circumstances in which it has to be applied, may have an effect merely of in-

68

creasing international discord and friction and of contributing to those very evils which it was designed to prevent.

"That is the position which His Majesty's Government feel bound to adopt in the case of Ethiopia.

It is the considered opinion of His Majesty's Government that, for practical purposes, Italian control over virtually the whole of Ethiopia has become an established fact, and that sooner or later, unless we are prepared by force to alter it, or unless for ever we are to live in an unreal world, that fact, whatever be our judgment on it, will have to be acknowledged.

"If this is so — and I say this with every consideration for the feelings of those most closely affected by these events — it is plain that the issue between those who would be disposed to take action by way of recognition of facts earlier and those who would take the same action later is one of political judgment and not part of the eternal and immutable moralities......... But no cause is served by vain lamentations over the past......... Meanwhile nothing is gained and much may be lost by a refusal to face facts.........

His Majesty's Government believe that these great issues may be affected by the treatment of the subject which is at present before the Council, and weighing all the considerations, political and moral, that arise, as fairly as I may, I cannot believe that it would be right to exclude the possibility of taking positive steps to secure the measure of good result for the world's peace.........

"It is for these reasons, Mr. President, that His Majesty's Government have thought it right to bring this matter before the Council and to express their views upon it.

"They do not, as I have said, ask for decisions on questions of principle nor do they suggest that the Council should impose on any Member of the League a particular course of action.

"They hope, however, that Members of the Council will share their opinion, that the question of the recognition of Italy's position in Ethiopia is one for each Member of the League to decide for itself in the light of its own situation and its own obligations."

Lord Halifax, representing as he did the United Kingdom, the greatest Power that had adhered to the League Covenant, had brutally and finally by this speech in the Council, brought down the curtain on collective security. Member States could retreat from the sacred pledge to support collective League action and decide to recognise Italy's loot as it suited their convenience. Hitler who had bolted from the League, and Mussolini who had defied it, were now given *carte blanche* to proceed to threaten and destroy the sovereignty of the European States. If it is true that Ethiopia's plight was made possible because of the unsettled political state in Europe, it seems equally as true that the unsettled state in which the Ethiopian question was left by the League of Nations involved, to a preponderant extent, the future of the Old continent. By 1940 Hitler had reduced it to a German colony.

What a painful experience it must have been to His Majesty the Emperor to listen to Lord Halifax when the British people were his friends, although the Tory Government surely did not support their view. Even after this tragic Council meeting, when the Emperor returned to Bath from Geneva, he said: *I still have faith in the League of Nations.........* *The British have always shown sympathy with my country and that attitude has not changed even today.* He heard with his own ears the betrayal — Ethiopia was to be abandoned to her fate as a mark of appeasement to the Italian Fascists. The British Government had closed the League chapter on Ethiopia by the Anglo-Italian Agreement, by Lord Halifax's Council speech, and by accreditting its new Ambassador to Rome, to the King of Italy as Emperor of Ethiopia.

His Imperial Majesty was next to address the Council. He declared:

Although only recently recovered from an illness, I decided to come myself to defend the cause of my people before the Council of the League of Nations. I hope, however, that the Council will be good enough to excuse me from reading the whole of my declaration and will allow H.E. Ato Lorenzo Taezaz, permanent delegate to the League of Nations, to read it in my place.

(The President: I am sure that Members of the Council will have no objection.)

Ato Lorenzo Taezaz (speaking on behalf of His Majesty): *The Ethiopian people, to whom all assistance was refused, are climbing alone their path to calvary. No humiliation has been spared to the victim of aggression. All resources of procedures have been tried with a view to exclude Ethiopia from the League of Nations, as the aggressor demands. Thus for three years there has been before the world and before the League the problem of international order: will law win the game as against force, or force as against law?*

Ethiopia, the victim of an inexcusable aggression, had placed her confidence in the signature of the States Members of the League, although the support that was due to her was given only in very incomplete measures. Since 1935 Ethiopia has with pain noted successive abandonments of signatures that had been appended to the Covenant.

Many Powers threatened with aggression and feeling their weakness have abandoned Ethiopia. They have uttered the cry of panic and rout. Everyone for himself! In the vain hope of currying favour with the aggressor, they have regarded themselves as freed from the undertakings they had assumed for general security. Thus they have themselves overthrown all the principles on which their very existence rests. They have torn up the treaties which ensured their own indepedence — the treaties of non-aggression, the Covenant of the League of Nations, the Pact of Paris. By what right will they themselves be able to invoke these undertakings if they regard as scraps of paper the treaties they have signed?

Aggressions have taken place in increasing number. The contagion has been propagated. Certain States are now engaged in full struggle, others are threatened. Fear reigns over the world. The present or forthcoming victims tremble for the future, and they think they may improve their

70

situation by flattering those whose aggression they dread. International morality has disappeared. The excuse of these weak peoples is their very weakness, the certainty that they would be abandoned as Ethiopia has been, and between two evils they have chosen the one which the fear of the aggressor leads them to consider the lesser. May God forgive them!

To those States which since the beginning of our trials have continued to give us their moral support, and have unfailingly asserted their unshakable devotion to the provisions of the Covenant, I would, on behalf of my people, voice an expression of our profound gratitude for their faithful friendship.

It is disappointing to the Ethiopian people to observe the attitude of the most powerful States in the world — States that have always proclaimed their devotion to the Covenant, asserted their respect for the undertakings embodied in international treaties, and recalled the sanctity of international contracts as the basis of international morality.

At the request of the most powerful State in the world, the Ethiopian question has been placed on the agenda of the present session of the Council. It has been set out in very indefinite terms: "The consequences arising out of the existing situation in Ethiopia." What is proposed, indeed, is really to ensure the execution of a note attached to the Agreement concluded at Rome on April 16th, 1938, in which the British Ambassador states to the Italian Minister for Foreign Affairs as follows:

'I have the honour to inform Your Excellency that His Majesty's Government, being desirous of removing any obstacle which may at the present time be considered as preventing the freedom of States Members in respect of the recognition of the Italian sovereignty in Ethiopia, intends at the forthcoming meeting of the Council of the League of Nations to take steps with a view to clarifying the situation of States Members in this respect.'

This Note is supplementary to the Protocol of April 16th, 1938, constituting the Anglo-Italian Treaty, and to annexes 5, 6 and 7 of the said Protocol. Annexe 5 contains a statement relating to Lake Tsana. Annexe 6 contains a statement relating to the military obligations of natives of Italian East Africa. Annexe 7 contains a statement relating to the free exercise of religion and the treatment of British religious organisations in Italian East Africa. By this Convention and by these annexes the British Government, so far as it is concerned, has, subject to certain conditions, assumed towards Italy an undertaking to recognise the Italian Government as de jure sovereign of the State of Ethiopia.

By the Note of April 16th, 1938, the British Government entered into a second and supplementary undertaking towards the Italian Government, and did so unconditionally. It undertook to use all its influence with States Members of the League of Nations in order to remove those obstacles which may at the present time be regarded as hampering the liberty of States Members in proceeding to the recognition of Italian sovereignty over Ethiopia.

71

The Council is asked to destroy the protective rôle laid down by the Assembly of the League of Nations on March 11th, 1932, and confirmed by the Assembly of July 4th, 1936, as follows:

'The Assembly of the League of Nations declares that the Members of the League are bound not to recognise any situation, any treaty, any agreement that may have been brought about by means contrary to the Covenant of the League or the Pact of Paris.'

That is how it is proposed to treat the principles of international law and Article 10 of the Covenant by which Members undertake to respect and maintain as against all external agression the territorial integrity and political independence of each Member.

Nevertheless, non-recognition of a conquest by aggression is the least onerous obligation in observing Article 10, since it involves merely a passive attitude. It does not call upon States Members to make any national sacrifice, nor does it lead them to incur any risk of war or reprisals.

Has this passive attitude become today too heavy a burden for those Governments which in order to take up once more with Rome what they call normal diplomatic relations, have thought it necessary to proclaim in one form or another, and always in a way that gives little satisfaction, their fidelity to the principle of the non-recognition of annexation of territory obtained by force?

Today it is the brutal abandonment of this principle which is contemplated, and which even seems to be called for by the powerful British Empire.

I greatly regret that I find myself here opposed to a Government towards which I have the most sincere feelings of admiration and of profound gratitude. It is that Government which in my distress, granted me its generous hospitality. I am forgetful of nothing of what I owe to Great Britain.

I also turn towards the French Government, whose powerful support I received fifteen years ago at the time of the admission of my country to the League of Nations. France has, at all times, been the desinterested adviser both of my predecessors and myself, the adviser whose advice was always listened to. How can I forget all that the past holds of friendship and loyal support?

But I, the sovereign of Ethiopia, have a more imperative duty than any other, and it is the duty to defend my oppressed people, which more than fifty nations of the world proclaimed less than three years ago, to be the victim of an odious aggression. Very respectfully but very firmly, I would ask the British Government itself — and everybody recognises the loyalty, generosity and humanity of that Government — to examine again its proposal regarding the situation of the Ethiopian people.

The interpretation of Article 10 must surely be the interpretation that has been given time after time by the Assembly, even so recently as on October 6th, 1937, with regard to another aggression. Barely seven months ago the Assembly confirmed the principle embodied in the Covenant in the following words: "The Assembly assures China of its moral support and recommends Members of the League of Nations to refrain from any action calculated to weaken the power of resistance of that country and thereby increase its difficulties in the present conflict and also to examine individually the extent to which they might be able to give aid to China."

Today the Council is being asked, in regard to Ethiopia, to recommend to Members of the League of Nations to associate themselves in a measure calculated to weaken the powers of resistance of the Ethiopian people, thereby aggravating its difficulties in its conflict with Italy, and that they should examine individually the extent to which they can assist the aggressor.

As against these defaults, and the proposals that are made, whatever the form they assume, I, legitimate Emperor of Ethiopia, address to all the nations of the world, on behalf of my martyred people, the most energetic protest.

In order to eventuate the flagrant violation of the Covenant, the suggestion made today to the Council invokes the de facto situation in Ethiopia at the present time.

But if it were true — and it is not so — that the invader has broken the resistance of my people, even if in fact he were occupying and administering effectively the territory of my empire — which is not the case — even in those circumstances the proposal submitted to the Council should be set aside without hesitation.

Did not the world hail as one of the most important marks of progress in international law, and as the most effective contribution to the organisation of peace between nations, the principle proclaimed a few years ago by the United States of America, namely, the refusal to grant juridical recognition to the results of aggression?

As sovereign of the Ethiopian people I invoke this principle, for it is my duty to defend the political independence of the Ethiopian people, the territorial integrity of Ethiopia, and at the same time the life, the property and the liberty of each of those individuals and each of those religious or civic institutions which make up the Ethiopian people.

Unhappily, it is true that my people can now expect from States Members of the League of Nations no material support. May I at least ask that the rights of my people should continue to be recognised and that, pending the moment of divine justice, Ethiopia may remain amongst you as the living image of violated right.

Do not say that the Ethiopian people will derive no advantage from that, and that the only result will be a disturbance of international relations. The greatest disturbance that may be caused in relations between peoples is the confirmation and consecration of a violation of right and of law, homage paid to the aggressor, the sacrifice of the victim.

Millions of men and women throughout the world are today anxiously following the deliberations of the League of Nations. They know that this is the tragic hour in which the destiny of the League is to be determined. Being responsible for ensuring respect for the principles of international justice, is the League of Nations about to end its own existence by tearing up, with its own hands, the Covenant which constitutes its sole reason for *existence? The magnificent edifice that has just been reared for the triumph of peace through law, is this henceforth to become an altar reared to the cult of force, a market-place in which the independence of peoples becomes the subject of trafficking, a tomb in which international morality is to be buried?*

My opposition to the suggestions put before the Council derives added force from the actual situation of fact today existing in Ethiopia.

As I have already stated to the League of Nations in my earlier communications, the Italian Government does not exercise control over the greater part of Ethiopian territory. Even in Tigré, which is the province nearest to Eritrea, the Italian base, the Italian troops control merely the towns and areas where garrisons have been installed. The remainder of the province is not under their domination. Garrisons can be supplied with provisions and munitions only by means of aircraft.

The same is true of the province of Begemder, where there is only one Italian garrison at Gondar, which is isolated from the rest of the province and which is fed with supplies by aircraft. In the province of Gojjam there is no Italian domination at all; in the province of Shoa, Italian garrisons are installed at Addis Ababa and Ankober and along the railway toward Jibuti.

In the province of Wallaga, too, Italian garrisons are encamped at Goré, Seyo and Lekempti, and these occupy merely the towns of those names, while the rest of the province is entirely outside their action.

In the provinces of Jimma, Sidamo, Borana, Bale and Wolamo, the situation is the same, only the towns of Jiram, Yirga-Alem, Mega, Goba and Ginir are occupied. All the rest of the territory has had to be evacuated under the pressure of our warriors.

In the province of Harar, only the towns of Harar and Jijiga are under Italian domination. The rest of the province is entirely removed from Italian action.

Finally, there is no Italian control at all over the provinces of Danakil and Aussa.

An annexe to the present statement contains the position presented by the Ethiopian warrior chiefs setting forth the situation and asking for the assistance of the League of Nations, and of the British Government. All those facts are well known. They are fully confirmed by the news that comes from the British and the French colonies that border on Ethiopia.

The Italian Government itself has had to confess that the expenses incurred by the occupation amount each year to thousands of millions of lire, without taking account of the expenditure in 1935 and 1936, which amounted to more than 27,000 million lire.

Despite this enormous expenditure, the exploitation of Ethiopian territory has proved to be impossible. The programme of road construction could not be carried out, not for lack of money, but because it was impossible to work in a country where guerilla warfare continues implacable, and will continue until the territory is evacuated by the Italians or until the Ethiopian people have been exterminated.

In order to break down the resistance of my people and its refusal to aban-

74

don that independence which it had enjoyed for more than thirty centuries, the Italian authorities are counting upon propaganda with the object of demoralising the people, and in this they make great play with the abandonment of Ethiopia by the League of Nations.

In Europe the Italian Government proclaims lofty indifference towards the attitude of the Powers and of the League of Nations, but in reality it is endeavouring to obtain the recognition of its conquests which it would then present to the Ethiopian peoples as a condemnation of Ethiopia by the League. Is not that a demonstration of the practical value of the principle of non-recognition by the League of annexation by force?

From the existing de facto situation, as it really is in Ethiopia at present, juridical consequences that are very clear follow. The fact is that war is continuing. International law in time of war grants the belligerent who occupies a certain point in foreign territory certain temporary, provisional and limited powers.

States outside the conflict have the right to maintain, with the military and civil authorities of the occupying Power, certain temporary, provisional, limited relations, concerned with the defence of the interests of their nationals resident in the occupied territories.

International law absolutely prohibits the belligerent making any annexation, and it prohibits any Power that is foreign to the conflict from recognising the occupant as the legal sovereign. Thus the de facto situation does strengthen and supplement the provisions of the Covenant and of the Pact of Paris, which in the most categorical way prohibit de jure recognition of annexation, which would be recognising the conquest of territory by force.

I am, of course, aware that to justify its action the British Government urges lofty preoccupations. Nothing less is at stake than action taken with a view to favouring general appeasement through the sacrifice of a nation, and this sacrifice is made dependent on the satisfactory settlement — satisfactory so far as England and France are concerned — of the Spanish question.

I would ask that this suggestion be set aside. Is it not absolutely incompatible with the spirit of the Covenant to sacrifice a State Member of the League in order to ensure the tranquility of other Powers? Is it thus one serves the international ideal to which the British and French Governments have so constantly proclaimed their devotion? Do not the small States see the risk by which they are threatened if they consent to creating so terrible a precedent?

Moreover, even supposing that the suggestion made to the Council by the British Government came within the competence of any organ of the League of Nations whatsoever, I would, in the most energetic way, dispute the suggestion that this is a matter that can be dealt with by the Council.

In a matter that is of vital importance both to my country and also to the League of Nations, in a matter where in fact what is at stake is a decision, a recommendation, a wish (or some other formula) tending directly or indirectly to free State Members from the obligation that they assumed when they signed the Covenant, to invite them in practice to recognise de jure the annexation of Ethiopia by Italy, I assert that a competent authority to discuss such a question is the Assembly of the League of Nations and the Assembly alone. In this respect Ethiopia would invoke the authority of the United Kingdom Foreign Secretary, who on December 16th, 1936, stated in the House of Commons: "The question of the recognition of the Italian conquest of Ethiopia and the exclusion of that country from the League of Nations is a matter for the Assembly of the League of Nations. It is the Assembly that must take a decision in the light of circumstances."

Ethiopia protests against all subtleties of procedure, the object of which would be to evade the rules of competence which are clearly written in the Covenant. As the delegate of Portugal said, nothing can be more repugnant and more hypocritical than the strangling of a nation by procedure.

Will the League of Nations agree to any such thing? The Covenant does not allow it.

I formally ask, as I am entitled to do, that the Council should refer this question to the Assembly of the League of Nations, before whom it is in fact already laid, and I ask, as is my right, that the Assembly of the League of Nations should proceed to this examination.

The distinguished representative of Great Britain has just put the question very clearly. He said there are at present two ideals in conflict, the ideal of devotion to a lofty aim, and the ideal of ensuring peace as a practical measure. He asserted that it is often difficult to reconcile what is ideally just with what is possible in practice. He asserted that it is the essential mission of the League to maintain peace. Yes, the League has as its essential object the maintenance of peace. But there are different ways to maintain peace, there is the maintenance of peace through right, and there is peace at any price. Ethiopia firmly believes that the League of Nations has no freedom of choice in this matter. It would be committing suicide, if, after having been created to maintain peace through right, it were to abandon that principle, and adopt instead the principle of peace at any price, even the price of the immolation of a State Member at the feet of its aggressor.

In concluding this statement, in which with all the strength of mind and heart at my disposal I have endeavoured to work for the defence of my people, I cannot refrain from reverting to the year 1923, the year in which my Empire was admitted to the League of Nations. I then assumed an undertaking to lead my people along the path of progress of western civilisation, which seemed to me to be something superior to the state at which my country had arrived. Since that time I spared no effort in order to ensure success. Important results had been achieved. I note with deep sorrow that all my work has been overthrown, blotted out by the Italian aggression.

But one unexpected result has ensued in Ethiopia, as indeed has been the case in other countries. The Italian aggression has brought the Ethiopian Chiefs more closely round their Emperor than at any other period. In the document that I am communicating to the League of Nations there are included letters of affection from Ethiopian Chiefs and from the people. As the Emperor of Ethiopia, basing myself on the faithful devotion of my chiefs, my warriors, on the affection of my people, being desirous of putting an end if possible to their sufferings, I repeat the declaration that I have made already in the League of Nations. I am prepared now, as I was previously, to discuss any proposal for a solution which, even at the cost of sacrifice, would ensure to my people the free development of their civilisation, of their independence.

But should this appeal remain without reponse war against Italy will be continued whatever happens, until the triumph of right and justice has been won.

I ask the League of Nations to refuse to take any step that may be asked of it with a view to encouraging the Italian aggressor by sacrificing his victim to him.

Excerpts from speeches of the delegates of Member States at the Council are here reproduced for they show how supine an attitude the League had taken to this fundamental question of collective security:

M. Bonnet (France): "Mr. President......... We are all grateful to Lord Halifax for the frankness with which he has reminded us of the facts of the problem and the reasons for the action that his Government took...... I will not attempt to conceal the feelings of profound sadness with which all Members of the Council have taken up and will conclude this discussion. The presence amongst us of His Majesty the Emperor Haile Selassie indeed, so far as it is possible to do so, increases the emotion that we feel. But there is another feeling that everything possible has been accomplished........."

M. Litvinoff (Soviet Russia): ".........One might go so far as to say that resolutions on non-recognition were adopted when it became obvious that Members of the League were unwilling to inflict more telling blows on the aggressor, or when other action undertaken against him was being brought to an end... When the British Government puts forward its motion to grant freedom of action to all League members, it bases its principal argument on the fact that many members of the League in violation of League resolutions, have already taken steps towards recognising the annexation of Ethiopia, and therefore the same opportunity should be afforded to others. This may be fair from the standpoint of equality of obligations......... If we once admit that principle, we may expect that it will be sufficient for one or a few members of the League to break one of its decisions — and that may easily happen, in the present state of international morality — for all other members of the League, one by one, to follow them. We cannot admit that breaches of international obligations are examples to be followed."

M. Petresco-Comnene (Rumania): ".........Like the representatives of the United Kingdom and of France, I consider that we should recognise clearly with regard to this question, that, in the present circumstances and in the very interest of the cause that we serve, it is essential to leave each State Member of the League of Nations free to appreciate for itself what decisions should be taken..."

M. Komarnicki (Poland): "Whatever may be the result of the present discussions they cannot in any way influence the attitude which the Polish Government has taken up in a question that comes within its own sovereignty and in the form that was deemed to be most appropriate. Nevertheless, as a Member of the Council, I desire to emphasise the view that the Polish Government is of opinion that an exchange of views between the Members of the Council with regard to the consequence to be deduced from the existing situation in Ethiopia may be of some value, more particularly if it contributes towards the dissipation of doubts which certain Members of the League still entertain in that connection."

M. Sandler (Sweden): "........The Swedish Government shares the idea which has just been expressed namely, that each of the Members of the League of Nations is entitled to determine its own attitude.'

M. van Langenhove (Belgium): "My Government was led recently, in conformity with the example of several Members of the League, to normalise its diplomatic relations with Italy........."

M. Garcia-Calderon (Peru): "........Taking account of this state of mind after having listened to the remarks made by the representatives of France and Great Britain, we are able to understand that the facts are there, that realities frequently command us........."

Mr. Wellington Koo (China): "........The principle of non-recognition of territorial changes effected by force is implicit in the Covenant. It is the foundation upon which we hope to build a new and better world order wherein nations will be able to live in peace and security under the reign of law........ The Chinese Government will content itself with reserving its position in regard to the question of the principles involved."

Mr. Jordan (New Zealand): "........The New Zealand Government cannot support any proposal which would involve, either directly or by implication, approval of a breach of the Covenant."

Mr. Costa Du Rels (Bolivia): "........ My country has also had an opportunity to state its adhesion to the principles which we consider to be fundamental for the settlement of conflicts, whilst voting for the Assembly Resolution of July 4th, 1936........."

M. Bahramy (Iran): "I have nothing to add to what has already been said. In the present circumstances my Government too will resume its freedom of action."

M. Munters (speaking as representative of Latvia): "May I ask the indulgence of my colleagues to make a very short statement in my capacity as representative of Latvia? The Latvian Government hold the view that since collective action in the Italo-Ethiopian dispute was explicitly abondoned, the question of the consequences arising out of the existing situation in Ethiopia is one for each Member of the League to decide for itself."

Mr. Munters (speaking as President of the Council): "........ We have been asked whether we share the opinion that the question of the recognition of Italy's position in Ethiopia is one for each Member of the League to decide for itself in the light of its own situation and its own obligations.

"Secondly, in regard to the question just defined, we have not been invited to take a formal decision......... It is, however, clear that, in spite of regrets which have been expressed, the great majority of the Members of the Council feel that, so far as the question which we are now discussing is concerned, it is for the individual Members of the League to determine their attitude in the light of their own situation and their own obligations."

His Majesty the Emperor, having returned to Bath where he maintained residence during his term of exile, continued through public protests both to the League and the world press to stress the need of justice for his country and, above all, consideration for the preservation of the League of Nations. In addressing the League of Nations on October 1st, 1938, His Majesty included in his letter to M. Joseph Avenol these words:

Ethiopia, despite her sufferings, considers it her duty in the present unsettled state of Europe, not to create fresh difficulties and to refrain from any act that might appear likely to complicate the international situation. Nevertheless, it is my duty to defend in every circumstance and on every occasion the cause of the Ethiopian people, which has not renounced, and never will renounce, its independence.

In His note to the same source on January 1st, 1940, again from Bath, the Emperor declared:

Nevertheless, at the moment when the two greatest Powers who are members of the League of Nations have courageously undertaken to oppose by their arms the accomplishment of a new abuse by violence, Your Excellency will understand that I recall with particular emotion the events of four years ago, of which my country was the victim.

The succession of acts of violence which since then have fallen upon Europe have clearly demonstrated that it was vain to hope to appease the appetites of aggressors by the sacrifice of the independence of one nation or another.

I have confidence that my people, who continue with indomitable courage to oppose armed resistance to the invaders, will find in the new organisation of peace which the entire world demands, guarantees sufficient for a free and happy existence.

The League abdicated its responsibility to Ethiopia, repudiated the stand it had originally taken to punish the agressor and, as future events showed, committed suicide. Thus another era in the search for an effective instrument for world peace ended in disappointment, especially for the small states, whose cause was so ably represented by His Imperial Majesty in the defence of Ethiopia.

CHAPTER 7

The Liberation Campaign

The liberation of Ethiopia, the first country to be freed in World War II, could be considered the opening stage in the series of victorious events leading up to the end of that world conflagration. There were several contributing factors which led up to this restoration, among them the position taken by the Emperor, even when the situation looked very dark.

The Emperor's activies through the League of Nations for the redemption of his country are dealt with elsewhere in this book; it is however known that they were unique and historic. He boldly and lucidly told the fifty nations and the world that justice must ultimately prevail. He indicated in words and his patriots demonstrated in deeds that League expediency was at best temporary. His Majesty devoted all his energies and prayed for the fulfilment of his dream that one day he would return to his country and people. He meanwhile studied plans for fulfilling his hope of liberation.

During the period of the League's committal to the case of Italy's aggression against Ethiopia, when member states tried to turn their backs against the country of the Negus — the victim — in addressing a message to the Secretary General on September 10th, 1937, from Bath, His Majesty the Emperor said:

Our faith in the League of Nations remains firm. However limited our power in respect of material resources, our moral strenght supports us. and we are confident that a day will come when the League of Nations will succesfully help us to return freedom to our country, and to see that it rises from its fallen state. When that is achieved it will mean that the League has established those rights which form the principal basis of peace.

The League, however did not rise to the occasion and died as a result.

In the other statements made by His Majesty the Emperor and also in his appeals in his exile in the United Kingdom these sentiments of hope in final justice and the cause of his country invariably characterised them all.

Taking cognizance of the changing world situation, His Majesty the Emperor watched the fulfilment of his prophecy before the League Assembly in 1936. Hitler in 1939 began to tear up the map of Europe while Mussolini basked in the sunshine of a temporary "Africa Orientale". The two totalitarian leaders endeavoured to merge their empires and their military might in a world war of further conquest. The stage was then set for the United Kingdom, which had so much part in the original downfall of Ethiopia, forced by circumstances, to lead in the

80

climax to the drama which changed the tragedy to a happy ending. Had His Majesty given up the struggle, had he despaired of the ultimate end, had he capitulated to the offers of Il Duce, and had he been swayed by the attitude of many of the League Members who considered Ethiopia's doom sealed, a *fait accompli*, no one knows what would have be the turn of events.

When the Emperor left Addis Ababa for Europe in voluntary exile on May 2nd, 1936, the reasons for his leaving were clear.

He expressed them on the stop-over in Jerusalem in his message to the Secretary General of the League of Nations, Mr. Eric Drummond, in which he said:

When the matter which arose between Ethiopia and Italy started, we made all the efforts we could that peace might not be disturbed. Until Italy poured down on us as it were a rain of poisonous gas, we fought for our country in a proper manner. But when poison came down like rain upon our army and upon our peaceful folk, we felt that we must recognise the impossibility of any strong defence against it. If we had put up a strong defence, the result would have been a vain annihilation by poison of the Ethiopian people. Therefore we request that the League of Nations may now continue for the future the support and efforts it has previously made to secure respect for the Covenant of the League; and that, in view of Italy's transgression of many and various obligations which have been accepted by the countries of the world, the League of Nations neither recognise as pertaining to Italy the territory she has seized by improper and outlawed force of arms, nor accept Italian claims to sovereignty over any such territory.

This could be considered, though remote, the first contribution to the campaign of liberation; for, had His Majesty the Emper bowed to conquest because of the overwhelming power of the enemy in the battlefield, his country would have been lost and the cause with it. Had he not with his own hands manned the guns and in person stayed with his men in the battlefield at Maichaw, and experienced the trials of war, he would not have been in a position to explain the situation accurately and in detail to the League of Nations and the world.

Maintaining his dignity and poise and also expressing his purpose to see achieved the liberation of his country, he further gave direction and meaning to the resistance at home. Constant contact, by word and through representatives such as Lorenzo Taezaz, Colonel Sandford and others kept the morale of his people. In fact, through Ethiopian intelligence which was very active and well organised, the Emperor knew from day to day what was taking place in Ethiopia during his exile abroad.

It is undoubtedly a fact that Ethiopian patriots were kept firm in their sustained campaign against the occupiers, primarily because of their belief that their Emperor would eventually return. His Majesty the Emperor, true to his trust had, by all means at his disposal, kept the fire of patriotism ever burning. This was one factor which the British allies openly recognised. Were the Ethiopian patriots and the resistance non-existent, not only would Italy have consolidated her ill-gotten gains but the chances of the East African Campaign in clearing the Italians from the Ethiopian soil would have been by far less. It would have upset the time schedule of the Middle East and North African campaigns and surely would have given aid and comfort to General Rommel in his North African assault.

The Ethiopians, like their Emperor, never gave up the hope of the day when their country would be finally free from the abuses of the enemy. In diverse ways His Majesty the Emperor kept in close touch with the Ethiopian patriots. They were promised a sign of his coming. Despite the hardships they encountered they were hoping for the day when they would see their sovereign in person.

The Italians, in their uneasy occupation, had to face the harassing of these patriots. Ras Ababa Aragai, Dejazmach Balcha, Nagash and other well-known patriot leaders kept the occupiers busy. The Italians also had to face the diplomatic combat which the Emperor posed for them, not only in the League of Nations, but in the arena of world opinion.

In June, 1940 the Emperor was flown out from England to Khartoum to assist in raising the inhabitants of his Kingdom against the Italians and to cooperate in a guerilla campaign which was being organised by Brigadier Sandford and Colonel Wingate (Major-General Orde Wingate, deceased) in Western Ethiopia. Arrangements were made for the Emperor to reside at Khartoum and there he stayed until the middle of January, 1941. He then entered Ethiopia from the west to join Brigadier Sandford who, with Colonel Wingate, had been in Gojjam since the previous August, organising patriot activities with the determination and gallantry since recognised as having contributed immensely to the campaigns of the British Armies under Generals Cunningham and Platt.

While the Emperor was in Khartoum preparing plans to activate the patriots in their important part in the liberation of their country, pioneering work had to be carried forward and completed.

Upon His Majesty's arrival in Khartoum on July 3rd, 1940 he found the British had not been wholly idle. Five depôts of arms, food and Maria Theresa Thalers (the then Ethiopian currency) had been established under the guard of an embryo frontier battalion. Major Cheeseman who was familiar with Gojjam had been appointed as special intelligence officier in Khartoum. The Emperor was thus at once able to make known his presence at the frontier, but many (until he actually re-entered his country) believed in the Italian story that he had died in exile. [1]

What joy was felt in the hearts of the people when, after arrival at Khartoum His Imperial Majesty made his first broadcast to his people from the Sudan!

---

[1]   Lord Rennel of Rodd, *British Military Administration in Africa.*

This voice that you hear is mine, your Emperor, Haile Selassie I. Heroes of my country!

Our fathers shed their blood and broke their bones in handing down to us our country in freedom, and for a long time now we have laboured that it might stride on towards a high degree of civilisation. Seeing this, our blood-thirsty enemy, Italy, violated our frontiers and waged aggressive war against us. This you all know. For our part, after putting up such defence as we could, we went to those countries which were our friends, to the League of Nations, to ask for help. During the time we stayed there, engaged in the consequent conversations, you heroes of Ethiopia, without sheating your swords, without turning your backs, without furling your flag, refused to be ruled by foreigners; making your natural valour your weapon, and trusting solely in the God of Ethiopia, you struggled bravely with a cruel enemy who far surpassed you in the quantity of his arms, persisting by day and by night, in the forests and in the ravines. As you can now see, you have made it possible for yourselves to witness the fruits of the efforts and of the sacrifices you have made in the course of this five years of continuous struggle.

At the time when Italy violated our frontiers and invaded our country, Great Britain and France acted in such wise that she might be punished by financial difficulties, so she has now under the wing of Germany, started war against them. And since they have given us their assistance, we have got what we wished for and come to your aid. The powerful air forces of England and France are flying in the air over Ethiopia, where the Italians hold sway; in Europe, Italy is receiving her repayment from aeroplanes and artillery. Her infantry too shall not escape you brave Ethiopians in whom I trust. Wherever you are, patriots of Ethiopia, fight the Italians vigorously. And my countrymen who are willy-nilly, under the Italian heel, do not believe the lying pretences which Italy puts across you, to the effect that England and France are going to be defeated. Those of you who from henceforth injure your country by being tools of the Italians will hand on to your posterity a curse which shall not be erased from the page of your history.

Criminal governments have arisen in the world. Therefore the age in which we live is a time when human beings are uprooted from their country, sundered from their kin, and chased like wild beasts. So do not forget the proverb which runs: "if threads are joined they can bind the lion." Great and small, adult and child, from border to border, lift up your arms against Italy!

In the same month in a proclamation to the people scattered by the British aeroplanes, His Majesty called them to the height of their responsibility to their country and in defence of their motherland. The message further reiterated that allies were behind Ethiopia and summoned all, even those who had gone over to the enemy, to join the liberating patriots. This proclamation, which brought a large number of deserters from the enemy camp, was to some commentators, the turning point of the deflection of the Italian native troops from the enemy vanguard. In part this proclamation said:

People of Ethiopia, chiefs and patriots.

*All the free peoples of the world admire the way in which you have con-
tinued during the last five years to contend with our enemy oppressor, in
courage and unceasing hope, with your strength ever unbroken. You have
gained their friendship. The tortures and sacrifices you have suffered, as
well as your courage and hope, have not been in vain. The day of your
deliverance has come.*

*As from to-day the government of Great Britain has offered us the aid
of its unrivalled military might, that we may obtain our complete freedom.*

I have, then, come to you.

*Let us praise God who has turned His face of mercy towards us. Then
let us praise and remember our heroes who fell on the field of battle, and
those Ethiopians, to the number of many thousands, whom the Italian
Fascists cruelly massacred.*

People of Ethiopia, chiefs and patriots.

*The government of Italy has begun to make war upon Great Britain. The
reason for his so doing is that, when our aggressive enemy invaded our
country, Great Britain prevented him from obtaining supplies and arms,
and further contended for the honouring of the principles of the League
of Nations.*

Now you know what you must do.

*All of you who have gone over to the enemy, help your country by
joining the Ethiopian patriots forthwith. Not one of you shall be a tool of
the enemy, whether by speech or by act. Make it impossible for the
enemy to move, by ambushing him wherever he is to be found and by
cutting his communications; and so weaken and crush him.*

The advance guard of the Emperor were quick to organise their counter-
propaganda machine under the direction of Mr. G. L. Steer, to give the
people the news of the Emperor's arrival. Besides, a dozen identical letters,
printed in Amharic script on stout linen and sealed by General Platt in
the name of the United Kingdom Government had been sent to the
District Commissioner at Gedaref shortly before the Italian declaration of
war. They were held in a secret envelope until the night of the 10th
June.

Then they were opened and despatched to eleven of the Ethiopian Patriot
Chiefs of Gojjam, Armacheho, Walkait and Begemder. They contained a
few simple sentences announcing war between Britain and Italy, and
offering arms, munitions, money and food to those Chiefs who would send
mules to the Sudan frontiers to fetch them. The runners were ready at
Gedaref to take them in their forked sticks to the high plateau of
Ethiopia.

There were already certain Chiefs on the frontiers of Gallabat, asking
for weapons and for news of the Emperor. The first single-shot Martini
rifles were issued to them — not wonderful firearms, but this was a time
when parts of the British Army in England were training with sticks. They

84

were invited to co-operate in attacks on the Italian post at Metemma, and did take part in two attacks. (²)

It was the task of the British Mission which entered Ethiopia on the 12th August 1940, to give news of the Emperor's arrival in the Sudan, to meet and instruct patriot leaders as to the most useful part they could play, to arrange a route for the entry of arms and ammunition and so to play on the nerves of the Italian forces in Gojjam as to discourage them from any offensive action against the Sudan or reinforcement of their troops elsewhere. In this way the revolt was to be spread at the fitting moment, neither too early nor too late, throughout the whole Ethiopian Empire. Disaster to the Mission was at all costs to be avoided, and it was considered that it would be better to send no mission at all than that it should be captured or in other ways liquidated by the enemy.

There were five British Members to the Mission; Col. D. A. Sandford, Capt. R. A. Critchley, Lt. C. Drew, R.A.M.C., as Medical Officer, Sergeant-Major G. S. Gray, and Signalman T. W. Whitmore. With them went as delegation from the Emperor, a remarkable group of young Ethiopians who have all since made their mark. (³)

Mangasha Jambare of Gojjam had already received General Platt's message with a *feu de joie* from all muskets, and with Dejazmach Nagash, the other leading Gojjam patriot, he rapidly beat the drums in the country villages around the Italian forts, levying hundreds of mules and men for the great convoy that would go down to the bad lands on the Sudan border. They had met Sandford on his way in and had fought with a strong Italian patrol a few days earlier. For a time the Italians believed that they had broken them up, but on a day late in August a dozen of them swam across the River Atbara and saw the young English District Commissioner on the other side.

These men were back in Gojjam in October carrying in their hands photographs of the Emperor and of the aircraft that he had stepped from. His proclamation was read in their market places. Gradually a people who after five years of the Italians had come to disbelieve every printed word, who had seen nothing but Italian aeroplanes, armoured cars and knew nothing for certain except that Kassala, Gallabat and Kurmuk (and probably Somaliland) had been taken by Italy from Britain, very gradually these people, tired by the hopeless tussle with the Italians, began to see that the opportunity for independence and the despoiling of the invader was at hand. (⁴)

On the 20th January, the Emperor Haile Selassie left his Vickers Valentia in a landing ground cleared at Omedla, walked a short distance with his cousin Ras Kassa, the Ichege Gabra Giorgis, and his two sons, the Crown Prince and the Duke of Harar, and found himself on the western bank of the dry bed of the River Dinder. Descending, he was saluted by a Sudanese Guard of Honour and a speech of dignified farewell and of good

(²)   H. M. Stationery Office, *Abyssinian Campaigns.*
(³)   Christine Sandford, *Ethiopia under Haile Selassie.*
(⁴)   H. M. Stationery Office, *ibid.*

wishes was read to him by a Senior Officer on behalf of General Platt, "detained by events on another front." They crossed the bed and on the other side the Ethiopian Flag was raised on Ethiopian soil by a Royal hand for the first time for nearly five years. A Company of the 2nd Ethiopian (Refugee) battalion saluted as smartly as they had been able to learn in the short time available, the management of their American Springfield rifles. ([5]) On this symbolic occasion His Majesty said:

Today when I tread the soil of our country, I beg you to convey my thanks to Major-General Platt, Commander-in-Chief of the Sudan forces, for the good wishes he has, through your instrumentality, sent to me in his own name and in that of the officers and men in his Command.

Great is my joy now that I go to my people, who with lifted arms and courageous breast have remained resisting the invader for their freedom's sake, waiting for five years the help which I bring on my return: and who expect me with yearning.

Please inform General Platt of my full confidence that my people will completely liberate my country with the help of Great Britain, who has lifted her mighty arms to restore to freedom at the cost of heavy sacrafice, those peoples who have been forcibly oppressed and have become the prey of Fascism and Nazism. Assure him that I and my people remain fully confident that the help we have secured from our ally Great Britain will break the wings of the common enemy of Ethiopia and of Great Britain.

When a task involving very great trial and trouble meets with succes, the taste of joy is very sweet to the performer. Please express the desire I feel at this time of trial for the people of both our countries, that we shall together rejoice to see that day which draws near for assuming the crown of victory — a day long awaited by my army, by all the forces of Great Britain, and not least by that well-tried army which is under the leadership, so fully competent and wise, of Major General Platt, whom I recognise as Commander-in-Chief of the forces in the Sudan, a neighbour of Ethiopia.

I hope too that you veterans of war, who are assembled here at the place where there begins a new history of community between Ethiopia and mighty Great Britain, you who are chosen to be chief participants in Ethiopia's deeds of warfare, will be participants in this good fortune.

Nor shall I forget the British commander and the officers with him, who came first to knock upon the gates of victory, and who are now to be found amidst my army.

At this present moment when I arrive at the confines of my country and rejoin my people, I recall to mind the splendid people of Great Britain, who comforted me with kind hospitality. My gratitude towards these people, who felt so deeply the plight of myself and of my people, and who comforted me with their sympathy at the time of my bitter trial, will never disappear from my heart.

And then I shall not forget the friendly welcome I met with during my

([5])   G. L. Steer, *Sealed and Delivered.*

86

stay at Khartoum, from the authorities, from the government officials and from the people.
I thank you too for the good wishes you have extended to me on your own behalf.

The Emperor issued a Decree pardoning all those Ethiopians who had betrayed their trust, which said:

Since God in His goodness has turned His face of mercy upon all of us, I pardon all of you your past faults wherein you have before now injured your country and your Emperor, whether by force or by consent, whether within the orbit of the Italians or without. So from border to border, lift up your arms against our enemy, who came with intent to destroy your race, to plunder your heritage, to obliterate your very name. Drive them clean out of Ethiopia.

Italy is being harried without respite by the armed forces of Great Britain, in the air, on the sea, and on land. And the soldiers of Italy who are in our country will not escape from the heroes of Ethiopia in whom I trust.

To the Government and people of Great Britain, who in our time of bitter trial received and helped me with such kindness as touches the heart, I express before the world, in my own name and in yours, my thanks and my undying gratitude towards them.

Omedla was the anti-climax of Italy's over half a century's dream of the conquest of Ethiopia. As the Frontier Battalion, No. 4 Company, brought the patriots arms and news of the coming of their Emperor, their hearts were full — they were overjoyed. It inspired their hope, strengthened their courage, and steeled their determination to continue the struggle. On that day when His Majesty the Emperor alighted from the plane and planted the flag in the dry bed of the River Dinder, and when the first Imperial Decree was issued under its shadow, the chances for the restoration of the ancient Kingdom were assured.

The dry ravine, a mere unnoticed geographical feature, on the border of Ethiopia and the Sudan, Omedla became, in 1941, a shrine made hallowed by the rehoisting of the Ethiopian flag to flutter in the free air of what was then to be a revived and independent country. Omedla was more than that; it heralded the succesful campaign of the liberation when Ethiopia, assisted by valiant allies, brought the Italian wolf to book.

All around, hidden from aircraft in the bush were thousands of camels of the Sudan plains about to be driven without mercy over the hard and unattempted mountains to accomplish the strangest restoration of modern times. They would have to be sacrificed; no other transport could carry the supplies into Gojjam to garrison her for the coming rains. (6)

The Italian flag, temporarily unfurled over Ethiopia, was about to be disdainfully pulled down. The uneasy occupation was tottering because of the news of the Emperor's coming. Their propaganda machine had told the people that their Sovereign was dead and would never return. Even this did not give them peace. The Patriot Movement which His Majesty and his allies were ready to exploit in the liberation of their country existed

(6) H. M. Stationery Office, *op. cit.*

primarily in the Amhara areas and was strongest in Gojjam, Armacheho and Begemder (the country round Gondar). This was the zone to which General Platt had already sent his letters offering arms to those who would go to the Sudan and fetch them and to which Wingate, of revered memory in Ethiopia, as Commanding Officer, blazed the trail. There was also revolt in Shoa, east of Addis Ababa, which was fed from Jibuti by men under General Le Gentilhomme who remained loyal to the cause.

The liberation campain and especially the part played by His Majesty the Emperor began under circumstances which were rather trying. In the Sudanese capital many months elapsed before things started to take place. The Emperor was given the promise and was flown to Khartoum with the clear purpose of stimulating a climactic resistance to dislodge the occupiers. He was also promised the necessary tools with which to do the job. His emissaries and a British Mission had informed the people of the Emperor's return. The rebellion which was always in the minds of his patriots was awaiting his arrival and was expecting effective action. The months spent in Khartoum without decisive action were not only distressing to His Majesty the Emperor, they added to the Emperor's anxieties. Deserters were coming across the frontiers; refugees in Kenya were prevented from coming to join their Emperor. Those who entered the Sudan were gathered into camps awaiting fitting up and training. Neither the many interviews with General Platt nor his complaints to Mr. Anthony Eden, who had at that time arrived in Khartoum for a military conference, left him optimistic of the situation.

It was not until Major Orde Wingate arrived in October that the drama started to move. Confirmed by General Wavell as Chief Officer for Rebel Activities, from the moment that Wingate reached Khartoum, he acted as a man charged with a mission of the rightness of which he was convinced. The first conference with His Imperial Majesty reads:

"I bring you most respectful greetings, Sire, and my warm personal ad-miration." He waited while this was translated into Amharic, and then went on:

"In 1935 fifty-two nations let you and your country down. That act of agression led to this war. It shall be the first to be avenged. I come as adviser to you and the forces that will take you back to your country and your throne. We offer you freedom and an equal place among the nations. But it will be no sort of place if you have no share in your own liberation. You will take the leading part in what is to come."

The Emperor reflected upon Wingate and his words. "What part can I play? he finally said. "Nothing is being done. They have even prevented my escaped troops from coming here from Kenya. I sit here and time passes. I am being used as a pawn."

Wingate said: "That is not so. You will play your part. I remind you of an ancient proverb: 'If I am not for myself, who will be with me?' You must trust to the justice of your cause."

Haile Selassie smiled. "Yes, Major Wingate. But can I also trust to the justice of your superiors?"

88

"You have my word upon it", said Wingate. (⁷)

General Wingate kept his word and took the initiative in assisting the Emperor to turn the patriots into a fighting force. He knew that the revolt was being organized within the Gojjam area by Brigadier Sandford and flew against personal hazards to Sakala to confer with him to ascertain the local conditions within Ethiopia. Less than a fortnight after consultations with Sandford, Orde Wingate left with General Platt and General Cunningham (commanding South and East African troops in Kenya) for a conference in Cairo with General Wavell. He outlined his plan of operation by which he believed he could take over Gojjam and harry the Italians. At the end of the conference General Wavell had agreed. Wingate was promoted to a Lieutenant Colonel and given official permission to proceed with his plan. Colonel Sandford was also promoted to Brigadier.

Facing many pressing problems Wingate espoused the cause, trained the Refugee Battalions, organized his campaign and led the patriot forces with camel transport up the steep cliffs to Gojjam and into the interior of Ethiopia proper.

The lorries carrying His Imperial Majesty and his retinue were led by Major Boyle, commanding the 2nd Patriot Battalion. The sufferings and hardships of the Ethiopian campain were borne resolutely by His Majesty the Emperor together with Wingate and his men. The Emperor even demonstrated how to fish in a pool with a mosquito net, providing the party with its supper one evening when they stopped at the 'Elephants' Water Hole. He never complained about the hardships, and put his shoulder to the chassis when a lorry overturned or stuck in the sand.

Gideon Force (as Wingate called his army for obvious reasons) consisted of four Sudanese Bren companies, four companies of variously armed Ethiopian Patriots, an Ethiopian mortar platoon of four three-inch mortars, a miscellaneous group of radio sets and signallers, the staff of Sandford's Mission, and three Operational Centres consisting of a British officer and a Sudanese platoon, stiffened with what troops they could pick up locally. In all, these came to a total of 50 British officers, 20 British N.C.O.'s, 800 Ethiopian troops and 800 Sudanese troops, plus the members of the camel transport company.

No aircraft was available after the first few days, and Wingate's pleas for air support were repeatedly ignored. There is no doubt that if planes had been forthcoming at one point in the campain, Gideon Force could have driven the 35,000 well-equiped Italian troops in the Gojjam into complete surrender and take over the capital of Addis Ababa, long before the troops of the conventional armies threatened it. For what may well have been reasons of policy, however, this aid from the air was not given; and Wingate resented it bitterly.

By the end of April Gideon Force had driven the whole of the Italian Army out of Gojjam, despite urgent orders to it from Rome to stand fast. When Wingate handed in his command, the total number of prisoners and

(⁷)   Leonard Mosley, *Gideon Goes to War.*

war material captured, areas cleared and casualties inflicted by his troops was: Prisoners — Italian nationals, 282 Officers, 800 Other Ranks and Colonial Troops, 14,500. Four Artillery field guns, 8 pack guns, 60 heavy and 161 light machine guns, 4 mortars, 12,000 rifles, 5 million rounds of ammunition, 4 radio sets, 2,000 mules and 300 horses. The casualities were: 1,450 killed and 2,125 wounded. [8]

When Mussolini decided to join Hitler in 1940 and declared war against the allies, it was after calculating on the strength he had amassed in East Africa. The necessity to free Ethiopia and limitrophe territories from the grip of the central powers was a prime one, and His Majesty's part fell in as an important act of the whole drama. This might, of necessity, had to be destroyed. The Ethiopian campaign of liberation was a far-reaching contribution. Italian military power in East Africa, according to the book, "The Abyssinian Campains", official story of the conquest of Italian East Africa, was broken by a gigantic pincer movement. The northern arm consisted of forces based on the Sudan under General Platt; the southern arm of the forces based on Kenya under General Cunningham; the northern arm which conquered Eritrea and broke the core of all Italian resistance in East Africa at Keren; the southern conquered Italian Somaliland, was the operative factor in the recapture of British Somaliland and opened Addis Ababa for the return of the Emperor. Simultaneously with the closing of the two arms of the pincer the Emperor entered Abyssinia across the Sudan frontiers and finally was received in his capital. These were the three primary movements in the East African campaign — the northern attack, the southern attack, the return of the Emperor. After these primary events, there were secondary campaigns but the great pincer and the return of the Emperor meant the military and political end of the Italian East African Empire.

General Cunningham would have found far greater difficulty in reaching Addis Ababa if General Platt had not reached Keren; but General Platt could not have fought his way so swiftly to Keren and might not have won his decisive victory there, if General Cunningham had not been fighting his way to Addis Ababa. For in spite of the drain on the garrison of the capital to defend Keren, General Cunningham found between 10,000 and 15,000 armed enemies in Addis Ababa alone; with seven further enemy divisions to the south of it — some within easy reach. The victories in the North and in the South were a joint victory, of which it is hardly possible to exaggerate either the local or the distant repercussions.

The joint victory removed most of the continent and a whole ocean from the strategical map. These victories made available in other threatres of war forces which kept alive the hope of victory in the Middle East and therefore the hope of victory in the war as a whole. General Wavell has taken upon himself the blame for his miscalculations which lost the ground but not by any means all the fruits of his conquest of Cyrenaica. All the more reason for giving him the credit for his calculations. If he

[8]   Leonard Mosley, *op. cit.*

90

enumerates the bricks he dropped, others must enumerate the bricks he made with so little straw. Not a man, nor a gun, nor an aeroplane, nor a tank was left one moment too long on any one battlefield.

So now, after Keren, only one division and a few guns and aeroplanes were left to drive the northern attack through to its end at Amba Alagi. The South Africans were already racing up the road to Dessie to complete their job and be released for service in Egypt. There were still forbidding posititions to take and fine exploits to perform. But all the rest of the campaign was essentially "mopping-up" operations.

Though the Emperor crossed the frontier on the 20th January, it was not until the 6th February that he arrived on horseback below his 9,000 foot headquarters, the Rock Belaya and that with a suite reduced to three British and three Ethiopian officers. All attempts to break through the bush with motor transport failed. (9)

A saga, if there ever was one, is the trek from the frontier into Gojjam. Fifteen thousand camels left the border carrying arms and food to support the Emperor's advance. The story is related in his manner by "The Abyssinian Campains", which states:

The lorry carrying the Emperor itself rolled over at one point, and on several occasions he and all his lords had to turn out to build stone or bush tracks over the almost impassable dry river beds. Days were passed without water, and the heat was very great. The 2nd Ethiopian Battalion led by Major Boyle followed behind, while on a converging and better route from the south the rest of the Sudanese Frontier Battalion made for Belaya. Among the paraphernalia of this great camel trek was an Amharic printing press to publish the Emperor's propaganda and decrees in many coloured inks, and megaphonists to "oyez" the enemy in battle.

Those who beat their way to Belaya through this hard country declare that a compass was not needed; one could orient the column by the stink of dead camels, of which on one day the Emperor's suite counted fifty-seven. A fine black hot dust hung over the tenuous track. Not a human being was seen until they came to the mountain.

Here a cave was ready for the Emperor and chiefs and retainers began to make ant-like for Belaya to pay him their respects. Italian aircraft came over, but bombed only the unfinished aerodrome. The Banda — uniformed Ethiopian irregulars — who had hitherto held the further escarpment east of Belaya for the Italians and were their watchdogs of the plateau, began now to fall away at the Emperor's presence. (10)

The Emperor's preliminary instructions were given to the various leaders while he was still in Gojjam. Ras Ababa Aregai, the great patriot leader who had kept resistance against the Italians simmering ever since the fall of Addis Ababa in 1936, was instructed to send five hundred men immediately to cooperate with the South African forces attacking Dessie.

(9)   H. M. Stationery Office, *op. cit.*
(10)   Ibid.

These men were dispatched by lorry within twenty-four hours of receiving the order and did most useful work during the attack on Dessie. The leadership of the patriot forces converging on Jimma was given to Cherassu Duké, another fighting soldier who had never surrendered to the Italians, Shalaka Mesfin and Azaj Kabbada (Sandford's colleague in Gojjam), commanded the patriots against Lekemti. To Ras Kassa the Emperor assigned the work of rounding up the Gojjam garrison, in conjunction with such of Wingate's force as could be spared.

The news of landing of a British plane at Sakala, the dropping of arms, ammunition, money, and stores by other planes a few days later at the same spot, and the bombing of the Italian garrisons, spread like wild fire over the country and created an enormous impression. The arrival of the "sign in the skies" which the patriots had been demanding from the Emperor for the past year seems to have been the turning-point of the Gojjam campaign. ([11])

Zalleka Birru, the important chief of the green land of Matakal where the track winds up the scrap to Central Gojjam, submitted with all his men. The Frontier and 2nd Ethiopian Battalions moved into his country, and by 23rd February the bulk of these two units with a mortar platoon of four pieces (their nearest and most effective approach to artillery) were in Enjabara, an Italian fortress under a great sugar-loaf mountain in the very middle of Gojjam, astride the Italian-made axial road of the province which runs southward from Bahrdar Guorgis on Lake Tana to Dangila, Enjabara, Burye, Dembacha, Debra Markos and Addis Ababa. Italy had abandoned Enjabara a few days before.

The brigade that had held Dangila, bombed by the R.A.F. and harassed by patriots, had also marched out to Bahrdar Guorgis and left the whole of Mangasha's country clean of Italians. The strain on these garrisons imposed by a hostile countryside and by rumours of a great enemy column, and the clamant need of General Nasi in Gondar for reserves, had led to the abandonment of Northern Gojjam.

Gideon Force, as this part of the Frontier and 2nd Ethiopian battalions, the mortar platoon and the propaganda unit were now called, therefore turned south.

They marched at night, for they had no close air support; in single file. With 700 camels and 200 horses and mules they went down the road to Burye through wakening Ethiopian villages. The column was four miles long, and was followed by the Emperor and his personal guard. Report flew, and gathered momentum in flying. The approach of an enormous force was announced to Colonel Natale, commanding the Italian brigade group at Burye, where there were 5,000 troops encamped in well-sited forts with artillery, cavalry, and a mass of light and heavy automatics. The Colonel could not know that the fighting men against him counted 450, with four mortars, a few anti-tank rifles, and a sprinkling of Vickers and Bren guns.

([11])   C. Sandford, *op. cit.*

92

On the afternoon of 27th February, Wingate engaged the enemy in one of the outer Burye forts with two platoons and the mortars, which small handful also repulsed a counter-attack by cavalry. The first blows in a memorable guerrilla campaign had been struck. One platoon continued to harass the fort all night. The Italians replied by firing a phenomenal number of shells and bullets at imaginary targets until dawn, and in two days they had abandoned the position.

On the 1st March platoons of the Frontier Battalion began to worry in their terrier style the easternmost fort of Burye, Mankusa, on the direct line of retreat from the Burye garrison to Debra Markos. The fort buildings were burned by mortar bombs and drilled by a Vickers gun, while propagandists yelled at the troops through megaphones in intervals of fire. There were many desertions. The Eritrean N.C.O.'s had to tie up a lot of the enemy troops. At a crucial moment two old Ethiopian ladies were mobilised to creep into the fort's cowfold, unlock the door, and drive out the entire cattle herd into the arms of the waiting Patriots. These bizarre tactics on a ubiquitous agressor were too much for Natale, and on 4th March, screened by low-flying aircraft and girdled by cavalry, his army came swarming out along the road to Debra Markos. They nearly overrun Gideon Force, who stepped aside in the nick of time. Wingate himself had to run miles. Then Boustead's Frontier Battalion — at this point only 300 strong — closed behind the Italian retreat and tickled up their tail.

Here was a moment when, if aircraft from our meagre resources could have been spared, the Italian army in Gojjam might have been blotted out. Chased by 300 Sudanese experts, with a population out to strip them of their rifles and their clothes, panting on either flank like African hunting dogs, they were marching straight on the 2nd Ethiopian Battalion which lay across the road on a river-bed just west of Dembacha. As it was, the 2nd Ethiopian Battalion had to take the blow of this great body without the final demoralising influence of the air to aid them. Individual platoons put up a very stiff resistance. One Ethiopian ran out into the road in front of the armoured cars that led the advancing horde, carefully laid his anti-tank rifle on the open ground and at short range knocked out two of the cars. He then removed the breech and ran away. The place was strewn with Italian dead, of whom 120 were later counted. But so small a force could not indefinitely stop Natale, who in the end flooded over and round them, breaking up their baggage train on the way. Indeed, the force was so small that the greater part of it was able to hide in bushes and water-pools, and to survive.

Very shaken, Natale abandoned Dembacha on the 8th, and Fort Emanuel on the 10th March, taking all the garrisons with him to Debra Markos.

The entire Italian army of the Gojjam, except for a battalion at Mota and the forces of Torelli now invested by other sections of the Frontier Battalion in the far north at Bahrdar Guorgis, was now concentrated at Debra Markos and in the powerful positions in the Gulit hills a few miles west of Debra Markos on the Burye road. They numbered more than

12,000 men, with the usual Italian proportion of mountain artillery. The 2nd Ethiopian Battalion after their harrowing experience, could no longer be accounted a combatant force; the fighting for Debra Markos fell upon the shoulders of 300 Sudanese of the Frontier Battalion, commanded by Lieut.-Colonel Boustead. It was now that they developed a new techniqque in organised guerilla warfare.

Following the enemy down the road, they had sniped at his camp fires every night from close range with light automatics, but now in front of Debra Markos, they took to bombardment on a grand scale.

They would lay off their camel transport at a respectable distance from the enemy cavalry, using mules and horses only for close carrying. The fighting men camped very near the enemy, under cover, and rested during the daytime — except for the officers, who reconnoitred new approaches to the enemy positions. At night parties, rarely more than 100 and often only 50 strong, went off quietly on an approach march well marked out. No talking was allowed above a whisper, and no reply allowed to the searching fire of an apprehensive enemy. The arms were rifle and bayonet, and two grenades a man, with Bren guns in support.

After midnight the Sudanese crept up the hills in line, and came within 10 yards of the enemy positions before they threw their bombs. There would be an attack with the bayonet; the position taken; the counter-attack beaten off, a silent withdrawal. In this way different positions were tackled every night, the Abina fort cleared, the Gulit line made intolerable. The enemy was forced on to his inner ring at Debra Markos, from which he was withdrawn across the Blue Nile by the High Command in Addis Ababa on 3rd/4th April, shedding deserters by the thousand, two days before Lieut.-General Cunningham's troops entered the capital.

And so on the 6th April the Emperor was able to raise the Ethiopian flag over the forts of Debra Markos. Ras Hailu, a diplomat of no mean order, had stayed behind with his Banda to stop looting, and now bowed to the ground before his old suzerain with surprising measured grace for a man of his seventy years and ambiguous past. His chest was a jewel-box of Ethiopian and Italian orders. In Debra Markos, as previously in Enjabara, Burye and Dembacha, there was found food enough for a force many times the size of Gideon. Moreover, by a staggering feat of engineering and endurance, new American trucks had been brought from the Sudan across the tousled Belaya foothills, had been dragged by ropes and hundreds of men up the escarpment at Matakal, and were now running on the axial road of Gojjam. So the problem of supply, hitherto moving only at the camel's pace, was solved. South African aircraft brought munitions and dollars.

There remained Mota, seat of the Italian 69th Colonial Battalion, to be cleared up. To tackle this last fort 300 men of the Frontier Battalion marched in their game, resistant, spindle-legged Sudanese style over the Chokey range, 14,000 feet high, in a blizzard, in their tropical outfit with one blanket a man. Recovered from their mountain sickness, the black plainsmen invested Mota. An order came from Headquarters to send

94

back all except two platoons (60 men) and the mortar. The remaining handful, under their Colonel, then gave Mota the pasting that they felt it deserved. The fort was mortared all night at given intervals, which were made more lively still with Bren gun fire. A British lieutenant was dressed up as a major and sent in with a letter ordering the enemy to yield. And yield he did, after a show of resistance. Four hundred troops got a shock when they saw two platoons file into the fort. Thus the whole of Gojjam except Bahrdar Guorgis in the far north was taken from the Italians; and Nasi soon withdrew the Bahrdar garrison across Lake Tana to strengthen his own position in Gondar.

By the treachery of a Gojjam chief, Colonel Maraventano, commanding the Debra Markos garrison, with the 8,000 troops and Italian government officials who had not deserted him, had been allowed to slip across the Blue Nile unharmed, and to destroy the pontoon in that colossal gorge. Addis Ababa had fallen, so he turned north along the east bank of the Blue Nile for Dessie. Dessie fell, so he turned further north, hoping to make Debra Tabor.

Gideon Force were determined not to let him go.

One hundred men of the Frontier Battalion, some 60 of the 2nd Ethiopians (now refitted and re-formed), and 2,000 Patriots under old Ras Kassa pursued him and pinned him down to fight in Agibar, a high tableland above the Nile. There, by a series of spirited and fierce attacks in the open, watched by the old Ras seated on a shooting-stick, and after a little more of the nightly nerve-war in which the regular platoons now specialised, they wore him out. For the loss of less than 200 allied troops killed, Colonel Maraventano on 22nd May put up the white flag over the biggest haul that Gideon made in Gojjam: 7,000 infantry, 120 light machine-guns, 7 mountain guns, 2 mortars, 15,000 mules, 300 horses, 700 Italian civil officials. The whole lot were disarmed under the scowl of three Bren guns, which were all that the British commander could spare for the operation. He was given the D.S.O.

Gideon had done his work. With the help of the R.A.F. and of a friendly countryside he had smitten the Italians hip and thigh. He had pestered them and cheated them, given them no rest or sleep, he had broken down their nerves, and, a flyweight himself, had knocked the self-styled champion of East Africa into a corner. He had taught the British army new lessons in guerrilla warfare.

It was therefore fitting that, on 5th May, 1941, when, five years to the day after Marshal Badoglio entered Addis Ababa, the Emperor Haile Selassie came down Mount Entoto into his old capital, the 2nd Ethiopian Battalion marched ahead of his car and the turbaned Frontier Battalion behind; and that another car carried the bald head of Mission 101 (Colonel Sandford), who in the hard days before arms and regular troops were available had maintained the prestige both of Britain and the Emperor in a tired Gojjam.

Two battalions, with a mint of optimism and fearlessness and with the compelling name of the Lion of Judah on their flag, had defeated and largely captured or dispersed four Italian brigades, with all their horse, foot, artillery and aircraft. The total odds in man-power against them were 10-1, the odds in fire-power far greater. They had shown how to overcome these obstacles by exploitation of night, of bush, of superior discipline, enthusiasm, silence and cunning. As they marched into Addis Ababa the last 50 faithful camels of their train, past further labour, were slaughtered on the hills above; you can find the bones of 15,000 of the rest all the way back to the Sudan.

The entry of the Emperor into Addis Ababa meant something more than the reversal of a four-year-old story discreditable to all except the victim. It meant the close instead of the distant co-ordination of the British forces coming from north and from south. For, before the Emperor entered his capital, British forces had reached it from the south, and were holding open its gates for his triumphal return. (12)

The rôle of Ethiopia's patriot forces was definite and telling in the liberation of their country. While no one can deny that the British forces, bcause of the line assigned to them by force of military necessity, and by their desire to expel the fascists and nazis from the Middle East and North Africa, directed the campaign to its succesful conclusion, success could not have come in Ethiopia except for the patriots' support.

The 5th Indian Division headquarters, under Major-General Heath, was set up at Gedaref, the obvious centre of communications by road and rail for the two offensive possibilities that were to present themselves to General Platt: either against Kassala, the gate of Eritrea, or against Gallabat, the gate of the Ethiopian rebellion and of the important Ethiopian province Amhara, whose capital is the ancient Ethiopian capital of Gondar.

General Platt wanted to stimulate the Ethiopian rebellion to the utmost. While Indian troops had been picked for this campain for their experience in mountain warfare, it was never believed that they would, even at a later date when a second Indian Division arrived, be able to break through the colossal ramparts of the Eritrean and Amharic escarpment and seal their victory on the inner plateau without the closest co-operation with the Patriot forces in the Abyssinian interior. (13)

The campaign for the liberation of the whole Middle East and North African sector devolved on wise British deployment of forces, execution of strategy and concerted planned action. The overall succes prevented Italy from contributing Africa, as Germany was contributing Europe, to the Axis spoils. Had this not been prevented by this succesful campaign, the British Empire would have been split by a hostile mass stretching from Narvik to Bulawayo.

It is impossible in this work to report fully on the entire campaign; but a major factor to the liberation of Ethiopia and a concomitant thereof was the spectacular battle at Keren. The success as wel as the doughtiness of the combined forces of the United Kingdom and the dominions has become a very noteworthy part of British military history. It could be said

(12)   H. M. Stationery Office, *op. cit.*
(13)   *ibid.*

that the campaign in Ethiopia and the battle at Keren were complementary in securing for Ethiopia its liberation.

His Imperial Majesty in October, 1952, on his first state visit to Eritrea when a memorial ceremony was held in honour of those who had fallen in the famous battle of Keren of 1941, stated briefly but concisely, the meaning of the Keren battle to this dramatic episode of Ethiopian's liberation.

In a solemn ceremony held at the cemetery where a monument and graves of the allied war heroes are found, His Imperial Majesty, in the presence of members of the diplomatic corps, princes, dignitaries, high military officers and many distinguished persons, declared:

The soil on which we are now treading is soil sacred to the memory of thousands of families throughout the world whose beloved sons here fell in the cause of justice and freedom.

During the sanguinary years of the Second World War, there have been many battlefields consecrated by the blood of heroes, of which, in the history of those world-shaking events, the battlefield of Keren is but one.

Let us cast our minds back over the history of those fateful weeks during the months of February and March, eleven years ago, when the vital line of communications through the Mediterranean and Red Sea remained closed to the hard-pressed British Armies in Africa which, with our help and that of the Free French and Belgian forces in East Afria, alone carried on the war against the Axis powers. The vast battle to the north of us, along the shores of the Mediterranean, continued to rage without decision. However, with the simultaneous victories under our leadership in Ethiopia, and the victory of Keren in that part of Ethiopia which has now been joined to its own land under Our crown, the first flashes of hope for the ultimate victory in World War II began to be seen, and Ethiopia, together with Eritrea, became the first territories to be freed from oppression.

The victory of Keren was, therefore, a victory of wide remifications and, indeed, it could not have been won, had not all the many forces brought into play, contributed selflessly and courageously to that end. With the prescience of genius, General Wavell, C.O.C. Middle East, not only pressed relentlessly for the execution of the campaign, but also withdrew from the northern front at Sidi Barrani, part of the heroic Fourth Indian Division to throw them into the assaults on the precipitous cliffs of Keren.

At the very same moment that the battle of Keren had taken shape, We Ourselves, as liberator, crossed the frontier of our beloved Empire and on the 6th of February, when the heroic Second Camerons and the Rajputana Rifles were baptisting with their names and blood the ridge henceforth known as the Cameron Ridge, and when the Fifth Brigade of the Fourth Indian Division was moving into position on the Acqua Ridge, We established Our headquarters at Belaya to the south from whence We pursued Our campaign of liberation. On 6th April, about 10 days after the final victory at Keren, We raised the glorious flag of Our Empire over the

97

fortress of Debra Markos. Had We not pushed on against all odds, the victory of the Keren might not have been possible, since the enemy had already withdrawn from the south all the forces that he dared, and could, even in his dire straits, withdraw no more from the hundreds of thousands of troops whom We Ourselves, faced to the south of Keren. Moreover, Our proclamations to the population of Eritrea immediately raised the flag of Empire and of revolt against the enemy and deserters began to flow in by thousands to our lines and those of our allies, resulting in 30 to 40 % depletion of some units.

The battle which developed during the months of February and March 1941, was therefore, one of unusual size and importance. Some measure of its scope may be assessed from the fact that no less than sixty-five enemy battalions were engaged and that the victory, after fifty-two days, counted no less than forty thousand prisoners and 300 guns: and from the fact that not only were the Fourth and Fifth Indian Divisions engaged as well as the Free French Forces including a battalion of the Foreign Legion and the Chad Battalion, but also Our forces led by General Orde Wingate to the south as well as the army of General Cunningham, coming up from Kenya, secured the victory.

During the fifty-two days of fierce struggle on the battlements of Keren, each crag and ridge assumed before history an eminence which all patriots may well commemorate. The present and future generations will remember with appreciation and with pride the sacrifice and devotion of these buried heroes of Cameron Ridge, of Flat Top, of Samana, of Sanchel, of Happy Valley, of Acqua, of Dologorodoc and of Brig's Peak.

The memory of places where deeds of valour were performed should serve to keep forever fresh the memory of those selfless heroes who performed them.

We have assembled here to do honour, before the Empire and before history, to the deeds of these brave and selfless men. Forever in Ethiopia will be hallowed the names of the Battalions and brigades of the Fourth and Fifth Indian Divisions; of the French Foreign Legion and the Chad Battalion; of the Highland Light Infantry, of the Fifth, Seventh and Eleventh Indian Infantry Brigades; of the West Yorkshires; of the Rajputana and the Punjab Rifles; of the Second Battalion of the Fifth Mahratta Regiment and of its fierce bayonet charge on Flat Top hill; of the Ninth Brigade of the Fifth Indian Division which stormed by surprise the heights of Dologorodoc; of the Tenth and Twenty-ninth Brigades of the same Division, and of their heroic and immovable stand against an encircling enemy when food and ammunition could be supplied them only by antiquated aircraft; of the frightful casualties suffered by the Third Brigade of the 18th Garhwal Regiment; of Skinner's Horse; of the Fourth Brigade of the Tenth Baluch Regiment and of the valiant Sudanese Forces. We shall not forget the countless heroes; Subadar Richpal Ram, V.C., the Sixth Rajputana Rifles; Generals Heath, Slim, Mayne, Beresford-Pierce, and General Platt and Cunningham and General Wavell himself.

Finally, since the days of Homer and the Siege of Troy, one may not forget the honoured dead who fought with soldierly qualities of courage and devotion. We cannot condone the cause for which they were fighting nor the sorrows and destruction wrought. We cannot, as have soldiers and statesmen throughout the ages, but testify before history to those qualities of courage and devotion which led these men to lay down their lives in response to the command of their leaders and the appalling casualties suffered by the enemy during the fifty-two days of the Keren battle, eloquently translate their response to that call. Before such acts of sacrifice and devotion the veils of history, of enmity and of suffering even, are drawn aside and all appear before their Creator, friends and foes alike, clothed in the imperishable mantle of courage.

The battle of Keren was, to adopt a modern term, a Combined Operation in every sense of the word, not only in the type of arms employed but also, and in particular, in the contribution from all fronts which were made towards the achievement of the victory. Today, that collaboration of eleven years ago is now being pursued on another and, thanks to God, a more peaceful plane. The blood shed on the battlefields of Keren, of Burye and of Debra Markos, has now borne its fruits in a people reunited under their Emperor; a people forever grateful for the blood of these heroes, come both from abroad and from the homeland, and who march forward, under Our guidance, on the paths of peace.

We invoke the blessing of Almighty God on the heroes named and nameless of the battlefield of Keren and now lay to their eternal memory Our wreaths on these hallowed graves. This place We shall always respect, and devote Our personal interest towards it.

CHAPTER 8

The Triumph

The liberation campaign with its dramatic beginning as outlined in the previous chapter and its equally dramatic climax from the north and south was practically won nearly two months before the Emperor's triumphant entry into Addis Ababa.

Although there were many active pockets of Italians in various parts of the country, the backbone of the Italian campaign was now completely broken. At this time the Emperor was at Gojjam where his patriots under General Wingate were bristling with joy over their defeat of the enemy.

Time and circumstance made it imperative that the campaign had to be pressed forward to its conclusion. The enemy had to be routed as part of the general strategy of the Middle East and North African campaign.

The fall of Keren on 26th March, 1941, the occupation of Addis Ababa by General Cunningham's troops on 6th April, and the entry of the Emperor into Debra Markos on the same day meant that the campaign was won and that the Italian East African Empire was in dissolution (1).

On the 6th April His Majesty delivered a speech at Debra Markos in which he tied up his joy with openly voicing his appreciation of the telling sacrifices made by the Ethiopian patriots, and especially the 2nd Battalion which had distinguished itself in the recapture of Gojjam:

To risk death for refusing to be ruled by aliens; to be exiled to the forests and ravines or to foreign lands; to suffer calamities; to hunger and to thirst —it is by such hazards that a man is enabled to see the object of his desire. And so you are now enabled to see in Gojjam the two signs which display and represent the liberty for which you have been struggling. And it is God in His goodness Who has vouchsafed that you may see, after so short a time, these two symbols of liberty; it must be accounted a miracle, for it is something never seen or heard of in the history of any other country; it is unique for past and future times alike.

It is incumbent on us all to be found worthy of the beneficence God has worked for us. And the way in which we should express our gratitude to Him is by forgetting rancour and revenge; by following the paths of love and fellowship, by serving our country, which has for five years endured agonies under a cruel oppressor, and so to bring it to a high degree of culture; and by ensuring that succeeding generations are saved from the trials of invasion. We shall not withhold our mercy and our bounty from any loyal Ethiopian who dwells beneath the shadow of our flag, loving his country and rendering honest service; we shall make no distinctions, and you shall know that this is the basis on which we shall work for the future.

(1)   Christine Sandford, *op. cit.*

*You must be energetic in watching out against the presence in the country
of any bandits, lest the land be ravaged and the people maltreated, and so
that the merchant may trade at will and the farmer plough. You patriots
of Ethiopia, rejoice that today you assume the crown of your deeds: and in
future you must contend for a still greater crown. No Ethiopian citizen will
forget the officers of the British Army—which is fighting for the freedom
of the world—who came into our country under the leadership of Brigadier
Sandford and Colonel Wingate to help in the cause of Ethiopia's freedom.
We are particularly pleased, you my soldiers of the 2nd Battalion, to speak
among your brethren of the valorous deeds you have recently performed in
routing the enemy, after waiting long in exile, through love of your country,
and for the honour of your Emperor and your flag. Your deeds are greater
than can be estimated from your numbers; and we do not forget those who
are separated from you by death. Patriots of Ethiopia, rejoice that you have
been enabled to see that which you have awaited as a sequel to your labours
—the flag of liberty waving before your Emperor and before yourselves, a
resplendent jewel in the Ethiopian air.
May Ethiopia live for ever in her freedom!*

There remained the rounding up of the enemy forces. These were now
split in two. In the north the Duke of Aosta sought to make a stand at Amba
Alagi, where, with the elements which he took with him from Addis Ababa
and which he gathered as he retreated up the northern road, and with the
defeated troops from Eritrea, he was able to collect a considerable army. He
was given little time, however, to organise a defence as British troops
followed hard upon the heels of the retreating enemy from north and south,
and after a heavy artillery bombardment Amba Alagi fell to General Platt
on the 20th May, 1941.

The clearing up of the south took longer. The enemy forces were scattered
over a very large area and General Cunningham, having detached troops
to pursue the Duke of Aosta northwards and to assist in the encirclement
of the enemy at Amba Alagi, had very limited means at his disposal for the
task of rounding up an enemy of greatly superior force. There was stiff
fighting in the region of the chain of lakes which lie along the direct road
from Nairobi to Addis Ababa. The enemy was finally dislodged and forced
back westwards across the Omo River about the middle of June. A converging movement from the north and east then took place on the town of
Jimma, a hundred and fifty miles south-west of Addis Ababa, which was
entered by Major-General G. C. Fowkes, commanding the 12th (African)
Division and the patriot forces under Fitaurari Gerassu Duké on 21st
June.

The only Italian forces now remaining in the field in the south were being
concentrated by General Gazzera in the neighbourhood of Dembi Dollo,
near the Sudan border, and about two hundred miles west of Addis Ababa.
The rains had by this time set in and the movement of regular troops with
their mechanised transport became increasingly difficult. Patriot forces
pushed out from Jimma westwards and a flying column of regular troops
and patriots was sent down the road from Addis Ababa through Lekemti
to make a turning movement from the north. These forces converging on

101

him from the east and north shepherded Gazzera into the arms of a small Belgian force under General Gilliert, who had entered the country from the Sudan at Gambela. Gazzera's army capitulated to the Belgians on 3rd July.

The whole country was now free of the enemy except in the north-west. Here at Gondar a remnant of the once formidable Italian East African Army held out for six months. It is perhaps truer to say they were allowed to remain unmolested. They were incapable of doing harm, and to undertake operations against them at the height of the rainy season would have entailed an effort out of proportion to the importance of the object to be achieved [2].

In all these operations the Ethiopian patriot forces bore a useful and indeed an essential part. Even before he left Gojjam the Emperor had gained touch with the Shoan leaders. Ras Ababa Aragai, who had throughout the Italian occupation kept a force in the field in eastern Shoa, in spite of strenuous efforts made by the Italians to crush him, was ordered to send a portion of his troops northwards to co-operate with the British column which was following up the Duke of Aosta. Fitaurari Gerassu Duké — fierce fighter and perpetual thorn in the flesh of the Italians in the districts just south of the capital — was directed to keep contact with the enemy, who had retreated south-westwards from Addis Ababa and were covering Jimma.

General Cunningham gave orders that the Emperor's journey to Addis Ababa was to be expedited, not only because it was fitting, but because it would be helpful to enlist his influence in stopping any excess or violence, if such were meditated by his people in the capital against the large Italian population, which had been much increased by refugees from neighbouring country districts. It was thought that for the Emperor to be in the country, at Debra Markos, and not in his capital, could only create an embarassing situation for all concerned. General Wavell accordingly informed London that General Cunningham was arranging to instal the Emperor in Addis Ababa [3].

It was obvious that the Emperor's place, for political as well as military reasons, was in the capital, where he could get the reins of Government into his hands and from whence he could most easily direct the movements of the irregular patriot forces who were growing in strength from day to day. There were practical difficulties in the way of the immediate entry into the capital, and moreover, the fear was entertained by the military authorities that the entry into Addis Ababa of a large patriot army flushed with victory, would be the prelude to acts of reprisals or worse against the Italian population of the town. These fears proved groundless.

After suitable arrangements had been made to relieve and disarm the Italian garrisons of the outlying forts, to replace the Italian police and to confine the Italian civil population of some twenty-five thousand in zones of segregation, the Emperor made his triumphal entry. The bearing and

(2)   Christine Sandford, op. cit.
(3)   Lord Rennell of Rodd, op. cit.

102

behaviour of the patriot troops and of the Ethiopians generally were exemplary (⁴).

His Imperial Majesty did not arrive in his capital without facing a great deal of rigours. After many vicissitudes and innumerable hardships, he reached his capital on May 5, exactly five years to the day after the entry of the Italians.

Mr. G. L. Steer in his book "Sealed and Delivered" gave such an accurate and dramatic description of His Imperial Majesty's journey from Debra Markos to Addis Ababa that we reproduce it fully here:

He set out from Debra Markos at the end of April, with the 2nd Ethiopian and half the Frontier Battalion. The rest were at Bahrdar Guorguis, or had broken east after crossing the Blue Nile to chase Maraventano's retreating column to Agibar, where they were to win a famous victory, taking over 7,000 prisoners and seven guns. Down the enormous gorge wound the Imperial host, escorted by the *arbenyoch* of Gojjam into the feverish Blue Nile bottom, a day's march from the summit of the divide. Here Leblanc and fifteen of his Sudanese had built a new bridge at Safartak to replace the old pontoon destroyed by the Italians in their retreat. The Sudanese advance guard of the Lion of Judah did not fail him. In thirty-six hours, working without respite in the icy water of night, up to their chattering chins in the young Nile, these fifteen men hauled by main force old forty-gallon petrol drums and iron traverses from the wreckage downstream until they had built the pillars and cross-pieces of a bridge 200 yards long. Work in the middle where the Nile was five feet deep was particularly hard, but by careful swimming and balancing they got the drums into place. Then the Sudanese crossed over and in four days cleared or bridged two large demolitions in the opposite cliff left by Maraventano. They were not engineers; they were lorry drivers and machine-gunners, directed by an automobile expert; they were our own magnificent Sudanese troops, the frank-hearted blend of Arab and African, capable of performing all the tasks of war toughly and cheerfully if well led, of marching anywhere, any height and any how and beating the enemy at the other end, incomparably the finest fighting stock in Africa, ready for trials and sudden diversions intolerable to European infantry. These fifteen were the tip of a spearhead of 1,000 who had blazed the track of an Emperor through twenty-three battalions of the enemy. After he had crossed the Blue Nile bridge laid by their art, and already awash in the turbulent promise of the great rains overspilling Lake Tana, and had climbed for a day up the other bank of the chasm with Ras Kassa and Ras Hailu, the Emperor ordered for the Frontier Battalion a feast at Debra Libanos. There, in the old refectory of the monastery that had been pillaged and burned by the Italians in 1937 because it housed a deep Ethiopian nationalist tradition, the Mohamedan soldiers sat cross-legged on the rush floor and were served with food and drink by Christian monks. The Emperor and his cousin Kassa prayed beside the dank grave of Kassa's murdered sons, victims of Graziani, Aberra and Wand Wassan, whom even the White Russian

(⁴) Christine Sandford, *op. cit.*

103

Konovaloff, most critical of the Ethiopians, had described as *noble princes*.
In Addis Ababa they were putting up shaven eucalyptus poles painted green, yellow and red along a road that I remembered. It came down Entoto past the Little Palace, and it was the road by which the Emperor and a handful of faithful members of his Guard had entered Addis Ababa after the crushing defeat at Lake Ashangi in April 1936.

The people of Addis Ababa, when they had bought up the coloured silk and cotton in the town, were painting their flag upon their houses, and making garlands of flowers in its colours. Though sheeting was rare and must be husbanded, there was a great washing of old clothes in streams that filter through Addis Ababa to the Akaki plain.

May 5th opened bright and clear. The Italians kept within doors, and the Ethiopian radio made a special announcement after playing the only surviving record of the Ethiopian national anthem, kept in reserve over five years by a far-sighted Armenian jeweller. Fifteen thousand patriots of Ras Ababa Aragai's forces came down Entoto with their quiet leader in the middle of the orderly mop-haired column, to line the streets of the capital along the processional way. The Ras, with a face no less modest for its scars, spoke in an undertone to his commanders. He was well equipped in machine-guns and even in mountain artillery; the old police chief of Addis Ababa was also returning to claim his own after five years of fighting in the wilds, never more than 150 miles from the capital. Slobbering droves of oxen went in dust up the winding highway in the eucalyptus to Entoto, where they would feast the Ras' men in the evening. Women passed, in men's clothes and bearing arms; the old Ethiopian warriors rode by on horseback with bandages round their heads and tilting lances in their hands and chanting; and priests passed in a daze under their silk umbrellas, holding high their flat, ornate silver crosses; and there were a few Italian prisoners in chains who, one had to explain to fellow South Africans, would not be eaten alive or even mutilated at the end of the day, but if they liked raw meat would get their fair slice at the banquet.

Towards midday the Emperor arrived at the summit of Entoto, where he prayed in the church of St. Mary, from whose other side he could see for the first time Addis Ababa floating in the billows of eucalyptus far below, like a mirage that might be stolen away.

The procession formed among the rocks. Ahead, a South African motor-cyclist; next my loudspeaker van flying the Ethiopian flag; six South African motor-cyclists abreast; three South African armoured cars; two red Italian fire-engines carrying a scramble of the Press; Wingate close-shaven, carrying a long leather whip on a white horse; the 2nd Ethiopian Battalion under their flag; a cloud of Ethiopian mounted police on white horses carrying carbines round a car containing the Emperor and Major-General Weatherall, commanding the Addis Ababa division; cars with the Princes, the Rases, the Itchege, Dan, Andrew, Lorenzo; the Sudan Frontier Battalion in clean turbans and grins, with rich green flag of silk sporting their badge, a golden lion; lorries of Ethiopian exiles, some more armoured cars. We moved slowly down the steep incline and through the crowded streets of Addis Ababa, through many thousands of waving flags and stooping bodies. Lij Yilma at my side called into the microphone, "Today, five years ago, the Italians entered our city to murder and pillage; today, five years after, our King returns, with the aid of a just God and of the English!" Looking through the sides of the van one could see the expressions of the crowd as we descended through the skirting forests. The shock of the first news; the recognition; the faces wrinkling up in a mixture of sorrow at memory, and of release from sorrow; tears starting suddenly from the faces of old people; wrinkled women raising their arms in ecstasy to the sky; lines of men and woman going flat on the ground and kissing it; dignified judges of the Quarters at one moment lifting high their inscribed silk standards and flowers, then bowing low till their foreheads touched the earth; before the centre of the town was reached and the streets were clogged, flocks of people running alongside the Emperor's car shouting proverbs and throwing flowers; old faces in the crowd that one had not expected to see again. Addis Ababa means the New Flower, and as the car entered the town somebody shouted, "The New Flower has flowered again."

The ranks were serried, the individuals were lost in the mass, the expressions grew more uniform, there was no room for bowing, the women only cried out like a swarm of bees on the wing, the men gave the short triple clap. At the gates of Menelik's old palace an artist encouraged by the propaganda section had set up a most horrible representation of the Ethiopian lion disembowelling the Roman wolf; and beyond waited Lieutenant-General Sir Alan Cunningham, G.O.C. East Africa Force, and a guard of honour of the King's African Rifles and a battery of captured guns, whose Italian ammunition was to be touched off twenty-one times as the Emperor mounted the rostrum to speak, and everybody fell flat as in the book of Daniel [5].

A journalist who accompanied the Emperor's force into Addis Ababa wrote the following description of his return:

"On the summit of Mount Entoto, above Addis Ababa, in the inner sanctuary of the Church of the Virgin Mary, Haile Selassie I kissed holy ground and gave thanks to God on the morning of May 5th for his return to Ethiopia. Tears welled in his eyes as he was leaving the dim sanctuary for the light of day. Outside, his second son, the Duke of Harar, affectionately passed his arms round his father's shoulders as he walked down the steps to the crowded courtyard of the famous mountain church.

"Priests, soldiers, and common people crowded in front of the Emperor, kissing the soil of Ethiopia on which he was treading after five years in exile.

"The mountain ceremony and the endless stream of the army of patriots, riding on mule and the great swelling crowd of white-clad singing women and children winding down the steps of the mountain road through the eucalyptus groves was the real centre of today's triumphant and touching entry of the exiled ruler.

"The acclamation died as the Emperor stood in dramatic silence and made

[5]   Christine Sandford, op. cit.

a speech in Amharic. After recalling it was five years since the Fascist forces entered the city, he said:

'It is with a sense of deep thankfulness to Almighty God that I stand today in my palace from which the Fascist forces have fled. It is my firm purpose to merit the blessing I have received. First, by showing gratitude to my allies, the British, for my return and for the benefit I have received by the release of Imperial troops for warfare on other front, and by my supplying them with armed forces wherever they may need them; secondly, by establishing in Ethiopia Christian ethics in Government, liberty of conscience and democratic institutions!'

"Then His Majesty the Emperor came down from Mount Entoto towards his capital. He was still escorted by the Gideon force (who earned the honour through the valiant part played by them in blazing the trail for the Emperor), with an Ethiopian battalion marching ahead and the frontier Battalion behind.

"Major General Wingate rode in front on a white charger (it was the Wingate who afterwards won immortal fame in the Burmese campaign and died in an aeroplane crash March, 1944).

"The Emperor sat speechless in his car with a heart that was brimming over with love for his subjects and filled with gratitude towards the Almighty. The streets were lined by about 15,000 patriots of Ras Ababa Aragai's army. And still more thousands of men and women, who jostled against each other in their eagerness to catch a glimpse of their beloved Emperor.

"Entering the city amidst the loud cheers of his jubilant subjects, the Emperor was welcomed by General Sir Alan Cunningham, the G.O.C., of the East African Forces, at the gates of the old Menelik Palace. While he mounted the old throne in the palace, the British fired a salute of 21 guns."

Then the victorious Lion of Judah mounted the rostrum to make a memorable speech which contained the following words:

No words of thanks spoken by human tongue are sufficient for that the good God has vouchsafed me this day to be in your midst, a thing that could be known or conceived neither by the angels of heaven nor by the hosts of earth. What I want to tell you all and to convey to you before everything, is that this day is the opening of a new era of history for a new Ethiopia: and in this new era there will begin a new task which it will be for all of us to perform.

If we wish to recall the sufferings that have befallen Ethiopia in past times, it is only in order briefly to speak of her history connected therewith. Ethiopia has existed for many thousand years or more guarding her liberty; Italy, whose aggressive designs date from long ago, arose to destroy that liberty, but in 1888 (1896) at Adwa Ethiopia preserved her independence through the battle waged by her heroes. It was not simply the treaty of Ucciali which was the reason why the battle of Adwa took place, but Italy, who before that time had maintained a constant desire to rule over Ethiopia, thought she had then found a pretext. After her defeat at Adwa Italy, resentful that truth had vanquished her, pretended in her words to be a friend of Ethiopia, while in fact she was making preparations against her; these were inter-

106

rupted by the previous great war in Europe, but have been revealed in the recent past.

When Italy waged aggressive war upon Ethiopia, although we were aware that we were no rivals in respect of armaments, it was our duty to resist an enemy who had come to snatch our country from us by violence, so we resisted with the resources we possessed. But as she was going to exterminate our people with poison gas, a weapon prohibited by international law, we went to the League of Nations to plead our cause and to obtain justice. However, as this dispute which Italy had started was liable to extend to the whole world, it was a time when all those responsible for the guidance of their nations were striving to save the world from the disaster which has now overtaken it; and they were engaged in efforts to secure agreement in the world, so that this conflagration might not be set off. At that period our sincere friend Great Britain extended to us a friendly welcome. There we remained at our task, never separated in thought from my countrymen shedding their blood at the unavailing hands of the unjust and ruthless Italians; nor from the monasteries and churches being pointlessly burnt down; nor from those who, exiled in alien lands or in the forests and ravines and wilds of their own country, were facing agony and suffering.

How many are the young people and the women, the priests and the monks, whom the Italians cruelly slaughtered during these years? In 1929 (1937) at the time of Yakatit Mika'el, in the town of Addis Ababa alone, during three days there were massacred, as you know, people amounting to many thousands. Those split by the spade and the shovel, the axe and the hammer those pierced by the bayonet or battered with sticks and stones; those consumed by fire in their houses, together with their infant children; those who perished in prison from hunger and thirst—their blood and their bones still raise their plaints. And no one is unaware that such deeds of barbarity and cruelty were not confined to the town of Addis Ababa but were committed on an even worse scale in the other parts of Ethiopia. One cannot find a person who has not been arrested and beaten up, trampled on, affronted or imprisoned.

Let us now pass on to the new history which is before our eyes. On this day exactly five years ago the Fascist soldiers entered our capital. Forthwith Mussolini informed the world that he had established the Roman Empire in our country of Ethiopia. When he told his people "I have made it your colony," he confidently thought the land would stay for ever in his hands. The valour of the Ethiopian people is known from history: but as we had no port whereby we could import them, it was impossible for us to get the modern weapons necessary for our people. Fifty-two nations condemned Mussolini's action: but he counted their judgement as nought; he gloried in this act of violence. The past five years were for you, my people, days of darkness. But you never lost hope; and, from gradual beginnings, you went out to station yourselves on the hills of Ethiopia. During those five years our enemy could never dare to come to the mountains where you, patriots of Ethiopia, were stationed, enduring every suffering and hardship, but guarding your liberty. Although he could not colonise the country thoroughly, he poured out thousands of millions of lire with the idea of "civilising" the part he held. But the expenditure of all this money was not for raising the conditions of the oppressed Ethiopian people, nor for rectifying the violence he had wrought; on the contrary, it was for planting Fascist "colonies" in our sacred land of Ethiopia, and for establishing a cruel regime in accordance with his own ideas. He endeavoured, indeed, to exterminate the Ethiopian race: he never contemplated administration as a mandate or protectorate, though even that might have been reckoned a heavy yoke for a free nation to bear.

But all that money, to be reckoned by many thousands of millions, and all the armaments that had been prepared, far from being used in the way Mussolini had intended, served a purpose he had by no means contemplated. When Italy, thinking to grab what she could from conquered France, declared her decision to go to war, the men she had despatched to Ethiopia, and the money and material she had sent thither, were immeasurable. The regular army she had assembled was not less than 150,000 in number; and in case she should be beleaguered she had accumulated supplies for many years. Confident in this great quantity of war material that she had prepared, she boasted that nobody could conquer her: so she began to establish in our land the totalitarian regime of the Fascist state. But events supervened which the Fascist state had not thought of. The fighting spirit, a chief essential in the warfare of the present day, became manifest in you.

In addition to your being the people, endowed with courage and pity, of a single country, your mutual co-operation and your knowledge of the art of war enabled you to destroy an enemy much superior to yourselves in arms and in military forces.

The British forces, who were fighting in other sectors for the right of mankind to freedom, needed time before they could be prepared and girded for helping and liberating Ethiopia. But you patriots of Ethiopia, by cutting our enemy's lines of communication and harassing him throughout Ethiopia, brought it about that he did not leave his strongholds. Despite the very large number of his troops, wherein he trusted, he soon realised that the Ethiopian people, in the length and breadth of the land, hated him and his regime, and he recognised the impossibility of living in such a country and among such a people. When his supremacy had been weakened at its heart, it became impossible for him to contemplate remaining, dropping poison-gas bombs and performing deeds of barbarity and cruelty according to his custom. He realised that the soldiers who everywhere held him besieged were opponents more powerful than himself. In engaging these opponents he used up all the small surplus of enterprise and money that he possessed. Afterwards, he tried to see whether he could find a good place in Ethiopia wherein to take refuge; but he found not one place of refuge.

When the time came, the great British Government, our ally and our aid, was ready properly to fight our enemy. When I knew this, I started with my troops from the Sudan, a distant land on our western borders, and arrived in the centre of Gojjam. Our enemy had in Gojjam strong fortresses, powerful troops, aeroplanes and artillery. If we estimate the numbers of troops of ourselves and of our enemy, the extent of his superiority would be about twenty to one: and moreover we had no artillery or aeroplanes at our command as we should have wished. My mere presence among my patriots attracted many thousands of men at a time: and the alarm and embarrassment of our enemy increased proportionally. My troops, advancing rapidly, cut the lines of communication of our enemy, and putting his soldiers to flight, followed them up beyond the Abai and across into Shoa and Begemder. While this was going on, I heard the joyful news that the British Imperial forces, hastening forward in an unparalleled manner, had taken our capital and were pushing on northwards towards Dessie and southwards towards Jimma. Similarly, the troops departing from the Sudan had with most amazing vigour smashed the fortress of Keren and completely defeated the enemy. As the time had come for me to enter my capital, I collected up my troops, who were scattered in various places chasing our enemy, and today I am here in my capital. That I have arrived thus far, leading my troops, with the enemy defeated all along my route, and that I have broken the power of our common enemy, my joy gushes forth without pause. The sincere thanks which I render to Almighty God are boundless, for my being here amongst you today in my palace, which the Fascist Government have abandoned in their flight.

People of my country Ethiopia.

This is a day when Ethiopia, stretching forth her hands to God in jubilation, presents her thanks and declares her joy to her children.

This is the day in which the children of Ethiopia are liberated from the grievous yoke of the foreigner and from eternal slavery; it is the day when we are vouchsafed to be reunited, after full five years of separation, with our beloved and longed-for people: therefore this day is honoured and sanctified, and one on which there shall be held every year a great Ethiopian holiday. On this day we shall call to mind our heroes who shed their blood and shattered their bones in sacrifice, refusing to betray the strict trust passed on to them from their fathers — the freedom of the country they loved, and the honour of their Emperor and their flag. The history of Ethiopia shall be a witness for these our heroes.

If we are to learn from the sufferings and agonies we have experienced in the past five years — endless to relate and to reckon up in detail — the principal lesson to be drawn is that you should have inscribed in your hearts industry, unity, fellowship and love, that you may be helpers in our plans for Ethiopia. Henceforth in the new Ethiopia we want you to be a people undivided, who have freedom and equality before the law.

You must become labourers together with us in the tasks at which we shall labour: the prosperity of the land; the wealth of the people; the development of agriculture, commerce, education and science; the security of the lives and property of our people; the complete reorganisation on modern civilised lines of the country's administration, and similar matters.

Now that God in His goodness has performed his work for us, it is our firm wish and our intention, first of all to express real gratitude to our ally and aid the British Government for what they have done on our behalf, by making it possible for the soldiers — the Imperial Troops as they are called — to be transferred to another war front so as to attack our common enemy, and by assisting them, should it be found necessary, with the aid of an army

109

secondly, to perform tasks beneficial to the people and to the country, by establishing a government which shall secure the respect and protection of religion in our land of Ethiopia, and by granting freedom to the people and to their opinions.

Now I end by telling you, my people, that today is a day of rejoicing for us all. Today is the day on which we have forged victory over our enemy. Therefore, while we all rejoice with full hearts, let it be in the spirit of Christ and not otherwise. Do not return evil for evil: do not act according to the inveterate custom of the enemy, who up to the very last moment performed deeds of cruielty and violence. Take care lest the good name of Ethiopia be soiled by such things as are a reproach to our enemy. We shall cause our enemies, after they have handed over the arms in their possession, to go back the way they came. St. George who killed the dragon is the patron alike of our army and of our ally's: so that we may be able to stand up against this cruel godless dragon that has newly arisen to afflict the human race, let us be bound to our ally in a firm and everlasting friendship and brotherhood: and I charge you to show them goodness and kindness, regarding them as your family and friends.

That evening there was national celebration and some wild scenes in the capital, but neither riot nor rape. At the palace where His Imperial Majesty was installed, a few of Wingate's officers gave the Emperor a small banquet, at which, towards the end, Wingate rose and gave a toast in these words:

"I and the British officers under my command did our share in this campaign together with the patriots, in the knowledge that in doing so we were helping in furthering the object for which Britain is fighting throughout the world—the right of every individual to freedom of conscience, the right of a small nation for a just decision at the tribunal of nations. Until the liberation of Ethiopia, the wrongs which brought this war in its wake had not been put right and there was no hope for victory to our arms in this war."

A message of congratulations from the British Premier Winston Churchill was received which read:

"It is with deep and unanimous satisfaction that the British nation and Empire have learnt of the reception given to Your Imperial Majesty on your return to your capital, Addis Ababa. Your Majesty was the first of the Sovereigns to be driven from his throne and his country by the Nazi and Fascist criminals, and you are the first to return in triumph. We shall not fail to transmit Your Majesty's thanks in due form to the Commander-in-Chief, Officers and soldiers of the British and Imperial armies who have helped the patriots to put an end by a total and final destruction to the military usurpation of the Italians. His Majesty's Government has the firm hope that Ethiopia will enjoy a long period of peace . . ."

110

CHAPTER 9

Post-Liberation Political Issues

His Majesty the Emperor, as seen in the preceding pages, had reached his capital on May 5th, 1941, in a high spirit of hope, thankfulness and gratitude. He left as monarch and returned as monarch. But he had sought and obtained the aid of the British ally in the prosecution of a war which concerned the interests of freedom in all parts of the world. Truthfully the success of the liberation campaign was, to a major extent, achieved by this spectacular allied aid. The military restored the freedom of the country from Fascist domination. Was this to be just a swapping of oppressors? This question was posed in its stark reality almost immediately after the Emperor's triumphant return to Addis Ababa.

From a military stand point no one could have doubted the ally's responsibilities. Had not these been carried out with efficiency, the transition to civil rule in Ethiopia would undoubtedly have been most difficult. In the heat of the conflict, however, there was no time to strike the lines which the ultimate political resolution after the liberation of the country would follow. This was a political matter which, in essence, concerned more the British and Ethiopian Governments than the military men whose authority was clearly delegated.

After a preliminary examination of the general picture in Ethiopia following the surrender of Addis Ababa, it was decided that the best method of establishing some form of administration which would meet British requirements and those of the Emperor, within the limitations imposed by necessity, was to divide the country into nine administrative units. These were to be as nearly as possible self-contained, and consequently to include, for instance, medical, agricultural and financial services. These groups of officers would form Political Missions under the central direction of the Deputy Chief Political Officer at Addis Ababa, but decentralised and working with the local Ethiopian Chiefs and surviving Ethiopian administrative officials. The officers composing these "Missions" would not themselves administer—they would guide and direct the local authority, whatever form it took.

The nine administrative areas in the first instance were: (1) Gondar—with the Mission at Gondar; (2) Tigré—at Axum and Adwa; (3) Gojjam—at Debra Markos; (4) Wollo—at Dessie; (5) Shoa—at Addis Ababa; (6) Wallaga—at Lekemti; (7) Sidamo—at Neghelli or Soddu; (8) Jimma—at Jimma (later changed into the Kaffa Province); and (9) Harar—at Harar.

It was subsequently decided to divide areas Nos. 7 and 8 into two, with headquarters at Mega and Kaji respectively. The Italians were still at Gondar, so this area could not come into existence until they had surrendered, and there were still Italians in the west. It was an essential part of the scheme that these Missions could remain as units in the centres selected, from which the officers could tour their areas. They would now detach officers in numerous provincial centres, in order to economise personnel and prevent young and enthusiastic officers trying to play the part of district rulers or to undertake direct administration.

As the military operations drew to a close in various parts of the country and the surviving Italian armed forces surrendered, the Political Missions took shape in the centres from which they were to work. Their arrival and beginnings were as a rule marked by the peaceful restoration, or the institution from local resources, of an embryonic local administration.

In a desire to get ahead with the civil administration of the country as speedily as possible, on 11th May, 1941, the Emperor appointed seven Cabinet Ministers and a Governor of Shoa, which included Addis Ababa. This move irked Sir Philip Mitchell, the Chief Political Officer so much that he asked for instructions from the War Office in London. The appointments meant little more than a formality, inasmuch as departments and staffs did not exist, and the Emperor, apart from gifts received and a grant towards a civil list from British funds, had no financial resources or means of collecting taxes. In order to overcome this misunderstanding and meet the Ethiopian authorities as far as possible, after the public announcement of these appointments, it was decided to regard the newly chosen Ministers as advisers, in their respective branches, to the staff of the Military Administrators charged with their subjects. In the outcome the advice of these Ministers proved of assistance to Brigadier Lush's officers, although the Ministers were hampered by the lack of Ethiopian departmental personnel. This misunderstanding regarding appointments accelerated the dispatch from London on the 17th May of a detailed instruction on the policy which was to be followed in Ethiopia.

It was the outcome of the deliberations of the interested departments of His Britannic Majesty's Government during the weeks which followed the return of the Foreign Secretary from the Middle East and was designed to be the authoritative basis for the relationship of the Chief Political Officer with the Emperor Haile Selassie I. It was made clear that while the re-appearance of an independent Ethiopian State was welcomed, the advice of the British Military authorities must be strictly adhered to by the Emperor while the existing military situation continued. Pending further decision by His Majesty's Government, Ethiopia was to remain under British military guidance and control. In areas occupied by British Military forces, to be notified by the Commander-in-Chief and liable to alteration in accordance with military exigencies, the Deputy Chief Political Officer was to be the political and administrative executive of the Commander-in-Chief.

On behalf of His Britannic Majesty's Government and the War Office the Chief Political Officer would exercise departmental control and administrative supervision, British Military Administration thus being operative in these areas [1].

(1)   Lord Rennell of Rodd, *op. cit.*

The British Government accepted Ethiopia as an ally. It was abundantly clear, even before the Emperor left the United Kingdom, that the Ethiopian campaign was part of the allied strategy to defeat the Axis powers. In the campaign the Emperor led his armies against the enemy in the field, and, as has been eloquently agreed even by the Italians, his presence alone had the most damaging effect of kinetizing the rebellion of the patriots who had never ceased to harass the enemy.

There could have been no doubt whatsoever about the status of the Emperor and of Ethiopia, neither in the war nor in its ultimate outcome. The new Anglo-Ethiopian relationship was definitely in no state of uncertainty. Most wisely and in a general measure due to His Majesty the Emperor's tact, patience and resolve, the situation subsequently cleared up with the signing of the Anglo-Ethiopian Agreement and Military Convention signed in Addis Ababa on January 31st, 1942.

Had things turned out differently because of the temporary misunderstanding which arose in the early days of the settlement, it would have been the tragic anti-climax to what His Imperial Majesty said at Omedla:

To the Government and people of Great Britain who in our time of bitter trial received and helped with such kindness as touches the heart, I express before the world, in my own name and in yours (the Ethiopian people), my thanks and my undying gratitude towards them.

And equally would it have smeared the picture which the Emperor painted in concluding his first speech in Addis Ababa upon his return, when he said:

St. George who killed the dragon is the patron alike of our army and of our ally's: so that we may be able to stand up against this cruel godless dragon that has newly arisen to afflict the human race, let us be bound to our ally in a firm and everlasting friendship and brotherhood: and I charge you to show them goodness and kindness, regarding them as your family and friends.

Since Ethiopia became an ally the previous recognition of the Italian conquest of this country became, for all purposes, null and void. The new relationship could have been founded on nothing short of a full recognition of the right of independent life and happiness of the Ethiopian people; full repudiation of the Fascist attempted conquest; and of the infamous Anglo-Italian agreement made in the disastrous days of appeasing the aggressors. This position was clearly established by the affirmative answer to Colonel's Wedgwood's question in the House of Commons, July 11th, 1940, given by Mr. Butler, then Under-Secretary for Foreign Office. The question asked was:

"Whether contact has been made between the lawful Government of Ethiopia now admitted to the full status of an ally in the present war, with assurances that Ethiopia's independence will be assured when the war is won . . ."

The curtain had already been raised on a new chapter of Anglo-Ethiopian relation, and in spite of everything it had to be written. The British Government was quick to react to a situation which could have had far-reaching repercussion, not only on the further prosecution of the war, but more so, within its far flung Empire.

His Imperial Majesty knew his responsibility to his nation and people. Although the situation was a delicate one, he handled it with *savoir-faire*. In a conference with the Chief Political Officer prior to his departure for London to discuss this problem, His Majesty the Emperor produced six points which he wished to be submitted by Sir Philip Mitchell to the War Office. These were: (1) He wanted to form an army as soon as possible; (2) He needed a prompt financial arrangement; (3) Advisers were needed at once for the ministries, especially Finance and Justice; (4) He wanted to establish his provincial administration; (5) He would like to see a draft treaty as soon as possible; and (6) How much did he owe for the campaign. Some of these points, as will be later seen, were included in the agreement signed on January 31st, 1942, which ended the system of dual control that emerged with the end of the liberation.

Sir Philip Mitchell flew to England, where he arrived on the 31st May. Between that date and the 15th June when he left London, all aspects of the Ethiopian situation and of Italian East Africa and British Somaliland were discussed with the departments concerned. At a meeting of the War Cabinet on the 9th June, to which Sir Philip Mitchell was summoned, he was instructed on his return to open discussions with the Emperor in order to come to a definite understanding on the lines laid down, pending the conclusion of an agreement between His Britannic Majesty's Government and himself. This was to be either at the end of the War or at such earlier date as might be found desirable.

On his return to East Africa Sir Philip Mitchell attended a conference, at which Generals Wavell, Platt and Cunningham were present, to discuss the policy to be pursued in Ethiopia in the light of the wishes expressed by the War Cabinet. The outcome of this conference was recorded by Sir Philip Mitchell as follows:—

"I reached Addis Ababa on my return on the 24th June and after a conference on the 25th and 26th at Asmara with General Wavell, General Cunningham and General Platt, made proposals to the Emperor for an understanding of which the following is a broad summary:—

(I)   The Emperor to agree to abide in all matters touching the Government of Ethiopia by the advice of His Majesty's Government.
(II)   Taxation and expenditure to require the prior approval of His Britannic Majesty's Government.
(III)   Jurisdiction over foreigners to be reserved to British courts.
(IV)   The Emperor to raise no objection if the Commander-in-Chief found it necessary to resume military control of any part of Ethiopia.
(V)   No armed forces to be raised or military operations undertaken except as agreed by His Majesty's Government's representative.

"If the Emperor should agree to accept the above conditions I was instructed that His Majesty's Government would be willing:—

(a) To provide funds to establish the armed forces, administrative and other services needed in Ethiopia;

114

(b) To provide expert advisers for the Emperor;

(c) To use their best endeavours to re-establish the Ethiopian Government;

(d) To operate the necessary communications;

(e) To examine proposals for a Treaty with the Emperor which would include a general financial settlement."

With Lord Rennell, who had also attended the Asmara Conference and had been acting as Chief Political Officer during his absence in England, Sir Philip Mitchell then proceeded to Addis Ababa to open discussions with the Emperor. These were to range over the whole field of administration of the country, including the vital subjects of finance, financial control, economic policy, and assistance from His Britannic Majesty's Government. From the outset negotiations were to some extent hampered and delayed by the material difficulties of language and lack of competent Ethiopian staff, the Emperor carrying on all the negotiations in person in Amharic through interpreters.

The Emperor was fortunate, however, in having as his European Political Adviser Brigadier Sandford, and with him a legal adviser, Mr. Charles Mathew, formerly Judicial Adviser to the Native Government of Buganda, seconded at the suggestion of Sir Philip Mitchell by the Colonial Office to assist the new administration on the Ethiopian side as distinct from the British Military Administration side. The first reply to Sir Philip Mitchell's *aide memoire*, drawn on the lines recorded, came on the 12th July. It disclosed only differences which could apparently be bridged. From the end of July onwards the main discussions dealt with points of detail of a proposed agreement. Among these were the subsidiary convention or agreement laying down the rights of British troops and foreign persons in Ethiopia including the judicial regime covering them, and the functions of a proposed British Military Mission which was to undertake the training and organisation of the Ethiopian Army—as the historical successor of the Military Mission which had trained and organised the Patriots for the campaign against the Italians [2].

It became momentarily apparent that His Imperial Majesty and his inherent authority became the centre of a divergence of views between himself and the Chief Political Officer. When it is remembered that the Emperor did not travel to Europe to bury his country, but had gone there to plead his just cause before the League, and that he led the campaign of liberation at the head of his own forces, the general view of occupied enemy territory could not have applied to Ethiopia.

On the 16th October, 1941, Sir Philip Mitchell was summoned to London to discuss the Anglo-Ethiopian Agreement which had been under negotiation since the Chief Political Officer's visit to England in the summer. In London he was met by his C.F.A., Lord Rennell, who had arrived a few days previously. After some preliminary talks had taken place with the War Office and other interested departments of His Majesty's Government, a Cabinet Committee, presided over by the then Lord President (the

[2]   Lord Rennell of Rodd, *op. cit.*

115

Rt. Hon. Sir John Anderson), was appointed and during the first ten days of November prepared material for a second submission on policy to the Cabinet. This submission was made on the 11th November and its directions were incorporated in the revised texts of an Agreement and Military Convention, which showed differences from the original drafts in several particulars.

These were mainly (a) in the degree and nature of budgetary control over revenue and expenditure in Ethiopia, (b) the amount and nature of the financial assistance to be granted by His Majesty's Government, (c) in the status and responsibilities of the British advisers, who were to assist the Emperor in setting up his administration, and (d) in the composition and duties of the personnel of the Ethiopian High Court. Furthermore, the material contained in the original drafts was rearranged so that all matters affecting military interests while British military occupation continued were, as far as possible, included in a Military Convention, while the Agreement proper was confined mainly to political relationships between the two parties.

One of the differences between the original drafts on which Sir Philip Mitchell had been working in his negotiations with the Emperor during the summer months, and those now taken back by him to resume discussion, was, as has been said, connected with financial control. Effective financial control in return for a grant of financial assistance from His Majesty's Government, had been regarded as probable by interested Political Branch Officers in Africa and it had been in anticipation of such a system being installed that the Deputy Controller of Finance and Accounts in Addis Ababa had begun to draw up his organisation of central and provincial treasuries, central accounting and a budgetary mechanism. In the November drafts, however, appeared the following formula (Article IV (c) of the Agreement):—

"His Majesty the Emperor agrees that there shall be the closest co-operation between the Ethiopian authorities and his British Advisers, to be appointed in accordance with Article II (a), regarding public expenditure." Thus no effective control of expenditure was now envisaged. The Agreement provided moreover that the grants would be made by His Majesty's Government to the Emperor directly without passing them through the hands of any financial controller or adviser.

In brief the policy put forward in London was to cut short the responsibilities of His Majesty's Government in Ethiopia as quickly as possible, and this therefore was the setting in which the Chief Political Officer, Sir Philip Mitchell, returned to Ethiopia to resume negotiations on the drafts of the Agreement and Military Convention. The Chief Political Officer reached Addis Ababa on the 12th December, 1941, and, as soon as the necessary translations of the documents into Amharic had been prepared, negotiations were resumed. With unimportant amendments the texts were put into final form for signature.

The signature of the Agreement and Military Convention took place on 31st January, 1942, with as much pomp and ceremony as was possible in the circumstances. The Council Room of the Imperial Palace was chosen as the appropriate place for the signature of the instrument, which in fact restored to the Emperor the sovereignty of his country. Two guards of honour, consisting of a company each of the King's African Rifles and of the new Ethiopian Army trained by the British Military Mission, were drawn up in front of the steps of the Palace on either side of the flagstaff which had flown the Italian flag until the surrender of the capital.

The British Representative, Sir Philip Mitchell, arrived first; his staff and the British Commander of the troops in Addis Ababa with his staff were on the steps of the Palace to receive him. The Emperor and his staff then arrived to find Sir Philip Mitchell and the senior British officers drawn up in the Council Room to meet him. The signature and sealing of the various documents took nearly an hour and the proceedings were terminated by appropriate honour as the Ethiopian flag was hoisted on the flagmast and the Ethiopian National Anthem was played. From that moment the Palace, where the Emperor had been living since May, 1941, became the official residence of the Sovereign of Ethiopia; the offices of the Deputy Chief Political Officer were installed in the old Fascist Headquarters; the duties of the Deputy Chief Political Officer and the Chief Political Officer, when in Addis Ababa, were transferred to the British Diplomatic Representative who should arrive to take up his functions.

In his semi-annual despatch to the General Officer Commanding-in-Chief, East Africa Command, for transmission to the Secretary of State for War, Sir Philip Mitchell, referring to the signature of the Agreement, wrote:—
"There is no doubt that, at that time, the instruments gave genuine pleasure and were warmly welcomed by Ethiopian Ministers and Notables."(3)

The negotiations were hard and tedious and demanded of His Imperial Majesty a great deal of patient thought. The Emperor was dealing with matters which touched the integrity and future status of his country and his government. While space does not permit a detailed analysis of the negotiations, the words of Sir Philip Mitchell, written in his book, *African Afterthoughts* should give an idea of what the situation was when these post-liberation political issues were being negotiated. He wrote:
"I was becoming very tired and irritable and so no doubt was the Emperor, but we remained on excellent personal terms. I ought to record here that as I got to know him I came to have a very high respect for him and recognised his qualities of courage and determination and his considerable wisdom, even when I wished he would be a little more forthcoming in negotiation. I hope, if he ever sees this, he will not mind my recording as much, and adding that I retain now only the most agreeable recollections of those days and of our long association in the course of the negotiations."(4)

The 1942 Treaty served its purpose. It was, in truth and in fact, purely a war measure. Fortunately for Africa, however, by the time of its expiry, the continent was fairly safe from the Axis strategy. In addition, Ethiopia had begun to move forward in her strides on the road to civil life and re-

(3)   Lord Rennell of Rodd, *op. cit.*
(4)   Sir Philip Mitchell, *op. cit.*

117

habilitation in 1944 which marked the end of the 1942 Agreement and Military Convention. To meet the new situation, another temporary agreement was, therefore, signed in Addis Ababa on the 19th December, 1944, and its preamble read:

"Whereas, on the 31st January, 1942, an Agreement and a Military Convention were signed at Addis Ababa between His Majesty the Emperor and the Government of His Majesty the King of the United Kingdom of Great Britain and Northern Ireland, with the provision that they should remain in force until replaced by a treaty for which His Imperial Majesty the Emperor might wish to make proposals;

"Considering that circumstances have changed since the said Agreement and Convention were concluded, but that while the war continues it is not opportune to negotiate a permanent treaty;

"Desiring, as members of the United Nations, to render mutual assistance to the cause of the United Nations and to conclude a new temporary Agreement for the regulation of their mutual relations;"

This 1944 Anglo-Ethiopian Agreement (text in the Appendix) was negotiated on a basis more in accord with normal international relations. In 1942, Ethiopia had been recently freed from the yoke of fascist aggression —thanks to British arms! Italian soldiers were still in the land and the continent was still a possible springboard for Axis domination of the world. A Member of the United Nations, pledged to the ultimate defeat of the Axis, Ethiopia was farther from the distress in which the Italian war had left her. The nature of the signatories had changed because of the intervening circumstances. The former Agreement had been negotiated, "to assist in providing the immediate needs of the country and to help His Imperial Majesty." The 1944 Treaty was entered into, "to render mutual assistance to the cause of the United Nations and to conclude a new temporary agreement for the regulation of their mutual relations."

While certain points in the 1944 Pact represented harsh concessions on the part of Ethiopia, it was the basis for normalising relations between the two countries. In so far as the terms of its predecessor were really superseded, Ethiopia was left with certain options, in the 1944 Agreement, more compatible with the essential nature of an independent and sovereign state. Unlike the previous Agreement, the new one was concluded without any financial assistance, although the country could, even today, use large sums for her long-term development projects. The nation's independence of political action so preserved, however, seemed to the Imperial Ethiopian Government and the people a better deal than the terms on which the United Kingdom had offered gratuitous and limited financial assistance.

The continuing aspects of the world war caused the Ethiopian Government, in its desire to shoulder its responsibility to the Allied and Associated Powers, to grant certain concessions. Article VII of this Agreement which was a carry-over from the former Agreement read:

"In order as an Ally to contribute to the effective prosecution of the war, and without prejudice to their underlying sovereignty, the Imperial Ethiopian Government hereby agree that, for the duration of this Agreement, the territories designed as the Reserved Area and the Ogaden, as set forth

118

in the attached schedule, shall be under British Military Administration."
Ethiopia was freed— the first occupied country to be freed. But German
and Italian troops (1942), under Rommel, were menacing Egypt, and the
British required a protected land route from the Sudan to the Red Sea.
This concession was part of the collaboration and mutual assistance for
the duration of the war for which the 1942 Anglo-Ethiopian Agreement
and Military Convention had provided.

CHAPTER 10

State of Country on Emperor's Return

On May 5th, 1936, after the dramatic episode from Walwal to Maichaw, which ended in the defeat of Ethiopia's unprepared and unorganised armies of defence, the Fascist hordes marched in Addis Ababa. A great deal of havoc was caused, the people were displaced, hearths and homes were destroyed. In a nutshell, ordered life for the Ethiopians came to a stand still.

The occupiers, in their unholy mission of "civilisation", tried desperately to present a convincing front to the world. They were in haste to build a façade to prove that finally, after years of trying, they had succeeded in conquering an empire to be constructed in a hurry, in order to maintain Italy's vaunted prestige. Except to utilise their labour and the country's wealth to this grandiose end, the occupation policy was, naturally, not in the interest of the Ethiopian people. Moreso, the continual plastering of the Ethiopian patriots retarded even this plan of empire building.

Within five years the counter-attack came. The Italians had neither time to consolidate their gains nor breathing space to use their ill-gotten booty. The reconquest had battered the ramparts of the paper citadel which Mussolini was attempting to build in Ethiopia and East Africa which, like the tottering walls of Jericho, fell down on his head.

The toll of two wars had, therefore, torn the nation to shreds — economically, socially and spiritually. The Emperor's task then, was equal to the destruction and dislocation that had taken place from 1935—1941, which had brought immemorable hardships to Ethiopia and her people.

After His Imperial Majesty reached Addis Ababa, May 5th, 1941, the operations against remaining Italian pockets at Gondar had yet to be carried out. This began at the end of the rainy season. Over the greater part of the country conditions of peace had to be rapidly re-established. The work that the Emperor and the British Military Authority had to tackle was enormous; before the war Ethiopia was in the melting-pot of progress. Some of the achievements of the Italians (those which were left) had to be included in the new structure. It was not a mere reconstruction of the past then, but more a rebuilding to meet the new situation. Military necessity and its stringency on supplies determined, to a telling extent, the pace of this reconstruction.

His Majesty the Emperor was naturally impatient to re-enter into full possession of his kingdom and his authority so as to proceed with the business of state. He also knew that his country was embarking on a new period of history with the heavy handicap of the decimation of the class of educated and trained officials and administrators. To restore to Ethiopia an independance more securely founded than that which she enjoyed before 1935, was his aim with the co-operation of his British ally. It surely was not a task to be easily achieved while the world war was raging even within the borders of his country. In addition, so long as Hitler threatened the world, any part of Africa was a potential part of the theatre of war.

The changes brought about by the Italo-Ethiopian war and occupation were, from the point of view of a sovereign state, completely disruptive. The occupiers, naturally, in their plan of "Africa Orientale", had designed Ethiopia to be a colony to support the central economy of the mother country — Italy.

It is a historic fact that the drive for empire, not only in the case of Italy, had economic causes. The occupiers, therefore, had, with much haste, and so far as their superior force could secure for them some respite for administration, attempted to change the Ethiopian empire into a first rate colony. Thus, the political, social, economic and psychological status left by the Italians had to be completely reshaped. In fact, the Emperor had to uproot the processes of Italy's five year colonisation and reinstate the foundation of an independent state.

When the Emperor came to the throne of Ethiopia in 1930, after having been Regent for 14 years, he spent his utmost effort in introducing various reforms. It was a heavy task, for his country, geographically isolated and cut off from the sea, lay outside the main stream of modern progress. The evident results of these internal reforms had excited Mussolini's desire to invade the country in 1935, come hell or high water. The billions of lire poured into the colonising enterprise from 1935—41 gave a hint as to how this policy of penetration was regarded by Rome. Conversely, it indicates the extent of the rehabilitation programme which His Majesty the Emperor had to face upon his return to the throne on May 5th, 1941.

What was the political and economic situation in Ethiopia then? To many it has been told that the Italian occupation of this country had done some material good. This is a premise based, to some extent, on the knowledge that Italy is a more advanced nation than Ethiopia. In fact, a great deal of money was poured into the Ethiopian adventure.

The restored Emperor was faced with a hard task. The Italians, during five years of uneasy domination, had set themselves to break the spirit of a proud people and turn them into helots. They had killed or confined all the leading men who had not fled; they took the schools, which the Emperor had erected, for their own children and excluded the Ethiopians. They set up an elaborate and venal bureaucracy; and their lavish expenditure — nearly £ 120,000,000 of capital with an annual contribution of £ 10,000,000 to the local budget — raised the cost of living without doing anything to fit the people for modern development. They invested over £ 80,000,000 in constructing motor roads, finely engineered but costly to maintain, and smaller sums in medical services, in the residential and industrial quarters of their colonists, in barracks and public works. When they were expelled they left little to benefit the country save the roads. The hospitals were without doctors, the schools without teachers, most of the factories without machines and workers, the offices without trained officials.

The Italian occupation, most decidedly, had both advantages and disadvantages for the restored regime of His Majesty the Emperor. The most important benefits were from the roads, radiating from the capital and linking it with the most important provincial centres. These, supported by the expansion of the system of telegraph lines, built originally by Menelik, aided greatly in simplifying the administration and preservation of order.

Among the most important of the other results of the Italian occupation may be accounted the modernisation of the principal towns: the construction of houses, shops, offices, and workshops on the European pattern. Harar, Dessie, Dire Dawa, and a number of smaller centres had been converted in this way to look like bits of Italy. Some of them contained useful industrial plants. The ubiquitous motor repair shops were the most obvious examples, but there were also sawmills, cement, brick, and other works, and factories for the production of such things as boots and coarser textiles. These various forms of investment, besides serving as an object lesson to the Ethiopians, provided some means of carrying on the development of the country. The maintenance of their capital value, however, was conditional. Some were taken over by Greeks or Armenians; some by those Italians permitted to remain in Ethiopia; and others were run by Ethiopians with European assistance; part of them, especially those which depended on Italian subsidies, inevitably fell into decay for lack of tenants or concessionaires.

The Italians paid great attention to the development of the mineral resources of the country. They had begun to mine lignite as fuel for the cement and other works. Gold and platinum were being extracted in small quantities, but probably the most attractive mineral proposition is a couple of mica mines which were in fairly promising production. With the mines may be classed the attempts made by the Italians to start, with Italian labour, intensive agricultural production of such things as cotton and vegetable fibre.

Like all conquests, that of the Italians in Ethiopia had left several scars on the country. As mentioned previously, they, for good reasons, killed the intelligentsia and liquidated many of the leaders on whom the Emperor should have depended. They had to destroy all opposition.

True, the five years had ushered in new ways, and by emulation, some of the people were influenced by the occupiers' manner of thought. Many old traditions were undermined and new standards were set up. In most of the economic, social and political detail, however, the nation was really stricken when the Emperor returned.

In these cataclysmic times memories tend to become short, and it is hard to remember how formidable the task which confronted him. There was no part of the country which had not been visited by the war in the six months preceding his entry, and many districts had been ravaged over and over again during the previous six years. Shattered buildings, broken bridges, and abandoned transport met the eye wherever one went. The country was full of rifles, machine guns, and bombs captured from, or flung away by, the fleeing enemy. These weapons were by no means all in the hands of the peaceful peasantry desiring nothing better than to get back to their ploughing. They were largely in the hands of disbanded soldiers of the Italian native army, or of patriot guerillas, who after years of outlawry would require time and opportunity to become absorbed again as members of a peaceful community. These unruly, or at least unsettled, elements of the population had to live, and they were in fact 'living on he country'. The Italian administrative machinery had of course disappeared. Means of communication had been dislocated and the roads were dangerous in more senses than one. Trade was dead, and in many districts there was a shortage of the necessaries of life — of salt, of clothing and, in large areas, even of food. (1)

Realising the heavy task which lay ahead, the Emperor, in laying his plans for reorganisation, was astute enough to make prior provisions. The Anglo-Ethiopian Agreement and Military Convention signed at Addis Ababa on January 31st, 1942, states:

"Whereas His Majesty the Emperor, true to His Coronation pledges not to surrender his sovereignty or the independence of his people, but conscious of the needs of his country had intimated to the Government of the United Kingdom of Great Britain and Northern Ireland (herein referred to as the government of the United Kingdom) that he is eager to receive advice and financial assistance in the difficult task of reconstruction and reform; and

"Whereas the government of the United Kingdom recognise that Ethiopia is now a free and independent state and His Majesty the Emperor, Haile Selassie I, is its lawful ruler, and, the reconquest of Ethiopia being now complete shall help His Majesty the Emperor to re-establish his government and to assist in providing for the immediate needs of the country:

"Have agreed as follows:" (See Appendix)

As stated in the preceding chapter, the Grants-in-Aid provided by

(1)   Christine Sandford, *Ethiopia under Haile Selassie.*

that agreement assisted in paving the way for the enormous task of reorganisation. They had a salutary effect on the new fiscal policy which was to unfold. Things had to happen in a hurry. There was the ministerial and administrative side to be taken care of as a first step in the revived state.

The reorganisation could not move fast, but progress was seen in a comparatively short time. Under the Agreement, the Emperor had the help of British advisers in the opening stages of the reconstruction. These were appointed to the ministries of Interior, Finance, Justice, Education, Commerce and Industry and Public Works. A few British were appointed to executive posts and two British judges to the Imperial Ethiopian High Court. British teachers directed some Boys' and Girls' schools. Moreover, two British agencies, independent of the Government, gave valuable and welcome service: The British Council opened an Institute to teach English to adults in Addis Ababa and in a few provincial towns; an Anglo Ethiopian Club fostered social contact. A Friends Ambulance Unit followed the army to look to medical, hygienic and social needs of the civil population. Some were doctors, some medical students, some had experience of teaching others were professional or business people trained in social service.

The Ethiopian people remained loyal and receptive in spite of this aftermath of war and occupation. The ravage of the occupation had displaced a multitude of them. Many homes were destroyed, families had to flee for refuge from one place to another before the systematic persecution of the district folk carried on in order to locate the connections of the patriots. Many of the educated class who escaped liquidation were still in exile. Those crippled by poison gas, wounded in battle and otherwise mentally deranged by the strain of privation swelled the ranks of the displaced. Then there were the orphans, the widows and the sick. Since the devastation was wide-spread as a result of two wars in six years, and over a country as extensive and topographically difficult as Ethiopia, the magnitude of the task o setting up the new administration could be easily appreciated.

The country was virtually littered with Italians whose evacuation could not be taken care of until after January 31st, 1942, when the Anglo-Ethiopian Treaty and Military Convention was signed. This was the major task of the British Military Administration. Immediately after the re-occupation of Addis Ababa the Italian civil population in the capital were segregated into four zones in the city. Those in outlying places were assembled in a few centres, whence, with those in Addis Ababa, they were evacuated by rail as far as Dire Dawa and then by road to the Somaliland coast. The able-bodied men were interned in British East African territories, the women and children and invalid or old men were repatriated to Italy in three waves of steamers sent from Italy for the purpose.

There were as well economic problems created from the fact of a

124

complete dislocation of the Italian norm, that attendant on the re-occupation, and the drive to erect the new economy.

As Sir Philip Mitchell has written:

The supply services of the forces found much Italian plant and many stores which they needed for the war and took them away, the Emperor protesting strongly at the removal of booty of war, which he hoped to turn to good use in the country. There were occasional incidents, sometimes involving loss of life, between British troops and Abyssinian irregulars. There were interminable arguments about money or currency; the Abyssinian currency had been the Maria Theresa Dollar, a bullion currency worth its face value as metal. We had arranged stocks of these for our own purposes and to support credit, but in the British taxpayers' interests were very sparing in the use of them. This did not commend itself to the new Ethiopian authorities, whom we financed with East African currency. These and many other things played their part in creating misunderstandings. And all the time the vast task of evacuating Italian prisoners of war and civilians in tens of thousands was going on, and of course often raising awkward questions about Italian property, as to which we were apt to be more particular than the Ethiopians thought necessary. (2)

Sources of Government revenue were non-existent and attempt at a fiscal policy extremely confused. At that time the Maria Theresa Thaler, the East African currency, the Rupee and Italian Lire were in circulation.

By the summer of 1941 the railway from Dire Dawa to Addis Ababa was restored; prior to this access to the sea from Dire Dawa had been maintained through British Somaliland, since the French Somali-land Coast was still in Vichy hands.

Economic conditions, however, improved rapidly during 1941; prices showed a substantial fall until the impending signature of the Agreement, when this trend reversed itself. Exchange rates were maintained stable without difficulty between all the currencies in use, except that the Italian lira had a tendency to fall below the rate of 480 to the Pound Sterling which had been fixed throughout these territories. During the period of British administration, the Maria Theresa Thaler fixed at 1s. 10½ d. per dollar on the prevailing price of silver remained steady, merchants preferring to trade in the East African and Rupee currencies. Little was possible in the direction of collecting revenues except from the Customs duties on imports. The Italian fiscal system had, of course, broken down completely, and, in view of the imminent evacuation of the Italian population, nothing could be collected from that source. The Ethiopians, naturally, considered that, with the change of regime, nothing further was payable on the Italian imposts. An attempt to set up a western financial system by the organisation of

(2) Sir Philip Mitchell, *op. cit.*

125

provincial treasuries, wherever British political officers were stationed in the provinces, also failed since the Emperor, from the outset, preferred to collect whatever was possible by the older methods which had existed before the Italian occupation, through local chiefs and officials, without assistance from the British Military Administration.

Arrangements were made by the British Military Administration with the Sudan Government and with the Military Administrations of Eritrea, British Somaliland and Italian Somaliland to collect custom revenues; in the case of the Sudan this was done at the Sudan Frontier Posts for a small commission. Facilities were made available for the resumption of trade with neighbouring countries and more especially with Aden the historic entrepôt for Ethiopia. In spite of Italian efforts to direct all Ethiopian trade to Italy, there remained a substantial merchanting connection between Addis Ababa and Aden in the hands of some Indian, Arab and Greek traders who had survived the Italian occupation.

A money remittance system through the treasury organisation of the Military Administration of Ethiopia, Eritrea and the Somalilands was made available to traders until such time as a British bank could be established at Addis Ababa, which was contemplated at the earliest possible moment. The pegged rates for all the currencies in use in Ethiopia and the neighbouring countries enabled merchants to remit freely for the first time for years to Aden and India without exchange risk. Though the occupied territories were not formally admitted to the sterling group of countries, permission was granted for these to be treated in practice as if they were in the sterling area. ([3])

The sums due from these collections were credited in the books of the political Branch against the cost of the Military Administration in Ethiopia until the country was over on the signature of the Agreement when the sums collected were credited to the Ethiopian Government.

The Customs tariffs were those in force at the moment of occupation, specific tariffs being converted to *ad valorem* equivalents to provide for depreciation of the lira currency in which they had been stipulated. The Franco-Ethiopian railway rates for civil passengers and freight were fixed at levels estimated to cover running costs.

The cost of the British Military Administration consisted in the main of the salaries and maintenance of the British Staff, a monthly grant to the Emperor for Civil List purposes, urgent maintenance and repairs on a very modest scale, the cost and maintenance of the Police Force in Addis Ababa, and a few grants to the Emperor for disbursement to Ethiopian Chiefs and officials for services rendered or other political reasons. No general grants-in-aid were made to the Emperor for administrative purposes, such as were provided for in the Agreement which, when they commenced, fell as a charge on Foreign Office votes. Receipts as stated were largely Customs. The cost of the

(3) Lord Rennell of Rodd, *op. cit.*

evacuation of the Italian population was separately accounted, so as to be recoverable from the Italian or other authorities.

While the Chief Political Officer, Sir Philip Mitchell and his staff were busy doing what to them was probably a routine job of Military Administration, His Majesty the Emperor was deeply preoccupied with methods of setting up his administration. After a series of negotiations with the Chief Political Officer, the Emperor and the British authorities, on January 31st, 1942, the Anglo-Ethiopian Agreement was signed.

Thereafter the Emperor was not operating in a vacuum, for the 1931 constitution was there as a blue print. He forthwith applied its provisions, and what was veritable chaos began, in a short period, to take shape. The Imperial Palace became the centre of a swift-moving administrative machine, His Majesty the Emperor taking a personal interest in the men, issues and problems which were essential to the present task.

Decrees and proclamations began to pour out of the press. The Negarit Gazeta started to appear with the laws, particularly administrative, which have been appearing ever since. As a prime necessity and deriving from the urgent need, education became the first line endeavour of the country. Men must be trained for the chores immediately ahead and to meet the growing responsibilities of the future structure of a modern state. For in line with the provisions of the constitution, His Majesty the Emperor was pledged to share the onus of government with his people.

Settled administration naturally, was the most important necessity. As aftermath of the occupation and the rout of the Italians, the country was flooded with abandoned arms. The people were uprooted, and unemployment threatened thousands who were turned from their hearths and homes by the previous conditions. Communications were cut, those who suffered under the restive rule by coercion were eagerly looking for the fulfilment of the new hope which they anticipated upon the return of their Sovereign. In brief, resolute and quick measures were required to turn the turmoil into tranquility, the chaos into order.

Central Government organisation was speedily undertaken. Eleven Ministries were created, namely: Interior with Dejazmach Makonnen Endalkatchaw as Minister, this Ministry was then divided into the departments of Public Security, Administrative Services, Lands, Health and Labour; the Ministry of War with Ras Ababa Aragai as Minister; Education with Ato Makonnen Desta as Minister; Foreign Affairs with Blatengeta Lorenzo Taezaz as Minister; Commerce and Industry with Nagadras Gabrezgier as Minister; Agriculture with Ato Makonnen Habte Wold as Minister; Post, Telegraphs and Telephones with Ato Balatchaw Yadate as Minister; Ministry of Pen with Tsahfe Tzezaz Wolde-Giuorgis Wolde-Yohannes as Minister;

127

and Public Works and Communications later with Ato Balatchaw Yadate as Minister with effect from the 15th July, 1942.

Ministerial co-ordination was provided by the institution of the Ministers' Council, comprising all the Ministers and the Vice-Ministers with His Imperial Majesty as its head. The office of Prime Minister was created in September 1942, with Dejazmach Makonnen Endalkatchaw as incumbent.

From among the small number of trusted men, His Majesty the Emperor, pressed with the task of reconstructing civil rule, got together his Government. Other subordinate administrative posts were filled as fast as the men could be found. But the officers of the twelve provinces had also to be named.

The avid search began, and in less than a year, Governors-General and other main suburban officials were named.

Security, the principal pillar of a stable government, began immediately to take shape. Assisted by the Anglo-Ethiopian Agreement and Military Convention (text to be found in the Appendix) in which His Imperial Majesty had arranged for the assistance of the United Kingdom government, the revived Ethiopian army and police force were brought into being simultaneous with the changeover from military to civil administration.

With the aid of the British Military Mission to Ethiopia a small but efficient regular army of men enlisted on a voluntary basis was created. This army comprised 10 infantry battalions, three batteries of artillery, engineers and signal units, an armoured car regiment and a mechanical transport corps. The Ministry of War later raised some 42 or more territorial battalions, also on a voluntary basis. In addition, three battalions of the Imperial Body Guard were mustered as a reliable reserve.

The regular police force was formed at the same time. Proclamation No. 6 of 1942, provided for the organisation, discipline, powers and duties of the police force. Article 4 (1) of the proclamation reads "The force shall consist of such number of superior police officers inspectors, non-commissioned officers and constables as our Ministry of Interior may from time to time direct, and to be subject to such conditions of service as the Commissioner may prescribe."

The Commissioner of Police was a Britisher who was assisted, a stemming from the Anglo-Ethiopian Agreement, by other British police officers. Ethiopians were recruited and trained in modern police craft to provide the necessary nucleus for the force. A division was made between the regular (nation-wide) police and those who were to be stationed in Addis Ababa. To meet the need for police security in the outlying parts of the Empire, local police, recruited more or less from members of the disbanded territorials, maintained law and order to the best of their possibilities.

Undoubtedly, there were problems in reinstating general security throughout the Empire where life was completely disorganized by the

128

war and occupation. The usual difficulties of a change-over of political organisation had also aggravated the situation. The security measures undertaken, therefore, were dependent for their success on the settling down of the population to peaceful living.

The Ministry of Interior started forthwith to build up its provincial administration. The authority of the central government had to permeate the whole country before an overall security system could have been effective.

In the capital itself, which had been the centre of all the unemployed, where those who were dislocated thronged to seek favours and opportunities, strong measures were called for. This caused the government to institute the curfew, and to be vigilant to prevent, and when necessary, stamp out, disorder. It is interesting to note, however, that crime was kept to its minimum, and the public peace was very little disturbed. In less than a year of His Imperial Majesty's return, public security in the capital was probably comparable to that of several large cities outside of Ethiopia.

The problem of prisons, so closely related to security, had to be tackled. Reorganisation under the authority of the Ministry of Justice started immediately. By reason of the fact that people were thrown in jail on the least pretext during the occupation, and that the Italians did not care to treat these prisoners humanely, the prison facilities, upon His Imperial Majesty's return, were deplorable. Because the resources at the disposal of the Government were rather slender at the restoration, not much could have been done to the project of penal reform. The government, however, did its best, under the circumstances, to modernise them. Thus, the prisons in the capital and in the larger towns saw some measure of reorganisation.

Again stemming from the Anglo-Ethiopian Agreement of 1942, His Majesty the Emperor made provisions clearly for immediate reforms in the Administration of Justice.

Forthwith to establish adequate machinery for internal security, completely disarranged as a result of the war, occupation and subsequent rout of the enemy, the Emperor immediately issued the Administration of Justice Proclamation. To indicate the measure of fore-thought given to an enlightened administration, the Emperor had consulted with the British authorities on this matter, and a draft of the proclamation became part of the Annexe of the Anglo-Ethiopian Military Convention of 1942.

The proclamation established four kinds of courts: (a) the Supreme Imperial Court; (b) the High Court; (c) the Provincial Court; (d) Regional and Communal Courts, and specified their Jurisdiction. The qualification of Justices and Imperial prerogative to choose them were provided for. Part II of the proclamation specifically stated: "The High Court shall contain such number of judges of British nationality as we shall consider to be desirable."

So essential to the maintenance of public order, the administration of justice appeared simultaneously with the other agencies of public security. The new system of courts (Regional, Communal, Provincial, High and Supreme, Imperial), was launched as soon as possible to ensure the speedy administration of justice to all persons in the Empire.

In Chapter 14 a fuller report of the administration of justice as it developed during the 25 years of His Imperial Majesty's reign will be found.

In the time of Menelik various Imperial edicts were published, but the written law as known today did not truly appear until the regency of the present Emperor. The first proclamation after the liberation, therefore, most appropriately, established the Negarit Gazeta. In it, all legislation, proclamations, legal notices of the Imperial Ethiopian Government are published. This was a tremendous step forward in Ethiopian Legislation. The proclamation that gave the Negarit Gazeta its legal basis contains a provision that no law or by-law is valid, and would come into force only when it is published in the Negarit Gazeta; furthermore, that the publication must be monthly. The first basis for codification of Ethiopian laws, according to modern practice, was laid down by this Negarit Gazeta proclamation — the first edict after the liberation.

It was expected that, apart from security which, because of the circumstances, was an imperative step in the early post-liberation, education should immediately emerge. Realising that the five years of occupation had completely up-rooted the embryo system begun during his regency and closely cared for during the four years of his ascendency as Emperor, His Majesty immediately set up the Ministry of Education. Material and personnel were, naturally, in short supply. This was, however, no barrier. Actually the situation had to be met and this most far-reaching reform swiftly got under way.

Perhaps the most significant and encouraging indication of the spirit in which the Ethiopian people faced the future was the immediate and insistent demand for education which arose on all sides and from all classes as soon as the Emperor's Administration was restored. The education of his people has always been the interest nearest to the Emperor's heart. Before the Italians invaded the country he had instituted excellent Government elementary and secondary schools in the capital, and had encouraged educational work by Missionaries and others all over the Empire. All that he had created was destroyed by the Italians, who not only swept away the schools but sought out and exterminated a large portion of the young men who had been educated. For five or six years, therefore, there had been no education in the country, and a little reflection will show what a setback that has meant to plans for staffing the professions and essential Government and other services, and to reconstruction generally. The section of this book dealing with education will show what strides have been made since the liberation and what is planned for the future, at this 25 years' mark of His Imperials Majesty's reign.

Among the primary problems tackled by His Majesty the Emperor when he returned after his arduous period of exile was the health of his people. One of the inevitable results of war is ill-health and disease. Ethiopia sustained two wars from 1935 to 1941. This meant excessive depletion of the physical and psychological energies of the people. Then again, the occupation years were ones of rigid exploitation, characterised by the occupier's desire to drain the resources of the country for his own benefit. The mental and physical wear and tear at the time of the liberation was enormous. Over 50,000 Italian settlers, outside the huge army, were brought in the country. And the normal lag between their entry and the development of adequate food resources necessitated a tightly rationed diet even for these immigrants. The plight of the bulk of the Ethiopians was one of near starvation during these fateful years — malnutrition was rampant. Health rehabilitation had to be taken care of immediately.

The organisation of public health services was the next most urgent problem. Diseases — due largely to war conditions and to malnutrition, and in some cases newly imported from abroad — were rife. Medical services, except in the capital, had disappeared.

Ethiopia faced severe difficulties in finding doctors, surgeons, radiologists, and bacteriologists. In addition, the problem of replacing medical and surgical supplies was fraught with difficulty.

Finance and a fiscal policy, were started after the liberation with the Grant-in-Aid from the British Government, which sprang from article IV of the Anglo-Ethiopian Agreement and Military Convention of 1942. The article provided that:

"(a)   His Majesty the Emperor, having intimated to the Government of the United Kingdom that he will require financial aid in order to re-establish his administration, the Government of the United Kingdom will grant to His Majesty the sum of Pounds Sterling one million five hundred thousand during the first year and Pounds Sterling one million during the second year of the currency of this Agreement. If this Agreement remains in force for a third year, (which it did not) the Government of the United Kingdom agree to pay to His Majesty the Emperor the sum of Pounds Sterling five hundred thousand in respect of such third year, and if for a fourth year then the sum of Pounds Sterling two hundred and fifty thousand shall be paid in respect of that year. Payments will be made in quarterly instalments in advance.

"(b)   His Majesty the Emperor agrees for his part that this grant shall absolve the Government of the United Kingdom from any payments in respect of the use of immovable property of the Ethiopian State which may be required by the British forces in Ethiopia during the war.

"(c)   His Majesty the Emperor agrees that there shall be the closest co-operation between the Ethiopian authorities and his British Advisers, to be appointed in accordance with Article II (a), regarding public expenditure.

"(d) In order to facilitate the absorption into Ethiopian economy of the funds to be provided under paragraph (a) above, and to promote the early resumption of trade between Ethiopia and the surrounding territories. His Majesty the Emperor agrees that in all matters relating to currency in Ethiopia the Government of the United Kingdom shall be consulted and that arrangements concerning it shall be made only with the concurrence of that Government."

With this money, for which His Majesty's Government has always been grateful, the new administration began its programme of rehabilitation. It was impossible to finance all the projects with which the new ministries were primarily concerned. Expenditure had to be confined to most essential services. A Budget for 1941—1942, was drawn up, but with inadequate cash resources, disbursements had to be strictly controlled. Ministerial expenditure had to be regulated by a system of quarterly allocations which hampered the formulation of any long term development schemes.

By Imperial decree of 25th November 1941, much of the archaic system of mediaeval Ethiopian financing was attacked. The banking system had to be revived and revised. A Canadian, Mr. A. S. Collier was assigned the job as Governor of the revived Bank of Ethiopia which then, because of the prevailing circumstances, introduced the East African currency which, together with the Maria Theresa Thaler were the accepted legal tender.

Transportation and communications and other essential phases of administration were tackled with vigour. Thus, a fresh start was made to reconstruct and rehabilitate the state, the activities of which were violently interrupted by six years of war and alien occupation.

Ethiopia is an agricultural country and the prosperity of her people depends on their crops and their livestock. The external trade of the country involves the exchange of agricultural produce, such as: cereals hides, skins, coffee, beeswax, and pulses, for manufactured goods imported from abroad.

During the Italian occupation, a great deal of land went out of cultivation and patriot activities interfered considerably with the export trade. This state of affairs was greatly aggravated by the blockade and the subsequent hostilities which led to the reconquest. On the restoration of the Emperor's Government, war-time deficiencies of supply and lack of transport made it difficult to apply remedies from outside, and for the first year of her regained sovereignty, there was insufficient food in considerable areas of the Empire.

The Government, by establishing public security, by reducing and remitting taxation, by the distribution of seeds and by securing higher prices for the produce of the country, did much to encourage the cultivators. The good harvests of 1942 and 1943 were reflected in

132

the quantity of foodstuffs which Ethiopia was able to export to assist her Allies in feeding adjoining territories. On the other hand, the United Kingdom through the Middle East Supply Centre, immediately made provision for diverting supplies of badly needed manufactures from other territories and lent considerable help in setting in motion the wheels of recovery.

As a result of war destruction and the very heavy traffic which communications had to bear, both before and after military operations ceased, the state of the roads constructed by the Italians throughout the Empire greatly deteriorated. In spite of the lack of funds, which would have enabled the Government to carry out a proper reconditioning of the road system and bridges, nearly all the main roads were in fact kept open.

Telephone communication was partially restored and where this had been impossible through lack of the necessary materials, wireless communication had been instituted with nearly all the provincial headquarters. Postal services had also been restored.

CHAPTER 11

The Imperial Palace

The Ethiopian Imperial Palace, situated in the heart of the city of Addis Ababa, is more symbolic than its name would signify. Apart from being the home of the Emperor, the head of the State and therefore of political significance, it is really the seat of the Government even in a physical sense. In this compound, spacious of ground and intriguingly landscaped, are located some of the important Administrative branches of the Imperial Ethiopian Government. Apart from the stately building where the Imperial Family lives and the newly erected marble building — the State Building of the Emperor — the place presents the aspect of being a huge co-operative encampment.

And so it is in more ways than one. The Crown Council chambers, the Council of Ministers chambers, the Ministry of Pen, His Imperial Majesty's Private Secretary's Office, the Headquarters of the Imperial Guard, the Palace Church and several subsidiary buildings are located there. And still when inside the Palace grounds some parts look as if the only inhabitants are the pines, evergreen, hedgerows and other vegetal sentinels which stand guard on its broad acres.

In other respects the place is a veritable beehive. For people of all sorts and conditions frequent the Imperial Palace. From the Ambassadors and Ministers Plenipotentiary, the Ministers Administrative and their many satellites, the public servants (and these very numerous), the public — the high and the lowly, the rich and the poor — all stream around daily either serving or seeking to be served. To one who has to do with Ethiopian Administration, it has become an official chorus to be told by the secretaries that His Excellency Mr. so and so has gone to the "Gibbi". And this is a verity; for there lies the hub of the Imperial Administration, since the Emperor keeps a very close and observing finger on the pulse of the whole administrative machine.

The reason for this continuous and active liaison between the Head of State and the Administration can be found in the fact that the constitutional forms under which the Government is run are of comparatively recent origin. Actual responsibility resides in His Imperial Majesty's Ministers; but the residual responsibility rests with the Emperor, who, as an active executive, keeps himself always informed about the working of all departments. As Bagehot said in *The English Constitution,* "The Emperor has to supply both the decorative and effective parts of government, since he is the monarch, the prime minister and even, to a large extent, the chief executive agent." In this, as in other ways, Ethiopia feels the strain of her sudden transition from the mediaeval to the modern.

134

And this makes his duties very exacting. Coupled with all this, he is a good husband, kind father, generous grandfather and a benefactor of very many of his people. Frankly his duties, official and unofficial, are such as to tax to a point of exhaustion any man of ordinary stamina. Yet the health of the Emperor is very good and he finds enough energy to tackle his multifarious duties.

A brief sketch of the regular routine activities of His Majesty will serve here to illustrate what is meant by the foregoing. Arising early in the morning, after prayers His Majesty is known to take up State matters even before his breakfast hour which is at 8 a.m. At 9 a.m., he is in his office where he remains up to 12 noon, receiving Ministers and other officials in the transaction of State affairs. From 12 noon to 1.15 p.m., through the Chamberlain he receives members of the public whose problems cover the whole range from land grants, to charity. After lunch which is served between 1.15 and 2.30, the Emperor takes a brief rest from 2.30 to 4.00 p.m. Re-entering his office at 4 p.m., he attends to official duties until seven or eight p.m., during which time Ministers and members of the Diplomatic Corps are received by appointment. Supper is usually served at eight p.m., after which His Majesty, who is a keen radio fan, listens to the radio. He then goes through matters which might have been left unfinished during the strenuous day's activities. It is reported that the most important business, which calls for personal care, is taken up before His Majesty retires, because of the calm which these hours afford. This routine is followed from Monday through Friday. In special cases he works on Saturday evenings; but invariably Saturdays and Sundays are his days of rest.

Haile Selassie I is a sportsman. Because of the pressure of work however, he does not of late, find much time to devote to his favourite sports. Tennis, horseback riding and hunting are the most important of these. His hobbies are photograph collection and horse raising. A great lover of horse flesh, it is reported that whenever His Majesty enters his stables the horses know him so well that their happiness is usually expressed by incessant neighing. Some of these horses are entered in the periodic horse races which take place at Jan Meda and from which His Majesty is seldom absent. His pets are lions, dogs and birds.

A keen interest and appreciation of the arts and of letters form part of the cultural leanings and activity of the Emperor. He is a lover of classical music and after the evening news usually listens with avid interest to the best classical programmes on the radio. He takes time to read (from his beautiful and well-stocked library), his specialities being Religion, History and Politics.

To those who have lived in Ethiopia, His Majesty's significant interest in Church affaires is well known. In the religious observances of the nation both Their Majesties are very devout. The Imperial Family makes substantial bestowals to the Church benefice and many are the hours spent in prayer by Their Majesties.

In true womanly co-operation the Empress, Itegue Menen, shares all the cares of the Emperor in the intricate governance of the Empire. She usually accompanies him on trips through the Provinces and exercises a true motherly vigil over the interests of her children, grandchildren and the host of other people who seek and graciously receive her succour and her aid.

Very often she takes a personal hand in the Palace cuisine. Flowers give her particular satisfaction and she takes great pride in all flowers both wild and cultured of which Ethiopia has a lavish share. Her taste for clothes is on the conservative but modern side and enough time and attention is given to her boudoir. The Empress is not a reckless believer in paints and powders and her taste for jewellery befits Her Imperial status.

In the field of education Empress Itegue Menen's interest is particularly great. The Itegue Menen Girls' School in the City of Addis Ababa, named after her, the Empress Menen Handicraft School and a school for the handicapped, opened under her auspices, receive her special attention, care and assistance. A good mother, she is solicitous of the welfare of children and has always been a gracious host to them at the Palace, which is the home and anchorage of the Dynasty.

The law determines that the Imperial dignity shall remain perpetually attached to the line of His Majesty Haile Selassie I, descendant of King Sahle Selassie, whose line descends without interruption from the dynasty of Menelik I, son of King Solomon of Jerusalem and of the Queen of Ethiopia, known as the Queen of Sheba.

His Imperial Majesty Haile Selassie I reigning head of the dynasty, Elect of God, Emperor, was born in Harar on July 23rd, 1892; he married Woizero Menen, grand-daughter of Negus Mikael of Wollo, on July 30th, 1911; succeeded to the throne on April 2nd, 1930, and was crowned Emperor at Addis Ababa on November 2nd, 1930. Their Imperial Majesties have issue:

1. Her Imperial Highness Princess Tenagne Worq Haile Selassie. Born, January 30th, 1913; married, November 16th, 1924, to the late Ras Desta Damtew who was killed by the Italians, 1937. Issue:
1. Princess Aida Desta; born April 8th, 1927.
2. Lij Amha Desta; born August 21st, 1928; died November 3rd, 1944.
3. Immabet Hiruta Maryam Desta; born April 20th, 1930.
4. Immabet Sable Wongel Desta; born August 29th, 1931.
5. Immabet Sofia Desta; born January 1st, 1933.
6. Lij Iskandir (Alexander) Desta; born August 6th, 1934.
Her Imperial Highness married, September 17th, 1944, Afa Mesfin Andargatchew Messai; Afa Mesfin has now the high title of Bitwoded, and is the Representative of His Imperial Majesty in Eritrea.
2. His Imperial Highness Merid Azmach Asfa Wossen Haile Selassie,

Group picture of the Imperial Family: Their Imperial Majesties with children and grandchildern

137

Heir Apparent, born July 26th, 1916, His Imperial Highness was declared Heir Apparent to the Throne of Ethiopia, November 2nd, 1930. The title of Merid Azmach was conferred on him, January 22nd, 1931. He married:

First, Her Highness Wolete Israel Seyoum, May 9th, 1932. Issue: One daughter, Princess Ejigayehu Asfa Wosen; born at Dessie on September 4th, 1934, and second, Princess Medferiash Worq Abbebe April 8th, 1945. Issue:

1. Princess Mariam Sena; born December 11th, 1950.
2. Princess Azeb; born December 10th, 1951.
3. Prince Abeto Yacob; born August 15th, 1953.

His Imperial Highness was educated in Ethiopia and England. He returned to Ethiopia with His Majesty the Emperor in 1941, and was present at the capture of Gondar, the last Italian stronghold. He is now Governor-General of Wollo Province.

3. Her Imperial Highness Princess Zannaba Worq Haile Selassie. Born on July 25th, 1917; married in 1932 to Dejazmach Haile Selassie Gugsa. Died in childbirth on March 24th, 1933.

4. Her Imperial Highness Princess Tsahai Haile Selassie. Born on October 13th, 1919. Educated in Addis Ababa and England. In 1937 Her Imperial Highness joined the Children's Hospital, Great Ormond Street, London, and was qualified as Nurse. She then joined Guy's Hospital where she gained further experience of nursing. After her return to Ethiopia she worked at Dessie Hospital and later with the Ethiopian Women's Work Association. Married to Colonel Abiye Abebe (now Brigadier General Abiye Abebe) on April 26th, 1942, and went to Lekemti where she supervised a hospital. Died without issue on August 17th, 1942.

5. His Imperial Highness Prince Makonnen Haile Selassie. Born on October 1st, 1923. Created Duke of Harrar on May 9th, 1933. Flew from England to the Sudan with His Imperial Majesty in 1940. Received military training in Soba (Sudan) under British officers. His Imperial Highness proceeded to Harar and resumed his governorship of the Province. He was educated in Ethiopia and England.

His Imperial Highness married Princess Sara on 10th February, 1946, and has issue:

1. Prince Wossen Seged, born 21st August 1947.
2. Prince Amde Iyasas, born 30th January 1950.
3. Prince Dawit, born 30th January 1952.
4. The youngest Prince, born 18th March, 1954.

6. His Imperial Highness Prince Sahle Selassie. Born on February 27th, 1931. His Imperial Highness was educated in Ethiopia and in England.

Succession on the bases of primogeniture has been assured as stated above when His Imperial Highness Asfa Wossen Haile Selassie was proclaimed Heir-Apparent to the throne in the coronation ceremony

on November 2nd, 1930. "Zekre Negar" reports this as the object of a special part of the coronation; when the author writes:
"Following the Coronation of the Emperor, the Crown Prince takes off his coronet and kneels at His Imperial Majesty's feet. The Archbishop accosts him:
"Are you willing to serve your father, the Emperor, throughout your life?"
"Aware as I am of the golden maxim, Honour thy father and mother, with all my heart I dedicate myself to the service of my father, the Emperor", replied the Crown Prince.
"The Archbishop continued: "Will you take great care not to associate yourself with those who in defiance like Absalom, and in hurry and anxiety, like Adonias, may ill-advice you to plot against your Emperor.'
"The Crown Prince answers: "I have been told that he who betrays his father is cursed and deserves (to be doomed to) death, I will, to the best of my ability, guard myself against association with such people and I will never plot against my father."
"In conclusion, His Holiness asks: "Are you willing, regardless of what evil-doers and outlaws might do and suffer the consequences, to respect the laws and decrees issued by your father, the Emperor's Houses of Parliament?"
"The Crown Prince replies: "Whatever laws or decrees that my father has, and will have, issued, I am willing to observe!"
"The Crown Prince having made his vows, the Emperor stretches forth his sceptre and addresses him: *May God make you heir to my power, authority, throne and Crown.*
"In acknowledgement, the Crown Prince says: "Amen, as you have said, let it be", and kisses the Emperor's hand." (1)
The Imperial Palace is quite an institution apart from the simple God-fearing life of the principal occupiers. The running of the place devolves on eight departments, namely: the Private Secretary's Office, the Aid-de-Camp's Office, the Special Imperial Treasury, the Office of the Equestrian, the Imperial Properties Office, the Chamberlain's Office, the Imperial Guard and the Master of the Household or "Azage." Of these His Majesty's Private Secretary's Office acts as the coordinating agency.
Two of these are pertinent to this brief sketch of the Imperial Palace organisation. As is expected an organisation as active and as expansive as this calls for divison of labour, accuracy, confidence, administrative ability, Court manners, honesty and integrity and the many other necessary attributes of high positions of trust.
No Imperial Palace exists but that receptions and banquets are many. The Imperial Ethiopian Palace is far from being an exception. Between the Aid-de-Camp's and the Private Secretary's offices the responsibilities for Imperial Receptions are shared. Concretely the former is

(1)   Balambaras Mehteme Selassie, *Zekre Negar.*

139

charged with the internal guests and their appointments and the latter with the foreign guests and their appointments.

The main functions of the Private Secretary's office are those of arranging and conducting audience granted by His Imperial Majesty, attention to the correspondence of the Imperial Family and generally all matters of confidence relating to the Imperial Household. Complete charge of all arrangements for the Imperial Receptions and all other functions, including interviews and protocol, is given over to this office with the A.D.C. performing his part in their successful execution.

Needless to add that the duties of His Majesty's Private Secretary are of a highly confidential nature. His department therefore is the smallest of all the sections of the Palace organisation. Despatch in the work however is achieved to a very high percentage of efficiency because the men are well chosen and they know their job and their responsibility.

The Office of the Aid-de-Camp has certain specific routine duties, among them being the arrangements of meetings of His Majesty with the Ministers, both special and regular, and on fixed or special feast days the A.D.C. makes the arrangements, prepares the list of invitees and sees that they have received their invitations. When Ethiopian Notables or Dignitaries die, the sending of the Imperial Condolences and the visitation of the bereaved are taken care of by this office. As mentioned before, in most of these duties the A.D.C.'s Office works in close collaboration with the Private Secretary's department.

When His Majesty decides to go out of the "Gibbi" on visits, missions or for other numerous causes, the A.D.C. makes arrangements for Guards of Honour, and other security posse for the safe conducting of the Imperial Functions. In such cases the A.D.C. informs the Commander of the Imperial Guard who provides the posse of men necessary to cover the mission.

CHAPTER 12

The Capital

Ethiopians have long possessed a common sense idea of community co-operation. In the olden days, the Grand Old Man of the community, with his wisdom and the grey hair that commanded respect, was the leader. No formal election was needed to accredit him as such. He, along with his group of elders (who likewise merited their social status by service to the group) was the champion of every cause which had to do with the welfare of the community. This *de facto* council of the village or district met as and when exigences arose: to build a road, to fell a tree that stood in the way, or to dig a well, in the common interests of the community. (Reminiscent of this is the system of arbitration by "shemogelis" — elders — that even today keeps many a dispute from reaching the court of law).

That was the beginning of civic co-operation born of the necessities of day to day life and a general realisation of the need for joint efforts to tackle common problems. The introduction of municipal administration in Ethiopia as it is understood in the world today, owes much to Emperor Haile Selassie I. An Imperial Decree issued on August 27th, 1942, under Article 11 of the Constitution, laid down a series of Administrative Regulations of far-reaching importance. Parts 71—77, Article 9, of these Regulations, relate to municipalities. These were subsequently amplified by a Proclamation issued on March 30th, 1945, under which one "Kantiba" (Mayor) was appointed for each of the towns of Addis Ababa and Gondar, and a Town Officer for every other town in the country. The "Kantiba" of Addis Ababa, who is also the Governor of the city, is the Chairman of the Municipal Council. The Council was then composed of representatives of the various Ministries and seven Ethiopian residents elected yearly by owners of immovable property.

The Municipality of the capital had to assume responsibility in several directions: registration of property; public hygiene; recording births, marriages and deaths; construction, repair and maintenance of water supply, light and roads; registration and grant of permits and licences for all vehicles; issuance of licences for theatres, cinemas, hotels, restaurants, public houses, shops, butchers, meat shops, stalls, etc.; maiantenance of the fire brigade; supervision and direction of new constructions so as to conform to the city planning; in sort, to carry on the good administration of the city.

To carry out its manifold functions, the Municipality must be assured of a steady flow of income. The Proclamation provided for revenues from a number of sources: a general rate on all immovable property calculated as a percentage of the rental value of the property; a water rate; licenses to carry on trades and professions; market stall fees and fees for the use of markets; fees for various municipal public services such as, sanitary services, slaughter house, fire brigade, surveying and registration of property, etc.

Control of epidemics and removal of other threats to public health such as contamination of water and food, constituted an urgent task especially in the years immediately after liberation. The danger to public health was greater then. The war had wrought havoc on the general health of the average citizen which resulted in decreased resistance to disease. Here then were in demand all the available resources of the Public Health Services.

The National Public Health Department had its beginning about the time of His Imperial Majesty's Corronation twenty-five years ago. It was a department within the Ministry of the Interior and catered to the needs of the whole country including, of course, the Municipal limits of Addis Ababa. The Department, in effect, was the forerunner of the present Ministry of Public Health which came into being in 1947. The Addis Ababa Municipality then established its own Public Health Services, functioning in close cooperation with the Ministry of Public Health in matters within its area. The Municipal Sanitation Office, set up in 1947, gave place in 1952 to the present Municipal Public Health Department with nine distinct sections whose names are self-explanatory: Office of Statistics; Communicable Diseases Control; Care for Mother and Child; Sanitation Offices; Industrial Hygiene; Mental Hygiene; Public Health Education; Laboratory Services; and Municipal Clinic. A remarkable feature is that all the services of the Municipal Public Health Department are rendered free of charge. It is estimated that about 1,000 patients per day are attended to by the various sections of the Clinic. Over 200,000 inoculations yearly are given by the Office for Communicable Diseases Control, operating in conjunction with the Ministry of Public Health. It took part in the B.C.G. anti-tuberculosis campaign carried on by UNICEF in 1953—1954.

As for sanitation, an effective safeguard against the contamination of water drains by sewage water has been found in the construction of separate, specially designed septic tanks. The sanitary needs have proportionately grown with the increase in the urban population. Measures have been taken to ensure prompt, regular collection of refuse matter, and its disposal outside the city limits.

Rules and regulations to ensure high hygienic standards are also rigorously enforced in the vegetable, meat and grocery markets. To meet the requirements, market stalls have been constructed anew. Public urinals and latrines have been provided and acts of public nuisance have been declared by law to be crimes punishable by fines and/or imprisonment. Cesspools have been set up in sufficient number at necessary points. For soil collection, three vehicles of capacities

A view of Haile Selassie I Square in the centre of the capital

ranging from 3,000 to 7,000 litres, with modern pumping systems are in daily operation. An abbatoir of the most modern type with incinerators attached, has been built at a cost of Eth. $ 2,500,000. Refrigerator meat vans are employed to transport meat to the various groceries and butcheries. The slaughter house, with a capacity to handle 600 animals a day, is large enough to serve the whole city. No animal is admitted for slaughter unless it is declared free from disease by the veterinary section of the Municipality. A corps of scavengers is on the permanent staff of the Addis Ababa Public Health Department. Stray street dogs, which may turn out to be carriers of rabies, are promptly and systematically disposed of. Following the expansion in the area of the city, cemeteries, which were thought safe within urban limits before, have now been replaced by two large ones in the suburbs. Additions to these health and sanitary service are constantly being made to meet the rapidly growing needs of the city.

143

Paradoxically enough, Addis Ababa, with plenty of rains, is still fighting the problem of water shortage. The problem is due to the inadequate facilities of the past, on the one hand, and the growing needs outpacing the development of the system on the other. Some years ago, the total quantity of piped water distributed was only 500 cubic metres per day. Twenty per cent of the population had to depend upon wells. Since then, schemes have been put through which have brought 300 cubic metres through a six-kilometre main from a reservoir at the foot of Mount Entoto; 1,500 cubic metres, through a two-kilometre pipe-line, from Medhane Alem fountain and the Kabana River; and 300 cubic metres, through an eight-kilometre line from the Addis Alem Road. Also, among the additions made since the liberation were: 820 cubic metres from the Addis Alem Road by installing larger pipe-lines; a further 300 cubic metres, from the same source, by diverting the water of the fountain situated sixteen kilometres away, through a line of eight kilometres, to supply the New Market area; 300 cubic metres by tapping Abbo Tabal fountain along a route of 960 metres; and yet another 400 cubic metres by building dykes and filtering installations on the Kabana River near to Villa Sahla Selassie, four kilometres from the heart of the city. The most important in this series has been the exploitation, in 1952, of Lake Gaferssa by laying a 14-kilometre-long main, and the building of a reservoir right in front of the Municipal building. Since then, a two-metre high dam has been built across the Lake, with a fence all round and guards to prevent men and animals from polluting the water.

As it enters the main from Lake Gaferssa, the water is filtered through gravel and is chlorinated. In the year 1952 a machine for ozonation was bought at a cost of Eth. $ 15,000. Besides completing the six wells, works on which commenced during the occupation period, thirty-four deep wells have been drilled in different parts of the city, costing over Eth. $ 420,000. Several tube wells have been bored to augment the water supply. The network of pipe-lines embracing the whole city has seen vast expansion, brought about by stages. About 100 roadside taps provide free water to the poor.

One of the essential requisites of any modern city, namely, the fire-fighting device, is provided adequately and efficiently by the Municipality. The vigilant Fire Brigade, on duty twenty-four hours a day and seven days a week, have a number of cases of spectacular service to their credit. Most modern machines are employed — three of them with a tank capacity of 5,500 litres and a discharge pressure of 1,500 litres per minute. They are fitted to serve the dual purpose of extinguishing fires and washing the streets.

Progress has been recorded since the liberation in the repairs to, and improvement of the streets. A number of streets have been widened, as necessitated by the considerable increase in traffic. New lanes have also been opened for traffic other than vehicles, and these have to some extent relieved the pressure on the main roads. The provision of several streets with sidewalks has been helpful in diverting pedestrian traffic. A proper drainage system, a necessity in a city with such a heavy rainfall, has been provided while constructing all new roads and sidewalks. At the same time the drains formerly built were given needed repairs.

Besides improved roads, well-laid squares, monuments and parks in appropriate places (the Zoological Gardens a most important addition) have lifted the face of the capital to an appreciable extent. A goodly number of modern buildings in concrete and stone have risen up to add to the beauty of the landscape of the town. Private buildings, some of them colossal ones, built to meet municipal regulations, are fast filling the available space in the heart of Addis Ababa. Among the outstanding public buildings to come up are the new Filowha Imperial Palace and the buildings of the Ethiopian Electric Light and Power (six-storeyed with elevators), headquarters of the Shoa Province, Princess Tsahai Memorial Hospital, Dejazmach Balcha Hospital, the Filowha Palace Hotel with annex, the Ras Hotel and others. Under construction are the Town Hall, Haile Selassie I University Building, the Headquarters of the Imperial Bodyguard and the Palace of Justice. The municipal stadium completed in the year 1947 is being rebuilt on a lavish scale at an estimated cost of Eth. $ 2,000,000.

By way of providing entertainment for the public, a municipal theatre and orchestra have been organized. The auditorium of the municipal building is often availed of by civic organizations to put on plays, concerts, boxing or wrestling matches, and other variety shows. The hall has also been the meeting place of several social functions. The Mayor's receptions in the hall, in honour of His Imperial Majesty's Birthday Anniversary and on the occasion of the New Year (with its highlight of international folk dances and music) are annual events eagerly looked forward to by the residents of the city.

On Great Days Addis Ababa is invariably decorated with flags, festoons, multicoloured electric lights and triumphal arches. As the Honourable Mayor of the Capital, it is his privilege to offer felicitations, on behalf of the citizens, to His Majesty the Emperor on special occasions.

A city grows by degrees, and in no other case is the saying more appropriate that "Rome was not built in a day." This adage has been particularly true of Addis Ababa which is moving step by step to her station as the capital city of the Empire. Politically, it sets the pattern for other municipalities in the country. On the 28th April, 1954, a new Addis Ababa Charter, befitting the present stage of the city's advance, was issued. The capital — the cultural, economic, and administrative centre of the Empire — was made the first self-administering unit in the country. All the necessary powers for a responsible execution of municipal affairs were granted to the city by this new Charter — a crowning step in the political evolution which began with the

Imperial Decree of the 27th August, 1942, and which was amended by the Proclamation of the 30th March, 1945.

By virtue of this Charter, the Municipality is empowered to attend to all public affairs in its interests, not defined by law to be within the responsibility of any other administrative authority. The number of elected Municipal Councillors is further increased to twenty, and the Council, if it deems it necessary, with the approval of the Emperor, may further increase this number. Meetings of the Council are open to the press and the general public. The responsibility for the peace and security of the city is vested in the Kantiba as President of the Council who, through the Chief Police Officer, is in command of the authorized Municipal Police Force. The Municipal Council now has wider financial authority and, like all modern city councils, may issue bonds and negotiate notes in anticipation of these bonds in order to finance the necessary projects.

With this fresh stimulus the Municipality has been moving at an accelerated pace towards execution of further measures aimed at turning Addis Ababa, in due course of time, into one of the most modern, most beautiful cities in the continent. Some concrete instances may be cited to reveal the accomplishments and the long-range planning since the promulgation of the Charter.

To assist the city's programme of hygiene and sanitation a modernly equipped town-cleaning unit was established in October 1954. Earlier the same year, in July, an agreement was reached between the United States International Technical Administration (Point 4) and the Municipality in a project to cooperate in studying the future possibilities of water supply and sewerage systems for the city. Whatever would result from this study will be done to meet the demand of the town planning which calls for first rate water supply and sewerage systems. The experts estimate that a sewerage system for Addis Ababa will necessitate a large investment on the part of the Municipality. This study and survey are progressing and within a reasonable time a modern type of this fundamental necessity of the capital would be provided.

The population rise of the capital, especially within the past ten years, has put undue pressure on the five thousand cubic metres of water per day which was the maximum up to six months ago. The axiom that the water supply should always be greater than the demand has caused His Imperial Majesty to approve some additional schemes to increase piped water to the city. Among them is the Lake Gaferssa project (now in execution) by which the lake catchment is to be increased to supply thirty thousand cubic metres of water per day by the elevation of its dam by six metres. In connection with this project the construction of a modern purification system at Gaferssa with a fifteen million daily cubic metre capacity has just been completed. Another move to relieve the water supply situation is the construction of two big reservoirs (5,000,000 cubic metre capacity

146

each) on Mesfin Harar Street and a third of 1,000,000 litre capacity in the Entoto region — all to be completed by the end of this year. To increase the flow, the present 200 mm. pipe line from Lake Gaferssa is to be replaced by one of 400 mm. by the beginning of 1956. Considerable enlargement of the pipes in the water supply network within the city is envisaged in order to cope with the proposed increased capacity of the mains. The technical and the administrative sides of the Municipal Water Supply Department have also undergone reorganization.

Street construction and repairs have seen extraordinary activity between 1954 and 1955. His Majesty the Emperor has approved the policy of extensive re-laying, construction and repair of the main squares and avenues of the city. Foreign technicians have been engaged to carry forward this work which has changed the traffic scheme considerably and added a more urban touch to the capital's road network. These highways are designed to fit in with the modern town planning project which will be dealt with later. To aid in the proper execution of the Municipality's plans and to assist its administration, foreign experts with proven experience have been engaged as advisers. In 1954, fourteen such persons, mostly technicians, were added to the city's personnel. In the spirit of the new Charter, reorganization in public administration and municipal finances are under active consideration.

Town planning has been taken up since 1946, when Sir Patrick Abercrombie, British town planning expert, was invited to Addis Ababa to study and recommend plans to redesign the city. His reports and plans were submitted but because of more urgent projects, execution was postponed. Re-invited last year, Sir Patrick arrived at the end of October and on the 9th December, 1954, resubmitted a report and final plans which have met with the Emperor's approval. The "Master Plan" is to construct a three-ring city surrounded by a green (vegetal) girdle, from the boundaries of which will extend four satellite cities. This modern idea in town planning, suggested by one who has planned some of the classic towns in post and pre-war years, will avoid an uninterrupted "ocean of buildings", undesirable within the city according to the modern concept of town planning. This new design demands an extension of the service area of the capital, since an average distance of fifteen kilometres will separate the centres of the proposed satellite cities from the heart of Addis Ababa. His Majesty the Emperor, who has evinced great interest in the whole project, has approved the annexation of the additional sub-urban area. Modern Addis Ababa of tomorrow is expected to exceed an area of 600 square kilometres.

As the cultural centre of the Empire, there has always been a series of events in Addis Ababa for the entertainment of the city's residents. The legitimate theatre has been the most prevalent. Troupes of students and adult actors and dramatists have usually provided the

147

public with a varied number of plays, mostly original, some recognised as notable. Ethiopians seem to be natural actors and it is never difficult to find characters suited to the various rôles — dramatic or comic.

The Addis Ababa Municipality has itself for some years now organised its own dramatic troupe and orchestra. On weekends and on Great Days their art has been an enjoyable supplement to the five cinemas which show British, American and other films. In November, 1954, His Majesty the Emperor approved the taking over of the unfinished ex-cinema Marconi building and the proposal to convert it into the future municipal theatre and opera. With a seating capacity of 1,200, this theatre is now ready to serve its new purpose. In February this year the theatre and music section of the municipality was reorganised on a bigger scale to prepare and offer special programmes for the Jubilee celebrations in November.

Another important development feature of the capital is its lighting system. The Ethiopian Electric Light and Power undertaking (wholly owned by the Ethiopian Government) with its headquarters in Addis Ababa, is responsible for generation and transmission of the city's current. The demand for light and power has grown to such an extent that the capacity of the sources supplying the city keep increasing. Thus, this year a 1,000 KW. installation was made and a 5,000 Turbo-alternator will be added early next year.

CHAPTER 13

The Ethiopian Church

Outside of the government the institution which claims the loyalty and support of the people most is the Ethiopian Church. More than a mere religious body, this is the instituted Church to which the Emperors must swear loyalty while assuming the mantle of becoming Head of State. There are several reasons for its unchallenged claim. Long before the administrative side of the Government had taken any universally accepted shape, the Ethiopian Church was wielding power — spiritual and temporal.

In Christendom in general this church takes pre-eminence above many. It was in the early fourth century that Christianity was embraced by the Ethiopians, and the Orthodox Church has been holding forth ever since that time. While Ethiopia is unlike most other African countries, in that it was never conquered and ruled by a foreign power, except for the brief pereiod of 1936 to 1941 during the Italian occupation, curiously enough, its ancient church remained under the tutelage of the mother church in Alexandria until very recently.

A jewel in the Jubilee Crown of His Imperial Majesty is the fact that it was through his intervention that this eight-centuries-old relationship was normalised. The Ethiopian church struggled long to gain its autonomy which came in theory in 1948 and factually in 1950. With the Church's liberation from dependence on the Alexandrian Patriarchate, it gained the complete national character which it sought since mediaeval times. Now the Ethiopian Church has its own Archbishop and twelve diocesan bishops.

Undoubtedly the successful negotiations with the authorities of the Coptic Church which resulted in the church's autonomy would fix the name of Haile Selassie I forever in Ethiopian ecumenical history. He did more. The reorganisation of the institution which is still going on, owes much to the inspiration and advice of the Emperor. Modern church administration, proper fiscal policies governing the benefice of the church and provisions for improving the educational standard of the clergy and the laity are among these reforms.

For administration the Ethiopian Church is divided into twelve bishopsrics corresponding to the twelve provinces or political sub-divisions of the Empire, one for Eritrea and one which heads the Ethiopian Monasteries in Jerusalem. There is a diocesan council in each of them which advises the bishop on administration. Effective consolidation is also provided for at the centre under the Archbishop, himself a diocesan, with his seat in the capital. The Episcopal Synod advises him in all matters of faith and order. An ecumenical Council consisting of both elected and appointed members from the clergy and the laity advises on matters of policy and general church administration.

When Haile Selassie I became Emperor there were only four Ethiopian bishops. Soon after, this number was increased to five by the consecration of the Ichegue (the temporal administrator) in Addis Ababa as Bishop by the Patriarch of Alexandria, Yohannes, who visited the country upon the Emperor's invitation. During the Italian occupation, the church was completely cut off from Alexandria, and the Italians got an Ethiopian bishop consecrated to head the institution. These actions of the Italians were not recognised by a restored Ethiopia. They, however made the Ethiopian faithful more determined to press home their long struggle for the liberation of their church.

One of the ancient oriental Apostolic churches, the Ethiopian Church has always been and still is the unifying influence in the Empire. It believes in and endeavours to preserve the Royal line, tracing its origin to Solomon and the Queen of Sheba. It guards zealously the maintenance of the Faith as handed down originally. Since the acceptance of Christianity the Emperor has always been the accepted defender of the Orthodox Church as he was the defender of the Old Testament church. There was never any clash between the church and the state, and the church has always stood steadily behind the monarch as long as he remained loyal and true to her. In fact, throughout, church and state complemented each other in all matters pertaining to the welfare of the people.

The Ethiopian Church, therefore, has been able to express and develop itself as a truly national and indigenous body, maintaining its prestige inside and outside the Empire. The faithful have thus been provided with a stronger incentive to work and live for the church and have been inspired to inculcate a missionary vision. Further, since its autonomy, people of African origin abroad have begun to look to the Ethiopian Orthodox Church with the view of seeking affiliation. The antiquity, Apostolic origin, indigenous character, with an independent ruler as its leader, as well as the orthodoxy of its faith, have attracted many people to the Ethiopian Church.

His Imperial Majesty, conscious of the fact that the church should keep in step with the secular progress of the State, has endeavoured to stimulate reforms within its administration. The Decree published in the Negarit Gazeta of November 30th, 1942 provides the legal basis of the temporal administration of the church.

By order of the Emperor translations of the Holy Bible and the Liturgy into Amharic have been made which have helped the laity in devotional life. The mysteries of the word of God and the blessed sacraments have thus been made open to a greater number of the faithful than heretofore. There is no need for an enquirer to attend a service in Ge'ez without understanding what is going on, as the

Amharic text is given side by side with the Ge'ez in the Liturgy. The Holy Bible, now made available in Amharic, by a more recent order of His Majesty the Emperor, will soon see a revised translation, now under preparation. The Church now has its own printing press for the publication of religious books and periodicals. This is aiding the laity tremendously in keeping up to date in religious thought and action.

The establishment of the central Theological School in the capital eleven years ago was designed to improve the education of the clergy. It was meant to keep clerical intelligence in line with the trend of the times. The effort began with the expressed desire of training deacons, educated in the church schools, in a more organised course of general education in a religious atmosphere. These young churchmen were taught the Holy Bible, Ge'ez and Amharic along with the art of preaching. In the higher classes the English language was used as the medium of instruction. As time went on the Ministry of Education's general curriculum for this level of instruction was adopted and at the beginning of this academic year a secondary section is opened. The idea was launched that this school should progressively raise its standard until it reaches that of a Theological College. It is thought that only when the secondary section is completed will the time be ripe for introducing theological teaching on a college level. It is envisaged that in the Theological College a special department for training youth workers and a missionary training centre will be included.

Many of the graduates of the present Theological School are occupying posts as religious teachers in the various schools inside and outside Addis Ababa. Some are also attached to the important churches in the city. When the Theological School reaches college level it is anticipated that its graduates will fill more and more responsible posts in the spiritual and temporal administration of the Church. The training at present is in its earlier stages, yet its impact has begun to be felt both on the clergy and laity.

The church is responsible for other theological institutions, like the Ras Makonnen Teachers' Training Theological School in Harar and Her Imperial Majesty's St. Paul's School in Kolfe. The former was established with the expressed purpose of training teachers and preachers in theological subjects. The latter is an elementary school giving instruction in theology and other subjects. It has been found that these two schools act as feeders for the central theological institution in Addis Ababa.

The Ethiopian Church, as is well known, has always maintained parochial schools throughout the Empire. At present there are 6,993 such schools with 30,045 students, sponsored and supported by the church. Practically every church has a school nearby, generally in the precincts of its compound. These schools are invariably used as a recruiting ground for church workers and for missionaries in

151

the outlying districts. Here the children master preliminary general religious knowledge, those with the inclination and opportunity for more than elementary education proceed to a regular parochial school, where they study one of the three main branches of religious learning, while taking part in the community life. These three branches are: (1) Church music; (2) Philosophy and Compositon; (3) Theology and History.

Up to the time that His Imperial Majesty came to power, these parochial schools were the main centres of learning, at least one attached to each Church. Advanced studies were given in the monasteries which included: Philosophy, Bible Commentary, Church Fathers and Ascetic Theology. It was after His Imperial Majesty's accession that the Government took the responsibility for higher religious education, recognising its importance to the modern progress of the church. (The teachers of local Church Schools are priests and in some cases the catechists.)

Church administration has taken a new turn since its autonomy. The central office is situated in the campus of the Archbishopric, with its various departments. The church has its own budget and separate sources of income in addition to the good-will offerings of the faithful. Church finance is administered from the central diocesan headquarters. The clergy is paid and all necessary liturgical vestments and vessels are owned by the church. Whenever necessary new buildings are constructed, a task in which His Imperial Majesty shares, in addition to the church funds and special donations from the faithful. The payment of missionary teachers teaching in both regular schools and Sunday schools, other Christian workers and the expenses for the publication of religious books and periodicals are also met from the church funds.

152

CHAPTER 14

The Constitution, Law and Justice

History agrees that the Ethiopian civilisation existed several centuries ago. The legendary basis of the ruling Ethiopian dynasty places it from a union between Queen Sheba and Solomon in 975 B.C. It is, therefore, reasonable to expect that the influence of law and justice in this country is of very remote origin.

After Menelik II completed the unification of the realm (as is reported, through military campaigns), it became necessary, in order to consolidate the social and political gains, that the laws of the country had to be revised. This revision, if it were to have any logical basis, must of necessity have been built around a central authority. With the Emperor as the centre of this authority which fanned out into the remote areas of the country, a new era in the constitutional and legal history of the country began to unfold.

Constitutional Government in Ethiopia, however, in the accepted sense of the term, dates from July 16th, 1931, when the written Constitution was granted by the present Emperor, Haile Selassie I. Since the nation existed as a polity prior to that date, it could be said that the Government was carried on through the customary rules, born of the centuries of its existence.

Divided into seven chapters, containing 55 articles, the Constitution provides the legal basis for the exercise of political and administrative powers. This fundamental law was given expressly to bring the people into the pale of constitutional practice, sharing part of the supreme power of His Majesty the Emperor which the document delegates to them.

This first Ethiopian Constitution could be considered the beginning of a new phase in the development of law in the country. The present generation must, of necessity, look upon the Constitution in a different manner to that of succeeding ones. Their need, it seems, is more to understand not to venerate nor so much to criticise it, for its *raison d'être* lies in the fact that it has ushered in the basis of a rule of law upon which future generations can build. While much has not been written by Ethiopians themselves heretofore to explain the political situation which obtained before Haile Selassie I, it is evident that, so far as the theory and practice of constitutional rule, as the term connotes, the 1931 Constitution supplies the first embryonic elements in the long history of the country.

Politics and administration were given a new framework in which, for these 24 years, a great deal of experience has been gained by those Ethiopians who have been chosen to fill the various political

153

and administrative posts in the life of their country. It has been als
beneficial to the people, whose relation to the Crown has been clearl
defined. In this new political condition one must give deserved cred
to His Majesty the Emperor and the political and administrative élit
with whom he has surrounded himself to put the Constitution i
practice. The measure of stability which has characterised the Ethiopia
Government since July 1931, is directly attributable to the way i
which the Ethiopian Constitution has been applied. This does no
exclude the problems attendant thereto. Formerly, direct rule wa
exercised by the head of State only on the basis of imperia
prerogatives. Today, and since July 1931, the Emperor recognise
certain definite rights belonging to the nation as well as the dutie
incumbent on it. The predominant idea seems to be the transitio
from purely direct rule to one by a constitutional monarchy. Th
students of constitutional Government must recognise the 1931 Consti
tution as the foundation stone of constitutional Government in Ethi
opia. The document indeed, is the basis for a unitary Government
supreme power, in essence, residing in the person of the Emperor
In time of State emergency, the Emperor may clothe himself with th
powers divested by Chapter III of the Constitution. (Chapter dealing
with liberty of person and property of Ethiopian subjects.) This i
a condition true to all heads of states, for in any emergency, actio
usually springs from a single or unristricted will.
It would seem that the best mode to comprehend the nature of the
Ethiopian Constitution and its application, during the years o
transition from a purely feudal Government, would be to look at the
country to which it has been applied. As Walter Bagehot said, in his
book *The English Constitution:*
"There is a certain common polity, or germ of polity which we find
in all rude nations that have attained civilisation. These nations seem
to begin in what I may call a consultative and tentative absolutism."
A concrete illustration of what is meant here could be taken from the
words of His Imperial Majesty in a speech which he made before the
Princes and dignitaries, the Bishops and principal clergy, on the
occasion of the signature of the Constitution on July 16th, 1931, when
he said:

*It may be useful to recall that in the past, the Ethiopian people, completely
isolated from the rest of the world and unable to benefit by the great
currents of modern civilisation, were in a backward state which justified
their Sovereigns in ruling over them as a good father guides his
children. But the considerable progress realised in all directions by Our
subjects at the present time, enables their Emperor to affirm that the grant
of a constitution is not premature and that the moment has come for
them to collaborate in the heavy task which, up to the present, their
Sovereign have accomplished alone.*
*It is essential for the modern Ethiopian to accustom himself to the
working of all the machinery of the state, and it is in this spirit that We*

154

Awaiting the arrival of the Emperor to open Parliament
on the 24th Anniversary of the Coronation, November 2, 1954

have resolved, in order that all who are worthy may participiate . . . . .
It is rare in constitutional history to hear of a constitution voluntarily
given by an absolute authority calling on its people to share in its
powers and prerogatives. This is exactly what happened when His
Imperial Majesty, nine months after his coronation as Emperor, bestowed on the people a constitution inviting them to share with him
the responsibilities of their governance.

The Constitution provides among other things:

1. A bicameral parliament,
2. That the law, whether it rewards or punishes, must be applied
    to everyone without exception,
3. That responsible Ministers will be entrusted with the duty of
    enforcing throughout the territory of Ethiopia, in accordance
    with the interests of the population, all decisions resulting from
    the deliberation of the Chambers (of Parliament),
4. That no Ethiopian subject may be arrested, sentenced or
    imprisoned except in pursuance of the law,
5. That no Ethiopian subject may, against his will, be deprived of
    the right to have his case tried by the legally established courts,
6. That judges, sitting regularly, shall administer justice in conformity
    with the laws,

155

7. That judges shall be selected from among men having experience of judicial affairs, and

8. That judges shall sit in public, and that in cases which might affect public order or prejudice good morals, the hearing may according to law, be held *in camera.*

A very interesting growth in the constitutional processes of the Government came into being as a result of the federation of Eritrea to the motherland in September 1952. By an Imperial Decree, the Ethiopian Constitution has been made applicable to Eritrea in consonance with the Federal Act, springing from the United Nations Resolution of December 2nd, 1950. As a corollary, the respective powers of Ethiopian Ministers were extended to Eritrea so far as the federal aspects are concerned. The function of this machinery is exercised through the Emperor's representative with his seat in Asmara. All bills passed by the Eritrean Assembly are referred to His Imperial Majesty as Emperor of the federation for his assent. Eritrea is represented as well in the Ethiopian Parliament.

The Emperor is assisted by a Parliament of two Chambers — a Chamber of Deputies and Senate. The members of the Senate are appointed by the Emperor from among dignitaries who have served for a long time as princes, ministers, judges or army leaders. The Deputies are chosen from among representatives of the local people. A constitutional committee has been studying amendments to the Ethiopian Constitution which, it is expected, will liberalise the method of selection of the members of Parliament.

Bills for the discussion in the two Chambers of Parliament invariably originate with the cabinet, commonly known as the Council of Ministers. These bills, subsequently submitted to the Parliament, are debated and their conclusions or resolutions cannot become law until approved by His Imperial Majesty. Time and again individual Ministers may appear before the Parliament to explain their bills, but only when resquested by either Chamber to do so.

These bills, and especially financial ones, are discussed and voted upon in the Lower House or Chamber of Deputies. They are then passed to the Senate. In the event of disagreement between the two houses, the bill reverts back to the Chamber of Deputies. Should further consultations fail to remove the disagreement, the Bill is placed before His Imperial Majesty with the respective views of the two houses. The Emperor has the right and prerogative of promulgating into law the view of either house or adjourning the matter. In some cases, subject to the consent of His Majesty the Emperor, either house may initiate legislation (this is, however, very rarely done). In the absence of a meeting of the Parliament, due to its adjournment or prorogation, the Emperor *alone* can issue laws by decrees.

Ethiopian laws are all published in the form of proclamations, while bye-laws are issued as legal notices or general notices signed by the appropiate Ministers.

156

As stated above the document provides for responsible ministers. The Government has taken the shape of one of Cabinet supremacy, its members appointed by His Majesty the Emperor. The Council of Ministers (Cabinet) and the office of the Prime Minister were, until 1943, not known in Ethiopia. In this respect a parallel may be drawn with England. In England too the office of the Prime Minister was legally unknown until the Treaty of Berlin. In the middle of the last century the Cabinet of Ministers was also legally unknown. In Ethiopia under Order No. 1 of 1942, when the powers and responsibilities of the Ministers, was published, most of the powers and responsibilities of the Prime Minister were wielded by the Minister of Pen.

The Council of Ministers which is composed of Ministers and Vice-Ministers, was presided over by His Imperial Majesty and in his absence, a Minister appointed by His Majesty the Emperor used to preside. By Order No. 2 of 1943 the duty of presiding over the Council of Ministers was given to the Prime Minister. The Prime Minister was also given the duty of convening the Council of Ministers at times that he deemed fit and it was for the Prime Minister to submit, under Order No. 2 of 1943, the minutes of the Council's business to His Imperial Majesty. Finally, under Order No. 2 of 1943, no administrative instruction issued by any Minister can be put into effect before it is presented to His Imperial Majesty by the Prime Minister.

The Constitution is the tree from which the branches of reforms in law and justice have sprung. It enjoins that no law can become effective unless passed by the Chamber of Deputies and Senate and confirmed by His Imperial Majesty. Significantly, all proclamations, so approved, begin with the words, "in accordance with Article 34 of Our Constitution, We approve the resolutions of our Senate and Chamber of Deputies and We accordingly proclaim as follows:"

Historically law and justice in Ethiopia are built to a great extent upon a religious than secular basis. The "Fetha Negast" of thirteenth century origin is a volume of religious laws compiled in Ge'ez. It dealt with both secular and religious subjects which were related to the personal status of the parties concerned. While this law has become archaic and relegated more or less into the realm of pure church law, it still commands general reverence as an ancient legal work written in the classical language.

This mediaeval legal compilation advocated, significantly enough, that the administration of law must be tempered by justice; the judges must be above reproach so far as corruption and partiality, and that court hearings must receive publicity. It would seem then that many of the salient features of law and justice, as known today, passed through the stream of Ethiopian culture. Even today when the question arises of ascertaining an old local custom, the courts have reference to the "Fetha Negast". As a further recognition of the usefulness of Ethiopia's legal history to present day legislation, references to the

157

"Fetha Negast" are made in the current Ethiopian criminal code. During the period from 1916—1935, which includes both the regency and the accession of Haile Selassie I as Emperor, the Ethiopian judicial system saw some measure of development. As is expected during the Italian occupation, owing to the change attempted, to transform what was an independent state into an Italian colony, the existing constitutional and legal system was set in abeyance. In its place laws were enacted and enforced primarily to strengthen the position of the occupiers. They did not spring from the wishes of the indigenous people and, therefore, when the Italians were expelled, the system of *lex Italo* crumbled.

Upon the re-establishment of His Imperial Majesty's Government, after his triumphant return on May 5th, 1941, the Ethiopian Constitution was immediately reapplied. The re-instituted Ethiopian Government abolished by decree all concessions granted during the Italian occupation, and to deal with lands then expropriated, special boards were set up. The revived Ethiopian judicial system came back into force, and since then has formed a fascinating phase of post-liberation activities.

By the very nature of the subject, any elaborate report on the judicial system of Ethiopia would occupy many volumes. To give a synoptic view of the system as it operates today in the Empire, the following summary is produced.

A. *ETHIOPIA*

    (1) *Supreme Imperial Court:* This court is composed of three judges. The Afa Negus is the President of the Court and he sits together with two other judges. "Afa Negus" means "the mouth of the Emperor" and is an old title given to the highest judge in the land. It is usual for a non-Ethiopian judge from the High Court to sit as a puisne judge in the Supreme Imperial Court. The Supreme Imperial Court sits in several divisions and apart from the Afa Negus as President, there are two divisions, each of which is presided over by a Vice Afa Negus.

    The jurisdiction of the Supreme Imperial Court is to hear appeals from the High Court only. Many appeals go from the Supreme Imperial Court to His Imperial Majesty sitting in his Chilot (the Emperor's special Court). This seems to follow an immemorial custom of Ethiopia.

    (2) *High Court:* The High Court consists of several divisions, viz:

        (a) one division for the hearing of appeals from the Provincial Courts;

        (b) several divisions for hearing criminal matters;

        (c) two divisions for hearing civil and commercial matters;

158

(d) one or more divisions for the hearing of land cases;

(e) one division for the hearing of cases brought against the Imperial Ethiopian Government, or cases brought by the Imperial Ethiopian Government against defendants.

A division is composed of a Presiding Judge and two judges. These divisions are arbitrary and were made for the convenience of the public.

There is no limit to the jurisdiction of the High Court. This court can hear cases of whatsoever value, and can hear criminal cases for whatsoever offence, whether such a case is a petty one or serious.

Sentences of death given by the High Court and confirmed by the Supreme Imperial Court in appeal, cannot be executed unless the sentence is confirmed by His Imperial Majesty.

(3) *Provincial Courts: (Taklay Ghizat Courts)*: The Taklay Ghizat Court is also composed of a Presiding Judge and two other judges. There are no foreign judges in the Taklay Ghizat Court, and the majority opinion of the Court also prevails there. Under Decree No. 1/42, the Governor-General of a province sits as the presiding judge of the Provincial Court of the City where such Governor-General has his residence.

The jurisdiction of the Taklay Ghizat Court in criminal matters is in offences where imprisonment does not exceed five years and fines do not exceed 2,000 dollars. It can also order 25 lashes. In civil cases, its jurisdiction extends to cases where the value of the subject matter does not exceed 2,000 dollars.

The Taklay Ghizet Court can also hear appeals from the Awradja Ghizat Court.

Apart from the Supreme Imperial Court, the High Court and the Taklay Ghizat Courts, the following courts exist and function:—

(4) *Regional Courts: (Awradja Ghizat Courts)*: The Awradja Ghizat Court is composed of three judges and their jurisdiction seems to be limited in criminal matters to a sentence of imprisonment not exceeding one year, and a fine not exceeding 500 Ethiopian dollars; and in civil matters, where the subject matter of the dispute does not exceed 500 Ethiopian dollars.

Under the law, a judgment passed in two instances is final. An appeal, therefore, lies from the Mektl Woreda Court (Sub-Communal Court) to a Woreda Ghizat Court. When a Woreda Ghizat Court sits as a court of first instance, then an appeal from such a court lies to an Awradja Ghizat Court, and from an Awradja Ghizat Court sitting as a court of first instance to a Taklay Ghizat Court, etc.

(5) *Communal Courts: (Woreda Ghizat Courts)*: These courts

159

seem to be composed of two judges. In case of disagreement between these two judges, the case is referred to the Awradja Ghizat Court. The jurisdiction of the Woreda Ghizat Court seem to be limited in criminal matters to a sentence of imprisonment not exceeding three months or a fine not exceeding 50 Ethiopian dollars; and in civil matters, where the subject matter of the dispute does not exceed 100 Ethiopian dollars. Under Decree No. 1/42, the "Misselenya" (District Officer) of the Woreda sits as Presiding Judge of a Woreda Ghizat Court
(6) *Sub-Communal Courts: (Mektl Woreda Courts):* These courts seem to be composed of only one judge and their jurisdiction is limited to a fine not exceeding 25 Ethiopian dollars in criminal matters and in civil matters, where the subject matter of the dispute does not exceed 50 Ethiopian dollars.

The growth of the Judicial System in Ethiopia can be seen from the fact that from a few courts created in 1942, in the year 1955, i.e 13 years afterwards, there are, a Supreme Imperial Court with three divisions; a High Court with eight divisions, apart from one or two divisions which are always going on assize or circuit in the provinces thirteen Taklay Ghizat Courts, one in each district; and from 62 Awradja Courts in 1942 there are 74 such courts in 1955. The same development can be gauged from the Moslem Courts. From 35 Moslem Courts in 1942 their number grew to 86 in 1955, apart from a multitude of lower courts known as "local judges courts" all over the country all are controlled by the Minister of Justice.
In 1942 there were 224 judges in the Ordinary Courts and 38 judges in the Moslem Courts; in 1955 we find 720 judges in the Regular Courts and 92 Mohamedan Judges in the Moslem Courts.
The Ethiopian Courts have dealt with and completed during the year 1946 E.C. (i.e. October, 1953—October 1954) about one hundred and thirty seven thousand five hundred and sixty criminal cases and about one hundred and thirteen thousand five hundred and thirty five civil cases.

Apart from the courts already mentioned, there are also the following

(I) Local Judges
(II) Military Courts
(III) Church
(IV) Mohamedan Courts.
(I) *Local Judges:* The jurisdiction of this court in civil cases extends to matters where the value of the dispute does not exceed 25 Ethiopian dollars; in criminal matters, where the sentence entails a fine, not exceeding 15 Ethiopian dollars.
(II) *Military Courts:* Apart from the ordinary courts of justice there are special military courts with special powers over

160

military personnel. Their jurisdiction is described under the "Imperial Army Proclamation 1944."

(III) *Legal Jurisdiction of the Church:* Apart from the temporal jurisdiction of the various courts in Ethiopia mentioned, the Ethiopian Church, the administration of which was reorganised by Decree No. 2/42 also retains, under the said Decree, certain legal jurisdiction it held before the Italian occupation.

(IV) *Mohamedan Courts:* The Ethiopian legislature has allowed the Mohamedan inhabitants of Ethiopia to retain their own courts in matters of personal status. They are courts set out by and under the control of the Minister of Justice and rules of court can be issued by him. In every district where there are Mohamedan inhabitants these courts function. An appeal from these courts go to Addis Ababa to the Court of Shariat. Their jurisdiction is in matters of personal status between Mohamedans, and the law applied is the Mohamedan Law. In 1946 E.C. (1953) these courts dealt with eleven thousand two hundred and three cases.

B. *ERITREA.*

The Supreme Court in Eritrea is divided into three branches:

(x) Commercial Court
(y) High Court
(z) Court of Appeal.

(x) *Commercial Court:* The Court is composed of one judge sitting alone. The jurisdiction of the said court is in suits and other proceedings arising out of, or relating to, any matters of bankruptcy, partnership and companies, insurance, carriage of goods, mercantile agency and usage, patents, trade marks, and copyright.

Under the Italian system of laws in Eritrea, matters of a commercial nature came exclusively within the jurisdiction of the Italian Commercial Courts even if the parties were Eritreans. Matters of a commercial nature are still heard by a court where at least one judge is versed in commercial law and usages.

(y) *High Court:* The said court is constituted of one or more judges as the President of the Supreme Court may, from time to time, direct. Until a special law directs otherwise, a High Court is properly constituted by one judge sitting alone. The jurisdiction of the High Court extends to the following matters:

(1) Actions based on administrative acts brought aigainst the Government of Eritrea or other public bodies including municipalities; and

161

(2) Criminal and disciplinary responsibility of judges for acts in connection with the discharge of their duties.

(z) *Court of Appeal:* The court of Appeal consists of such judge or judges as the President of the Supreme Court may, from time to time, direct to sit in such court.

On the recommendation of the President, the Chief Executive may appoint one or more District Judges, who have been appointed to administer customary and Mohamedan Laws, to be *ad hoc* judges of the Supreme Court for the purposes of disposing of any particular appeals or class of appeals.

In the following matters, the composition of the Court of Appeal is one judge sitting alone:

(a) an appeal against a judgment or order of a District Judge appointed to administer Customary or Mohamedan Law;

(b) an appeal against a judgement or order of a Conciliatori; and

(c) if an appeal arises directly or indirectly out of the proceedings of an arbitrator, provided that by law such right of appeal exists.

Civil appeals are heard by a court constituted of two judges. Where the two judges are of a different opinion, the appeal with their opinions is laid before another judge, and such judge, after such hearing as he thinks fit, delivers his opinion and the judgment or order follows such opinion.

The Court of Appeal has jurisdiction to hear appeals from orders and judgments of:

(a) a judge of the High Court exercising original jurisdiction;

(b) a district judge appointed to administer the customary law; and

(c) a judge conciliatori;

but only in a case where an appeal lies under the Italian Code of Civil Procedure. The said Court also has jurisdiction to hear appeals from judgments but not from orders (unless where the law expressly provides for right of appeal against orders or where there is an error defect or irregularity in such order and such objection has been raised as ground of objection to the judgment);

(d) a district judge appointed to administer the customary law;

(e) a district judge appointed to administer the Mohamedan law;

C. *FEDERAL SUPREME COURT:*

By Proclamation No. 130 of 1952, federal judicial powers in Ethiopia were given:

(a) to all existing Ethiopian Courts created under Proclamation No. 2 of 1942, and

(b) to a special court to be created in the territory of Eritrea which was incorporated into Ethiopia.

Lately some cases in Eritrea against high officials and the administration of Eritrea have been tried by the Federal Court under the Human Rights Proclamation issued by the Emperor.

162

Now this Proclamation was later amended and the powers of the Federal Courts were given in far greater detail in Proclamation No. 135 of 1953.

The Supreme Imperial Court in Addis Ababa, which was created under Proclamation No. 2 of 1942 before the federation of Eritrea with Ethiopia, exercises federal judicial power when sitting as "The Federal Supreme Court". The said Court, however, when exercising such function, has one judge of Eritrean origin on the Bench. In 1953 the Federal High Court in Eritrea dealt with two hunderd and sixty seven criminal cases and twenty-seven civil cases.

PROSECUTIONS

The old system (some of which still prevails in some parts of the Middle East) of considering offences committed against individuals as being private affairs between the victim, his relatives and the offender, and that therefore it is up to the victim or his relatives to settle or prosecute the offender, was superseded in 1943 by introducing the office of public prosecutions. Thus, Ethiopia recognised that offences against individuals are the concern of the people and the State. The Department of Public Prosecutions is under the Advocate General who is responsible to the Minister of Justice. All prosecutors are appointed by His Imperial Majesty directly. One or more public prosecutors, depending on the amount of work, are attached to every court. Police Prosecutors have their share in prosecutions and lately the Ministry of Finance had a number of its officials appointed by His Imperial Majesty as prosecutors in tax evasion cases. All of them, however, slowly, but surely, co-ordinate their work under the auspices of the Advocate General.

SOME POST-LIBERATION REFORMS

By a treaty of 1906, known as "The Klobukowaski Treaty", between Emperor Menelik and the French, the French, in legal issues between themselves, were not amenable to the Ethiopian courts. In disputes between the French and Ethiopians, the only court of jurisdiction was a special court, known as "The Special Tribunal". The latter was composed of an Ethiopian judge as chairman and a French consular agent as judge. Foreigners of other nationalities also invoked this Treaty in their favour. The inherent problem of a so constituted "Special Tribunal" became intense. There seldom used to be a judgment of concurrence between the two judges and remote was the practicability of executing a judgment. Such ex-territorial rights enjoyed by foreigners constituted a matter of hindrance to the Ethiopian Government in its legislative work. The question of remedying this situation is one of those that claimed the personal attention of His Imperial Majesty in the post-liberation period. From the text of

163

the Anglo-Ethiopian Agreement of 1942, (see Appendix), one learns that all privileged positions of foreigners in Ethiopia vis-a-vis Ethiopian Courts and law are no longer enjoyed. The only company that still enjoys ex-territorial rights in Ethiopia is the Franco-Ethiopian Railway.

Before the Italian occupation, there was no official Gazette in which laws could be published. These, along with other matters, used to appear in an illustrated weekly called "Berhana Salam". All the laws enacted could not find a place in this. Some edicts were simply stuck to the gates of the municipality or made known to the people concerned through the governors of various districts. The courts are sometimes called upon now to decide whether a law said to have existed before the Italian occupation was actually promulgated or was only a bill. Since the Restoration, all the laws, subsidiary laws and appointments are invariably published in the official gazette, the Negarit Gazeta", in Amharic as well as in English. The first proclamation to appear in this provided that all laws and regulations must be published in the the "Negarit Gazeta". Since 1942, over 140 proclamations dealing with legislation in all fields have been published.

Among the important legislation passed since the Restoration can be mentioned the following:

A law setting out the powers and responsibilities of the various ministers; a law creating and defining the provincial administration of Ethiopia; the Human Rights Proclamation; Federal Legislation (relating to Ethiopia-Eritrea Federation of 1952); the re-organization of the Ministry of Health; the organization of the Defence Ministry; the Maritime Law and Coast Guard Administration as well as the setting up of various statal and para-statal organisations, such as the Ethiopian Air Lines Corporation, the Mining Board, the Board of Education and Fine Arts, the Scrap Iron Board, the State Bank of Ethiopia, the Y.M.C.A., the Addis Ababa Chamber of Commerce, National Ethiopian Sports Confederation, the Ethiopian Aero Club, Ethiopian Red Cross Society, etc., to mention some of the earlier laws. But since the liberation the following have appeared: "The Slavery (Abolition) Proclamation" which appeared among the first Proclamations in 1942 — makes it an offence punishable either with imprisonment or death for any person to deal with, or to transport, or to prevent any slave from asserting his freedom; "The Administration of Justice Proclamation" which fixes the division of the courts and their respective functions; "The Currency and Legal Tender Proclamation" which introduced a new currency of Ethiopia's own in place of the East African Shillings and Maria Theresa Thalers; "The Transport Proclamation" which introduced modern laws for traffic and licences; a modernised and comprehensive Customs Duty Proclamation; the Health Proclamation which set out the various Health Boards and their respective functions in different parts of Ethiopia; an Educational Tax Proclamation which is a special tax levied for educational

164

purposes; a Municipal Proclamation which divided the cities in Ethiopia into Municipalities and Townships and also set up Municipal Boards giving their various functions and mode of election; the Imperial Army Proclamation which set out in detail the constitution, duties and discipline of the Imperial Army, etc.

The historic federation of Eritrea with Ethiopia in 1952, brought suddenly for both a train of opportunities for advancement, and with it the urgent need for measures to avail of these. The contact with the outer world through this newly federated maritime province became more direct and easier. Such contact brought in its wake an industrial, commercial and social awareness; and commercial, financial and social life goes on with an ever mounting tempo. New industries and commercial undertakings are being opened constantly. All this required new legislation. Special legislation was published giving the Minister of Commerce and Industry the power to issue regulations for factories, and for Workmen's Compensation in cases of accidents. Legislation was also published with a view to attract foreign capital into Ethiopia, such as; exemption from the payment of income tax for five years, facilities for repatriation of capital and profits, exemption from customs duties and other taxes on industrial and agricultural machinery, etc. Thus, foreign capital is gradually finding its way into Ethiopia to take part in the industrial and agricultural development of the country.

New legislation, as said, was published, but, in the nature of things, it could not keep pace with other developments. It was quickly found, for instance, that the Ethiopian Penal Code of 1930 had too many lacunae to deal adequately with the new tempo of events. It was also quickly found that the commercial and civil laws of the country were totally inadequate to cope with the situation. Admiralty laws also had to be published. At the Emperor's personal urge to introduce at once new criminal, civil and commercial codes, three savants, two from France and one from Switzerland, were engaged in the beginning of the current year (1955) to prepare such codes. These codes translated from French into English and Amharic will go to Parliament and to His Imperial Majesty for enactment. When this book goes to press, the Criminal Code and part of the other codes will already have been translated into Amharic and enacted.

Behind every move for modernisation and development of the country is the untiring drive of His Imperial Majesty. So in matters of legislation too, he has been taking a hand. A respecter of the law himself, he demands respect of it from others. It is universally known in the country that, at times, he confronts a clash between duty to enforce the rewards of law and a high sense of humanity towards the guilty. He took the initiative in putting an end to the once prevalent practice of cruel punishments, such as physical mutilation upon criminals. It was he who introduced much needed prison reforms. Anxious that capital punishment should never be meted out if a lesser would meet the situation, he has ordained that no execution of a death sentence shall take place without his confirmation. He retains the prerogative of pardon and revision of all judgments and sentences given by the highest court in the Empire. The condemned always looks up to him with hope, not very often in vain. Commutation of sentences and amnesties are regular features on important occasions such as the anniversary of his birthday or coronation. He is accessible to any petitioner with a grievance, when he is at his special court known as "Chilot". He has set aside two days of the week for his judicial duties.

It is indeed no easy task for a country that has suffered a devastating enemy occupation — that had to build from the ground up — to put up a structure of proper judicial system in the course of a decade and to keep pace with fast changing times in promulgation of laws. Yet, what has been accomplished is a tribute to the guiding hand of His Imperial Majesty.

166

CHAPTER 15

Agriculture in Ethiopia

The economic history of most developed countries revolves around agriculture as the beginning. Such industrial giants as the United States, Soviet Union and others could never have reached their present position except for their broad agricultural base. Since the Industrial Revolution, however, the existence of purely agricultural economies has dwindled to the minimum. This is due, primarily, because the application of technology to agricultural projects has accelerated the development of all-round economic production. With an estimated land area of 350,000 square miles, over 50 % of it arable, Ethiopia has a very promising chance of developing into a rounded industrial economy. The essential factors such as abundant rainfall, variety of soil and variety of climate are present. The Ethiopian people have traditionally always lived near the soil. With the introduction of modern scientific methods as has been evidenced during the twenty-five years of His Imperial Majesty's reign, the stage is set for making the maximum use of Ethiopia's agricultural and industrial possibilities.

It has been recognised by authorities and by Ethiopians themselves that agriculture forms the base of the nation's economic and political life. In this certain definite periods may be seen. We have the pure agrarian stage which existed during the period of the country's isolation; with the opening up of the country to foreign contacts, the emphasis began to change — crops and their by-products such as beeswax, civet, and hides and skins took on a different relation. During the occupation not only were new crops introduced but the farmers were indirectly exposed to the influence of modern agricultural techniques. With the restoration and the evolution of His Imperial Majesty's new plan to make the country as selfsufficient as possible has come yet another phase of the economic productive life of the country.

It is during the last fourteen years that this modern productive advance has been most pronounced. His Imperial Majesty in re-establishing his Government after the restoration, took particular pains to charge the Ministry of Agriculture with the responsibility of fostering, in all directions, the extension and development of this, Ethiopia's greatest industry — agriculture. It is reasonable to say that even before the Italo-Ethiopian war plans had been envisaged to help the Ethiopian farmer increase his production. Whatever national plan there was in this field was completely upset by the occupiers. Their objectives were to develop the Ethiopian economy, including her agriculture, for the benefit of the Italians. The Ethiopian farmer, therefore, was not accepted as an equal participant in the scheme of agricultural development. In fact, the old and tried primitive methods which he used to meet the limited demand for aggregate production were disturbed. Ethiopian farmers were forced to leave their lands, probably never being able again to return to them because of the exotic plans of the Fascists. The responsibility of the Ministry of Agriculture after the liberation was not only to re-introduce the original plan on a scale to suit the new conditions; it had, as it were, to re-settle the Ethiopian farmers on the land.

Although it cannot be said that Ethiopian agriculture is completely modernised, a great deal of mechanisation has been adopted which, together with the age-old uses of the land, presents the present agricultural picture. This does not mean that Ethiopia's production has lagged behind. In the war years Ethiopia's grain, through the Middle East Supply Centre, was depended upon to relieve food shortage in the Middle East area. Ethiopian exports, the great majority of which is either purely agricultural or semi-processed agricultural items, have grown to very reasonable proportions. In fact all phases of national life, whether it be moral or material, depended and still depend on the country's agricultural production. Constituting the greatest activity of the Ethiopian people, agriculture may be considered the greatest national industry, and there is no doubt that it will continue to be so for many years. And, it must be remembered that not only does it supply the food requirements of the nation; agricultural products, as referred to above, are basic to industries, banking, customs, and the entire fiscal policy of the nation. Why? Because surplus agricultural products provide foreign credits by which imports are financed. From agricultural production are also financed other agencies, both public and private, the services of which are essential to national progress.

Education, for instance, one of the main objectives of the Emperor's plan for modernising the nation, especially in the provinces, depends on a land tax. This means the tax on the yield or the agricultural production of the land. If, as is universally accepted, education of the right kind, can solve any problem, then it is easy to see the importance of agricultural production to the national life of the country. On a high standard of education depends the whole social and economic activity of the community.

No wonder His Imperial Majesty's interest in the development of Ethiopian agriculture has been so deep and constant. During the past fourteen years the spread of education has been phenomenal. Primary and secondary schools have increased considerably. Specialised and technical schools are being rapidly established; a University College, established in 1950, has begun to produce graduates since last year. Hundreds of students are receiving advanced training in foreign educational institutions, some of them in agricultural sciences. If our original premise is correct that agriculture still lies at the bottom of

168

the financing of the national life of the country, its importance may be further readily seen.

In the educational field this major national industry has also had its fair amount of attention. Prior to the Italian occupation, there was the Ambo Agricultural School. Naturally, this was upset by the war and occupation. Since His Imperial Majesty's return not only has the Ambo school been revived, provision for the training of agricultural technicians, experts and scientists has been made. In co-operation with the Foreign Operations Administration of the United States

His Majesty the Emperor visiting the Agriculture Pavilion in the 1951 International Exhibition held in Addis Ababa

(Point 4), the Jimma Agricultural Technical School has been operating now for over two years; under the same arrangement, another school of this type is projected to be set up at Bishoftu. These schools are designed to train farmers, farm leaders, school teachers and extension workers to extend and perfect the nation's agriculture. In addition, and this should be the capping stone of agricultural education in the country, Point 4 is co-operating with the Imperial Ethiopian Government in the establishment of the Imperial Ethiopian College of Agriculture and Mechanical Arts. The campus, buildings and equipment will be ready for the coming school year. Realising the urgent need to train leaders in agricultural administration, agricultural college teachers, experimental and research officers, specialists in crop pro-

169

duction, livestock husbandry, horticulture, crop protection, botanists, entomologists, veterinarians, and all others needed in this extensive field, agricultural college courses leading to a degree began two years ago in the Jimma Agricultural Technical School. Young men selected from secondary schools are taking courses and will continue their senior years in the halls of the new agricultural college.

As an industry, agriculture in Ethiopia not only supports but depends on certain other factors of the national life — on Education, as previously indicated, transport, government administration, the financial status of the country. The plans for the construction and maintenance of suitable roads are definitely tied up with the transport of people and agricultural products. Crops must be brought from farms to rail heads and ports for foreign exportation. The Franco-Ethiopian railway and certain trunk highways date back to the reign of Menelik II. During the Italian occupation there was marked highway development; unfortunately the war of liberation has caused disproportionate destruction of most of the roads. During the last fourteen years much advance has been witnessed, culminating with the formation of the Imperial Highway Authority which has been responsible for keeping the main arteries of transport open. Air transport to all centres in Ethiopia now speeds deliveries, and fleets of modern trucks take agricultral products to markets. It is planned that railway facilities will be extended to other parts of the Empire, at this time only served by surface transport. All these together are elements making ready the way for a sustained development of agriculture as an industry in Ethiopia.

The structure of the Ethiopian Government which was revived after His Imperial Majesty's return in 1941, makes it possible for other contributing agencies to assist the country's agriculture. The Imperial Decree of 1942, which forms the basis for provincial administration has made it possible for a unified co-operation between the provinces in this vital field. For instance, the State Bank of Ethiopia was established and is the most dynamic agency essential to domestic and foreign trade. The many arms of the Government, such as customs, postal services, telecommunications and the like are all contributory and have become, to some extent, indirectly parts of the agricultural activites of the country, past, present and future.

A further point which illustrates the importance of agriculture may be gleaned from the position of exports and imports during this period of twenty-five years and especially in the past ten. The country has no internal debts; her external debts are small and easily negotiable. Changing from a deficit annual trade balance, Ethiopia now has a substantial favourable balance of trade. Ethiopian exports are almost 100 % agricultural raw, or processed, products, and if her imports are analysed in the light of future agricultural development, there is an extensive field of expansion possible. We note that in 1953, 50 % of the total imports consisted of raw or

170

manufactured materials of an agricultural nature, most of which could be grown and processed in Ethiopia. Forty per cent of the total imports are of raw or manufactured fibres; cotton, wool, jute and sisal. Of the remaining 10 % of imported agricultural products, we note sugar, canned meats and fruits, vegetables and fish, fruit, wines and tobacco, all of which can be produced locally. It would seem then that the future of Ethiopian agriculture could be based on an accelerated production plan so that the foreign exchange utilised in the imports detailed in this paragraph could be freed and applied to other phases of industrial and social life.

Picture of the irrigation scheme of the H.V.A. Sugar Estates at Wonji, about 100 kilometres from Addis Ababa

Crop production, its growth and future prospects: The Ethiopian farmer continues, with excellent effects, to cultivate the traditional crops grown in Ethiopia for centuries. They have adopted a system of cultivation which has served their forefathers before them and, though in the estimate of modern specialists these methods could be improved, the aggregate agricultural yield has been to a great extent satisfying. The excellent conditions of the soil in most places, after centuries of use, attest to the sensible methods applied by the Ethiopian farmer in these places. Great pride is taken in the soil and in preventing erosion. It is true, however, that in the interests of maximum

171

production and variety of crops which could meet expanding export demands, modern scientific methods should be applied.

Varieties of improved types of crops were recently introduced, some of which have become popular with the farmer and are here to stay. Among these are such new varieties in cereals as Kenya and Montana wheat and maize. Then there are crops in the leguminous category such as oilseeds, including linseed, groundnuts, chick peas, lentils and soya beans. Some new species of potatoes were also introduced. In addition, fruits like grapes, oranges, mangoes, etc. were improved — the original types yielding to amelioration.

Agricultural production in Ethiopia, therefore, has a sound historical basis, for the original crops, through succeeding years, have always been produced without any danger to the supply of the local needs. In addition, the exports, during the last world war, which met the war food needs of other countries in the East, were undertaken without the application of any new and modern appliances. The contribution has been recognised by the allied and associated powers. The principal products which supplied home consumption and exports and which are today the subject of improved agricultural technique might be briefly mentioned here:

Coffee: This has been and still is the most important crop harvested as a basis for revenue and employment. Even before 1935, coffee exports amounted to 10,000 to 20,000 tons per year, of which 50 per cent was plantation coffee from Harar and the other 50 per cent forest coffee from the west. Many excellent plantations fell into disuse during the war years; yet in 1941, 20,000 tons, by 1946, 35,000 tons; and in the bumper year, 1953, over 43,000 tons were the respective yields. The greatly increased world coffee prices were responsible for the accelerated picking of wild coffee which, in turn, was a greater factor in the increased production than any addition of plantation acreage or improved care of plantations. Much as Ethiopia may be proud of the growth in coffee exports and revenue, two factors remain: 1) The country could economically increase coffee production and exports ten times or more. 2) Should world coffee supplies result in a great surplus and prices decline, then, other countries marketing superior quality of the product will have a great priority over the Ethiopian coffee, unless steps are taken to improve the quality of her coffee exports. Measures are now being taken to solve this major problem.

Cereals and Pulses: Cereals include teff, sorghums, maize, barley, wheat and rice in about that order of production. Pulses include chick peas, beans of three types and peas — all of important production. The modern system of taxation which has replaced the tithes has had some influences on the methods of cultivation as well as on the types of these crops grown. So also have improved transport facilities and market demands. Although the types of cereals and pulses still remained fairly constant during the past years, certain factors have

172

influenced increased exports. It became recognised and continues to be recognised during recent years that only the clean and pure product can find the best world market. New methods for cleaning and grading for export which have been adopted are also responsible for this upward export trend.

Great improvement in seeds has been also recognised. It is now generally accepted that to improve the chances of Ethiopian cereals and pulses in the world market impure and mixed types should be eliminated. Improved quality of seeds has, therefore, become a mark of policy of the Ministry of Agriculture to guarantee a place for the country's cereals and pulses in world markets. It is interesting to note the amount of export of cereals and pulses during recent years. It reached a peak in 1948 of 1,246,000 quintals; declined in 1951 to 482,206 quintals; but in 1953 again reached 1,000,000 quintals. World surpluses and distribution are essential factors in this fluctuation; but Ethiopia has come to realise that, as in the case of coffee, the greatest factors in holding a stable market continue to be high quality and a constant supply.

Wheat Products: World shortages after World War II made heavy demands for flour and macaroni paste, and the years 1945 and 1946 saw a heavy export of wheat from Ethiopia. World surpluses, however, of high quality, caused Ethiopian wheat and wheat products to almost disappear from the market.

Oilseeds and Vegetable Oils: Because of exceptional soils and variety of climates, Ethiopia is in the happy position of being able to produce some ten different varieties of vegetable oils. Although greatly used in the domestic market, world demands have remained firm. Foreseeing foreign market needs, wise Government policy has stimulated oilseeds and vegetable oil production. As a result, export of oilseeds, which in 1945 was only 1/40th that of cereals and pulses, has, in 1953, equalled half the quantity of cereals and pulses, or a total of 47,300,000 kilograms, with a value of 14,000,000 Ethiopian Dollars, just a little short of the entire value of cereal and pulse exports. The wisdom of this policy of expanded production in these items is apparent and future years will still further demonstrate its value.

Horticultural Crops: Although not stimulated by any special Government policy, growth in the production and the domestic consumption of horticultural crops may be illustrated by the volume and value of vegetable exports which reached a peak of 3,019,000 kilograms, valued at nearly 1,000,000 Ethiopian Dollars. Spices and peppers also now assume an increasingly important place in export values. But the variety of climates of the country offers opportunities as well of improved quality and greatly increased quantities of all tropical fruits. Improved transportation on land, air and sea will, without doubt, see the exports of citrus and other fruits expanded in the near future.

Sugar: The value of sugar as an economic good was naturally recognised in the consideration of improved nutritional standards.

173

Cotton: This crop has been grown in Ethiopia for many years, but the quantity produced has never been sufficient to meet the country's requirements. With increased prosperity, more and better cotton clothing and household materials are used. Foreign credits are utilised to import cotton piece-goods and the shortage is met in this way. Imports of cotton piece-goods have increased considerably and statistics show that 1,543,000 pieces of grey sheeting at a value of 24,000,000 Ethiopian Dollars were imported in 1953. Imports of cotton yarn have quadrupled, and at present 3,273,000 kilograms are imported at a value of 10,000,000 Ethiopian Dollars. Cotton blankets costing about 6,000,000 Ethiopian Dollars are imported. In addition, imports of cotton have trebled and the present figures show that 1,840,000 kilograms are imported at a value of 4,000,000 Ethiopian Dollars. Thus, it will be seen that the imports of cotton and cotton fabrics cost about 44,000,000 Ethiopian Dollars per annum which figure represents about 33 per cent of the total imports into the country.

During recent years, the cotton industry has received much attention. The Dire Dawa cotton mill has been modernised and its capacity has been doubled; it now has 22,500 spindles and 320 looms. Recently a new mill was established in Addis Ababa. At the same time attention is being paid to the question of increasing cotton production in the country and a plan in this direction is now under consideration, which envisages the cultivation of cotton in four more areas favourable to cotton cultivation.

Livestock: This is given the important place it deserves in the sphere of agriculture. This particular item cannot be neglected as long as there is demand for milk, meat, wool, hides and skins, etc. Permanent soil fertility also depends on a livestock policy. But the dangers of drought affecting food supplies, animal diseases, overstock, and over-grazing, inducing erosion of soils and other factors, are also well-known. Hence the improvement of livestock in Ethiopia has become a very major programme during the past twenty-five years.

According to available information we see that:

1. According to official Italian estimates published in 1938, the population was: cattle 7,000,000, sheep and goats 18,000,000, horses 1,600,000.
2. The U.S. Technical Mission estimated in 1944 as follows: cattle 15,400,000, sheep 14,000,000 and goats 12,000,000.
3. Estimates made in 1952 show: cattle 19,000,000, sheep 18,000,000 and goats 13,000,000.

In the absence of a proper census, the accuracy of these figures is doubtful, but the volume of exports of hides and skins is a fair index of the population growth. Exports of livestock during the past twenty-five years have been small. Exports of hides and skins and leather have grown in value from 4,000,000 Ethiopian Dollars in 1945, to a peak of 30,000,000 Ethiopian Dollars in 1951, and a yearly recent

174

average value of nearly 18,000,000 Ethiopian Dollars, which, as an export commodity, is second only to coffee.

In volume of materials the maximum export of cattle hides was 10,314,500 kilograms in 1951 and about 6,800,000 kilograms per annum since. Exports of sheepskins reached a maximum of 215,700 kilograms in 1953 and also goatskins, 392,300 kilograms in the same year. It will, therefore, be seen that between the years of 1945 and 1953 there has been an increase four times in the export of cattle hides, over twice in sheepskins and thrice in goatskins. The 1952 populations are fairly representative of the growth since human population and domestic uses have also increased.

The following remarks are appropriate in connection with livestock population of Ethiopia:

1. His Imperial Majesty the Emperor is fully aware that a large and balanced livestock population is a wise national investment.
2. With its growth, the nation is better fed on meat, milk and eggs.
3. Animal and poultry health is associated with human health and food supplies.
4. Surplus meat, milk products and eggs are needed for the under-nourished millions of people in Eastern countries.
5. An export trade of finished animal products is now a major programme to answer foreign needs, to improve the quality of all livestock, and to prevent soil erosion and fertility depletion by overstocking.

Advances of great national importance have taken place during the past ten years which are here briefly mentioned.

Meat Exports: The recent establisment of two large exporting units for frozen and canned meats, with freezing and shipping facilities, is a most important national development. These are located at Asmara, Massawa, Dire Dawa and Jibuti. It is expected that other similar plants will soon be added.

Animal Health: Control of animal diseases has been a national programme for the past eight years. A nation-wide vaccination pro-gramme with the co-operation of FAO and now Point 4, conducts a free vaccination campaign against rinderpest and C.P.P., while other animal diseases and parasites also are being given all attention possible.

Leather: Establishments to meet internal requirements are seen in seven tanneries and two leather manufacturing plants in Addis Ababa and numerous others in Eritrea.

Wool: Although imports of woollen goods annually amount to 4,000,000 Ethiopian Dollars, yet the possibilities of producing all domestic wool needs are fully recognised. The great sheep population include mostly hair producing kinds. However, the importation of Merino wool type sheep during the past twenty years has now created three large flocks of this type, numbering in all over 3,000 head. The new policy of distributing animals from these flocks for crossing on native breeds to improve both meat and wool, will soon alter the wool situation and be basic in establishing domestic arts in manufacture. The Point 4 Organisation is now taking a very keen interest in this original scheme of the Ministry of Agriculture and the two bodies have now cooperatively chalked out a common programme in this direction. It is also noteworthy that in addition to this scheme of improvement through Merino blood, a new important venture in a similar manner is now underway, namely, introducing the Caraculs as a means for enriching the fur industry.

Quality Improvement: This period of great expansion in production has brought with it the lessons of competition on and the requirements and demands of foreign markets. Realising the needs for improved quality in goods exported, His Imperial Majesty's Government has established by decree, cleaning and grading standards and other necessary plants to meet existing domestic and export needs. We now find twenty-five licensed cleaning plants in Ethiopia with a capacity of 134,000 tons. This equipment is used for coffee, cereals and oilseeds.

But high quality of all these crops depends on the parent seeds, methods of production and harvesting and the processing, before final cleaning and grading. The joint programme with Point 4 to improve coffee quality illustrates the fact that the Government is not unmindful of this important factor.

Agricultural Research and Experimental Work: The Government has for many years been aware of the need of the basic knowledge of Ethiopia's soil, crops and livestock, and of methods of improvement and protection. Some recording work was started previous to the Italian occupation. The Italians also started experimental work on several stations to explore the possibilities of introducing new varities of crops. It is advisable to follow up this activity. It is very important that this particular item in the general programme, that is, of research in experimental work on several stations, is fully continued as soon as a sufficient number of qualified Ethiopian officers are available when they have come back from their studies in foreign countries.

With the co-operation of the FAO, seeds of many varieties of crops were imported and distributed to farmers who would co-operate in these experiments. An expansion of such experimental work, however, should await the arrival here of qualified personnel.

Now, however, experimental work is well established at the agricultural schools at Ambo and Jimma, at a station at Alamatta, and in co-operation with the Sudan Interior Mission at Shashamanna. Preparations are being made for more expansive work at Harar and Bishoftu, where the agricultural college and school respectively are being built. Extensive experimental demonstrations are also being held with regard to cotton cultivation at Alamatta, Jimma, Shashamanna and at least two other areas, such as Awash and Soddu. Plans are completed for more extensive experimental work at Jimma in coffee production and

176

in a less intensive manner at several smaller stations. Point 4 is giving major leadership in much of this agricultural work, while the FAO continues to co-operate in an advisory way where specialists are available. And so the structure is being built for research, centred around the agricultural colleges and schools, with the broader phases of experimentation at special stations and with co-operating farmers and other agencies.

Co-operating Foreign Aid: Realising that a large proportion of educated and trained leaders in administrative and scientific work had been lost in the war, His Majesty the Emperor sought assistance where it might best be found.

The U.S. Technical Mission of 1944 made valuable surveys and reports. UNRRA contributed much information and materials for demonstrations in many phases of agriculture, including also livestock, poultry, dairy machinery and other equipment.

However, these experts were here but for a short period. Hence experts were sought from FAO, first in a programme of animal disease control. Early in 1951, a more complete agreement with FAO brought in other foreign advisers, and with later agreements in the following fields: —

Ministerial adviser: 3 Veterinarians; Veterinary Biology Officer; Forestry; Coffee; Cotton; Home Economics; Seeds and Crops; Hides and Skins; Farm Tools and Machinery. (The last three have completed assignments.)

It may be stated briefly that each Adviser of this group has contributed in laying a pattern for the future programme of the Ministry. Meanwhile the Ambo Agricultural School had graduated two classes of young men who worked under these foreign advisers for further training.

Point 4 (now Foreign Operations Administration of the U.S.): With characteristic keen foresight His Majesty the Emperor saw the ever increasing needs for education in agriculture, administrative training, teachers, experimental and research workers, extension officers, as well as for farm leaders of the future.

The agreement with Point 4 (1952) and the later agreements have given great stimulus towards this end. The Jimma Agricultural Technical School is already a successful institution. The Harar Agricultural College is now already in its second year and has been temporarily housed at Jimma. It will soon be transferred to its permanent location at Harar, where the construction of the buildings and the campus are nearing completion. Another agricultural technical school is expected to be established at Bishoftu. Also through joint funds, and otherwise, many projects are being attended to, viz:

Crop improvement and experimentation; Animal disease control; Animal breeding; Coffee improvement; Cotton development; Water and irrigation development; Agricultural machinery.

In undertaking the above mentioned projects, the objective is not only to bring about an improvement in the agricultural industry as a whole, but at the same time, to put enthusiasm into farmers for embracing the right methods of cultivation of crops and to train farm leaders and technical and administrative hands.

Scholarships: Ethiopian students have obtained scholarships in order to study agricultural science and administration over the past many years, but the students so trained in foreign countries have not been sufficient in number to fill the requirements of the country. Consequently, the FAO and the Point 4 Organisation are granting increased scholarships, enabling students to get training in the different departments of agricultural science. Today there is a complete dearth of veterinarians, biologists, soil and forestry experts and other trained agricultural scientists and this, naturally, points to the need of an increased number of scholarships. It is hoped that with the development of the Agricultural College and the University a greater number of scholarships will be available to deserving students.

Ministerial Organization: The proper organization of the Ethiopian Ministry of Agriculture itself has taken some little time owing to the numerous impediments brought on first, by Italian occupation, and secondly, by the war, when the country was rid of the Italian occupation and its aftermath. However, the organization of the Ministry has been accomplished in the shortest time possible, and the Ministry has been very quick in absorbing both trained staff and graduates from the Ambo Agricultural School. The Ministry has a Veterinary Department, Animal Breeding Department, a Forestry Department and an Agricultural Economics Department. There is also a Locust Control Department. These departments are collaborating very closely with the FAO and Point 4 in organising and carrying out their activities in the provinces.

Settlement Programme: Plans are underway to introduce coffee and cotton cultivation in sparsely populated areas which are highly favourable to the cultivation of these crops. The whole policy involves size of holdings, aid for establishment, guidance and supervision organised roads, marketing facilities, water supply for domestic use and agriculture, and the very important factors of education and social life.

The Development Bank and the Farmer: It has long been recognized that advanced methods to be adopted by our farmers will involve some additional capital, which if wisely spent under guidance, can and will quickly repay itself in increased production revenue. Hence the establishment of the Agricultural Bank which was later converted into the Development Bank with a greater capital and an increased scope of activities. The usefulness of this source of help to farmers is now being understood, and its future is assured. The Development Bank covers not only the production of coffee but all other agricultural products.

Eritrea: The return of Eritrea to the motherland is another great step

178

in agricultural advancement. The outlet to the sea is definitely a very important factor, and the roads and transport facilities are naturally a great national asset. Associated with these are such industries as meat canning and freezing plants, sisal production and manufacture, cotton production, manufacture of leather and leather goods, and other products.

The people of Ethiopia and Their Response: This is but a brief and incomplete review of the phenomenal progress in the agricultural field in Ethiopia during the short period of fourteen years. His Imperial Majesty has established the administrative machinery of the Government with keen forethought and foresight. For Government machinery to be successful it must have the energetic and enthusiastic co-operation of the people, and this the Government has enjoyed in full measure. The progress made bears testimony to this fact. The students are playing their part; their thirst for knowledge is very great. On the leaders and workers which the future generation will produce, Ethiopia places her faith so that with the help of these leaders and workers she may assume her rightful place in the family of nations, as a country having high moral and living standards. It is her earnest desire and hope that she will always have a surplus of agricultural products to enable her to aid less favoured countries or countries in distress as a result of natural calamities as occured during the war years.

CHAPTER 16

Education

INTRODUCTION

"Will Your Imperial Majesty found education institutions for the promotion of the spiritual and material welfare of your subjects?" asked the Archbishop at the coronation ceremony at St. George Cathedral *"Yes, I will, conscious as I am of the benefits that education holds out not only for the Church but also for the State,"* replied Emperor Haile Selassie the First, with a hand upon the Holy Bible.

That coronation vow has been amply honoured, and the results are not far to seek. The advances made, against heavy odds, in the educational field in the quarter century of his reign are strikingly apparent. As against Eth. $ 879,413 spent on education in 1943—1944 (1936 Ethiopian Calendar) — just two years after the liberation — a sum of Eth. $ 10,319,545, representing 8 % of the national budgetary expenditure, was spent in 1950—1951 (1943 E.C.), and as against these, Eth. $ 18,709,809.38, representing 17 % of the budget was spent in 1954—1955 (1947 E.C.). There were 508 Government schools in 1950—1951 (1943 E.C.) with a student population of 56,305 (7,000 of them girls); in 1954—1955 (1947 E.C.), the 425 schools had a total enrolment of 79,533 (11,370 of them girls). In addition, over 300 students were studying abroad. The number 425 does not record any diminution, *in fact,* inasmuch as to this number should be added some 177 primary schools transferred to the church administration through educational tax readjustment. And, these figures do not include the institutions run by the Ethiopian Church itself, by foreign missions and other agencies.

The department of education is a proverbial drain on the state revenues. Under the Emperor's programme of encouraging literacy and higher learning, education, for the most part, is free. The following Table 1 of budget allocations for education is revealing:—

TABLE 1 BUDGET ALLOCATIONS ON EDUCATION

Year	Budget
1943—1944 (1936 E.C.)	Eth. $ 879,413
1944—1945 (1937 E.C.)	Eth. $ 1,772,451
1945—1946 (1938 E.C.)	Eth. $ 6,963,397
1946—1947 (1939 E.C.)	Eth. $ 8,107,363
1947—1948 (1940 E.C.)	Eth. $ 10,178,600
1948—1949 (1941 E.C.)	Eth. $ 10.530,797
1949—1950 (1942 E.C.)	Eth. $ 10,337,105
1950—1951 (1943 E.C.)	Eth. $ 10,319,545

180

Constantly keeping the goal of universal schooling before him, the Emperor has declared that the needs of the Ministry of Education shall enjoy top priority. This dictum of his was again underlined in his opening address to the Board of Education and Fine Arts set up in the year 1947 *to function in direct contact with him and under his personal direction.* The Emperor said:

The work that you are now ordered to achieve is above all the various duties of Our Government that will give to Ethiopia and her children life . . . . By education We shall be able to preserve Ethiopia's famous history, her liberty and her independence which Almighty God has graciously vouchsafed her . . . . The Ministry of Education has been notified of Our point of view this Ministry should be .well organised and developed even more than any other arm of the Government Administration in order to raise Ethiopia's standard of education . . . .

Giving concrete shape to his determination to aid the Ministry, the Emperor issued a proclamation in November 1947, providing for the levy of a special tax on lands. By another proclamation, he threw open a supplementary source of funds through a tax on goods imported. Further, with a view to carrying forward effectively the movement of educational resuscitation, the Ministry instituted in the year 1953 a committee charged with the task of conducting a survey of the thirteen years' progress and of making recommendations for the future development. The committee, designated the Long-Term Planning Committee, early this year submitted recommendations in the form of a ten-year plan of expansion for the educational system. The plan, since approved with necessary modifications, is being put into execution. This is reflected in the number of moves for expanding the existing schools, construction of new ones, amendments to curricula, etc., referred to later in this chapter.

Not content with this material encouragement in the cause closest to his heart, the Emperor, accompanied by the Empress, lends his inspiring presence at every educational function, be it the annual school-closing day or the track and field meet. By sudden visits to institutions, without waiting for occasions, and gladly seizing now and then an hour in between his numerous state duties, the Emperor encourages teachers and students to do their best.

To appreciate the magnitude and complexity of the problem of switching the nation, with its roots deep in an age-old civilisation, over to the road of modern education, and steering it through to the goal speedily enough to catch up with time, it would help to have a look back at the near past, then into the present, and finally at the long way ahead.

THE ETHIOPIAN EDUCATIONAL SYSTEM

The history of formal education in Ethiopia may be divided into four distinct periods — traditional; the first modern period (before 1935, the year of Fascist invasion of the country); the period of Italian occupation (1936—1941); and the period since the liberation of the country (post-1941).

(a) *Traditional*

As one of the few countries in the world that could rightly boast an ancient civilisation, Ethiopia is heir to an alphabet and literature of her own. Ge'ez, the classical language of Ethiopia, has from early times been occupying the same place in the Ethiopian Orthodox Church as Latin in the Roman Catholic Church. The Ethiopian Church has for centuries now been training the priesthood in Ge'ez, and at the same time imparting instruction to the laymen in reading and writing Amharic. The latter contribution of the Church provided an essential form of basic education in the country. Today, the Church, with its 6,993 schools for the laity, is moving to widen the traditional curricula hitherto practically limited to the teaching of reading and writing. The Mosques also provide school teaching Arabic and the basic doctrine of Islam.

(b) *First Modern Period, Pre-1936*

The establishment, by Emperor Menelik II, of primary and secondary schools, adopting the Western curricula and French or English as the language of instruction, ushered in the modern system of education. This has been carried successfully forward by His Imperial Majesty Haile Selassie I ever since his debut on the administrative arena as Regent. Scientific advancement having broken the natural barriers to communications, Ethiopia now was accessible to all, and could share the benefit of the educational work of foreign Christian missions and other public agencies. Also, the road was now open for selected Ethiopian youngsters to further their studies overseas by means of scholarships and government grants.

(c) *Italian Occupation, 1936—1941*

Then came the Fascists upon the country, unleashing a train of destruction. The chapter would not be complete without a passing mention that the first fruits of the modern era in education — products of the State- and Mission-schools, and students educated abroad — were systematically massacred by the invaders. During the enemy occupation of the country, the buildings, once places of learning, were turned into barracks. And the hands of the clock set years back.

(d) *Modern Period, Post-1941*

Such was the dismal state that looked up for urgent relief to the august Patron of Education as he re-entered his liberated country in 1941. The special attention of the Emperor again went to the field of education, notwithstanding the innumerable problems of the post-liberation period. He threw himself heart and soul into the re-organisation and development of the educational system. The Ministry

182

Their Imperial Majesties at School Closing exercises.
Emperor hands prize to a small school boy

of Education was re-established in 1943. The schools that had been closed by the enemy were reopened, and new ones sprang up one by one.

SYSTEM OF ADMINISTRATION

The Board of Education and Fine Arts, referred to earlier and composed of persons of eminence in public life including a representative of the Church is invested by the Emperor with supreme authority in the matter of education. It receives advice from the Ministry and supervises the progress of schools. To it has been entrusted the responsibility of laying down or endorsing all major policies, the implementation of which is the responsibility of the Ministry.

The elementary schools in each province are financed from the Education Tax collected in that province. To see that this is duly done and also to make suggestions and recommendations, a local board of education exists in each province. The local board submits reports and requirements to the Ministry. The latter, with the approval of the

183

National Board of Education, causes the expenditure and development schemes to be carried out through the provincial education officers. The expenditure on secondary and higher education in the provinces as well as all, including elementary, education in the capital is met from the central pool of revenues.

EDUCATION IN ERITREA

At this point, a reference is called for to the system and administration of education in Eritrea, which was federated with Ethiopia in the year 1952. Under the Federal Act, all matters relating to education in Eritrea are left to the Eritrean Government. Nevertheless, the welfare of this integral part of the Federation remains the personal concern of His Imperial Majesty. This is clearly evidenced by the fraternal co-operation between Ethiopia and Eritrea in more than one way — in basic and higher education, in the allocation of seats for Eritrean students in Ethiopia, in the training and provision of certain teachers, etc. As a concrete instance, a secondary school of the most modern type and costing over a million Ethiopian dollars has been built in Asmara, since the federation, as a gift of the Imperial Ethiopian Government. Eritrean students, who hitherto had come te Addis Ababa for secondary school training, will now have facilities for this close at hand in Asmara. In 1950, an elementary school, founded by a loyal Eritrean subject, by name Kekia Pasha, and named after His Imperial Majesty, was inaugurated in Argiko, near Massawa. A special course in port administration was organised in the University College of Addis Ababa during the academic year 1951—1952, the aim being to prepare young men for immediate work concerning maritime commerce, in the ports and in ministerial departments. This was to meet the needs arising out of the federation that connected the Eritrean ports to Ethiopia. Even before the federation, Eritreans who had sought knowledge through studies here and abroad under the sponsorship of the Emperor, had always been welcomed. Living witnesses to this are some of those Eritrean proteges of the Emperor who are serving under him in high offices.

EDUCATIONAL ACCOMPLISHMENTS SINCE LIBERATION

Primary Schools

In the Ethiopian educational system, the first four grades of schooling are now designated as the "Primary School", grades 5 through 8 "Middle School", and 9 through 12 "Secondary". The primary school is eventually to be replaced by the community school for basic education. At present Amharic is the medium of instruction in the first and second grades. English is introduced as a subject in the third grade, and gradually thereafter replaces Amharic in the teaching of most subjects. As an important complement to the schooling in basic

184

and academic subjects, special attention is paid to manual training and to the needs pertaining to a country the bulk of whose population is directly or indirectly concerned with agriculture.

There were at the end of 1952—1953 (1945 E.C.), 412 Government primary schools, 168 of these teaching the complete four grades. Compared with 52,467 students in that year in all grades, the number was 62,387 in the following year, taught by 1,541 teachers. The rapid growth of student enrolment and the increasing ratio of students to teachers are evident from Tables 2 and 3 below:—

TABLE 2 NUMBER OF STUDENTS ENROLLED IN PRIMARY SCHOOLS IN THE COUNTRY

Year	Enrolment
1949—1950 (1942 E.C.)	49,077
1950—1951 (1943 E.C.)	43,608
1951—1952 (1944 E.C.)	45,649
1952—1953 (1945 E.C.)	52,467
1953—1954 (1946 E.C.)	62,387
1954—1955 (1947 E.C.)	79,000

TABLE 3 NUMBER OF STUDENTS PER TEACHER IN GOVERNMENT PRIMARY SCHOOLS

E.C.	1944 1951—1952	1945 1952—1953	1946 1953—1954	1947 1954—1955
Numbers of Teachers	1,375	1,514	1,541	2,799
Number of Students	45.649	52,467	62,387	79,533
Students per Teacher	33	35	40	28

There are only two *sources of primary school teachers* now under the administration of the Ministry of Education: (1) the Haile Selassie I Day School special one-year teacher education programme, and (2) the Handicraft School special one-year teacher education programme. The former will have an output of approximately 200 teachers in the current year. To make possible the expansion of the primary schools proposed, it is estimated 2,185 teachers will be required. The present primary school teacher education programme, continued in operation at maximum capacity, should be able to meet that need by the end of the ten-year period of the plan adopted by the Government.

For several years, beginning from 1947 (1939 E.C.), vacation training courses at different levels have been officially organised for teachers serving in Government schools. The main emphasis of these courses has hitherto been on professional preparation, but academic instruction has also been included. Special courses have been held for handicrafts, physical education and science teachers, and for school dressers.

It is a false notion prevalent in many countries that teachers in the

185

primary grades need less preparation than those who teach in the middle grades, or that they can teach larger classes just as effectively. Ethiopia is exceptional (according to a visiting educationist) in the sense that the average preparation of her primary school teachers is much lower and the size of the classes they teach is much larger. In her thoroughly modern salary schedule, however, primary school teachers who have equivalent preparation are paid the same salary as teachers who teach at any other level of the school system. Therein Ethiopia provides a brilliant example to many fully developed countries. This favourable provision is bound to do much in facilitating the up-grading of the primary school teachers by making teaching as attractive financially at the primary school level as at any other level.

Besides the training and provision of adequate numbers of teachers, there is another problem that the 10-year plan is designed to solve. The Government is concerned at the evident overcrowding of the primary grades and the resultant health hazards to the students and loss of efficiency in teaching. For the teachers, the position is aggravated by the need to teach continuously in overcrowded classes throughout the whole of the school day. To remedy these conditions, it has been decided that the primary school class size should be limited to 40 students — until such time as the increased supply of teachers permits a lower maximum.

As steps towards reduction of the present class size and teaching loads, it is proposed, first, that students who are six years or more over-age for their grade should not be admitted to the regular classes, if their presence would result in overcrowding. Instead, they should be provided for in a special programme outside the regularly scheduled classes. Secondly, school directors should be authorised to suspend or to transfer to the special programme any students who are persistently irregular in attendance. This expedient is all the more called for, because the class size problem is almost unavoidably accompanied by a class-room space problem; school buildings are not normally constructed to house such large classes.

As educational tax has not been paid on church lands, the Ministry of Education has been obliged in the past to transfer some 177 Government schools to church administration. It is proposed that church-owned land should be subject to the payment of the provincial education tax. Also, it is intended that those schools which have been transferred to the church should eventually be re-established as Government schools where this is in accordance with long-term plans for the expansion of Ethiopian education.

Also under preparation are proposals for the improvement, within the ten-year period, of the primary school curriculum — content, methods and materials. According to the policy which has been accepted, the projected new system of community schools is to absorb the present primary schools. These will be converted into community schools for

186

basic education as rapidly as teachers and teaching materials become available.

Middle Schools

The term "Middle School" is now used to designate grades five through eight in the Government school system. From the eighth grade, selection is made of students to enter various types of high schools, upon the results of the country-wide, final examination. Preparation of these high school entrants has been seen as constituting the chief purpose of the middle school.

There are at present 119 Middle Schools in operation, out of which 60 teach the full four grades. In the year 1953—1954 (1946 E.C.), 344 Ethiopian and 172 foreign teachers and directors (headmasters) were employed to staff these 119 schools.

Under the 10-year plan, the above mentioned 60 complete schools are to be continued, the remaining 59 incomplete ones to be completed and at least 22 additional ones to be established. Thus, at the close of the ten-year period. Ethiopia will have not less than 141 complete Government Middle Schools with an estimated output of 2,500 to 3,500 students annually completing eight grades of elementary education.

It is believed that an additional 250 to 350 students may be graduated at this level from non-government schools. The resultant annual output of 2,750 to 3,850 students will prove adequate to supply, even with the application of relatively high selective standards, the various schools and programmes operating at the secondary school level.

As against the 344 Ethiopian and 172 foreign teachers and directors in 1953—1954 (1946 E.C.), the expansion programme outlined above will, in seven years, require up to 833 new teachers, including replacements for those who leave the profession. This target is excepted to be reached within seven years. It has been provided that courses in arts and crafts and in physical education be taught to all students at the Harar Teacher Training School.

The expansion programme, in regard to Middle schools, calls for construction of new school buildings in a number of provincial areas, according to model building plans prepared by the Architectural Department of the Ministry of Education. The total cost of the ten-year expansion programme, additional to present expenditure, will approximately be Eth. $ 11,354,000.

Secondary Schools

Secondary education normally covers the four grades nine through twelve. The secondary schooling falls under five main categories — academic, technical, commercial, agricultural and professional (teacher preparation). In addition to the Teacher Training School and Medhane Alem Secondary School at Harar, the Agricultural

Secondary Schools at Jimma and Ambo, and the Public Health Centre at Gondar, there are seven Government secondary schools in Addis Ababa. Others are to be established in the chief provincial centres.

Academic Secondary Schools

The chief function of the academic secondary school is the preparation of candidates to enter the various colleges and other institutions of higher learning. The Government's primary concern is providing an integrated education which shall prepare students for life in Ethiopia. At the same time, it is not unmindful of the desirability of conformity of its basic educational standards with those of other lands. With this end in view, academic secondary students are enabled to sit for the London University General Certificate of Education Examination. in culmination of their courses here in the twelfth grade.

In the year 1954—1955 (1947 E.C.), seventy-seven foreign teachers and school directors are employed by the Ministry to serve in the academic secondary schools. Sixty-seven additional teachers will be needed to staff the school under the proposed expansion programme. Every opportunity is being taken by the Ministry of Education to assign Ethiopians of high potential capacity in administration and curriculum, to work with the co-operative education specialists of the Ministry. With the resultant on-the-job experience and subsequent foreign study, they are enabled to qualify themselves to take over the work as responsible Ministry officials.

The understandable over-zealous education drive that followed in the wake of liberation resulted in one unexpected development, in that the superstructure of the school system was built up far more rapidly than the foundation. Consequently, these higher institutions operate at excessive costs with a rather limited student enrolment. As explained hereunder, it is apparent that by 1960 (1953 E.C.), the needed expansion of the output of the academic secondary schools will have been reached for the purpose of supplying higher institutions with the needed number of students. After 1960 (1953 E.C.), the number to be graduated annually will be temporarily stabilised at 525 graduates. The task confronting the academic secondary schools, therefore, is to expand and to make other adjustments as soon as possible so as to produce 525 graduates annually. This is an important task to tackle for which the 10-year plan is well prepared.

Within the next ten years secondary school graduates will be needed to enter the College of Agriculture and Mechanical Arts at Harar, the College of Engineering, Institute of Building Technology, Technical Institute, Marine Training Institute, Military Training Institute, Public Health College and Training Centre at Gondar and the University College of Addis Ababa. It is possible also that other post-secondary institutions will be founded during the period. For those listed it is

188

*Students welcoming Their Imperial Majesties on an informal
visit to the Empress Menen Girls' School, Addis Ababa*

estimated that no less than 525 entering students will be needed each
year from 1960 (1953 E.C.).

Of the institutions mentioned above, University College of Addis
Ababa, College of Engineering and Public Health College and Training
Centre at Gondar were established in 1950, 1952 and 1954 respectively.
The rest are definitely projected for establishment within the 10-year
period, as follows: Institute of Building Technology in 1955 (1948
E.C.); College of Agricultural and Mechanical Arts, Harar, in 1955
(1948 E.C.); (pending completion of the Harar buildings, college
classes are being taught at Jimma), Marine Training Institute in 1955
(1948 E.C.); Institute of Technology in 1957 (1950 E.C.); and Military
Training Institute in 1957 (1950 E.C.).

To provide the 525 secondary graduates for these higher institutions,
the 10-year plan provides for expansion of the existing secondary
schools and the establishing of others. This involves a building
expansion programme to provide additional dormitory facilities, to
prepare the Medhane Alem School of Addis Ababa to receive secondary
students and the opening of three secondary schools, one each at

189

Gondar, Dessie and Ambo. The Gondar unit will receive Grade 9 students from Begemder and Gojjam; the Dessie unit from Tigré and Wollo; and the Ambo unit from Shoa and Wallaga. Provisions are also made to progressively increase the number of students of these secondary schools planned to bring them up to the maximum capacity of 200 students each.

The completion of this proposed building expansion programme will provide facilities for the accommodation of 2,500 students, the anticipated maximum annual secondary school enrolment over the 10-year period to 1964—1965 (1957 E.C.).

For the total period of 10 years, the estimated cost of the expansion programme, above and additional to the present annual expenditure, is estimated to be Eth. $ 13,975,000.

University College of Addis Ababa

Being the first of the higher institutions here, and the highest one in academic training yet, the University College of Addis Ababa deserves a little detailed mention of its origin, scope and activities. In March 1950, His Imperial Majesty decreed its foundation, in February 1951, formally inaugurated it.

Staffed by a team of 25 qualified personnel, under the direction of the President, the College aims at providing Ethiopian youth with a sound academic background, leading to professional studies abroad and, eventually, at the projected Haile Selassie I University in Addis Ababa. The language of instruction is English. There are a Faculty of Arts, offering four-year courses, and a Faculty of Science, offering three-year courses. The Faculty of Arts has an Extension Department offering evening courses in subjects related to the work of the sections of the Faculty, such as Education and Administration. The Extension Department caters to persons already employed by various Government ministries and agencies and by public and private corporations. The courses in Education are offered to teachers in service, to headmasters and supervisors.

Attached to the Faculty of Arts is the Berhane Zarie Neo Institute, an evening institute of adult education which prepares candidates for the Extension Department, and also offers any course of study in demand in the field of adult education. The University College Law School is yet another department of the College designed to meet the special requirements of the country. It has been established to give sound theoretical legal training to practising lawyers, police officers, civil servants and young men engaged in trade and the liberal professions. The more immediate aim of the School is to fill the temporary gap between the present moment and the founding of a permanent Law Faculty. The courses are conducted in the evenings, and the full course consists of four years of study. During the academic year 1951—1952, a special course in Port Administration was organised

190

at the College to meet the immediate needs that arose as a result of the federation of Eritrea, with its Red Sea ports, with Ethiopia. Facilities for the teaching of science include seven laboratories for personal work and research by members of the teaching staff. The College library, of the open-stack type, now contains more than ten thousand volumes, and is increasing at a rate of over two thousand volumes per year. A section dealing specifically with Ethiopia is being built up and now contains more than seven hundred volumes.

The College, together with the College of Engineering and the College of Agriculture and Mechanical Arts (under development at Harar), will constitute integral parts of the Haile Selassie I University, now in the course of construction and organisation in the capital.

TECHNICAL EDUCATION AND TRAINING

College of Engineering

The College of Engineering has now completed its third year of operation. In regard to the training of engineers, it has been felt best at first 20 to 30 a year, so that the existing system might absorb them without disruption, and also so that they might obtain the necessary on-the-job experience under professional supervision. The College's physical plant is now set up to accomodate 50 new students a year. But, for the reasons just mentioned, the present enrolment has been restricted to 30, while the number of applications has far exceeded it. Admission to the College is based upon the Ethiopian School Leaving Examination.

Eight qualified second-year students have been sent to the United States for higher education. In the opinion of the staff, all qualified and experienced foreigners, the standards of the College are comparable to those of first-class institutions of the same type in Great Britain and the United States. It is also thought by them that these eight students, whose achievement will be watched with great interest, will make a very creditable showing abroad.

According to the last estimate unofficially made, there are approximately 600 foreign engineers and technicians occupying responsible positions in Ethiopia. These engineers and technicians were engaged in planning, designing, management and supervisory activities. (The figure does not include foreigners employed as mechanics and skilled workers). Assuming the accuracy of this estimate, there is an immediate need for at least 600 Ethiopian engineers and high-level technicians. If training were started at once with 25 students each year, it would be 28 years before the present demand could be satisfied.

In Ethiopia, the efficiency of the professional engineer is seriously impaired by his inability to obtain competent sub-professional technical assistance. If sufficient numbers of well-qualified technicians were available, the number of professional engineers needed might be reduced by as much as 50 per cent. Technicians could be trained in

two years. Professional engineers require at least four years' training
and some additional years of experience under professional super
vision before they are qualified. Ethiopia's present need for technical
personnel may be summed up as follows: —

Professional engineers   200 to 300
Sub-professional technicians   1,500 to 2,500
Skilled workmen   50,000 to 100,000

In regard to training of engineers, as mentioned earlier in this chapter
it is considered best at first to prepare 20 tot 30 a year. The Engineering
College, which is the available source of engineers at present, i
scheduled, within the ten-year period ahead: to develop its civi
and industrial engineering sections according to the existing four-yea.
programmes; to ensure an enrolment of 40 or more in civil and
industrial engineering and to add a new curriculum in electrica
engineering; and to add eventually additional curricula which wil
make it possible to restrict the sending of students abroad for studies
in special fields. Among the other projected high technical institutions
are the Institute of Building Technology and the Institute of Tech
nology, scheduled to be completed in 1955 and 1957, respectively.

The Technical School

The Technical School provides training in nine different trades and
technical skills. Students are assigned by the Ministry of Education
on the basis of the Eighth Grade General Examination results as wel
as on a special aptitude test. At present, the courses of study are
three years long, but a further year is to be added. The institution
in a way, is a combination of a Technical Institute and Trade School
Three of the nine departments, radio, electricity and auto mechanics
require a rather high level of technical achievement. Normally, such
training would not be considered feasible for Eighth Grade graduates
But the graduates, according to teacher's reports, have done well in
their jobs, and some of them have risen to positions of responsibility.
In three other departments, forging and welding, machine shop and
foundry, the required technical achievement is not so high. The
building construction programme has been in operation for only one
year, and is now to be taken over by the new Ethio-Swedish Institute
of Building Technology. The remaining two departments, cabinet-
making and painting and finishing are taught as skills at the trade
school level.

The current enrolment of 225 is made up of 100 first year students
50 second year and 75 third year. During the past three years, fifty-
three Technical School students and graduates have been sent abroad
for apprenticeship courses in mechanics, carpentry, radio engineering
printing, etc. With the equipment and staff that are available in the
Technical School, training abroad is considered unnecessary except

192

to prepare the best talent for specific jobs, and then only if there is assurance that the training involved will enable the student to move at least one step upward in his level of technical employment.

Under the ten-year plan, the Technical School standard is to be raised as rapidly as the availability of qualified students permits, with the ultimate goal of establishing a true technical institute. And, to complete the pattern of technical training in Ethiopia, there is an urgent need for the establishment of trade schools. The objective of the trade schools should be the teaching of a specific skill. The courses would normally cover a year, and as soon as suitable teachers can be trained, all instructions will be in the Amharic language in the trade schools.

Because of the shortage of trained personnel, several Government agencies have found it necessary to establish their own schools or in-service training organisations to provide their own specialists. These schools and programmes are helping to alleviate the extreme shortage of specialised technical personnel in Ethiopia. Until the present Technical School can be converted into a true technical institute, it is considered best for the Ministry of Education to co-operative with separate agencies, such as Civil Aviation, Tele-communications and the Air Force, in the operation of their own training schools for specialised personnel; the matter of co-ordinating such programmes and of meeting special needs is receiving consideration in the long-term planning.

COMMERCIAL EDUCATION

The Commercial School

With the development of governmental and commercial activities in Ethiopia since the liberation, there has been a very great demand for trained and competent administrative and office personnel. This demand has not been completely met, but the need has been partly covered from two main sources. The first and regular source of recruitment is from the Government Commercial School, established twelve years ago. The numbers of graduates from this school proving insufficient, however, promising students have been drawn off from various levels of the Government academic school system and a number of teachers have also left their profession to take commercial or administrative appointments.

The Commercial School ranks with the academic secondary schools, offering a full four-year secondary programme. For several years, a three-years course has been provided for girls. With the exception of Amharic typewriting, the commercial subjects are taught in English. Students are admitted to the Commercial School on the basis of their performance in the Eighth Grade Examination, their expressed interest, and a personal interview. One hundred and thirty-five boys and

193

thirty-four girls constitute the current enrolment. During the past ten years, the school has graduated 220 students. Graduating students are prepared to sit for the Royal Society of Arts Examination in appropriate subjects as well as for the internal school examinations. In addition to the regular day time programme, the school plant is used for regular evening classes.

Of the thirteen staff members (including the Director), two are Ethiopians (teaching Amharic and Amharic typewriting), and eleven are foreigners. Nationalities represented on the staff include Ethiopian, Egyptian, Indian, American, Canadian, British and Persian.

A modern building for the Commercial School, in a central location is to be constructed as early as possible in the ten-year period. This will increase the capacity of admission and will avoid discipline problems arising from students housing in another place. The current budget of the Commercial School is Eth. $ 215,500 and the estimated cost of the expansion programme is Eth. $ 6,536,300.

COMMUNITY SCHOOL FOR BASIC EDUCATION

The decision by the Ministry of Education to establish community schools for basic education is a great step forward in the development of Ethiopian education — perhaps, the most fundamental step that has been taken since the establishment of the Government school system. This national educational movement aims at achieving functional literacy in a single language (Amharic) among the entire population. It is designed to develop basic abilities which will enable every citizen both young and old, to meet more effectively his problems in everyday living. He also will be enabled to make a great contribution toward the advancement of his community and the Empire. These proclaimed objects may help, to some extent, to explain the significance of this project.

It has been decided that the chief vehicles of mass educational expansion in the future should be community schools, teaching normally a four-year programme. Candidates for community school training will be recruited from the ranks of experienced school teachers. The teachers' work will be largely in the community outside the classroom primarily with adults on problems of the individual and of the community — on the farm, in the home, at the village well, with the cattle, in the forest, and elsewhere, wherever improvement is needed

Beginning in 1957, at least thirty-five community schools are to be opened each year. Of these schools, twenty-five will be entirely new and ten will be established by converting primary schools at present in operation. The establishment of a special training school for the preparation of community school personnel has already been approved During 1955—1956, selection is to be made of thirty-five teachers having a minimum of two years of teaching experience, and thirty-five having

194

a minimum of one year of teaching experience for preparation as community school leaders and teachers.

AGRICULTURAL EXTENSION

Pending the full prospecting and exploitation of the nation's mineral resources and industrialisation of the country, agriculture stands out as the most important source of wealth of Ethiopia. Endowed by nature with an extensive area of fertile soil, abundant rainfall and ideal climate for vegetation, the Ethiopian farmer has never before missed the aids of modern methods of agriculture. But, in the world of today, Ethiopia as a potential "Granary of the Middle East", could be an effective contributor to the world economy at large, and to her own benefit in return. Hence the interest of the Government in scientific methods and devices to boost up the country's agricultural possibilities.

The Agricultural School at Ambo, the Agricultural Technical School at Jimma and the College of Agriculture and Mechanical Arts at Harar (under development), among others underway, are designed to teach Ethiopian students the scientific theory and practice of this hereditary occupation of the majority of the people. It will, of course, be up to these youngsters, with the hall-marks of degrees and diplomas, to pioneer and guide the use here of improved and modern methods of agriculture.

At the same time, and as an inseparable adjunct to the said training, it is necessary to carry on demonstrations of improved methods where the actual tillers of the soil cannot miss observing these. This has been found — and the finding confirmed at the Agricultural Experimental Station at Bishoftu and elsewhere — to be the best way of carrying to the farmers the practical benefits of improved farming, without burdening them with a heavy load of theoretical instructions.

It is this and related extension work that form an essential part of the new Joint Agricultural Programme being implemented by the Ministry of Agriculture with the United States Technical Co-operation Administration. Incidentally, the Food and Agriculture Organisation of the United Nations, even before the advent of the United States T.C.A. personnel in Ethiopia, have also rendered significant assistance in this field.

STUDENTS OVERSEAS

While the University College of Addis Ababa and the Engineering College mark great advances in higher education, development of a full-fledged, self-sufficient educational system in Ethiopia must take its due course of time. Meanwhile, many students in the past years have been sent overseas for further studies. There are at present approximately four hundred of them. More than three hundred of them are under the direct sponsorship of the Ministry of Education, and most of these in Great Britain and North America.

Now, it is the policy of the Ministry that no student need be sent abroad for studies which are already provided for by the facilities at home. The necessity which once existed for acquiring in foreign countries secondary schooling, not to speak of higher education of the standard provided by the University College and the Engineering College now at home no longer exists. That alone should serve as an indication, in part, of the progress that has been achieved in these few years. The growth of the national system and the provision of facilities which the students are urged to avail themselves of to the best of their abilities, serve as an unprecedented testing ground for recruiting the most promising, the most deserving ones. Such students, with their sound educational background and more mature development of mind, may be depended upon to benefit better from specialised foreign studies and experience.

TEACHING STAFF AND FOREIGN ASSISTANCE

Foreign

As stated earlier, the swing of Ethiopia towards modern education took place relatively late in world history. Started by Emperor Menelik II, the movement was carried forward by Emperor Haile Selassie I, vigorously at the beginning but restricted later by insurmountable forces — the consequences of Italo-Ethiopian War and its aftermath. As a result, Ethiopia has had to draw heavily upon the services of foreign instructors to achieve the progress that has been achieved.

Ethiopia has gladly welcomed not only the help given by individual teachers and administrators but also that provided by some specialised Agencies of the United Nations and certain friendly nations, particularly the United States of America under Point 4 Programme (now Technical Co-operation Administration) and the Swedish-Ethiopian Technical Mission. Apart from the members of the United States T.C.A. staff and the Joint Fund personnel, there are at present about 369 foreign teachers and administrators employed in the service of the Ministry of Education, representing many different nationalities.

It is, of course, a logical development to be expected that this reliance on foreign assistance will gradually become less and less as more and more Ethiopians highly qualify themselves, and as the national higher education system attains maturity.

Ethiopian

There are at present 2,080 Ethiopian teaching personnel attached to

196

primary and middle schools. The secondary schools, with very few exceptions, and the higher institutions are staffed by foreign nationals. Under the Teacher Training Programme of the Ministry of Education, the following types of instruction are provided:—

(1) A four-year secondary course at the Teacher Training School in Harar.

(2) A four-year secondary course at the Haile Selassie I Day School in Addis Ababa.

(3) A special one-year course at the Haile Selassie I Day School in Addis Ababa.

(4) A special one-year course at Her Imperial Majesty's Handicraft School in Addis Ababa for prospective handicraft teachers.

(5) Courses in Education at the University College of Addis Ababa. (These may be considered the nucleus of a most important source of future recruitment for the profession.)

(6) Annual vacation courses, averaging six weeks, organised in Addis Ababa and the chief provincial centres, for academic and handicraft teachers; Physical Education instructors; and School Dressers. (These courses are to be attended by all teachers in Addis Ababa and in the provinces.)

Simultaneously as efforts on the above lines are being directed towards training indigenous personnel for the national educational system, and pending the full development of these to meet the higher needs, some Ethiopian students are undergoing special courses abroad in Administration and Education.

Other Specialised Institutions

For administrative convenience, certain special institutions are administered by ministries and departments other than the Ministry of Education. As already mentioned, the Air Force, Civil Aviation, Telecommunications Board, and a few others, provide schools and training centres to train their technical personnel. There are schools for specialised training of police cadets, military cadets, air force cadets, civil aviation cadets, public health workers, nurses and dressers. Her Imperial Majesty's Handicraft School at Addis Ababa is administered by the Ministry of Commerce and Industry. The Agricultural Technical School at Jimma and the Agricultural School at Ambo are both run by the Ministry of Agriculture. There is the Theological School that imparts both general and specialised education to prospective entrants to the priesthood.

Training by non-governmental agencies

Among the agencies that apprentice young Ethiopians and, at suitable levels, finance their studies abroad, both theoretical and practical, first mention perhaps is due to the Ethiopian Air Lines. It is part of the long-range programme of Ethiopianisation of the Air Lines' staff. The Civil Aviation School, under the joint sponsorship of the Ministry of Communications and the International Civil Aviation Organisation,

197

is operated by the latter. The State Bank of Ethiopia, another present and potential employer of Ethiopian personnel with its network of branches, is concerned in the provision of special courses in the Extension Department of the University College in subjects such as Money and Banking, Economics, Book-keeping and Accountancy and Business English. The Bank, in deserving cases, also sends young Ethiopians overseas for higher studies of special interest to banking in general.

Private Schools

Christian Missions in the country (apart from the Ethiopian Church) run schools, following the official curriculum of the Ministry of Education. The resultant advantage is that students from these schools may easily fit into the national system of education at appropriate levels. French cultural ties are maintained through the Alliance Française and the Lycée Gabremariam. The British Council, active here for some years after the liberation in the fields of culture and education maintains a valuable connection with Ethiopia by supplying personnel to staff the General Wingate Secondary School. Private schools of high standing are maintained by several of the foreign communities in Addis Ababa, including the Armenian, British, Greek, Indian and Scandinavian. Naturally, these are designed primarily to serve their respective communities, but the English School, for instance, has a sizable number of Ethiopian students on its rolls.

Mention should be made of the Nazareth School in Addis Ababa recently opened on September 8th, 1953. This is a private effort begun with the original idea of founding a Girls' School by Catholic Sisters. (Now it has enrolled some boys under 9 years old). Recognised by the Ministry of Education and Fine Arts as a private school giving assistance to the national education effort, the institution is self-supporting.

The staff consists of six Catholic Sisters: one French (Headmistress) three Canadians; one United States citizen and the other from Chile Seven other teachers were engaged locally which includes three Ethiopians, one Egyptian, one Indian, one Maltese and the other European. Children representing nineteen nationalities are in attendance.

The Ethiopian Women's Welfare Work Association runs schools that fill a real need. Another welcome contribution is made by the classes in general education organised, for their own personnel, by branches of the Imperial Government, including the Army, Air Force, Police and the Ministry of Public Health.

Adult Education

In the sphere of adult education, special mention is merited by the

198

evening classes conducted in many of the schools in the provinces and in the capital, by the Extension Department of the University College Faculty of Arts, by the American Institute and the Berhane Zarie Neo Institute in Addis Ababa.

The American Institute is a private philanthropic venture that owes its origin, in 1946, to a handful of public-spirited Americans resident in Ethiopia. The Berhane Zarie Neo Institute, founded in 1948 as a library, reading and study hall, holds evening classes. Since 1953, it has been attached to the University College. The Institute building also houses the headquarters of the Ethiopian Teachers' Association. The United States Information Service provides, in the city of Addis Ababa, a Reading Room with study facilities, the hall of which also serves as an auditorium for periodical lectures and instructive film shows. The USIS also supplies educational films and other materials which act as visual and auditory aids to education.

CONCLUSION

The foregoing represents a modest attempt at outlining some of the salient features of the educational system in Ethiopia. That system is still in its infancy, and many years of growth and development will be needed to bring it to full maturity. But, what has been done in a short period of less than fourteen years has been described by a foreign educationist as revealing "accomplishments which are more spectacular than the re-establishment of the school system in the war devastated countries of Europe following the Second World War."

The beginnings of an educational system here were in the making prior to the Fascist invasion in 1935 (1928 E.C.). During the years of the occupation, organised education did not exist. School opportunities, except for the Church schools, whose programmes were of an extremely elementary character, were limited to those who fled the country and continued their education in schools in foreign countries.

Most of the young Ethiopians who had advanced educationally by studies abroad prior to 1936 (1928 E.C.), and who did not leave the country during the years of occupation, or who were not successful in remaining underground, were liquidated. These were the potential teachers for the post-liberation period. At the close of the occupation in 1941 (1933 E.C.), the Government schools systems had to be built from the ground up.

By 1954 (1947 E.C.) the Government school system enrolls more than 70,000 students from the kindergarten through four years of college; operates more than 425 schools and institutions of higher learning; and has more than 400 students studying abroad. That is an achievement, and it is at the same time evidence of the intense desire of the Ethiopian for educational opportunity. A student walking up to two hours daily to come to school is no unusual sight.

The Ethiopian Government has borne the brunt of the task of building the educational system, in the trying periods of the post-war years in particular. In tracing the progress above, due credit has been given as far as space has permitted, it is believed, to the assistance rendered the Government by outside individuals and agencies. The success achieved has been described as phenomenal by foreign observers who have been here, or who have followed with sympathetic interest the history of Ethiopia under the regime of Emperor Haile Selassie I. They have paid warm tribute to His Imperial Majesty for this achievement which he inspired from the outset, which he personally directed and in which, with his sagacity and broad outlook, he induced the said international agencies and elements also to participate. It is in line with that progressive outlook that the Ministry instituted a Long-Term Planning Committee on education in October, 1953. It is the Committee's recommendations, since approved, that constitute the ten-year plan of educational expansion. If the past record of His Imperial Majesty is any indication, successful consummation of the plan may be taken as a thing assured.

200

CHAPTER 17

Finance and Fiscal Policy

The Ministry of Finance, in any country, is a key portfolio in the administrative machinery. So in Ethiopia. On finance depends every measure of progress, be it constructive work within or useful contacts without. The forward march of Ethiopia in the various fields of national life — thanks to His Majesty the Emperor — is indicated, inadequately perforce, in other chapters of this book in the limited space available. That all-round progress is in itself a reflection of the growth of the Ethiopian Ministry of Finance, both in its efficiency and its sphere of activities.

The need for the direction of the fiscal policy of the country from the centre was little felt centuries ago when each village was virtually an isolated, self-sufficient, self-supporting unit with barter as the medium of trade. The need has steadily become more and more pressing and vital with the introduction of a currency, the unification of the country by the Emperor Menelik II, and presently in the reign of His Imperial Majesty Haile Selassie I, when a modern Ethiopia has her economy tied up with that of the world. Ethiopia is a member of the International Monetary Fund, and the International Bank for Reconstruction and Development and ties of commerce, friendship and diplomacy connect her with various nations. Her position as a member of the comity of nations rests on her strength derived in the main from the pursuit of a sound financial policy. That this position has been acquired, maintained and is having a healthy growth is in no small measure due to the influential rôle of the Ministry of Finance which had a humble beginning in the year 1907-8. It has the semblance of an organised institution created for the purpose implied in its name. Its scope and functions, however, were limited. Calls on its services were far fewer than in Ethiopia of today. When the present Emperor entered the administrative field as Regent of the Realm, a new era of reforms was ushered in. Public finance being one among them, he planned and saw to the execution of the new financial policy as the resources of the country permitted, paying special attention at the same time to strengthen and increase these resources in order to permit, in turn, increased national activities. The success in this two-fold programme was amply evident by the year 1935. It was in this period that the Bank of Ethiopia was nationalised with note issuing powers.

Nothing much need be said about the period of enemy occupation of the country. The fiscal policy of the colonialists could never have been for the benefit of the country as would be the case under a national government. Along with the revival of other arms of the Ethiopian Government, the Ministry of Finance was re-established in 1941 with a legacy of problems, and little means to solve these Reformation of the financial system of the Empire was the primary task. The logical steps to be taken in this direction were the centralisation of the system, the standardisation of taxation and effective control by the Central Treasury of all its branches in the provinces These were done as fast as could be humanly possible for a Government so hard hit by the ravages of war. In this revival, grateful acknowledgement must be made of the assistance given Ethiopia by her ally, the United Kingdom, in the administration of the country in the initial months after the liberation. Starting with an empty treasury at the end of war, His Majesty the Emperor realised the need for monetary help as well. Thanks to his far-sightedness and to the friendly co-operation of Great Britain, provision was made in the 1942 Anglo-Ethiopian Agreement for grants-in-aid of Sterling £ 2,500,000 to Ethiopia. As stated previously, these grants-in-aid assisted greatly in the enormous task of re-organisation.

Hardly six months after the liberation — on November 25, 1941, to be exact — His Imperial Majesty issued a Decree by which a reformed land tax was introduced. By this and subsequent laws, the tax on land came to be the most important of direct taxes. The tax is collected through the provincial treasuries and their sub-treasuries. The size of the land, on the one hand, and the categories according to fecundity of the soil, on the other, constitute the basis for levying the land tax.

Registration and classification of land — a colossal job in a vast country like Ethiopia — has proceeded to an appreciable extent during recent years, primarily because of the steady expansion of communications and the spreading out of the network of the Ministry's agencies.

In the same year was abolished the toll gate, a proven barrier to the free flow of internal trade. Tax payment in kind and corvée was done away with. To match the reforms in revenue, improvements were made on the expenditure side. Through a system of budget allocation and regulation of the Government finance, strict control of the Central Treasury was extended to the whole State expenditure. This achievement cannot be under-estimated in the face of the fact that no established system in this regard had been left when the enemy made his exit. Incessant harassing by the patriots of the underground movement had made it impossible for him to impose any kind of comprehensive taxation.

Article 55 of the Constitution of Ethiopia provides: "The law determines that the receipts of the Government Treasury, of whatever nature they may be, shall only be expended in conformity with the annual budget which fixes the sums placed at the disposal of each Ministry. The annual budget shall be framed on the basis proposed by the Minister of Finance during the deliberations of the Chamber of Deputies and of the Senate, whose resolutions shall be submitted for the approval of His Majesty the Emperor." The internal regulations of the Ministry are also provided by law. The Financial Regulation of 1942 regulates: financial and accounting responsibilities, the annual estimates, classification and control of receipts and payments, the custody of government funds, accounts, book-keeping and auditing, among other functions. In the authority it has thus obtained, in the functions it thus executes, may be seen the Finance Ministry's unique position as the centre around which other Ministries operate.

As the paying officer for all materials and services of the State, the Minister of Finance is also the controlling officer to maintain effective checks against the occurrence of fraud, embezzlement or negligence. This he does through the Chief Treasurer in the capacity of the Chief Accounting Officer. With the Ministry having its seat in the capital, a system of Provincial Treasuries extends throughout the Empire, like spokes radiating from the central part of the wheel. The Provincial Treasurers are the official representatives of the Minister of Finance. In his duties and responsibilities, a Provincial Treasurer is a prototype of the Chief Treasurer.

As already said, under Article 55 of the Constitution, the Minister of Finance is responsible for drawing up the budgetary estimates. The estimation of the budget for any year begins in the last quarter of the previous year. Ministries and departments are required then to submit their estimated budgets to the Budget Department of the Ministry of Finance. This is done by a general statement including the anticipated financial position, how the estimates have been arrived at and a filled-in schedule giving in detailed items the sums needed for the financing of the year's activities. After a careful study by the Ministry, invariably with subsequent conferences with the ministry or department concerned, the budget is set up under the following headings: (a) defined and undefined expenditure; (b) salary and working expenses. A special Budget Committee then examines the estimates in comparison with those of the preceding year.

As to the revenue estimates of the subject ministry or department, the following procedure is taken: a study of the past year's income and the current year's estimates to determine which is greater; examining those sections in which income was more or less than their previous estimates; seeing where new activities have been sanctioned by proclamation that might constitute new sources of revenue; taking into consideration the over-all national revenue estimates; and by ascertaining the continuing or discontinuing income sources in the light of the general Government estimates.

These estimates with explanatory details the Minister of Finance presents to the Council of Ministers. Upon its approval, with the necessary modifications, the draft estimates are presented to the Legislature. The draft Appropriation Law emanating from the Parliament is submitted to His Majesty the Emperor. Thereupon, the estimates for the year become effective, after certain prescribed rules granting the Minister a General Warrant for Expenditure. This procedure through which the budget becomes law ensures a healthy check on the powers of the Ministry of Finance and collective responsibility for the spending of State funds. The years past have proved the workability and virtues of this system, the broad lines of which were so thoughtfully laid down in Chapter VII of the Constitution that was born twenty-four years ago.

As in any modern polity, taxation constitutes the main source of the revenue in Ethiopia. A series of one hundred and fifteen sources are operative. Their yields may be summarised under four broad categories: (1) duties, taxes, licences, etc.; (2) receipts from, or in aid of, specific Government services — such as hospital fees or hospital receipts; (3) receipts from undertakings of a commercial character; and (4) revenue from Government property, such as land, houses and investments.

Simultaneously as the registration and classification of land has been making headway since the Liberation of the country, further reforms were introduced in land tax. First, Tithe Tax, which used to be paid in kind before, is now collected in cash. The rates vary according to the classification of land. This new system has obviated the difficulties which were once experienced before 1944. Secondly, in 1947, bearing in mind that the financial needs of the expanding education programme were on the increase, and land tax was a source that could still bear being tapped, an additional tax known as the Educational Tax was introduced by Proclamation. The tax so collected in a province, is spent exclusively on education in that province.

The Land Tax being the most important of direct taxes, the importance of the Department of Land Tax Revenue cannot be over-emphasised. As an arm of the Ministry of Finance, it is concerned with taxation on land and with land tenure. The land tenure falls into two types: (a) those in the relatively newly developed areas; and (b) the communal lands in the older areas measured by the *Geber* (fixed tax). The first type is taxed on the basis of *Gasha* (approximately 40 hectares), while tax of the second type is assessed on communal units. Of the rates now existing on the basis of fertility there are three types. The Tithe is paid on land that is tilled, the amount payable being one-tenth of the current value of the produce. Government-owned land, which is administered by the Department of State Domains, also pays land revenue.

The steady increase in the revenue from land tax is a clear indication that more and more land is being brought under the plough. For instance, land revenue of Eth. $ 3,000,000 in 1942—1943 increased by more than double (Eth. $ 6,200,000) in the following year, four-fold (Eth. $ 12,000,000) in 1945—1946, five-fold (Eth. $ 15,500,000) in 1947—1948, and nearly six-fold (Eth. $ 17,000,000) in the next year.

204

To have a comparative idea of the three constituent parts of the amount, the last sum of Eth. $ 17,000,000 was composed of land tax, Eth. $ 4,800,000; Tithe Tax Eth. $ 7,700,000; and Education Tax Eth. $ 4,500,000.

Another reform under consideration is assessment of Education Tax on church lands, free from this until now. For this exemption, the Church took over the maintenance of certain schools located on, or in the vicinity of church lands. Now, the proposal is to levy education tax on church lands and to bring back to government administration the schools, about 177 in number, earlier handed over to Church administration. The advantage, when this is done, will be greater equalisation of the taxation procedure on the one hand, and of regularisation of the school system on the other.

Another source of revenue is the Inland Revenue Department, concerned with income-tax, excise and stamp duties. Keeping pace with the growth in commerce and industry and the increased earning power of individuals and organisations, the Department of Inland Revenue has greatly advanced since its establishment in 1944. With very few exception, income-tax is payable by all persons (except foreign employees on contract) and businesses in Ethiopia. With a view to providing an incentive to industrial, transport, mining development, enterprises in these fields involving long-term investment of not less than Eth. $ 200,000 in the first investment year, enjoy tax exemption for a period not exceeding five years.

The tax payable on salaries amounts presently, to approximately 5 per cent, while for businesses a tax of 15 per cent is levied, on net profits. It is to be noted that both these two rates do not provide any extra taxes on larger incomes. As a first step in the simplification of assessment of income tax, and until adequate accounting facilities are available, a considerable number of businesses are paying income tax on a basis of fixed rates established by a committee set up for that purpose. The second, and the latest step in the same direction, is that income tax on businesses is charged on estimated profits: the importer or exporter having to produce the respective invoices. A certain minimum percentage of profit according to the invoice value is assumed and taxed accordingly. Although the estimates of profit in this way might be under-estimations from the actual eventual profits in many cases, and hence a reduction in revenue, the over-weighing considerations are the simplification and, what is more, reduction in the number of tax evasion cases. Revenue from income tax rose from about Eth. $ 800,000 in 1943—1944 to about Eth. $ 2,500,000 in 1946—1947.

Accounting for nearly half of the Government's total ordinary revenue, the Imperial Ethiopian Customs Administration is the most important source of revenue. The difficulties of organising such an administration in a country with an area of 350,000 square miles and an approximate population of 15,000,000 should be imaginable. The industrial, agricultural and commercial centres are scattered all over the vast country, according to the suitability of demographic and climatic conditions, not to speak of the availability of transport means.

Following a study of the main traffic roads and the general movement of commerce, steps were taken to set up Customs stations in several border towns. Still these were not adequate to cover the extensive boundary areas. More stations are continually being opened as exigencies reveal. Another main difficulty was that of communications between the border stations. With the recent improvement in this respect, the situation has eased a little; but the easing, on the one hand, has been offset by the growth of commerce on the other. As against the fourteen stations in 1944, there are today 43 stations. Notwithstanding these impediments, the Ethiopian Customs Administration is reckoned as one of the best administered of the Government agencies.

Prior to the Italo—Ethiopian War, the Customs Department was a branch of the Ministry of Commerce. It was then concerned with the collection of all forms of revenue due from taxation. The tremendous increase in the Customs work alone has led to the present giant stature of the Department. The Customs Tariff law and Regulations, promulgated on June 30, 1943 was an important measure leading to the present improved organisation.

Customs revenue rose from Eth. $ 6,000,000 in 1942—1943 to more than double (Eth. $ 13,600,000) in 1946—1947 and was more than quadrupled (Eth. $ 26,500,000) in the following year. It has never since gone below this level; on the contrary, it has registered slight increases.

The Petrol Tax and Road Tax have naturally brought steadily increasing revenue, because of the expansion in the road system of the country, the increase in the road traffic and the number of vehicles and the resultant increased consumption of petrol. Now the proceeds amount to not less than Eth. $ 4,000,000 a year, and these are set apart exclusively for repairs and maintenance of roads and bridges. A minimum of Eth. $ 4,000,000 from these sources of revenue, together with an additional Eth. $ 6,000,000 per year is placed at the disposal of the Imperial Highway Authority for the maintenance of the roads and highways of Ethiopia. This road building organisation came into being in the year 1951, following a loan of Eth. $ 12,500,000 granted to Ethiopia by the International Bank for Reconstruction and Development.

About Eth. $ 3,000,000 in all is derived per annum from other indirect taxes which include salt tax, alcohol tax, stamp duty, entertainment tax, etc., in the order of their importance.

A subsidiary department of the Ministry of Finance, the Department of State Domains administers Government-owned real estate. The Department sublets these — buildings or lands — or develops them as business enterprises. The net results of its activities are turned over to the Ministry of Finance. The Department is also in charge of workshops and other State owned enterprises, not falling within the purview of other Ministries. The Department has an annual income of around 1,000,000 Ethiopian Dollars.

In the year 1944—1945, sales of gold yielded approximately Eth. $ 10,500,000 — the highest figure ever attained, but the revenue from this source has been in a vicinity of Eth. $ 4,000,000 per year for the past ten years.

The Tobacco Regie is a State monopoly incorporated by the Imperial Government to do business on its behalf. It fetches between Eth. $ 1,000,000 and Eth. $ 1,500,000 per year. A Tobacco Factory was started in 1942 with thirty workers and a monthly production of about 100,000 cigarettes. Within two years, the factory boasted more than 300 workers and an output of more than 2,000,000 cigarettes per month. The first industry of its kind here, it meets a real need. Tobacco cultivation has been extended and the native tobacco blended with a small amount of imported leaves is yielding cigarettes with a special flavour. The policy of the management is that Ethiopia should not try to imitate some of the popular foreign brands but introduce, standardise and popularise some quality brand cigarettes which could compare favourably with some imported ones and which will sell under their own proud trade and patent marks. That ambition has been almost fulfilled today, after thirteen years of the industry's prosperity. The modern machinery installed in the new factory turns out in a day 1,000,000 cigarettes. Two of the varieties, "Ketel Work" and "Faraseena" are in demand and popular among both Ethiopians and foreign residents in the country.

The services of the Ministry of Posts, Telegraphs and Telephones yield to State revenue an additional Eth. $ 1,000,000 to Eth. $ 1,500,000 while Court fees and fines bring in a handsome Eth. $ 1,500,000 annually.

If an index is necessary to show the development of Ethiopia's economy, one could surely rely on the figure of the national budget. National income in 1934, the year before the Italo—Ethiopian war, stood at Eth. $ 17,904,000; the estimated revenue for 1954—1955 (1947 Ethiopian Calendar) is Eth. $ 108,170,000. To give an idea of the steady progress and expanding economy since the liberation, the following table has been inserted:

The Annual Budget from 1941 to 1955

Year			Amount	
1941—1942 (1934 Ethiopian Calendar)			Eth. $	12,047,000
1942—1943 (1935	,,	,,)	,, ,,	25,095,000
1943—1944 (1936	,,	,,)	,, ,,	26,313,000
1944—1945 (1937	,,	,,)	,, ,,	39,156,000
1945—1946 (1938	,,	,,)	,, ,,	50,515,000
1946—1947 (1939	,,	,,)	,, ,,	49,202,000

1947—1948	(1940	,,	,,	)	,,	,,	48,923,000
1948—1949	(1941	,,	,,	)	,,	,,	52,182,000
1949—1950	(1942	,,	,,	)	,,	,,	72,017,000
1950—1951	(1943	,,	,,	)	,,	,,	68,217,000
1951—1952	(1944	,,	,,	)	,,	,,	71,726,000
1952—1953	(1945	,,	,,	)	,,	,,	103,119,192
1953—1954	(1946	,,	,,	)	,,	,,	121,295,606
1954—1955	(1947	,,	,,	)	,,	,,	108,170,341

A striking feature of the fiscal policy of the Government under the directives of Emperor Haile Selassie I has been to move very cautiously in the matter of incurring foreign debts. As far as is feasible and found to be expedient the aim is to depend largely on the internal revenue of the country. Nevertheless, when loans held out definite benefits for the country — as, for acceleration of progress with clear prospects of repayment — His Imperial Majesty has exercised his practical wisdom. Ethiopia has been always prompt in meeting her payments on any loans contracted for. When, in the year 1944, the United Nations offered assistance for the relief of the havoc of war in the country, the Emperor's broad outlook prevailed, and Ethiopia preferred to let the assistance go to nations in greater need. And today, after some years of waiting, Ethiopia has welcomed assistance from the United Nations, not necessarily in cash but in the form of technical assistance. From the International Bank for Reconstruction and Development, Ethiopia has borrowed the equivalent of US $ 7,500,000 which is giving dividends in the improved highways, telecommunications and the establishment of a Development Bank — schemes partly financed by Ethiopia herself. Under Joint Fund projects with America, the International Technical Co-operation Administration (Point 4) is co-operating with Ethiopia in the development of the country.

The Swedish technical assistance organisation, on the lines of the American one, though on a smaller scale, recently entered the field in Ethiopia. Ten years earlier, in 1945, the Swedish Government gave Ethiopia a credit of Swedish Kronor 5,000,000 which later was augmented by a further 2,500,000. About 45 per cent of this loan was to be utilised for the purchase of certain equipment in Sweden, mostly for hospitals and schools, and the remaining for travelling expenses and home salaries of Swedish personnel employed by the Ethiopian Government, Swedish Kronor 2,000,000 was repaid as per December 31st, 1950, and the balance by the end of 1951.

From the International Monetary Fund, in 1948 and 1949 Ethiopia obtained a total of US $ 600,000 against the equivalent deposit of Ethiopian dollars to the Fund's credit with the State Bank of Ethiopia. By 1951, Ethiopia had settled her dues fully in this connection. In 1950—1951, three loans were secured from the I.B.R.D.; US $ 5,000,000 for highway building, US $ 1,500,000 for development of telecommunications and US $ 2,000,000 for the establishment of a Development

208

Bank. Repayment is due to start in March next year, to be spread over a 15-year period.

Ethiopia has no internal debt. Her international debt is at present Eth. $ 31,037,705 (US $ 12,415,082) which includes the three International Bank for Reconstruction and Development loans totalling Eth. $ 21,250,000 (US $ 7,500,000), borrowed between 1951 to 1952 to undertake the specific modernisation projects referred to above. These three loans must be considered against the background that the Imperial Ethiopian Government has itself matched these sums and, in the case of the Imperial Highway Authority, for instance, the I.B.R.D. loan constituted less than 20 % of the total cost of the first six years of operation, the remaining 80 % having been supplied from current revenues of the Government. The rest of the nation's debts outstanding are: a balance of Eth. $ 93,749,95 from the Eth. $ 749,999,95 borrowed from the Import-Export Bank, Washington, for the purchase of machinery, mining equipment and the printing of Ethiopia's dollar currency in 1945; the United States Government Lend-Lease commodity settlement of Eth. $ 496,894,00 of which a balance of Eth. $ 193,954,83 remains unpaid; and a United States Government Lend-Lease silver loan to be returned in silver of 5,400,000 Pounds Sterling.

In the meantime Ethiopia has invested a total of more than Eth. $ 10,000,000 in four institutions of great public utility — State Bank of Ethiopia, Ethiopian Air Lines, Ethiopian Hotel Company Ltd., and the Tobacco Factory.

The improvement in the favourable balance of trade, which is conclusive proof of a country's financial prosperity, has been strikingly visible in the years following His Imperial Majesty's return to his liberated country. Internal stability restored, agricultural produce increased, communications improved, coupled with an intelligent fiscal policy which encouraged exports — these have all contributed to a sound Ethiopian economy.

The Finance Ministry's move in establishing the central bank, namely, the State Bank of Ethiopia, has played a prominent part in stimulating development and, at the same time, providing the banking connections abroad conducive to foreign trade. These eminently and in time assisted, advantage being taken of the changing conditions of world trade. In the wake of the cessation of World War II, the prices of primary products shot up more than the prices of manufactured goods. Here then was Ethiopia's golden opportunity, and proper direction of the financial policy was not lacking to exploit the situation.

By the beginning of 1950, a tendency towards reversal of this position of vantage was discernible. Before this could get very far, the Korean War turned the switch backwards, and Ethiopia's position as producer of raw materials and basic foodstuffs, brightened up again. It proved beneficial that Ethiopia did not take part in the currency devaluations of 1949 — a decision looked back upon with satisfaction until today. The wisdom of this course is reflected in the following table of exports and imports, given in units of million of Ethiopian dollars: —

Ethiopian Trade since 1945

Years Sept.	Merchandise Exports	Merchandise Imports
1945	38	36
1946	53	59
1947	74	84
1948	77	95
1949	71	87
1950	70	73
1951	116	104
1952	106	115
1953	169	137
1954	160	160

Definite steps are being taken to favour the development of industry, which must bear fruit before long. As for mining, geological experts have forecast that prospecting must uncover rich deposits of various metals that should make the economy of the country yet sounder stabler and brighter.

Ethiopia's improved trading position could be seen in Chapter 18 which deals with modern banking in Ethiopia. The State Bank's monetary gold holdings rose from 4,85 million Ethiopian dollars at the time of prevalent currency devaluation in 1949, to 8,19 million in the following year a clear 70 per cent increase. For the past decade the bank has registered a high level of earnings derived largely from commissions on foreign exchange transactions. Last year's earnings which were a record saw 53 per cent of this income coming from this source.

The currency reform of 1945 with the State Bank acting as the agent of the Ministry of Finance has assisted greatly the free flow of trade.

Under the Currency and Legal Tender Proclamation the State Bank became the house of issue. The new currency called the Ethiopian Dollar, as different from the M.T. Dollar, was given a par value with gold (5,52 grains of gold) which has been maintained up to the present.

By this Currency Proclamation the M.T. Dollar ceased to be legal tender. It was bought as silver bullion. The central bank offered to buy those that remained distributed in the country. The people reluctant before to surrender them, gradually began doing so as the purchasing value of the new currency won their confidence. It was a daring move to replace such a coin as the M.T. Dollar, so universally favoured, so widely distributed. The success in doing so, which has added to the stability of the country's economy, in so short a time, is a success for the Ministry of Finance.

The State Bank's issue department suffered a loss in the year 1945 owing to the heavy initial expenses in printing, transport, and distribution of new notes, and the gathering and repatriation of the East African Shillings. But since 1947 it has been making a net profit and the country has been building a gold reserve.

The most important departments of the Ministry are: Head Office, Accountancy Administration and Control Section, General Treasury, Customs Main Office, Income Tax Department, Budget and Finance, The Mining Board, The Tobacco Monopoly, State Domains, Inspection Section, General Office of Accountancy, Purchase and Distribution Agency, Registry and Documents Preparation Department, Personnel, Civil List Direction, Land Tax Revenue Department, Alcohol Tax, Shop and Commodity, Army General Stores Section, Government Transport Garage and Workshop, Finance Guards Section, and General Government Revenue Office, which includes the office of the Finance Advocate.

CHAPTER 18

State Bank of Ethiopia

Banking, in the modern sense of the term, like many of the reforms in present-day Ethiopia, is of comparatively recent date. Menelik II, who started his country on the road to international contact, established, in 1905, the Bank of Abyssinia. This bank was opened under an arrangement with the National Bank of Egypt.

Haile Selassie I, in the first year of his reign as Emperor, 1931, removed the Bank from Egyptian control and an institution purely Ethiopian in character, was established in its place. After nearly four years of successful operation, like all other modern efforts of the State, the bank was closed by the aggression against the country in 1935.

The Banking business fell into the hands of the occupiers who set up their own banks, branches of the Banco di Roma. This temporary banking empire was completely broken up with their expulsion in 1941 by the Ethiopian and allied forces and the return of the Emperor. A branch of the Barclay's Bank (D. C. & O.) was opened in the capital to meet the banking emergency of the new situation. Naturally, the new, expanding economic and commercial life of the restored nation necessitated some permanent banking institution. The establishment of an Ethiopian State Bank was the answer.

An Imperial proclamation of August 26th, 1942, set up the new institution. Its charter, which was published in the Negarit Gazeta of November, 1943, outlined in detail the powers and functions of the State Bank of Ethiopia. It became the central bank of the Empire empowered to issue bank-notes and coins as agent of the Ministry of Finance, which had subscribed the whole amount of the original capital investment of the Bank in the form of Maria Theresa Thalers 1,000,000 the currency then in use along with the East African Shillings brought in by the Military Administration. Upon the subsequent withdrawal of the Barclay's Bank, the State Bank of Ethiopia became the sole bank in the country to engage in normal commercial banking activities. A branch of the "Banque de l'Indo-Chine" was opened in February 1943, which offers limited banking facilities.

The State Bank first opened its doors to the public in April, 1943, under a Canadian governor, Mr. C. S. Collier. With Mr. Collier's transfer to the position of Comptroller and Auditor General of the Imperial Ethiopian Government, an American, Mr. George A. Blowers, was given the post, and it was under the latter's direction that the 1945 currency reform was effected. Mr. Blowers was succeeded in July, 1949, by another American, Mr. Jack Bennett, who left at the end of 1952 after guiding the Bank through three of its most successful

212

years. A new governor, Mr. Walter H. Rozell Jr., assumed the leadership of the bank in December, 1953.

From a modest beginning the State Bank has grown remarkably. When the bank first began operations, activities were conducted on a rather small scale, and the number of employees totalled only about fifteen. Services offered included current accounts, issuance of drafts, mail and telegraphic transfers, letters of credit, and the granting of loans against mortgages, merchandise, and personal guarantee. Overdraft facilities were also extended to a few firms. The bank's early years were marked by rapid growth, reflecting a concomitant expansion in all phases of economic activity, both government and private. Nevertheless, the bank showed a loss for the year 1943, due largely to non-recurrent costs involved in starting operations and in the opening of branches. During succeeding years the bank has earned a profit in each fiscal period.

Correspondent accounts were opened with numerous banks abroad, and today there are 34 correspondents in 17 countries throughout the world. An Issue Department was added to the bank in July, 1945, by virtue of the Currency and Legal Tender Proclamation of that year, and customer services and the number of branches were gradually increased. Savings accounts were made available to the public by the Head Office in January, 1946, and since that time have been extended to most branches. From a small beginning in that year savings deposits have grown to today's total of over Eth. $ 3,000,000, a sure index of the country's prosperity.

The extension of banking facilities into the various provinces of the Empire has been an important development in banking in Ethiopia — a development greatly encouraged by His Imperial Majesty. One month after the opening of the Head Office at Addis Ababa in April, 1943, the first branch was established at Dessie, and this was followed in August of the same year by another branch at Dire Dawa. Both cities are important commercial centers of the Empire. In April of the following year a third branch was opened at Jimma, capital of Kaffa province. Additional branches to a total of fifteen have since been established throughout the country, plus a transit office in Jibuti, French Somaliland, although it was realised that commercial activity in some areas was not sufficient to ensure a profit. Nevertheless, it has been the policy of the State Bank to maintain branches in these areas on the principle that in this way the public will become acquainted with and develop confidence in the currency of Ethiopia and the use of its banking facilities.

In bringing the bank to the people, the organisation in the outlying districts is kept under constant control of the Head Office. Each of the branches is under the direct supervision of a branch manager who, in turn, is responsible to the Supervisor of Branches at the Head Office in Addis Ababa. Branches in Eritrea are controlled through the Manager of the Asmara Branch. The branches provide all general

213

banking services, such as current accounts, loans, mail and telegraphic transfers, letters of credit, and deal in the sale or purchase of foreign exchange with the approval of the Head Office. In addition, all except two extend savings account facilities to the public. The opportunity to safeguard their funds in such accounts at an attractive rate of interest (currently 4 % per annum) has had a wide appeal among the people, of whom an increasing number are coming to realise the advantages of regular savings. Current accounts have likewise grown from a small beginning in each of the branches, becoming approximately four-fold since the war's close in 1945.

The outstanding feature of branch operations in the last few years has been the opening of three new branches in Eritrea, at Asmara, Assab, and Massawa followed by the opening of a fourth, at Tessenei early in 1953.

The unique circumstances attendant upon the opening of the Eritrea branches deserve special mention.

Prior to the federation of Ethiopia and Eritrea on September 15th, 195? banking services in Eritrea had been provided through the branches of four foreign institutions: Barclay's Bank (D. C. & O.), (since closed) Banca di Roma, Banca di Napoli, and Banca d'Italia. The establishment therefore, of branches of the State Bank of Ethiopia in Eritrea brought the Bank for the first time into direct competition with other banks of long standing. Federation also imposed upon the State Bank the urgent necessity of replacing the former Eritrean currency — the East African shilling — with the national currency of Ethiopia, an operation that called for careful planning and execution. A further difficult task was the problem of organising and exercising an efficient control over foreign exchange in Eritrea. The extension of the State Bank activity into Eritrea, it will thus be seen, posed problems of a nature more complicated than had hitherto been encountered in branch operations. Despite difficulties, however, a complete measure of success has been achieved. The Ethiopian Dollar has successfully replaced the former East African currency as a medium of exchange, and the State Bank is securing the co-operation of the Eritrean merchant and foreign banks.

The growth of branch banking in Ethiopia has played a major role in strenthening commercial activity and in acquainting the people with the many advantages that a sound banking system can bring the community. Following is a list of branches of the State Bank Ethiopia and the total assets of each as of the end of April, 1955.

BRANCHES OF THE STATE BANK OF ETHIOPIA

Name of Branch	Assets, April 30th, 19
Asmara	Eth. $ 14,801,618.9
Dire Dawa	,, 8,943,490,7
Jimma	,, 3,394,201,5

Assab	. . . .	,,	1,953,203.55
Goré	. . . .	,,	1,910,463,40
Dessie	. . . .	,,	1,875,236,40
Jigjiga	. . . .	,,	1,407,737,78
Massawa	. . . .	,,	1,376,868,06
Gondar	. . . .	,,	1,299,502,56
Lekempti	. . . .	,,	1.051.703,90
Gambella	. . . .	,,	1,026,690.91
Addis Katama	. . . .	,,	907,908,05
Nazareth	. . . .	,,	518.187.40
Tessenei	. . . .	,,	263,819,82
Jibuti	. . . .	,,	235,522,10
Wardair	. . . .	,,	225.410,65
		Total Eth. $	41,491,566.52

Organisation:

The State Bank of Ethiopia is a corporate entity whose capital is entirely subscribed by the Ministry of Finance. As mentioned above the original capital investment of the bank was Maria Theresa Thalers 1,000,000 which was converted to an equal number of Ethiopian dollars at the time of the currency reform in July, 1945. Since then the capital of the State Bank has been raised several times and now totals Eth. $ 5,000,000.

The charter of the State Bank vests final control of the Bank's affairs in the hands of the Government, since its capital is owned by the Ministry of Finance and the Board of Directors is chosen by the Crown. The State Bank is officially designated as the bankers of the Imperial Government. While the sole right of issuing currency is by law invested in the State Bank of Ethiopia, the latter acts in this capacity "for and on behalf of the Imperial Ethiopian Government".

Active direction of the Bank's affairs is in the hands of the Board of Directors and its policies are decided by that body. The chief executive officer of the bank is the Governor, who is personally appointed by the Crown.

Bank Services - Domestic:

Savings Accounts and Time Deposits.

Through the medium of savings accounts and time deposit facilities offered by the State Bank the people are becoming acquainted with the advantages of regular savings. Funds kept in regular savings bank accounts earn interest at the rate of 4 % per annum, compounded semi-annually. Time deposits held for twelve months or longer earn interest at 3½ %, for six months, 2 %. Savings accounts may be opened with an initial deposit of as little as Eth. $ 5.00, and thereafter deposits of Eth. $ 1.00 and up will be accepted. At present such accounts are limited to Eth. $ 5,000 per person, but there is no limit on the amounts that may be placed on time deposit.

215

In the case of regular savings accounts withdrawals are restricted to two per month and are limited to 25 % of the amount standing to the credit of the account unless, of course, the depositor decides to close the account, in which case thirty days notice may be required. Interest is calculated on the minimum monthly balance and credited to depositors' accounts half-yearly. To earn interest, a minimum balance of Eth. $ 25.00 is required.

The money deposited by the public with the bank in savings accounts is not permitted to lie idle, but is put to work in the form of loans, portfolio investments, and other interest-bearing uses. It is, in fact, only through the active employment of such funds that the bank is able to pay interest to its depositors.

Current Accounts:

Current accounts have always been one of the most important services extended to the public by the State Bank of Ethiopia and its branches. Payment by check has become increasingly popular in the larger cities of the Empire, because of ease and convenience. An initial deposit of at least Eth. $ 250.00 is required, but thereafter no minimum balance need be maintained.

Loans:

A primary source of a bank's income is interest on loans. Loans are often needed to start a new business or to help an established concern through difficult times; to enable a merchant to buy supplies; to finance the purchase of land or the construction of buildings; to advance funds needed by a farmer or industrialist to buy machinery and equipment; and, in general, to provide the money needed to finance worthwhile ventures in anticipation of profitable returns. Without the aid of loans commercial activity would be severely restricted and the prosperity of the community curtailed.

In the matter of serving the public through loans the State Bank of Ethiopia holds a predominant position. It is the only financial institution of size and strength sufficient at present to meet the financial need of the Ethiopian business community.

What are the sources of these loan funds? As previously indicated they arise in the main from customers' deposits, current savings and time.

Five main types of loans are made by the State Bank. These are:

1) *Mortgage loans,* made against real property, land, or buildings. Such loans are usually extended for a period of from one to six years and bear interest at the rate of 8 % per annum. Mortgage loans are normally the major type of loans in terms of money involved.

2) *Merchandise loans* are normally made against a pledge of merchandise by exporters to obtain an advance on payment of goods shipped abroad. The duration of such loans averages about three

216

months, and interest on them is payable at 7 % per annum. Naturally, this type of loan is heaviest during the main export season which extends from January to July. Merchandise loans generally are limited to 50 % of the value of the goods.

3) *Guaranteed loans* are made against the personal guarantee of a third party, who bears liability in case of default. The period covered is usually no longer than one year. Interest is at 9 % per annum. Individual loans in this category are limited to Eth. $ 25,000, but in practice the amount advanced rarely exceeds Eth. $ 5,000. Guaranteed loans are frequently made to finance small purchases, such as a small piece of property, an automobile, or other durable consumer goods.

4) *Overdraft facilities* are granted to reputable and wellknown clients of long standing with the bank. Overdraft facilities are usually extended for six months at a time, but may be renewed. Facilities granted vary with the capital position of the applicant. Interest accumlates at 7 %.

5) *Merchants' promissory notes and other commercial paper* are discounted by the bank at 9 % per annum. Collection is then made by the bank from the signatory.

In order to avail himself of the lending services of the State Bank of Ethiopia a prospective borrower has only to visit the Loan Department of the bank and discuss the matter with a bank official. In most cases any difficulties that arise can be readily settled and helpful advice given. Approval of every loan, however, must await the decision of the Loan Committee and the Governor.

Other Services:

In addition to these services the bank has facilities for the safe custody of clients' valuables and provides expert appraisals on real estate at nominal charges.

Bank Services - Foreign:

One of the other important functions of the State Banks, is its rôle as a link between merchants at home and abroad. In the sphere of foreign trade the bank renders a vital service to the nation through its sale or purchase of foreign exchange, for which purpose it maintains a relationship with 34 correspondent banks throughout the world. By virtue of its many contacts abroad, it is able to help both exporters and importers to receive and meet payment for their foreign services and obligations. For this purpose it maintains a Foreign Department which is open to serve the public every day except Sunday. This Department is responsible for issuing foreign exchange, and is in daily contact with the foreign correspondents of the State Bank through whom the sale and purchase of exchange is conducted.

Exchange Control:

The establishment of an effective system of exchange control came

217

about in September, 1949. Legally, some form of control had existec since October 31st, 1942, and this was considerably strenghthened b an amendment of June, 1948, to the Currency Proclamation of 1942 However, no formal control had been set up. By legal Notice No. 12 of 1949 this situation was altered. Detailed instructions were lai down on the mechanics of control; the State Bank of Ethiopia wa declared the sole authorised dealer in foreign exchange; and, i accordance with this provision, an exchange control office, under a Exchange Controller, was set up in the bank. This office is activel engaged in administering the new currency regulations and in settin up rules and methods of procedure for foreign traders.

The central point of exchange control as it has been practised sinc September, 1949, is that all persons exporting goods from Ethiopi must undertake to transfer all of the foreign exchange proceeds fro such sales to the State Bank of Ethiopia. Equivalent compensation i of course, made in local currency. Ethiopia's exchange control ma be described as a system of quantitative restrictions based on individu allocations of foreign exchange.

There are no import licenses, but payments outside Ethiopia for impor require exchange licenses. These exchange lincenses are at prese freely granted for all goods in the appropriate currency of the countr of their origin, or in a softer currency when ordered through a thir country.

Payments abroad for "invisible" imports also require exchange license Exchange for such purposes as charity and maintenance is grante in moderate amounts to residents not permanently domiciled Ethiopia for remittance to their own country. Exchange for educatic is granted to permanent and temporary residents based on eviden of necessity and amount. The transfer abroad of dividends and oth current earnings due to non-residents is allowed within limits.

In order to obtain exchange to pay a foreign shipper, the Ethiopi importer must file an application with the Exchange Controller. Th application, when approved, becomes an exchange license and assurance to the importer that he will obtain the necessary forei exchange for payment, if available, either against documents aft arrival of the goods or against a letter of credit. An export lincens similarly obtained, is required for the shipment of goods abroad, a serves as a check on the surrender by exporters of 100 % of t receipts from foreign sales to the Exchange Controller. In the ca of coffee — Ethiopia's main export — present regulations requi the exporter to surrender at least 50 % of the proceeds in U.S. dolla and the balance in sterling. Exchange control has markedly affect the pattern of imports in the direction of a greater proportiona volume of those items which may be loosely described as of industrial nature, or satisfying in the main industrial, constructic or transportation needs. The change has taken place largely at t expense of textile consumption, which has declined corresponding

218

Relatively speaking; the absolute value of textile imports has risen by more thans 50 % since 1945. Within the general framework of exchange control, the volume and value of Ethiopia's foreign trade have continued to increase. The country has enjoyed a healthy surplus in its overall balance of payments with the rest of the world in recent years, and has been able to build up large reserves of United States dollars to further its capital development.

Currency:

Although some form of money had been in use in Ethiopia for many hundreds of years, the present widespread acceptance of a paper currency is of recent origin. The use of a gold, and later a bronze, coinage is reported from very early times but it appears that much of the internal trade of the country was for long carried on by means of barter with blocks of salt, lengths of cloth, and iron. About the middle of the nineteenth century the large silver coin known as the Maria Theresa Thaler, first minted in Austria in 1751 under the reign of Maria Theresa, came into circulation, and remained the coin most generally accepted throughout the country until the currency reform of 1945. It was esteemed not only for its intrinsic worth, being 83.33 % silver, but for its decorative and easily recognisable design as well. About fifty million of these coins were estimated to have been in circulation on the eve of the Italian invasion in 1935. Neither the issuance of an Ethiopian metal coinage under Menelik II and Haile Selassie I nor the printing of some notes by the Bank of Ethiopia prior to 1935 met with any appreciable success in replacing the silver Maria Theresa Thalers.

In 1941 the currency situation became more confused than ever, as the British troops brought with them a large quantity of East African Shillings. A third currency was thus added to the two others in circulation, the Lira and the Maria Theresa Thaler, and all three were declared legal tender.

The difficulties of the Ethiopian Government were increased by the limitations placed on its control of the currency in the Anglo-Ethiopian Agreement of 1942. A second agreement in December, 1944, removed these restrictions and opened the way for the establisment of a new, and purely Ethiopian, currency. That this was a vital necessity was becoming increasingly evident with the disruption of trade and the substantial fluctuations in value of the several currencies in terms of each other. In addition, there existed a strong tendency to hoard Maria Theresa Thalers and to ship them out of the country, in view of the rising price of silver world markets. By the end of 1944 this rise had caused the exchange value of the Maria Theresa Thaler to increase to three East African Shillings on the free market, although it had been legally pegged at only two shillings in 1943.

To straighten out the difficulty the Government of Ethiopia, with the help of a large silver loan under Lend-Lease arrangement with the

United States, began the issuance of a new currency on July 23rd, 1945
The details of this reform had been published the previous May in
the official Government journal, the *Negarit Gazeta*, under the titl
of "Currency and Legal Tender Proclamation", No. 76 of 1945. The
new law established the Ethiopian Dollar, equal in value to 5,52 grain
of fine gold, as the single monetary unit of the country. The Dolla
is based on the decimal system and is pegged at 40.25 United State
cents. The sole right of issue is vested in the Issue Department of
the State Bank of Ethiopia, acting on behalf of the Ministry of
Finance. For this purpose the State Bank of Ethiopian maintains a
currency fund, consisting of gold, silver, and foreign currency ban
balances or readily covertible prime securities, originally to a minimum
extent of 75 % of the fund, and Imperial Treasury obligations to
maximum of 25 % of the fund. The fund, under terms of the 194
law, constituted a reserve for redemption at full value of the note
outstanding.

In 1950 the legal coverage for Ethiopian dollar notes was reduced
In an amendment to the currency proclamation of 1945, the require
holdings of gold, silver, and foreign assets were lowered from 75 %
to 30 % of the currency fund. Imperial Treasury obligations ma
now comprise a maximum of 70 % of the note cover, and an
themselves secured by a pledge of fixed assets of the Imperial Treasur
to a value equal to 110 % of these obligations. This step was take
after careful deliberation of the needs and resources of the countr
had indicated that it was no longer necessary to hold such a larg
proportion of the nation's gold and foreign exchange reserves in
idleness. The Ethiopian Dollar, since its introduction five yea
earlier, had proved its stability, had successfully replaced the variou
competing currencies, and, in general, had gained a wide measur
of confidence and acceptance throughout the land. Prior to th
reduction in the note cover, the Ethiopian Government had been almo
alone among the governments of the world in undertaking to kee
so high a proportion of its monetary reserves immobilised to secure i
currency. The action released a total of Eth. $ 21 million of foreig
exchange for use in the support of imports and permitted a great
degree of flexibility in the money supply to meet the seasonal need
of the country's foreign trade.

After the introduction of the new currency in July, 1945, East Africa
Shillings continued as legal tender for another six months, but Mar
Theresa Thalers were immediately demonetised and called in fo
redemption by the State Bank at the rate of 1½ Ethiopian Dolla
to every Maria Theresa Thaler. As of July 10th, 1950, the increase
purchasing power of the Ethiopian Dollar had made it possible
lower the redemption rate between Maria Theresa and Ethiopia
Dollars to parity. The demonetised Maria Theresa Thalers a
treated as silver bullion, and constitute a part of the legal backin
for Ethiopian Dollar notes. The East African Shillings in circulatio

at the time of the currency reform have been gradually redeemed by the State Bank at the rate of two Shillings for one Ethiopian Dollar. Almost 60 % of the original currency reserve arose from the redemption of these notes for sterling balances in London, which were later invested in gilt-edge British Empire securities. The remaining 40 % of the original reserve came from the normal expansion of foreign exchange balances of the State Bank acquired through merchandise exports and the sale abroad of newly mined gold.

The note fund reserve at the end of a little less than 1½ years operations under the new currency (December 31st, 1946) covered a total issue of Eth. $ 39,885,000 in notes, composed of the following: Foreign securities, 84 %; Foreign balances, 9 %; Silver bullion in the form of Maria Theresa Thalers, 5 %; and Ethiopian Treasury bills, 2 %. By December 31st, 1954 the total issue of notes had grown to Eth. $ 115,747,100 and was backed by foreign securities, 13 %; foreign balances, 12 %; gold, 9 %; silver, 13 %; and Ethiopian Treasury Bills, 53 %. Thus although a minimum backing of 30 % in gold, silver, and foreign assets is required by law, in actual fact 47 % of the note issue was covered in this manner as of the end of 1954. The coin issue has grown from Eth. $ 14,499,201 at the end 1946 to Eth. $ 35,239,073 as of the end of 1954. In addition, gross bank deposits have expanded from Eth. $ 36,562,133 as of December 31st, 1946 to Eth. $ 119,801,764 as of December 31st, 1954 so that the total money supply — cash in circulation plus gross deposits — today aggregates Eth. $ 238.5 million, compared to Eth. $ 79.3 million eight years ago.

This large expansion of the money supply, in conjunction with the greater purchasing power of the Ethiopian Dollar today at home and abroad, is indicative of the success which the post-war currency reform has enjoyed. While the hoarding of silver fifty-cent pieces is, even today, not uncommon among farmers in the provinces, the traditional hold of the Maria Theresa Thaler on the economic life of the people has been broken, and a wide measure of confidence now exists in the national currency.

Conclusion:

Looking back over a decade of growth and service to the nation, the State Bank views with pride its record of the past ten years. During this period its total assets have increased from approximately Eth. $ 16 million in 1944 to over Eth. $ 300 million today. Total deposits have similarly increased to a record level of about Eth. $ 120 million. The bank has earned a profit in every year except the first, and in the last three this has climbed to impressive proportions.

Private loans increased substantially in 1954, but loans to Government declined, resulting in a net rise in loans and advances to Eth. $ 21,759,780 as of December 31st, from a level of Eth. $ 19,606,573 the year before.

Largely as a result of another surplus in Ethiopia's balance o
International payments, note issue was expanded by some Eth. $ 1.
million during 1954, raising the total issue of notes and coins t
Eth. $ 151.0 million at the close of the year. This amounts to a ris
of 11 % over the same date a year earlier.

Over the past decade the number and quality of bank employees ha
risen steadily. At present the total staff at Head Office and branche
numbers close to 600, compared with 481 at the end of 1953. Nc
only has the staff gained invaluable practical experience during th
years, but it has been the policy of the Bank to send promising youn
Ethiopian personnel abroad for further training and study. It has als
been management's policy to encourage the employment of Ethiopia
citizens in key positions, and thus gradually to reduce the proportio
of non-Ethiopians in the bank. These policies are coming to bear frui
as indicated not only by the fact that the percentage of Ethiopia
employees has been rising steadily, but by the increasingly responsib.
positions which Ethiopians are assuming.

In conclusion, it should be said that the rapid development of bankin
in Ethiopia, particularly in the past ten years, has been due in n
small measure to the continuing encouragment and support of H.I.N
Haile Selassie I, Emperor of Ethiopia, who has on numerous occasio
expressed his keen interest of seeing the establishment of a tru.
modern banking system.

CHAPTER 19

Commercial and Industrial Progress

A comparative study between the commercial and industrial position of Ethiopia today and twenty-five years ago, reveals great change both in volume and value of trade, as well as in the variety of items with which this trade is concerned. The cause has been twofold. First, there has been, during this time, a greater awareness on the part of Ethiopians and the Ethiopian Government, of the necessity to expand commercial and industrial activity. They have come to realise that commerce, both national and international, holds the key to the country's progress. Just as in other fields of national striving the older and lethargic ways were found unsuited and insufficient to meet the newer ways ushered in by the Emperor's many reforms, commerce also felt the impact. Secondly, an expanding economy was recognised as the keystone of progress. Manufactured goods, not made locally, had to be imported to feed and support these reforms; international trade provided the best means of doing so.

Certain traditional agricultural items, such as coffee, hides and skins, beeswax and cereals had always found their way into world markets. It became necessary, however, because of the new impulse, to produce these items on a wider scale. As reported in the chapter on Agriculture, efforts were made and energy released to make agriculture an industry. Farm crops with merit in world marts were put on a basis, related not only to local consumption, but with emphasis on creating exportable surpluses. Plans were therefore laid to aid the farmer to increase his production; he was encouraged to stress the production of crops and other farm products suitable for export. Measures were put into effect to see that certain acceptable standards be obtained in them to meet modern market demands. In other words, agricultural production became keyed to commerce and trade — a factor which has been responsible for the favourable balance of trade experienced, especially in recent years. Nothing explains this new rôle of agriculture in the national economy than the fact that Ethiopian exports today are almost 100 % agricultural raw or processed products.

A similar trend has been noticed in the field of industry, although with a different emphasis. Even before His Majesty the Emperor's accession to the throne, such industries as saw-mills, flour-mills, oil-mills, soap manufacture, tanneries and a few others existed on a small scale. A new economic situation was called for and created. The motto was, to see that national industrial production, within available limits, served to reduce the volume and value of imported goods which could be locally made. In 1953, 50 % of total imports consisted of raw or manufactured materials of an agricultural nature, most of which could be grown and processed in Ethiopia. Os a coronally to utilising the country's agricultural potential

in terms of attainable self-sufficiency in these items, secondary industrie
were encouraged and their number has increased and continues to increase
The schools have been recruited to better the ancient arts and crafts and
the Government has sought, through technical training, to provide artisan
and technicians in preparation for industrial development.

The guiding hand in these two vital fields of national life fell to the
Ministry of Commerce and Industry which came into being at the be
ginning of His Majesty the Emperor's reign. With six departments, the
Ministry performs several important functions. It controls the imports and
exports of Ethiopia; takes all necessary steps to promote native industrie
and handicraft; keeps contact with the trade agents established abroad
organises commercial and industrial exhibitions; encourages foreign
investors in the exploitation of the country's resources, among many
others.

In 1930, when His Majesty ascended the throne, the country's export
stood at a low ebb and were far exceeded by her imports. But today, the
situation is reversed, since the exports exceed the imports by a handsome
margin, to the value of Eth.$ 16,668,600. The import and export tonnage
of 1954 are respectively four times and ten times those of 1930, while the
import and export values of 1954 are respectively eight and a half time
and twelve and a half times those of 1930, as shown in the tell-tale table
given below:

		Tonnage	Value
Imports:	1930	42,162 tons	Eth.$ 18.287,62
	1954	179,100 tons	,, 155,175,40
Exports:	1930	24,950 tons	,, 13,593,66
	1954	249,130 tons	,, 171,844,00

The imports in the 'thirties' consisted mainly of grey sheeting, cotton yarn
cotton piece-goods and salt. These items were still in demand in 1954
but new items too had captured the market. From the point of view o
demand, the importance went to motor-cars, spare-parts and tyres, which
exceeded the other items in total value. Among the other items, Ethiopi
imported sugar, silk, benzine (petrol), cotton-yarn and corrugated iron
sheets, in that order.

Table 1. *Ethiopia's Import Commodities, 1930 and 1954*

(Years ending Sept. 10th of years stated)

		Quantity		Value (Eth.$)	
		1930	1954	1930	1954
Grey Sheetings	tons	5,116	6,268	$ 6,425,000	$ 10,964,40
Other Cotton					
Piece-goods	tons	785	4,921	2,150,400	16,055,40
Cotton Yarns	tons	1,702	1,564	3,652,740	4,931,00
Silk and Art. Silk Goods		—	—	198,400	6,230,10
Corrugated Iron Sheets	tons	2,096	6,483	181,380	3,848,10

224

		Quantity		Value (Eth.$)	
		1930	1954	1930	1954
Motor Cars, parts and Tyres	tons	284	6,340	268,600	22,713,200
Sugar	tons	2,113	22,263	278,480	7,076,400
Salt	tons	19,314	5,554	1,515,240	564,900
Kerosene	tons	2,222	6,904	556,960	1,020,800
Motor Spirit (Benzine)	tons	628	18,673	352,620	5,072,000
Other	tons	7,902	100,130	2,707,800	76,699,100
Total	tons	42,162	179,100	$18,287,629	$155,175,400

As regards the commodities of export, only four items were worthy of mention in 1930: these are coffee, hides and skins, beeswax and cereals. But today, with the development of communications throughout the Empire, with the vast strides of progress made in agriculture, and with the return of Eritrea to Ethiopia, the number of new commodities and the amount of old commodities exported from Ethiopia have increased several times beyond their 1930 level. From the point of view of revenue, the most important items today are coffee, hides and skins, oil-seeds, "chat", cereals, frozen meat, fruits and vegetables, oil-cakes and ground-nuts, in that order.

Table 2. *Ethiopia's Export Commodities, 1930 and 1954*
(Years ending Sept. 10th of years stated)

		1930	1954	1930	1954
Coffee beans	tons	14,412	37,219	$ 8,085,700	$112,371,000
Cattle hides raw	tons	5,752	6,231	3,038,400	6,742,000
Goatskins	tons	1,203	2,409	946,520	6,924,000
Sheepskins	tons	662	973	372,900	3,612,000
Beeswax	tons	346	398	355,360	645,000
Ghee or clarified Butter	tons	77	67	—	136,000
Cereals	tons	1,344	17,983	—	2,359,000
Flour (wheat)	tons	129	237	—	84,000
Pulses	tons	—	64,122	—	9,940,000
Oilseeds	tons	—	40,562	—	10,982,000
Salt	tons	—	20,566	—	73,000
Fresh Fruits and Vegetables	tons	—	3,421	—	1,141,000
Meat (frozen)	tons	—	1,446	—	1,303,000
Fish (dried)	tons	—	1,109	—	328,000
Fish meal	tons	—	2,824	—	781,000
Edible Oils	tons	—	1,007	—	249,000
Groundnuts in shell	tons	—	2,361	—	1,067,000

		1930	1954	1930	1954
Chat	tons	—	1,139	—	3,918,000
Civet	Kgs.	—	1,722	—	679,000
Oilcake	tons	—	15,214	—	1,078,000
Cotton raw	tons	—	265	—	675,000
Other miscellaneous	tons	1,025	27,855	794,780	6,257,000
Total domestic exports	tons	24,950	249,130	$13,593,660	$171,844,000

When Ethiopia was liberated in 1941, the country's economy was found to be in a disintegrated state. The country's imports and exports had practically come to a stand-still. Her industries had received a crippling blow from the Fascist invasion and occupation. Under these circumstances the Ministry of Commerce and Industry had to adopt strict measures of control over the internal trade to prevent illegal profiteering.

Soon after the liberation, however, Britain recognised in Ethiopia a regular producer of food and primary products. As a result of the negotiations between Britain's Minister of State and Emperor Haile Selassie the United Kingdom Commercial Corporation undertook a transport service from Dire Dawa to Berbera, in British Somaliland, facilitating the export of the grain supplies from Ethiopia to the Middle East Supply Centre. (By the end of 1942, the supply arrangements in Eritrea were also handed over to the U.K.C.C.). The figures available at present are only for the latter half of 1941:

Imports		In Value	In Metric Tons
a) Vegetable and Animal Products .		£ 96,004	3,562
b) Manufactured Products		£ 79,477	n.a.
c) Mineral and Other Products . .		£ 27,311	n.a.
	Total	£ 202,792	

Exports		in Value	In Metric Tons
a) Grain		£ 2,611	151
b) Other Foodstuffs		£ 22,110	n.a.
c) Other Goods		£ 573,474	n.a.
	Total	£ 598,195	

As soon as World War II ended, the commercial situation began to improve. With the ever-rising standard of living, with the ever-increasing purchasing power in the hands of the public, and with the establishment of new enterprises in Addis Ababa and elsewhere, scarce import goods began to flow increasingly into the country. And Ethiopia was not slow in improving her terms of trade.

The rise in the general standard of living is particularly visible in the following fields of consumption:

226

	Import in 1930	Import in 1954
a) Cotton piece-goods other than Abujedid	785 tons	4,921 tons
b) Silk and Art. Silk goods . . .	E$ 198,400	E$ 6,230,100
c) Sugar	2,113 tons	22,263 tons
d) Corrugated Iron Sheets . . .	2,096 tons	6,483 tons
e) New Passenger Motor Cars . .	300 No. (estimated)	1,669 No.
f) Motor Spirit (Benzine) . . .	628 tons	18,673 tons

Other items like the consumption of radios, leather shoes, metal furniture and pharmaceutical products must have all shown substantial increases, although the corresponding figures for 1930 are not available.

The following list shows the most important suppliers of Ethiopia's principal imports:

a) Cotton raw: U.S.A.,
b) Cotton Piece-Goods, Yarns and Manufactures: India, Japan, Italy, U.K., U.S.A.,
c) Woollen Yarns and Manufactures: U.S.A., Italy, U.K.,
d) Rayon and Silk Yarns and Manufactures: Japan, Italy,
e) Gunny Bags: India,
f) Motor Vehicles and Other Metal Goods: U.S.A., U.K., Italy, Germany, Belgium,
g) Rubber Tyres and Tubes: U.S.A., U.K., Germany,
h) Petroleum Products: Saudi Arabia, Egypt, Iran,
i) Sugar: U.K., Holland, Belgium, Germany, Czechoslovakia,
j) Salt: French Somaliland.

Ehiopia's balance of trade and balance of payments have generally been favourable since 1946 as shown below. The particularly favourable position since 1950 can be attributed partly to the larger quantities of coffee exported at higher prices during those years and partly to the Exchange Control system enforced by the State Bank since 1949. As a result of the exchange control, Ethiopia's gold and dollar reserves are adequate enough to enable her to meet the demands of international payment:

	Balance of trade (Surplus + 1)	Balance of payments (Surplus +)
1945	+ 5.1	— 3,1
1946	+ 7.4	+ 2.9
1947	+ 10.3	— 18.9
1948	+ 2.8	+ 5.7
1949	+ 1.7	— 2.6
1950	+ 15.3	+ 8.1
1951	+ 38.2	+ 15.3
1952	+ 15.6	+ 4.9
1953	+ 63.9	+ 42.4

In recent years, the Ministry of Commerce and Industry have done their best to secure greater standardisation of export commodities and to guarantee proper grading and cleaning of such items. For this purpose, a number of grading and cleaning machines has been imported and legislation for the protection of the prospective exporters and the traders has been projected. Cereals and other commodities are being brought under this reform and the improving of the qualitiy of hides and skins has begun.

A National Coffee Board was set up in 1954 to supervise all stages of production throughout the country. The programme also included technical assistance to coffee growers through demonstration centres; training for research in the coffee districts; and the assembly of information about the costs of establishing and operating commercial plantations. A coffee expert from the Food and Agriculture Organisation of the United Nations is working in conjunction with the F.O.A. (Point 4) Mission who have devised, in co-operation with the Government, an overall programme for the improvement of the quality and quantity of coffee produced. The Mission provides plant, materials and demonstrations. A coffee centre has been established at Jimma and there are plans for establishing five more during this year.

About five years ago the Ethiopian Grain Board was formed to encourage better production of grain. Since then, both the local and foreign consumers of Ethiopian grain, pulses and oil-seeds have been assured of a higher standard of quality in these commodities.

Ethiopia's industrial potential, like in many other countries, lie in her natural resources. The United States Technical Mission of 1944 made a general survey of the country, but as yet no comprehensive geological survey of Ethiopia has been made. The extent of mineral deposits is therefore unknown. Exploration is hindered by the difficulty of travel and the lack of communications. A Mining Board, recently set up, has been charged with the responsibility of making arrangements for an air survey but it is still considering how it should be tackled. The Board is also responsible for the issue of mining concessions and a draft law to govern prospecting is in course of preparation. A number of foreign firms have shown interest in these. The Ethiopian Government is anixous to encourage mineral development and would welcome new enterprises.

Known mineral resources include:

(a) Occurrences of non-bituminous sulphur mainly in the Danakil area which have been surface-mined intermittently in a small way. In 1954 production was 1,200 tons. The fact that there are several such occurrences suggests that unproved reserves may be greater;

(b) Potash deposits also in the Danakil area, mainly sylvinite and carnallite. These also are surface-mined but are not thought to be extensive. In 1953/54 production was 2,400 tons;

(c) Salt is manufactured on the Eritrean coast by the solar evaporation of sea water, and there are substantial salt deposits in the North Danakil area, accompanied by gypsum, which are also exploited;

(d) Platinum, mined at Yubdo;

(e) Indications of copper and tungsten at Benishangul;
(f) Gold, also at Benishangul, an ancient mining district; extensive alluvial gold mines at Adola and Assosa; and alluvial gold on the Acobo River, which the Government are currently investigating;
(g) Indications of antimony, copper, graphite, pyrites, mica and vermiculite in the Harar Province;
(h) Elemental silver in the mountains of the Awash valley;
(i) Lignite at Memdi and Chelga;
(j) Tin near the borders of British Somaliland;
(k) Limestone, distributed fairly widely throughout the country.

Industrial enterprises number 126. Most of these are of comparatively recent origin, and wholly or partly owned by foreigners, and almost all are small with a very modest output. Cotton textiles form the most important group. A flourishing hand spinning and weaving industry in and around Addis Ababa uses local tree cotton, and a modern factory, re-equipped since the war, imports its cotton at present mainly from the United States of America. Good quality hessian ropes and coffee bags, manufactured from *musa ensette,* largely meet local requirements. A new factory, attached to the Dutch sugar plantation at Wonji is now producing about 15,000 tons of refined sugar a year. It is hoped that within the next two years the output will have been increased to 24,000 tons and that production of cube sugar will begin. One thousand persons are employed in the plant, most of the executives being Dutch.

The capital invested is 100 % Dutch and the project, which has received every assistance from the Ethiopian authorities, has achieved considerable success in a very short time. There are ten tanneries and the production of hides and skins is one of the more important industries. The number of coffee-cleaning and grading establishments has increased considerably since the coffee boom, and there are various plants for seed-cleaning and oil extraction. Some building materials are produced. There are four brick and tile factories, and a cement manufacturing plant at Dire Dawa with plans for establishing another at Massawa. There are two cigarette and tobacco factories, one in Addis Ababa and the other ad Asmara. Both are owned by the Government tobacco monopoly and use home grown and imported tobacco. Eight factories produce 60 % of the country's requirements of soap, and two make boots and shoes. A factory established about three years ago at Asmara produces frozen and canned meat. Other industries include wood-working and furniture making, basketry, brewing, alcohol distillation, production of foodstuffs and beverages, beeswax refining, flour milling, silversmithing, and the manufacture of jewellery, glassware, matches, buttons, candles, paper and carpets.

Mention should be here made of the International Exhibition of 1951, held in Addis Ababa. It served the useful purposes of studying the industrial and commercial potentialities of the country as well as giving opportunities for the exchanging of ideas between the exhibitors and the visitors. This is evident from the fact that the number of commercial and industrial enterprises (of foreign origin), established after the Exhibition, is on the increase.

229

As seen in Table 2, coffee accounted for 65 % of the total domestic exports in 1954. The Ethiopian Government, recognising that the country's economy is too narrowly based for security and that some reduction of her dependence on world coffee prices is very desirable, are seeking to broaden its foundations, on the one hand by making her self-sufficient where this can be done by the better use of her natural resources, e.g., by growing tea, rice, tobacco, rubber, cotton and other fibres, and exploiting minerals; and on the other by encouraging the establishment of manufacturing industries. A list of fields which are considered to have suitable opportunities for industrial expansion was recently published. It included textile, plastics, paint, ceramics, food canning, building materials, furniture, paper, meat packing and leather industries.

It is the policy of the Imperial Ethiopian Government to encourage the inflow of foreign capital into all possible fields of commerce and industry. In order to achieve this object, the Government has adopted positive measures such as follows: exempting newly-established investment pojects from taxation for a period of five years; exempting imported capital goods from customs duty; granting resident visas for technicians and managers; permitting the regular remittance of savings, profits, etc., to foreign countries; and facilitating the "repatriation" of foreign capital.

Year after year, Ethiopia's foreign trade is increasing in quantity and value. Both the imports and exports are showing a favourable upward trend.

The major suppliers of Ethiopia's import commodities are India, U.S.A., Great Britain, Italy and Japan, in their order of relative importance. Together they supplied 66 % of the total value of imports during the period of 1949—52. (In 1953, this percentage rose to almost 70 %). As regards metals and engineering products, not less than 75 % was supplied by U.S.A., Great Britain, Italy, Belgium and Germany during the same period. (In 1953, the figure rose to 82 %). Egypt and Iran supplied about 90 % of the petroleum products imported in 1949—52. U.S.A., and Great Britain together supplied about 80 % of the rubber tyres and tubes imported during the same period.

Until the reunion of Eritrea with Ethiopia, a major share of the export trade had been carried on through the neighbouring countries — Sudan, Eritrea, French Somaliland and the Aden Protectorate. During 1949—52, about 72 % of the total coffee exports passed through those territories. In 1952—53, Aden, French Somaliland and the Sudan together handled about 48 % of the total exports and particularly 62 % of the coffee exports. The percentage of trade through those channels fell considerably after the federation of Eritrea with Ethiopia in September 1952.

The Ethiopian-Eritrean Federation has brought two seaports into the service of the Empire. Of the two ports, Massawa feeds the northernmost part of the Empire, while Assab feeds the hinterland in the south-west. A large number of deep sea ships call at these Ethiopian ports.

The river-port of Gambeila (on a tributary of the Nile), in Western Ethiopia, takes care of the commercial traffic in that part of the Empire. Cargo-laden ships can reach this port during a good part of the year.

230

The Agricultural Bank

The Agricultural Bank of Ethiopia (the fore-runner of the Development Bank of Ethiopia) was established by the Imperial Proclamation of 29th April 1945 as a measure designed to stimulate agricultural production. Its objectives were to aid the small farmer to increase his yields as a means of getting higher farm income, part of the general economic drive to raise living standards, instituted by the government in its reconstruction programme.

The capital of the Bank was authorised at one million Maria Theresa Dollars, subscribed by the Government Treasury. Thirty per cent of the said sum was paid to the Bank, by the Treasury, as paid-up capital; and the remainder was to be paid to the Bank by the Treasury, as called upon from time to time.

The Bank was empowered: (a) to lend, advance, or discount money, and to grant mortgages on the security of agricultural realty, lands, buildings and agricultural chattels and crops growing and/or cut, and/on cattle or other farm animals; and to lend money and grant mortgage to and on agricultural products and agricultural enterprises, as well as industrial and commercial enterprises relating to agricultural production; (b) to cancel at its discretion, any loan, advance, discount or mortgage, where the borrower was not exploiting the agricultural realty, lands, buildings or other security given to the Bank, in accordance with standards established by the Ministry of Agriculture to the satisfaction of the Bank; (c) to borrow money, float loans, and issue bonds or other evidences of indebtedness, and to give security for the same; (d) to take all measures necessary to protect the security on which loans, advances, discounts or mortgages were made, and to take all necessary measures, either by foreclosure or otherwise, subject to existing legislation, to realise and collect the value of such security; (e) to employ the funds of the Bank in all types of agricultural enterprises, and/or industrial and commercial enterprises relating to agricultural production, and to manage, sell, or otherwise dispose of such enterprises, by way of protection of the interests of the Bank, as provided by sub-section "d" of this Article; (f) to act as agent or representative in Ethiopia of manufacturers of farm equipment and implements, and of insurance companies; (g) to establish such branches and sub-branches as may be requisite in Ethiopia and abroad; (h) to open and maintain accounts with Banks and Banking Correspondents in Ethiopia and abroad.

The Agricultural and Commercial Bank

According to the Imperial Proclamation of 30th September 1949, the name of the Bank was changed as shown above.

The Bank was authorized to undertake general banking business including the acceptance and receipt of time and demand deposits.

The Bank was required to maintain, at all times, as a reserve on deposit with the State Bank of Ethiopia fifteen per cent (15 %) of the amount

231

of the demand deposits and five per cent of the total sum of its time deposits.

The Bank was further required to submit, on demand at any time by the Board of Directors of the State Bank of Ethiopia, its books and records for inspection and examination by auditors designated by the State Bank of Ethiopia.

With the limited means at its disposal, the Agricultural and Commercial Bank was not able to finance the larger agricultural schemes. Its capital was hardly sufficient to satisfy the most urgent needs of small farmers and it had to confine its activities to the Province of Shoa only. Most of the agricultural loans granted to the Bank were to small farmers and rarely exceeded one thousand Ethiopian Dollars, mostly for the purchase of a few pairs of oxen for ploughing.

His Majesty's Government was not satisfied with this state of affairs as it was at the beginning of the year 1951.

The Development Bank of Ethiopia

In order to achieve a greater measure of success in the economical uplift of the country, the Development Bank of Ethiopia was created by the Imperial Proclamation of March 9th, 1951. The Agricultural and Commercial Bank of Ethiopia was merged into, and consolidated with, this new enterprise as from the date of the Proclamation.

The aims of the Development Bank are: (a) to assist in the development of industrial and agricultural production; and (b) to foster the investment of private capital for productive purposes.

The new Bank started its operations on May 15, 1951.

The authorized capital stock of the Bank is Eth. $ 13,000,000, of which 11 million Ethiopian Dollars is ordinary stock subscribed by the Government, and 2 million Ethiopian Dollars is preferred stock to be sold on conditions determined by the Board of Directors of the Bank.

The Board of Directors

1. H.E. Balambaras Mahtemeselassie Wolde Maskal, Minister of Agriculture, President.
2. H.E. Ato Makonnen Habte Wold, Minister of Finance, Director.
3. H.E. Ato Getahun Tessema, Minister of Commerce and Industry, Director.
4. Mr. Nathan Marein, Advocate General, Director.
5. Mr. W. H. Rozell Jnr., Governor, State Bank of Ethiopia, Director.
6. Ato Araya Okubagzi, Director-General, Commerce Department, Ministry of Commerce and Industry, Director.
7. Mr. A. Abel, Managing Director.

H.E. Ato Yilma Deressa, one of the sponsors of the project of establishing the Development Bank of Ethiopia and a member of the Board since the beginning, resigned when he was appointed Ambassador in Washington

232

n August 1953. Dr. L. Baranski, the first Managing Director resigned in
uly 1953 and was succeeded by Mr. A. Abel, until then Deputy Ma-
aging Director and formerly Governor of the Agricultural (and Com-
nercial) Bank of Ethiopia. The post of Deputy Managing Director is
now held by Dr. G. Nowak.

The Imperial Ethiopian Government has established an overall development programme (which includes, among other services the development
of communications). The Development Bank, being a link in this overall
programme, was designed to help in developing the agriculture and industry of the country. Thus, the Bank has two major fields of activity:
1) financing projects benefiting agriculture; and (2) financing projects
or industrial development.

In co-operation with the International Bank for Reconstruction and
Development (I.B.R.D.), the Ethiopian Government organised the Imperial Highway Authority to take care of the re-construction and development of roads, and the Telecommunications Board to build the essential
links of local and international radio and telecommunications.

Proceeds of the International Bank loan are intended to be used to
finance loans granted to industry. Whenever any amount is withdrawn
from the loan account opened by the I.B.R.D., the equivalent, in Ethiopian
Dollars, of the amount so withdrawn is to be credited to the Imperial
Ethiopian Government as a payment of the subscription of the ordinary
tock.

Agriculture

The Bank is continuing to grant small loans, ranging from Eth.$ 500 to
 1,500 to farmers on liberal terms with repayment stretched over a
period of three years. Development loans granted to individual land-
owners for the improvement of their properties have also been increasing
teadily. The total number of such loans (including the small loans men-
ioned above), by the end of 1954, was 496, amounting to Eth.$ 1,290,000.
The Bank has established a branch office in Jimma, the capital of Kaffa
Province, to co-operate with the Government in carrying out its long-
erm coffee development programme by clearing and bringing under cul-
ivation the immense wild coffee forest regions in the south-west of
Ethiopia. At this branch office, the Bank grants individual loans up to
Eth.$ 5,000, repayable over a period of 3 years, and in certain cases,
 years. In addition to this, coffee experts employed by the Bank in Jimma
are sent out to inspect the properties of the customers periodically and to
dvise them how to improve their holdings.

Besides the agricultural loans, the Development Bank maintains an investment, ranging from Eth.$ 1,000,000 to Eth.$ 1,500,000, in agriculture
hrough its subsidiary, the Ceres Company Ltd. This Company has
branches in the provinces and works on a commission basis for third
parties, helping in the stabilisation of the prices of a number of agricultural
products.

Industry

The Bank has been a blessing to every branch of industrial activity existing in Ethiopia — cotton mills, oil mills, flour mills, tanneries, a fibre factory, a wood-cutting enterprise, a macaroni factory, an enterprise for exporting meat in refrigerated vans, and many other enterprises. Loans in this field were granted partly to existing enterprises (for the modernisation of equipment and expansion of production) and partly to promoters of new industries.

By the end of 1954, the Bank had granted 53 industrial loans amounting to a total of Eth.$ 5,600,000.

At present, the Bank has a number of important loan applications under active consideration.

The Future

During the first two-and-a-half years of the Bank's existence, the operating costs were high in comparison with its income, since the Bank's funds remained unemployed while investment opportunities were being explored. By the end of 1954, however, the initial losses had been absorbed and a surplus of Eth.$ 53,671,34 had been realized.

The Management of the Bank is convinced that the Development Bank will have an important rôle to play in the country's economic progress. They find grounds for this optimistic view in the abundance of the country's natural resources, in the sound programme of improving communications, in the efforts to explore the mineral wealth, in the increasing phases of higher education and in the general expansion of agriculture, commerce and industry.

Transport

The Franco-Ethiopian Railway carries agricultural products from central Ethiopia to the deep-water port of Jibuti (Djibouti) and brings miscellaneous import commodities from Jibuti to the capital. This French port still deals with a good deal of Ethiopian Commerce.

The Ethiopian Air Lines Inc., is also playing a vital role in the development of trade and industry. The cargo-planes of the E.A.L. carry about 3,500,000 kilos of freight annually.

Power

Ethiopia has abundant *timber*, though it is difficult to assess, but no known *oil* resources of any size. Prospecting for oil has been continuing in the Ogaden Province since 1947, so far without success; it is also in progress on the Dahlac Island off Massawa in the Red Sea.

Electricity

Generation. Power is derived partly from thermal stations using charcoal gas or imported oil, and in some cases equipped with diesel driven units, and partly from hydro-electric generation. The Ethiopian Electric Light and Power undertaking (wholly owned by the Ethiopian Government) is responsible for generation and transmission and, through its subsidiary companies, owns stations at:

(I) Abbasamuel: a 6,600 kW hydro-electric plant situated about 25 miles from Addis Ababa, which takes the bulk of its output. It was recently enlarged and is producing 20 million kWh a year. There is an old charcoal gas and diesel standby station of 1,500 kW in Addis Ababa itself, the output of which is now only about 800 kW.

(II) Harar: a 450 kW diesel set in poor condition, operating only at about 50 % efficiency.

(III) Dira Dawa: a 420 kW hydro-electric station in good condition established two years ago, and an older 300 kW thermal station.

(IV) Jimma: a 120 kW hydro-electric station and an old 200 kW thermal set now giving only 140 kW at peak.

(V) Nazareth: a 320 kW hydro-electric station.

(VI) Ambo: a 170 kW hydro-electric station.

(VII) Dessie: a 200 kW thermal station, reported to be too old for effective operation.

(VIII) Debra Berhan: a 90 kW hydro-electric station.

(IX) Wolliso: a 40 kW hydro-electric station.

The Swiss-Italian Societa Elettrica del'Africa Orientale operates a 300 kW diesel station at Massawa, a 900 kW diesel station at Asmara, 3 other stations in Eritrea, of 1,000, 640, and 600 kW respectively, and 2 small hydro-electric stations producing 625 kW.

Consumption. Except in Eritrea, where it has fallen by about 10 % since 1950/51 and is now steady, consumption is rising by about 20 % a year. Current requirements are about 19 million kWh a year, and in excess of capacity. Future development is likely to be divided between one major scheme (the Coca Dam) and a number of small expansions to existing installations:

(I) *Coca Dam*

The F.O.A. (Point 4) Mission has completed topographical, geo-physical, geological and other surveys in connection with the proposal to construct a dam and power plant on the Awash River at an estimated cost of Eth.$ 23 million (£ 3.3 million). An engineering report is now being prepared and a Swedish engineering consultant is advising the Government. The proposal is for a dam of random masonry construction with dressed masonry facing. The height of the dam was given as about 36 feet, the

235

falls below it as 90 feet. A 30,000 kW plant is planned to cover an estimated base load of 10,000 kW, and a number of other possible hydro-electric schemes downstream would benefit from the storage provided by the reservoir at Coca Dam. For some considerable time the Italian and Ethiopian Governments have been discussing the construction of the dam and hydro-electric station by the Italians as part of their war reparations. It is understood that no agreement has yet been reached. Calculations suggest that, to avoid a serious power shortage, this station must be in operation within seven years.

(II) the expansion of capacity at Addis Ababa: a 1,000 kW installation is being supplied by a British firm and should be in operation in June, 1955; and a contract for a 5,000 kW turbo-alternator is about to be placed;

(III) a new 280 kW steam turbine plant is being installed at Dessie

(IV) the expansion of existing hydro-electric stations, e.g. at Jimma

(V) modernising the installations and increasing the installed capacity at Asmara and Massawa, at a cost of Eth.$ 2,5 million (£ 0.3 million).

There exist also long term plans — drawn up by a British consulant — for hydro-electric development on the Blue Nile at Bahrdar, near Lake Tana. No decision to proceed with them has yet been taken and in view of the distance from the load centres and the poor communication their implementation appears to be rather remote.

Transmission. Generation and consumption are at present localised and no grid system exists. When the Coca station is in operation it may be economic to link it with Addis Ababa, Dire Dawa and Harar, as such a line would run through a fairly populous area, but in general the policy is to expand local stations where hydro-electric power is available, rather than to attempt to carry from the Coca station.

The Chamber of Commerce of Addis Ababa was created by Imperial Charter, in April 1947, to aid the progress of commerce and industry in Ethiopia. The Board of the Chamber of Commerce has powers to consult and submit to the Minister of Commerce opinions about commercial practices and recommendations in connection with public service.

CHAPTER 20

Ethiopia's Foreign Policy

For a country which has relatively recently emerged from isolation, it is remarkable what strides Ethiopia has made in the international field during the past twenty-five years. Most undoubtedly, this position has been achieved through the personal direction given to the nation's foreign policy by His Majesty the Emperor. Ethiopia's present status in world affairs, intervening circumstances notwithstanding, has been no chance affair.

A keen student of history and western civilised progress, since he was Regent of the Realm, foreign affairs held out the most fruitful field for the exercise of the energies of His Imperial Majesty. It was, as well, a field of endeavour in which he was personally interested. He had studied the Treaty of Versailles and its background and was quick to realise the particular interest shown in the humanitarian aspects of the League of Nations. This was particularly so concerning slavery. He was familiar with the conditions existing within Ethiopia and foresaw the possibility of foreign interference in the slavery question as it affected his country. With the abolition of slavery as a condition for Ethiopia's League membership, after his formal application, he was convinced that the institution had to be eradicated. Based on his previous preoccupation on this matter, he was quick to take steps to stamp out slavery in Ethiopia. The 1924 (March 31st) Slavery Proclamation was the direct result. Ethiopia's admittance to the League of Nations, September 28th, 1923, was a triumph for the Regent's policy of destroying the country's previous state of isolation. It also justified his fears that slavery might have been used as a pretext for foreign intervention into his kingdom — League membership made this difficult, as later events illustrate.

In line with the desire to orient his country with the west, the Regent, at the invitation of Britain, France, Germany, Italy, Greece and Egypt visited Europe and the Middle East. This tour confirmed his own ideas and plans for the advancement of his people and the progress of his country along modern lines. From England, during this visit, he brought back the crown of King Theodore which was taken from Magdala by the Napier Expedition of 1868.

The Regent's new foreign policy began to bear fruit two years after Ethiopia's admission to the League of Nations. League membership thwarted the Anglo-Italian deal to divide Ethiopia into spheres of influence.

The two parties signed an exchange of notes in December 1926, and in accordance with their obligations as Members of the League published their contents. The Regent was quick to see and resent the action of the two Great Powers in thus interfering with the property of the Ethiopian people, without any effort to consult them, and appealed to the League for protection against such discourtesy. He gained this point. The two offenders hastily disclaimed any intention of infringing the sovereign rights of a fellow Member to dispose of her own concessions, and the Regent, having insisted that his protest should be published alongside the notes, was content to do no more. He had very properly administered a deserved reproof and had shown, by his protest and the way in which he represented it, that statesmanlike dignity and moderation which he was to display later in his appeals to the League, when invasion threatened and took place.

After the admission of Ethiopia to the League of Nations, the Regent added his signature to the Kellogg-Briand Pact in 1928, and followed up this policy of friendly contacts by signing a treaty of perpetual friendship on August 2nd, 1928, with Italy, the only one of the three Powers from whom he felt he had anything to fear in the way of territorial aggression. This provided that "there shall be constant peace and perpetual friendship between the kingdom of Italy and the Abyssinian Empire." Practical results of an economic character were sought by an annexe which gave to Ethiopia a bonded warehouse in the port of Assab, in Southern Eritrea, subject to the construction of a road from that port to the town of Dessie, which was to be a joint enterprise of the two signatories.

Ethiopia's position with her immediate neighbours brought her into direct touch with France in French Somaliland, with Great Britain in Kenya, the Uganda Protectorate and the Anglo-Egyptian Sudan, and with Italy in Eritrea and Italian Somaliland. The most dramatic phases of the nation's foreign policy revolved around the designs, attitudes and interests of these contiguous neighbours.

At the Emperor's coronation, November 2nd, 1930, there existed on the diplomatic record a series of treaties and agreements, indicative of Ethiopia's neighbourhood position.

1894: On March 9th, 1894, Emperor Menelik granted a concession to a French Company for the construction of the Jibuti-Addis Ababa Railway, a measure which manifested the French economic interests in Ethiopia. The French thought that, by building the railway, they could direct Ethiopia's traffic through Jibuti.

1896: On October 26th, 1896, the Italians, after their defeat at the Battle of Adwa, signed a Treaty of Peace with Ethiopia, by which, the Treaty of Ucciali was renounced and Ethiopia's absolute independence recognised by the vanquished. Until her very defeat Italy had looked upon Ethiopia as her protectorate, a position which she had assumed after the conclusion of the Ucciali Treaty which the Italians interpreted as giving them complete control over Ethiopia's foreign relations.

1897: On March 20th, 1897, a Convention was signed between Ethiopia and France with respect to the frontier between Ethiopia and French Somaliland. In April of the same year a mission under Mr. (later Sir) Rennell of Rodd arrived in Ethiopia. On May 14th, 1897, there was signed an Anglo-Ethiopian Treaty of Amity and Commerce, supple

238

ented on June 4th by an agreement which accepted as the frontier
etween Ethiopia and British Somaliland the line laid down in Menelik's
ircular letter of April 10th, 1891, thus recognising both Harar and the
)gaden country as within the Emperor's domain.
900: On July 10th, 1900, the frontier between Ethiopia and Eritrea
which was settled in Ethiopia's favour in a supplementary agreement of
897, was revised by an agreement signed in Addis Ababa.
902: On May 15th, 1902, there was signed in Addis Ababa the Anglo-
thiopian Treaty regulating the frontier between the Sudan and
thiopia, and giving Britain water rights in Lake Tana which was of
nmense political importance for the British in the Sudan and Egypt as
ne of the main sources of the Nile. This same treaty also allowed
ritain to construct a railway west of Addis Ababa. On this same day,
n Anglo-Ethiopian Treaty was signed, defining the boundary between
he colony of Eritrea, the Sudan and Ethiopia.
903: On June 27th, 1903, the boundary between the Sudan and
thiopia was definitely laid down in accordance with the Treaty of
May 15th, 1902.
905: In 1905 the National Bank of Abyssinia was established under
concession granted to the National Bank of Egypt.
906: On July 21st, 1906, a commercial treaty was signed at Addis
Ababa between Ethiopia and Italy, confirming friendly relations with
Menelik and securing to Italian commerce the establishment of consuls
r other representatives at all commercial centres in Ethiopia.
)n December 13th, of the same year, a tripartite agreement was signed
t London between Great Britain, Italy and France, which carefully
efined the interests of the three countries in this part of Africa, delimited
he East African possessions of the signatories and recognised to each
f them certain zones of influence in Ethiopia. In this they stated that it
vas their common interest to maintain the integrity of Ethiopia and
greed that in the event of a break up or division of the Empire, because
Menelik's health was declining and there was no obvious strong successor
o follow him, that they would respect their existing agreements and
everal interests. These were for the French, the railway from Jibuti;
or the British and her Egyptian partner the control of the Tana and
lue Nile waters; while Italy was recognised as having an interest in
uilding her two colonies across Ethiopia.
y an additional agreement signed on the same date, the three Powers
ngaged to "exercise a rigorous surveillance over importation of arms
nd munitions" into Ethiopia.
907: In February 1907, the agreement of May 15th, 1902, defining
he boundary between Eritrea, the Sudan and Ethiopia was finally
pproved, as a result of the frontiers having been marked out on the
round by the respective boundary commissions.
)n December 6th of the same year the Ethiopian Government signed
  Treaty with the British Government defining the frontiers between
ast Africa, Uganda and Ethiopia.
908: On January 10th, 1908, Ethiopia concluded a treaty of commerce

239

with France, which contained such matters as the rights of French citizens in Ethiopia, criminal and civil cases involving French subjects, the Jibuti railway, and the importation of arms.

On May 16th, of the same year Ethiopia signed with Italy a convention defining the frontiers between Ethiopia and the Italian Somaliland. (I was this Treaty which Italy violated in occupying Walwal, in the vicinity of Italian Somaliland).

1909: On April 13th and May 12th, Ethiopia and Great Britain exchanged diplomatic notes with respect to import duties.

1928: On August 2nd, 1928, Italy and Ethiopia signed a twenty-year Treaty of Friendship and Arbitration, in which each Government undertook not to engage under pretext "in action calculated to prejudice the independence of the other."

In the same year an agreement was made between Ethiopia and Italy to construct a motor-road from Assab to Dessie, each country carrying out the work within its own borders. (This plan was never carried out.)

1930: In 1930 a Treaty was signed between Ethiopia and the three Powers (Great Britain, France and Italy) which provided for the regulation of the import of arms, subject to the promise not to refuse transit if arms were needed by the Ethiopian authorities to maintain public order. Despite this agreement the signatories imposed an embargo upon arms in 1935, even though this meant disaster for Ethiopia.

The story of the Italo-Ethiopian conflict of 1935 has been briefly dealt with in Chapter 4. The detailed moves chronologically stated here should aid the reader in following the events as they developed from the standpoint of Ethiopia's foreign policy under His Majesty the Emperor.

Ever since Italy took a foothold on the Benadir Coast, it had attempted to enlarge its possessions, first by forced negotiations, and when this failed, by illegal occupation of Ethiopian territory.

Soon after the Fascists rose to power in Italy, the pressure on the frontier became intense and on December 5th, 1934, Fascist Bandas provoked an incident at Walwal, way inside Ethiopian territory. On December 8th, 1935, the Italian Government presented a protest to Ethiopia. The latter replied that the dispute should be submitted to arbitration under the terms of the Italo-Ethiopian Treaty of Friendship of 1928. In notes of December 12th and 14th, 1935, the Italian Government asked compensation for the incident and rejected the proposal of the Ethiopian Government that the dispute be referred to arbitration.

On January 3rd, 1935, the Ethiopian Government requested the League to take action under Article 11 of the Covenant. On January 17th, the Council of the League met to discuss the dispute and asked Ethiopia to withdraw her protest as Italy declared willingness to arbitrate.

On March 17th, Ethiopia referred the dispute to the League under Article 15 and called attention to Italian military preparations. Five days later Italy denied that such preparations were being made or that Article 15 was applicable. Italy consented to the appointment of an arbitration commission. On March 29th, 1935, Ethiopia transmitted a note to the League urging that the dispute, together with the whole question of the Italo-

240

Ethiopian frontier in the Benadir, be submitted to arbitration within thirty days. Ethiopia also requested that no military preparations be made while the case was being heard.

On April 3rd, 1935, Ethiopia requested the Council of the League that the dispute should be considered at its next extraordinary meeting. The Council, however, decided to postpone discussion till May. On April 14th, Italy informed Ethiopia that it was prepared to make arrangement for arbitration. Ethiopia replied that arbitration must deal with the whole question of the frontier as well as the incident of Walwal and others.

On May 25th, 1935, the Council adopted two resolutions as to the procedures of arbitration by which frontier incidents since December 5th, 1934, were to be submitted to arbitration. Italy withdrew her objections to Ethiopia's arbitrators which she had made earlier.

On June 6th, 1935, the Conciliation and Arbitration Commission held a preliminary meeting. The Commission began work on June 25th, 1935, but suspended its meetings because it could not agree whether or not to examine and decide the ownership of Walwal.

In the extraordinary meetings of the Council of the League in July and August is was decided that the ownership of Walwal was not within the competence of the Arbitration Commission and the members of the Commission were to designate a fifth arbitrator without delay. The Council decided to meet in December 4th, 1935, to examine the situation again. The Commission resumed its work in August 19th and Mr. Politis was appointed as the fifth arbitrator. On December 3rd, 1935, the Commission decided unanimously that the Italian Government and its agent on the spot could not be held responsible for the Walwal incident and that the Ethiopian Government and its authorities on the spot could not be held responsible either.

At its meeting of September 4th—6th, the Council appointed a Committee of Five to seek a peaceful solution of the dispute. On September 18th the Committee laid its proposals before Italy and Ethiopia. Ethiopia accepted the proposal as a basis for negotiation. Italy rejected all.

The Council, on September 26th, 1935, adopted the report of the Committee of Five and appointed a Committee of Thirteen to draft a report envisaged by Article 15, paragraph 4, of the League Covenant. On October 5, the Council discussed the report of this Committee and appointed a Committee of Six to study the situation. The latter Committee came to the conclusion that Italy had resorted to war in violation of her obligations under Article 12 of the Covenant of the League. The Council unanimously adopted the reports of the Committee of Thirteen and of Six. The Italian representative dissented.

At the October meetings of the Assembly all Members, except Albania, Hungary, Austria and, of course, Italy, acquiesced in the findings of the Council. The Assembly created a co-ordinating committee to study the measures under Article 16 of the Covenant.

The Co-ordinating Committee appointed a smaller committee, Committee of 18, which drafted a proposal concerning arms embargo, financial measures and economic sanctions.

The proposals of the Committee of 18 were communicated to the Co ordinating Committee which in turn communicated them to Members o the League and other States. The Committee of 18 met again on Octobe 31st to November 2nd to consider execution of its proposals and the Canadian delegate proposed that the embargo should be extended to oil coal, iron, and steel. In the meeting of the Co-ordinating Committee, the proposals of the Canadian delegate were adopted in principle. On Novem ber 18th, 1935, economic sanctions came into force against Italy.

In December 7th and 8th Sir Samuel Hoare visited Paris and agreed upon a dismemberment plan for Ethiopia with M. Laval. When the plan wa. published in the French Press, there was widespread criticism of it authors. The plan was rejected by Italy and the Council abandoned it a its meeting of December 18th—19th.

In January 1936, the Council of the League met and on the 22nd approved the conclusions of the second Committee of Thirteen reaffirming Italy'. aggression against Ethiopia. The Committee decided to study the econo mic aspects of oil sanctions.

On March, 21st, 1936, the Committee of 18 of the League met and Mr Anthony Eden (now Sir) informed it that his Government were willing to apply oil sanctions against Italy if the other Governments were also willing to do the same. Two days later the Committee adjourned for an indefinite period. The Committee of Thirteen met in Londen on March 23rd, 1936, but arrived at no definite decisions and failed to give con sideration to poison gas bombing by Italy.

In March 1936, His Imperial Majesty led in person his troops into the battle at Maichew and fought with them.

In April 1936, the Emperor believing that further resistance without the assistance of the League was to sanction the slaughter of his people decided to go to Geneva in person and make his appeal to Membe: States of the League. On May 2nd, 1936. His Majesty left Addis Ababa and on May 5th, 1936, Italian forces entered the Ethiopian capital. On May 6th, 1936, the Italian Government issued a decree placing Ethiopi under the sovereignty of the King of Italy.

On May 10th, 1936, His Majesty appealed to the League of Nations to cointinue its efforts to ensure respect to Covenant obligations and request ed it to refuse to recognise Italy's alleged sovereignty over Ethiopia.

In June 1936, His Imperial Majesty arrived in London and began pre paring his appeal to the League. On June 30th, 1936, His Majesty went to Geneva and made his appeal to Members of the League.

At Geneva His Majesty the Emperor proposed two resolutions: One concerning financial assistance to Ethiopia and the second concerning non-recognition of Italian conquest of Ethiopia. The first resolution wa covered by a draft resolution of the General Committee regarding with drawal of sanctions, non-recognition of annexation and suggestions to reform the League. The draft was adopted by 44 votes to 1, with four abstentions — only Ethiopia voted against. The second Ethiopian reso lution was presented alone and was defeated by 23 votes to 1, with 25 abstentions.

On July 6th, the Co-ordinating Committee recommended that sanctions should cease to apply as from July 15th. At the Seventeenth Session of the Assembly, after a memorable fight in the Credentials Committee, Ethiopian delegates retained their seats for that current session.

When His Majesty the Emperor was in exile at Bath, he was on a foreign policy mission. He deployed his efforts to prevent recognition of Italian annexation of Ethiopia by States Members, especially Britain and France. He endeavoured to maintain Ethiopia's League membership. He exploided every opportinuty to make known to the world the brutality of the Fascist military occupation of his country. He continued to study and interpret events of the moving international scene. Thus, when the appropriate moment came, he was in a capital position to exploit those phases germane to the liberation of Ethiopia. The Emperor encouraged and kept alive the national resistance within the country to this end. The diplomatic struggle was succesful as is detailed in Chapters 7 and 8.

The United Kingdom Government had recognised the illegal Italian conquest of Ethiopia, but when Fascist Italy declared war against her in 1940, she was forced to withdraw this recognition. His Majesty the Emperor was able to secure Britain's agreement to accept Ethiopia as an ally. An arrangement was arrived at by which the Emperor proceeded to Cairo and thence to Khartoum to head the patriots in Ethiopia and to co-ordinate their military activities in the campaign of liberation with the co-operation of British forces.

Ethiopia's liberation posed some unpredictable problems for the nation's foreign policy. His Imperial Majesty's triumphant return to his capital on May 5th, 1941, raised some urgent and pressing questions. How long would the British forces remain in the country; financial assistance had to be procured from friendly Powers to provide the necessary administrative services; technical and expert services and advice to establish viable civilian life after the occupation and two successive wars had to be obtained. Some of these were regulated by the Anglo-Ethiopian Agreement and Military Convention of 1942; the Lend-Lease Agreement with the United States in 1943; and the Anglo-Ethiopian Agreement of 1944. (See appendix).

Civilian life restored, the object of the nation's foreign policy was to normalise international relations. This was most evident in the diplomatic struggle to re-unite the lost provinces of Eritrea and ex-Italian Somaliland, support of the United Nations and its Specialised Agencies, approval of international measures to better the living standards of the peoples of under-developed countries, co-operation with the United Nations humanitarian agencies for the settlement of refugees of the Middle East and other parts of the world, support of United Nations machinery for collective security, the expansion of Ethiopia's diplomatic contacts, and the development of commercial and cultural relations with other States.

Of paramount importance is Ethiopia's attitude to the United Nations. It was no vain expression made by the Secretary General of the United Nations when he said to the Emperor on the latter's visit to the United Nations Headquarters on June 1st, 1954: "Your Majesty stands in the

243

perspective of the history of our time as a symbolic landmark, a prophetic figure on the path of man's struggle to achieve international peace and security through concerted international action." From 1923, when, as Regent, His Majesty the Emperor formally applied for Ethiopia's membership to the League of Nations, to to-day, marking the Silver Jubilee of his reign as Emperor, this country has remained a staunch supporter of world co-operation. The experience of Ethiopia with the League, though of a rather sombre tone, still found the Emperor's ready response given to the League's successor — the United Nations. Ethiopia adhered to the United Nations on July 28th, 1942, and accepted the invitation of the sponsoring Powers to participate in the fifty-nation conference to organise the world body. As a member of the United Nations, Ethiopia has regularly met her annual financial obligations towards the United Nations which amounts to an average of US$ 36,000. She receives technical and financial assistance from the United Nations which helps to implement her development programme. The phase of Ethiopia's foreign policy that deals with the United Nations is so compelling that it has been dealt with separately in Chapter 21.

Apart from the bilateral treaties named earlier to which Ethiopia is party, could be cited over twenty-two multilateral agreements entered into by the Imperial Ethiopian Government, since the restoration. The new look in Ethiopia's foreign policy, which has meant so much to the economic, social and political evolution and the development of the country, springs from the continued outlook of His Majesty the Emperor, which has manifested itself since his earliest entry into public life.

The Anglo-Ethiopian Agreement and Military Convention of 1942, the first instrument negotiated after the liberation, formed the basis of a working agreement between Ethiopia and the United Kingdom Government, after the liberation, as allies and members of the United Nations. It was superseded by a new temporary agreement in 1944. The generous financial aid afforded by Great Britain to Ethiopia according to the terms of the 1942 Agreement — a free gift of £stg. 2,500.000 — provided the first impetus to the internal stability of the country. Several British advisers were, as the result of this Agreement, provided in important administrative fields. The British Military Mission to Ethiopia gave invaluable assistance in the building and reorganisation of the Ethiopian Army of Defence. Personnel for and advice to the Ministry of Education were provided by the British Institute.

Through the Mutual Aid Pact signed between the United States and Ethiopia in Washington D.C. on August 9th, 1943, the country benefited from Lend-Lease by items of communications and transport supplies. A United States Technical Mission, 1944—1945, made a thorough survey of the country's economic, social and industrial potential. Subsequently, the United Nations Relief and Rehabilitation Administration sent a similar mission to Ethiopia.

A general economic and friendship treaty as well as a mutual defence assistance agreement with the United States are among the more recent pacts signed by Ethiopia.

244

In order to accelerate her economic development, like many under-developed countries, agreement was entered into with the United States of America in Addis Ababa on June 16th, 1951, to obtain Point Four's co-operation, the objective of which is to enhance the national incomes of the said countries, and directly raise their peoples' standard of living.

To realize the above policy, the Imperial Ethiopian Government and the Government of the United States of America agreed, according to Article I, paragraph 1, of the Agreement to "co-operate with each other in the interchange of technical knowledge and skills in related activities designed to contribute to the balanced and integrated development of the economic resources and productive capacities of Ethiopia." Consequently, the scope of work which Point Four is undertaking in Ethiopia is quite wide. So far its activities have extended into the fields of education, agriculture, public health, water-resources development, commerce and industry development and locust control.

In the field of education many measures have been taken on a co-operative basis by the Imperial Ethiopian Ministry of Education and Point Four to raise the standard of education in Ethiopia. The co-operative programme of education which has been introduced by the Imperial Ethiopian Ministry of Education and Point Four is a very good manifestion of international co-operation. In this respect Point Four is providing technical experts and specialists in the field of education in the college, secondary and elementary levels.

Because Ethiopia is predominantly agricultural the Ethiopian Government, with the assistance of Point Four, has established agricultural institutions, for example, Jimma Agricultural Technical School, with the aim of training indigenous agricultural experts who are quite indispensable for improving the working condition in the rural areas. Moreover, a supplementary agreement was reached between the Imperial Ethiopian Ministry of Agriculture and Point Four to establish a "Co-operative Machinery Pool" which will be used as an inventory, repair and distribution centre for equipment supplied by the said Ministry to aid the Ethiopian farmer to improve his standard of cultivation by the application of modern machinery. Other projects are being executed too in the field of agriculture by the help of Point Four. For instance, the co-operative coffee development project, since the further development of coffee production would undoubtedly have a positive impact upon the economic development of Ethiopia.

Great efforts have been made by the Imperial Ethiopian Ministry of Public Health with the assistance of Point Four to develop an improved public health in Ethiopia. To realize the said objective, the Imperial Ethiopian Ministry of Public Health with the further assistance of Point Four, WHO and UNICEF through their co-operative action, have established a Public Health Centre in Gondar and a Nurse and Midwife Training School. These institutions prepare Ethiopians for public health work — Ehtiopians who will be attacking the major disease problems of Ethiopia in the future.

Realizing the fact that there is water shortage in certain parts of Ethiopia, for instance, in the Ogaden area, as well as the need for the development of water resources for the building of hydro-electric power plants for future industrial development, the Imperial Ethiopian Government requested the help of Point Four to study the water resources of Ethiopia. This study includes a project of demonstration and teaching techniques of drilling wells as well as the study of the Imperial Ethiopian Government's plan for a multipurpose dam at Coca and irrigation surveys in the Awash Valley.

In the field of commerce and industry, Point Four has extended its help to assist Ethiopia in improving the efficiency of the present plants by encouraging private investments in new technique, furthering expert assistance in their development, stimulating improved methods of marketing and by providing technical training and similar activities. The technical staff which Point Four provides to the Imperial Ethiopian Ministry of Commerce and Industry is assisting it by providing management and industrial engineering services to existing industrial and commercial enterprises, as well as by rendering technical assistance to new enterprises in getting underway and by studying existing marketing methods in Ethiopia and suggesting improvements.

The Technical Co-operation Adminstration's assistance has been extended to Eritrea too, as a result of the exchange of notes between the Government of Ethiopia and the United States of America which was signed on March 30th, 1953. The said Governments share equally the cost of expenditures which result from the expanded programme of assistance in that area. The local Government of Eritrea makes available the necessary land, building and the services for the projects envisaged. The planned projects which are to be executed, some of which have already begun in Eritrea, include a survey of irrigation and power facilities, the establishment of a vocational trade school, a school for nurses and midwives and agricultural extension services and soils analysis survey.

During the period covering the twentyfive years of His Imperial Majesty's reign, another notable feature of the country's foreign policy is in the field of diplomatic contacts. Before the Italo-Ethiopian conflict, there were seven legations — Great Britain, France, Italy, the United States, Belgium, Russia and Germany and three consulates — Japan, Egypt, and Greece. After the liberation, diplomatic relations expanded to twenty-six missions — embassies: Egypt, France, Great Britain, Greece, India, Italy, the United States, and Yugoslavia; legations: Austria, Belgium, Czechoslovakia, Denmark, Germany, Iran, Iraq, Mexico, Netherlands, Norway Poland, Portugal, Spain, Sweden, Switzerland, Union of Soviet Socialist Republics, Venezuela and Yemen.

In addition to consular representation in the above countries, consulates are to be found in Aden, Brussels, Marseilles, Jibuti, Athens, Jerusalem, Beirut, Valletta, the Hague, Zurich, New York and Kenya, besides a Liaison Officer in Khartoum.

Ethiopia Shares Technological Advance
Point Four Programme in Ethiopia

Under the impulse of modernisation set in motion by His Majesty the Emperor since he came to public life, Ethiopia has been and is undergoing continual moral and material change. Among them, the most remarkable has come through the country's foreign contacts. During the Haile Selassie I era there has been an uninterrupted search to benefit by the influence of the west. That the Emperor travelled to Europe and the Middle East, in 1924, sent Ethiopians even then to study abroad, engaged foreign advisers in the 1920's and continues to follow the same pattern up to today, explains the depth of his conviction to open his country to westernisation. In this vein friendly nations have always been invited to share in the development of Ethiopia. A glance over the preceding pages of this chapter on Ethiopia's foreign policy and a study of Ethiopia's international engagements support this observation. There could be no wonder then that mutual aid agreements have more recently been concluded between the United States, Yugoslavia and Sweden.

The United States Foreign Operations Mission (Point 4) activity in this country, hereunder briefly recorded, fall within this broad plan of seeking technical assistance from Ethiopia's friends in her modernisation.

It was a happy augury for Ethiopia then that soon after the end of World War II the U.S. Congress launched a basic technical co-operation programme for "the less developed areas" of the world. The programme was aimed, particularly, at training personnel, and at helping to develop strong, competent, technical institutions in the countries concerned. On the whole, the work of the U.S. technical mission was, and is, intended to be a joint co-operative enterprise as between two independent, friendly nations. In its early days, the programme was known as Technical Co-operation Administration, and now, as U.S. Foreign Operations Mission, or more popularly, as Point Four.

His Imperial Majesty has always been anxious to establish an Agricultural College of high standard in Ethiopia. When Dr. Henry G. Bennett visited Ethiopia in May 1951, the Imperial Ethiopian Government decided to accept his offer to help establish a college and to provide general technical assistance through the "Point Four Programme", of which he was the Administrator until his untimely death in December 1951.

A General Agreement for Technical Co-operation between the United States Government and the Imperial Ethiopian Government was signed on June 16th, 1951 and a Special Technical Services Programme Agreement on April 21st, 1954. Since then several Project Agreements have been concluded with various Ministries and Departments which have requested the technical services and training programmes that Point 4 is

247

designed to offer. The General Agreement set forth the following aim and ideals:

(1) to promote and strengthen friendship and understanding between the peoples of Ethiopia and the United States of America and to further their general welfare;

(2) to aid the efforts of the people of Ethiopia, to develop their agricultural and related resources, to improve their working and living conditions, and to further their social and economic progress;

(3) to this end, to facilitate the development of agricultural and mechanical arts education activities in Ethiopia through co-operative action

(4) to stimulate and increase the interchange between the two countries of knowledge, skills and techniques in the field of agricultural and mechanical arts education.

The agreement was signed by H.E. Ato Aklilou Habte Wold, the Foreign Minister, for Ethiopia, and H.E. J. Rives Childs, the U.S. Ambassador in Ethiopia, for the United States of America.

The first Director of the Point Four Programme, Mr. Marcus J. Gordon arrived in Ethiopia in June 1952; and the project of the proposed Imperial Agricultural College was taken up immediately afterwards. The first batch of agricultural specialists arrived a few months later. Specialists in other fields have been arriving, ever since, individually and in small groups. At present there are 103 U.S. personnel working in Ethiopia on various projects together with a staff of 781 Ethiopians. There is also a large number of trainees and students benefitting by the various fields of Point Four activity.

By the end of the past U.S. fiscal year (June 30th, 1955), the United States Government had spent a total of U.S.$ 7,000,000 for its share of the Point Four Programme in Ethiopia. The Imperial Ethiopian Government contributed approximately the same amount to this cause.

These expenditures fall under two main headings: (a) salaries, travel and other expenses for U.S. personnel; and (b) cash contribution to "Joint Funds", to carry out projects and to purchase the necessary equipment.

The Jimma Agricultural Technical School may be considered as the forerunner of the proposed Imperial Agricultural College. The School is now in its third year. It has an excellent, well-equipped physical plant and about 200 students receiving both practical and theoretic training. College instruction as well as secondary-level training are being given at this school. The vast amount of information collected about Ethiopian agriculture, at Jimma, ought to serve as a basis for the curriculum of the future college.

It has been finally decided to build the *Imperial College of Agricultural and Mechanical Arts* at an excellent site near Lake Haramaya, on the highway between Harar and Dire Dawa. Detailed plans for the buildings were prepared by the Architectural Department of the Oklahoma Agricultural and Mechanical College, and construction is proceeding as scheduled. The college will open at the beginning of the 1956—57 academic year.

Meanwhile, the *Jimma Agricultural, Technical School* is training the

248

young Ethiopians in various ways: classroom instruction is given in general agriculture, including livestock, poultry, soils, vegetable crops, plant diseases and insects, farm-machinery and coffee. Along with general academic training, the students receive practical farm experience in the care and management of farm-machinery by working on the school farm. Here experiments on better breeding are being carried out with cattle, swine, poultry and sheep.

One of the most important experimental projects under way is the Jimma Coffee Programme. In connection with this project, many varieties of young coffee plants are being cultivated under varying conditions of cultural practice, pruning, spacing etc., to determine the most promising varieties and the most satisfactory methods for Ethiopia.

Another important project is the *Co-operative Coffee Programme*. which will be concentrated in the provinces of Kaffa and Ilubabur. This project lays emphasis on (a) seedling producing and distribution, (b) full development of existing forest coffee, (c) encouragement of plantation coffee on unforested lands, and (d) educational work in the best methods of planting, cultivating, pruning, harvesting and processing.

An *Agricultural Improvement Centre* has been established at Alamata (Tigré Province) "to carry on educational and demonstrational work among the farmers of the Gobo-Alamata plain area to help them improve their agricultural practices". Here, special attention is given to seed improvement, soil conservation, insect control, pasture improvement and allied activities.

One Point 4 Agricultural Engineer and several Ethiopian assistants are working on the project of setting up an *Agricultural Machinery Pool*, with the co-operation of the Ministry of Agriculture. This is to train Ethiopian farm-mechanics to repair, adopt and utilise stores of tools and agricultural machines in the possession of the Imperial Ethiopian Government.

Two trained Ethiopians are now working as *agricultural extension agents* among the farmers of the Assella and Fitche areas in an effort to solve their problems and improve their practices. These agents are expected to introduce improved seeds and tools, eggs for local hatching and "wool sheep" for breeding purposes.

A plant introduction and field testing programme was conducted at Shashamana during 1954. Here, large varieties of corn, cotton, legumes, milo maize and pasture grasses were planted in an attempt to discover the most suitable and the most productive types.

Land has been set aside at Bishoftu for the establishment of a *Central Agricultural Experiment Station*, which is expected to start work in 1955. The *Soil Testing Laboratory* started operating in 1954; and several hundreds of soil-samples have already been analysed as to texture, content of salts, organic matter content, phosphorus level, conductivity, permeability and water-holding capacity.

The Ministry of Agriculture is receiving valuable assistance from both Point Four and the F.A.O., in the programme of *Animal Disease Con-*

trol. Point Four is contributing funds as well as the services of two veterinarians.

Another field in which Point Four gives assistance is that of *locust control.* Two aeroplanes and pilots as well as insecticides were provided during 1953 for air-spraying demonstrations. Point Four has also provided the Ministry of Agriculture with an experienced entomologist to assist in the development of an effective Pest Control Section within that Ministry.

The first organized Ethiopian Locust Control team from the Ministry of Agriculture, went into action in the May-June locust breeding area (along the railroad) in 1954. Some experimental spraying, with insecticides new to Ethiopia, was carried out during this compaign with most satisfactory results. It is hoped that this method of locust control can replace the more expensive one of poisoned bran bait.

Commerce and Industry Development Service

This Service is being carried on by a small group of experienced industrial engineers and marketing and investment specialists, located within the Ministry of Commerce and Industry. These men are expected to advise and assist the Ministry in its effort to stimulate and guide the commercial and industrial development of Ethiopia.

One of the main functions of the Service is to attract foreign and native capital towards Ethiopian industry and to assist the potential investors in working out proposals agreeable to themselves as well as to the Imperial Ethiopian Government.

Another important function is the development of the sales and distribution of goods throughout the Empire.

Co-operative Education Programme

This project is run in close co-operation with the Ministry of Education and Fine Arts, which can now claim the services of a well-qualified staff of specialists in various aspects of education.

In November 1953, H.E. The Vice Minister of Education established a *Long-Range Planning Committee,* with the help of his Point 4 specialists and advisers. This Committee has submitted many far-reaching plans and recommendations, most of which have been approved by the Vice-Minister and the Board of Education.

Another important achievement is the development and approval of a modern *salary schedule* for teachers and other school personnel.

The Co-operative Education Programme has paid particular attention to *teacher training.* At present more than 600 students are undergoing training, of whom 280 teachers are expected to complete their education this year.

The other important activities of Point Four in connection with education, include the following: (1) the preparation and printing of Maps of Ethiopia on 21 different topics; (2) the writing of a series of geography text-books for the elementary schools; (3) the development of a highly-efficient audio-visual education system; (4) the introduction of objective educational measurement in the public schools; (5) the adaptation of well-known American intelligence tests for use in Ethiopia; (6) the preparation of a new book under the title, "USE BETTER ENGLISH", for helping the secondary school students to improve their English; (7) the establishment of a Co-operative Education Press; and (8) the launching of a permanent educational materials exhibit, at the Ministry of Education.

Public Administration

Having received requests from several Ministries for expert assistance in solving problems of administration, Point Four entered into a contract with the Public Administration Service of Chicago, which provides experts acceptable to both the Point 4 Director and the Imperial Ethiopian Government.

Assistance in various administrative problems has been, or is being, given to the Ministries of Agriculture, Commerce and Industry, Education and Interior, as well as to the State Bank of Ethiopia and the Imperial Ethiopian Air Force.

Public Health Activities

As far as public health is concerned, Point 4 renders a two-fold service in Ethiopia: (1) as advisers to the Ministry of Public Health, and (2) as trainers of Ethiopian youth in health, sanitation and allied fields. In addition to this, Point 4 specialists are co-operating with school authorities to develop a health education programme among the students.

The major achievement in this field has been the establishment of a *Public Health College and Training Centre at Gondar* in October 1954. The purpose of the College is to train and turn out, as fast as possible, medical, nursing and sanitation personnel for the whole country. These personnel will be trained to staff the *Rural Health Centres* to be established in all the provinces in due course.

The College is a unique project, because Point 4 and the World Health Organisation provide the staff, the Ethiopian Government contributes money, and the United Nations International Children's Emergency Fund (UNICEF) aids with supplies, equipment and financial grants.

As a part of the Point 4 Program, assistance is being given to the Medical Services Department of the Eritrean Government in the training of nurses. The first *School of Nursing* started functioning early in 1955. Assistance has also been granted by the Public Health Joint Fund to the four schools of nursing already existing in Ethiopia.

In March 1955, two new agreements were signed between the Ministry of Public Health and Point 4. The first of these provides for a *Malaria Study and Control Programme,* to make a thorough study of the malarial mosquitoes in Ethiopia, where malaria is endemic in some areas and

251

epidemic in others. Areas selected for study are those where agricultura
or public health projects are already in progress.

The second agreement deals with a *Public Health Centre for Addi
Ababa*, to provide the citizens of Addis Ababa with all kinds of healt
services including health education, sanitation, public health nursing
maternity and child health, venereal disease and tuberculosis control, an
an out-patient clinic for emergency ceses.

Special Technical Education

In addition to the educational assistance given to the public schools o
Ethiopia, Point 4 is contributing to the progress of vocational trainin
and technical education.

Her Imperial Majesty's Handicraft School has been supplied with addi
tional equipment and helped to make considerable progress.

A modern *vocational trades school* has been established in Asmara, an
more than 100 students are now receiving training.

A specialist has been provided by Point 4, to assist in the expansion an
administration of the Technical School in Addis Ababa.

A Joint Fund has been established with he Ministry of Commerce an
Industry, for the establishment of *Rural Arts and Crafts Centres* in th
provinces. The first of these is about to start work at Assella, utilisin
the local wool in making rugs, carpets and blankets.

Water Resources Activities

In 1954, Point 4 carried out topographic *surveying* of the Coca Dam an
the Reservoir Area. Concurrently with this work, the hydrologis
established *staff gauges* on the Blue Nile near Safartak, on the Mill
River near Tandaho, and on the Awash near Awash Junction.

Soil reconnaissance has been carried out in Eritrea and in the Ogaden
Ground-water surveys have been made in those areas where *well-drillin
is in process. This well-drilling programme is meant for both human an
animal consumption in those areas of Ethiopia and Eritrea, where wate
is scarce. Well-drilling rigs are now in operation in different parts o
Ethiopia.

The new project agreements were signed between the two co-operating
Governments in June of this year. The first, signed on June 20th has a
its object the establishment of a co-operative programme of technica
guidance to the Imperial Ethiopian Government's land resettlement and
community development efforts, as administered through the Ministry o
Interior.

The project, to which the Point 4 will provide a Director and such other
specialists in the fields of agriculture, health, education, public administration and resettlement, will be carried forward on a demonstration basis
and through the development of plans for the conduct of a broad resettlement programme by the Ethiopian Government. In the related fields
in which Point 4 will provide technical assistance, Ethiopian personnel
will be trained with the objective of taking responsibility for the operation
of the programme and of specific resettlement projects.

The second, signed on June 22nd, has the object of furnishing specialised
advisory services to the Department of Civil Aviation. It will bring civi

aviation technicians to the Department of Civil Aviation as may be mutually agreed upon by Point 4 and the Department. These technicians, in accordance with approved plans, will carry out demonstrational and training activities in the various fields represented, will furnish advice and consultation to the Department, as requested, on any problem within their specialised fields. Ethiopians will be trained to assume responsibility for administrative and technical positions in the field of civil aviation.

The Ethio-Swedish Institute

Through a bilateral agreement between the Royal Swedish Government and the Imperial Ethiopian Government signed at Addis Ababa on the 13th October, 1954, the Government of Sweden is also participating in the technical assistance programme in Ethiopia. The Ethio-Swedish Agreement is for technical assistance in the field of vocational and technological education. This aid specifically concerns the Institute of Building Technology under associated Ethiopian and Swedish direction. The activities of the Institute, as well as any other activities developed under the Agreement are designed to fit in with existing educational programmes of the Imperial Ethiopian Government and will fill an important gap in the technological training of the country. The current moral and material advance of Ethiopia and the plans on foot for an extension of building and construction make this Institute a very timely asset.

On the same pattern as joint fund programmes under Point 4, the Royal Swedish Government will supply technical experts and top-level instructors for the Institute. The Imperial Ethiopian Government will provide suitable buildings and premises for the Institute, their maintenance, necessary furniture and equipment over and above that provided by the Royal Swedish Government, and the necessary funds for maintaining the functions of the Institute of Building Technology. Provision is also made for a total of not more than 15 scholarships, each of 6,000 Swedish Crowns, for Ethiopian students to study in the technological field in Sweden.

As could be found in the next chapter several Specialised Agencies of the United Nations are taking part in technical assistance of the Imperial Ethiopian Government. It has been and continues to be an important part of His Imperial Majesty's policy to permit Ethiopia to benefit by sharing world technological advance through arrangements with friendly nations. From this brief report of International co-operative activities in the country it is evident that His Majesty the Emperor's position in international co-operation bids fair to accelerate the nation's progress in many vital fields. Not only is this aid destined to increase the material resources of the country; most important, it will elevate the standard and increase the number of technical hands so essential to the development and extension of the social and cultural advance of the country.

CHAPTER 21

Ethiopia and the United Nations

In May 1945 when the Axis powers in Europe and Africa were defeated and the allied nations were meeting at San Francisco to formulate the Charter of the United Nations, His Imperial Majesty made the following assertion:

May it be taken as Divine significance, that, as we mark the passing of the Nazi Reich, in America at San Francisco, delegates from all the United Nations, among whose number Ethiopia stands, are now met together for their long-planned conference to lay foundations for an international pact to banish war and to maintain world peace. Our churches pray for the successful triumph of this conference. Without success in this, the victory we celebrate today, the suffering that we have all endured, will be of no avail.

To win the War, to overcome the enemy upon the field cannot alone ensure the victory in peace. The cause of war must be removed. Each nation's rights must be secure from violation. Above all, from the human mind must be erased all thoughts of war as a solution. Then and then only will war cease.

The United Nations came into being after sixty-three days of strenuous labour and the Charter was subsequently signed in this Western U.S. City by fifty nations. The Ethiopian Delegation for the San Francisco Conference was headed by H.E. Bitwoded Makonnen Endalkatchew the Prime Minister, and included H.E. Ato Aklilou Hapte Wold, Vice-Minister of Foreign Affairs, H.E. Ato Ambaye Wolde Mariam (deceased), Vice-Minister of Justice, Ato Emmanuel Abraham, Director General of the Ministry of Education, Ato Menassie Lemma, Director-General of the Ministry of Finance, Mr. John H. Spencer, Adviser to the Ministry of Foreign Affairs, and the Secretary of the Delegation Ato Petros Sahlou. The Ethiopian Minister to the United States, H.E. Blatta Ephrem T. Medhen, and the First Secretary of the Legation in Washington, Ato Getehoun Tesemma joined in the party. On June 26th, 1945, the day of the success and completion of the United Nations Organisation, His Excellency Ato Aklilou Hapte Wold, Ethiopia's Vice-Minister of Foreign Affairs, since Minister, and acting Chairman of his country's delegation to the conference, signed on behalf of Ethiopia.

For Ethiopia, the new world organisation answered, to some extent, the desire of the country for some international force which could retrieve the situation created by the defunct League of Nations. More than any other of the fifty nations who laboured diligently to build this new world security organisation, Ethiopia's history has a definite significance. As elaborated in Chapter 6, His Majesty the Emperor, as leader of Ethiopia, even after the League had failed to guarantee the security of his country, still held out hope that the principles of the covenant could be preserved. In this spirit were the Ethiopian delegates sent to San Francisco, and in this spirit, as well, was the United Nations Organisation accepted by his country.

It could be safely said that the conditions which prevailed in world politics between 1935 and 1945 — this significant decade — was the inspiration that led to the founding of the new organisation. The great powers, impelled by a world public opinion against war as a policy of settling international disputes, called the San Francisco meeting to incorporate the wishes of the majority of mankind in terms of an instrument which could attain these aims.

This was reflected in the welcome speech of President Truman to the delegates to the conference when, in a radio speech, he said: "At no time in history has there been a more important conference or a more necessary meeting than this one in San Francisco which you are opening today...... With ever-increasing brutality and destruction, modern warfare, if unchecked, would ultimately crush all civilisation. We still have a chance between the alternative of the continuation of international chaos or the establishment of a world organisation for the enforcement of peace."

The Ethiopian Minister to the United States, H.E. Blatta Ephrem Tewelde Medhen, a member of his country's delegation, addressed a plenary session in the War Memorial Opera House in the city of San Francisco where the United Nations conference was held, and said: "The Nations gathered here must ensure that the United Nations security organisation they are setting up be enabled and compelled to vote not resolutions or recommendations, but decisions, not only of principle, but for immediate action to ensure the maintenance of peace."

It is interesting to note that international co-operation was the pillar of Ethiopia's post-war aims from the day, May 5th, 1941, that His Imperial Majesty returned to his capital. Ethiopia offered to place a brigade of the Ethiopian Army at the disposal of the Allied and Associated powers, and it was the hope of all Ethiopians that their troops would take part in the operations leading to the defeat of the Axis powers.

In 1943 Ethiopia had sent her delegates to participate in the Food and Agricultural Conference in Atlantic City; and subsequently to war-time conferences at Bretton Woods, Montreal, Philadelphia, Chicago, London, Geneva and Cairo. Tons of cereals had been forwarded to the Middle East Supply Centre. A vast quantity of machinery, which was introduced by the Italians for the development of the country, was re-exported for use by Ethiopia's allies in the successful prosecution of the war. War material, although urgently needed for the equipment of the Ethiopian military forces, was sent instead to the allied armies in the field, the Ogaden and Reserved Area were put under British Military Administration to aid in the successful prosecution of the war. The Ethiopian Government assisted the allied effort by providing a temporary home for one thousand four hundred Greek refugees. In addition, through a process of reverse lend-lease, other materials were furnished to assist the allied campaign for the restoration of world peace.

Many of the principles of the United Nations were part of the post-war foreign policy envisaged by the Emperor after the liberation. That is why, as stated above, for instance, in her interests as an agricultural country, Ethiopia sent delegates to the United Nations Relief and Rehabilitation Administration in 1943; her representatives were at the Monetary and Banking Conference held in July 1944 at Bretton Woods. After the formation of the United Nations Organisation, the country subscribed to the charters growing out of these conferences and co-operated, undertaking her full share of the responsibilities. That is why when on March 5th, 1945, the Ethiopian Ministry of Foreign Affairs received from His Excellency the American Minister an invitation on behalf of the five Great Powers to participate in the San Francisco Conference, it was readily accepted and delegates immediately selected to represent her at that conference. The official opinion of the Ethiopian Government then was expressed in these terms:

"It is the sincere hope of all peace-loving nations that this Conference may lay the basis of an effective international organisation for the maintenance of peace and security. No country in the world attaches greater importance to the realisation of that objective than does Ethiopia.

"Ethiopians stood firmly for the principle of collective security throughout the interval of 20 years between the two Great World Wars. It was in the firm conviction of the validity of that principle that she took up arms in 1935. Her reverses in the struggle against a vastly superior enemy were at the same time reverses for the League of Nations and the principle of collective security.

"Today her liberation as the first of the United Nations is a shining vindication of the validity of those principles of collective security and of the right of all nations to a free and independent existence.

"At San Francisco, Ethiopia will collaborate whole-heartedly and to the maximum of her capabilities for the realisation of the highly idealistic and, at the same time, practical objectives of the Conference."

Not only has Ethiopia adhered to the principles of the United Nations since its formation, His Majesty the Emperor pleaded even in 1936, for an organisation that would live up to the high principles of international morality and in which member states would honour their words. As a Charter Member, Ethiopia has in many ways defended her right to be a member and has upheld the principles of the Charter in more than lip service. Ethiopia's position on the United Nations could hardly be better illustrated than in the Emperor's own words when he said: *Our collective efforts must not be limited merely to participation in organisations of an international character. However numerous and strong, such organisations cannot preserve a peace that is not founded upon justice.*

For these ten years Ethiopia has faithfully attended the General Assembly and has subscribed to several of the Specialised Agencies. At present she is a member of the following United Nations Specialised Agencies: Food and Agriculture Organisation, (FAO); International Civil Aviation Organisation, (ICAO); World Health Organisation, (WHO); Universal Postal Union, (UPU); International Telecommunications Union,

Mr. Andrew W. Cordier of the U.N. visits with Commanding Officer of the 7th Division the Commander and officers of the Ethiopian Battalion (Kagnew) in Korea

lTU); World Meteorological Organisation, (WMO); International Monetary Fund, (IMF); International Bank for Reconstruction and Development, (IBRD); and United Nations Educational, Scientific and Cultural Organisation, (UNESCO). Ethiopia has signed several conventions dealing with the progress and security of mankind. The question of the problem of the ex-Italian colonies, in which Ethiopia had a major interest, brought this country and its delegation in very active contact with the workings of the United Nations and with the delegates of the member nations. His Imperial Majesty directed the policy, the attitude and the approach of Ethiopia to this ticklish problem which in the end was peacefully solved. The question of the return of Eritrea is dealt with at length in Chapter 31 in which an appreciable view could be gained of this activity in the United Nations. The Emperor has had occasion frequently to address the United Nations and has taken a very keen interest in the workings of the organisation. He has always taken a very wide and statesmanlike approach to the well-being of the world body and has frequently expressed his hope for its success. In his message to the fourth assembly of the United Nations we find the following words:

On the occasion of the opening of the fourth regular session of the General Assembly we desire to convey to you our earnest wishes for success in your important deliberations. We have no doubt that for these vital issues, on which depends the destiny of millions of human beings, you will endeavour to find just and equitable solutions. Among these, and still long outstanding, is the settlement of the former Italian colonies Needless to say that further delay to settle the question of the return of Eritrea and Somaliland to Ethiopia will not enhance the confidence of the peoples of the world and of these territories in particular.

It is a mark of policy that on United Nations Day in Ethiopia, the anniversary of the birth of the world organisation is always duly observed In schools and other educational institutions, the students are taught to know more about the United Nations and, invariably, radio programmes about the activities and the nature of the organisation are being broadcast in several languages. Arrangements have been made with the United Nations Radio Department so that on Tuesday, every week, reports of the United Nations activities are broadcast in Amharic and relayed to the Ethiopian people by Radio Addis Ababa. Time and again, His Imperial Majesty has sent other messages to the Secretary General of the United Nations reiterating Ethiopia's adherence to and support of the principles on which the United Nations was founded.

Ethiopia has unceasingly made her contribution and given her support in order to strengthen this successor of the League of Nations. In 1950 however, the occasion came when Ethiopia, among the fifty-nine member states, distinguished herself as an active and concrete supporter of the principle of collective security, denied her by the League in the 1930's.

The Republic of South Korea apprised the Security Council that an aggression was perpetrated against her by the North Koreans. The Security Council, whose functions as stated in Article 24 of the Charter read: "In order to ensure prompt and effective action by the United Nations, its Members confer on the Security Council primary responsibility for the maintenance of international peace and security, and agree that in carrying out its duties under this responsibility the Security Council acts on their behalf," called on the Member States for assistance to stem the tide of aggression in Korea. The appeal was addressed by the Secretary General.

In response to the United Nations Secretary General's request, the Ministry of Foreign Affairs sent a telegram approving the Security Council's recommendation and endorsing the efforts of member nations to better the immediate position and render assistance to the Republic of Korea. The Ethiopian Government reaffirmed its unswerving loyalty to the principles of collective security and its prompt application to limit and control aggression in order to secure and maintain international condition that will permit the self-determination of peoples.

Ethiopia's response to the United Nations request for contributions to

258

the United Nations Command in Korea was to offer 100,000 Ethiopian Dollars for medical supplies and to state that Ethiopia would give other military and economic assistance.

Secretary General Trygve Lie released a letter from the Ethiopian Foreign Affairs Minister expressing Ethiopia's intention to aid the United Nations in putting down Communist aggression against the Republic of Korea.

"Fully aware of the incredible suffering resulting from the aggression." the letter said, "His Imperial Majesty has ordered the transfer to your use of one hundred thousand Ethiopian dollars in order to provide medical suppies for alleviating the sufferings of victims of aggression and to honour these heroic victims of aggression."

Lie was advised also that Ethiopia is "considering the practical problems involved in contributing foodstuffs."

After fulfilling the stated economic offers to support U.N. action in Korea, His Majesty the Emperor further agreed to put a battalion of Ethiopia's armed forces under United Nations Korea Command. At the end of the necessary time for preparation of the troops, the first contingent of 1,153 officers and men left Addis Ababa for the Korean peninsula on April 14th, 1951.

At Jan Meda His Imperial Majesty, Thursday morning, April 12th, 1951, presented battle colours to the Ethiopian battalion which was going to Korea. He made a stirring speech to the soldiers, as follows:

You are today on the point of leaving Ethiopia on a voyage half way round the world in defence of the liberty and of the principles to which all members of the United Nations stand committed . . . .

We have personally come here in the presence of the highest officials of the nation which is honouring you today and of representatives of other nations participating in this momentous undertaking, to bid you a fond farewell and God-speed on your mission and to hand to you your Regimental Colours. These flags you will carry in valour throughout the compaign. You will, we are sure, bring them back to Your Emperor and Commander-in-Chief, to whom you have sworn allegiance, as cherished battle standards, glorified by your exploits and heroism.

. . . . When we and our people were called upon to fight, we did not fail in our fierce resolve, and today, Ethiopia has again resumed her rightful place amongst the United Nations . . . You are departing on a long crusade in defence of that very principle for which we have so long fought — freedom and respect for the freedom of others.

. . . . You are also representing and defending in far corners of the earth, the most sacred principle of modern international policy — that principle of collective security with which the name of Ethiopia is imperishably associated.

Of all the nations of the world, the name of Ethiopia has been most closely associated with that principle. Our undaunted defence of collective security in the League of Nations, our own appeal to that august body, our fierce and unaided struggles throughout the darkest hours preceding the last World War, the courage of our patriots, the unending

259

sacrifices of our families, have given to Ethiopia an imperishable place in the history of that principle in modern times.

That is why, as Sovereign Head of Ethiopia and as Commander-in-Chief of the Ethiopian Armed Forces, we did not hesitate immediately to respond to the appeal for collective assistance launched by the United Nations following the aggression in Korea.

. . . . . Not only did we promise military assistance, but also immediately transmitted funds to the United Nations to help in the collective effort.

. . . . . So new was that principle in 1936 that Ethiopia could only hope for the most basic economic sanctions to restrict aggression, and urgent measures to bring to an end the use of asphyxiating gas . . . .

It was fifteen years ago today that the Council of the League of Nations finally and formally declared its inability to meet these essential requirements of collective security . . . .

Today it is no longer a question of asking for simple economic sanctions. Korea asks of the United Nations and receives from it collective security in the form of military assistance . . . .

Remember that you are about to pay a debt of honour for your homeland which was liberated, thanks not only to the blood of her patriots, but also to that of faithful allies, likewise members of the United Nations. Remember also that, in paying this debt, you are laying the basis for a universal system of collective security in behalf of your own homeland as well as of all nations of the world, be they great or small, powerful or weak.

May God protect you, give you courage to acquit yourselves as heroes and bring you back safely to your beloved homeland.

Named the "Kagnew" Battalion, the Ethiopian expeditionary force distinguished itself very creditably in fulfilment of the orders of its Commander-in-Chief. News published by the leading newspapers of the world carried high praise for Ethiopia's fighting men defending the principle of collective security in the Far East. High officers of the United Nations Command also testified to the prowess, bravery and discipline of these Ethiopian soldiers. A typical release runs something like this:

"Ethiopia's Kagnew Battalion continues to win high tribute from United Nations Military Officials for its part in the Korean campaign. Praise for the Battalion has been expressed by Lt. Col. William A. Dodds, who commands the regiment to which the Ethiopian unit is attached.

"The Regiment is extremely proud of the Kagnews assigned to us," he said, "They are excellent fighters and are anxious to engage the enemy. I consider our Regiment fortunate to have them fighting at our side.

"The Battalion arrived in Korea a year ago. It consists of volunteers from the Ethiopian Imperial Guard.

"Since their arrival, the Kagnews have taken all 37 objectives assigned to them, and have sent out 113 combat patrols. They have accounted for many enemy casualties.

"Kagnew, the Ethiopian name given to the Battalion, means 'to make order out of chaos'. U.N. Officers say the Kagnews are living up to their name."

The President of the United States, the President of Southern Korea and

260

the Commander-in-Chief, U.N. Command, all cited many of the Kagnew men and gave them military awards for the way in which they bore their share in the defence of this high principle.

A typical citation is here given to illustrate the manner in which the military exploits of the Ethiopian soldiers on the Korean battle front were regarded.

The President of the United States of America has awarded the Bronze Star Medal to Major Tadesse Wondimagegnehu, Imperial Ethiopian Body Guard, for meritorious service in ground operations against the enemy in Korea.

The citation for Major Tadesse reads:

"Major Tadesse, Imperial Ethiopian Body Guard, distinguished himself by meritorious service as Commanding Officer, Kagnew Battalion, in Korea, from 27 June to 4 October 1951. Through aggressive leadership, astute judgment and keen foresight, he rapidly oriented the men of his unit in new and different equipment and unfamiliar tactics, and led the Battalion to outstanding success in their first encounter with the enemy. Despite language differences, he skilfully integrated his command into United Nations operations, making the Battalion a highly effective element of the 32nd Infantry Regiment and achieving singular combat successes during decisive phases of the Korean conflict. Major Tadesse's unrelenting devotion to duty and achievements contributed materially to the success of the United Nations campaign in Korea, and reflect credit on himself and the Military service."

New York Herald-Tribune correspondent, Homer Bigart, reports that U.N. Command Officers consider the Kagnew Battalion of the Imperial Ethiopian Expeditionary Force the best of the smaller national units fighting communist aggression in Korea.

In a dispatch published by the newspaper, Bigart says that the Kagnew Battalion has never yielded a position or a prisoner and has suffered only relatively light losses despite three recent sharp encounters with the Communists. The correspondent says the Ethiopians live up their name of Kagnew which means "fix it."

One of the Battalion's Commanders, Colonel Asfaw Andarge, is quoted as saying that his unit never retreats "as long as we have ammunition." Only the wounded, according to the Colonel, are allowed to leave their positions. "Our men," he added, "have orders never to be taken prisoner."

While Ethiopia's contribution in the military sphere in the defence of self-determination and freedom of South Korea remains very outstanding, considering the size of the Ethiopian army and its distance from Korea, it marks a significant change in the attitude of States to this principle, signally absent in 1936. As the Christian Science Monitor said, "There is something stirring in the thought of soldiers coming from Haile Selassie's country half way across the world to help in a collective campaign against aggression. How different the course of history might have been if the free world had taken a comparable stand at the time of Mussolini's Ethiopian aggression."

Ethiopia's contribution in the defense of the United Nations Charter and support of the principle of collective security as a means of maintaining world peace was not a chance affair. It sprang from an ideal which had long been the cornerstone of the country's foreign policy as directed by His Imperial Majesty the Emperor. In his throne speech in 1951, when the Kaqnew Battalion had just begun to test its mettle on the Far East battle-field, His Imperial Majesty said:

On our part, no sacrifices have been great enough to prevent us from upholding these principles. We have endeavoured, in every way, to support this sacred ideal in order to help build up international co-operation and justice. The realisation of these ideals and the achievement of world co-operation can only come through an effective system of collective security.

The next year on the same occasion, Ethiopia's position was again reaffirmed, when His Majesty the Emperor said, referring to Ethiopia's participation in Korea:

In so doing, Ethiopia is but re-affirming her loyalty to the principle of collective security for the defence of which she has been contributing to the United Nations in its struggle against aggression in Korea. The sacrifices are made by our troops in support of a principle hallowed by the blood of many nations. Through its application, isolationism is called upon to disappear and the world itself, to be united in firm solidarity. By our deeds we have manifested to the world our conviction that world peace can be founded only upon this principle. Moreover, our soldiers, detailed to defend collective security in Korea have, by their gallantry on the battle-field inscribed with their blood, Ethiopia's testimony to the validity of that principle, her hatred of aggression and the bravery of her people.

Another fascinating aspect of Ethiopia's relation to the United Nations is the settlement of the ex-Italian colonial problem which resulted in the return of Eritrea to the motherland. From the moment that the Great Powers decided that the settlement of the question should revert to the General Assembly, His Majesty the Emperor, in high statesmanship, directed the course of his country's discussion in a manner which led to the agreeable climax. Because of his belief in the efficacy of the world organisation, and supported by the justice of his cause, the Emperor never became impatient. The decision reached by the General Assembly on December 2nd, 1950, is, therefore, not only a credit to the United Nations Organisation as an effective agent in the peaceful settlement of international problems; it is, as well, a tribute to the ability of His Imperial Majesty in obtaining a solution which has enhanced the position of world peace, satisfied the aspirations of the people and brought justice to Ethiopia's cause.

In accordance with the idea inherent in the Emperor's approach to the development of his country, U.N. Specialised Agencies are participating in the development and modernisation of Ethiopia. Some of these agencies, such as WHO, FAO and ICAO, have missions in Ethiopia which furnish technical assistance to Ethiopia in various services of the Government. These missions are regulated by agreements entered into between the agency concerned and the appropriate Ministry of the Government. The World Health Organisation has now for several years been participating in co-operation with UNICEF, in lifting the health standards of the Ethiopian people. The Food and Agriculture Organisation, in the formulation of which Ethiopian delegates participated, has, in co-operation with the Imperial Government, assisted greatly in developing the agricultural resources of the country. In other fields of modern development, the International Bank for Reconstruction and Development has aided through loans to the Imperial Ethiopian Government in the repair and maintenance of the nation's roads and highways, through the Imperial Highway Authority; in stimulating the nation's agricultural and industrial development, through the Ethiopian Development Bank; and in modernising the nation's telecommunications service through the Imperial Board of Telecommunications. The International Civil Aviation Organisation, co-operating with the Ethiopian Department of Civil Aviation is aiding in the training of Ethiopians in Civil Aviation techniques and administration. Unceasingly for ten years of the existence of the United Nations, an organisation in which Ethiopia has played her relative part from its inception, the country has lived up to its obligations. Her delegates have always taken a position which expressed the unwavering faith in Ethiopia in international co-operation and in the lofty principles for the maintenance of world peace couched in the United Nations Charter.

In the opinion of the Ethiopian Government the rôle played thus far in the interest of peace and security and in economic and social progress, by the United Nations may not have been a success *in all* its aspects. But weighing the difficult post-war situation or state of affairs, they are of the opinion that the U.N. cannot be considered a failure. Because the United Nations always seeks collective solutions to any particular problem, the political, social and economic problems it has this far attempted to settle could not have satisfied every Member. Such is the very nature of collective decisions. Results of negotiation and compromise do not always satisfy everyone concerned — particularly when the negotiators are as many as 60 States. But they provide the best that can be had under the circumstances.

If there are failures in the United Nations attempts, these cannot be attributed to the U.N. as a corporate entity. They must be attributed to Member States without whose determined assistance the U.N. cannot function. With greater assistance from every Member State, the U.N. can easily make greater achievements. Weighing all the circumstances under which it has operated this far, it is the belief of the Government that it has justified the hope which they have placed upon it. The Government is particularly appreciative of the effort and success of the United Nations in preventing a major World War.

On this Jubilee of His Imperial Majesty's reign, it is more than an encouraging commentary that Ethiopia, which had suffered from the abscence of faith in the Covenant of the League of Nations, should remain a bright star among those nations which repose confidence in those principles that failed her in the hour of her tragic distress in the 1930's.

263

CHAPTER 22

Public Health

It is beyond question that among the most important reforms which characterise the quarter century of His Imperial Majesty's reign, the fight against illiteracy and superstition through education and the campaign against diseases through public health stand out as most significant. His Majesty the Emperor in strengthening his country and providing means for Ethiopians to share in her progress has always felt that a healthy and intelligent nation is a prerequisite to everything else. Thus even during the period of his regency, concrete plans were laid to establish an effective system of public health administration in Ethiopia.

Before 1930, comprising the activities of a department in the Ministry of Interior, Public Health services were directed by a Public Health Commission of three doctors and one pharmacist. In those days, the main aims of the Department were to cure and control the diseases occurring within the Empire. After the liberation, however, the functions of the Department were widened to include the preventive and sociological sides of public health. Thus the new programme embraced the problems of sanitation, medical training, national diet, and educating the public on matters of health.

When His Imperial Majesty returned in 1941, the general health and medical facilities of the country were in a deplorable state. Some of the not very numerous well-equipped hospitals and clinics which existed prior to the Italian invasion had been destroyed or looted more than once by succeeding armies, as well as those built by the Italians during their occupation. The invaders had built many barrack type, temporary and semi-permanent hospitals and clinic buildings and supplied them with adequate medical and surgical equipment; but war damage, looting and the transfer of these supplies and equipment to other theatres of war left most of the towns and provinces with inadequate medical facilities. To curb epidemics and to meet emergency medical needs the remaining medical supplies were assigned to the Ethiopian medical authorities and some forty Italian doctors along with twenty nurses and laboratory technicians were allowed to remain in Ethiopia to assist in the task of taking care of an estimated population of fifteen millions.

By February 1945, there were 47 physicians in the whole country, thirty-eight of them then in Government service, seven in private practice and two in mission services. The picture in this important and vital field was really gloomy then, especially as a result of the withdrawal of the Friends' Ambulance Unit which necessitated the closure of some hospitals and clinics until personnel replacements could be secured from abroad. When it proved impossible for the great Allies to spare medical personnel for Ethiopia because of the war emergency, Emperor Haile Selassie I despatched a mission early in 1945 to Sweden to procure a selected medical and nursing staff. Between November and December of that year these persons and equipment began to arrive for the Public Health Department. Since the beginning of 1946 there has been a marked and steady improvement in Public Health organisation, personnel and hospital rehabilitation. The Medical Directorate, as it was then called, had a Vice-Minister appointed to head it, who remainded under the Minister of the Interior. In 1947, it was elevated by Imperial Decree into a full Ministry. A separate spacious building was acquired and renovation and reconstruction started immediately.

The Ministry of Public Health was created by the Public Health Proclamation of August 1947. The new Ministry was made "responsible for the care and promotion of Public Health in the Empire of Ethiopia". According to the above proclamation, the Minister shall establish a General Advisory Board of Health, consisting of not less than 11 persons, to give "the expert view" on matters of public health. The Board is expected to co-opt as many experts as may be necessary for the conduct of its business.

The Minister is to carry out his duties through an executive body, known as the "Department of Health". The duties of the Department of Health include the following:

(1) the study of the state of the Public Health and of sanitary conditions throughout the Empire, and the devising of measures for the promotion of healthy standards of living;

(2) the general administration, supervising and control of public Health units and the maintenance of professional discipline;

(3) the enforcement of Public Health legislation;

(4) the taking of adequate measures for the protection of Public Health in an emergency;

(5) the registration of surgeons, physicians, dentists, pharmacists, midwives and nurses, and all other medical practitioners;

(6) the supervision and control of the philanthropic institutions engaged in Public Health activities;

(7) the establishment of procedures for the collection and compilation of such statistical data, concerning Public Health as may be required;

(8) the organisation of medical and sanitary education and the issuing of qualification certificates.

The following table shows the progress achieved by the Ministry in taking the necessary steps for the care and maintenance of Public Health:

	Institutions	In 1934	In 1954
a)	General Hospitals	13	38
b)	Leprosaria	2	3
c)	Government Clinics	28	105
d)	Mental Hospitals	—	1
e)	TB-Sanatoria	—	1
f)	Nurse Training Centres	—	4
g)	Central Research Laboratory	1	1

265

Though most of the General Hospitals have their own laboratories, the central research institute, known as "Institut Pasteur d'Ethiopie", deserves special mention. It was established in September 1951, in the buildings of the former Tafari Makonnen Hospital in the outskirts of Addis Ababa. The "Institut Pasteur d'Ethiopie", originally directed by Dr. M. A. Chabaud, consists of six departments:

(1) the Dept. of Bacteriology - Parasitology;
(2) the Dept. of Chemical Research;
(3) the Dept. of Entomology;
(4) the Dept. of Serology;
(5) the Dept. of Typhus; and
(6) the Veterinary Department.

The Institute has set apart, at the disposal of the World Health Organisation, special rooms for TB vaccination service.

The Institute has also launched an educational project to train Ethiopians as laboratory technicians.

In addition to all this, the "Institut Pasteur d'Ethiopie" is engaged in scientific research in the following fields:

(1) advanced study on rabies;
(2) new aspects of Rickettsial infections;
(3) different treatments for leprosy; and
(4) the physiological and bio-chemical study of certain venoms.

The Red Cross Society was first established in Ethiopia, in 1935, with international recognition. Having been suppressed during the Italian occupation, the Red Cross was revived and re-established in 1947. A detailed account of its activities can be found elsewhere in Chapter 29.

According to the Public Health Proclamation of August 1947, Municipal Public Health Services shall be organised in such towns as the Minister may decide, on the recommendation of the Governor-General of the Province in which the town is situated. Since the Mayor of Addis Ababa has more or less the same powers and responsibilities as a Governor-General, the Municipality of Addis Ababa was given its own "Public Health Department" to be run in close co-operation with the Minister of Public Health.

Originally known as Municipal Sanitation Office, this department was gradually expanded and improved to meet the rising population. Today it deals with the following fields of public service:

(a) Office of Statistics
(b) Communicable Diseases Control
(c) Mother and Child Care
(d) Sanitation Office
(e) Industrial Hygiene
(f) Mental Hygiene
(g) Public Health Education
(h) Laboratory Service
(i) Municipal Clinic.

All the services of the Municipal Public Health Department are rendered free of charge. Two important problems — water-supply and town-

266

planning — have already been undertaken. Plans are afoot for a modern stadium, public parks and swimming pools. In short, the Municipal Public Health Department is doing its part in maintaining Addis Ababa as a healthy place to live in.

After the liberation, it was found that there were practically no youths, left alive, with the basic education necessary for medical training. So the Government had to pick the most promising and intelligent of the un-educated "Orderlies" working in various hospitals for a period of training at the Menelik II Hospital.

As soon as candidates with the necessary education became available, the Red Cross Society started the first Nurses Training School in 1949. In the years which followed, three other training schools were started in the following hospitals: the Tafari Makonnen Hospital, the Empress Zauditu Memorial Hospital and the Princess Tsahai Memorial Hospital. Every year an increasing number of nurses is coming out of these training centres.

In 1954, the Ministry of Public Health started the "Medical College and Public Health Training Centre" at Gondar, in co-operation with the W.H.O., the U.S. Operations Mission and the United Nations International Children's Emergency Fund. The College is expected to turn out Public Health Officers, Sanitary Officers, Community Nurses and other auxiliary personnel necessary to staff Rural Health Centres.

The Princess Tsahai Memorial Hospital plans to start midwifery training as soon as a sufficient number of qualified nurses is available.

At present about 15 Ethiopian students are studying Medicine abroad — most of them on W.H.O. fellowships.

In this connection, it should be mentioned that some of the international agencies have given valuable support to the Ministry of Public Health in Ethiopia. Among them, the *World Health Organisation* has helped in the following fields, besides sending a Field Mission to Ethiopia to establish a medical education programme:

1. A Fellowships Programme for the training of medical personnel.
2. Anti-Leprosy Work.
3. Anti-VD Work.
4. The B.C.G. Mass Vaccination.
5. Anti-Malaria Campaign.
6. The Medical College and Public Health Training Centre at Gondar.
7. Public Health advisory services.

The UNICEF has given financial assistance for the following projects. (1) anti-VD work; (2) the B.C.G. Mass Vaccination; (3) the Gondar Medical College; (4) Maternity and Child Welfare.

The Russian Red Cross is staffing and maintaining a well-equipped hospital, known as the Dejazmach Balcha Memorial Hospital in Addis Ababa. There are other hospitals run by Christian missions of American and European origin. The Indian Community in Addis Ababa has established the *Gandhi Memorial Hospital* (to commemorate the name of a saint-statesman, who is revered throughout Ethiopia) on a site gra-

ciously presented by His Imperial Majesty. All these private medica
institutions are supervised by the Ministry of Public Health.

The U.S. Operations Mission (Point 4) has signed separate agreement
with the Ministry of Public Health to give aid in the following projects
(1) the Anti-Malaria Campaign; (2) the Gondar Medical College; anc
(3) Public Health advisory services.

Menelik II Hospital

The history of the oldest Government hospital in Ethiopia goes back tc
the first Italian invasion, in 1896. During this invasion, the Russian Czar
Nicholas II, had sent a Military Medical Mission to Ethiopia in demonstration of his friendship for Emperor Menelik II. When the woundec
soldiers were transferred to Addis Ababa after the victorious Battle o
Adwa, the Emperor chose a place in the north-eastern sector of the capital as a base-camp of the Russian Medical Mission. This base-camp, ir
course of time, grew to be a general Hospital, which was officially inaugurated in 1910.

Up to the year 1906, the administration of the Hospital was in the hands
of Russian doctors. Dr. Wladikine was the first Director. When the
Russian Medical Mission finally left in 1906, French doctors undertook
the direction of the Hospital.

Soon after the liberation, this Hospital was transferred to the control of
the British Miltary Mission to Ethiopia. It remained a military hospital
(admitting civilians occasionally), until the beginning of 1946, when it
came under the jurisdiction of the Directorate General of Public Health.
In 1947, Menelik II Hospital held an Elementary Dressers' Course, at
the end of which 40 dressers received diplomas.

In 1950 an Elementary Dentistry Course was conducted and about 10
Ethiopians were trained as dental assistants.

The vast progress achieved by Menelik II Hospital, within a decade, can
be noted from the following table:

a)	Out-patients	1944	1955
1.	General Medical Consultation	1,284	3,222
2.	Eye Diseases	852	2,180
3.	Surgical Cases	384	980
4.	Ear, Nose and Throat Dept.	—	695
5.	Dental Clinic	—	572
6.	Gynaecology and Obstetrics	—	350
7.	First Aid	—	1,242
	Total Average of Patient in one month . . .	2,520	9,241

b)	In-patients		
	Total number of Beds Occupied	180	394

268

Haile Selassie I ("Beth Saida") Hospital

This hospital was established in 1924, under the direction of the Swedish surgeon, Dr. Hanner, and his assistant Dr. Nystroem. In the beginning, the Hospital had only 30 beds, ably looked after by the Swedish nurses, Varna Hagman and Vera Bostrom.

The original building and its various installations were planned by a German architect. A part of the original building is now used as a training-centre for young Ethiopian nurses.

Today the Haile Selassie I Hospital has developed to be one of the major hospitals in the capital. Today it has 180 beds and a staff of nine doctors, including a dentist. There are special consultation-hours, every day, for those suffering from ear, nose and throat diseases. The other important departments are the Surgical, the Internal Diseases, the Maternity and Gynaecological, the Eye, Ear and Nose and the X-Ray Departments. It is the only hospital providing deep Therapy treatment in Ethiopia.

Not long ago, His Imperial Majesty graciously made a gift of 60 milli-grammes of Radium to the hospital for the treatment of Cancer and other fatal diseases. This is the only instance of Radium for treatment known to exist in Ethiopia. It should be mentioned that this is also the first hospital to establish a *Blood Donor Bank* in Ethiopia.

Imperial Guard Hospital

The Imperial Guard Hospital owes its origin to the reorganisation of the entire Imperial Guard in 1943, two years after the triumphant return of the Emperor to Ethiopia.

Starting as a small clinic-cum-dispensary, having only 40 beds, today it has become a fully independent, general hospital, giving free treatment to all members of the Imperial Guard and their families. The free treatment includes major operations and X-Ray examinations.

During the Korean War, this hospital served as the home base for the Ethiopian soldiers sent to Korea. The Imperial Ethiopian Air Force and the Imperial Ethiopian Navy are also making use of this hospital for the examination, treatment and hospitalisation of serious cases.

Princess Tsahai Memorial Hospital

The Princess Tsahai Memorial Hospital has a romantic history as be-fitting the treasured memory of the Ethiopian princess, who is deservingly known as "the Florence Nightingale" of her country. The Princess Tsahai Memorial Hospital Fund was started in England, where the princess had four years of vigorous training as a nurse and where she had made several good friends among the high and the lowly. The financial contributions from the British people alone approximately amounted to £ 57,000 (Eth.$ 400,000), thanks to Miss Sylvia Pankhurst's painstaking devotion to the cause. This amount was sufficient to cover the cost of purchasing and shipping the complete medical equiment required for the hospital. This

269

hospital continues to receive equipment bought by the Princess Tsaha Memorial Hospital Fund from donations solicited in the United Kingdom and other countries. Its operation and maintenance, however, is the full responsibility of the Ministry of Public Health. The main building was planned, and its construction supervised, by Mr. Selby Clewer, a British architect.

The Princess Tsahai Memorial Hospital stands on a spacious site (10,000 sq. metres), graciously donated by her august father, the present Emperor, on General Smuts Street, facing the airport. The hospital was officially opened by His Imperial Majesty on November 2nd, 1951; and it began taking patients in December of the same year. It has five main wards, named after the following personages: (1) Princess Tenagne Worq ,the eldest sister of the late, lamented Princess; (2) Miss Sylvia Pankhurst, the editor of "New Times and Ethiopian News", published in England; (3) Lord Davies, a British philanthropist who gave substantial support to the hospital; (4) Dr. John Melly, a popular physician, reputed for his pioneering services in Ethiopia; and (5) General Orde Wingate who led the liberation forces in 1941, and "whose memory is always vivid in the minds of the Ethiopian people."

The Princess Tsahai Memorial Hospital offers its services in the following fields:

(a) Child Care
(b) Gynaecology
(c) Maternity
(d) Outpatients Clinic
(e) Nurse Training
(f) General Surgery
(g) Free Medical Care for the Poor.

St. Paul's Hospital

This hospital was built by the Italians as Officer's quarters. In 1947 the buildings were remodelled for a hospital and in 1948 His Imperial Majesty named it "The St. Paul's Hospital" with the instruction that it be used solely for the poor. The hospital is independently run by a Board of trustees appointed by His Imperial Majesty, and financed by the proceeds of the present Palace Hotel and other land revenues. It has about 200 beds with a staff of 5 physicians and about 15 dressers and nurses.

The Ras Desta Hospital

This hospital, built by the Italians before the invasion, seemed to have been premeditated. They wanted a hospital for their officers after the conquest of Ethiopia, so they built the present Ras Desta Hospital around 1934, but it was not used as such till after the occupation, 1936. During the occupation it was named "The Italian Hospital" (Ospedale Italiana).

270

Their Imperial Majesties open Princess Tsahai Memorial Hospital, Addis Ababa

After the liberation this hospital was remodelled and named: "The Ras Desta Hospital". It is entirely run by the Ministry of Public Health. It has at present about 100 beds, and 6 physicians, two sisters and several dressers on its staff.

Empress Zauditu Memorial Hospital

The Seventh Day Adventist Mission in 1934 built and operated a Maternity Clinic and named it "The Empress Zauditu Memorial Hospital" in honour of the late Empress Zauditu. The land and buildings were given to the Mission by the Government. Today the Zauditu Me-

271

morial Hospital has about 94 beds, 5 physicians and 5 European Nurses on its staff.

It is run and operated entirely by the Mission. With the consent of the Ministry of Public Health the Empress Zauditu Memorial Hospital opened a School of Nursing in 1950, located in its compound and bearing the same name, which has already graduated 17 nurses.

The expansion of hospitals, clinics, sanitation and medical education both in Addis Ababa and the provinces is going on. Addis Ababa has 11 hospitals and 6 clinics, and Harar has 2 hospitals. In all there are now functioning in Ethiopia no fewer than 44 hospitals and 153 clinics. Patients suffering from tuberculosis and other communicable diseases such as VD, etc., are treated free of charge if they show that they cannot afford to pay. The number of patients treated in hospitals and clinics last year was over 800,000.

Leprosy Control

Twenty-five years ago, there was only one hospital, in Ethiopia, to take care of leprosy patients. It is still functioning in Harar, under the direction of its founder, Dr. Feron.

In July 1933, a new leprosarium was founded in Addis Ababa by Dr. Lambie of the American Mission to Lepers. It was named the Princess Zenneba Worq Hospital, the cornerstone of which ("Jesus Christ, Himself, being the Chief cornerstone") was laid by His Imperial Majesty. This and the Harar Leprosarium treated about 600 patients during the Second World War.

His Imperial Majesty has graciously given the necessary land to the American Mission to Lepers; and they have established two Leper Colonies, with facilities for modern treatment of the disease. Of the two settlements, one is at Shashamanna (Arussi) and the other is near Dessie.

A leprosy specialist from the World Health Organisation has done important research work in Ethiopia to find out most effective ways of controlling the disease in the future. Nowadays more and more patients are flocking to the various centres, voluntarily, as a result of the propaganda carried out by the co-operative efforts of the World Health Organisation and the Ministry of Public Health.

His Imperial Majesty has also helped to set up a *preventorium*, where more than 100 children of leper parents are brought up and educated under the most favourable conditions.

CHAPTER 23

Internal Administration

The point explained in Chapter 1 about Menelik's succesful efforts to unify Ethiopia has a direct bearing on the internal administration of the Empire. The unification brought together in one political organism all the provinces under a central direction. Its concomitant was the establishment of central institutions with enough authority to command the respect of the subjects in the far-flung corners of the country. Such institutions, conditioned by the stage of internal communications, began under Menelik, but the improved system in operation today was introduced by Haile Selassie I. Needless to say that it was a tedious task, primarily because of the historical and traditional relics of the days of the (Mesafint) rule of the princes. Effective administrative control was secured gradually and by the piecemeal introduction of modern methods. During the period 1930—1935, for instance, administrative areas of the country, set up as provinces, were still allotted to princes, rases, dejazmaches and other members of the aristocracy. They were permitted to keep troops which they led and, by the central Government, they were allowed to levy land and other taxes within their areas to meet administrative expenses. It is of historical significance that it was during this period that His Majesty the Emperor granted the Imperial Ethiopian Constitution (1931) which gave birth to the parliament. He also introduced the Criminal Code and provincial courts, more modern forms of taxation, schools, hospitals and other reforms bearing directly and indirectly on the new type of internal administration.

Among the first steps for establishing effective provincial administration which were introduced at that period by the Emperor was revenue control. By Decree the Governors of provinces, sub-provinces, counties and districts were called upon to make strict account of revenue collected from taxes levied on land and markets against numbered receipts. Such income was to be deposited directly into the Government treasury and allocation made for the payment of local officials and the maintenance of local security forces. At the outbreak of the war, 1935, this fiscal reform had taken root in such areas as Shoa, Harar, Chercher, Bale, Kafa, Jimma, Wallaga and Kellam.

The Governors General at this time were directly responsible to His Majesty the Emperor; in their administrative functions, however, the Minister of the Interior was the fountain-head. For swift contact with the central authority, provincial officials utilised the posts and telecommunications system. This was done when unusual problems arose; but normally, Governors General had possessed delegated authority to act. The provinces of Shoa, Wollo, Harar, Begemder, Gojjam, Tigré, Wallaga, Kaffa, Ilubabur and Sidamo were headed by princes and rases.

Such areas as Gamu Gofa, Arussi, Bale, Kanta, Kullo, Kambata, Wollamo, Yeju, Wadlana, Delanta and others were governed by Dejazmaches and other ranks under the overall supervision of Governors General.

In the early days a security force like the present police was very little required. As the majority of the men were born into the soldier's life, they, more often than not, sought military honour. Whenever a quarrel arose between two parties and one of them swore by the name of the King, it was the duty of any third party hearing the words, "ba Negus," (by the King), to see that the parties were taken to the court. Even today this custom of taking an oath in the name of the Emperor is prevalent throughout the country. After the founding of the capital, Addis Ababa, a security force was formed known as "zabagnas" (guards) which wore no uniform or distinctive dress but was allowed to carry arms. An Ethiopian police force, as the term implies today, was begun during the period of His Imperial Majesty's Regency when foreign instructors were invited to train recruits and develop such a security force. When Italy struck in 1935, modern police organizations existed in Addis Ababa Harar, Jimma, Debra Markos and Bale.

In line with their plan to integrate Ethiopia, Eritrea and Somaliland in "Africa Orientale", the occupiers had redivided the Empire into six major provinces: Shoa, Amhara, Harar, Galla-Sidamo, Eritrea and Somalia. Reorganisation after the liberation saw a new phase of progress in internal administration. Twelve provinces, seventy-four sub-provinces 360 counties and 1,122 districts were established as the revived administrative units.

The machinery of Provincial Government is clearly set forth in the Provincial Regulations which, in addition to outlining the organisation, provide for Provincial Councils. These Provincial Councils are composed of senior officials of the Administration, senior representatives of the other Ministries who function there and other local persons of prominence Their function is primarily to discuss and advise the Governor General on matters relating to the welfare of the inhabitants and the prosperity of the province; they sit as a Council three or more times annually. In broad outline, the Provincial Administration under the headship of the Governor General is responsible for the maintenance of public security and the proper administration of justice throughout the province; for the supervision of tax collection and the expenditure authorised by the Annual Appropriation Proclamation. Only taxes and dues legally fixed by the Government may be levied.

The Governor General, his assistants and the Council are reflected in the administrative set-up of the other sub-divisions. Their functions are similar on a lower level and they bear the greater share of rural administration. Their work is of enormous importance, especially because of the present state of communications in the country. In fact, their importance can be readily appreciated when it is taken into consideration that the Provincial centres are small in the aggregate, compared with the wide expanse of the country broken up into the districts and villages.

The Administrative Order sets forth the rules for the appointment of all key provincial officials from the Governors General, Directors' Councils, Principal Secretaries of the Governors, District Officers, Mayors of Municipalities, Town Officials, Provincial Judges, and officers to command the military forces necessary for the security of the provinces. Purely administrative personnel are appointed by His Imperial Majesty upon the recommendation of the Minister of the Interior, while those concerned with special services are named upon the seconding of the appropriate Minister involved.

The Governor General, who is known as the *Taqlai Agara Gazhi* of the Province (Aurajja), exercises general supervision over all officials, named to his province by the other Ministries and by the departments of the Ministry of Interior. Within the province there are a number of sub-divisions, termed *warada*, each of which is administered by an *Agara Gazhi* or Governor. Each warada or sub-division is broken up into a number of districts each administered by a *Mislanye*, or District Governor. This system, it is reported, dates back to 1890, after Menelik II started the unification of the country. The concept, however, is of ancient origin, going as far back as the pre-Christian era.

The old system of levies by Governors General was done away with and a system of taxation based on tax laws enforced by the central Ministry of Finance was substituted. Thence forward all revenues from any part of the Empire went into the central treasury, the Ministry of Finance maintaining a corps of officials under the immediate control of the Governors and Chiefs of the internal areas. Salaries for all administrative personnel were provided for in the national budget and paid in accordance with central treasury allocations. A strict system of book-keeping and accounts was put into operation with Government auditors making periodic checks. The system of land tax, which constitutes the main source of provincial revenue, was revised and made more equable. Land survey and registration have been introduced and the categories of the holdings for the purpose of estimating the tax have been ascertained in a substantial part of the Empire. Taxation in kind has been substituted for by levies made and paid in cash.

Internal administration has been further improved through better communications and transportation. Goods and persons are more easily transported from one area to another, and through the use of the facilities of posts and telecommunications contact on all levels has been facilitated. Quite a change from the "zabagnas" (guards) who formed the embryo of security forces and were stationed in comparatively few locations before the Italo-Ethiopian war, today the national police force is a modern establishment. The Minister's definition of powers, Order 1 of 1943, states: "The Minister of the Interior shall supervise security throughout the Empire. All Governors General, Governors and Police shall carry out their duties under his orders."

The administration of the Police, of prisons and the control of aliens and their movement within the country is in the hands of the General Director of Public Security, one of the departments of the Ministry of the Interior.

275

The regular Ethiopian Police is under the command of a Commissioner of Police, with headquarters in the Ministry in Addis Ababa. This police Force, centrally administered and disciplined, is responsible for the policing of the capital, the provincial towns and the frontier districts. Formerly, local administrations in the provinces and districts of the country were policed by irregulars recruited and administered on the spot. Today, however, with the increase of officer personnel and with the increase of patrolmen, the Police Headquarters in Addis Ababa is in control of the policing of the whole nation.

The whole of the provincial administration receives its authority from the Central Government. Thus, the sectional Police work in conjunction with the local Governors General and Governors, but their administration moves forward by directives from the Headquarters. Organised on modern lines, in addition to a small number of foreign engagees, a large corps of Ethiopian Police Inspectors and Captains form the leadership of the Force. Ethiopian Police receive their powers through the Police Proclamation of 1942, their ordnance, in the main, imported from foreign countries. In line with the general trend, there are schools and media of instruction carried on continuously to train the Ethiopian Police in the art of the maintenance of law and order.

In the reorganisation of the Police a significant step has been the Aba Dina Police Staff College at Gullale. In the spacious and modern compound, all the buildings have been renovated, redecorated and equipped to house a student body of 120. Organised some time ago, the College opened its doors in October, 1946, has an enrolment of over eigthy regular full-time students, holds classes for active service officers who attend in the mornings for special subjects and evening classes for others who have enrolled for the full-time course on a part-time basis. The qualifications for entrance are a secondary education or its equivalent, good character and an apititude for training to take on responsibility. It is hoped that from this group of men will come the Police administrators to take full charge of the nation's Police Force.

The professional aim of the College is to make experts of the students in the various fields of crime prevention and detection and the maintenance of civil peace and security. The courses offered are intensive, and fall under the following heads: Police Peace Service, Criminology Service, Report Writing, Witness and Examination Psychology, General Criminal Psychology, View Points on Criminal Investigation, International Criminal Police Activities, Athletics and Gymnastics, Civilian Air-raid Precautions and Care of the Sick. Appropriate examinations are held after the two-year duration of the course to determine the successful absorption of the subjects taught. Those who pass with distinction are selected for a six-month course in special fields leading up to the rank higher than 2nd Lieutenant of Police granted to these cadets on completion of the course at Aba Dina. There is a school for the training of the rank and file known as the Kolfe Police Training School.

CHAPTER 24

National Defence

A substantial part of Ethiopia's history, ancient, mediaeval and modern, is the dramatic story of self-defence. And this activity has moved from the primitive stage of fighting with spears and shields, with little or no organisation, to that of the use of modern weapons under modern military establishments. In all these stages one characteristic has remained unchanged — the unconquerable fighting spirit of the Ethiopian soldier. His Imperial Majesty's words to the graduation class of air force officers at Harar Meda last February vividly recalled this fact, when he said:

The Ethiopian people, since the founding of their independence, have managed to withstand waves of trials without losing their flag — this symbol which they gloriously protected until Our reign. It is Our sincere hope that you also will safeguard this flag with the same heroism and ardour inherited from your forefathers, who, under their successive Emperors, were able to protect it with great devotion and sacrifice.

A modern army of defence in Ethiopia was in the early plans of His Majesty the Emperor. Even though the supply of arms and munitions was controlled and virtually prohibited by adverse conditions, he knew that such military establishments were a prime requisite in the defence and preservation of his country's independence. That is why in 1929, a Belgian Military Mission was secured to undertake the task of training the Imperial Body Guard. His Majesty the Emperor opened the Ganat Military School (later renamed Haile Selassie I Cadet Training School) in 1933, with a staff of five Swedish and one Ethiopian officers as instructors to train military officers for the Imperial Ethiopian Army.

Some of the partially trained Imperial Body Guard cadets of exceptional promise were sent for training to the Academy of St. Cyr in France. Some of them returned as qualified officers to take part in the new military programme, then fairly on the way. The Fascist invasion arrested this training programme, but it is significant to note that as the result of these projects, thanks to the Emperor's foresight, a modern trained and equipped army of 7000 officers and men was ready to be thrown into the unprovoked struggle. After the restoration, the revived Ministry of War was charged with the organisation, training, and administration of the Ethiopian army. The Imperial Guard remained under the direct command of His Imperial Majesty. The Haile Selassie I Cadet Training School and the Imperial Body Guard Cadet School were also reinstituted to take care of military training. Today these institutions are functioning in full swing and producing officers who are filling responsible positions with credit.

In pursuing the aim to provide Ethiopia with adequate defensive military weapons, and realising that modern military establishments are vitally necessary for the maintenance of this defence and for national and international security, His Imperial Majesty, through the Anglo-Ethiopian Agreement and Military Convention of 1942, obtained the services of a British Military Mission to Ethiopia. This Mission was responsible, in co-operation with the Ministry of War, for the effective training and development of the Ethiopian army. The work of the Mission ended in 1950; simultaneously Swedish military instructors were engaged to continue the training of officers for the Imperial Body Guard.

A significant part of the advance in the modern development of the military training programme of the country is that after the British Military Mission ended its task, instruction in the Haile Selassie I Cadet Training School was taken up by trained Ethiopian officers. Today the programme is entirely in the hands of these officers who are in every way proving their worth and their ability. The same is true of the Imperial Body Guard Cadet School in which all but one of the instructors are Ethiopian officers trained in the same school.

There has been a marked elevation in the levels of instruction and of entrance to both of these military institutions. Formerly cadets were admitted after completion of the elementary school. Now they must offer a secondary school background. The Haile Selassie I Cadet Training School for two years now, has been offering courses in higher and advanced leadership within the Ethiopian army. Another forward step in His Majesty the Emperor's future plans for military training is to elevate the standard to a higher academic level so that college graduates might be attracted to make their careers as top-ranking officers in the army.

The Ethiopian Armed Forces of today began with the armies of liberation, the nucleus of which came from Ethiopians exiled in Kenya and the Sudan, and from the multitude of others who spent five years in the hills resisting the enemy. When His Imperial Majesty, with the aid of His British allies, crossed the Sudan Frontier and entered Ethiopia, the refugees from Kenya and the Sudan and the veterans were grouped together and trained by a British military mission. They made up four brigades — the First, Second, Third and Fourth. The First brigade joined the British Army under General Cunningham and reached Addis Ababa. There a new brigade of Ethiopian volunteers was recruited and trained. The Second and Third brigades accompanied His Imperial Majesty under the command of the British army from the Sudan border through Gojjam and Gondar to his triumphant entry into Addis Ababa on May 5th, 1941.

Immediately thereafter a military mission, styled, "General Direction Mission", was established in the compound now used by the Imperial Ethiopian High Court, as a temporary measure. After the signing of the Anglo-Ethiopian Agreement and Military Convention on the 31st January, 1942, the Ministry of War came into being. By order of the Emperor, former trained officers were charged with drafting the provisions for the reorganisation of the Ministry which then had its headquarters in the compound of the Imperial Palace. On the 5th May, 1942, the Ministry of War was transferred to its permanent headquarters and started its ever-growing functions.

278

Reorganisation of the army was then undertaken, consisting of two parts: an army staffed and trained by the Ministry of War; a second staffed and trained by the British Military Mission to Ethiopia, the historical successor to the Mission which prepared the Ethiopian army of liberation.

The use and appropriation of the veterans of the war and of the liberation campaign was an initial problem in the early post-liberation days. It became the responsibility of the Ministry of War to utilise them to the best advantage. Since these men had varying degrees of military training, it was necessary to classify them into officers and the ranks and to separate them in squads, regiments, etc. In accordance with their ranks and their military accomplishments during the war and the campaign, several among the patriots were made regimental and brigade commanders, while those of less important record were posted elsewhere in commensurate ranks. The principal pre-war graduate officers were detailed to the several brigades to train the new army which was divided into fifteen regiments as follows:

The 1st and 15th, located at Addis Ababa; 2nd, at Nazareth; 3rd, at Ambo; 4th, at Debra Berhan; 5th, at Begemder; 6th, at Tigré; 7th, at Gojjam; 8th, at Dessie; 9th, at Harar town; 10th, at Wallaga; 11th, at Sidamo; 12th, at Arussi; 13th, at Kaffa; 14th, at Ilubabur. The 2nd regiment was later transferred to Gamu Gofa. The training programme was extended to all these units which included veterans, patriots and new recruits.

All the officers of the veteran army remained non-commissioned officers, until in 1945, by the approval of His Imperial Majesty, they were awarded classified ranks depending on the capacity and the apitude shown during the active training period. To keep the officers who received their commissions in actual combat rather than from special training, the Ministry of War admitted them to special courses in the military school. After prescribed training and a passing grade in a set examination, their ranks were re-classified. They received diplomas from His Imperial Majesty. In April, 1944, His Majesty the Emperor, in order to strengthen the national police, ordered the transfer of 14,157 trained army personnel to the police force under the Ministry of Interior.

Further consolidation of the army became necessary in order to make it more well-knit and to aid in providing better conditions for training and administration. The organisation which began in Kenya and the Sudan was then redeployed into eleven brigades and sent to the following outposts: the 1st, to Gondar, Azezo; the 2nd, to Debra Markos; the 3rd, to Jimma; the 4th, to Gorgora-Gondar; the 5th, to Dessie; the 6th, to Ada-Tigré; the 7th, to Asba Tafari; the 8th, to Tigré-Maichew; the 9th, to Harar; the 10th, to Alamata; and the 11th was stationed at Addis Ababa.

The British Military Mission, which had undertaken "general direction" then moved from its temporary headquarters and took over a large compound opposite the Addis Ababa airport. There its main departments were established — office of the Commander of the Mission, Department of General Direction, and a department including administration and stores.

Each of the units of the Ethiopian army, both those trained and administered by the British Military Mission to Ethiopia (BMME) and those under the Ministry of War, had a British officer at its head. It was later decided that in the interest of uniformity, the training of all the units of the Ethiopian army should be put under the supervision of the BMME. As a result, a department, — "General Army Direction," under the overall direction of the General Headquarters of the Ministry of War was established. This department was maintained by British and Ethiopian officers. The training of Ethiopian officers was intensified with the view to making them ready in due course to replace their British tutors.

The drive for uniformity brought on a delineation along Divisional lines — the whole army was then broken up into three Divisions: the First at Addis Ababa; the Second at Dessie; and the Third at Harar. This move brought about further consolidation. All commanding personnel were brought under a single direction, the brigades put under Divisional commands thus: 1st Divisional Army, including 1st, 2nd, 3rd and 4th brigades; 2nd Divisional Army, including 5th, 6th, 7th and 8th brigades; and 3rd Divisional Army, including the 9th, 10th and 11th brigades. The 12th brigade was established in Eritrea, 1952, following federation. The following auxiliary units were also organised: artillery, tank, engineering, communications, general stores, supply and transport, driving and correspondence school, clinical, medical and veterinarian.

Part of the fifteen regiments, during the early period of rehabilitation of the army, was partially equipped by the Imperial Ethiopian Government with such arms as Belgian machine guns and rifles and with some equipment captured from the enemy. The several barracks left in many parts of the Empire by the former occupiers were taken into use by the army.

The re-equipping of the Ethiopian Army, which had constituted one of the barriers to the country's defence in the Italo-Ethiopian war in 1935, has experienced beneficial advances in the post-war period. Before the 1st and 4th brigades left the Sudan and Kenya to take part in the liberation campaign in 1941, they were equipped with American Springfield rifles. During the period of post-liberation military reorganisation, the 5th to 11th brigades were equipped with rifles captured from the enemy. In 1951 His Imperial Majesty established the small munitions factory in Addis Ababa to supply the army with small arms. Springing from the Mutual Defence Treaty between Ethiopia and the United States of 1951, the army is now equipped with modern weapons.

In 1947 His Majesty the Emperor, through negotiations with the British Government, transferred the general direction of the army from the BMME to the Ministry of War. The officers of the BMME who remained were absorbed in various capacities until 1950 when the Mission's term ended. The Head of the Mission remained until then as adviser to the Ministry of War, while the British officers served as regimental advisers and instructors in the Haile Selassie I Military School. After the term of the British Military Mission to Ethiopia ended in 1950, the armed forces were further reorganised and consolidated and, as stated above, previously trained Ethiopian officers took over the entire training of cadets at the military school.

The Ministry of War was thereafter organised into four major departments: General Headquarters, a department for organising and improving the strength of the army, administration, Ministry of War properties and accounts. The entire responsibility for running the organisation of the nation's armed forces was then undertaken by the Ministry of War. The Imperial Ethiopian Government sought and obtained, through the United States-Ethiopian Mutual Defence Treaty, the assistance of American officers and instructors of the Military Assistance Advisory Group (MAAG) to advise the Ministry and train military personnel in modern methods.

As regards the part of air support in defence, the lack of which we ourselves had experienced, we should like to remind you that the lack of modern air force which would co-operate with land and naval forces in modern warfare constituted an insurmountable handicap for effective national defence. The (Ethiopian) air force would undoubtedly be valuable assistance for the land and naval force ...... These were the words of His Majesty the Emperor to a graduating class of the Imperial Ethiopian Air Force Training Centre. In this observation all modern strategists are agreed. Without doubt the air arm is and will remain a very significant part of modern armed forces as has been eloquently supported by World War II.

The Ethiopian Air Force with its Training Centre at Harar Meda, Bishoftu, forms the nucleus of Ethiopia's military air arm. After the Ganat Military School was opened by His Imperial Majesty in 1933 to train Ethiopian youth in the art of modern warfare, air force training followed almost immediately. It was the Emperor's wish and the Ethiopian Government's plan that the two services might grow to be defenders of the country's liberty. This phase of military preparedness was eclipsed by the war — the nation's fighting men facing the enemy without adequate air protection. The Italian Chief Officer in Charge, in his account said: "We were alone in the sky." Ethiopia's population and the defenceless army were easy victims of the invaders' planes. This experience was uppermost in His Imperial Majesty's mind, for in 1944 air force training was revived. The Haile Selassie I Air Force Training Centre, formerly at Akaki, was reorganised in 1947 and moved to the aerodrome at Harar Meda, Bishoftu. The air force is being trained by Swedish instructors invited into the country for this purpose. The organisation has made steady progress and consists at present mainly of headquarters, attack squadron, transport flight division, flying school, technical department, ground school, signal department and a meteorological station, each divided into several specialised sections. Development of the air force is rapidly taking shape. Besides expanding its number of wings it has been engaged in surveying for an auxiliary aerodrome and new permanent air fields and bases. A part of its squadrons is based at

281

Asmara. Annually, His Majesty the Emperor witnesses air force manoeuvres and awards wings to pilots and certificates to other categories of military airmen. There is a number of trained pilots, radio operators, and ground crews, which has received training in the Air Force Training Centre.

Although primarily established to train air force personnel, the Haile Selassie I Air Force Training Centre has been also a contributing factor to the nation's civil aviation. As stated elsewhere in this book, being the only institution which trains pilots, the Ethiopian Air Lines has been able to secure its first Ethiopian pilots from the Air Force Training Centre. At present eight such pilots, after receiving air line conversion training, have been absorbed into the pilot ranks of the Ethiopian Air Lines.

With federation of Eritrea to Ethiopia which was finalised in September 1952, Ethiopia once again became a maritime nation. Ethiopia's ancient seaports — Massawa and Assab — were returned. The immediate responsibility arose of providing the necessary machinery to take care of the nation's maritime pursuits. Eleven months before legal provisions were proclaimed by the Emperor — on His State visit to Massawa, these were His Imperial Majesty's words: *In order to utilise to the maximum the resources of the two ports of Massawa and Assab, we have given orders to Our Government to undertake an ambitious programme of rehabilitation and improvement in the installations at Massawa and Assab. Moreover, and this has taken place well before the date of the federation of Eritrea with Ethiopia, we have already commenced important projects for the repair and improvement of roads linking these two ports with Eritrea and Ethiopia.*

For this reason, the occasion of Our state visit to Massawa at this time marks the beginning of a period of profound significance for the development and the future of the Empire of Ethiopia. Not only will access to the sea join Ethiopia to the outer world but also this same access to the sea will serve at the same time to join, by bonds of mutual and reciprocal interests the economies of Eritrea and Ethiopia.

Order No. 12 known as the Maritime Order and published in the Negarit Gazeta of September 25th, 1953, brought into being the Department of Marine under a Director General. Organisation, management and development of harbours; supervision, development and control of merchant shipping; supervision and development of fisheries in the Red Sea and in the inland waters; organisation, management and supervision of the coastguard which is intended to untertake the responsibilities normally vested in a navy in other countries in addition to preventive maritime services; and supervision of the light-houses and aids to navigation are among the most important responsibilities of the Department of Marine.

One of the more recent administrative agencies, it is evident that the most primary task is one of training Ethiopians in its various fields — in seafaring, port administration, coastguard activities, etc. Plans for such education were promptly devised. As found in the chapter on education, a special course in port administration was organised in the University College during the academic year 1951—1952. Young men were thus being prepared even then to take part in work pertaining to maritime commerce in the ports and ministerial departments. Lij Alexander Desta, grandson of His Majesty the Emperor is under training as a naval officer with the Royal Navy in England; eight trainees were tutored in Holland in marine engines, their running and maintenance; four men are undergoing similar training in England. A coastguard college and technical training establishment for technicians to serve in the coastguard are planned to start in the beginning of January 1956, apprenticeship courses for which began on October 1st, 1955. Eight candidates for deck personnel and engine room training were sent to Yugoslavia, and to the United States, two for port engineering and two for harbour management. Various other training programmes are under consideration by the Government.

Since the federation, commercial traffic from the two ports has begun to be developed and it is expected that in the course of the normal progress of the commercial, industrial and social life of the Empire it would continue to do so. Ethiopian exports can now reach world markets without paying tribute; imports demanded by the progressing national economy can find ready access.

The port of Massawa has the necessary facilities to handle the available trade with a surplus capacity to be utilised when the trade of the Empire is further developed. The Assab harbour is too small for the present and future needs, and a plan for its development has been worked out and is for consideration by the Imperial Government. Each port is controlled through a harbour master.

Port Statistics

Massawa

Year	Ships	N.R.T.	Gross Tons	Import	Export	In	Out
						Passengers	
1942	174	496204	909303	33350	131250	No	Record
1943	216	954195	1640948	63750	20750	,,	,,
1944	174	279351	472284	53513	57576	,,	,,
1945	177	230971	403985	60680	97750	,,	,,
1946	258	242000	419614	88159	40408	,,	,,
1947	382	550073	971294	87984	100502	,,	,,
1948	499	727168	1230145	95301	120108	4809	7465
1949	459	792761	1323591	87207	126731	2444	5108
1950	415	772933	1339795	85390	77614	3860	6283
1951	371	659742	1127871	77257	145451	3099	4043
1952	470	795390	1399678	98578	144819	2111	4918
1953	436	766093	1307583	81790	99861	1190	2649

Assab

Year	Ships	N.R.T.	Gross Tons	Import	Export	In	Out
						Passengers	
1952	205	173259	293875	17241	57842	443	428
1953	286	327382	528763	21952	49256	380	242
1954	412	426972	716134	46059	106372	498	361

The 800 kilometres of seacoast is a valuable addition to the Empire's economic and commercial activities. Besides providing means of international communication, it has brought back the potential of fisheries. The Department of Marine is charged, as mentioned above, with the development of this industry. The United States Operations Mission (Point 4) has agreed to undertake a proper survey of the fisheries possibilities along the Eritrean coast. In the overall development of the Department's functions, when the fisheries become established, it may serve the purpose also of providing Ethiopians with seafaring experience. Fishing was one of the principal occupations of the New England colonies — fishing fleets have continued, even today, to be a training school for American seamen.

At present both the civilian and defence sides of Ethiopia's maritime interests come under the Department of Marine. This seems to be a normal consequence of the fact that this is a new enterprise necessitating economy of personnel and co-ordination of training. Originally part of the Ministry of Public Works and Communications, His Imperial Majesty has recently made the Department of Marine part of the Ministry of National Defence.

The Imperial Ethiopian Ministry of National Defence was created by Proclamation published in the Negarit Gazeta of September 25th, 1953, known as the Ministry of National Defence Order of 1953.

The new Ministry is intended to meet the new situation of national and international security created by the return of Eritrea and, in turn, that of the 800 kilometres of Ethiopia's ancient sea coast on the Red Sea. The Federal Act provides that, "the jurisdiction of the federal government shall extend to the following matters: defence, foreign affairs, currency and finance, foreign and interstate commerce and external and interstate communications, including ports."

To meet this new situation the Ministry of Defence brings together the Imperial Ethiopian Army and Air Force which existed before federation and the newly formed Imperial Ethiopian Marine.

CHAPTER 25

Public Works and Communications

The increase and perfection of communication facilities remain one of the chief characteristics of present day civilisation. In this expansive and indispensable field, transportation is absolutely essential. The Imperial Ethiopian Government, particularly since the reign of Menelik II, took cognisance of this fact. As stated in Chapter 1, the Franco-Ethiopian Railway, still one of the main arteries of the country's transportation system, was conceived in 1894 by Emperor Menelik II. By 1930 when Haile Selassie I came to power, appreciable progress had been made in highway transportation, then the twin factor with the railway for the inland transportation system of the Empire.

Mr. Adrien Zervos in his book, "L'Empire d'Ethiopie — The mirror of modern Ethiopia — the period from 1906 to 1935" (which is exactly up to the year of the launching of the hateful Fascist aggression), affirms that there were already in this period 4,000 kilometres of roads and tracks for cars, not taking into account the innumerable caravan tracks. The plan then was to complete the network in a few years so as to render all the provinces of the Empire accessible by road. Already a contract for the construction of the road to Kurmuk, projected to assure direct communication between Ethiopia and the Anglo-Egyptian Sudan, had been awarded to a construction company and some 745 kilometres of this road had been completed.

During the last twenty-five years the system of roads and highways has not only been sizably extended but aviation has also been added. It can be safely said as this chapter is intended to show, that the position of inland transportation today shows a great deal of improvement in comparison to what it was in the year of His Majesty the Emperor's accession.

Some countries are particularly favoured by having ample water transportation to serve their basic needs. Ethiopia was for many years land locked and had no such natural advantages. Two Ethiopian ports, Massawa and Assab, have recently been made available to serve the Empire. The western part of the country is inadequately served by the Baro River, which for a few months only during the year joins up with the Nile. It is navigable only a short distance inside the western boundary.

Ethiopia is a very rugged country and the construction of heavy duty highway and railroad outlets is difficult and costly. This has tended to slow the development of land transportation facilities and to preserve many of the aspects of an isolated internal economy.

The Italian occupation gave a boost to road construction in Ethiopia. Apart from improving the network which the occupiers found, they constructed other highways as a part of their plan of speedy penetration; they sought to connect the capital as much as they could with the important production areas of the country. That the roads and bridges left by the occupiers were useful war booty is somewhat questionable, for the scheme was too grandiose for Ethiopia's early post-liberation revenue. As a result a very substantial part of the Italian highway system in Ethiopia (that part which survived the liberation campaign) deteriorated from lack of maintenance. The best thing possible was to keep open the most important highways, thought to be indispensable and within the strict priorities of a balanced programme of reconstruction. When it is considered that the construction and maintenance of the main highways of the country are strictly central treasury debits, there can hardly be any wonder why an early post-liberation highway development programme had to wait.

His Imperial Majesty and his Government never lost sight of the fact that such a programme was inextricably tied up with the all-round progress of the country. This can be supported by the fact that the first loan sought by Ethiopia from the International Bank for Reconstruction and Development in 1950 was to be applied to the nation's highway system.

Proclamation 115 of 1951, signed January 26th, 1951, was the culmination of many plans, and a long series of conferences and negotiations between the International Bank for Reconstruction and Development and the Imperial Ethiopian Government. These plans and conferences were aimed at the establishment of a highway organisation with the initial objective of repairing and opening up a main road system in Ethiopia. The Imperial Highway Authority was created by this proclamation — a new, autonomous organisation which, under Ethiopian Law, could enter into contracts, hire personnel and do the great variety of things a modern highway organisation is called upon to untertake.

Financing of the initial three-year programme was based on a loan of US.$ 5,000,000 from the International Bank for Reconstruction and Development. This sum was used primarily for the purchase of road-building machinery and services of American engineers and specialists. Repayment of the loan is to be made from Ethiopian Government funds. Payments, including interest, extend over a twenty-year period. A minimum additional sum of Eth.$ 23,000,000 was pledged by the Imperial Ethiopian Government for the initial three-year programme; the amount actually appropriated was Eth.$ 23,324,725.50. Funds were provided by direct grants to the Authority and from imposts on motor fuels, oils and greases.

The work of the Imperial Highway Authority was carried through the fourth year, ending February 28th, 1955, by a direct appropriation of Eth.$ 8,000,000 from the Imperial Ethiopian Government. The programme for the fifth and sixth years will be controlled by an overall budget of Eth.$ 20,000,000, appropriated by the same source. Thus, it is apparent that the initial loan of US.$ 5,000,000 has constituted less than 20 % of the total cost of the first six years of operation, the remaining 80 %

286

having been supplied from current revenues of the Imperial Ethiopian Government.

American engineers and equipment specialists familiar with American construction methods, maintenance practices, and road machinery, were provided under a contract concluded with the United States Bureau of Public Roads for the management of the Imperial Highway Authority. An American engineer was named as Director of the Authority and a Member of the Board of Commissioners. The Board is under the Chairmanship of the Minister of Public Works and Communications. Other Members are the Vice-Minister of Finance, the Vice-Minister of Commerce and Industry, and a fifth Member oppointed by His Imperial Majesty.

Original Programme

In establishing the original work plan the Imperial Ethiopian Government and the World Bank wisely agreed to limit the first efforts to a selected system of primary roads so that there would be a concentration of effort. The completion of this initial network would provide a basis on which to build a future expanded system of highways that would extend into the heart of the provinces and provide direct service to the rich agricultural and mineral resources of the Empire. This initial primary system of roads consisted of the following routes:

Termini	Kilometres
Addis Ababa-Eritrean Border (Assab)	802.8
Addis Ababa-Jimma	335.0
Addis Ababa-Lekempti	331.4
Combolcia-Eritrean Border (via Adigrat)	554.8
Quiha-Makalle	10.7
Adigrat-Adi Abuna	103.0
Gorgora-Gondar	65.7
Gondar-Adi Abuna-Eritrean Border (Mareb Bridge)	414.1
Bishoftu-Nazareth-Awash Bridge	179.2
Erer-Dire Dawa	58.0
Dire Dawa-Jiggiga	160.0
Nazareth-Assela	76.3
Addis Ababa-Blue Nile	213.0
Blue Nile-Lake Tana	365.0
Modjio-Wondo-Adola	400.4
Wondo-Dilla	33.1
Irgalem Spur	5.9
Total	4,108.4

Upon the federation of Ethiopia and Eritrea, September 15th, 1952, a system of Federal roads in Eritrea was taken over by the Imperial Highway Authority for maintenance. An initial organisational appropriation of Eth.$ 75,000, plus a regular monthly budget of Eth.$ 48,000, were provided from the Treasury of the Imperial Ethiopian Government. In 1954 there was a supplemental appropriation of Eth.$ 300,000 for the repair of flood damage which occurred during the 1953 rainy season. The following Federal Roads were included:

Termini	*Kilometres*
Asmara-Massawa	115
Massawa-Archico (Shell Plant)	6
Asmara-Solcotom	152
Asmara-Mareb Bridge	115
Decamere-Nefasit	40
Asmara-Sabderat	392
Eritrean Border-Assab Airport	74
Total	894

Recently the 74 kilometres on the Assab Road from the Eritrean Border through the town of Assab to the Airport have been transferred from the Eritrean system, which is still under a separate and rather low maintenance budget, to the primary Ethiopian system. This was a practical change which enabled the regular highways maintenance crews working out of the Direct Headquarters at Combolcia to care for the portion of the Assab road in Eritrea, this section being isolated from and quite inaccessible to the remaining Federal roads in Eritrea which are handled from the District Office in Asmara.

Initial Problems

The first tasks of the Imperial Highway Authority were to staff the organisation, procure equipment, and undertake emergency repairs on the most critical sections of road in order to revive and free traffic, which was virtually at a standstill in 1951.

As referred to above, the Imperial Highway Authority inherited an extensive road system built by the Italians throughout Ethiopia, but this system had deteriorated to and beyond the point of complete disintegration over most of the system. Extensive slides and washouts cut the roads. The thin bituminous surface had deteriorated to a point where only the extremely rough Telford base was left on many sections. Continued use by trucks had caused base failure that frequently required trucks to unload and reload in order to get past a mud hole. During the rainy season trucks were often stuck in mud holes for two to three months at a time. So great was the need for transport service that trucks continued to travel on roads which were virtually impassable. The penalties were high rates for transportation and long delays.

The first basic problem which confronted the Imperial Highway Authority was that of providing adequate drainage for the heavy annual rainfall which is concentrated during the months of July, August and September

His Imperial Majesty laying cornerstone of one of the several
public structures of the post-liberation period

n most areas. This single word "drainage" means providing side ditches,
ateral furrow ditches and special drains to conduct surface water away
rom the road so as to keep its surface and base intact. It involves
also the repair, reconstruction, construction and maintenance of bridges,
culverts, retaining walls and similar structures. During the past four
years many millions of dollars of expensive structures of this character
have been restored to service and saved from imminent failure due to
basic design faults which in many cases involved wholly inadequate
foundations under existing culverts, bridges and retaining walls.

289

The second equally important problem, of more obvious interest to the travelling public, was the necessety for restoring road surfaces which not only had deteriorated but had completely disintegrated and disappeared on many sections of road. This problem was tackled by first strengthening and repairing base failures and holes which were encountered everywhere along most of the roads of the Empire. These holes trapped eight-ton trucks for days, weeks and even months at a time, and made the highways wholly impassable for passenger vehicles during the rainy season.

After repairing the underlying base, the surface was restored by one of three methods: (1) patching and sealing portions of the old bituminous surface which were still intact in 1951 and 1952; (2) constructing a new bituminous road-mixed surface course by crushing new hard stone and adding this material to existing base stone; and (3) constructing a new traffic-bound surface of crushed stone and selected material over sections where only the old, denuded, and very rough Telford base remained. These base and surface repairs were visible improvements which contributed to smoother riding, reduction in travel time, and less wear-and-tear on tyres and transport equipment. This is the type of improvement which the travelling public sees, feels, and appreciates.

Progress

On the 4,100-kilometre primary system approximately 330 kilometres of old bituminous surface have been salvaged by patching and sealing, with some additional patching only on other sections. At other selected locations, totalling about 165 kilometres, a new road-mixed bituminous surface has been constructed. In the main, however, the new surface material has consisted of traffic-bound crushed stone and selected material, approximately 2,370 kilometres of this type of improvement having been now completed. These improvements have resulted in striking benefit to highway transport during the past four years.

The 860 kilometres between Addis Ababa and Assab have been virtually completed. Trucks are making the run from Addis Ababa to Assab in two to two and a half days and are making the return trip from sea level to 8,000 feet in three days. Formerly it took two to three weeks in good weather.

While the rehabilitation of the Assab Road has been given top priority, the Authority has accomplished substantial improvements on the Lekempti and Jimma Roads. On the former, the 125-kilometre section to Ambo has been completed, and forces are now concentrating on the section between Ambo and Lekempti, which includes building a new road between Sire and Goute, 29 kilometres, where some Eth.$ 625,000 were expended during the third year for new structures. The section of road from Addis Ababa to kilometre 150, beyond Ambo, now has a relatively smooth surface, and can be traversed easily in three hours in a passenger vehicle.

The increasing importance of coffee shipments from Jimma warranted assignment of a high priority to this road. Equipment and personnel were concentrated here during the fourth year, and the reconstruction of this road is now virtually completed. Trucks now require one day for the trip from Jimma to Addis Ababa instead of five days or more before the road was improved. Passenger cars make the trip in six hours.

The maintenance work accomplished on other roads has greatly facilitated travel. Such roads as Gorgora-Eritrean border, Adi Abuna-Adigrat, Combolcia-Eritrean border, and Addis Ababa-Blue Nile, have been reopened to traffic. Slides have been removed, and are continuing to be removed, in the mountainous areas. Ditches, culverts and bridges have been cleaned, repaired and reconstructed. Base repairs have been made and holes filled. As much surfacing material as possible has been placed over rough sections of base, but long sections still remain to be surfaced when funds and time permit.

Organisation

When the operations of the Imperial Highway Authority began in 1951, initial efforts were directed entirely toward making improvements that would reopen the roads to traffic. These early efforts constituted what might be called the "reconstruction phase". As initial improvements were completed it became necessary to divert more and more equipment from large reconstruction projects, such as on the Assab and Jimma roads, to establith a maintenance organisaton, with many smaller crews, to "hold the line" and keep the roads already constructed from reverting to their former condition. During the fourth year, a major shift in forces and equipment was made from "construction" to "maintenance". The remaining "construction" forces are now concentrated on the uncompleted section between Ambo and Lekempti.

The regular maintenance of the 4,100-kilometre primary network is handled from six District Headquarters under the direction of six Dictrict Engineers. Each District organisation consists of a small administrative and clerical staff, a service unit consisting of a central garage and machine shop at the District's Headquarters, and a number of separate maintenance crews along the highways.

The value of good roads

The need for an adequate system of roads and the dependence of the Empire on such a system is often taken for granted by planners, economists and engineers, for it is true that the life and development of any community, province or nation are intimately tied to transport and communications. The economic necessity for a good road system is quite obvious to everyone, who gives thought to the matter. Highway improvements already made have resulted in very substantial reductions in the cost of transporting goods, as will be mentioned later.

Additional improvements and the extension of good roads into agricultural areas will result in further reductions in transport costs. This will stimulate the greater production of agricultural products for export and will bring back to Ethiopia foreign currencies that will make possible further developments in such fields as transportation, communications, education and public health. During this past year when world coffee prices were depressed below those which existed in previous years, the improved condition of the highways in Ethiopia made it possible for Ethiopia's coffee to reach world markets at prices which insured ready sale. Without the benefits of the improved highways, and lower transport costs from the coffee producing areas to the seaports, much of Ethiopia's coffee would have remained on the trees during this past year, with consequent stifling of production incentive and serious damage to the Empire's economy.

An extensive and well-maintained road system not only benefits the Empire economically, but socially and politically as well. Good roads afford an opportunity for the inhabitants of one community or province to visit friends and neighbours in other areas, to exchange cultural ideas of mutual benefit to all citizens, and to understand and appreciate more fully their fellow-countrymen. Free economic and social intercourse welds political unity which comes with greater understanding among separate communities and with ready access to the several seats of government for all citizens. This access is a two-way channel which also enables government officials and administrators to reach, understand, the citizens of the Empire, and to effectively carry out their duties and responsibilities.

The quantities of motor fuel imported and consumed annually is one index of the recent increase in motor travel and motor transport. For the five years 1948—1952 the average importation of gasoline (petrol) was about 8,100 tons annually. The figure for 1953 was 16,500 tons, and for 1954, 18,700 tons, an increase of 13 % over the 1948—1952 average. Similarly, the importation of diesel fuel averaged approximately 11,000 tons annually during the period 1948 to 1952, and jumped to 23,900 tons in 1953 and 32,100 tons in 1954.

Studies have shown that reduction in hauling rates, primarily due to improvement of the Addis Ababa-Assab Road, both by highway to Assab and by the competing railroad to Jibuti, resulted in a saving of about Eth.$ 4,000,000 in 1954 on the transport of exports and imports. This saving was computed by comparing 1954 hauling rates and tonnages from Addis Ababa to Assab and Jibuti with 1951 rates. This substantial saving in one single year, which undoubtedly will be much greater in future years, may be compared with an average annual expenditure of Eth.$ 2,800,000 per year, during the past four years, for reconstruction and maintenance on the 860 kilometres of road between Addis Ababa and Assab.

This is but one striking example of the economic benefits to be derived from an improved highway system.

Bus Transportation

In 1951 there was very little transportation of persons. Some trucks carried passengers as supercargo, limited to five people per truck. A small bus line operated near Dire Dawa, and a bus made the trip from Addis Ababa to Asmara once a month. The general conditions of highway transportation were characterised by high cost, long weeks and even months en route, and heavy damage to equipment caused by incredibly rough roads, detours and washouts. With the free movement of truck-transportation on the main roads throughout the Empire, it is gratifying to see an increase in the movement of people. Per capita income, for Ethiopia normally does not permit the purchase of an automobile for personal transportation by a large number of the people. However, the Central Ethiopian Transport Company is now operating the following regular round-trip schedules, with capacity loads:

Addis Ababa—Fitche		Twice daily
,,	,, Debra Markos	Twice weekly
,,	,, Guhazion (beyond Debra Markos)	Twice weekly
,,	,, Ambo	Twice daily
,,	,, Lekempti	Three times per week
,,	,, Wolliso	Twice daily
,,	,, Wolkitte	Twice daily
,,	,, Jimma	Daily
,,	,, Debra Berhan	Daily
,,	,, Debra Sina	Four times weekly
,.	,, Adwa	Twice weekly
,,	,, Asmara	Weekly
.,	,, Shashamanna	Twice daily
,,	,, Neghelli	Weekly
,,	,, Soddu	Weekly
,,	,, Alaba (Soddu Road)	Weekly
,,	,, Butagira (Soddu Road)	Twice weekly

In addition to these regularly scheduled buses of reasonably modern design, there is a great number of individually owned or group operated truck-buses and jeep and land-rover buses operating throughout the Empire.

Future Plans

On February 28th, 1955, the Imperial Highway Authority celebrated its fourth Birthday. Arrangements have been completed for the U.S. Bureau of Public Roads to continue in responsible charge of the management for another two years. Activities are to be confined to the initially approved 4,100-kilmetre (2,550-mile) primary system, plus the 894 kilometres in Eritrea.

As improvements to this system are completed it is anticipated that there will be extensions to include other primary routes and to connect with a system of secondary or feeder roads designed to serve all of the rich agricultural areas, mineral deposits and market centres of the vast Empire. The development of such a system cannot be attained in a few months

293

or years. It will be accomplished through a sustained long range programme. The Board of Commissioners and the management of the Imperial Highway Authority are now actively engaged in making studies, establishing priorities, and developing a programme for the further extension of the primary network and the development of a system of secondary roads. It is expected that these studies and plans will lead to the adoption of a new large scale highway improvement programme by the Imperial Ethiopian Government. Such a programme will involve difficult problems of finance, yet to be solved.

Ethiopia is entering an era in which the impact of highway transport will change the lives and habits of the entire population. The Imperial Ethiopian Government has recognised and is meeting the challenge that is presented by the need for an improved and extended highway system. Real advances have been made in the past four years but these improvements will be merely stepping stones for future accomplishments which ultimately will provide convenient and ready access to every community, farm, school, church and home in the Empire.

In addition to the Franco-Ethiopian Railway, the Imperial Highway Authority, the Baro River waterway System, as discussed in the chapter "Ethiopia and the Air Age", the Imperial Ethiopian Government included civil aviation to serve her transportation interests. Complementary to the Ethiopian Air Lines and as well supplementary to it, the Civil Aviation Department was established, attached to the Ministry of Public Works and Communications. Charged with the technical and economic administration, regulation and control of civil aviation in the Empire, this department fills an important need in Ethiopia which entered the air age during His Majesty the Emperor's reign. Such functions as establishing a meteorological service, providing radio and navigational aids, the construction of airports throughout the land, negotiating and signing international air agreements and training Ethiopians in civil aviation techniques and practices are the responsibilities of the Department of Civil Aviation Bilateral agreements facilitating the operations of the National Carrier (the Ethiopian Air Lines) have been signed with Pakistan, Egypt, Greece and Netherlands, and those with the United Kingdom and Yemen are now being negotiated.

It seems necessary here to note some of the important civil aviation accomplishments so far. Under the auspices of the Department and in co-operation with the Ethiopian Air Lines, there are to-day twenty-four aerodromes in Ethiopia, fifteen of which are regularly operated by the Ethiopian Air Lines. Four of these — Addis Ababa, Asmara, Assab and Dire Dawa — are international airports. Extensive survey by a British consulting firm has been undertaken in the vicinity of Addis Ababa to determine a more suitable site for Ethiopia's main international air terminal in the capital. Growing out of studies made by the technical division of the Department of Civil Aviation, a contract for the construction of the new air field with cement alongside the present runway at Dire Dawa has been awarded to a Norwegian construction company. Work has begun and completion is anticipated within a year. A project for the

294

construction of an air field in Harar is under study and the Asmara airport is being improved for international use. Alternative airports at Awash and Massawa are used for refueling stops to relieve the effect of high altitude.

The future programme for extension and development of an airport network throughout Ethiopia calls for fifteen all-weather runways. The planning, construction, maintenance and the inspection of airports are among the functions of the engineering section of the Department. An aeronautical information service and a committee of inspection are now being formed. International Civil Aviation Organisation Annexes are

The Blue Nile which rises in the Ethiopian mountains cuts its way through to neighbouring territory

strictly followed in civil air operations in the country; Ethiopia, however, being mostly a highland, calls for special techniques.

The rapid progress made in aviation throughout the world and the growing dependence on this means of transportation, both in times of peace and war, has influenced extensive training here in this highly technical field. Upon His Imperial Majesty's initiative, the Department of Civil Aviation introduced a civil aviation training programme to fit Ethiopia to share in the responsibilities of the air age.

Up to five years ago but a handful of Ethiopian nationals was employed in responsible positions in the civil aviation services of the country. The Imperial Ethiopian Government discussed with ICAO the possibility of

295

participation in the United Nations' technical assistance programme. Early in 1951 seventy young men were recruited from the secondary schools to be trained in a civil aviation school which was then established. An ICAO mission consisting of a head of mission and experts has been operating here since.

The school, based on the on-the-job training policy, has been functioning since with gratifying results. Even early in their courses the seventy boarding-students began to contribute to the various aviation services of the country. Some students in meteorology completed observer training by mid 1952 and were assigned to the provinces to set up weather stations from which three-hourly reports by radio are transmitted to the main station at the Addis Ababa airport. These reports are amalgamated by trained Ethiopian meteorologists aided by students of the school and then sent out on the international radio circuits for use by world aviation. Incoming reports are also decoded by the students who are also taught to plot the information on a synoptic map and to forecast the weather. New classes for meteorological observers are opened annually. At present there are sixty-five observers trained by the Civil Aviation School with an immediate goal of one hundred which is estamined as a reasonable number for the service. To secure economy in personnel, meteorological observers are also trained as radio operators to provide in the provinces persons qualified for both fields.

Radio communications including electronics and radio maintenance are taught. Twenty students are studying aeroengines and airframes, spending half their time in class work and the other half in on-the-job training with the Ethiopian Air Lines. With regard to air traffic services, through ICAO co-operation an expert in air traffic control and radio operation has been provided who gives instruction in civil air operations. Air traffic controllers so trained will serve both Ethiopian's civil and military aviation.

The training of civil air personnel has not been confined only to the Civil Aviation School. Five Ethiopian pilots who received initial training in the Imperial Ethiopian Airforce Training Centre, under the ICAO scheme, received a one and a half year's course as air line pilots abroad. Together with three other pilots from the Imperial Airforce who were given airline conversion training by the Ethiopian Air Lines, they have been absorbed into the pilot ranks of the National Carrier.

Fellowships for advanced training in aviation fields have been awarded to Ethiopian personnel by the U.S. Foreign Operations Mission and the International Civil Aviation Organisation. For instance, under FAO fellowships, two Ethiopians are studying meteorology; three, radio maintenance; and two, aircraft maintenance in the United States. The students have benefited by ICAO fellowships abroad, one each in meteorology and radio maintenance, whilst one in the latter field is studying radio engineering in London under the auspices of the British Council.

The Franco-Ethiopian Railway Company (Compagnie du Chemin de Fer Franco-Ethiopien de Djibouti) extends from the capital to Jibuti, French Somaliland. Built by French capital, the construction of the railway started in 1897 and was completed in 1917. It serves Ethiopia only. The foreign and internal trade of Ethiopia are its only *raison d'être*. There is substantially no traffic handled for French Somaliland or for elsewhere than Ethiopia. It is meter-gauge, 784 kilometres long, with single-track line on steel cross-ties. It crosses very little built up, cultivated, or otherwise valuable land and thus obviates the need for right-of-way fencing. The use of rather high maximum grades and sharp curves makes practicable the use of a profile line (i.e. a line which lies on or near the surface of the ground), and requires relatively few heavy cuts or expensive engineering works. The general maintenance of the line is good. The maintenance of equipment was difficult during the war years and no new equipment was available during that time by purchase or otherwise. Practically no spare parts, stores or space tools were then available. Operating equipment was maintained on a day to day basis. The personnel for maintenance and operation was sufficient in numbers but lacked trained men for mechanical supervisory and administrative positions.

To deal with the considerable increase in traffic since that time, additional equipment, stores and tools and some additional trained personnel have been supplied. No great amount of increased construction was required, but some new rails have been laid and some bridges rebuilt, including the Awash bridge.

Since the railway serves only Ethiopia it ought to be of interest to note the progressive increase of commercial tonnage from 1930 to 1953, excluding the war-occupation-liberation period. With 89,617 tons in 1930, in 1946, when the Ethiopian economy began to regain normalcy, it rose to 162,665 and in 1953 the commercial tonnage stood at 303,933 tons.

The property is essentially an economically located railroad which serves as a carrier of agricultural products from mid-Ethiopia to the deepwater port of Jibuti and of miscellaneous imports in the other direction. It has not developed major related or subsidiary interests or activities. It is the only railroad that serves Ethiopia, exclusive of Eritrea.

The extent by which the actual length of line exceeds the airline distance between the principal control points is shown by the following table:

Section	Jibuti to Dire Dawa	Dire Dawa to Addis Ababa
Railway length	311 km.	474 km.
Airline distance	262 km.	347 km.
Excess of railway length over airline distance	18.7 %	36.3 %

From Dire Dawa to Awash a considerable amount of grain is brought each year to the railway for shipment, but all of this is from the plateau 15 miles or more to the south. There is very little cultivation close to the railway.

The Eritrean Railway is operated by the Government. It consists of 306 kilometres of track, largely one way traffic, from Massawa up the 7,000 feet escarpment to Asmara and thence to Keren and Agordat, with a road link from Agordat to the Sudan border at Tessenei. It operates both diesel car passenger services and steam passenger and cargo services, carrying about 500,000 passengers and 120,000 tons of goods annually. The track has been maintained in good order but the rolling stock and equipment are in need of modernisation. There is also a ropeway from Massawa to Asmara, but it has not been in operation for some years.

Within the functions of the Ministry of Public Works and Communications also falls the authority to supervise the construction of edifices and buildings. "The Minister of Communications and Public Works shall engage the necessary workmen and technicians, undertake authorised Government construction and repair work and enter into necessary contracts whether by tender or otherwise; shall supervise contracts to be entered into by other Ministries for authorised works and certify that the proposed expenditure is necessary and reasonable."

After the liberation and the revival of this Ministry, the execution of its duties and responsibilities, so far as buildings generally are concerned, presented some problems. Construction materials and technicians were not in ample supply, and the mode of building and architectural transition was rather unsettled in the early post-liberation years. The buildings and construction which fell directly under the Ministry were to be found in the towns and centres where Government agencies were installed. For instance, in the capital the repair of the Palace, the reconstruction of the Parliament building, the repair of schools, hospitals, military buildings, including the Ministry of War, the National Library, the construction of the new buildings for Public Works and Public Health, etc., were among the first projects tackled.

In the ensuing years the erection of monuments in such places as at Axum where the old Mary of Tsion Church has been restored; at Adwa where a monument commemorating the 1896 victory has been laid; the several monuments in the capital; the Abbai bridge; and other construction work of a national character has been executed.

It developed, however, that some of the Government agencies, like the Ministries of Finance and Education and the Addis Ababa Municipality created their own works and architectural departments charged with carrying forward their own programme. These did not usurp the authority of the Ministry of Public Works and Communications but were complementary to it.

All architects, engineers and contractors must by law be registered with the Ministry by which the rules governing construction have been worked out and laid down. The standard of building materials is also a Public Works Ministry responsibility. All plans for any major construction projects stand to benefit by the examination of the experts of the Ministry who readily supply the required data. In this way the Ministry of Public Works and Communications exercises an overall supervision in the type of buildings and building construction carried out in the Empire.

Authorities believe that historical architecture in Ethiopia could be divided into three main periods: the Axumite style, developed contemporaneously with that of Ancient Greece with which it exhibits some

298

affinity. The early mediaeval period represented by a number of churches of which records exist. The third historical style shows the influence of the Portuguese Jesuit Mission of the Seventeenth Century which was invited by Emperor Libna Dingal. There seems to be, therefore, very much background to assist in arriving at a standard present-day Ethiopian architectural style. The architecture of the last twenty years has been somewhat influencel by the rapid if unsubstantial building programme of the occupiers between 1936 and 1941. This has made the present type varied, both in quality and in style. The cold climate of the plateau has led to the development of a type of building which is not far different from its counterpart in Europe. Before the Italian invasion the influence was predominantly late Nineteenth Century French — of this the façade of the railway station in Addis Ababa is a good example. This style could be seen in a picturesque local variant in the numerous two or even three-storey town houses with their lower flat built in masonry and the upper with overhanging balconies in wood and mud plaster. Here of late, however, and particularly in the capital, a building boom has been going on, the majority of the houses being of the villa or chateau type.

There is no dearth of the primary elements for the manufacture of building and construction materials in Ethiopia. It is known that the mineral possibilities of the country have not been exploited. The cement factory in Dire Dawa, tile and brick factories in Addis Ababa and its suburbs indicate a trend toward the possibility of development of a building and construction material industry. Until such industries are developed to the extent that these products can be put on the market at a price reasonable enough to accord with the earning power index of the masses, a general type of Ethiopian architecture, particularly for houses in the low income bracket will be delayed. Through His Imperial Majesty's encouragement possibilities to meet this important need are taking shape.

Two of the hostesses of the E.A.L.

CHAPTER 26

Ethiopia in the Air Age

Among the several delegations that represented their respective countries in the coronation ceremony in 1930 was one from the United States of America. Assigned by the Emperor to accompany the U.S. delegation, during their visit, was Ras Gugsa, the then Governor of Tigré Province. In a casual reference, an eye-witness of the coronation ceremonies remarked that "it took as long for Ras Gugsa to reach Addis Ababa from his isolated province as for the American Mission to get there from New York!"

This casual, but exaggerated friendly remark is pregnant with significance. Like Tigré, 800 kilometres (500 miles) from Addis Ababa, outlying parts of this extensive Empire were virtually isolated from one another and from the capital, then. Communications were difficult, except for the Franco-Ethiopian Railway established by Menelik II which traversed the northeasterly section through the province of Harar to the Port of Jibuti. Mules, horses or camels were the only available means of carriage connecting the capital to the vast hinterland of the Empire. Even their capacity was limited by the rugged terrain of the land of mountains, rivers and ravines.

Not these internal barriers alone. The Ethiopian plateau, studded with peaks stretching at points as high as 17,000 feet into the sky, rises abruptly from the wastes of equatorial Africa. The surrounding belt of wilderness for centuries had isolated Ethiopia from the rest of the world.

This isolation, today, is a thing of the past. Thanks to the Ethiopian Air Lines, Inc. (EAL), that owes its birth to the initiative of Emperor Haile Selassie I, provinces like Tigré that took days to reach in pre-Coronation days, are now but hours' flight from Addis Ababa. Ethiopia is no longer the impenetrable mountain land that it was. The air routes thrown open by the EAL, over the mountain peaks and across unbridged rivers and unbridgeable gorges, connect Ethiopia to every part of the world.

Prior to April 1946, when the EAL was born, travellers to Ethiopia by aerial navigation were few. Rare visitors by air were officials fortunate enough to obtain priority on the services of the British Overseas Airways Corporation, which were restricted here by the demands of war upon their aircraft. The war then was still going on in Europe and the Far East. Previous to this, there never existed regular air transportation facilities to Ethiopia. Such stray instances as the arrival by plane of the Duke of Gloucester, to represent His Britannic Majesty King George V at the Imperial Coronation here in 1930, were events looked upon as out of the ordinary. His Royal Highness's plane landed on an air-strip provided by the spacious grounds of the British Legation in Addis Ababa. It was a sensation of the first magnitude to thousands of people who watched the first Ethiopian Government aircraft fly over Addis Ababa on August 13th, 1928.

Up to April 1946, passengers had to come through the Red Sea port of Jibuti, taking the railway terminating at Addis Ababa. As against the eight hours' flight to Cairo and three to Nairobi from Addis Ababa, as at present, seven to ten day's plodding was the lot of travellers then.

The Establishment of E.A.L.

At the invitation of His Imperial Majesty, a Technical Mission from the United States visited Ethiopia in 1944, to study and report on ways and means to rehabilitate the war-devastated country. Among its findings was recognition of the urgent, imperative need to increase the transport facilities. The over-worked, 500-mile long, Addis-to-Jibuti railway stood in need of other supplementary means of transporting persons and goods to the main centres. In the absence of adequate roads and highways, aerial transportation offered the most practicable solution.

In the spring of 1945, an Aviation Commission headed by General Wilson Middle-East General Director of the Trans World Airlines (TWA) of America, visited Ethiopia. This led to the conclusion of a contract between the Imperial Ethiopian Government and the TWA on September 8, 1945, for the establishment of an airline of Ethiopia, in Ethiopia. The TWA was to supply the management and technical assistance, including air crews for an initial period of seven years. This period has since been extended. The Government put forward an authorised capital of Ethiopian Dollars 2,500,000 (equivalent to Sterling Pounds 357,429, equal to U.S. Dollars one million). Six Douglas C-47 cargo planes and a supply of spare parts were purchased. Thus was born the Ethiopian Air Lines, Inc. (EAL)—the Government-owned, first national airline of Ethiopia.

The planes were bought from the surplus stock of the American Army. The arrival of the first lot of five aircraft in the country was considered as a historic event, with all the concomitant joy and pride of the man on the street and a legitimate feeling of gratification by the Government at the achievement under His Imperial Majesty's guidance. The extended Addis Ababa air-port, in proper trim for the occasion, received that Friday morning of February 1, 1946, the units that bore the name, "ETHIOPIAN AIR LINES INC.—The Wonderland Route," in bold letters on the flanks along with the insignia of the "Lion of Judah" and the national flag painted in its three colours of green, yellow and red—all proudly announcing that here at last were some airliners that Ethiopia could call her own.

A large gathering of people, including cabinet ministers, high-ranking civil and military officials and members from the diplomatic corps, filled the available space at the air-port to welcome the Douglas C-47 units that were to constitute the nucleus of the EAL fleet. Douglas C-47's, for over two decades now, have proved reliable and safe in the United States, Europe, South America, China and many other countries. They were used throughout all theaters of war by the Allies, and proved their worth.

The primary object of the EAL, as stated at the outset, was to serve the

301

country internally. In order to stimulate interest among the population local flights in and around Addis Ababa were conducted in the beginning The enthusiasm evinced was above expectation and regular flights were organised. So striking was the popular response that it was decided, after only two months' trial, to initiate flight services to foreign countries. The first of the regular flights beyond the national boundaries commenced on April 8th, 1946. The large-sized Douglas Sky-train took off from Addis Ababa and landed in Cairo after eight hours in the air, except for a brief stop-over in Asmara, Eritrea.

Two months afterwards — on June 6th, 1946 to be precise — a scheduled weekly flight to Jibuti, French Somaliland, was commenced. Soon thereafter, this route was extended to Aden, touching Dire Dawa and Jibuti With the beginning so well made, attention now was switched over to the development of services within Ethiopia, in addition to the opening of a service to Nairobi, Kenya.

Three of the aircraft, converted into De Luxe type DC-3's were put in commission in the autumn of 1947, maintaining regular connections between Cairo, Asmara, Addis Ababa and Nairobi. Thus, Ethiopia, with its own airline, was offering first class air transportation between Egypt and East Africa, specifically providing regular services from Ethiopia to these points.

The inauguration of direct connection to Athens, Greece, in April 1954 was another landmark in the history of EAL. The frequencies have been increased to four flights per week on two different routes, namely, Addis-Asmara-Cairo-Athens and Addis-Khartoum-Wadi Halfa-Athens.

It has from the beginning been the policy and objective of the EAL to provide the maximum in comfort, dependability and performance for its passengers. In the nine years of its existence, this policy has been fully implemented. Conversion of the above mentioned three Douglas aeroplanes by the Scottish Aviation Company in Prestwick, Scotland, provided aircraft as fine as any in their class. The 21-seater planes, with comfortable reclining seats, had two of the seats removed to provide more luggage space for the convenience of the passengers. A steward (hostess) is a member of the flying crew to attend to the passengers with a courtesy, diligence and efficiency that conforms to the highest standard set up anywhere in the world. Hot coffee, tea, lunches, drinks and other refreshments are served in flight.

In keeping with this policy of providing comfort, speed and dependable performance, it was decided in the early part of 1949 to purchase new equipment. Two Convairs-240's, the world famous product of Consolidated Vultee Aircraft Corporation of San Diego, California, were placed into scheduled operation on January 15th, 1951. These twin-engined, low-wing transport planes have been specially provided with "Jato" (jet-assisted take-off), the EAL being the first airline using Convairs to install "Jato" as standard equipment. The Convair Liners incorporate many of the most modern features of design, performance and comfort in use. Spacious cabins provide room for 40 comfortable chairs. The cabin is attractively arranged and lined with material that keeps out much of the sound of the

ngines. Equipped with loud-speaker system, passengers may listen to
ews broadcasts, music and announcements by the Captain. In addition,
here is the luxury of cabin pressurization. Large engine-driven, air com-
ressor pumps draw in the thin cold air at high flying altitudes. They pass
he clean cool air through heaters that bring it up to comfortable temper-
ture. The air is pumped into the sealed, air tight cabin until the pressure
n the cabin is equal to the atmospheric pressure that exists at altitudes
everal thousand feet below the smooth cruising flight of the airplane.
Accurate automatic controls operate valves and heaters to maintain both
ressure and temperature at desired values. Measuring 91 feet 9 inches

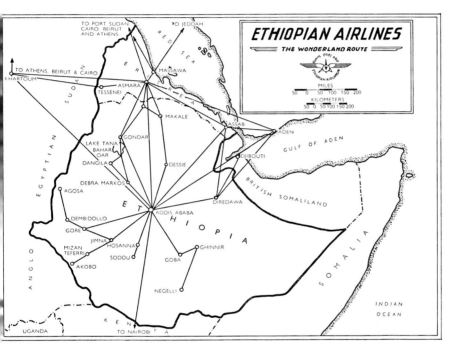

rom wing tip to the tails, weighing 41,790 lbs. when loaded with passen-
jers, mail, cargo and gasoline, this giant carrier has a top speed of 512
ilometres per hour (307 m.p.h.) and the amazing capacity, for a transport
lane, to climb to 25.000 feet on two engines! The acquisition of these
Convairs has enhanced the prestige of the EAL as the one providing the
inest service ever flown between Cairo and East Africa.
While this improvement in international flights continued, great strides
vere also taken towards providing the best possible transportation system
o internal Ethiopia. With this end in view, the EAL built new fields,
nstalled its own communications system, and at the same time, and in spite
f rising costs, brought down rates and fares to an absolute minimum
Today, the net-work of scheduled operation embraces twenty-three air

303

fields within Ethiopia. Many of these fields, such as Goba, Ghinner, Misan Tafari, Magi and Hosana are almost inaccessible by any other means of modern transportation.

Utmost safety is ensured by installation of EAL's own point-to-point and air-to-ground communication system, for the control of the flow of traffic as well as the actual control of the aircraft at any point throughout Ethiopia. After two years of operation experience and steady introduction of improved devices, it was decided to do away with the normal communication system then in use in Europe, the Middle East and Africa. It was decided to dispense with radio operators, transmitting Morse Code, and to rely on voice communication exclusively. Now, Radio Operators have been excluded from internal flights, and pilots carry on their direct communication by radio telephone with the ground stations at all times.

Each year since the beginning of operations in 1946, new routes and new stations have been added to the EAL's internal network. The planned expansion programme has as its objective the gradual linking of Addis Ababa and every important community in Ethiopia where facilities exist for the preparing of an air-port. Today twenty-three communities in the Empire, including Eritrea, are inter-connected and served. The number of flights has been gradually increased on the more important internal routes. There is at present a daily service operating between Addis Ababa and Jimma, the chief coffee growing centre of Ethiopia. A total of eleven flights is in operation on the Addis Ababa/Dire Dawa sector as part of the international route to the Red Sea ports of Jibuti and Aden. Other routes with less volume of traffic but with none the less need for air communication have their frequencies of service related accordingly. For instance, one station — Neghelli — needs air service but does not need it more frequently than once a month. On other routes, there are two or more services per week according to the demand.

Having spared no pains to make the flight operations the best possible, the EAL concentrated on another department essential for the successful and efficient operation of the airline—maintenance facilities for the inspection repair and overhaul of aircraft and accessories. During the early months of the operation of the new-born airline, reliance was placed on TWA's maintenance shops in Cairo for major inspection and maintenance work. This was not only expensive but also entailed the loss of considerable airplane time. The next logical step was the establishment in Addis Ababa of the minimum requirements for service, maintenance and inspection. The EAL set up shops and facilities for everything except the major overhaul of aircraft engines and the larger accessories.

By the end of 1949, three aircraft that needed overhauling had to be sent to the Scottish Aviation Company in Scotland, the nearest facility then available. When the fourth one was ready for major overhaul, it was the proud privilege of the EAL's workshops in Addis Ababa to handle the job. Since then the progress has been so marked that Addis Ababa could accomplish such important operations as air frame overhaul and even technically complicated modifications of aircraft configuration. The only practical consideration against setting up an engine overhaul shop here

304

An ancient castle of Gondar, one of the oldest cities of the Ethiopian Empire

was the limited number of engines, which would not justify the equipment and maintenance of such a shop. As a result, engines are still sent abroad for overhaul. As the EAL operations continue to grow and as more airplanes are acquired, it will be found economically feasible to erect the shop and set up equipment for engine overhaul.

After perfecting the arrangements for flight operations and aircraft maintenance, attention was paid to the organisation and staffing of other departments. The complicated nature of airline accounting called for special, detailed training of personnel for the Accounts Department. Then followed the organisation of a Sales Department to sell the air transportation that the EAL was now in a position to offer in increasing volume to the business and travelling public. Personnel were employed and trained for duty at airport stations to handle loading, unloading, clearance and despatch of flights. The next to be created was a Food Service Department to handle

305

preparation of inflight food service and other passenger service facilities, running its own kitchen and purchasing its own food supplies. A Purchasing Department came into being to handle purchase, shipping, storing and issue of everything that an airline needs—from paper napkins to aircraft engines. The EAL now holds a stock of materials running into 14,000 items and amounting to a value of Eth. $840,000.00.

It had been the avowed policy of the EAL, when it engaged the supervisory and technical assistance of the TWA, that in due course of time, and by gradual process, the staff should be completely Ethiopianised. Remarkable has been the achievement in this direction during the past decade of EAL's history. In 1955, 415 Ethiopian employees are in the service of the EAL, many of them holding responsible supervisory positions. To name a few, the Director of Accounting in the Treasury Department, the Assistant Director of Accounting and the Supervisors of the sections of the Accounting Department, the Station Managers and District Sales Managers at all stations within Ethiopia (excepting Addis Ababa and Asmara), District Sales Manager in Addis Ababa, Supervisors of the City Ticket Offices and the Reservations Office—are all Ethiopians who have proved themselves to be second to none in their jobs. As an illustration of the importance of the positions held by these young men, mention may be made of the duties of one who is a Senior Flight Despatcher in the Operations Department. He has the responsibility for clearance and despatch of all aircraft movements in the air in Ethiopia, while on duty. He must maintain up-to-the-minute knowledge of position and routing of aircraft, weather conditions, status of radio aids and communication facilities and any other data pertinent to safe and efficient flight operation.

In the Stores Department, the supervisors in charge of all sections are Ethiopian personnel who, with the last few years' training, have proved themselves square to their posts. They have given evidence of possessing a good working knowledge of the intricate business of airline provisioning and supply. Young trainees in aircraft maintenance are bidding fair to be rated as master mechanics. Three junior aircraft mechanics have been sent to the United States for two years of advanced training on scholarships sponsored by the U.S. Point 4 (International Technical Co-operation) organisation. The Radio Operators in charge of the 11 radio stations operated by the EAL are Ethiopians who have received most of their training and experience in the service of the airline.

Seven Ethiopian First Officers have acquired knowledge and experience, in flight operations, that have put them on the road to qualify as airline captains. The senior pilot in this batch has started his captain check-out training. Four out of a total of six Flight Radio Operators are Ethiopians. Among the flight hostesses, three are Ethiopian girls. More are under training to fill the cadre. Five Flight Attendants, employed for local and international flights, are all Ethiopians.

In the enthusiasm and quick grasp of work of this corps of Ethiopian personnel lies the hope of early fulfilment of the policy of Ethiopianising the entire staff of the Ethiopian Air Lines.

For the steady implementation of this policy, of providing adequate on-

Ethiopian Air Lines Convairs on the station ramp at Addis Ababa Airport

he-job and in the classroom training, the EAL has established its own raining department. Training ranges from review of mathematics and English and elementary physics to the construction and operation of an aircraft instrument. The Civil Aviation School conducted by the Civil Aviation Department of the Government, is doing yeoman service. The Technical College in Addis Ababa turns out young men educated in the mechanical sciences who constitute excellent material for training in aircraft maintenance and engineering. The Commercial School graduates are found to be useful assets to the clerical and accounting cadres of the EAL. Suitable graduates from the University College of Addis Ababa and from colleges abroad are looked upon as future candidates for initiation into the managerial positions of the EAL.

The TWA has extended its co-operation, in the matter of training, by making arrangements on a share expense basis for taking groups of Ethiopian employees on familiarisation trips through TWA offices in Europe and the U.S.A. Four groups of employees have already benefitted from such trips.

The EAL's fleet of 10 planes consists of two Convair 240, three Douglas DC-3's and five cargo type carriers. With Addis Ababa as the nerve centre, the ramification of the EAL routes stretches to many points of Ethiopia. The map on page 303 is highly illustrative.

As at June of the current year (1955), the EAL is operating 3,750 unduplicated route miles on its internal system. On its international route pattern—which includes service to Nairobi, Jibuti, Aden, Khartoum, Port Sudan, Cairo and Athens—its flight covers 9.504 unduplicated route mileage. From a humble beginning of one schedule per week to Cairo and a few flights internally, the EAL today boasts a schedule of 84 flights per week, flying an average of 210,000 miles per month. Since its beginning, it has flown approximately 14 million airplane miles with a fortunate record of no accident involving any casualty. Eloquently illustrative of the progress of the EAL are the following tables showing the increasing air miles and passenger miles and sound financial position.

Each year the airline's air miles have increased over the year before. The following table shows the steady progress that has been attained.

Description	1948	1949	1950	
Revenue passengers carried	12,486	16,937	22,347	
Revenue freight carried kgs.	1,312,393	2,423,949	3,065,979	
Revenue passenger miles	6,212,995	8,989,307	9,782,022	
Revenue freight ton miles	409,498	957,290	1,089,852	
Airplane miles flown	938,245	1,265,830	1,305,725	
	1951	1952	1953	1954
Revenue passengers carried	36,795	40,806	58,603	66,02C
Revenue freight carried kgs.	3,823,590	3,365,765	5,168,607	4.570,518
Revenue passenger miles	16,099,506	17,765,005	18,869,520	25,721,798
Revenue freight ton miles	1,132,273	1,115,257	1,443,631	1,431,654
Airplane miles flown	1,606,755	1,632,655	2,006,970	2,287,08C

The airline has during the course of its history, managed to operate within its own revenues. It has not received moneys in the form of a direct subsidy from the Imperial Ethiopian Government. The Government has given substantial assistance to the airline for the purchase of aircraft but it has required the airline to pay for all its operating expenses out of its revenues. The following table furnishes a picture of the airline's financial performance beginning with the year 1946:

	Operating Revenue Eth. $	Operating Expense Eth. $	Operating Profit (Loss) Eth. $	Non-Operating Net Eth. $	Net Profi (Loss) Eth. $
1946	1,106,344	1,703,979	(597,635)	—	(597,635)
1947	3,012,481	3,663,086	(650,605)	(333,291)	(983,896)
1948	3,081,746	2,948,557	133,189	(234,505)	(101,316)
1949	3,956,799	3,656,581	300,218	(148,183)	152,035
1950	3,675,027	3,523,908	151,119	34,787	185,906
1951	5,156,723	5,658,888	(502,164)	53,670	(448,464)
1952	5,586,215	6,278,213	(691,998)	64,821	(627,178)
1953	6,413,099	6,760,325	(347,226)	25,675	(321,551)
1954	7,900,492	7,652,055	248,437	143,845	392,282

The losses shown for some of the years have amounted to less than the reserve charged to depreciation of aircraft and equipment.

308

The Tchis Isat Falls, one of the natural beauty spots of the Ethiopian landscape

EAL is a member of the Multilateral Interline Traffic Agreement sponsored by the International Air Transport Association, thereby participating, with 65 other major airlines of the world, in the interchange of ticketing and reservations facilities. Under the agreement, an EAL ticket bought in Addis Ababa is good for travel to any part of the world. The General Sales Manager of EAL attends the annual conventions of International Air Travel Agents—a convenient forum for familiarising the leading travel agents with Ethiopia. EAL is a member of the Red Sea Operators Conference. With all these connections, EAL has come to be reckoned as a most modern airline of international repute.

The decade past has seen substantial progress in the commercial and technical phase of the EAL's activity. Even greater progress has been made in the extent to which the airline has become closely integrated in the political, social and cultural life of the Empire. It has brought even the remote provinces of the 350,00 square mile country within convenient travel time from Addis Ababa. It has helped to extend the direct and beneficent influence of His Imperial Majesty's Government in steadily expanding circles across the land. A greater number of people have been given the opportunity to see and hear their Emperor. The establishment of new schools, missions, medical centres, police posts and communication stations has been greatly facilitated by the transportation services provided by the EAL. Emperor Menelik has been recorded in history as the unifier of the Empire by bringing different parts under a central regime. It has been the proud achievement of Emperor Haile Selassie I to consolidate this unification and to maintain the Empire as a well-knit unit by means of the most modern of communications—namely, air transportation.

CHAPTER 27

Posts and Telecommunications

It is beyond question that communication is the life blood of civilised communal, national and international contacts. By reason of improved methods in this vital social field, the nations of the world have become next door neighbours. Distance has been inconceivably shrunken and time does not any longer constitute an agent of delay.

Menelik II, after instituting the programme for national unity, sought to make his country share in modern communications. It was he who originally instituted the Ethiopian postal and telecommunications system.

The Ministry of Posts, Telegraphs and Telephones first came into existence in March 1894, by an Imperial edict of Menelik II. But this nation-wide reform, like many others, was brought to its fruitful climax during the reign of Emperor Haile Selassie I.

Ethiopia had become a member of the Universal Postal Union as early as November 1908. During the Italian occupation she ceased to be a member; but, soon after the liberation she joined the Union once again. It should be mentioned here, that some of the valuable suggestions put forth very recently by the Ethiopian Postal Administration have been accepted by the Union.

During the early days of the postal set-up, mail was carried by men and mules, while today, mail is being distributed throughout the Ethiopian Empire by bus, train and plane. As regards her foreign mail, today Ethiopia is linked with the whole world (with a few exceptions such as Nepal, Tibet, etc.) by means of an efficient fleet of planes operated by the Ethiopian Air Lines Inc.

Since the advent of the aeroplane, the speed and regularity of postal delivery has improved considerably. At present, mail is being despatched on every week-day to Dire Dawa, Jibuti and Aden, and twice a week to Khartoum, Cairo and Athens. Internally, the planes deliver the mail at all important towns, which are beyond reach by ordinary means of transportation.

The new General Post Office, removed to its present site after the liberation, remains open from 8 a.m. to 8 p.m. every week-day, for the purchase of stamps and other accessories, for the registration of out-going mail and for the collection of in-coming mail.

From the philatelic point of view, the Ethiopian stamps issued in recent times are far more attractive and popular than those issued before the invasion. The Ethiopian Postal Administration was represented at the Philatelic Congress held at Brussels in 1952, and is now ready to present several new ideas and to submit new resolutions at the next International Congress.

The first set of Ethiopian stamps was printed in Paris and was first placed on sale, in January 1895, in the provincial capital of Harar. They portrayed the profile of Emperor Menelik II as well as the heraldic Lion of Judah. These stamps were exhibited at the Philatelic Exhibition in Paris in the year 1900. Soon after Ethiopia's admission into the Universal Postal Union, a new set of stamps was issued, bearing the inscription "Postes Ethiopiennes." The Coronation of Empress Zauditu, the arrival of the first government aeroplane, and the Coronation of Emperor Haile Selassie I were also commemorated as philatelic events. Most of these early issues were destroyed or damaged, when the General Post Office of Addis Ababa was bombed by the Italians.

Among the post-liberation issues, special mention must be made of the five "Obelisk" stamps (1943) commemorating the 13th Anniversary of the Emperor's Coronation; the five "Roosevelt" stamps (1946) commemorating the Emperor's meeting with the great U.S. President; the two large sets of ordinary and Air Mail Stamps (1947), showing the beautiful natural scenery of Ethiopia; the four "U.P.U." stamps (1950) marking the 75th Anniversary of the Universal Postal Union; and the five sets of nine stamps (1952), commemorating the re-union of Eritrea with Ethiopia.

Begun by Menelik II, telecommunications in Ethiopia are little over a half century old. Compared with some of the more advanced countries in this important field of tele-contact, this is very young. As stated above, telegraph and telephone circuits within the Empire were introduced by Emperor Menelik II in his programme of introducing western ways to the country. This means of communication, which originated in the capital, crossed the provinces in several directions and reached some of the important borders of Ethiopian territory. The installations, however, were constructed according to the tele-technique known in the early 1900's and were not modern from the standpoint of present day technical development in the field. Nevertheless they served their limited purpose. Even long distance calls were then made whereby the operators were used as "repeaters."

In the early 1930's between 100 to 200 telephone subscribers existed in Addis Ababa. They were connected to a manual exchange with two switchboards. Connections with the outside world depended on a telegraph circuit between Addis Ababa and Asmara for which the Italians had a concession. (A telegraph circuit existed between the capital and Jibuti.)

The new Emperor, Haile Selassie I in the early days of his accession, took the initiative in starting to develop telecommunications in Ethiopia. He engaged foreign experts in this field who were attached to the Ministry of Posts, Telegraphs and Telephones. At the same time His Majesty the Emperor ordered radio installations to be placed between five and seven kilometres south of Addis Ababa, namely, the "Akaki" Station for transmission and the "Ras Kebede" Station for reception. On the completion of the installations, for some reason they were not made available for the use of the Ethiopian Government. The Ministry of Posts, Telegraphs and Telephones, therefore, at the turn of 1933-34, erected a Radio Station within the compound of the General Post Office in the centre of

312

His Majesty the Emperor leaving the Palace in Asmara

313

the town, and opened direct circuits with Cairo and Jibuti. Most of the radio telegraph traffic was done in this latter station.

At the beginning of 1935 the previously constructed Akaki and Ras Kebede installations were taken over by the Ethiopian Government and inaugurated by His Imperial Majesty. Additional radio telegraph circuits to London and Aden were opened. Not only did these installations serve commercial radio telegraph traffic, they were used as well for radio broadcasting to different parts of the world. It is from the Akaki Radio Station that His Majesty the Emperor, at the time of the beginning of the Italian conflict, broadcast his famous speech to the world. During the war the existing telecommunications system was completely destroyed.

An automatic telephone exchange of 1,500 lines in Addis Ababa and one of 1,200 in Asmara were opened during the Italian occupation. A large number of iron pole routes were also constructed in different parts of the country. By using telephone operators as "repeaters" telephone connection between Addis Ababa and Asmara was made possible. Some telegraph and telephone stations were erected.

During the campaign of liberation many parts of the telecommunications plant were completely spoiled. Reconstruction was therefore urgent and necessary. The World War, however, having embraced practically the whole world, made it almost impossible to obtain telecommunications experts and materials from abroad for some time. The wire lines and telephone exchanges were however restored. In Eritrea the British Military Administration took over the responsibility for telecommunications; in Ethiopia the responsibility fell on the Ministry of Posts, Telegraphs and Telephones. Radio telegraph circuits were opened in Asmara connecting London and Aden. The British Military Administration erected a wire circuit between Asmara and Khartoum; Ethiopia's telegraph traffic was relayed through Aden, Jibuti, Beirut and Tangiers. There was also terminal traffic with Khartoum and Yemen.

The telecommunications administration, which was re-organized in 1941, was confronted with many difficulties because of lack of funds and skilled personnel. Equipment existing in the country, despite the efforts of the Ministry of Posts, Telegraphs and Telephones, deteriorated, with a corresponding effect on the service rendered. At the same time the demand for telecommunications services kept growing because of the rapid economic, cultural and political development of Ethiopia. A fair amount of repairs and extensions was undertaken by the Ministry, but this could not keep pace with the demand for essential empire-wide services.

Complete re-organization of the telecommunications system and authority thus became pressing. As part of the general plan of reconstruction and rehabilitation, the Imperial Ethiopian Government sought and obtained financial assistance from abroad. A loan from the International Bank for Reconstruction and Development was obtained for the rehabilitation and extension of the country's telephone and telegraph system.

Through Proclamation Number 131, published in the Negarit Gazeta of October, 1952, His Imperial Majesty established the Imperial Board of Telecommunications of Ethiopia to be responsible for telecommunications

314

Emperor tours Asmara

throughout the whole Empire. This new organization, an autonomous governmental agency, undertook to provide the country with telephone, telegraph and broadcasting facilities. The funds at the disposal of the Board are partly provided directly from the Imperial Ethiopian Government and partly from the loan referred to above from the International Bank. One of the important responsibilities of the Imperial Board of Telecommunications of Ethiopia, as a corporate enterprise, is to arrange the rates for telecommunications services in the Empire in such a way that the organization becomes financially self-sustaining.

As this new institution was formed it had to keep in repair the old system which it took over and at the same time busy itself with securing new and modern equipment to install a modern and efficient system. The automatic telephone exchange in Addis Ababa, which had been operating since its installation in the 1930's, was found unable to cope with the heavy traffic. It was in poor mechanical order because of lack of spare parts. In addition, because of the absence of adequate maintenance, the cables and lines were in a bad condition which, especially in the rainy season, caused many subscribers' telephone lines to function unsatisfactorily. This condition was also true of equipment all over the country.

315

The Board, however, began immediately to overhaul the lines and the old equipment and to train essential personnel as first steps. As soon as funds were made available new equipment was ordered from abroad. By the end of 1955, the telecommunications facilities in the whole country will be completely changed, since a considerable part of the new equipment ordered will have been installed.

The following accomplishments, among others, could be credited to the Imperial Board of Telecommunications since it began to function on January 1st, 1953.

July 23rd, 1953:	The overhauling of the telephone line—Addis Ababa to Asmara was finished and the telephone circuit (a single line channel carrier circuit) opened for public use.
April 21st, 1954:	A new modern interurban exchange was put into service in Addis Ababa.
July 1st, 1954:	The Telecommunications Board took over the equipment and operation from Cable and Wireless in Asmara. From that date all public telecommunications services in the Empire are handled through the Imperial Board of Telecommunications of Ethiopia.
July 14th, to 21st, 1954:	New radio telegraph circuits, Addis Ababa to London and Addis Ababa to Rome were opened.
October 2nd, 1954:	His Imperial Majesty officially inaugurated the two radio telephone circuits: Addis Ababa to London and Addis Ababa to Rome. Today most places in Europe are available by telephone from Addis Ababa.
March 12th, 1955:	His Majesty the Emperor officially inaugurated the two new automatic telephone exchanges in Addis Ababa: The number of subscribers lines can now be increased from 1,500 to 4,800. A new Central Warehouse for the telecommunications organization was taken into use at the same time.

The greatest event from the telecommunications view point at the end of 1955 will be the opening of Addis Ababa new receiving station, situated close to Akaki Village, and Addis Ababa new transmitting station, situated at the same place as the first Akaki transmitting station, inaugurated in 1935. These two new radio stations will be equipped with modern single side band transmitters and receivers, etc. and when they are in use Ethiopia will have one of the most modern existing radio installations. New radio telephone circuits will then be opened with Aden, Beirut, Cairo, Nairobi and later probably a radio telegraph circuit with Bombay.

As for the domestic radio telephone circuits they will also be improved very much through the new radio stations in Addis Ababa and through new installations out in the country. Nine places which earlier have had no telephone connection will be linked to Addis Ababa through radio telephone, among them, Assab, Goré, Soddu, etc. Many new radio telegraph circuits will be opened later.

316

The now existing transmitting station in Addis Ababa, close to the airport, will in the future be used as the Addis Ababa broadcasting station. Technical arrangements will at the same time be made whereby several programmes may be transmitted at the same time and there will be stronger signals, which will facilitate the reception. The improvement of the broadcasting facilities throughout the country (from a technical viewpoint) is an important field for the Telecommunications Board.

Work is going on at present with telephone exchanges and with local networks, radio stations, telegraph equipment, etc., all over the country; for example, in Addis Ababa, Asmara, Assab, Dessie, Jimma, Harar, Gondar, etc. Longlines services especially, will reach a much higher grade of efficiency at the end of this year.

The Board's reorganization of the nation's telecommunications system has been thorough. Personnel in all branches have, through a series of rules and regulations and through the new organizational plan, been brought to realise their responsibilities to the Government and the public. Telecommunications traffic has been made to conform with international rules. One of the most important branches of the Board's programme has been the training of personnel. For it has not been only interested in installation of adequate modern equipment for the nation's telephone, telegraph and radio services. Through help from the United Nations Technical Assistance Administration, a Training Institute has been established. Since 1953 about 25 courses have been arranged for telephone operators, linemen, radio operators, radio technicians and high administrative staff.

From 1,179 employees taken over by the Board, the personnel now stands at 1,387. Of these, the number of foreign employees has dropped from 96 in 1953 to 74 at the beginning of 1955 and is expected to be about 55 at the end of the current year—a fact attributable directly to the training programme which the Board has stressed from its inception. One of the main policies of the Imperial Board of Telecommunications of Ethiopia is to have a self-contained staff in which foreign employees will be reduced to their minimum as early as practicable.

The Imperial Board of Telecommunications of Ethiopia published a new telephone directory which included, for the first time, the whole Empire, and was distributed between the months of March and April, 1954. A classified section was included to aid subscribers and the public to find the addresses of various business, professional and trade services.

As a going concern, the operations of the Board have two important aspects: they must provide adequate, swift, dependable services at reasonable rates; they must be financially self-sustaining. Within the range of the Board's operations, since January 1953, the first aspect is well underway. The second phase is being also achieved. Revenue, for 1955, is expected to show a balance over expenditure.

With the organisation of its administration into Headquarters and six regions: Addis Ababa, Asmara, Dessie, Dire Dawa, Jimma and Gondar, which was effected early in 1953, the whole Empire experiences dependable supervision and co-ordination.

Future plans have been laid to carry further the extension and development of the nation's telecommunications system. Under preparation is a detailed programme for the years 1956 to 1958, primarily as a base for future investment budget. To give a glimpse into the future, the following operations are planned: Wire circuits will be continued between Lakempti-Ghimbi-Goré-Jimma; Jimma-Soddu-Irgalem-Nazareth-Addis Ababa; Harar-Deder-Asba Tafari, etc. Reconstruction and installation of exchanges and networks in pre-federated Ethiopia will continue. The Asmara exchange and network will be reconstructed, as well as all other exchanges and networks in Eritrea. New automatic exchanges in the more important towns are planned together with coast radio stations in Massawa and Assab. Broadcasting will see a station in Asmara and a powerful shortwave broadcasting station in Addis Ababa, and others.

The reconstruction of a telecommunications system is a long-term enterprise. Although a great deal remains to be done before the goal is reached much progress has been made, and the Imperial Board of Telecommunications of Ethiopia has begun to play a fair part in serving the development of the Empire.

CHAPTER 28

The Ethiopian Press

Among the indispensable factors in the life of modern Ethiopia is its press, which began at the dawn of the century. In 1902. "L'Aimro" (Intelligence), the pioneering Ethiopian journal of this over-fifty-years of publications, appeared, named by Emperor Memelik II. It began not unlike the central European banking houses letters in the early history of the press, written by hand, since at that time there was no printing press. This weekly, from the small number of 24 with which it began, rose to over 200 by the aid of a mimeograph machine. It progressed until 1916 when it had to cease publication. "L'Aimro" was revived in 1924 by the assistance of the Ethiopian Government and appeared every Friday for several years after.

Taking account of the need for improving the printing technique, and realising the necessity of establishing a national press, His Imperial Majesty, then Regent, established the Berhanena Salam Printing Press, today the largest and best equipped in the country. At his own expense and giving his personal attention, His Highness Ras Tafari laid the foundation for the future and encouraged modern printing technique. The first official Amharic newspaper of the same name as the printing press, "Berhanena Salam" (Light and Peace), appeared in 1923 and reached a sizable circulation to all parts of the Empire. The Regent took a keen hand in the editing of this newspaper. He checked many proofs and sent them back to the printing press for page insertion. He encouraged apprentices to take up the printer's trade and watched the increase of equipment and efficiency of the institutions. Many of the older hands still remember receiving proofs marked with the Regent's O.K. to be included in the columns of the "Berhanena Salam."

But even during the interval of 1902 to 1923, when modern printing was introduced, the Ethiopian press kept moving forward. Successive steps, in terms of several newspapers were made. Each publication could be considered a link in the unbroken chain of Ethiopia's 20th century press progress. In 1905, "Le Semeur d'Ethiopie" (the Ethiopian Sower), in French, appeared; in the year of the First World War, 1914, "Yetor Ware" (War News), in Amharic, came out; "Le Courrier d'Ethiopie" (the Ethiopian Messenger), in French, was issued; in 1917, "Goha Tsebah" (the Dawn), in Amharic, was published. As stated above, the next seven years culminated in the publication of the "Berhanena Salam" from a printing press using modern equipment and technique.

From 1923, with the appearance of the new printing press, to 1936, a question of 13 years, six publications, which claimed the public interest and dealt in news and information, came out; "Aithiopicos Kosmos" (Ethiopian World), in Greek, 1925; "L'Ethiopie Commerciale," in French,

1932; "Atbia Kokab" (Morning Star), in Amharic, 1934; "Kasate Berhan' (Revealer of Light), in Amharic, 1935; "Ya-Ityopya Damts" (Voice of Ethiopia), in Amharic, from 1934 to 1936—the voice which was stifled by the enemy until 1941 and the liberation.

The Regent's interest in the press and in printing was intended, most certainly, to lay the foundation for a national press which would keep pace with the development of his country. Whatever was done was, most certainly, fathered by the thought that a rule of law can only prosper in a climate of enlightened public opinion. This view formed a significant part of the plan of reforms which was instituted during the period of the Renaissance of this country. It reached its climax by the formulation and establishment of the Press and Information Department which took definite shape after the Emperor's return.

To serve usefully the campaign, mostly to give the patriots and the people the long awaited news of His Majesty the Emperor's return with the co-operation of his British allies, the revival of what was later to be a fresh page in the history of the Ethiopian press began. The Italian propaganda machine had told the people that their Sovereign was dead and would never return. The advance guard of the Emperor were quick to organise the counter propaganda machine, under the direction of Mr. G. L. Steer, to give the news of the Emperor's arrival. There was need to tell the people of the campaign planned and of how they were expected to co-operate in their liberation. The great camouflage which broke the nerve of the enemy had to have publicity at a strategic moment. The news of Italian defeats in other points and the fate that awaited their soldiers in Ethiopia had to be spread. Mussolini's new position on the side of the Axis had been broad-cast. How was all this done? By the Amharic printing press which travelled on camel back and by which the publication "Banderachen' (Our Standard), in Amharic, was printed.

And the Ethiopian press, now guided by the Press and Information Department established in 1942, under the Ministry of the Pen, continued to flourish. "Sandek Alamachin" (Our Flag), Amharic and Arabic, and "Addis Zemen" (New World), Amharic, started on May 5th, 1941; the Negarit Gazeta, in Amharic and English appeared in 1942; the "Ethiopian Herald" (an English language weekly) came out in 1943; "Ya-Eritra Damts" in Amharic and Tigrinya, the organ of the Ethiopico-Eritrean Unionist Association; the "Ethiopian Review," a monthly review in English; "Berhanera Salam," in Amharic, a monthly review, were publish-ed in 1946. "Zana Bete Kristyan" and "Nuro Bezede," and "Tekle Haimanot," all in Amharic, 1947; the "Daily News Bulletin," in English; "Alamna Tebab" (the World of Culture), in Amharic and "Progrés Eco-nomique" in Amharic and French, all in 1950; "L'Ethiopie Contempo-raine," a periodical in French, printed in Cairo, in 1951; "L'Ethiopie d'Audjourd'hui," Amharic and French, 1952; and more recently, the counterpart of the English Daily News Bulletin in Amharic, rounded out the post-liberation publications. Several periodicals of a departmental nature have also been published in the current period, such as the "Ethio-pian Commercial, Industrial and Agricultural Journal," a monthly report of the State Bank of Ethiopia, the Quarterly Bulletin of the Ministry of Commerce and Industry; the Year Book of the Ministry of Education; several reviews on specific festal occasions and expositions; parochial bulletins and student organs of the highest educational institutions should be considered as part of this profuseness of the nascent Ethiopian press. Of the newspapers named above, five (all weeklies) are still appearing regularly and their circulation continues to increase.

The contributions of the Eritrean press, subsequent to federation, formed part of the combined journalistic effort of the Empire. The following publications may be cited: "Ethiopia," "Unione et Progresso," "Il Quotidiano Eritreo," "Giornale dell'Eritreo," "Il Lunedi," "Il Bolletino" and several monthly and quarterly reviews.

The Ethiopian press has over half a century of history; still it is a growing press. Its obligations, however, are not limited by these conditions. Its duty to the readers—in fact, to the state and community—is to translate to the public and the students of affairs the implications of local and foreign news. As Harold J. Laski said:

"The press, in a sentence, is a fundamental weapon in the social conflict, national and international, in which we are all, despite ourselves, combatants. We shall have truthful news when untruthful news does not pay, but it will not pay only when the majority of causes of social conflict, national and international, have been removed."

The effort spent by His Majesty the Emperor since his regency to establish a worthy Ethiopian press has been hedged about with certain obvious difficulties. The press still remains, to some extent, a controversial effort in the modern evolution of the country. A sustained adverse approach by the foreign press to Ethiopia has had a rather damaging corollary in the growth of the local press, it has vested it with the cloak of fear. This makes the national journalistic approach rather doctrinaire. In the introduction to Dr. Desmond's "Press and World Affairs," Mr. Laski further said:

I suggest, that so long as there is an unequal interest in the result of what impact the news may make, just so long will it pay the purveyors of news to report events with an emphasis deliberately calculated to serve those interests in a position to influence its supply. Our news system, in a word, is a reflection of our social system; there will be no vital change in the one unless there is also a vital change in the other." This is true of all national presses.

In Ethiopia, however, the problem is aggravated by diplomatic nuisances in which several missions use their diplomatic immunity as a bogey to muzzle the freedom of the local press. Strangely, some of these representatives, whose home presses are declared free, strain every inch of protocol to heckle the Ethiopian press at the slightest pretext—under the untenable claim that the newspapers are Government operated. This uneven opposition, in addition to other circumstances, tend to make the Ethiopian press timid and fearful in its approach to the news. In another aspect the local press has not as yet the confidence of the general public. Many people sometimes regard this publicity agency as un unnecessary evil, a "tell-tale" institution to which the least told the better. The inevitable consequence

of the position of the Ethiopian Press is that the literary talents, especially
of the educated élite, must observe an undue caution which is the bane of
original literary adventure. Yet, as indicated later in this chapter, there
has been some literary expression. Since the press, like other institutions
is imperfect, even in those countries where it is dubbed "free," there is
every hope that in due course the Ethiopian press, as an agency for social
and cultural progress, will come into its own.

On this Jubilee, it remains true that it is through the insight and the social-
mindedness of His Majesty the Emperor that the Ethiopian press has
evolved to its present level. Isolation did not support the need for newspapers, periodicals and other means of publicity and information. While
the press was coming of age in Europe and in America, which dates to no
more than little over a century, from 1838, when Mr. Bennett set up his
skeleton foreign correspondence staff in Europe, Ethiopia was still in
murky isolation. For the 53 years of its birth, however, within prescribed
limits, there has been constant growth in the service of information
provided for the public, thanks to His Majesty the Emperor's views about
the press. In a speech in Washington on his recent state visit to America
the Emperor praised the American press for reporting so exhaustively and
objectively. *"This objectivity was important,"* the Emperor said, *"because
all nations must have a clear concept of America's problems and attitudes."*

There has simultaneously been also an attempt to consolidate the means of
information in the Empire, not only through the press but through its close
ally, the radio. Prior to the Italian invasion His Majesty the Emperor had
visualised the necessity of a Radio Centre in his Empire. A Radio Station
was installed in the suburbs of Addis Ababa which connected the capital
with the large and important Radio Centres of the world. This was no
used for broadcasting programmes. Outside news was received thereby
and for commercial traffic wireless cable was established. Though the
pioneering services were headed by foreign experts many Ethiopians were
trained to operate this large station and smaller ones for internal use where
practicable.

The Press and Information Department at the liberation, took over the
equipment left by the Italians and began broadcasting radio programme
on what became Radio Addis Ababa. The equipment of the Akaki Radio
Station seemed to have suffered from the "scorched earth" policy of the
routed enemy. It was completely put out of order and could not be used at
His Majesty's return in 1941.

The programme of Radio Addis Ababa has been sustained since. What
began, with the assistance of the British Ally as an interim programme
soon blossomed into the regular scheduled programme, broadcasting news
views and comments in Amharic, English and Arabic. The musical side
of the programme, formerly provided by loans of records, has broadened
to include the station's own library, a great deal of in-person appearance
and a catalogue of national songs and musical airs which have become
standard features of the broadcasts. An interesting part of Radio Addis
Ababa's activities comprise programmes on feast, national and other com
memorative days and anniversaries, when special programmes are broad

322

cast and the language medium might include French, Greek and others. The national orchestra and singers of the Patriotic Association (Hager Fikir Mahaber) are responsible for the national songs and music used, assisted time and again by the various military bands.

In order to further build the service of information by radio, the Imperial Ethiopian Government entered into agreement with the International Bank for Reconstruction and Development, for a loan in 1950 to improve the Telecommunications service of the Empire. In 1953 the Imperial Board of Telecommunications of Ethiopia was established. Charged "to rehabilitate, extend, repair and maintain Telecommunications facilities of Ethiopia (other than military)," the radio facilities of the Press and Information Department have been completely overhauled. Future plans call for more powerful and modern radio stations in the Empire, when radio news gathering and dissemination would be further advanced.

Literature and Fine Arts
by Mr Stephen Wright

The close relation between religion and art has always been evident in Ethiopia, where geographical and political circumstances have tended to perpetuate and to accentuate such a connexion as was characteristic, for example, of the mediæval period in Europe. This is not the place for a full history of Ethiopian art and literature—a subject for which the materials are in any case difficult of access and as yet imperfectly studied. Developments of the last few decades can however be examined well enough with only slight reference to previous trends, for they reflect the radical changes that have come about in the present century—movements towards greater independence of thought and secularization of expression.

Ethiopia has a long literary tradition, and her people have great respect for the written word. Sufficient education to be able to read was always indispensable not only for the clergy and the lay clerks but for everyone who aspired to a life beyond that of the humble peasant or soldier. The language of literature and education was however not the vernacular— whether Amharic or a local language like Tigrinya or Gurage—but the "classical" Ge'ez ("Ethiopic"), a pure Semitic tongue to which Amharic is related somewhat as French to Latin, or English to Anglo-Saxon (though such resemblances must be regarded as rough analogies, not as strict philological parallels). It is five hundred years or more since Ge'ez was in use as a regular spoken language, though it still persists in the Church services, just as does Latin in the Roman Catholic Church. But it long remained the normal vehicle for literary composition: besides the theological works which constitute the bulk of Ge'ez literature, official annals, and formal letters and documents were, until a century and a half ago, generally written in the old language.

Amharic uses the same script as Ge'ez, with the addition of a few modified letters. The earliest surviving works written in Amharic are again mostly theological—translations of, and commentaries upon, Ge'ez texts. Its first extensive secular use was probably at the hands of two ecclesiastics at the court of the Emperor Theodore (reigned 1855 to 1868), named Zanab and Walda-Maryam; but their writings, of necessity, circulated only in the old form of parchment manuscripts. Meanwhile, however, printed Amharic literature was beginning to emanate from various missonary societies; this too was, of course, theological in character, if with a somewhat different bias. The texts, biblical and otherwise, were largely the work of Europeans whose Amharic style could not be expected to equal their devoted enthusiasm; moreover the books were mostly printed in Europe with founts that were rather clumsy and unpleasing. It was only in the opening years of the twentieth century that some small printing presses were established at Addis Ababa, and even these were incapable of producing any substantial books.

When in 1916 the present Emperor became Regent, he was acutely conscious of the unsatisfactory state of literary affairs. Even the missionary books, apart from the translations sponsored by the British and Foreign Bible Society, were now difficult to obtain; while the standard Ge'ez works were available, as ever, only in manuscript copies, far too expensive for the purse of the ordinary man. Secular Amharic texts, even on the newspaper level, were practically non-existent. As early as 1920 the Regent imported a printing-press capable of firstclass work on a comparatively large scale. Immediate necessity, policy, and the limited capacity of available writers combined to bring it about that the first books produced were traditional religious works; but now the Ge'ez texts were generally accompanied by Amharic translations or commentaries, sometimes from the hand of the Regent himself; and they were priced low enough for the average citizen to be able to buy them. Very soon a few entirely secular books appeared—accounts of the journeys of the Regent to Aden and to Europe and of his Consort to Jerusalem; a treatise on government administration; educational works on geography, history and arithmetic; and a few purely literary works by Blatengeta Heruy, the devoted collaborator of the Regent in this enterprise, and the virtual founder of Amharic literature. By the time of his accession to the Imperial throne in 1930, the Emperor could boast of some thirty books to the credit of his press.

The importance of this achievement cannot be over-emphasised, though it may be difficult for citizens of the western world to appreciate it. Within a decade Ethiopia had been transformed from a land where literary culture existed, indeed, but in a rarefied and almost inaccessible form, to the beginnings of a modern civilisation where intellectual ideas could be expressed in their own right. The old traditions had by no means been superseded: the writings of Solomon and Ezekiel and St. John Chrysostom were printed in their hallowed Ge'ez texts, but vivified by Amharic explanations, and made accessible to the clergy and the laity at large. And at the same time the way had been opened to a whole new world of knowledge—influenced, admittedly, by western ideas, but expressed in the Amharic of everyday usage—an Amharic which could, as Blatengeta Heruy and others had demonstrated, become the vehicle of a new, exciting, Ethiopian culture.

Once securely enthroned, the Emperor was able to pursue this line of

324

progress with added vigour, though the multifarious cares of state now limited his personal rôle to that of encourager and patron. The brief five years before the Italian conquest saw an increasing number of books being produced. It would be foolish to pretend that a new literature has sprung, Athens-like, full armed from the brain of a presiding deity—some of the works printed at the government-sponsored presses (there were now two) were perhaps more enthusiastic than profound; but the renaissance had begun, and it was no idle coincidence that *Goha-Sebah*, "The Dawn," was the name alike of one of the first printing-presses and of Blatengeta Heruy's earliest considerable work.

During the brief occupation of the country, the Italians did not fail to recognise the capacity of the populace to respond to the printed word; but their policy was, in this as in their whole attitude towards Ethiopian national sentiment, destructive rather than constructive. While suppressing and confiscating such books as might be considered detrimental to their regime, they sought to produce a substitute in Amharic newspapers and magazines full of propaganda extolling the glories of Fascist "culture." It was not likely that such procedure would destroy or replace the desire for independent expression of a people who were quietly conscious of their ancient literary heritage, and who had become aware of its incipient renaissance. Despite the Italian interlude, then, that renaissance was neither stillborn, nor strangled in its infancy; indeed, as soon as liberty was restored, it proved to have been restlessly awaiting the day when it could exercise itself—all the more vigorously, perhaps, for a period of repression.

On the very day the Emperor returned to his capital, two newspapers were issued for the first time: *Addis Zaman* ("The New Era," entirely in Amharic) and *Sandaq-alamachen* ("Our Standard," Amharic, with a section in Arabic). Both have appeared regularly every week since then. Besides general and local news, they carry a good deal of literary matter, and provide an opportunity for embryo writers to try out their talents, if within a somewhat restricted scope.

Only a month or two later came an indication that serious literature was not going to fall behind the other progressive movements inspired by the restoration of freedom. This was the publication, in the summer of 1941, of *Yaddis zaman mazmur*—its full title in English is "Hymn of the New Era," composed by young writers of Ethiopia for the glory of liberty. It was a substantial book of 150 pages, containing poems by thirty-five authors. The quality of the work is not specially remarkable, as was only to be expected in a book so hurriedly produced, and with two exceptions, the contributors have not published anything since. Its chief importance lies in the preliminary prose essays by Yilma Deressa and Berhanu Denqe, the former being a reasoned call for the development of a modern Ethiopian literature. Coming so soon after independence had been regained, this book was an inspiring encouragement to those who felt that they had a voice and something to say.

Publication, however, was not an easy matter. There was a desperate shortage of paper, and the presses were overworked with the printing of essential stationary, official forms, the newspapers, and schoolbooks for the Ministry of Education, which were very properly given prior consideration. Moreover there was no publishing house to undertake the production and marketing of books, and few authors were prepared to pay to have their works printed. The Department of Press and Information alone had at its command, and that only on a limited scale, the necessary funds and machinery. No books other than those officially sponsored, therefore, had much chance of appearing as yet. Today there are still no commercial publishing businesses, and although bookselling has much increased in volume, it is doubtful whether many independent authors have reaped a financial profit from their work, or even covered their expenses. It is well known that several writers, besides those officially employed, have received grants towards their printing expenses from the imperial purse: the Emperor is indeed a patron of letters in every sense of the word.

The first books in Amharic commissioned by the Ministry of Education after the restoration were two on "Physiology and Hygiene" and three reading-books entitled *Tarik-enna mesale* ("Story and Parable"). Despite certain faults (the Amharic too often bears the marks of translation from European languages) all these books have continued in use, and some have gone through several editions. One of them, the third of the *Tarik-enna mesale* series, is of outstanding merit; although many of the pieces (which are in prose and verse) are again clearly derived from foreign sources, the Amharic is clear and simple without being infantile, and unfamiliar ideas are paraphrased, not slavishly translated. Unlike the other two volumes of the set, this third one is not annonymous, but bears the name of Kabbada Mika'el, who had already contributed to *Yaddis zaman mazmur,* and had also produced two small books, an elementary school reader called *Majam-mariya ermeja* ("First step") and a collection of poems entitled *Berhana hilina* ("The Light of Intelligence"). In the preface to the last-named work (which has recently been reprinted) the author explains that he has paraphrased extracts from foreign books that he had copied down when at school: but he has recast them into an Amharic verse truly Ethiopian both in vocabulary and in syntax.

It is not surprising, therefore, that Kabbada Mika'el has, in the course of the last fourteen years, developed into the leading exponent of Amharic style. He is equally at home in prose and in verse, in *belles-lettres* and in didactic essays. It is a pity, perhaps, that for his subjects he largely relied, directly or indirectly, upon foreign sources; but in the present stage of Ethiopian literary development this is neither to be wondered at nor altogether to be deplored. His plays (all of them in verse) include *Ya-tinbit qataro* (translated and published in English as *Fulfilment of Prophecy*) and a paraphrase of Shakespeare's *Romeo and Juliet;* among his other works may be mentioned a book of biographies of "Great Men" (ranging from Homer to Napoleon) and a World History which is due to appear.

Another writer already mentioned as contributing an essay to *Yaddis zaman mazmur* is Berhanu Deneqe, who has a deep feeling for Ethiopian traditions and ways of life. His output is so far small: two little books for children, a verse play, and three historical works, the children's books are *Ya-kis Mastawat* ("A pocket mirror"), advice on good behaviour in the form of simple verses, and *Ya-hesanat mesale* ("Parable of childhood"), a collection of the subtle allegorical riddles in which Ethiopian children delight. The play, *Negest Azeb* ("The Queen of Sheba"), is a short dramatization of the legend of the Queen's visit to Solomon; the "bedroom scene," fraught with such historical consequences for the future dynasty of Ethiopia, is treated with ingenuity and tact. Of the historical works the most important is *Ya-ltyopya achir tarik* ("A short history of Ethiopia"), a succinct and clearly written account which has gone through three editions.

A more ambitious historical writer is Takle-Sadeq Makurya. He has produced two volumes on Ethiopian history, one covering the period from Lebna-Dengel to Theodore (1508-1860), the other carrying the story thence up to the restoration of 1941. He has a clear grasp of the principles of historical writing, and makes full and intelligent use both of European sources and of Ethiopian tradition, quoting extensively many of the witty and ingenious *gitim,* folk-poetry written to commemorate remarkable events or personalities. His style is vigorous and lucid, and it is not surprising that both volumes have gone through more than one edition. Takle-Sadeq is less successful in his other works, *Ka-ta'ot amleko wada Krestina* ("From Paganism to Christianity"), a more or less encyclopedic survey of ancient religions, and *Ya-sau tabai-nna abro ya-manor zade* ("Man's nature and the art of communal life"); relying largely upon foreign sources, their achievement does not equal their pretensions.

The most mature of contemporary writers, and one who may be regarded as a legitimate successor to Blatengeta Heruy, is the Prime Minister, Bitwadded Makonnen Endalkachau. His works, fairly numerous by Ethiopian standards, are mostly composed of a mixture of dramatic dialogue and straightforward narrative, and verse interpolations are not infrequent; all are characterized by philosophical reflections, allegories, and a certain didacticism. Thus both in form and in content they recall the writings of Blatengeta Heruy; and perhaps the ultimate model of both authors may be found in Bunyan's *The Pilgrim's Progress,* which was the first considerable work of European literature, apart from the Bible, to be translated into Amharic. It was indeed a happy inspiration that led the Swedish Mission in Eritrea to publish, in 1892, the version made by Gabra-Giyorgis Terfe: Bunyan's style and argument alike could not fail to make a strong appeal to the Ethiopian mind which, tending as we have observed to regard art and literature primarily as handmaids of religion, delights in parables and in stories of spiritual struggle typified by material trials. One of the most popular types of Ge'ez literature has always been the *gadl,* stories of the "strivings"—against temptations, persecutions and so forth—of individual saints, the prose narrative being usually followed by a poem relevant to the subject. Bunyan's religious fantasy therefore pointed the way to an Amharic literary form at once original and imbued with elements deeply rooted in Ethiopian tradition. Consciously or unconsciously, several authors have followed this indication, and the *libb wallad tarik*—"story born of the imagination"—has become, in the hands of writers like Blatengeta Heruy and Bitwadded Makonnen, one of the most successful and most distinctive productions of modern Amharic literature.

327

While Bitwadded Makonnen sometimes writes for a cultivated and sophisticated public, most of his work may be readily appreciated by any intelligent man-in-the-street. His settings are varied and always vivid—in *Ya-dahoch katama* ("The City of Poor Folk") an Ethiopian business man travels extensively in Europe and America; *Asab-enna sau* ("Man and his thought") is a dramatic presentation of an episode at the court of the biblical David; *Salsawi Dawit* ("David the Third") relates to an Ethiopian Emperor of the early eighteenth century, and includes a long episode illustrating the downfall, through acquaintance with a frivolous woman, of a humble coachman. In all his moralities his message is fundamentally clear and simple—a plea for sane, honest and sober ways of life and thought. His style is appropriately quiet and restrained, if sometimes a little involved and "literary." From the purely dramatic point of view he has been very successful in *Ya-dam dims* ("The Voice of Blood"), a play in prose, for the most part frankly realistic, depicting the execution by the Italians of Abuna Petros, one of the Ethiopian patriot bishops. It goes well in the theatre, and though the mixture of patriotism and religion may strike the western mind as a little strange, the theme is movingly treated, especially in the last scene, where Ethiopians of different provinces and races are discussing the emotions that the sight of the martyrdom has aroused in them; they are interrupted, to their alarm, by a Moslem woman who they fear has been eavesdropping and will inform against them; but she confesses to an even greater spiritual and patriotic fervour than theirs.

The Ethiopian stage is as yet in its infancy, but already some plays of merit have been written besides those mentioned above. The best, perhaps, is *Tewodros* ("Theodore") by Germachau Takla-Hawaryat, a drama in verse on the life of the nineteenth-century Emperor, who is presented as attempting prematurely to restore the national solidarity and effective unification of Ethiopia—a task in which he failed owing to a lack of patience and a tendency towards violent means: there is a passage in which the success of the present Emperor—patient and pacific—is fortold. The play suffers a little from some undramatic repetition, for example of Theodore's pleas for support in his schemes, and of his resentment at not receiving it; and the verse is not always impeccable by rigorous literary standards. But it acts very well. In the final scene Theodore, from his lofty fortress of Magdala, nostalgically surveys, in a quiet soliloquy which contrasts well with his previous rantings, the land he has lost through his own violence; he had imprisoned sundry foreigners, and as the revenging British troops arrive he shoots himself rather than fall ignominiously into their hands; his wife makes the traditional lament over his corpse, which the British formally salute as the curtain falls.

Germachau Takla-Hawaryat has also published a highly successful novel, named after its hero *Ar'aya*, an Ethiopian boy who goes to France for higher education; on his return (this is before the Italian occupation) he is disillusioned in not being able to serve his country as he had hoped, owing to hostile reactionary influences in the Ministry where the Emperor had appointed him to an administrative post. The book is written interestingly and with feeling; and the fact that it has been issued in a second edition at Addis Ababa (the first was printed in Asmara) is a sufficient rebuttal of the charge sometimes voiced that publication of books at all critical of domestic politics is forbidden.

A novel bearing some superficial resemblance to *Ar'aya* is *Ag'azi,* again the name of an Ethiopian who goes to Europe; but it is from the more optimistic and less sophisticated pen of Walda-Giyorgis Walda-Yohannes, a professional writer of the Press and Information Department, and was originally serialised in the newspaper *Addis Zaman.* Walda-Giyorgis Walda-Yohannes (who must not be confused with his namesake who was until a few months ago Minister of the Pen) and his colleague Yared Gabra-Mika'el are responsible for many official publications, including souvenir booklets and broadsheets issued in celebration of the Emperor's birthday and coronation anniversaries and similar occasions; they are, as a rule, verse resumés of the ancestry and activities of the Imperial family. Both writers have produced more substantial books, but their preoccupations are utilitarian rather than aesthetic. Thus Walda-Giyorgis, in his *Bilsiginna ba-gibirnna* ("Wealth in Farming"), exhorts the countryman in familiar prose interspersed with verse; and in *Ka-sira Bahwala* ("After work") he provides children with another set of allegorical riddles. Yared Gabra-Mika'el gives advice on marriage in a poem called *Ine-nna anchi* ("I and Thou")—with a preliminary prose essay on traditional marriage customs which includes the text of some old wedding-songs.

At a time when new ideas are making rapid headway it is urgently necessary to see that the lore of older times does not fall into oblivion. So it is satisfactory to find that the advantages of print are being utilised to perpetuate much of interest and value that is in danger of disappearing. The Emperor himself has often stressed the desirability of preserving all the best elements of Ethiopian traditional culture, especially when enthusiasm for western ways and for technological progress might tend towards a denigration of indigenous art, science and philosophy. Credit must be given to Balambaras Mahtama-Sellase, who has made two notable contributions to this end: *Yabatoch gers* ("Relics of our fathers"), a collection of over 3800 Ethiopian proverbs and metaphors; and *Zekre Nager* ("Remembrance of things"), a voluminous record depicting the complicated organisation of the imperial household in the early years of the century, and the general administration of the country on the eve of its transition to a modern bureaucracy. Traditional Ge'ez literature also enjoys the benefits of printing: besides official publications of the Church Council, the activities of Tasfa Gabra-Sellase should be mentioned: he has edited standard texts like the Psalter (with its Ethiopian appendices) and *Doctrina Arcanorum,* and a large number of *Malk'at,* hymns in verse, many of them fairly ancient, addressed to Deity and to various saints. Tasfa Gabra-Sellase has recently acquired his own press, and one of the first fruits is an edition of the *Sayfa Sellase* ("Sword of the Trinity") composed in the fifteenth century by Abba Giyorgis of Gassecha—a work not otherwise easily accessible.

The wide range of the literary renaissance is in fact remarkable. In this short survey it is impossible to specify more than a fraction of the numerous works that have been published, on all sorts of subjects, by some eighty writers, among whom many walks of life are represented (¹), and there are many books in manuscript awaiting a favourable opportunity for publication. A few of the more important writers have already been discussed in some detail, and mention can be made only of one or two others who, though as yet they have publised little, may eventually rank among major authors. First there is Blatta Sirek Walda-Sellase son of Blatengeta Heruy, who has done a scholarly translation of Johnson's *Rasselas,* and is reported to have other works completed. Tamrat Amanuel is a savant whose short biography of Mahatma Gandhi does not adequately represent his wide talents. A younger writer, Asaffa Gabra-Maryam, shows considerable promise in his first novel, *Enda wattach qarrach* (²), written in 1949 but not published until 1954. Almost the only humorist, and for that reason worthy of remark, is Mattewos Baqqala, whose little comedy *Der biaber anbasa yaser* ("Joined threads can bind the lion") points the way to a literary form which should prove highly congenial to the Ethiopian love of wit and satire: it is a pity that more writers do not realize that humour can be a potent means of pointing the morals they are too often apt to labour somewhat sententiously.

Women have furnished their quota to the output. There were two women contributors to *Yaddis zaman mazmur;* since then Senedu Gabru has published two verse dramas in her *Yalibbe mashaf* ("Book of my Heart"); and Romana-Warq Kasahun is responsible for a play, *Mahtota Tebab* ("The Lamp of Science"), about Princess Tsahai, the Emperor's daughter, who died just as she was beginning to utilize the nurse's training she had received in England. Romana-Warq has also written a manual of domestic science, *Tidar ba-zade* ("Planned economy"); distinctively feminine too is *Yamoya minch* ("Source of household tasks") in which Maqdasa-Warq Zallaqa has collected three hundred recipes, mostly for dishes exclusively Ethiopian in character.

Since there were few precedents for Amharic writing, all this literary activity would not have developed so smoothly had there not been earnest students of the language who laid the basis for good style. Foremost among these is Blatta Mars'e-Hazan Walda-Qirqos, whose *Ba-addis ser'at yatasanadda ya-Amarinnya sawasew* ("Amharic Grammer arranged on new principles") was originally written in 1927 and remains a standard and widely used work on the subject. A younger teacher who has interested himself in stylistic questions is Takla-Maryam Fanteye, whose *Hohta Tebab za-sena sehuf* ("Door to the art of good writing") has achieved a second edition. Interest also attaches to *Ya-and qwanqwa edgat waim Amarinnya enda tasfafa* ("The growth of a language, or how Amharic developed") (³), by Ba'emnat Gabra-Amlak, a succinct study of the development of Ethiopian language generally, with special reference to the vocabulary of modern

(¹)   A fairly full, but not exhaustive, bibliography is to be found in the *Guide Book of Ethiopia* issued by the Chamber of Commerce, Addis Ababa (1954).
(²)   No close translation of this title is possible; perhaps it might be paraphrased as "The fatal step."
(³)   Recently printed.

Amharic, which has inevitably incorporated a large number of foreign words.

But the prime mover of the Ethiopian literary renaissance, and the source from which every writer derives his place therein, is the Emperor, Haile Selassie. Not only has he provided the material conditions, in every detail, whereby writers can produce their work, but he has set a practical example, and encouraged with his guidance and support many adventurers in the new field. To reconstitute a national literary culture in a new, less esoteric, medium required both imagination and the faculty of transmitting that imagination to others; and if the Emperor has been fortunate in finding so many competent people to develop his ideas, that is in large measure due to his simultaneous creation of a general atmosphere of patriotic sentiment and dedicated endeavour. One can feel no surprise that much of the new literature is preoccupied, explicitly or implicitly, with national prestige and the imperial dignity. After all, the *Aeneid* is a glorification of Rome, and the *Faerie Queene* a eulogy of Queen Elizabeth; and while no one would pretend that Amharic already has its Vergil or its Spenser, the enthusiasm and confidence which characterise the Ethiopia of Haile Selassie form the best of nurseries for a young and growing literature.

Since his accession, the Emperor's direct contribution to literature has mostly been confined, not unnaturally, to oratory. His speeches, whether political pronouncements or homely addresses to his people or to some particular audience (the *mari qal,* "words of guidance," are treasured by every school or other institution he visits), are invariably couched in an Amharic appropriate to the occasion. Their style is always tempered to the speaking voice; in print they sometimes seem involved, even obscure—there will be a baffling ambiguity, an ingenious anacolouthon, completely effective in speech, but grammatically as hard to resolve as anything in Pericles's famous oration. The frequent happy word or phrase, the apt allusions, make these speeches models of their kind, and they are justly regarded as examples of Amharic *pur sang.* A small selection was issued in 1945 as *Germawi Negusa Nagast Qadamawi Haile-Selassie baya-gizew ya-tanagaruachaw qalat* ("Speeches delivered on various occasions by His Imperial Majesty Haile-Selassie I"); a much larger collection, under the title *Fre kanafer za-Qadamawi Haile-Selassie Negusa Nagast za-Ityopya* ("Fruit of the lips of Haile-Selassie I, Emperor of Ethiopia"), appeared in 1952 (¹).

Of an importance not primarily literary, but liable to exert great influence upon all types of writing, is the revision of the Amharic version of the Bible. The Emperor has always had this very much at heart. The first translations, made by, or under the direction of, European missionaries a century ago, were never wholly satisfactory, and by the Emperor's command a new text was prepared, tentatively, by Ethiopian churchmen. The manuscript of this, completed shortly before the Italian invasion, was

---

(¹) An English translation of the first four sections of this book is in the press. The famous address to the League of Nations in 1936 has been printed several times in English, French and other versions.

brought to England, where photographic copies were made; a few of these were issued, but unfortunately the bulk of the stock was destroyed during the London "blitz." Soon after the restoration the Emperor, in order to establish a final text, nominated committees for the Old and for the New Testament, foreign scholars being represented upon each of them. Three books of the Old Testament, and two of the New, were issued at intervals between 1949 and 1951, mainly so as to obtain criticism from responsible quarters. The whole of the New Testament has now been completed, and is in the press; the Old Testament should follow within a year or two. Apart from its religious significance, the "authorised version" of the Amharic Bible may well have a literary influence analogous to that felt in England ever since 1611; in any event, it will remain one of the major achievements of the reign of Haile Selassie I.

One literary matter remains to be mentioned, affecting letters in the narrower sense: the possible "reform" of the Ethiopian syllabary. The complexities of the system tend to be much exaggerated by those who do not realise that the 250 or so characters are not all entirely different, but follow regular patterns quite easy to grasp. The average Ethiopian child masters his *fidal* as rapidly and effectively as the European child his ABC. At the same time there are some features which make its adaptation to the typewriter and the linotype machine somewhat awkward and expensive, though there is no reason why these difficulties should not be resolved much more easily than those occurring in, say, Japanese. The question of simplification came to a head when Dr. Laubach, the celebrated apostle of mass literacy, visited Ethiopia in 1947 and decided immediately that his projects demanded some modifications of the syllabary; and he presented his requirements forthwith. No little interest was aroused, for in the previous year a commission of five savants had met to consider proposals submitted by Ras Imru, Ato Abbaba Retta, and Blatta Mars'e-Hazan Walda-Qirqos ([1]). A larger commission now met, under the auspices of the Ministry of Education, to review the whole question. A report was issued under the title *Fidalen mashashal* ("Improvement of the Syllabary"), giving full explanations of all the systems; but no positive recommendations were made. It would indeed be difficult to evolve any useful modifications that might prove universally acceptable; and most students of Ethiopian languages, whatever their own mother tongue, would agree with the verdict of the great scholar Dillmann, that the existing fidal is "a highly perfected syllabary, which for completeness and effectiveness leaves little to be desired." As is the case with Semitic cultures in general, literature occupies in Ethiopia, proportionally to the other arts, a far more predominant position than

---

([1]) Blatta Mars'e-Hazan had evolved a scheme for the possible adoption of the Latin alphabet. The transliteration of Amharic into Latin character is a problem of great complexity; a rough and ready system has been in use by the telegraph services for many years, but it is far from satisfactory, being in several respects inconsistent and ambiguous. Any logical and accurate system requires the use of many diacritical marks, which create psychological as well as typographical difficulties, as Blatta Mars'e-Hazan's system demonstrates. In the present sketch some attempt has been made to avoid the grosser solecisms, but Amharic scholars will detect many uneasy and erratic compromises.

in, for instance, the European or the Indian civilizations. The present Emperor has encouraged music and the graphic arts when possible, but there is neither the scope for wide development nor the immediate practical benefit which literature affords.

The theatre, however, with its literary affinities, should make rapid strides towards a flourishing future. One has only to watch the grace and vigour of gesture, and to hear the expressive vocal range, employed by every participant in village law proceedings to appreciate the histrionic talent latent in every Ethiopian; while certain church ceremonies, and the old-style parades which are unfortunately fast disappearing, display a genius for spectacle. So far, stage performances in Amharic have been practically limited to the activities of the Patriotic Association, *Ya-agar fiqir*, who have a small regular theatre for danced and mimed songs, with occasional play-lets, and of the Addis Ababa Municipality, which sponsors a dramatic company who give occasional performances. Many schools put on dramatic shows, but these are often in English. Bigger developments may be seen in the near future: not only are special dramatic performances being arranged at the Jubilee Exhibition, but a new, properly equipped theatre is under construction in the centre of Addis Ababa. The creation of a national drama may well prove to be yet another achievement of Haile Selassie's reign.

It is scarcely likely that the youngest of the arts, the cinema, hedged round as it is by economic factors, will develop in Ethiopia in the near future; but it is significant that a film competition is to be a feature of the Jubilee Exhibition, and although the participants (including amateurs) will doubt-less be mainly, if not entirely, foreign, it may represent a first foreshadow-ing of an Ethiopian contribution to cinematographic art.

Ethiopian music, both vocal and instrumental, is in its way highly develop-ed; but as yet it is practically confined on the one hand to the Church, and on the other to folk-music. Both *genres* would repay study, and in partic-ular it is to be hoped that an Ethiopian Cecil Sharp or Rimsky-Korsakov will appear, to collect and preserve the rich heritage of folksongs, many of them extremely elusive, and sometimes, it would seem, deriving from church hymns. Folk music continues to be created: new popular songs appear from time to time, notably on Radio Addis Ababa, but the com-posers are generally anonymous; even *Anchi lij*, the tune which for the last dozen years has been a favourite of Ethiopians and foreigners alike, has an origin so obsure that half the provinces of Ethiopia lay claim to it. If music develops as a personal artistic medium in Ethiopia it will probably be under foreign influences—and until the right influences are available more harm than good might come of attempting to force the growth of an art so abstract and so easily corruptible.

Painting and drawing, however, as being capable of directly expressing concrete ideas, are more congenial to the realistic and somewhat didactic temperament of the Ethiopian. Churches have always been extensively decorated with pictures, as a rule traditional in subject and styles; and illuminated manuscripts of religious texts are fairly common. Secular paintings, portraying historical subjects (especially battles), hunting scenes, banquets, and (less commonly) scenes of domestic life, are also produced on quite a large scale by artists who are bound to tradition both in training and in outlook. The treatment even of new subjects (like the battles of Mai Chau in 1936 and of Gondar in 1941) is strictly in accordance with conventions designed for the expression rather of hard facts than of aesthetic emotion. At the same time a good deal of shrewd observation may find its way into the composition, and sometimes the balance and colouring are strikingly good. Of the living exponents of this traditional style, Yohannes Tasamma probably displays most individuality; but certain others, notably Solomon Balachau, might be considered more characteristically Ethiopian. While painting of this kind is more of a craft than a medium for conveying individual artistic ideas, foreigners who have taught graphic arts in Ethiopian schools have been impressed by the instinctive talent shown not only in technique but in the expression of individual feeling. Already there are several young people who have persevered on their own and are capable of very competent work.

Only one or two Ethiopians, however, have pursued serious art studies abroad. Agenyahu Engeda, who worked in Paris for several years, and who was beginning to produce work of high quality, was the untimely victim of a road accident in Addis Ababa. More recently, Afawarq Takle had a brilliant student career in London, at the Slade School and elsewhere, and has subsequently, with the Emperor's constant support and encouragement, acquired a first-hand acquaintance with the best works of art in Europe. Afawarq's first exhibition in Ethiopia was held at the Addis Ababa Municipality Hall in 1954. It is too early to judge the lines along which his work will develop—he is still in his twenties—for he has been feeling his way among a variety of styles; but it is already clear that a deep feeling for his own country will not be submerged beneath his foreign experiences, since some of his best productions so far are those inspired by Ethiopian physiognomies and Ethiopian scenes.

Foreign influence is more evident in the work of Ema'ilaf Teruy, although his technique was acquired within Ethiopia. His bold canvases of religious subjects in particular display a confident approach and considerable technical skill.

The literary activities of the Prime Minister, Bitwadded Makonnen Endalkachau, were mentioned earlier; he also possesses skill as a painter—not the only Prime Minister who has found art not to be incompatible with politics.

It must be emphasized again that this survey of developments in literature and fine arts during the reign of Haile Selassie I is intended merely to provide an indication of their general character, not a comprehensive account of all the work that has been produced. Nor does it attempt to record the activities of foreigners, whose many performances of drama and music, exhibitions of works of art, and other contributions to cultural life have always enjoyed the Emperor's sympathy and patronage, and have doubtless had effects beyond the circle of their own communities. In matters of the mind and spirit, influences are not so easy to assess as in material affairs. But we can be quite certain that the cultural advance that

334

the Ethiopian people have made in the last twenty-five years would have been impossible had not their sovereign provided them with fertile fields for new endeavour, and with constant aid and encouragement to work them. In the long run, the renaissance of Ethiopian art and letters may prove to be the most significant, the most permanent, and the most benefi-achievements of the reign and effort of Haile Selassie I.

CHAPTER 29

Civic, Social and Welfare Organisation

The cultural advancement of any country depends on the number, as well as the nature, of the social and welfare organisations which take root in that country. Side by side with her agricultural, commercial and industrial progress, Ethiopia has been paying considerable attention to the establishment and encouragement of such world-wide organisations as the Red Cross, the Boy Scouts, and the Y.M.C.A. Ethiopia's waxing interest in these organisations can be traced to the following factors: (1) the spreading of education throughout the country; (2) the steadily rising standard of living; and (3) the growing need for organised group-activities, especially among the youth.

His Imperial Majesty's Government has always been eager and willing to lend a helping hand to international agencies, which wanted to set up their branches in Ethiopia. Whenever occasion demanded, His Imperial Majesty has even freely and most generously contributed to such deserving causes from the Privy Purse. Most of these civic organisations continue to enjoy the gracious patronage of the Emperor or the Empress, or some member of the Imperial Family.

In the midst of numerous State functions and activities, His Imperial Majesty has always found time to lay the cornerstone of one organisation, to inaugurate the activities of another, or to pay an official visit of encouragement to a third. No wonder then, that several social and welfare organisations are found to be flourishing in Ethiopia.

The Boy Scout Association

The Boy Scout Movement was introduced into Ethiopia even before the Italian invasion; but it was only officially recognised when the Boy Scout Association of Ethiopia was chartered by an Imperial Proclamation of July 28th, 1950, as published in the "Negarit Gazeta" No. 11.

In August 1948, His Imperial Majesty had ordered the formation of an Executive Committee, under the Chairmanship of Dr. R. N. Thompson, to re-organise the Boy Scout Movement in Ethiopia. This Committee was responsible for conducting short courses in Scout leadership, to qualify young Ethiopians for their future duties as Troop Leaders and Scout Masters.

The governing body of the Association consists of a Chief Scout appointed by His Imperial Majesty and a National Council composed of seven members. The Chief Scout, at present, is His Highness the Duke of Harar, who was the first to enroll as a Boy Scout in 1934.

The National Council has the power to appoint the National Commissioner and to fix his Deputies. The present office-bearers are: the National Commissioner: H. E. Ato Yilma Deressa; the Deputy Commissioner: H. E. Ato Akalaworq Haptewold.

The annual meeting of the National Council is held once every year, in Addis Ababa, during the month of January, in the presence of the Chief Scout. At this meeting, the annual report of the preceding year is presented to the Council by the National Commissioner.

The main purpose of the Boy Scout Association of Ethiopia is the further-ance of the International Boy Scout programme and the Boy Scout methods which train its members in good citizenship, self-reliance and firmness of character.

The initial supply of materials, including books and badges, were purchas-ed from the Boy Scouts Association of Canada. The World Brotherhood Edition of "The Boy Scout Handbook" has been officially recognised as the manual for the Boy Scouts of Ethiopia. Lord Baden-Powell's "Scout-ing for Boys" is also widely used.

Today the Boy Scouts have become part and parcel of the civic and social life in the country. The practice of the Scout Law makes them friendly, courteous, loyal and co-operative. They frequently take part in parades on public occasions. They help to maintain order and discipline at public functions. At least one Troop in the Capital has endeared themselves to the public by distributing fruits among the patients in hospitals. Others have done, and are doing, their share of "good deeds" whenever opportunities arise.

It may be mentioned here that many of the young men who fought for the defence of the country, during the Fascist invasion, belonged to the first few Troops of Ethiopian Boy Scouts organised in 1934.

During the Spring, every year, the Boy Scouts in Addis Ababa and the main towns of Ethiopia approach the public for voluntary contributions to the Boy Scout Fund. Two-thirds of the total collection is divided among the various Troops, while one-third of it goes to the Headquarters of the Association.

The figures for the total collection in Addis Ababa, in recent years are given below:—

Year	Total
1951	Eth. $ 5,015.17
1952	Eth. $ 6,377.50
1953	Eth. $ 5,138.31
1954	Eth. $ 5,187.35
1955	Eth. $ 5,369.99

A National Boy Scout Jamboree was held in Addis Ababa, in May 1953. Twenty-seven Troops participated in the Jamboree, consisting of 630 Boy Scouts and 52 Girl Guides. The Jamboree was organised by the Ethiopian Boy Scout Association, to make the public familiar with the scouting activ-ities. During the Jamboree, His Imperial Majesty was presented with original gifts made by the Boy Scouts and the Girl Guides. Later, the Scouts gave demonstrations in bridge-building, signalling, staff drill and fire rescue work.

At the close of 1954, there were 72 Troops in Ethiopia, consisting of about 2,400 Boy Scouts. The Girl Guide Movement has also begun to take root in the country. At present there are five Troops of Girl Guides in Ethiopia, consisting of about 150 members.

The Boy Scouts of Ethiopia have, fortunately, several interesting places to choose as their camping-grounds. Some of the most favourite camping-grounds are the lake-district of Bishoftu, the valleys of the Awash and the Blue Nile, the Rift Valley lakes of Arussi and the extinct volcano, Mt. Zuquala.

The Young Men's Christian Association in Ethiopia.

On the occasion of laying the cornerstone of the first national Y.M.C.A. in Addis Ababa, on November 2nd, 1949, His Imperial Majesty Haile Selassie I declared: *Our help shall always be forthcoming to this movement here in Ethiopia in order to enable it to fulfil its mission of moulding the youth of Ethiopia in harmony with those of the world, towards advanced living — spiritually, materially and morally.*

The story of the Y.M.C.A. in Ethiopia actually began in 1947, when two senior Y.M.C.A. Secretaries arrived here from Egypt to investigate the possibilities of starting work in this country. They came at the request of the World's Alliance of Y.M.C.A.'s, which had received several appeals from Ethiopia for establishing a Y.M.C.A. in Addis Ababa. The two gentlemen were received by His Imperial Majesty, who indicated his keen interest in the movement and promised his invaluable help in getting the work started.

Soon afterwards the National Council of the Egyptian Y.M.C.A. secured the services of Mr. Michel Wassef of Egypt to do the pioneering work in Ethiopia. Mr. Wassef arrived in Addis Ababa in April 1948. With His Imperial Majesty as the Chief Patron, and with H. E. Col. Tamrat Yiggezou as the President of the Board of Managers, the first national Y.M.C.A. began to function in November 1949, in a temporary building magnanimously lent by the Ethiopian Patriots' Association. The Y.M.C.A. was officially recognised by the Imperial Proclamation of 28th February, 1950. Thus Ethiopia became the 74th country to welcome this world-wide organisation.

Membership

As in other countries, the Ethiopian Y.M.C.A. can proudly claim a membership roll, which embraces different races, religions and nationalities. Besides a predominant number of Ethiopians, there are Arabs, Armenians, Americans, Egyptians, Europeans, Indians, Syrians and Sudanese among the members of the Addis Ababa Y.M.C.A.

The annual Membership Fees are as follows:

Student Membership	Eth. $ 2.50
Adult Membership	Eth. $ 15.00

338

The Y.M.C.A. Membership has been steadily increasing. At the end of 1953, the membership consisted of 43% students and 57% adults. Several interesting activities, such as lectures, debates, film-shows and stage performances, attract large numbers of the public; and so the total attendance has always exceeded the total membership, as shown in the following chart:

Year	Total Membership	Total Attendance
1951	58	10,000
1952	127	459,133
1953	261	720,023
1954	349	919,377

The World's Alliance Meeting in Denmark

In August 1950, the Ethiopian Y.M.C.A. was represented by Mr. Michel Wassef at the Plenary Meeting, in Denmark, of the World's Alliance of Young Men's Christian Associations. At that Meeting, Mr. Wassef had the honour of reading the following inspiring message from Emperor Haile Selassie I.

It gives us great pleasure to send our most sincere greetings and best wishes for the success of the Plenary Meeting of the World's Alliance of Young Men's Christian Associations. The work of the International Young Men's Christian Associations and of the national associations with their many branches throughout the world, enjoys and should enjoy even greater international support for faithful service to the most pressing needs of young men everywhere.

We would express to you our appreciation for the interest the International Y.M.C.A.'s have taken in their work in Ethiopia. The influence of that work is being more and more widely felt among Ethiopian youth and we are hopeful that additional branches may be established in Ethiopia. The devoted implementation of Christian principles to which the Y.M.C.A. give constant testimony is making its humble contribution to the creation of the Kingdom of God on earth and we join with you in our prayers for its success.

In grateful acknowledgement of the above message, the World's Alliance President, Mr. John Forrester Paton, and General Secretary, Mr. Tracy Strong, cabled the following reply to His Imperial Majesty:

"The World's Committee of Y.M.C.A.'s, having with deep gratitude received Your Imperial Majesty's most gracious message, begs to thank Your Majesty for the active interest you have shown and the very great assistance you have given to the young Y.M.C.A. in Ethiopia. May God's blessings rest upon Your Majesty and Your Empire."

Unity in Diversity

Toward the close of the year 1953, the total membership (including boys and contributors) was 261.

The analytical table of Membership, given below, presents an interesting study of the Addis Ababa Y.M.C.A. in its early stages.

339

Analytical Table of Membership

Occupation

Business men	67
Government and private employees	110
Students	84
	261

Religions

Christians	229
Moslems	17
Hindus	10
Jews	5
	261

Nationalities

Ethiopians	116
Egyptians	32
Greeks	29
Indians	22
Armenians	21
Arabs	14
Americans	7
Britons	5
Italians	5
Dutch	2
Danes	2
Lebanese	2
Austrians	2
Germans	2
	261

In December 1951, Mr. Michel Wassef left Ethiopia, to continue his training in the United States of America; and Mr. Merlin A. Bishop became the General Secretary. Mr. Bishop, with his experience in the training of youth, is eminently fitted to carry on the work started in Addis Ababa by his younger predecessor.

The Board of Managers

The Addis Ababa Y.M.C.A. is guided by some of the outstanding citizens, who form the controlling body:
1. H. E. Col. Tamrat Yiggezou (President)
2. H. E. Col. Kifle Yirgetou (Vice-President)
3. Ato Emmanuel Gabre Selassie (Vice-President)
4. H. B. Abouna Theophilos
5. H. E. Ato Akaleworq Haptewold
6. H. E. Blatta Marsie Hazan
7. H. E. Ato Menassi Lemma

340

8. H. E. Ato Imru Zelleke
9. Ato Yohannis Redaegzi
10. Col. Mebratu Fesseha
11. Dr. David A. Talbot (Ag. Treasurer)
12. Mr. I. Menezes
13. Mr. Berdj Babayan
14. Mr. C. M. Makris
15. Mr. Abdulla Baagil
16. Mr. Alfred Abel
17. Mr. Elias Djerrahian
18. Mr. Merlin A. Bishop (Gen. Secretary)

In July 1953, the Plenary Meeting of the World's Committee was held in Geneva, commemorating the 75th Anniversary of the Committee. It was attended by 160 representatives from 38 countries, of which Ethiopia was represented by Mr. Bishop. Soon after the Plenary Meeting, Mr. Bishop made an extensive tour of the Y.M.C.A.'s in the Mediterranean region before he returned to Ethiopia. During the three months of his absence, Mr. Charles A. Isaac acted as the General Secretary.

Permanent Headquarters

Recognising the need for a permanent building of its own, the Addis Ababa Y.M.C.A. launched a Building Fund in 1951, while Mr. Michel Wassef was the General Secretary. His Imperial Majesty granted a site for the building (between the Ministry of Education and the Holy Trinity Church) and blessed the fund-raising campaign with a generous donation of Eth. $10,000. Since then His Imperial Majesty has kept a constant interest in the association and lent it added material and moral support. Thanks to the earnest efforts of the Board of Managers, and thanks to the co-operation of all the different communities in Addis Ababa, the new building was completed by May 5th, 1955, when it was officially opened by Their Imperial Majesties.

Programme Activities

Realising that an individual must show Spiritual, Mental and Physical growth in his day-to-day life, the Y.M.C.A. has adjusted its activities to suit this all-round development of its Members. The following chart should give one a general view of the Addis Ababa Y.M.C.A. at work.

Analysis of Programme Activities for 1954

Activity	Number of Meetings	Attendance
Organised Groups	1,518	103,652
Unorganised Groups	1,407	762,181
Committees	541	3,541
Leadership Training	309	1,350

Major Attendance Categories

Activity	Number of Meetings	Attendance
Clubs	343	83,145
Lectures	65	25,604
Debates	7	2,421
Community Singing	24	7,687
Adult Education	146	84,795
Religious Services	83	16,112
Amateur Nights	9	3,314
Athletics	1,788	643,419
Informal Music	255	97,599
Social Events	20	1,307
Dramatics	21	15,299
Handicraft	431	1,618
Special Events	84	35,919

Distinguished Visitors

The Addis Ababa Y.M.C.A., can claim the honour of receiving several distinguished visitors from abroad, within the short period of its existence. Among those foreign visitors were: Dr. Tracy Strong, General Secretary of the World's Alliance of Y.M.C.A.; Mr. D. F. Meclelland, the Secretary-at-large for the Y.M.C.A.; the late Miss Sara Ghacko (one of the Presidents of the World Council of Churches at the time of her demise) and Mrs. Kamaladevi Chathopadhyaya from India; Dr. A. A. Hoveyda from the United Nations Organisation; Mr. Herbert Lansdale, the Executive Secretary of the International Y.M.C.A. Committee; Dr. W. A. Visser 't Hooft, the General Secretary of the World Council of Churches; Bishop R. C. Lawson from New York; and the Hon. Chester Bowles, the former U.S. Ambassador to India.

Financial Position

The money needed to operate the budget of the Addis Ababa Y.M.C.A. comes from two main sources; Membership and Contribution.

The income from Members covers only a small percentage of the account necessary to operate the ever increasing budget. Hence the major part of the income is derived from contributions from the general public—from those who believe in youth and want to provide facilities to create happy and responsible citizens.

Summary of the Y.M.C.A. 1955 Budget

A.	Boys Department	Eth. $4,040.00
B.	Young Men's Department	7,585.00
C.	Adult Education	13,565.00
D.	Physical Education Department	4,765.00
E.	Handicraft Department	855.00
F.	Leadership Training	4,835.00
G.	Coffee Shop	1,750.00
H.	Library	3,105.00
I.	General Administration	4,995.00
J.	Property Upkeep and Maintenance	3,000.00

Total 48.495.00

Emperor lays cornerstone of Y.M.C.A. building in Addis Ababa

In a special programme held in July 1955, the Addis Ababa Y.M.C.A. awarded special Plaques of Recognition to the Board of Managers for their devoted service to the Y.M.C.A., and in recognition of their work in completing the new Y.M.C.A. building debit free. These Plaques, it should be mentioned, were made by the young men in the Handicraft Department of the Y.M.C.A., and were a combination of ceramics, wood-work and metal-work.

At the Y.M.C.A. World Centennial in Paris (August 12th-24th) Ethiopia was represented by Mr. Merlin Bishop and three laymen, from the Addis Ababa Y.M.C.A.

Having found the Ethiopian boys eager, alert and responsive, the Y.M.C.A. offers a wide range of activities in order to create loyal and intelligent citizens out of them. Their lives have been enriched by lectures, debates, discussion groups, religious services, social events, film shows and com-munity singing. The Handicraft Department encourages them to create things with their own hands. The Y.M.C.A. Library provides them with a large variety of books, mostly presented by the International Y.M.C.A. Headquarters at Geneva. The Physical Education Programme keeps them healthy and teaches them the ideals of sportsmanship. In short, the Addis Ababa Y.M.C.A. is proving itself successful in "its mission of moulding the youth of Ethiopia in harmony with those of the world."

Ethiopian Women's Welfare Work Association

The Ethiopian woman has a place of honour in society and plays a rôle of great responsibility at home. She used to take her rightful place in social life, long before female education became the order of the day. All along the course of Ethiopian history, she has played and worked and fought and served, shoulder to shoulder with her male counterpart. Ethiopia has produced great warriorqueens like Itegue Taitu and valiant women-patriots like Waizero Shoa Regued. She has produced talented artists like Waizero Elizabeth Tesfai and gifted writers like Mme. Senedu Gabru. But however high they might rise, Ethiopian women have always striven for the uplift of their humbler sisters. Hence the origin of the Ethiopian Women's Welfare Work Association in August 1935.

The welfare programme and general constructive activities of the Asso-ciation had to be postponed due to the outbreak of the Italo-Ethiopian War. Nevertheless, during the war, the Association used to despatch bedding, food, tents, medicines, bandages, gasmasks and water-bottles for the Ethiopian soldiers on the battlefront. Their services in this field won due recognition not only from the Emperor but also from the Red Cross Societies abroad.

During the Italian occupation, the E.W.W.W.A. continued to function in England, giving aid to the Ethiopian refugees, wherever they happened to be.

After the liberation, the E.W.W.W.A. was re-organised in September 1941, under the Presidency of Her Imperial Highness Princess Tsahai. When she passed away in 1942, H.I.H. Princess Tenagne Worq was

344

chosen as the new President. In the same year the Association founded a Home for War Orphans, now known as the "Tensae Birhan Orphanage." Her Imperial Majesty Empress Menen has always had the progress and welfare of women at heart ever since she became the consort and counsellor to Emperor Haile Selassie I. So, when the Ethiopian Women's Welfare Work Association was re-organised in 1941, Her Majesty began to take a keen interest in the activities of the Association, while the active presidency is in the hands of H.I.H. Princess Tenagne Worq. The Vice-President is Her Highness Princess Ruth Desta, an enlightened young lady who was educated in England.

The Charter of the Association was granted in November 1953. According to its Article 2, the purposes of the E.W.W.W.A. are, "to relieve the distress of the destitute, the sick and afflicted, the widow and the orphan; to foster improvement in child care and welfare; to contribute to the advancement of women as homemakers; and to do all things necessary or appropriate thereto."

In order to achieve the purposes mentioned above, the Association is empowered "to accept gifts of money and property; to sponsor, promote, conduct and engage in benefit performances, sales and money-raising activities of all kinds; and to do all things necessary or appropriate to the accomplishment of the purposes of the Association."

Present Activities:

1. *The Tensae Birhan (Light of Resurrection) Orphanage* which is situated in the Urael district, provides a home for 60 boys and girls. Of these, the younger children are educated within the Orphanage, while the older ones attend public schools, considering the Orphanage as their home. The Orphanage is dependent on the generous support of the public.

2. *The Princess Tsahai Memoral Clinic* was started in 1943, in the same district, meant for outpatients and maternity cases. This project received considerable financial support from the English people, who paid for the employment of doctors and the cost of medical equipment for the first three years. At present, however, a part of its expenses is borne by the Ministry of Public Health.

3. *The Adult School for Women* provides training in child care, housekeeping, handicrafts and Home Economics. The present strength of the school is 150 students who are also given elementary education in English, Amharic and general knowledge. The course of their training is planned in such a way as to enable them to improve their own living standard and to obtain better employment.

Occasionally, the Ethiopian Women's Welfare Work Association present popular programmes, in order to raise funds for the various deserving causes mentioned above. It should also be recorded that the response from the public has always been quite generous.

The Ethiopian Women's Welfare Work Association has a branch in Harar. This branch has been enabled to carry on its good work through funds supplied from sales of hand-made articles, contributed by its members. The first and foremost aim of this institution is to take care of the orphans, who lost their fathers in the battle-fields, until they are able to support themselves.

The Rotary Club

Rotary has been described as "a world fellowship of business and professional executives, who accept the 'Ideal of Service' as the basis for success and happiness in business and community life." Ever since the first Rotary Club was organised in Chicago (U.S.A.), in February 1905, the Rotary ideals of fellowship and service have spread from pole to pole and have won more than 414,000 followers in 92 countries of the world.

Rotarians everywhere try to live up to their mottos, "Service Above Self" and "He Profits Most who Serves Best." Since Rotary does not seek to interfere with the religions and political beliefs of its members, every Rotarian is expected to be faithful to his own religion, and loyal to his own country.

The establishment of a Rotary Club links its members to a world-encircling chain of cities and towns, where other men have organised Rotary Clubs to express their desire to serve. ROTARY INTERNATIONAL is the association of Rotary Clubs throughout the world and has its offices in Evanston (U.S.A.), London (U.K.) and Zurich (Switzerland).

Rotary, because of its laudable aims and purposes, has gained a firm foothold in Ethiopia. The initiative for forming a Rotary Club in Addis Ababa was taken by Dr. M. B. Chiati, a former Egyptian Ambassador to the Imperial Court of Ethiopia.

The inaugural luncheon party, held at the Egyptian Embassy on 28th December 1954, was attended by 35 gentlemen from different walks of life, among whom there were eight old Rotarians. At this party, Dr. Chiati outlined the purpose of the Rotary International and gave a brief history of the organisation. During the course of the same meeting, a Nominating Committee was formed to recommend names for the various offices of the Club.

The first official meeting of the Rotary Club was held on 4th January 1955 at the Filwoha Palace Hotel. This meeting was attended by 40 prominent men, representing sixteen different nationalities. Seven office-bearers were elected during the course of the meeting, including the President, H. E. Blatta Dawit Ogbagzie, Vice-Minister of Foreign Affairs.

In January 1955, Mr. Fernand Zananiri, the District Governor of the Rotary International for the Middle East, visited the newly-organised Rotary Club of Addis Ababa. He conferred with the executives of the Club and also addressed its members at a luncheon party in the Filwoha Palace Hotel.

Fourteen new members were inducted into the Rotary Club of Addis Ababa, at its 30th mid-day meeting held on 26th July 1955.

At present the Rotary Club has members representing 18 different nationalities resident in the city.

The present President of the Rotary International, Mr. A. Z. Baker, per-

*His Imperial Majesty shows interest in a blind youth taking
Braille dictation in Blind school*

sonally presented a Charter to the Rotary Club of Addis Ababa during the
course of his visit to the city in September 1955.

The presentation ceremony took place at a special "Charter Night" dinner
at the Ras Hotel, in the presence of a distinguished gathering of invited
guests, including high-ranking Government officials.

With the acquisition of the Charter, the Rotary Club of Addis Ababa has
become a full-fledged member of the Rotary International, which is composed of more than 8,700 similar clubs in different parts of the world.

Sports and Games

In common with ancient nations that have produced men of valour and
strength in the course of their chequered history—of struggles against
invaders, territories lost and regained—Ethiopia can reasonably be proud
of her men and of a high standard of national stamina. Endowed by nature
with sound health, the average Ethiopian has, for centuries now, according
to his characteristic native genius, given proof of his interest in sports and
games as pastime and for physical culture.

Unlike the ancient Greek and Roman models, depicting a massive structure
of shapely muscles, a typical Ethiopian athlete has been, and is, noted
for his relatively light but solid-like-steel constitution, permitting agility

347

of limbs, amazing strength, and power of endurance. Aptly illustrating this fact is one of the Ethiopian folk dances styled "War Dance" in which the dancers with their head-dress and collar of the mane and skin of the agile baboon, and armed with spear and shield, exhibit their acrobatic skill and stamina.

No wonder the Ethiopian soldiers, who rank among the world's best, have displayed their mettle in the past, doing a creditable job despite the handicap of lack of equipment. With modern weapons today, in the Korean War they have annexed a number of medals with citations for "outstanding valour and skill" in the battle field. As in war, so in peace-time, in pursuits of hunting and in other sports and games, the athletic qualities of the Ethiopians have been manifest. They have been first class hunters with bow and arrow, spear and shield, they remain good, using modern guns.

Use of the sling in Ethiopia is of ancient origin. It has been cultivated to a high degree of perfection in some parts of the country. It is wielded to scare birds away from grain fields. It was put to an ingenious use during the Italo-Ethiopian War by some guerilla fighters — to transmit written messages, tied to stones, to comrades-in-arms in positions at more than a stone's throw.

Horse-riding is compulsory, in northern parts of the country in particular. "Gugs" is a sport, akin to joust, in which the participants, on horseback, try to knock down one another with a pole which has replaced the lance. A shield made of rhinoceros or oxhide is the only defence. "Wana" (swimming) is a favourite pastime. Wrestling has been in practice for centuries, the technique and rules varying slightly from place to place. Among the variety of ball games is "Shimmeth," the ball being made of rags and fibre and covered with cloth or hide. "Shimal Girfiye," wielding the staff for offence and defence, is a duel requiring skill and vigilance. "Genna" is very much similar to hockey, and of a far earlier origin. Both the stick, L-shaped at the end, and the ball are made of wood. The game, which is known all over the country and played during the Christmas season, has a legend behind it. It is said that the shepherds and peasants in Bethlehem were the first to play the game—on the day Jesus Christ was born. Among the other games are "Koo-la-loo," a form of hide and seek; "Kilebush," resembling Jacks; "Inglis Bandera," involving movement of men into sections like chequers; "Sany Maksanyo," a type of hopscotch; and "Satan and the Angel," similar to a game of London Bridge.

These and other national games and sports have of late, in urban areas, tended to give way to modern ones. His Majesty the Emperor, while encouraging this tendency in so far as it goes to benefit the people and to enable them to take part in international contests, is keen at the same time on development and standardisation of the national games.

Several of the modern games and sports, introduced in the current reign of the Emperor Haile Selassie I, have now taken root. Young men show a preference for football, tennis, polo, volley-ball, basket-ball, etc. while girls favour the last two, for the most part, and also participate in some of the field and track events. Cricket and hockey have been introduced in some schools, but have not yet attained the popularity of some other games.

348

Physical Education in Schools

As part of physical culture, and the attendant development of mind and character, gymnastics and games have been introduced in all educational institutions in the Empire. Besides the Physical Training Instructor on the staff of each school, there is a Physical Training Director attached to the Ministry of Education who co-ordinates the activities in this field. The proper organisation in this sphere at the schools has formed the right foundation for the eventual organisation of sports and games on a national scale, since the youth of today are the citizens of tomorrow. Among the games taught are some native and some modern such as foot-ball, basketball, volley ball and ping-pong. An excellent swimming pool has been provided at the Haile Selassie I Secondary School. Periodical contests, both intra- and inter-school, have done much to stimulate healthy competition and the elevation of athletic standard. Each school has an athletic association and there is a supra Inter-school Athletic Association to regulate the various sports. The annual field and track meets, conducted by this Association, have served to illustrate the progress made year after year, and to underline the highly significant remark of the Duke of Wellington that he won the Battle of Waterloo (against Napoleon) in the "playing fields of Eton" (his Alma Mater). Among the important events in the track and field are: 100 and 200 metre dashes; 100, 800 and 1,500 metre runs; 1,600 metre relay; shot put, broad and high jump; pole-vault, for the boys; and, 40 metre dash, 200 metre relay and basketball throw, for the girls.

Sport and Games among the Public

Football: No other game, perhaps, has a greater appeal to the Ethiopian public than the manly game of football. Record crowds invariably turn up to watch football matches, both internal and international. With their athletic constitution, natural skill and good running capacity, the Ethiopian youth seem destined to be among the world's best footballists in course of time. Football is still young in Ethiopia. It was after the liberation that a serious attempt at organisation was made. At first a five-man committee was set up for the purpose. Later, delegates of the various clubs in the capital formed a committee which functioned under the name of Addis Ababa Football Federation. In 1951, the Ethiopian Football Federation was founded, with widened scope for organisation and control of the game in the country. Further expansion has been called for, following the federation of Eritrea with Ethiopia. Steps are under way for revision of its statutes and for its re-organisation in general, so that all regional federations and leagues may have adequate representation.

The standard of Ethiopian football has remarkably improved as a result of experience gained from international matches. Among the foreign teams of repute that have visited Ethiopia may be mentioned: N.K.F. Nor-copping and A.I.K. Stockholm, from Sweden; Panyonos from Athens; Red Star of Belgrade; Hellenic Athletic Union from Alexandria; the Egyptian Athletic Club from Port Said; "Admira" from Austria; and "Hilal" from the Sudan. The national Ethiopian team has also played these teams, in return, at their respective home grounds.

Other Games and Sports: Coming next in popularity, but steadily growing in importance, are Lawn Tennis, Table Tennis, Basket Ball, Volley Ball, Boxing, Wrestling, Cycling, Motorcycling, Motor Car Racing, etc. Separate "Associations" have been organised for control and development of each of these. Periodical competitions in these events have become regular features. Indoor games, and boxing and wrestling are the most favourite pastimes during the long rainy season of Ethiopia. With a view to possible future participation in international contests, strict adherence to established international regulations is also enforced in all these and other events. In boxing, the switch in general has been towards Feather-Weight, Light-Weight, Welter-Weight and Middle-Weight — naturally so, remembering the characteristic body build-up of the average Ethiopian. Among the recent organisations to come up, in the sports field, is the Amateur Shooting Association. Markmanship is a natural gift of Ethiopians; as such, shooting as a sport, has a bright future, and has now come under proper organisation.

Horse Racing and Polo: The people of Ethiopia, with a background of horsemanship typified in the sport of "Gugs," have always shown great interest in racing and polo. Appreciating this, His Imperial Majesty, early this year desired that the Imperial Racing Club, which had existed before, should be revived and developed on a large scale. Consenting to be the Chief Patron, he made a generous monetary donation for the rehabilitation of the old race course and to help towards the construction of a new Club building. The "King of Sports" has been revived, and the first race meeting just held has been a success beyond all expectations. The success is an unmistakable assurance that the sport has come to stay and it has a future. Several fine horses were run at this meeting, under international regulations of the turf.

Unlike horse racing, polo has suffered no interruption and so has enjoyed a steady rise in standard since the memorable victory, in 1951, by four goals to none over the British team from the Aden Protectorate.

Golf: Another notable addition during the year has been the Imperial Golf Club which enjoys the patronage of His Imperial Majesty. This, together with the Racing Club, has enhanced the prestige of the Empire in introducing and promoting modern sports of universal favour.

Athletics: Carrying forward the fruitful organisation of athletics in schools, Addis Ababa Amateur Athletic Association was set up two years ago. Besides the Army, Police and Air Force that have produced some of the best athletes of international standard, there are the various clubs among the civilians with their welcome contributions. The group of athletes that visited Athens in 1952 drew praise from the popular athletic daily of Greece, "Athlitiki Iho" (Athletic Echo). In the 5000-metre and 1500-metre races, the Ethiopians stood second, while in 1500-metre $\times$ 4 race, they came out first with a creditable record of 17 minutes, 20,3 seconds. As early as May, 1944, in the athletic contest held in Ethiopia between selected teams of Ethiopians, Britons, Greeks, Armenians and Italians (all residents of the country), Ethiopians were the second, Britons being the first.

In the recent field and track meet in the capital, records have been set which compare favourably with world records. The scores were:

1) 200 m: Laguesse Bayene (Aba Dina Police College) in 23.1 s.
2) 400 m: Laguesse Bayene (Aba Dina Police College) in 50.8 s.
3) 1,500 m: Nigoose Zike (Imperial Ethiopian Army) in 4 m. 12.2 s.
4) 5,000 m.: Tadesse Demissie (Imperial Ethiopian Army) in 15 m. 39.6 s.
5) 10,000 m: Bekele Makonnen (Imperial Body Guard) in 33 m 11.4 s.
6) 110 m Hurdles: Zawdie Shifaw (Imperial Body Guard) in 16.8 s.
7) Relay 4 × 400 m: (Imperial Body Guard) in 3 m. 38.6 s.
8) Hop, Step & Jump: Ayalew Seileke (University College) in 12.58 s.
9) Shot Put: Askale Ayele (Imperial Ethiopian Army) with 12.25 m.
10) Discus: Askale Ayele (Imperial Ethiopian Army) with 30.88 m.

National Ethiopian Sports Confederation (NESC): Of the various measures taken under His Imperial Majesty's initiative in the field of sport undoubtedly the most important is the establishment of NESC by an Imperial Charter issued on the eve of the 18th Coronation Anniversary, 1948. The Confederation was set up with the declared objectives of promoting, organising and developing sport in general and physical education in the Empire. The NESC functions through a Board of Directors and receives Government subsidies from time to time to aid the accomplishment of its purposes. Also, it receives from the various sport federations a percentage of their income. By another provision of the Charter, the large Haile Selassie I Stadium, which is being rebuilt at an estimated cost of Eth. $2,000,000, has been entrusted to the NESC for its proper maintenance and use.

All the sport federations are affiliated to the NESC. It has the supreme authority and responsibility in all matters of sport in the country. It has put the sports organisations on the same basis as in other countries, adopting international rules and regulations. A historic landmark in its growth has been its recognition by the International Olympic Committee as the Ethiopian Olympic Committee.

Ethiopia and the Olympics: Ethiopia has been officially invited by the Organising Committee of the XVIth Olympiad to take part in the games to be held in Melbourne next year, and the NESC is presently busy arranging Ethiopia's participation. The participation this time may be more symbolic than active. It is believed, however, that Ethiopia will take part in track and field events, in cycling and shooting. Marathon race is regarded by some experts as an event worth trying. The first Marathon race, held in the country in May this year, gave clear evidence of the lung capacity and power of endurance of the Ethiopian runner. The distance of 42,195 metres was covered in 2 hours and 45 minutes. In recent tests, a 23-year young man has beaten his own record. Another event in which Ethiopia would compete is football. But, she must first take part in the preliminary contests aimed at eliminating all but the world's best 16 teams —the maximum number allowed in the Olympiad.

Whatver may be the extent and final results of Ethiopia's rôle in the greatest sport meet of the world, the historic aspect has its value. The Ethiopian flag will flutter proudly, for the first time on one of the Olympic poles, along with those of other nations.

CHAPTER 30

Tourist Resources of Ethiopia

A subject which is growing more and more interesting these days is that of tourism. Indeed the sizable income in foreign currencies arising from this activity has made it part of the economic planning of many countries. There are countries which are natural tourist resorts because of the attractions found in them. Among these Ethiopia could easily be placed as this brief account is designed to show. As a concomitant of the modern trend in the life of the country, more people have become and are becoming interested in this country. During recent years Ethiopia has begun to recognise tourism as of high cultural value to her modern outlook.

Situated in the African Continent, and although near to the equator, Ethiopia enjoys a temperate climate during the whole of the year because of its high altitude. On the high plateau the rainy season lasts from July to October. During the rest of the year, however, there is an even temperature, distinctly fresher during the night and comparable to the end of Spring in Europe.

On the whole the country has almost unparalleled varieties of beauty and attraction. From the Danakil region, covered with brown lava, to the green valleys of the high plateaux, from the enchanting panorama of the Blue Nile to the tropical forests to the west, from the high mountains of the north to the lakes of the south appears the same characteristic Ethiopian atmosphere. Majesty and vastness of space, impressionable solitude with a clarity of air permitting exceptional visibility for long distances the rising and setting of the sun with their alternations of light and shade provide unique natural beauty.

The extreme richness of the flora and fauna of Ethiopia is proverbial. A large variety of flowers can be seen everywhere; there are giant sycamore mimosa, acacias and eucalyptus groves.

Ethiopia can be considered a paradise for hunters; almost all African varieties of animals and birds abound in fairly large numbers. Found far from dwelling centres and according to seasons and types of region are lions, leopards, elephants, giraffes, zebras, rhinoceros, crocodiles, hippopotami and several species of fish in the rivers and lakes. There are also wild boar, monkeys, antelopes, gazelles, guinea fowl and partridges everywhere and in abundance. It should not be forgotten also, that Ethiopia is among those countries which possess a great variety of aquatic birds marabout, pelicans, flamingos, herons, colibris, etc.

Archaeological and artistic remains of considerable interest reveal Ethiopia's ancient civilisation, so closely linked with the outside world. Trace of the culture and civilisation of ancient Axum, where archaeological investigations are at present being carried out by the Imperial Archaeological Institute, are to be found. The architectural marvels of the monolithic churches at Lalibella, unique in the world, and of the old castles of Gondar are landmarks in Ethiopian history. There are numerous stellae scattered around the lakes in the Sidamo province and at Axum that still retain the secret of the civilisation which existed during the time of their erection.

Ethiopian art, essentially based on the religious motif, reveals itself in the church architecture, in ritual paintings, in illustrations of manuscripts and in the ornamentation of precious metals.

At Gondar, the old historic capital of Begemder and Semien an exhibition illustrating part of the history, art and antiquities of the Empire has been arranged. The exhibits are drawn from all parts of that province which includes Lake Tana with its numerous monasteries and other places closely associated with the history of both Church and State. While a long list could be made of places of particular interest to visitors, since antiquities are to be found in several regions of the country, Gondar should prove of particular interest both to students and to the average visitor.

Assembled by the Governor General of the province as part of the Imperial Jubilee Exhibition, many objects have been collected—crowns, coronation and other vestments, furniture with historical associations, ancient weapons, ecclesiastical vessels, and, in particular, many pictures and manuscripts.

Enquiries in various remote churches and monasteries have uncovered many relics of great interest, both ancient and comparatively modern. For example, a huge red cloak, obviously of Arab origin or inspiration, reputed to have belonged to Ahmad Gran, the Moslem invader of the sixteenth century; coronation robes, a state chair, and an elaborate silk standard, of the Emperor Yohannes (1872); the crowns of the Emperors Na'od (1494), Fasiladas (1632) and Theodore (1855); a hand cross of purely Ethiopian design but bearing a Chinese inscription (the origin of which has yet to be determined); and many manuscripts dating from the fifteenth century (or earlier) to the eighteenth, including some enormous and some finely illustrated specimens.

Lake Tana noted for its island churches and monasteries has supplied many treasures for this exhibition. There is, for instance, a cross of Palestnian workmanship, doubtless brought to Ethiopia in the reign of David I (1382—1411) at the same time as a fragment of the True Cross; the sword of Zar'a Ya-qob (1434—1468); and a magnificent chair of Fasiladas (1632—1667)—all of these brought from Daga Estefanos; the porcelain bowl in which the bones of the Emperor Sartsa-Dengel (died 1597) were conveyed from the Sudan (brought from Rema Madhane-Alam); and some remarkable paintings on parchment folded concertinawise between boards, dating perhaps from the 14th century, from Tana Qirqos; also many fine manuscripts, some of them written in hands of a very antique style.

The exhibits are displayed in the splendid halls of the Fasil Gimb, the oldest of the Gondar castles. The whole ensemble of castles and associated buildings has been discreetly restored, and the enclosure cleared of ugly barracks and temporary huts erected by the Italians during the occupation. Tourist lore, in the real sense of the term, has only partially been gathered and catalogued in Ethiopia. Almost everything has to be discovered and surprises abound amidst an originality and a beauty which are the true characteristics of the country. Ancient Ethiopia, wrapped in mystery and legend, possesses an infinite charm, which attracts the attention of the visitor as well as the curiosity of the scholar.

In the northern part of the country, principally at Axum, capital of ancient Ethiopia, is to be found a wealth of historic monuments whose secrets are yet untold. Still in the north are the "Ambas" a sort of very steep rocky hills cut in the shape of tables, which were either fortresses or prisons. The most famous of them is at Magdala, scene of the heroic and tenacious resistance of the Emperor Theodore.

In the south the antique town of Harar infinitely picturesque and enclosed in its ancient ramparts is of entirely another type. There are only a few of the numerous regions of Ethiopia which are not certain to be of interest to the tourist or the seeker.

A more detailed description of these places so full of mystery and of historical associations, ought to interest the most fastidious visitor.

Without any exaggeration one could confirm that, apart from the interest excited by its archaeological treasures, this ancient kingdom of Ethiopia, which dates back to King Solomon and to the fabulous Queen of Sheba, possesses a permanent and unlimited attraction to the tourist. The scenery of Ethiopia, majestic in its splendour, and the variety of its natural beauty spots join together to fascinate tourists. The vast space where silence and solitude create that serene atmosphere which carries the visitor, as it were, into an immaterial world; placid lakes, some of them in the form of craters, others bordered by a carpet of grass; the thick forests resembling those of tropical jungles should all be kept in mind when picturing tourist adventure in Ethiopia. Let us examine briefly some of the regions:

Entoto is only ten kilometres from Addis Ababa. Three thousand metres above sea level this place was the temporary capital of Ethiopia at the end of the 19th century. On the road from Addis Ababa to Entoto, an imposing panorama is offered to the visitor at each turning of the road. The capital, Addis Ababa, lies at the foot of the mountain hidden in a forest of eucalyptus; the plain of Akaki with its lake at the foot of Mount Furi, flanked by the Errer Mountain and embraced at a distance by the majestic Zuquala Range can be clearly seen. Colours vary according to the season, the end of the rains showing the most unexpected contrasts. On the whole this panorama depicts the vivid harmony of a variety of striking scenes.

The Blue Nile: At 175 kilometres from Addis Ababa is found the small village of Goha Tsion, along the Nile Valley where the separation of the Nile presents a very remarkable spectacle. Rising at Lake Tana, the Blue Nile turns widely to the south before leaving Ethiopia. From the village which is at the same level as the Nile, the scenery is fantastic. The Yellow River can be noticed rolling in a deep gorge, breaking through enormous blocks of basalt and flowing titanically, really recalling the divine origin of the Nile. This combination of enormous power and extraordinary scenery creates a strong, almost religious, impression on the viewer.

Lake Tana: On the opposite side of the Blue Nile the road continues across the Province of Gojjam towards Gondar and Lake Tana which forms a small interior river with its banks and islands. The lake takes the shape of a heart, 85 kilometres long from the north to the south and 65 kilometres wide from east to west, with an area of 3,630 sq. metres and a maximum depth of 14 metres.

The source of the Blue Nile is the Lesser Abbai, a river flowing into Lake Tana from the south. The fearless population of these districts are mainly hunters of hippopotami and fishermen with their small picturesque boats or "tanqua." As noted above the numerous islands of the Lake, surrounded by a mysterious charm, contain monasteries and churches which date from the 14th to the 16th century and which are of important archaeological and historical interest. Ancient and rare manuscripts are found in the libraries of these monasteries. The mummified body of Negus Fasiladas, one of the builders of the town of Gondar, can also be seen on one of these islands. A long enough stay will permit a complete visit to the lake and to the town of Gondar which lies at a distance of 40 kilometres from Lake Tana. The journey from Addis Ababa to Gondar can be made in two hours by Ethiopian Air Lines. The distance to Gojjam by road is 800 kilometres.

The Tarmabar: One of the greatest panoramas of Ethiopia is afforded by the north east valley of the Danakil region immediately adjoining the high plateau. The main road from Addis Ababa to Asmara (Eritrea) by way of Debra-Sina and Dessie follows the ridge of the high plateau at 165 kilometres from the capital, over Tarmabar. The road, well constructed, descends under the rocks through a passage 587 metres long, 8 metres wide and 6.30 metres high. Coming out of this passage the traveller is struck by a staggering spectacle. From a height of 3,000 metres, the view stretches to an immense valley which continues to the desert. The road is good and the atmosphere wholesome and agreeable. The vegetation, quite rich, is eclipsed by the originality and the immensity of the panorama.

Metahara: This desert, of a volcanic nature, torrid in temperature, of insupportable dryness, fascinates the traveller attracted by the tropical nature of Africa. Should it be during the hottest hour of the day, when the intensity of the light gives to the landscape a particular brightness, unreal and indescribable, or during the few minutes preceding sunrise, or during sunset, the quality of the colours and the clearness of the air change this arid spot into an enchanting and unforgettable scene. In the midst of this ravaged plain, the Awash River winds around in bands of dark green shade and forms the thick ribbon of the real jungle. The high trees conceal a number of monkeys and a large variety of birds. This region can be reached by road or rail. The distance from Addis Ababa is 200 kilometres.

The Region of Lakes: The attraction which Ethiopian lakes afford is proverbial. Near to the capital, at a distance of 45 kilometres by road or train, a number of craters are found of volcanic origin and, separated one from the other, they form five beautiful lakes. The largest, the Bishoftu lake, particularly attracts the swimmer. At a distance of 7 kilometres to the south, is found the Green Lake which is attractive for its atmosphere of quietness. The other three lakes have their particular charm. A number of large lakes continue to the south.

Hora Robi and Bereket at 105 kilometres from Addis Ababa, are interesting because in them hippopotami can be found at this relatively short distance from the capital. *Lake Zwai* that follows has a surface of approximately 400 sq. metres. It is inhabited by hippopotami and crocodiles, and its borders of basalt rocks prove its volcanic origin. It has a great deal of similarity with Lake Tana because on it there are five islands inhabited by fishermen.

At a distance of 190 kilometres from Addis Ababa can be found lakes Abaida, Langano and Scialia of different dimensions from 200 to 300 square kilometres with diverse characteristics. They are all found in the Arussi Province which has great agricultural possibilities. Here is found abundant vegetation of a wild nature, large stretches covered with various kinds of mimosas, acacias and giant euphorbia candelabrum. Lake Abaida is at a distance of 210 kilometres from Addis Ababa; Langano at 220; and Scialia at 232.

One of the natural sights, considered as very marvellous in Ethiopia, is undoubtedly Lake Awassa, situated in the centre of an extremely rich country. The beauty of this lake, which stretches its water over an area of 150 square kilometres, is so captivating that His Majesty the Emperor anticipates that a tourist centre, provided with a small airport will be built there. The circular road makes it possible to see the lake from all directions. From its banks various aspects can be seen: now a brilliant sandy beach; then attractive vegetation. The neighbourhood of the lake is well known for its fertility. Two large plantations produce the famous Sidamo Coffee. At 30 kilometres from the lake the large market of the town of Shashamana 338 kilometres from Addis Ababa is an important agricultural centre.

From this locality to Soddu, a distance of 153 kilometres, and from there to the extreme north of Lake Marguerita is a region reminiscent of the large lakes of central Africa. With a length of 70 kilometres, a width of 224 kilometres and an area of 1,256 square kilometres Lake Marguerita is surrounded by a circle of mountains approximately 4,000 metres high. Spread out at the foot of fertile slopes, rich in tropical agriculture, this large lake is considered one of the best sites in Ethiopia. Nevertheless, access is difficult and the climate unsuitable for many people.

Kaffa: The typical zones of tropical forests are found in the Kaffa region. A traveller who has been around the world recently said, after having visited that region, that no other existing scenery could be compared to that of this region. This is probably due to the extraordinary vegetation and the numerous shades that this corner reflects, of the beauty of its plants, of its thick forests and of its abundant fauna.

From an abrupt reef which slowly descends, cut through by a number of picturesque river valleys, always flowery and green, where everything appears to grow naturally, Kaffa, a real dreamland, resembles a picture, conceived by mediaeval travellers, of the celestial Eden that they imagined to be in Ethiopia. The region can be reached by the Jimma road, and lies at a distance of approximately 500 kilometres from the capital.

Half way along the road the traveller will be attracted by an imposing spectacle that should remind him in part of the tributary of the Nile; it is the descent to the Omo Valley, a river crossed by a bridge on the Jimma road, at a distance of 180 kilometres from Addis Ababa. This unique view surprisingly appears at the turning of a road hung on to a cliff. The impression is extraordinary and, correctly speaking, is awesome. At the bottom of the valley, marked by gorges and dry rocks in the centre of which the Omo washes through, is the road which goes down 15 kilometres along the mountain side before reaching the bed of the river where one can see crocodiles.

Thermal Waters: The tourist will find that among the thermal resources are many curative waters rich in chemicals. In Addis Ababa at Filoha are hot springs (71 degrees) of alkaline and carbonated waters. Miraculous legends are connected with the springs of Ambo, 125 kilometres from Addis Ababa. These waters springing from 52 different springs are sulphurous, ferruginous and bi-carbonated with sodium. They are considered extremely curative and, from the hotels and restaurants there, are easily available. On the Jimma road 112 kilometres from the capital, the springs of Walliso are well known for their medicinal qualities, especially in connection with skin diseases. To the south of Errer, at approximately 70 kilometres from Dire Dawa, the hot water springs are well known for the treatment of rheumatism.

Hunting by Regions: The entire Danakil Region which extends between the high Ethiopian plateau, the high Somali plain and the sea coast of the Red Sea has great possibilities for hunting. It forms a desolate desert plain except for the depression of the Awash River which shows the only sign of fertility. The heat is at its limit and it is a spot where the highest degree of dryness in the Empire is encountered. Nevertheless, this location compensates for lack of fertility by abundant game. In this region can be found oryx, small and large gazelles, and a variety of antelopes, from the tiny dik-dik to the large kudu with huge horns, zebras, the wild ass, ostriches, leopards and lions.

In the plain at the foot of Mount Fantale in the region of Lake Metahara, 200 kilometres from Addis Ababa, large flocks of oryx and kudus can be found. Pink flamingos, crocodiles and hippopotami are found in the Awash River. These places can be reached partially by railway and by road.

South Region: This is the region of lakes which stretches between Addis Ababa and the Kenya frontier. The country is rich, verdant and extremely fertile with a warm and agreeable climate. The cliffs and rivers that follow among the large lakes give the impression of an unlimited aquatic horizon. The flora and fauna vary according to seasons. For hunting, the thick covered regions of Arussi, the banks of Lakes Zwai, Abaita, Langano and Scialia should be explored for interesting results. It is after Lake Awassa that large game appears in the growing region of Sidamo-Borana. In the Arussi region it is possible to meet the nyala, a rare species of large African antelope. The Sidamo road leads to all regions.

Lake Bereket, oval in shape, a distance of about 105 kilometres from Addis Ababa, has many crocodiles and hippopotami. Fish is also found in abundance. In the same region are found several kinds of gazelles and complete families of wart-hogs.

Lake Zwai which follows immediatedly looks like a miniature sea studded with small islands inhabited by a population of fishermen and farmers. Hunting is concentrated on hippopotami and sometimes on crocodiles. Swarms of aquatic birds, mainly the flamingo, are found there.

Towards the south, between Lakes Awassa and Marguerita, the region of big game is reached. This is also extremely rich coffee country. The population is dense and the climate warm and healthy. Starting from Soddu (452 km) towards Lake Marguerita, lions, elephants, buffaloes and a large variety of antelopes and gazelles may be hunted. For large game it is necessary to organise a safari of mules starting from the villages of Soddu and Javelo. The distance from Addis Ababa to Soddu is 453 km and to Javelo 623 km.

West and South West Region: The most specifically tropical region of Ethiopia, not only from the standpoint of climate and vegetation but also from that of game, is incontestably Gimira and Kaffa. Cultivation is extensively carried on, and the variety and density of plants and forests are probably due to the moisture resulting from the long rainy season. Precautions against malaria should be taken.

Important rivers and their tributaries run through the country. Coming from Addis Ababa, the Omo River is reached, where there are swarms of crocodiles and hippopotami. In the tropical region of Bonga the Godjeb River also abounds with crocodiles and hippos. The further one goes from the capital the more game increases. Starting from the Omo, large numbers of antelopes, kudus and gazelles may be seen, and near the river banks it is common to meet with the python. In Gimira and Kaffa, besides antelopes and gazelles, lions, buffalos, giraffes and the black panther, well known for its fur, are found.

The town of Jimma may be reached by road and from that point onward to Bonga the road is usually crowded with mule caravans. The region interesting to hunters is situated between approximately 200 kilometres (the Omo Valley) and 500 kilometres from Addis Ababa.

North Region: Though interesting from a touristic and archaeological point of view, this region is less so as regards game. In this part of Africa are found the highest mountains (Semien Region 5,000 metres). The tropical climate at an altitude of 3,000 metres permits a rich flora in kakis, wild jasmins and orchids, and becomes almost alpine at even a higher altitude where roses and buttercups and a characteristic plant of the Semien, the lobella, are found.

The usual game of this region consists of antelopes with straight horns. The road is excellent and leads from Addis Ababa to Asmara a distance of 1,080 kilometres.

Other Aspects: While scenery and game are among the main attractions for tourists visiting Ethiopia, another aspect will strike the visitor. That is the contrast between an ancient and traditional country and present day Ethiopia marching by large paces towards modern progress.

In Addis Ababa, a city 100 sq. kilometres in area, are wide asphalted roads and avenues with modern buildings providing all the necessary comforts for living. Numerous cars, some of the latest model, are to be seen in the capital.

Among the hotels in the city, the Ras Hotel, the Itegue Hotel and the Filowha Palace Hotel are outstanding for their accommodation and comfort. The rate for full board varies between $10 to $12 Ethiopian per day $1 U.S. = $2.50 Ethiopian). The menu of these hotels is different from that of the Ethiopian menu, consisting largely of European and American dishes.

There is great diversity in the typical Ethiopian dishes which consist of a large number of very palatable sauces. A minimum of 30 different kinds of spices are needed to make the best type of these dishes known as "watt." Ethiopian meals are usually served with the national drinks: the "talla," being a sort of beer prepared with barley and "geisho" a special plant that grows in Ethiopia, and the tedj, a sort of wine (mead) made with honey and the leaves of the same "geisho." The national bread (injera) is principally made of teff (millet) or maize, barley, etc. It is a sort of pancake, sometimes 40 cms in diameter, baked on an iron sheet heated very slowly.

CHAPTER 31

The Return of Eritrea

The return of Eritrea to the motherland stands out as one of the most important accomplishments of His Majesty the Emperor during the twenty-five years of His reign. The historical, political, and social significance of this event, directly the result of the Emperor's statemanship, will remain for centuries. In fact, Eritrea's return has started a new era in the life of Ethiopia.

The struggle for the return of Eritrea, which ended in September 1952, had its roots in the old game of colonial expansion into the continent of Africa. What represented the cradle of the present day Ethiopian empire up till 1890, became the subject of imperialism and remained so until, with federation, it returned under the sovereignty of the Ethiopian Crown. The story is long and interesting.

First came the Rubattino Shipping Company in 1869; the Italian Government followed with the flag and its naval and land forces. These were forerunners of infiltration deeper into Ethiopian territory by force of arms. Menelik II arrested this trespass by the Adwa defeat of the Italians in 1896, but unfortunately, did not press his military advantage home. Eritrea (so named by the Italians) was to be the spring-board for southerly expansion. Since military penetration was stopped at Adwa, the Italians adopted other methods. Treaty making was tried — the famous treaty of Ucciali — the hidden design of which was scotched by Menelik II.

Returning to Eritrea, the Italians consolidated their interests there. The process of alienating the Eritreans from their brothers in Ethiopia was rapid and deep and not at all difficult. Eritreans were armed in preparation to kill their brothers across the Mareb River, in the march of and for the interest of the Italian imperialists. Italianisation and mercantilism held sway. Superficial quiet prevailed down to 1934. But the campaign of expansion into Ethiopia was not shelved, as later events illustrated. Chapters 9 and 10 have dealt with the climax of this continued campaign. It is *a propos* to state here, however, that in the all-out war by Italy to follow up the 1896 failure, Italian forces moved from their bases in Eritrea, and following the same line of attack, bombarded Adwa and Adigrat in the opening phases of aggression against the country. Italy won a temporary victory until 1941.

When the fortunes of war changed, Eritrea, smug in the hands of the occupiers, saw the rekindling of the flame of fraternity of the Ethiopians with their brothers across the Mareb River — a flame which the Italians had for over half a century striven to stifle. These new masters sought to crush the Eritrean traditions and culture and to impose on the people the Italian way of life. Although the change had to be expected, this caused considerable dissatisfaction among the people in general and the patriots in particular. But any kind of opposition was quite impossible as the colonisation of their country had become an accomplished fact. The Eritreans, however, entertained the hope that some day they would be able to shed their oppressors and the long term of imposed separation.

The first gun was fired in the struggle for Eritrea's final return to the motherland by His Majesty the Emperor when He issued the decree dropped by the Royal Air Force over Eritrea in 1941, encouraging the population to join their brethren in the liberation of their country — Ethiopia. *People of Hamasien, Akalaguzai, Seraie, Beni Amer, Habab and Mensa, whether you are on this side of the frontier or over in Eritrea, you must be united with your Ethiopian brothers; not one of you must be a collaborator with the Italians ... When Ethiopia regains her independence, it is Our wish that you will live together as one people,* was part of this decree.

The Italians were defeated in 1941 — the motherland and Eritrea were rid of the fascists. After the famous battle of Keren put an end, for all practical purposes, to the stranglehold on Eritrea between February 2nd and March 22nd, British troops quickly reduced Eritrea to British control and established a British Administration there. His Imperial Majesty returned to His capital, Addis Ababa, on May 5th, 1941. But the situation did not present, as one might have thought, an easy solution. The British Military Administration of Eritrea hit wide of that avowed concept which seemed to have existed when the war of liberation was taking shape in 1940, or even in 1941, after the fall of Keren which brought Italian East Africa crumbling as a house of cards. Nor for the last seven years preceding federation did the Eritrean Administration accord with the official British Government view as expressed by Sir Anthony Eden (then Mr. Anthony Eden), who declared in the House of Commons that under no circumstances could the United Kingdom admit that after the war any of the ex-Italian colonies in East Africa be returned to Italy. It would seem normal then that for Eritrea the logical course would have been its simple and direct return to Ethiopia; but this was far from being so. A long, confused, and laboured struggle developed on the Eritrean people and on Emperor Haile Selassie's Government to attain this aspiration.

And there were war-time pledges which made this long-drawn-out struggle seem even the more illogical.

A proclamation by the Emperor Haile Selassie I specially addressed to the people of the Italian colonies of Eritrea and the Benadir (Somaliland) was also showered down by the R.A.F. It read:

Eritrean people and people of the Benadir! You were separated from your mother, Ethiopia, and were put under the yoke of the enemy, and under the yoke of the enemy you still remain.

I have come to restore the independence of my country, including Eritrea and the Benadir, whose people will henceforth dwell under the shade of the Ethiopian flag.

The people of Ethiopia's lost seaboard province were deeply stirred by these promises of liberation and by the hope that they would soon be reunited to their ancient Motherland from which they had been torn by foreign conquest fifty years before. Eritrean soldiers in the Italian armies deserted *en masse*. Forty battalions, the cream of the Italian colonial army, dispersed and were never seen again.

Meanwhile, behind the front in Khartoum, Perry Fellowes began the publishing of "Banderachin," the first airborne newspaper of the war against the Axis. It was dropped in the Kassala—Tessenei—Sabderat triangle of Eritrea.

This propaganda was found extremely efficacious in Eritrea. British intelligence thereupon analysed the grievances of the Eritreans and began dropping the following leaflet, under the British Royal Arms:

"Soldiers of Eritrea! Listen!

"Our cowardly Italian enemy robs you of your fertile land.

"One English army is standing before Keren. A second army stands before Arresa and Adi Ugri. A third English and French army has taken Cubcub. Soon the Italians in Eritrea will be completely cut off by land as well as by sea.

"In Gojjam the Emperor Haile Selassie has driven the Italians back from Dangila and Enjabara to the Blue Nile. Those who wish to fight under the flag of Haile Selassie or under the English Flag will be allowed to do so."

To aid the Keren offensive which was to begin on the 15th March, 1941, with all the artillery and aircraft in the Sudan and two Indian Divisions scaling the hills, two replicas of the Ethiopian Flag were prepared, one of them bearing the likeness of His Majesty the Emperor, and millions of these flags were dropped over Eritrea.

G. L. Steer reports that the deserter flood at once increased. From the other side came more and more reports "not only of insubordination among the Amhara but of disobedience of the long-service Eritrean N.C.O.'s who had hitherto been Italy's most faithful soldiers." (1)

On the face of things, both the Emperor and the Eritrean people, in good faith, believed that, as was the case in the motherland, the British Military Administration in Eritrea would be temporary. In fact, it could not logically have been otherwise, except a complete *volte face* was taken. As the Administration became entrenched, however, both parties became more and more dismayed. An impracticable and ill-advised colonial attitude was developed by the British Administration. It became oppressive to the rights and aspirations of the Eritrean people. At a particular stage, the Administration seemed to have been run in the interests of the Italians to the dire distress and frustration of the local inhabitants. One of the greatest blows to the Eritrean cause came when Sir Philip Mitchell, who later signed the Anglo-Ethiopian Agreement and Military Convention in 1942, as Chief Political Officer for the occupied enemy territories, issued a memorandum which read:

"Italian law and regulations, territorial and municipal, should be maintained as far as possible, and if Italian Judges and Magistrates are willing to remain in office, they may be permitted to function with such safeguards as may appear desirable."

(1)   E. Sylvia and Richard Pankhurst, *Ethiopia and Eritrea.*

362

The decision as set out in Sir Philip Mitchell's memorandum was in striking contrast to the pledges of liberation from Italian yoke enunciated in the leaflets which so recently had been showered upon the people, but in the early days the Eritreans did not understand that a policy totally opposed to that of the leaflets was to be operated.

Furthermore, in the early days, after the Italian defeat, the people were far from anticipating that the British would remain for a lengthy period. On the contrary, they had taken quite literally the promises to liberate them from Italy and to reunite them to Ethiopia, which had been conveyed to them in leaflets, distributed by the British Royal Air Force, and repeated to them by loud-speakers from the British lines; to doubt the validity of these pledges would have been to doubt the honour and good faith of the British liberators, and that, in those first days of rejoicing and gratitude, was unthinkable. (²)

The situation in which the United Kingdom Government found itself was rather unfortunate. It had, regrettably, to select Eritrean administrators from among colonial civil servants. The training and activities of these men, while suitable for the British colonies which Eritrea oddly was not, seemed ill-appropriate to the new task. These men however, might have been considered efficient and sincere in their approach to their task. Peradventure they were experts, but the facts calmly and eloquently illustrated that they were out of tune with the wider issues involved in Eritrea. They were empire builders; Eritrea was not designed to be part of the empire which they were meticulously trained to build and preserve. Sylvia and Richard Pankhurst give the following account of the officialdom which was responsible for the administration of occupied enemy territories, including Eritrea:

The officials to administer the "Occupied Enemy Territory" were mostly Colonial Civil Servants imbued with the practice of white supremacy and African subordination.

The following held the key posts:

Sir Philip Mitchell,	Governor of Uganda, became Chief Political Officer for Occupied Enemy Territories. (Later signed the Anglo-Ethiopian Agreement of 1942 for the British Government).
Mr. R. H. Hone,	Attorney-General of Uganda, became Chief Legal Adviser.
Hon. Francis Rodd,	(afterwards Lord Rennell of Rodd), became Controller of Finance and Accounts.
Mr. B. Kennedy Cooke,	Governor of the Kassala Province of the Sudan, was given the rank of Brigadier, and was installed as Governor of Eritrea, under the title "Deputy Chief Political Officer."
Lt. Col. D. C. Cumming,	also a Sudan Civil Servant, became Secretary to the Administration.

General Frusci, the Italian Governor of Eritrea had gone and the leading

(²) E. Sylvia and Richard Pankhurst, *op. cit.*

Italian official left behind was the Secretary-General, Signor Barile. This man took over Italian administration under British control at the request of Brig. Kennedy Cooke.

Italian administrative officials were retained in the following three divisions:

Asmara and Hamasien (Asmara Division)
Serae (Adi Ugri Division)
Assab (Assab Division)

and Italian "extra commissioners" were maintained, in municipal functions only, in the following further divisions:

Eastern Plains and the
Seaport, Massawa (Massawa Division)
Keren (Keren Division)
Akele Guzai (Adi Caieh Division)

From the areas mentioned above, it will be seen that the educated and the politically conscious Eritreans were again brought into close contact with Italian officials. On the other hand, the uneducated and the nomadic people were removed from Italian control.

Lord Rennell, who was intimately concerned with decisions as to administration, explained:

"British propaganda among the Eritrean population before the campaign had led to expectations which were not fulfilled. The maintenance of Italian administration in the urban centres and on the plateau, and the mere existence of Italian civilians in the provinces, even though they exercised no judicial functions, was not understood by the native inhabitants."

The British Military Administration, having no adequate police force, determined at the commencement of their rule in Eritrea to make use of the Italian police force, the Polizia Italiana.

Zapti was the name of an Eritrean police force which occupied a very inferior status during the Italian occupation. The British re-enrolled both the Italian police force and the Zapti, and gave a superior status to the Italian force.

The fact that the Italian police force was still there between the British and themselves was very resentful to Eritreans who might have had some satisfaction had the British eliminated the Italians at least on a gradual scale, or had the British put some of the Zapti men in responsible positions.

Maltreatment of Eritreans by Italians became a regular feature in the capital, Asmara, and its suburbs. Consequently, a large number of Eritreans marched to the British Administration Office and placed their grievances before the authorities. The British authorities promised to look into their grievances and have them redressed, but instead, issued a proclamation forbidding the assembly of more than five persons and the display of the Ethiopian flag or any badge concerned with Ethiopia.

What was most resentful to the Eritreans was that Italians were still occupying positions of power. The continuance of discriminatory treatment to Eritreans in cinemas, cafes, etc. added fuel to the fire.

364

*His Imperial Majesty ratifying the Eritrean Constitution
in the Imperial Palace*

About the time the British issued the proclamation, they instructed the Eritrean people to select 12 representatives from the various provinces of Eritrea, to form a Native Council, which the British Senior Civil Affairs Officer would summon monthly, to receive the instructions of the British Authorities and to bring before them any difficulties or grievances of the Eritrean population. The Eritrean representatives of the Native Council, soon afterwards, presented a written report to the British Senior Civil Affairs Officer, Colonel White, advising the removal of the Italian officials. ([3])

Because of the background of these administrators, what was the legitimate expression of a normal reaction towards their policies and, even more, a national movement, was repressed. The express objective was to keep the Eritreans and their brothers across the Mareb River divided and, if possible, to partition Eritrea.

([3])   E. Sylvia and Richard Pankhurst, *op. cit.*

Stimulated by opposition to the trend of the British Administration policies, and in an effort to provide an organisation for the representation of their views and to make known their aspirations as a community, the Eritrean Unionist Party emerged. The organisation founded in April 1941 by the Eritrean patriots, later inspired Eritreans resident in the mother-land to form a party on similar lines. It was clear from the outset that the Unionist Movement was a challenge to the administration's policy o trying to perpetuate a colonial regime in Eritrea. These significant state ments were found in a British memorandum of June 28th, 1941:

"......Since the Italians are to a large extent dependent on the native for supplies, and since the Italians have the lion's share of capital and com merce, relations between the two races must not be allowed to become too bad.

"The urban natives have behaved as we anticipated. Those with some education have their heads in the clouds and are inclined to attach un-warranted significance to Haile Selassie's return to Addis Ababa. The movement will probably grow, and will no doubt be stimulated from Ethiopia.

"Our leniency towards the Italians must be dictated by our own interests and we are not here to strive after a native Utopia, although our ad-ministration should not be so open to criticism that it adversely affects British prestige in neighbouring countries."

Not only were the Eritreans wary of these Administrators' overt inclina-tions to suppress their spontaneous desire for reunion, they were also feeling the economic pinch. Eritrea's economic condition, however, was not a creation of the British Military Administration. The Italians had built up a fictitious economy in the country designed primarily for their intended war exploits against Ethiopia.

The condition of Eritrea and Somaliland as the British found it is vividly portrayed in "The First to be Freed," a pamphlet written by A. C. Gandar Dower, who accompanied the British forces, and issued by the British Ministry of Information. It describes them as "two over-capitalised, bank-rupt semi-deserts, which had never been self-supporting and which had never been intended to be self-supporting. The territories had developed no industries and little agriculture, their imports for years had greatly exceeded exports, they had been maintained hitherto only by enormous grants-in-aid from Italy."

To quote from official reports, "until 1935, the colony was a normal African territory, supporting perhaps 5,000 Europeans; by 1941 it was containing but not supporting 60,000 civilians, in addition to the armed forces."

"Asmara," declared *The First to be Freed*, "was a remarkable levitated white elephant, which Fascist grandiosity and engineering skill had con-jured into existence at 7,800 feet, in the midst of a country that lacked the means to support it. In this strange city lived 45,000 Italians who could not obtain enough fresh milk for their children and imported vegetables from Rome, and 100,000 natives, largely crowded into a latrineless native

366

quarter, which lacked enough water even for their unambitious needs."
To quote from official reports, "At Asmara and elsewhere, the Italians had established factories and engineering shops. There is an impressive transport equipment, there are air-fields, aircraft engineering shops, and electric light and power. But there is nothing for which all these facilities can be used except to supply the needs of an army campaigning south-wards against Ethiopia. The elimination of that army brought to an end the only purpose of the greater part of the organisation and equipment of the Italian colony, with the resultant problems of unemployment, sup-ply and subsidy which have caused us, and are continuing to cause us, the gravest difficulties." (4)

What made matters worse for the native Eritrean population was the fact that preference — economic and otherwise — was shown towards the Italians and that the Administration, though costly both to the British Government and tax-payers was, as it were, using the silver whip to bend the will of the Eritreans to accept a policy of self-determination alien to the wishes of the majority of them. Some of the Italians who were put in administrative positions did more harm than good to the Administration and to British prestige. From "Ethiopia and Eritrea," already cited, we read:

The relationship between the Italian Administration and the British was continuously dominated by the claim of the Italians that they must not be humiliated "in face of an inferior race." This claim, it must be regret-fully admitted, evoked considerable sympathy from the British colonial officials. Accustomed to deal with large African populations in Kenya, the Sudan and elsewhere, they had been trained to believe in the almost sacred necessity of upholding white prestige.

It was argued that the Hague Rules rendered it necessary for the local authorities of an occupied enemy territory to be permitted to function as long as they refrained from endangering the occupying forces. As we have seen, however, the Hague Rules were only maintained on the high-land plateau adjacent to Ethiopia, where the Christian population enjoyed close relations with the Ethiopian motherland to which they were ardently desirous of reunion; in the Western lowlands and in Massawa, where political feeling was much less intense, the local Italian authorities were almost immediately removed.

The reason for this marked difference seems, in part at least, to be that it was already the policy to partition Eritrea, awarding the Muslim areas to the Anglo-Egyptian Sudan.

British Colonial officials had concurred in the Maffey Interdepartmental Report which had been sympathetic to the proposed Italian conquest of Ethiopia; it was therefore natural that they should have one policy for the Eritreans, whose geographic proximity to Ethiopia made them an inte-gral part of the pan-Ethiopian movement, and another for Somaliland, which was relatively far off from the Ethiopian motherland and inacces-sible therefrom. In Somaliland, the indigenous population was given a

(4)   E. Sylvia and Richard Pankhurst, *op. cit.*

part in the administrative machine where the Somalis were far less advanced than the Eritreans, whereas Eritreans were not encouraged to hold identical posts in Eritrea.

A graphic picture of the first phase in British-occupied Eritrea is given by the American Commander, Edward Ellsberg:

"......What kind of topsy-turvy war was this where conquerors went about defenceless while their prisoners roamed the street at large, armed?" he said.

Ellsberg was informed by Major Goff that it was "all a matter of Italian honour. An American can hardly understand its nuances......"

Much softness was shown to the vanquished Italians and care was taken to guard their "honour" in spite of the fact that many Italians still hoped for a German invasion which would re-establish Fascist Rule; they were deliberately planning to assist the Germans when the opportune moment came, in the meantime they were organising sabotage and guerila warfare. (5)

Many sections of the population knew that it was vitally necessary for the salvation of their country that they should unite for the common good. In a long statement to the British Authorities in the early phases of the Administration, Abuna Markos, Head of the Ethiopian Orthodox Church in Eritrea, pointed out the hardships the Ethiopian people were undergoing. Dr. Spicace's (Commissioner of Adi Ugri) tyrannical way of administering that province was noted. So also did the Eritrean Unionists address two documents to the British: one reassured support to the British and expressed sentiments regarding reunion with Ethiopia; the other openly stated their grievances, particularly against the power given to the Italians.

It was clear that the Unionist Movement was growing, receiving its impetus and gathering momentum from the pitiful attitude of the Administration to the legitimate and spontaneous wishes of the people. The Movement clearly did not enjoy the Administration's approval.

A British Report issued during the month of April, 1942 said:

"... The unconcealed support of Abuna Markos for the cause of reunion to Ethiopia was also a source of complaint.

"Abuna Markos's intrigues have not met with much encouragement at our hands, and he is therefore flirting at present both with the Italians and with the Emperor.

"The 'politically minded' section of the community is 'very small' and mainly composed of a number of disgruntled ex-Government employees, a few leading merchants and a small number of Coptic priests. The vast majority of the people is exclusively concerned with the none-too-easy problem of how to earn the daily bread."

Political Officer for Native Affairs, Asmara, reported:

"......there has been an increase of propaganda in favour of the Negus and a bigger Ethiopia......"

A British report issued during the first half of January 1943 said that the year 1943 opened with increased unionist activity.

(5)   E. Sylvia and Richard Pankhurst, op. cit.

368

A British report covering the period February 16th to 28th, 1943 declared: "in his farewell audience Abuna Markos told the Emperor he hoped the Ethiopian flag would soon fly over Asmara. The Emperor replied he hoped it would happen within a year."

The Abuna's pro-Ethiopian sentiments were regarded with disfavour by the British. (6)

And there were strong efforts besides those used to make the Eritreans yield to administrative pressure to divide this small border territory. The colonialists were very active in Eritrea and outside with schemes based on race and religion to have the territory partitioned. They were even so bold as to suggest that parts of the Motherland (Ethiopia) also be taken in the divisionary plan.

Information received from Eritrean sources about the month of August 1943, referred to a British report which disclosed that the Chief Administrator, Brigadier Longrigg, had initiated a curious sort of propaganda. He visited Adi Caieh and there called together the representatives of the people and invited them to express their views of the future of Eritrea, promising to forward their views to London.

The Chiefs were reluctant to express their true desire, which was reunion to Ethiopia. They feared that by answering frankly they might incur the anger of the Brigadier, whose opposition to the reunion cause had already been disclosed. Longrigg's belief, as he himself averred, was that the "Muslim tribal areas adjoining the Anglo-Egyptian Sudan should be included in that country. The central Christian highlands of Eritrea, with the port of Massawa and the Smhar and the Sao tribes, should form part of a United Tigré state or province, which should be placed under the nominal sovereignty of the Emperor of Ethiopia but be administered, in his name by a European Power for either a stated or unstated term of years. The Dankali country, with Assab, would be assigned unconditionally to the Emperor. Eritrea would cease to exist." (A Short History of Eritrea, Stephen H. Longrigg). Ethiopia was thus to be deprived of her Tigré Province which would in effect be placed under British administration.

That Longrigg's propaganda was part of a concerted plan has since been clearly revealed by the publication of Sir Douglas Newbold's correspondence wherein he states that in 1942 he was "investigating possibilities" of the Sudan "taking over" Western Eritrea and that he and General Platt discussed this project at the Middle East War Council in 1943.

The British Administration was still unwilling to believe, far less to admit, that the desire for union to Ethiopia was strongly cherished by the people of Eritrea. On January 30th, 1944, Ethiopian flags were displayed on many houses. Posters demanding union with Ethiopia were displayed. The British were devoting considerable attention to counteracting the activities of the Unionists.

On February 5th, 1944, the Eritrean police threatened to resign if the authority of the Italian officials over them was not removed. The result

(6)   E. Sylvia and Richard Pankhurst, *op. cit.*

of the threat given by the police was that 150 Eritrean police were dismissed and replaced by Takrurs from French Equatorial Africa and Arabs from Yemen. Eritrean police officers were interned.

As a result of Brigadier Longrigg's efforts to obtain a vote against union with Ethiopia, Eritrean patriots began to organise a plebiscite in favour of union. On the 24th February, 1944, twenty-four notables were arrested.

The British Administration was busy in pushing Brigadier Longrigg's scheme for Eritrea. From Agordat a British report stated:

"The Beni Amer are not in favour of being included in a post-war Ethiopian Empire, the Diglal complaining that subordination to any other African ruler is repugnant to himself and to his people; the future of this territory is bound to the Sudan." ([7])

The ramifications of the administration of Eritrea were many. It cost the United Kingdom Government a great deal of money and effort which would probably be charged up to the responsibility of being a great Power. His Britannic Majesty's Government carried out the task in a manner creditable in certain respects, and in others, the appraisal will have to be made by history and the coming generations. The position taken by the Administration, however, had intensified the struggle and certainly left some grave doubts on its motives, even up to 1950, when the United Nations made the final decision to federate Eritrea to the Motherland.

The ultimate liberation of Eritrea and her return to the Ethiopian Crown devolved primarily on the Imperial Ethiopian Government and revolved around the Eritrean people before the conscience of the world. It was a diplomatic struggle which included the Big Powers, Ethiopia, and His Imperial Majesty's Government, Italy, many friends of justice and finally the United Nations. For attaining this success His Majesty the Emperor Haile Selassie I distinguished himself by guiding his country's policy with patience, tact and resolution.

After the defeat of Italy and her expulsion from Ethiopia and North Africa, the problem of the former Italian colonies, including Eritrea, became an important world issue. In June, 1945, at the San Francisco Conference the Ethiopian Delegation formally made all necessary reservations concerning these colonies. These reservations were solemnly recorded again at the first session of the General Assembly of the United Nations at London in February 1946.

Of all ex-Italian colonies, the return of Eritrea was the most baffling. The Longrigg theory of partition plagued the conferences which dealt with this question to the very end. It, however, failed in the face of the facts and before the brilliant light of justice. Italy and her friends tried to scuttle Ethiopia's legitimate claims for the return of the territory.

In 1945, a year before the Peace Treaty with Italy was signed, President Roosevelt, Mr. Churchill and Marshal Stalin met at Potsdam and decided to establish a Council of Foreign Ministers of Britain, the United States, Russia, China and France, and that this Council should consider

([7])   E. Sylvia and Richard Pankhurst, *op. cit.*

370

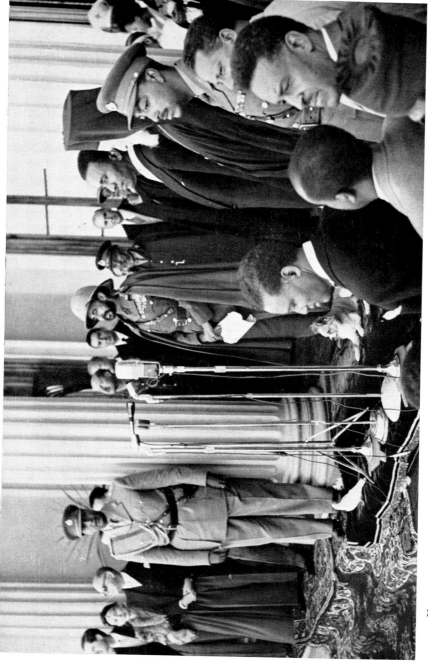

Emperor making historic speech at Asmara Palace on first State Visit to Eritrea after federation

the disposal of the ex-Italian colonies. As the first meeting of this Council was fixed for September 14, His Majesty the Emperor Haile Selassie I informed the British, American and Russian Ministers in Addis Ababa that Ethiopia attached a special interest to the consideration of her claims as the first victim of aggression. Although Italy was called to the meeting to state her case, Ethiopia was refused this courtesy, despite the fact that she had asked leave to be present. The Conference was attended by India, Yugoslavia, Australia, Canada, New Zealand and South Africa. The Council referred the matter of the ex-Italian colonies, after a brief discussion, to their Deputies for detailed study and they were to arrange to send a Commission to ascertain the wishes of the Eritrean people.

Strangely enough, Mr. Gladwyn Jebb (now Sir Gladwyn Jebb), for the British Delegation, promised British support in the Council of Foreign Ministers for Ethiopia's claim to Eritrea. It was on the proposal of the British Delegate that the matter was referred to the General Assembly of the United Nations.

The Emperor continued to make public protests. A written statement to the Council demanding the restoration of the colonies of Eritrea and Italian Somaliland to Ethiopia, not as a recompense but because they had been wrested from Ethiopia, was despatched.

A Peace Conference was called by the Council of Ministers at Paris in June 1946. Twenty-one countries, including Ethiopia and Italy, participated. Italy formally renounced all her rights to Libya, Eritrea and ex-Italian Somaliland. Article 23 of the Peace Treaty with Italy provided that the final disposal of these territories would be determined by agreement among France, Great Britain, the United States and the U.S.S.R. In paragraph 3 of annexe 11, the Treaty provided that if the four Great Powers did not come to an agreement within a year, this matter should be submitted to the General Assembly of the United Nations for recommendations to the four Great Powers.

The coming of the Four-Power Commision to Eritrea excited a great deal of activity on the part of the Administration and Italy's friends. There was definitely a cause. All the machinations of the local authorities had not diminished the ardour of the Eritreans to see their dream of reunion fulfilled. The "divide and rule" policy had brought forth some fruit, however. The lines of race and religion had set Moslems against the Christians to some extent. But it was unmistakable that the majority of the people, cutting across racial and religious lines, were for reunion with a smaller number of followers of the Moslem League, which was organised to express Moslem opinion.

Political demonstrations began to increase. Many were held in Asmara Addis Ababa and other centres both in the motherland and in Eritrea Regrettably, the disorders common to political demonstrations which took place brought only the Unionists afoul of the law. Many arrests were made among their ranks which led to imprisonment and even flogging. But the Unionists' manifestations were spontaneous and could not be smothered. A Youth Movement called "Andinet" (union) was formed at Asmara which, although suppressed by the Administration, came as a supplement to the Unionist Movement and aided greatly in strengthening the Unionist Party. "Rewards (ranging from £ 200 to £ 500) were offered by the British for the capture of Eritrean militants." A British-Italian Society was formed to fight for Italy's return to Eritrea. Suddenly an Italian Commission was permitted by the Authorities to come into Eritrea to settle back pay and gratuities to native Eritrean soldiers who had served the Fascists. Eritrean mercenaries were financed by Italy to go to Lake Success to plead for the return of their ruthless masters — they formed the Independence Bloc, which independence was meant to form a vacuum in Eritrea for Italy subsequently to fill. Interestingly, on their way back from Lake Success, members of the Independence Bloc visited Rome. One of their members was even sent to Pakistan to address public meetings there. The issue was now really joined, it being clear where the two loyalties lay.

When the Four-Power Commission arrived in Eritrea, it became most evident that the Authorities had held to their original stand against reunion. The Commission was informed by the Administration that arrangements had been made for its travelling to various parts of the country.

The programme was designed to enhance the comparative size of the separatists who were assigned urban areas and places of easy access, whereas it was proposed that the Unionists should gather their adherents to meet members of the Commission in odd localities, often in areas difficult of access to a large number of persons.

"By good fortune this plan failed; the Enquiry Commission told the Authorities that they could and would follow no programme which had not been made by the agreement of the Commission themselves." [8]

In order to make their investigations as impartial as circumstances would permit the Commission politely refused the "hospitality and solicitude" of the Administration. Their work was carried into all the five administrative divisions of Eritrea. The Commission, in each district, interviewed representatives regularly elected by the inhabitants of the particular locality, who expressed the desires of the people on the political future of the territory.

Disturbances prevailed and attacks were made against the Unionists and these attacks were encouraged. Deliberate attempts were made at all places visited by the Commission to keep the Unionists away from the Commission — Unionists were arrested and punished in several places. At the end of the enquiry, the Unionist Party followers found that they and their leaders had been arrested, fined imprisoned and punished in every possible way.

The Four-Power Commission stated that:

"With the exception of the Unionist Party, which was formed immediately after the restoration of Ethiopian independence, the other parties were essentially formed with a view to the arrival of the Com-

[8]   E. Sylvia and Richard Pankhurst, op. cit.

mission of Investigation. The main purpose of the leaders was, from that time, to recruit as many adherents as possible."

The Commission visited fifteen selected centres.

The percentage of support for the Unionist Party in the whole of Eritrea was estimated at 44.8. The Muslim League was given 40.5 per cent, the Liberal Progressives 4.4 per cent. The Muslim Leage represensatives relied mainly on their leaders; they wanted trusteeship by a power selected by their leaders; pending independence. (9)

The Commission's Report was submitted to the 3rd Meeting of the Council of Foreign Ministers in May, 1948, which examined it in London. Ethiopia again submitted her claim, the Head of the Delegation, H. E. Ato Aklilu Habte Wold, sharply criticising some parts of the Report. The Four Great Powers were, however, unable to agree as to the disposal of the three former Italian colonies and the whole matter was referred to the United Nations as formerly agreed.

The Italian Foreign Minister, Sforza, managed to get Mr. Bevin to agree to a plan of his which was sponsored by the British Delegation as a resolution. The solution suggested that for:

1. LIBYA: A United Nations Trusteeship for 10 years; Cyrenaica to be administered by Britain; and Tripolitania to be administered by Italy.

2. ERITREA: The East to be united to Ethiopia and the West to the Anglo-Egyptian Sudan.

3. SOMALILAND: To remain under Italian Trusteeship.

The British Resolution was referred to a Sub-Committee of the United Nations Political Committee. Annexation of Western Eritrea to the Sudan was not accepted. The rest of the proposal was accepted. It was, however, discovered that the Sub-Committee was not representative of the United Nations as a whole.

When the resolution was put to the vote in the General Assembly, there was a 37 to 11 majority in favour of union of Eastern Eritrea with Ethiopia. The return of Somaliland and Tripolitania to Italy and the annexation of Western Eritrea to the Sudan were turned down. After that what remained of the whole solution, namely, the question of Eastern Eritrea and Cyrenaica was put to a final vote and there, due to the South American *volte face*, it now failed to get the two-thirds majority.

Then Count Sforza spoke of independence for Libya and Eritrea. The Eritreans who had been taken to Lake Success to plead Italian trusteeship and the Eritreans who asked for Italian rule outright were hastily formed into a party called the "Independence Bloc" referred to above.

At the Fourth General Assembly, Bevin said the U.K. Government was supporting Ethiopia's claim to Eritrea except the western province. Acheson supported the division of Eritrea between Ethiopia and the Sudan.

Sir Zafrulla Khan, of Pakistan, who had formerly opposed Italian Trusteeship for any of the former colonies, now accepted the idea of Italian Trusteeship for Somaliland and turned his batteries against Ethiopia.

(9)   E. Sylvia and Richard Pankhurst, *op. cit.*

Brushing aside all the statistics ever published on the ex-Italian colonies, he declared he was not convinced that the economic deficiencies of Eritrea were any greater than the deficiencies of Ethiopia herself, and doubted whether Ethiopia had progressed further than Eritrea, even in political development.

Blatta Ephrem Tewelde Medhen, speaking with considerable emotion, protested that Sir Zafrulla Khan's observations had come as "a rude surprise to a people who for centuries had maintained the closest bonds of friendship and sympathy with the people of Pakistan.

"The Pakistan delegate," Blatta Ephrem suggested, "would not be content that the question of joining Kashmir to Pakistan should depend on a unanimous vote being recorded for it in the plebiscite to be taken on that question, yet that would seem to be the position he had adopted, not for Pakistan, of course, but for Eritrea." A fine note of sarcasm crept into the grave tones of the Ethiopian delegate at this point.

The Resolution which emerged from the "conciliation" Sub-Committee proposed; for all Libya, independence after three years; for ex-Italian Somaliland, Italian Trusteeship, leading to independence in ten years unless the United Nations should decide otherwise at that time; for Eritrea, postponement of all solutions till the next Assembly, a Commission to visit the territory in the meantime.

The United Nations Commission of Enquiry on Eritrea was composed of five Member States: Burma, Mr. U. Aung; Guatemala, Mr. Carlos Gracia Bauer; Norway, Mr. Erling Quale; Pakistan, Mr. Miam Ziauddin; South Africa, Mr. F. H. Theron.

After several months of consultation in Eritrea and several days in Ethiopia where it obtained the views of the Imperial Ethiopian Government, the Commission travelled to Rome. It submitted two reports to the Interim Committee of the United Nations on June 28th — a majority and a minority report.

The majority of the Commission, that is, Burma, Norway and South Africa, submitted their findings to the effect that there were strong ties of affinity between Eritrea and Ethiopia; that there were common strategic interests; that it was impossible to envisage an independent Eritrea capable of establishing a viable economy — this factor was considered decisive; that a political association of Eritrea with Ethiopia alone could further the well-being of the Eritrean population and assure peace and security in Eastern Africa. In view of these findings, the Burmese and South African Commissioners proposed a federation of Eritrea with Ethiopia under the sovereignty of the Imperial Crown of Ethiopia, and the Norwegian Commissioner, unconditional union of all of Eritrea with Ethiopia.

In His Throne Speech before a joint session of the Imperial Ethiopian parliament on the occasion of His Twentieth Coronation Anniversary, November 2nd, 1950, His Imperial Majesty pronounced the following:

The Commission of Enquiry, which the United Nations at their last year's session decided to send to ascertain the wishes of the Eritrean people, has now submitted their report, and it is hoped that the present session of the General Assembly will examine the matter and reach a decision. We have given clear and definite instructions to Our Delegation to deal with the question. It is with great admiration that We follow the efforts of the Eritrean people in their unflinching determination to achieve their consecrated aim to reunite Eritrea to its Motherland. For Our part, We shall never relax Our efforts for the reunion of Eritrea. It is vital to the security of Ethiopia.

Ethiopia stands for justice, has sacrificed herself before injustice. Now she asks for, and expects, justice from the United Nations.

From the reports of the second Eritrean Commission, the trend leading up to the Federation of Eritrea with Ethiopia under the Ethiopian Crown, was fixed. The Eritrean people sustained their vigilance in the protection of their rights. They did not only through petitions, telegrammes and other constitutional manifestations make this clear, but their delegations were present at the Fifth Session of the General Assembly in which the issue was decided. Quoting from one of the statements made to the Political Committee of the General Assembly by an Eritrean representative, this is what he said:

"For those of you to whom such basic factors of mental and national outlook are insufficient and who seek for some practical or tangible explanation in present-day life for this deep dependence which we feel upon Ethiopia, I could readily point out to you various factors of an entirely practical nature which indicate such a result. First of all, as the reports of the Commission of Investigation makes it clear, we Eritreans are unable to grow enough food on the plateau to sustain ourselves, the plateau alone containing the arable land of Eritrea. In consequence we must import from Ethiopia the wheat, the teff, a form of millet, the barley and the other grains which we Eritreans habitually consume and which are grown in Ethiopia alone. In addition, due to the poverty of our lands in Eritrea, and notwithstanding the declaration of the spokesman of the Moslem League, to the effect that the Tigré or Northern Ethiopia is a poverty stricken area of no interest to Eritrea, thousands of our people must pass many months of each year with their cattle in the Tigré of Ethiopia as well as in the Gondar area. Tigré thus affords the necessary grazing lands for the people of the low costal regions in the Eastern portion of Eritrea and Gondar for the large Mohammedan population in the Western Province of Eritrea. So it is that both Christians and Moslem, the Moslems of both Eastern and Western Eritrea, of both the Massawa Province and the Western Province, depend for their livelihood on Ethiopian pasture lands.

"Furthermore, Eritrea is so poor and lacking in agricultural and grazing lands that already far more than 100,000 Eritreans live permanently in Ethiopia. Were they obliged to seek their livelihood in Eritrea, they would starve to death.

"Eritrea, depending as it does upon the import of foodstuffs from Ethiopia in order to keep the population alive, it goes without saying that we have nothing to export except small quantities of salt. In consequence, our trade and commerce, both overseas and inland, consist for the most part in transit with Ethiopia or in trade destined solely for the supplying of the necessary foodstuffs for Eritrea. Without such trade with Ethiopia, Massawa would cease to exist, as would the commercial community of Eritrea.

"As mentioned, in addition to these practical economic factors, by far more important and intimate to outlook and mentality is the basic fact that for over 3,000 years our ancestors have formed an integral part of Ethiopia. Our common origins, traditions, languages, religions, and interests make that attachment too profound to express adequately or even clearly in words. It is that profound sentiment of nationality on which Mazzini based his appeal to the peoples of Italy, that same profound sense of nationality that makes the Scots, British."

Further evidence of the support of Eritreans to the union of Eritrea with Ethiopia is given in an appeal to all delegations of the United Nations against any further delay in the settlement of the ex-Italian colonial issue made by Eritreans living in Ethiopia.

"We, the nearby 200,000 Eritreans living in Ethiopia, have our brethren and relatives living in Eritrea. Their hardships are many and they are daily being pressed by the abnormal situation there. In fact, it must here be mentioned that the majority of trained Eritreans have had to flee this distress and are now enjoying a fair amount of freedom and self-development in the Mother country. Not only is our separation hard, but to know that our kith and kin are suffering privations and repression just across the border is heart-breaking.

"We appeal therefore for an urgent settlement of the matter of the reunion of Eritrea to Ethiopia. Too long have our filial hopes been dissipated by the continued delay; too long have we lived under the shadow of this gloomy separation; too long have we longed for the right of self-determination and the right to pursue the happiness which free peoples enjoy and for which our blood has been equally shed.

"This appeal is sent to you in the hope that, realising the dignity of the human personality, knowing what it is to have liberty, you would not fail in vouchsafing the same elementary right to the Eritrean people, clamouring for reunion with the Mother country, and to support the laudable principles of the United Nations Charter which the General Assembly meets yearly to implement."

The divided report of the United Nations Enquiry Commission in Eritrea was taken up in the Interim Assembly which began on July 13th, 1950. The Commissioners defended their positions; the minority, Guatemala and Pakistan, proposed a United Nations trusteeship over Eritrea for a period of ten years after which the territory would become independent. Both majority and minority opposed any partition of Eritrea such as was considered the previous year. This development assumed considerable importance during the course of the discussion at the Fifth General Assembly. The majority opinion was greatly elaborated by Mr. Jordaan, delegate from the Union of South Africa, who thought that the best solution should be federation of Eritrea with Ethiopia. The majority was of the view that trusteeship would be costly and impractical.

During the session of the Interim Assembly the Ethiopian Delegation fought vigorously in the defence of unqualified union of Eritrea to Ethiopia. H. E. Ato Aklilou Habte Wold opposed both independence and federation and gave strong grounds for his opposition. He pleaded for freeing the discussion from political opportunism and urged that only union with Ethiopia would meet the wishes of the population, including complete guarantees for the minorities and would insure peace and security in Eastern Africa. As the debate continued during the month of July, it became more and more clear that opinion in the Interim Committee was strongly moving in favour of the federal solution of the problem, in spite of the tenacious opposition of the delegates of Pakistan, Guatemala and certain other states.

Because of that opposition, however, the Interim Committee was unable to submit any recommendation to the Fifth Session of the General Assembly which opened on the 19th of September, 1950.

In the course of the debate on the 20th October, 1950, at the ad hoc Political Committee of the General Assembly, the Ethiopian delegation termed a United States suggestion for federation under the Imperial Crown of Ethiopia as a "positive contribution". Thus, after extensive discussion, the United States delegation in association with thirteen other delegations, presented to the ad hoc Political Committee on the 20th of November a draft resolution proposing the constitution of Eritrea as an autonomous unit to be federated with Ethiopia under the sovereignty of the Ethiopian Crown.

On the 22nd of November 1950, H. E. the Ethiopian Foreign Minister, and head of the Ethiopian delegation, conscious of the complications and the difficulties which the federal proposal imposed upon his Government, stated that Ethiopia was, nevertheless, prepared to accept federation as a possible solution in spite of the heavy concessions which it required, since it was the only solution which seemed capable of obtaining the necessary two-thirds majority. In his speech, the following paragraphs are found:

"......For its part Ethiopia, which more than any other country has at heart the aspirations of the Eritrean population, which is profoundly convinced that the overwhelming majority seeks to return to the homeland, and which maintains and defends as always that conviction, has, at the same time, too close at heart the interest of her brothers in Eritrea to wish to see them deprived of any solution by this Assembly. Consequently, although the compromise formula does not entirely correspond to the desires of the inhabitants or to the claims of Ethiopia, or to the feelings of justice on the part of the populations of Ethiopia and Eritrea, the Ethiopian delegation, for its part, does not wish, alone, to bar the route toward the adoption of that formula which alone, under present circumstances, can obtain the requisite majority so as to be adopted by the United Nations — that is to say, that formula which has just been submitted to us by fourteen delegations.

"I hope, that the United Nations will appreciate the extent and the sincerity of the efforts of my delegation when I state here that if the

Assembly adopts the formula in its present form, and subject to that condition, Ethiopia will accept and adopt it in all loyalty and sincerity. She will further exert all her efforts to bring about its accomplishment and to have it respected in the interests of the population in question, of peace and security in East Africa." H. E. the Foreign Minister took pains to stress the fraternal ties between the people of Eritrea and Ethiopia in the following terms:

"The essential fact — that I trust you will pardon me for repeating it again — is that Eritreans are our brothers, brothers of the Ethiopian people. Brotherly love will embrace them, bless them in any association with Ethiopia, and will always fructify the relations with our brothers of Eritrea, be they Unionists or members of the Moslem League, be they powerful or weak, be they Moslem or Christian."

On 25th November 1950, the ad hoc Political Committee of the United Nations brought the proposal to a vote and with 38 for, 14 against, and eight abstentions, recommended that Eritrea should be constituted an autonomous unit within a federation with Ethiopia under the Crown of His Imperial Majesty. The incorporation of Eritrea was to be accomplished not later than September 1952. The recommendation of the Committee was finally approved by the General Assembly on 2nd December 1950, by 46 votes for, 10 against and 4 abstentions.

Before the final vote, the proposal was formally accepted by H. E. Ato Aklilou Habte Wold, the Minister of Foreign Affairs, in the name of Ethiopia. He declared in summary that Ethiopia would accept federation in a spirit of conciliation, particularly in view of the grave international situation of the moment and of the fact that federation was the only solution that could obtain the necessary two-thirds majority and thereby avoid a crisis in Eritrea.

His Excellency's statement follows unabridged:

"Mr. Chairman, Fellow Delegates,

"I have asked for the floor in order to make a short explanation of vote in behalf of the delegation of Ethiopia.

"The serious events of the present hour require that we all set forth as briefly as possible our respective points of view and give evidence of a sincere spirit of conciliation in all our statements and discussions. It is in this spirit that I shall limit myself to a simple explanation of vote, in order to facilitate the work of the Assembly, although the question of Eritrea is of vital concern to my country and is of the greatest possible importance to it. I shall therefore be obliged to refer to my previous statements in the ad hoc Political Committee.

"In the course of these statements I had the occasion to remind the Committee that the findings of the two Commissions of Investigation sent to Eritrea have fully confirmed the claims of my country. According to these claims the great majority of the population, as well as economic factors and considerations of peace and security in East Africa, require the return of this territory to its homeland, Ethiopia.

"Consequently, as I have already had occasion to point out, the compromise formula presented by the fourteen Powers does not in our view, entirely respond to the aspirations of the majority of the population or to the claims of my country. It is a formula of conciliation between divergent desires of the majority and the minority of the population, and certainly the serious events of the present hour require that all of us give evidence of a spirit of conciliation, whatever be the questions with which we are concerned.

"As I have already stated in the *ad hoc* Political Committee, Ethiopia has too deeply at heart the interests and welfare of the population of Eritrea to see it deprived of any solution by this Assembly, especially after three years of discussion by the United Nations. Although the compromise formula presented by the fourteen powers does not entirely satisfy the aspirations of the population, or the claims of my country, the delegation of Ethiopia accepts it as being the only solution which, under the present circumstances, could obtain the necessary majority to be adopted by the United Nations.

"If the formula of the fourteen Powers is adopted in its present form, Ethiopia will respect it and will loyally exert all its efforts to bring about its implementation.

"I repeat again here that my Government readily accepts the necessary provisions for reassuring all indigenous and foreign minorities in Eritrea.

"The members of the Moslem minority in Eritrea can be assured of the fullest respect for their rights and privileges. They will be called, exactly as all other Eritreans, to all posts in Eritrea and in Ethiopia, where they will be able to enjoy all civil and political rights. On the other hand, political attitudes adopted by any groups in Eritrea will, in no wise, be the occasion for bitterness or discrimination.

"As I said in the *ad hoc* Political Committee, the essential fact is that Eritreans are brothers, brothers of the Ethiopian people. Brotherly love will enfold them, will bless them in every association with Ethiopia and will fructify forever the relations with our brothers of Eritrea, be they Unionists or members of the Moslem League, be they powerful or weak, be they Moslem or Christian.

"As regards the Italian minority, I have the honour and pleasure to reaffirm again that the Italians in Eritrea will continue, as in the past, to enjoy all their rights and privileges, and, moreover, they will be considered as friends, since the way is now open for a sincere and loyal collaboration between former enemies.

"In substance, there will be no majority or minority. There will be no Moslems or Christians. There will be no former political adversaries. There will be no former enemies. There will be only brothers of Eritrea and former enemies become friends who, all together, will collaborate with us, Ethiopians, in writing a new chapter in history, a chapter which will bring to an end a long epoch of exile and sufferings and which will demonstrate, in these critical hours of world history, the profound verity and justice on which is based the work of the United Nations."

The news of the United Nations decisions to federate Eritrea with Ethiopia was received with great joy and enthusiasm by the Eritrean and Ethiopian people. It was widely celebrated officially and unofficially. The

380

His Majesty the Emperor visits the Port of Massawa

4th December 1950 was declared a National Holiday. This continuous popular rejoicing, witnessed on the day when the resolution was passed, was re-enacted, renewed and intensified. The national flag was flown over public buildings, business houses and private residences besides Government offices.

At 10.30 a.m. on the 4th December, His Majesty the Emperor addressed

381

a mammoth gathering of his people, Ethiopians as well as Eritreans, assembled in the courtyard of the Imperial Palace. The speech, which was relayed by radio Addis Ababa, was as follows:

As all Our people know, the restoration of Eritrea to the motherland has been Our unfailing concern throughout Our reign; we therefore have to announce to Our beloved people in Ethiopia and Eritrea, the present results of Our efforts.

On 24th Hedar, 1943 (2nd December, 1950) the United Nations Assembly finally reached a decision concerning the aspirations of the Eritrean population and the just claims of Ethiopia. By this decision the United Nations has at last recognised the justice of Ethiopia's basic claims, as well as the desire of the majority of the Eritrean population to be rejoined to Ethiopia.

During their long years under foreign domination, the people of Eritrea have remained faithful to their homeland, Ethiopia, and it is with profound emotion that We now announce to the people of Ethiopia and Eritrea that their patience and devotion have not been in vain. And We must also pay tribute to the countless Eritreans who sacrificed their lives and shed their blood in serving their motherland Ethiopia.

We have consecrated many years of Our life and devoted much of Our thought, attention and energies to the long struggle for justice for Ethiopia and Eritrea.

The final stage of Our struggle began at the Peace Conference in Paris in 1938 (1946 A.D.) when it was decided that should the Great Powers fail to reach agreement, the question of Eritrea, along with those of Libya and Somaliland would be submitted to the United Nations for decision. It was under the compulsion of these circumstances that, having at heart the interest of the inhabitants of Eritrea who, by their devotion and by so overwhelming a majority have called for their return to Ethiopia, We personally undertook and directed the long and delicate negotiation of Our Delegation, headed by Our Minister of Foreign Affairs, with the world powers and with the members of the United Nations to obtain justice for the people of Eritrea and Ethiopia.

Thanks to Almighty God and Our faith in the profound justice of Our cause and of the cause of the people of Eritrea, and thanks also to the loyal support of the three Great Powers, the United Kingdom, the United States and France, and to the loyal support of many States, friends of Ethiopia throughout the world, the United Nations has now recognised the basic justice of Our claims and has agreed to a solution for rejoining Eritrea to Ethiopia.

The formula as adopted by the General Assembly does not entirely satisfy the wishes of the vast majority of the Eritreans who seek union without condition, nor does it satisfy all the legitimate claims of Ethiopia. However, after three years of discussions it became obvious that this formula was the only one that could obtain the necessary two-thirds majority for approval by the United Nations, and that unless it could be adopted, the inhabitants of Eritrea and their brothers in Ethiopia, who have anxiously waited for forty five years would be called upon to wait

382

still longer for justice. It was therefore Our clear duty to the peoples of Ethiopia and Eritrea to bring the problem to a solution.

Much remains to be done before that solution can be practically achieved. Many details must be elaborated. The Federal Act and the Constitution for Eritrea will require Our careful study and approval before the formula adopted by the United Nations can go into effect. This will require some months. However, the solution has been adopted and the principle accepted. The peoples of Eritrea and of Ethiopia are henceforth assured of being one again, and Ethiopia is to be granted her long denied access to the sea. Thus we would express the joy of Our peoples that their long standing and legitimate aspirations are finally recognised.

Last year We denounced and deplored before the world the disorders and bloodshed in Eritrea. Alas, at that time the future of Eritrea was uncertain. To-day, after the decision of the United Nations, We raise Our voice in appeal to all Eritreans to realise their common responsibilities for their own future and to collaborate in the work that lies ahead, so that the solution adopted may be in force as soon as possible. Ethiopians and Eritreans alike must now unite in brotherhood and mutual support for their common future.

To-day the world quivers under the threat of a new world war at the very moment when remedies are yet to be found for the damage of the last world war. The decision for Eritrea was achieved at the United Nations in the midst of their search for means to strengthen world peace, and at a time when a meeting of the Great Powers had been proposed. For her part, Ethiopia will not fail to fulfil her international duty to further the cause of peace.

We pray God's blessing upon the consummation of Our efforts to unite our peoples and for God's guidance for all men everywhere who are labouring to avoid war and catastrophe and struggling to achieve and maintain world peace.

To implement the United Nations Resolution of December 2nd, 1950, whereby Eritrea, as an autonomous unit, should be federated with Ethiopia under the sovereignty of the Ethiopian Crown, it was resolved that a United Nations Commissioner should proceed to Eritrea. The Honourable Dr. Eduardo Anze Matienzo of Bolivia was appointed United Nations Commissioner for Eritrea. He arrived in Eritrea on February 9th, 1951 with experts to take up his duties.

The terms of reference of the Commissioner were couched in the 1950 Resolution. He was charged to prepare a draft Constitution for Eritrea in consultation with the Administering Authority, the Government of Ethiopia and the inhabitants of Eritrea. The draft Constitution was subsequently submitted to a representative assembly of Eritreans chosen by the people and convoked by the Administering Authority.

Before going to Eritrea to take up his assignment, the Honourable Commissioner for Eritrea was invited to the United Kingdom and to Italy where he received the assurances of these governments, after informal talks, of their determination to stand by the terms of the United Nations Resolution. En route to Eritrea he also flew to Addis Ababa to pay a courtesy visit to His Imperial Majesty the Emperor of Ethiopia and the Ethiopian Government. There, after unofficial conversations, with the Ethiopian Government, the Commissioner left for Eritrea.

Friendly expressions of desire to collaborate in the implementation of the United Nations resolution were exchanged, and on his return to Asmara, the Commissioner informed the Eritrean Press that he felt that he had reached full agreement with the authorities in Addis Ababa on the broad lines of policy and objectives. He added that he was relying on the under-standing and co-operation of the Ethiopian Government for the success of his mission.

The part played by the Ethiopian Government in the United Nations in bringing a workable settlement of the Eritrean issue is well-known and equally as well exemplified through the statements made by its delegat-ion to the General Assembly. Moreover, His Imperial Majesty has con-sistently held to the view that the rights and interests of the Eritrean people were co-existent with those of Ethiopia, their protection devolving on the Eritrean people as alike on the Ethiopian Government and people. The spirit of conciliation and compromise evinced (for three years), by Ethiopia in the long and arduous deliberations in the General Assembly, which eventually led up to the acceptance of the formula of federation, made it possible for a settlement to be reached in December 1950.

The deep interest in the welfare of the Eritrean people was the guiding factor in Ethiopia's struggle for a speedy settlement of the problem. Dr. Matienzo, therefore, in his statement to the Eritrean people on his arrival in Eritrea to begin his tedious task had this to say:

"You now have new hopes for the future on which to build. This new spirit has been already shown in the discussions at Lake Success, when all the interested countries showed a remarkable spirit of compromise, and gave assurances that they would carry out the plan adopted and aid the United Nations Commissioner. In these discussions the General As-sembly was deeply impressed with the sincerity and tenor of the statement made by the Ethiopian Foreign Minister. He stated before the assembled United Nations that, while feeling that the recommendation would not entirely satisfy the hopes of the Eritrean population or the claims of Ethiopia, his country would respect them and would loyally exert all its efforts to bring about their implementation. He also stated that the Ethiopian Government had deeply at heart the interests and welfare of the population of Eritrea; that Moslems in Eritrea could be assured of the fullest respect for their rights and privileges and would receive equal opportunities for posts in Ethiopia and Eritrea; that no bitterness or dis-crimination would be shown towards any political group in Eritrea; that Italians would not be treated as former enemies, but as friends, and, in fact, that all Eritreans irrespective of their former political attitude, would be brothers with the Ethiopian people, thus bringing to an end a long epoch of exile and suffering."

Ethiopia's sincerity and her regard for the high principles of justice and right highlighted the atmosphere in which the Commissioner for Eritrea began his work. Shortly after his arrival in Eritrea on February 9, 1951,

384

he embarked on a series of personal visits to various parts of the territory. The visits extended over a period of eleven weeks, from the 29th February to the 12th May 1951, inclusive. The purpose of these visits was to gain a first-hand impression of the inhabitants, their way of life, the character of the country and its agricultural and other resources, while at the same time to learn something concerning the problems of the inhabitants, their hopes and aspirations.

These visits also gave the people opportunity to meet the Commissioner and to express their views concerning the plan for federation as well as to permit the Commissioner to explain in some detail the background of the General Assembly's recommendation for federation. They gave him a chance to explain also the nature of his task and the future status of Eritrea federated with Ethiopia under the sovereignty of the Ethiopian Crown.

In the consultations provided for in the United Nations resolution on Eritrea, with the three parties: the Administering Authority, the Ethiopian Government and the inhabitants of Eritrea, meetings were held by the Commissioner. This was necessary to carry out his primary responsibility in preparing a draft Eritrean Constitution to be submitted to the Eritrean Assembly.

On the 27th June, 1951, formal consultations with the Administering Authority were inaugurated on the subject of the draft Eritrean Constitution. These consultations were preceded by informal discussions between the Commissioner and the Chief Administrator, together with the Special Adviser to the latter.

The consultations began with a paper prepared by the Commissioner setting forth a detailed examination and interpretation of the provisions of the resolution as a basis for discussion. After certain amendments which were accepted by the Commissioner, the Chief Administrator stated that he considered the document to be a responsible interpretation of the United Nations resolution. Such points were raised as the difficulties in creating an Eritrean Administration without a prior knowledge of the constitution; the setting up of machinery for the settlement of jurisdictional disputes which might arise out of the Federal Act; the responsibility of the Administering Authority to hold elections bringing about federation according to the mandate of the United Nations resolution.

In accordance with paragraph 12 of the resolution, the Commissioner opened formal consultation with the Government of Ethiopia, represented by His Excellency Ato Aklilou Habte Wold, Minister of Foreign Affairs, in Addis Ababa on May 28th, 1951, on the subject of the draft constitution for Eritrea.

Meetings were held on 28th and 30th May, 1951, respectively and on 3rd July, 1951; two further meetings between the Commissioner and the Ethiopian Minister of Foreign Affairs were held in Asmara. In addition, a series of informal discussions took place in Addis Ababa and in Asmara between the Commissioner and members of the United Nations staff, on the one hand, and the Ethiopian Minister of Foreign Affairs and or, in his absence, the Vice-Minister of Foreign Affairs and their advisers.

385

These informal discussions were for the purpose of exchanging views and reaching agreement on constitutional questions, principally of a technical or non-controversial nature.

Pertinent phases of federation were gone into, the Commissioner making a detailed exposé of the basic elements which, in his view, should be incorporated in the draft constitution. The Minister of Foreign Affairs submitted a number of observations on the exposé presented by the Commissioner, together with the views of the Ethiopian Government on certain fundamental principles which should be taken into account in the preparation of the draft constitution.

General agreement was reached on a number of constitutional questions. In several informal discussions a recapitulation was made on the several points involved.

Consultations with the inhabitants, one of the important axes of the question of federation next followed. Early in April, 1951, a comprehensive plan was drawn up for consultation with every section of public opinion in Eritrea. The programme, however, was not put into effect until the end of June 1951, when the Commissioner, at a meeting at Asmara, on the 29th of that month, to which was invited the Press, civic, religious and political leaders and other notables, publicly announced the initiation of consultations with the inhabitants. At that time, the Commissioner formally presented a summary of an exposé of his detailed examination and interpretation of the United Nations resolution. The exposé was subsequently translated into Tigrinya and Arabic and, printed in bilingual form, being given wide distribution in advance of the meetings in various divisions, through the good offices of the Administering Authority.

At the time of the announcement, the Commissioner issued a communique inviting all the inhabitants to nominate delegates, according to their traditional methods, to act as their spokesmen in the open meetings which he would hold in all parts of the territory in order to hear an authentic expression of public opinion on aspects of the constitution. The communiqué was published in the press and given widespread distribution in Tigrinya and Arabic, in leaflet form throughout the territory, through the medium of the local authorities.

The methods used in consulting the inhabitants were designed to receive representative opinions and to encourage the people to work together and to listen to different views with tolerance. Alternate meetings were arranged and invitations for meetings on specific days were sent to all political parties, religious leaders and heads of foreign communities. Plans were also succesfully carried out to free the inhabitants from official pressure, with the Administering Authority co-operating fully to see that this was done.

The fifteen officially registered political parties were invited to the Palace at Asmara for consultations. These meetings took place during the period 11th to 20th July, 1951. A written memorandum was submitted which, together with the Commissioner's summary of his basic document, formed the basis of the consultations.

Naturally, there were many divergent opinions from these political parties

386

based on their points of view and their interpretation of the United Nations resolution. There were also fundamental points on which the majority of them agreed. The same could be said of the economic, cultural and professional organisations which, through a press release of July 1st, 1951, were invited to submit their views to the Commissioner.

The five divisions of Eritrea were visited in turn by the Commissioner. These hearings followed the same general pattern throughout the territory. The original plan was to separate the views of the political parties from those of the population by hearing the former in Asmara and the latter throughout the territory.

The views of the political parties ranged then from outright and unqualified reunion of Eritrea to Ethiopia, through separation of the Western Province under trusteeship, to the immediate independence of Eritrea. They differed then on some fundamental aspects of the Eritrean Constitution which were later resolved in the course of the Commissioner's findings and finally settled and agreed to by the Constituent Assembly.

Nor was the political situation among the political parties in Eritrea any more stable after the United Nations resolution. The position remained fluid to the extent that the published agreement of the "Peace Congress" held in December, 1950, by all the Eritrean political parties jointly, saw some fundamental changes during the formal consultations in certain sections of the territory. Differences on constitutional issues became so wide that the Commissioner on October 17th, 1951, expressed himself in the following terms:

"Although various political parties appeared to be determined to maintain their former differences of view and had not shown the expected spirit of conciliation, the inhabitants, whom the Commissioner met during the course of his consultations, displayed a spirit of brotherhood and tolerance and helped to establish his great faith and hope in the future destiny of the country. It is in this spirit that the Commissioner has found a renewed stimulus which enables him to carry on his work with a feeling of optimism, of faith in the resolution of the United Nations, and with confidence in the future of Eritrea.

"Confident that existing differences offer no serious basis of disagreement which cannnot be settled by conciliation and collaboration, I do not consider it necessary to ask the General Assembly of the United Nations to review the question of Eritrea. It is however my intention to present a progress report for circulation among the Member Nations of the United Nations at the coming meeting of the Assembly to be held in Paris."

Under the then prevailing circumstances, the framing of the Eritrean constitution was a job which taxed to their capacity the known principles of a federal form of government. The triangular consultation provided for by the United Nations resolution could not have been complete in all the aspects relating to the Eritrean Constitution, nor the many facets attendant to the federal plan. The realities of the situation, therefore, made the task of the Commissioner, in some respects, very difficult. As he said in his progress report, "To the extent to which the resolution of the General Assembly leaves it to the Commissioner to decide, he will take into consideration the prevailing local conditions, the opinions of the Administering Authority, the opinions and wishes of the Government of Ethiopia and of the inhabitants of Eritrea, whom, according to the resolution, he has to consult."

The Eritrean constitution is therefore what has resulted from the interpretation of the text of the resolution and the incorporation of the wishes and opinions of the interested parties as mentioned in the resolution. It is new to the Eritrean people who must for the first time undertake to govern themselves; it is new to the region.

In such a finely balanced mechanism its proper functioning is not automatic. The responsibilities and obligations are heavy. Attempting as it does to reconcile the ideas of both autonomy and attachment, the latter particularly arising from the cold facts of economic, ethnical, historical and strategic considerations, faith, goodwill, mutual understanding must be its essential allies. To what measure it satisfies the aspirations of the Eritrean people and meets the legitimate rights and claims of Ethiopia will emerge from its successful operation. The formal federation of Eritrea with Ethiopia under the sovereignty of the Ethiopian Crown, opened a new era of fraternity in this region of East Africa.

Thus, an issue which engaged the attention of the world for a very long time and especially since it was referred to the General Assembly of the United Nations in accordance with the provisions of the Treaty of Peace with Italy, was concluded. The part played by the Ethiopian Government in the defence of the rights and aspirations of the Eritrean people, her unchallenged spirit of co-operation, conciliation and open mindedness in assisting the United Nations Commissioner in his difficult task, could be taken as a guarantee of *bon esprit*. Moreover, the broad humanitarianism and deep interest of His Imperial Majesty in the welfare of His People are there as the moral force for the successful consummation of federation.

The Eritrean Constitution which was prepared by Dr. Eduardo Anze Matienzo, United Nations Commissioner in Eritrea, in consultation with the Administering Power, the Government of Ethiopia and the inhabitants of Eritrea and which was, on the 10th July, 1952, adopted by the Eritrean Assembly, and on the 6th August, 1952, approved by the United Nations Commissioner, was ratified by His Imperial Majesty at 4.30 p.m., August 11th, 1952. The ratification ceremony which took place in the Throne Room of the Imperial Palace, Addis Ababa, was held in the presence of Members of the Imperial Family, Their Excellencies the United Nations Commissioner in Eritrea, the Chief Administrator, Eritrea, the British Ambassador to Ethiopia, the President and Vice-President of the Eritrean Assembly, Members of the Crown Council and the Ministers' Council and the highest officials and dignitaries, as well as members of the Eritrean Association.

His Imperial Majesty, in placing his seal on the document must have recalled the undivided interests of Ethiopia and Eritrea, the mutual pains which the separation had caused and the stamina with which the people

388

withstood the hardships and privations attendant thereto, when, in his speech, he said:

By our Act of Ratification of the constitution of Eritrea we have today completed an historical phase in the life of the people of Ethiopia and Eritrea . . . . . . Two years ago the United Nations recognised the life-long aspirations of the brothers of Ethiopia and Eritrea for their reunion by recommending joining under Federation . . . . . . This present Act of Ratification has the significance of constituting the solution of federation, not as an imposed solution, but as one based upon and achieved through the expressed consent of the peoples concerned. . . .

Speeches were made by His Majesty the Emperor Haile Selassie I; H. E. the Ethiopian Foreign Minister, Ato Aklilou Habte Wold; the United Nations Commissioner in Eritrea, Dr. Eduardo Anze Matienzo; the Chief Administrator, Eritrea, Mr. D. C. Cumming, and the President of the Eritrean Representative Assembly, Ato Tedla Bairu.

On Thursday, September 11th, 1952, in a historic ceremony in the great Palace, Addis Ababa, His Majesty the Emperor affixed his signature to the Federal Act, the final move that returned Eritrea to the Empire of Ethiopia. H.E. the Minister of Foreign Affairs, submitting to His Imperial Majesty the instruments of ratification of the Federal Act and the Proclamation of the Federation of Eritrea with Ethopia, made a speech in which he said:

"In this solemn moment in the history of our three-thousand-year-old Empire, it is not without deep emotion that, as Minister of Foreign Affairs of the Imperial Ethiopian Government, I humbly inform Your Imperial Majesty that the aspirations and the fate of millions of human beings, at this moment, await the will and the decision of Your Imperial Majesty."

In ratifying the Federal Act making Eritrea and Ethiopia into one federal Union, His Imperial Majesty made a very historic pronouncement, reproduced in full in the appendix. A significant paragraph of that address reads:

To-day, there has been fulfilled the exact words of that message which, during the struggle for liberation twelve years ago, We transmitted to Our faithful Subjects of Eritrea when by proclamation broadcast throughout the land by the help of Allied aircraft, We announced the return to Our beloved homeland, stating: "I have come to restore the independence of my country, including Eritrea . . . . . . whose people will henceforth dwell under the Ethiopian flag." That promise, We have, to-day, kept to the very letter, but twelve years of struggle, sacrifice and self-abnegation have separated its utterance from its now glorious fulfilment. Eritrea was one of the first territories to be freed during the last war. In consequence of the long struggles and opposition to the expressed will of the people of Eritrea and Ethiopia, it is now the last to receive its solution.

A communiqué on the event issued by the Ministry of Foreign Affairs reads:

389

"To-day, 11th September, 1952, in the presence of the Members of the Imperial Family, Princes and Ethiopian and Eritrean Dignitaries, Ministers and Members of the Diplomatic Corps, His Imperial Majesty ratified the Federal Act and proclaimed the establishment of the federation of Eritrea with Ethiopia under the Sovereignty of the Ethiopian Crown.

"By this act, in fulfilment of the recommendations made by the United Nations two years ago, His Imperial Majesty rejoined Eritrea to Ethiopia after a separation of nearly three-quarters of a century and after many years of diplomatic struggle for recognition of the common aspirations of the Ethiopian and Eritrean peoples.

"With the re-establishment of Ethiopian Sovereignty over Eritrea, the British Administration which has been reponsible for the government of the territory since its liberation in 1941, will withdraw and the territory will be administered locally under the federal jurisdiction of the Imperial Ethiopian Government.

"His Imperial Majesty plans a state visit to the territory in the near future."

Their Imperial Majesties' Historic State Visit to Eritrea

Their Imperial Majesties' State Visit to Eritrea, which began actually on October 4th, 1952, following the federation of Eritrea with Ethiopia, was the fulfilment of an important part of Their Imperial Majesties' duty and prerogative, born of the attachment of the Ethiopian Crown to the final liberation of Eritrea and its people. The United Nations, in recognising the impelling facts of the situation, provided the letter; their Imperial Majesties' State Visit to Eritrea supplied the spirit of this restoration.

The importance of the event could be gathered from the fact that Their Imperial Majesties' State Visit took them away from the seat of Government for nearly a month. An elaborate programme was arranged which began on October 2nd, 1952 and extended to October 28th, 1952. The itinerary took Their Imperial Majesties from Addis Ababa to the historic city of Axum, thence to Adwa, across the Mareb River to Eritrea. State visits were made to important parts of that territory, Their Imperial Majesties returning to the capital southwards through the provinces of Tigré and Wollo.

The historic visit of Their Imperial Majesties in Eritrea began with a morning ceremony on the southern bank of the Mareb River on Saturday October 4th, 1952. This river, for over half a century, was used as an artificial boundary between the dwelling places of brothers. His Excellency Bitwoded Andargachew Messai, His Imperial Majesty's Representative in Eritrea and His Excellency Ato Tedla Bairu, (now Dejazmach), Chief Executive of Eritrea, pronounced the official welcome. They stood under a triumphal arch erected on the approaching end of the Mareb bridge, surrounded by hundreds of people and other leaders of Eritrea.

In his speech of welcome, His Excellency the Emperor's Representative said:

"Your Imperial Majesties!

"I should like to thank Your Majesty for permitting me to talk in the presence of Your Imperial Majesties on this historic and memorable day.

"I feel deeply the singular honour of being fortunate enough to become Your Majesty's first Representative in Eritrea and to welcome Your Imperial Majesties as You, our Sovereign, cross this Mareb River which divided Ethiopia and Eritrea and which no Ethiopian Emperor could cross while Eritrea was under foreign domination. But through Your Majesty's leadership and constant struggle, Eritrea once again has been joined to Ethiopia.

"For many years past this river constituted a boundary that separated people of common descent into two unnatural communities. Your Imperial Majesty has to-day removed this obstacle through sustained efforts and infinite patience. History observes to-day the crossing of what was so long an impassable river boundary.

"I express my heart-felt gratitude to God, Who alone granted You this privilege and led Your Majesty to this historic hour, and I gladly welcome

Your Imperial Majesties. Your Eritrean subjects have for many years longed for Your arrival.

"May I be permitted to present to Your Majesty Ato Tedla Bairu, the Chief Executive of Eritrea, who has come to express his feelings of joy and to welcome Your Majesties on behalf of the Eritrean people and himself.

"Long live Your Imperial Majesties!

"Long live Ethiopia!"

The Chief Executive declared:

"In a moment when the slavery of past years is cancelled and a new life opened, in this historic place, on behalf of Your faithful subjects, I beg Your Imperial Majesty to let me present a welcome.

"The people of Eritrea, who worship the great name of Your Imperial Majesty with great desire and love, since they knew of the arrival of Your Imperial Majesty in Eritrea, have longed for the hour they may be able to see the enlighted face of their Sovereign.

"Your Imperial Majesty, who has never been separated from the Eritrean people either by thought or by action, in setting Your foot, in this historic hour, on our territory to visit it, gives us confirmation of how much love and benevolence is shared on our behalf.

"Your Majesty's paternal protection and highest and unequalled statesmanship, which led us to this honour, shall constitute an unforgettable memento for the future Eritrean generations."

Accepting the welcome of His subjects, before cutting the silk ribbon and unveiling the bronze plaque, symbolic of changing the status of the Mareb River and of His historic entry into Eritrea, His Majesty the Emperor said:

With thankfulness to the Almighty for His direction and aid during the long years of struggle which We have led to obtain justice for the people of Eritrea. We, for the first time in Our life, as Sovereign of the rejoined peoples of Ethiopia and Eritrea, enter Eritrea. By crossing the Mareb River, We are doing away not only with the barrier which had for so long separated brother peoples but, at the same time, are bringing to an end a long period of suffering and struggle to achieve justice. The regions through which We have just travelled are among the most ancient territories of Our 1,000-year-old Empire, composed of Ethiopia and Eritrea.

Likewise, in crossing to-day the Mareb River, We have fulfilled an historic task. Upon the day when We Ourselves, took command of the armies to liberate Eritrea and Ethiopia, We gave thought to this historic river which separated two brother peoples. At that time (July, 1940) We declared: "Whether on this side or on the other side of the Mareb, join in the struggle by the side of your Ethiopian brothers to throw off the yoke of foreign domination. Your destiny is bound up with that of the rest of Ethiopia in the strictest sense of the word. I have come to restore the independence of My country, including Eritrea, whose people will henceforth dwell under the Ethiopian flag." As of this moment, these words assume new significance, for, by virtue of Our presence,

392

the Mareb no longer plays the rôle of separating brothers. This ceremony signifies the elimination once and for all of all barriers between Our peoples. As stated in the Federal Act which We have accepted and ratified in the name of the peoples of Ethiopia and Eritrea, "There shall be no barriers to the free movement of goods and persons" throughout the Empire. By Our action to-day the brothers of Eritrea will enjoy full rights and privileges like their Ethiopian brothers and return with full rights to their Ethiopian family.

Our state visit to Eritrea, which commences at this moment, demonstrates to the entire world the sacred and eternal character of the close relations We have just re-established between the two brother peoples.

Long live the reunited people of Ethiopia and Eritrea!

Accompanied by the Imperial party, Their Imperial Majesties crossed the bridge and set foot on Eritrean soil amid the resounding cheers of the large number of people who had gathered there to witness the ceremony. From that time, the Mareb River no longer constituted a dividing line between the territories of brothers. It became a link of community interests, a bond which again joins the fate and future of Eritrea with the fate and future of Ethiopia, the Motherland. There and then the decision of the United Nations to take into consideration the wishes and welfare of the inhabitants, the interests of peace and security in East Africa and the rights and claims of Ethiopia became, in truth and in fact, a reality.

At that moment a new page in world history was about to be written. The United Nations decision for the re-affiliation of Eritrea, the processes worked out for the implementation of the formula — the legalistic and the constitutional — had each their significant part to play in bringing back Eritrea to its ancestral connection. But no one, not even the conceivers of the plan, nor those delegated to delineate the lines of the picture, could have surmised where the capstone of the edifice, the flesh and blood of the skeleton, would come from. Their Imperial Majesties' visit to Eritrea was the unknown element, it brought a happy solution to the equation.

Their Imperial Majesties, after the Mareb ceremony, rode to Asmara, the capital of Eritrea. It was along this 116 kilometres of route that the great revelation came. The phenomenal welcome accorded by the Eritrean people all along the tour held the answer. In full view of the world, the decision of the United Nations was upheld by the inhabitants of Eritrea; Their Imperial Majesties rode triumphantly, accepting the plaudits of the thousands of Eritreans of all classes, religions, and nationalities, who stretched from the Mareb to the Asmara Palace.

Triumphal arches were constructed all along the route. With drums and enthusiastic songs, the people hailed His Majesty the Emperor. Flowers, flags, bunting, religious and group emblems, prepared signs of welcome, all the paraphernalia of a grand welcome marked the transcendent ovation which all the people of Eritrea gave to Their Imperial Majesties, who had come as Sovereign of the Federation and

393

as a Monarch who had never abandoned them in the struggle, the happy end of which Their coming signified.

Their Imperial Majesties' State Visit to Eritrea was a peace mission, Ethiopia and Eritrea are again joined, not through blood and sword, but through the act of the United Nations. It was evidence of one of the basic principles of the United Nations Charter upheld, that of the peaceful settlement of international disputes and problems. The enthusiasm with which Their Imperial Majesties were received by the Eritrean people, besides being a triumph for His Imperial Majesty, always a firm believer in peaceful world co-operation, was equally a triumph for the United Nations, through whose dispassionate decision Eritrea had been restored.

The welcome was so heart-warming that Their Imperial Majesties stopped several times, His Majesty the Emperor accepting the greetings of His people, speaking to them and bestowing on them gifts. In the two towns of Adi Ugri and Adi Quale, along the Imperial route, special arrangements had been made. There Their Imperial Majesties tarried to receive the warm greetings of the many thousands of their people, gathered together with their leaders. Bouquets and other tokens of welcome were showered on the Sovereign who accepted with benign gestures the stirring ovations of the people.

The crescendo was reached at the city limits of Asmara and grew as the crowds on the streets became larger and larger. People crowded windows, roof tops, some even on trees, most of them holding small Ethiopian flags and other tokens of welcome. Upwards of 500.000 persons from all parts of the territory comprised the milling throng, of all shades and complexions of Eritrean life.

Policemen were posted along the route, but the multitude was orderly; their only aim was to have a chance to personally lend their voices and their emotion to this, the greatest mass demonstration of affection in the history of Eritrea. There was no other traffic but of Their Imperial Majesties' train — and this was the focus of the attention of all. As Their Imperial Majesties rode through the spacious entrance of the Asmara Palace, the official reception party waited in tense expectancy. While church bells rang and Ethiopian Air Force planes dropped leaflets, a 101-gun salute heralded the Imperial entry. There were heads of diplomatic missions, Eritrean leaders — secular and religious — and many foreign friends who had come to join the significant and historic occasion.

The Ethiopian National Anthem was played by the Imperial Army Band and Their Imperial Majesties received bouquets of beautiful flowers from children and young ladies. After receiving the official welcome and inspecting the Guard of Honour, His Imperial Majesty ascended the dais before the Asmara Palace and delivered the following historic speech:

For the first time since Emperor Yohannes, Your Sovereign and Supreme Chief makes His appearance in the territory of Eritrea as Emperor of Ethiopia and Eritrea. At this solemn and historic moment,

We invoke the benediction of Almigthy God to Whom We address humbly Our prayers in thanksgiving.

In crossing the Mareb, which for so many years constituted a barrier separating so unjustly two brother peoples. We have demonstrated that the obstacle of a border no longer exists and that the two peoples will, in the future, live as they did throughout thousands of years before, as brothers in one family.

The whole history of Ethiopia and Eritrea demonstrates the profound truth of this unity. Even if We go back in the history of Ethiopia three thousands years, We see that this unity and identity of Eritrea with Ethiopia already existed. In fact, it has been only within the last sixty years that the word "Eritrea" has been employed for territory previously identified with Our Empire. Thus it was that in 1884, on the eve of the Italian occupation, the tripartite Treaty with Ethiopia, the United Kingdom and Egypt, recognising Our sovereignty over Eritrea, did not use this designation.

For three thousand years the territory of Eritrea provided for Ethiopia, as it now again provides, access to the sea. Up till the eighth century of our era, the port of Adulis was the outlet for Our Empire. After that period Massawa gave us access to the sea, even through the most troubled periods of Our history, when incursions from abroad were directed against this port. Notwithstanding these events, the local chiefs in the region of Massawa continued to recognise the sovereignty of the Emperors.

Exactly 1,022 years ago the Emperor Dilnead, Our Predecessor, moved the capital of the Empire from Axum to Shoa where Our dynasty established its seat. From this capital Our August predecessors, among them Yekuno Amlak, Amda Tsion and Zara Yakub, continued to reign over the entire Empire, including the territory of Hamasien, known to-day by the name of Eritrea.

Quite naturally, therefore, the Emperors of Ethiopia have always taken to heart the defence of Eritrea against attacks from abroad, attacks which commenced in the middle of the 14th century and continued for two hunderd years. We cite as examples the victories of Assab, Tajura and Hegera by Emperor Amda Tsion in 1331; of Dawaro on 26th December, 1445, by Emperor Zara Yakub; of Dahano by Emperor Malak Sagad Sertza Dingale in November, 1589 and later at the Mareb River.

Since that time, the people of Eritrea have never ceased to recognise the sovereignty of the Emperors of Ethiopia, nor did in the 18th and 19th centuries Ras Suhul Mikael and Dejazmach Ubie. Finally, Emperor Yohannes, crowned 1872, played a very important rôle in the history of Eritrea, as did his liege Ras Alula who established the city of Asmara.

It was, therefore, only 67 years ago that this thousand-year-old unity was broken and Our beloved subjects in Eritrea were called upon to experience a period of foreign occupation to which the events of World War II and the present days have brought an end.

During all this period, Our faithful subjects of Eritrea have never been shaken in their devotion to the Emperor and to the people of Ethiopia, notwithstanding the trials to which they were subjected during all of these 67 years.

From the moment when We Ourselves, assumed the high direction of Our Empire, We have never ceased to defend Our subjects in Eritrea and to seek to achieve for them their most profound aspirations. Already before the Great War and the invasion of Our Empire, We had laboured without respite to obtain the assistance of the Great Powers in achieving justice for the brothers of Ethiopia and Eritrea. Thus it was that We Ourselves undertook a long journey through Europe to solicit the assistance of friendly countries. Unfortunately, the events, which will always be remembered in history, put an end to these endeavours. If, since the Great World War, Our subjects in Eritrea have finally seen the achievement of their most profound aspirations, it is due to the strength of Our Creator, Almighty God.

However, at the price of the greatest efforts and sacrifices on Our part and through the exercise of all Our personal prestige, We were able to obtain justice for Our beloved subjects in Eritrea.

Although Eritrea was one of the first territories to be freed, by reason of the stubborn resistance provoked by international politics, alien to the interests of Our Eritrean subjects, it is only to-day that We can celebrate the settlement of this question. Not without the greatest anxieties, We and Our Ethiopian and Eritrean subjects, who worked so closely together, saw the piling up of delays and years without the achievement of justice. If we had not personally persisted, all would have been lost. Thus, We sent Our representatives to no less than twenty international conferences to discuss the question, and We Ourselves, personally consulted with President Roosevelt and Mr. Churchill. We have, alone carried on the struggle in your defence up to the moment when We were able to convince Our friendly allies abroad of the profound justice of the aspirations of the brothers of Ethiopia and Eritrea and obtain their support.

During this long period of struggle for justice, Our beloved subjects in Eritrea remained faithful to Us, as is testified by the numerous desertions of Eritrean soldiers during the war and the campaign of liberation and by the expressions of joy with which Our proclamations were received. Still more important: throughout that period, Eritreans, by the thousands, came to set up their homes in Ethiopia. It was, therefore, quite normal that We Ourselves should personally have taken in hand the education, not only in Ethiopia but also abroad, of Eritrean subjects and that nearly all of those loyal Eritreans, who have studied abroad or who have acquired experience in governmental functions, are already to-day, and have been for a long time, in the service of the Imperial Ethiopian Government. Here was a completely unique situation: already before the promulgation of the provisions of the Federal Act, Eritrea was already represented in that Government which will be for it the Federal Government. Thanks to the solution of this question which We have been able to give to the peoples of Ethiopia and Eritrea, We are now in a position

396

to manifest Our sovereign and paternal affection toward Our faithful Eritrean subjects who have exemplified their loyalty through devotion, notwithstanding all the hardships.

As We have always promised, We will provide, by all possible means, for the welfare of the population of Eritrea. We have given the order to the Imperial Ethiopian Government to assist with its financial resources the schools and hospitals of Eritrea. On the other hand, Eritrea will be called upon to participate in the economic and social progress of Ethiopia. The Ethiopian dollar, which is a hard currency and much sought after, will henceforth be the currency of Eritrea and will permit you to purchase imported products which up to the present have been lacking in the economy of Eritrea. We are actually promoting the full development of the two ports of Massawa and Assab, and already the Imperial Highway Authority is repairing the roads linking these two ports with the rest of Eritrea and Ethiopia. Eritrea may profit directly from all the transit trade passing between Ethiopia and foreign countries. We have also signed an agreement whereby Eritrea may profit from the services of the Point 4 Programme which the American Government is so generously offering to promote the social and economic welfare of all the inhabitants of Eritrea. Thus, a new era is opening up for our beloved subjects in Eritrea who will, after so many years of distress, enjoy the economic and social benefits of federation.

Finally, We take particular pleasure in announcing that We have just given orders for the immediate establishment in Eritrea of a hospital, a school and an orphanage, all three of which will be entirely free and placed at the disposal of our beloved subjects in Eritrea in commemoration of this day.

The Constitution We have recently granted to the people of Eritrea reflects clearly the intimate co-operation between the various elements of the population, and the Federal Act We have just proclaimed demonstrates to the entire world the close co-operation based on fraternal affection which will henceforth and forever mark the relations between the two brother peoples. The long struggle which We, personally, undertook to obtain justice for you, Our Eritrean subjects, notwithstanding imperialistic intrigues and stubborn opposition from abroad, constitute the incontestable proof of the affection which will always inspire the actions of your Sovereign towards you and your devotion to Us.

It is true that during the long struggle certain alien political elements, some belonging to the population itself, had thought another solution to the question was possible. However, all that is now a part of history, and We retain no bitterness towards those elements which, most probably, pursued their aims in all sincerity. There will be no longer any division, whether geographic, ethnic or religious, in Eritrea as in the past. All the provinces of Eritrea should, in accordance with the resolution of the United Nations, disappear in favour of the general interests of Eritrea with Ethiopia. The common interest alone should inspire the actions of all the inhabitants of the Empire of Ethiopia and Eritrea.

Several hours ago, in crossing the Mareb, We destroyed forever the

397

frontier barrier which had so long separated the two brother peoples. In this historic moment, We appeal to all elements of the population of Eritrea, Christians and Moslems, Ethiopians and Eritreans, Ethiopians and foreigners, to consider that no longer does a geographic frontier exist between Ethiopia and Eritrea and that the frontiers of religion, of politics, of nationality, even of hatred, have been effaced to-day. We desire that you retain no bitterness towards each other.

With the aid of Almighty God and under Our high direction, all the inhabitants of the Empire of Ethiopia will collaborate together, as brothers, for the mutual welfare and progress of all.

We thank Almighty God for having blessed our efforts, for having guided Our hand and for having sustained Us throughout the long struggle to obtain justice for Our beloved subjects of Eritrea, now re-united with their brothers of Ethiopia.

May God bless the reunited people of Ethiopia and Eritrea!

After His Majesty the Emperor's speech which was loudly applauded, a toast was drunk in champagne. In the evening of the same day, a State Dinner was given at the Asmara Palace attended by Princes, Dignitaries, Ministers, Heads of diplomatic missions, Eritrean leaders and high personalities. The first phase of Their Imperial Majesties' State visit to Eritrea ended on a note of joyous and tremendous welcome by the Eritrean people. From that time onward, His Majesty the Emperor, whose presence had captivated the hearts of His people in Eritrea, plunged into State activity.

Early the next morning, Their Imperial Majesties attended service at the St. Mary's Church. It was an impressive ceremony in which many bishops participated, His Grace Archbishop Basilios leading. Although it was early, the streets, squares and avenues were crowded with cheering people, an aspect of the welcome which was sustained until the early morning of the 18th of October, when their Imperial Majesties departed from Eritrea to Adigrat on the return journey to Addis Ababa. Throughout the State visit which was prolonged two days beyond the scheduled time, His Imperial Majesty took pains to receive Eritrean leaders, to visit the Eritrean Assembly and the Administrative buildings, institutions and establishments and to find out at first hand all that was possible about the life and interests of His people. Schools, hospitals, charitable institutions, farms and industries were graced by his presence. In all these, His Majesty the Emperor showed minutest interest, enquiring into their progress and their problems.

The port city of Massawa was visited on Tuesday, October 7th, by Their Imperial Majesties, who, accompanied by Their entourage, were greeted by thousands throughout the trip. The city was filled with joy and enthusiasm, eager to see and welcome the Sovereign. On the arrival of Their Imperial Majesties, high officials of the city gave the official welcome, while bands played and the populace sang, danced and shouted in a manner reminiscent of what had taken place on the Mareb-Asmara road.

This part of the visit has its particular significance in the restoration

of Eritrea. Throughout the long and arduous debates in the United Nations General Assembly, and as well through the past 67 years of Ethiopia's existence, outlet to the sea for Ethiopia was pivotal. In the United Nations resolution of December 2nd, 1950, paragraph (c) of the preamble states significantly:
"taking into consideration:
"The rights and claims of Ethiopia based on geographical, historical, ethnic and economic reasons, including in particular Ethiopia's legitimate need for adequate access to the sea."
Their Imperial Majesties' visit to Massawa signified the fulfilment of the aspirations of the Eritrean and Ethiopian people in their union, and it added the realistic touch of the formal and legal return of the Red Sea Ports of Massawa and Assab to Greater Ethiopia. It testifies not only to the fulfilment of the principle of self-determination observed by the United Nations in its decision to re-attach Eritrea to its ancient setting, but honours the legitimate claim for elemental justice to Ethiopia in the return of the means of normal international contact.
After the ceremony of welcome by the people of Massawa, His Imperial Majesty made the following speech which ties together the important facts regarding Ethiopia and her access to the sea.
With profound emotion We, by Our presence in this historic city of Massawa, on this occasion, mark the Empire of Ethiopia's access to the sea.
From the earliest periods of recorded history, statesmen and poets have rendered homage to the sea which unites the peoples of the world. Those nations which have been deprived of the right of access to the sea are not, properly speaking, in a position to participate on a basis of equality in world commerce and trade, in as much as they utilise intermediate countries and render them tribute. From the fact that it is entirely free and the property of all mankind, the sea alone is qualified to assure to each nation equality of rights and to assure commerce among peoples. None other than Queen Elizabeth I of England in the sixteenth century declared: "The use of the sea and air should be shared by all." For this reason, in the earliest years of modern times, the great jurists of international law recognised the right of access to the sea as the birthright of every free and independent state (jus communicationis).
For this same reason the resolution of the United Nations, recommending the federation of Eritrea with Ethiopia, stressed particularly this birthright of Ethiopia. It declared that the settlement of the question of Eritrea should be based upon "geographical, historical, ethnic and economic reasons including in particular, Ethiopia's legitimate need for adequate access to the sea."
The birthright of Ethiopia to have access to the sea is the more necessary and just in that Our Empire enjoyed that privilege throughout thousands of years. Several miles to the south of Us are to be found the ruins of the ancient port of Adulis which for thousands of years provided access to the sea for Our great Empire. After the destruction of Adulis in the seventh century, the present port of Massawa, which bears a poetic name

meaning "harbour of the shepherds", was the port of Our Empire for another thousand years, and indeed during the most troubled periods of the Middle Ages. Thus it was that the governor of the territory, recently known by the name of Eritrea, always bore the title "Bahr Negash". At the present time Massawa and Assab together provide access to the sea for the Empire of Ethiopia, although they do not of themselves suffice to meet the needs of the ever expanding economy of Our Empire.

In order to utilise to the maximum the resources of the two ports of Massawa and Assab, We have given orders to Our Government to undertake an ambitious programme of rehabilitation and improvement in the installations at Massawa and Assab. Moreover, and this took place well before the date of the federation of Eritrea with Ethiopia, We have already commenced important projects for the repair and improvement of the roads linking these two ports with Eritrea and Ethiopia.

For this reason, the occasion of Our state visit to Massawa at this time marks the beginning of a period of profound significance for the development and the future of the Empire of Ethiopia. Not only will access to the sea join Ethiopia to the outer world, but also this same access will serve at the same time to join, by bonds of mutual and reciprocal interest, the economies of Eritrea and Ethiopia.

Thus, through access to the sea, Ethiopia and Eritrea are called upon under Our high guidance to participate on a basis of equality, to progress with the modern world and to enter as brothers upon a new era of development and welfare.

The visit to the Port City of Massawa was one of great international importance. International contacts for Ethiopia, through the sea lanes of the world, are now assured, free from interference. In recognition of this fact, two sister nations, the United States of America and France had, as a gesture of friendship, despatched two warships to the harbour of Massawa to greet the Sovereign there. These were the U.S.S. Greenwich Bay No. 41, flagship of the United States Middle East Naval Force and the French warship La Gazelle 736. Both ships were visited by Their Imperial Majesties who took occasion to sail on them on the Red Sea.

Boarding the U.S.S. Greenwich Bay, Their Imperial Majesties and Their escort were taken for a cruise on the Red Sea. This cruise, a goodwill gesture of the United States Government, was arranged to coincide with Their Imperial Majesties' State visit to Eritrea in connection with the federation of Eritrea with Ethiopia.

As His Excellency Mr. J. Rives Childs, American Ambassador to Ethiopia, boarded the ship, a 19-gun salute was fired in his honour. When Their Imperial Majesties went aboard, a 21-gun salute was fired and Their Standard, the Ethiopian flag with the Coat of Arms, was raised on the main mast. The Imperial cruise got under way at 11.30 o'clock.

The U.S.S. Greenwich Bay steamed at fifteen knots with Their Imperial Majesties and Their escort aboard. After a little over two hours, motor boats were lowered to take His Majesty the Emperor ashore to visit Nakura, one of the Eritrean islands in the Red Sea. The island is of historic and sentimental importance. To Nakura many Ethiopian prisoners were sent from 1935 to 1941. Nakura island was bedecked with Ethiopian flags, and the inhabitants were ready at the small pier to receive and welcome their Sovereign. After speaking to them through their leaders and bestowing on them gifts, His Imperial Majesty left as they cheered vociferously.

Their Imperial Majesties' visit to the Port of Massawa, Their cruise on the Red Sea, and His Majesty the Emperor's call at the island of Nakura recall the era of "Bahr Negash", the time when Ethiopia had her ancient sea coasts and was a maritime nation. This visit was, therefore, an event in the new era of the history of the nation. As Head of the Federation of Eritrea with Ethiopia — of Greater Ethiopia, the presence of the Sovereign at Massawa and on the Red Sea was more than symbolic.

When Their Imperial Majesties returned to the harbour at 6.20 p.m. with the Imperial party and accompanied by the British, French and American Ambassadors, They had enjoyed the hospitality of a friendly power and had cruised the Red Sea to which Ethiopia now has finally gained legitimate access. His Imperial Majesty took the occasion to bestow Imperial decorations on the Commander of the United States Middle East Naval Force, Rear Admiral F. M. Hughes, the Commander of the flagship, and his deputy and to give a memento to each of the crew.

Arriving too late to take the pre-arranged cruise on the French battleship, La Gazelle, Their Imperial Majesties boarded it in the evening of the same day for a few minutes and promised to sail the next day. Appropriate arrangements were made, and Their Imperial Majesties made a two hour cruise on this French ship the next morning.

With His Excellency M. Henri Roux, as host, the French ship La Gazelle sailed towards the Gulf of Zula with its Imperial guests. His Imperial Majesty was pleased to observe, through binoculars, the islands on the Red Sea, especially the famous Ras Gedam. In the evening (at a dinner party) at the Massawa Palace, His Majesty the Emperor decorated the Commander of the French battleship, Capitaine de corvette Millet and the two officers next in command.

The next day His Majesty the Emperor addressed the chiefs and elders of Massawa:

We consider the occasion proper and fitting to invite you to-day to be presented to Us and to be received in audience by Us. You have been fortunate enough to witness the completion of the restoration of Eritrea with Ethiopia. The unity achieved should manifest itself through deeds. One deed is characterized by devotion, the other by indifference. Yours, in particular, should be characterized by devotion.

Among you who are present here to-day are chiefs and elders, but whether you are chiefs or elders, you are leaders of the people; you are intermediaries and instruments of the people in their relation to Us and Our relation to them. Despite the fact, however, that chiefs are above the people, they are in reality servants of the people. Beginning with Ourselves, Our ministers and officials are servants of the people. One should realize that We Ourselves are servants of the people. Unless We serve the people nothing belongs to Us. If We serve the people faith-

fully, the people in turn are bound to serve us two or three times as well. What We demand of you now is to be instruments between Us and the people in order that We may belong to the people and the people to Us. Both chiefs and people naturally recognize those who serve them with zealous attachment. Unless you follow the advice which We have given you, the union of Ethiopia and Eritrea will have been in vain.

Our country will be considered a just country only when We carry out Our respective administrative responsibilities in the interest of the people. There may be among you some who might have entertained in the past a political opinion different from others. Men, of necessity, cannot have the same opinion. There are bound to be differences. On the occasion of Our arrival at Asmara, We deemed it proper, to grant an amnesty to consolidate the unity of the people, which unity would enable you to start afresh to serve your country in harmony and brotherly love.

Now that the country which was taken by alien bands has been once more restored to Us, it is necessary that We should work with increased energy and zeal.

You can bring to Us any grievances and complaints. To-day things are not as they were. There are greatly improved means of communication. There is no barrier, and you should know that there is a house in Addis Ababa whose door is always open to welcome you. There is no reason to think, from your past experience, that you will be discriminated against by anybody. You are welcome when and as you like.

We have informed you without reservation what is in our mind. You should know that it would be to your advantage to accept this advice and to your disadvantage if you fail to accept it.

After the conclusion of His Imperial Majesty's speech, one of the elders present said that the people of Massawa were most happy about the visit paid by His Imperial Majesty to their part of the country and to the city of Massawa.

The tone and substance of the speech pleased His Imperial Majesty so much that he made the following remarks:

We are pleased to note what you have just said. It will be more gratifying when Our words and yours manifest themselves in deeds.

At Arkiko, 16 kilometres from Massawa, Their Imperial Majesties went to visit and inspect the Haile Selassie First School, Arkiko. This school was established by Saleh Ahmed Kekia, one of the Eritrean Moslem leaders and dedicated to His Majesty the Emperor long before federation. Their Imperial Majesties received a fitting welcome by the pupils of the schools which had arranged a special programme, and by the people of Arkiko.

Their Imperial Majesties motored back to Asmara in the forenoon of October 8th. There, as Head of State and symbol of the unity of all his people, His Imperial Majesty visited the Mosque of Asmara. The streets and squares were crowded; and an enormous body of people surrounded the space in front of the Mosque.

Members of Islamic societies, children from Moslem schools, Sheiks, Kadis and other Moslem leaders were present. Decorations were lavish, the Ethiopian tricolour fairly covered the stand prepared for the reception of the Sovereign. Are religious differences evident in Eritrea? Sheik Ibrahim Moctar, the Mufti of Eritrea, gave adequate answer in the following speech:

"Your Majesty!

"That Your Majesty is pleased to visit this mosque is a great honour to the Eritrean people and particularly to us Moslems. On this occasion, in welcoming Your Majesty on behalf of the Eritrean Moslems and myself, I am filled with unbounded happiness and pride. We had never thought we would see Your Majesty in person here among us. However, Almighty God has enabled Your Majesty to visit us, and in our interest.

"In the year 608, A.D. one of the Ethiopian kings offered hospitality to the disciples of Mohammed, the Prophet, who pled for a place of exile. In granting this request, the king performed an extraordinary act, an act unprecedented in the history of Christian kings. And to-day Your Majesty has renewed this reputation for humanitarianism among all the Islamic countries.

"We believe this beneficial act will strongly unite Your subjects, Christian and Moslem brothers. We realize that the Christian and Moslem religions have the same aims, and we believe that co-operation between Christian and Islam brethren is essential.

We pray Allah that this co-operation between Eritrean and Ethiopian brothers, under Your Majesty's leadership, will bring us an era of peace, friendship, prosperity, civilisation and justice.

"Long live our Emperor Haile Selassie I!

"Long live the Empress!

"Long live the Imperial Family!

"Long live Ethiopia and Eritrea!"

His Majesty the Emperor, whose policy towards religion is well known and whose public pronouncements and every act dispel any fear of religious intolerance in Ethiopia, answered in these words:

Since We crossed the Mareb, We have been greatly pleased by the welcome given Us by all the Eritrean people, Christians and Moslems. And now Our pleasure is greatly increased as We note the hearty welcome that you accorded Us when We appeared at this place.

The fact is well known that Christians and Moslems can live as brothers, without distinction.

When man was created, he was one in flesh, blood and soul, and these three can serve as an excellent example to him. When a man serves his country with his mind and body, he may also use religion to serve God spiritually. Thus, there is no conflict between serving one's country materially and serving God spiritually.

Both Christians and Moslems believe alike in God spiritually, and as God is always with those who believe in Him, there is harmony in man who is one in flesh, blood and soul. Therefore, Ethiopians are all one, and they do not differ one from the other. We are all one in Our belief in God. As we revere Him and believe in Him so do you. Christianity and Islam are not the only religions in the world; there are many differ-

ent religions. However, among believers, there are no differences when they serve their country, and We respect everybody's religion without partiality.

Did we not respect the Moslem, We would not have come to this place to visit this mosque. As prayers are said in churches, the same is done in mosques. The house of God is open and welcomes those who come with charity. Following this principle, since as Moslems and Christians all are loyal to Ethiopia, what has just been said is not new.

It is well known that during the invasion of Ethiopia by the enemy, there were many Moslems and Christians who defended their country, and We rewarded them, not the Moslems or Christians only, but both.

Hence, if anybody says that differences exist between Moslems and Christians, that person is an enemy of Ethiopia. We would not have come to your mosque if such were the case.

We thank you for your exuberant ovation and for the hearty welcome of all the Eritrean people. May God protect both Ethiopia and Eritrea!

The State visit took His Imperial Majesty next to Keren, famed for the battle which took place there in the campaign that led to the liberation of Ethiopia, and which contributed so much to the final victory of the Allied and Associated Powers against the forces of aggression in the Second World War.

The grand welcome and enthusiastic ovation of the Eritrean people for Their Imperial Majesties seemed now to have become the general pattern. On the 91 kilometre route from Asmara to Keren, this scene of a famous battle, over ten stops were made by the Imperial car. Their Imperial Majesties received the good wishes of Their people amid palms, triumphal arches, flags, flowers, signs in many languages and folk songs. With these songs, chanted with hearts brimful with joy and bodies and voices filled with enthusiasm, the people, tens of thousands of them, vividly expressed their emotion in welcoming their Sovereign.

Keren is predominantly Moslem. There, Their Imperial Majesties, the symbol of the unity of Ethiopia and Eritrea, took occasion to commune with the people. Schools, hospitals and other institutions were visited, the leaders of the people were received, and His Imperial Majesty reciprocated the warmth of their affection which was made evident in many ways.

The welcome at Agordat eludes accurate description. Over 8.000 people had gathered in a large paddock facing a pavillion erected for the Imperial guests. On the outer edge of this sea of people were camels, about 300 of them, mounted by men dressed with white turbans and differing costumes. Then there was a ring of people standing, and in front of them, were about 450 mounted horsemen. On the north corner were hundreds of tribesmen who had come from the interior, with their festive dress and bearing sticks and spears. In the foreground were school children from the Middle and Elementary schools, many of the women were veiled and others showing their beautiful and smiling faces. There, in the brilliant sun, flags, flowers, ribbons and green twigs contributed to the colour of the spactacle. Drums, flutes and other local instruments provided

404

the strains for the lively folk songs which went up in the crescendo of the ovation given to His Imperial Majesty.

Soldiers, the Military Bands, uniformed policemen mounted on camels were there; all a picture of colour and enthusiasm.

Particularly picturesque were the dresses of the women — they seem to prefer bright coloured prints — they sang, danced and shouted in their familiar ways, presenting a medley seen only once in a life time.

The formal reception at Agordat was similar to those given in other parts visited by His Imperial Majesty. The people presented tokens of their affection; speeches were made by their representatives and His Imperial Majesty replied fittingly.

Folk entertainments were in store to show the people's joy. The tribesmen and their women danced with vigour, rhythm, and spirit. This was followed by several groups, each trying to outdo the other. Then came the riding displays. Fine horses and equally deft horsemen ran and performed; there were camel races. All efforts were combined at Agordat to welcome His Imperial Majesty in a style which was plain grand!

His Majesty the Emperor returned to Keren after enjoying this unusual, sincere and genuine festival, provided by the people of Agordat to show their love and adoration. The stream of welcomers seemed to have waited on the route, for the ovation was sustained on the return trip, and at some places had even heightened. Haile Selassie I, Emperor, had charmed their hearts and they wished to see Him with their own eyes.

Again at Keren, His Imperial Majesty received the leaders of the local population and with his usual care and solicitude, took interest in the life of the people. Hospitals, churches, the mosque, the Catholic orphanage and industrial enterprises were visited. In all these, His Majesty the Emperor gathered from the people facts about their problems and progress and inspired in them hope and confidence.

Returning to Asmara, His Imperial Majesty busied himself with affairs of State, receiving persons and groups and visiting places of interest in the Eritrean capital.

The aspects of Their Imperial Majesties' State visit to Eritrea that are of significant interest are many. Two of them are particularly so: 1. the unanimous acclaim of the Eritrean people; 2. the unifying influence which the visit of the Sovereign had made manifest among them.

On the streets and side-walks the people were joined, and in unison welcomed Their Imperial Majesties. In the Palace Court, in every place that was visited, were seen Moslem Sheiks and Christian priests conversing and communing in perfect harmony. Communities representing the heterogenous population, of whatever race, sect or nationality, must live together in Eritrea. They all came and were received by His Majesty the Emperor, whom they recognize as the symbol of their political and constitutional unity.

Throughout his tour, His Majesty the Emperor listened attentively to the plaints and pleas of his people and responded in a manner which has inspired their mutual and common trust, their loyality and their allegiance. Their petitions, large or small, received His Imperial Majesty's attention.

405

Openly and by mute expression, all the people of Eritrea pledged their loyality and support in the tasks that lie ahead, under the enlightened leadership of His Majesty the Emperor.

In a visit to the Eritrean Assembly, the sentiment of the Eritrean people were voiced by their chosen representatives.

Sheik Mohammed Mousa Ali Radai, President of the Assembly, in his speech to His Imperial Majesty said:

"Your Imperial Majesty,

"First of all, I express my thanks to the Almighty God who enabled us to reach this stage, and, before starting with my speech, I beg to have Your Imperial Majesty's permission to do so.

"Your Imperial Majesty,

"When Your Imperial Majesty's visit to Eritrea was announced, all the members of this Assembly resolved to meet you at the Mareb, where you marked a historical event when Your Majesty broke the artificial barrier which was dividing two brothers and proceeded peacefully and with great honour to Asmara. On your way, all of them stayed in their respective constituencies and took part in your progress with joy.

"Throughout Your Imperial Majesty's journey from Mareb to Asmara, Massawa, Keren and Agordat we continuously took part in the joyful events arranged by the people which showed our happiness and gratefulness at Your Majesty's coming. The Eritrean people have, in the past, undergone sufferings and have now shown themselves to Your Imperial Majesty to be true citizens, and this heartfelt feeling of theirs will persist in the future.

"Before the future of Eritrea was settled and on the coming of the two Commissions to consult the inhabitants, the Eritrean people, despite the sufferings they were being subjected to, took all chances to show loyalty and love to Your Imperial Majesty. I am herein referring to Eritrea's march from death to life, and its people who have achieved this stage fully realise that this was possible to be so achieved, thanks to their full confidence in your high leadership, and I say this merely to assure that there is no one who does not realize this.

"Your Imperial Majesty,

"In addition to your great efforts and achievements to save us, and now that Eritrea is united to Ethiopia on the basis of federation, Your Imperial Majesty, without delaying for even a year to pass by, has been graciously pleased to honour us with your visit; this will remain carved in our hearts for eternity.

"Although you have huge tasks to deal with in the main capital for the welfare and greatness of the whole of Ethiopia, the fact that, in such circumstances, you have honoured us with a fatherly visit here, I beg, in the name of the Eritrean Assembly, to express my humble gratitude.

"In future, we humbly beg Your Imperial Majesty that you will graciously be pleased to grant us aid to solve difficulties arising out of the task entrusted to us by our people for the greatness and prosperity of Eritrea, whenever we may happen to ask for it through our beloved and chosen Head of Government."

406

To this, His Majesty the Emperor replied:

At this hour of Our visit to the Representative Assembly of Eritrea, We are pleased to give some advice.

But first, as the President of this parliament mentioned in his speech, We have been deeply moved by the enthusiastic welcome given us by the Eritrean people everywhere, since We crossed the Mareb River.

Since We were chosen by God to rule over Ethiopia, We have nurtured Our wish for the welfare of the Eritrean people, and Our persistent efforts for their federation with their Motherland, by abolishing the artificial frontier, have been recognized by Our people who long yearned for Our coming.

To-day, while We are here to visit Eritrea, remembering that We permit Eritrean representatives to sit in the Ethiopian Parliament to share fully with the people of Ethiopia the progress and the benefits of welfare, which is Our wish for the people of Eritrea, We perceive that this will make possible the disappearance of the geographical barrier that has heretofore existed between the two countries, and thus the united countries can pursue their common interests and seek common goals in a spirit of co-operation.

Since you, the representatives in the Assembly at Asmara, were chosen by the people of Eritrea, it ought not to be forgotten that by thus being elected you are to be the mirror of their wishes and ideas. In performing your parliamentary duties, fruitful results will be seen when the wishes of Our Eritrean subjects are put into effect. The responsibility for the protection of the Eritrean people's interest, their right to be Ethiopian and to see the accomplishment of their wishes, rests with you. It is important to remember that discharging this responsibility of your office demands enormous effort and vigilance.

May God give you the light of knowledge which will direct you to the right and true path in your work.

As told by the Chief Executive and also after observing for Ourselves that this parliament building is incomplete, We are pleased to allocate the necessary funds for its completion.

The federation of Eritrea with Ethiopia under the sovereignty of the Ethiopian Crown marks another important stage in the United Nations effort towards the settlement of world issues by peaceful means. It was inspired by the principles of San Francisco, embodied in the United Nations Charter, which found their expression in the United Nations resolution of December 2nd, 1950.

In full view of the world, and after a full cycle of debates, conferences and discussions, this formula was accepted by all parties concerned. Ethiopia, the most vitally interested party to this issue, exemplified throughout the deliberations a spirit of democracy. His Imperial Majesty, whose State visit to Eritrea, is here sketched never failed to prove this position. The enthusiasm and sincerity with which He was welcomed by the Eritrean people on this State visit is a fitting tribute to the high prestige of His Majesty the Emperor.

Not only have the manisfestations of the Eritrean people, during this

407

historic visit which climaxed the restoration, vindicated the bases of the United Nations decision, they were expressive of the incontrovertible spirit of unity which characterizes the fraternal ties between the Eritrean and Ethiopian people. Rallying around Their Imperial Majesties as they did throughout the whole of Eritrea is indeed a happy augury to the close association of the Eritrean and Ethiopian people toward their future common destiny.

In his concluding statement to the General Assembly on December 2nd, 1950, His Excellency the Ethiopian Foreign Minister significantly said: "In substance, there will be no former political adversaries. There will be no former enemies. There will be only brothers of Eritrea and former enemies become friends who, all together, will collaborate with us, Ethiopians, in writing a new chapter in history — a chapter which will bring to an end a long epoch of exile and suffering and which will demonstrate, in these critical hours of world history, the profound verity of justice on which is based the work of the United Nations."

The tremendous ovation accorded Their Imperial Majesties in Eritrea on their first State visit after federation, saw the people giving eloquent meaning to this statement. There was no section of the people omitted from the acclaim of Their Imperial Majesties as Head of the Federal Union of Eritrea with Ethiopia. His Majesty the Emperor in His attitude to the people, their problems and their progress testified to the fact that this statement would reach its fulfilment under his enlightened guidance and leadership. The clamour and pomp with which Their Imperial Majesties were received by Their people in Eritrea is demonstrative of one factor, above all else. It was the true answer to the fact that Eritreans feel oneness with their Ethiopian brothers. To see Their Imperial Majesties was like seeing parents from whom they were separated through no wish or desire of their own. Like the deep sentiments which characterize a family reunion, the Eritrean people, oblivious of what others thought to the contrary, were happy, in the fullest sense of the term to be back under the protecting arm of the mother country, where their forefathers longed and yearned to be.

Secondly, and contributory to this great ovation is the fact that now, once and for all foreign domination, under which they knew no respite, has been banished forever. The dismal period of uncertainty, which hung over the Eritrean people and which gave them no opportunity to order their own affairs in a constructive manner, has given way to the opportunity for Eritreans themselves, together with their Ethiopian brothers, to work for their common and mutual good.

Moreover, Haile Selassie I, Emperor, who had shown them so much care and solicitude in the honour of their separation, who had made their difficulties his, who had taken the patience to battle in the world diplomatic arena for their ultimate redemption, who had fathered so many of their brethren, now free participators in the life and progress of the mother country, and who, in many more ways, has shown them his love and devotion in their every problem, had come in person to bind their wounds and pledge continued aid.

His Imperial Majesty, who guided the cause through the morass of disputes, arguments and deliberations, has been chosen by the United Nations as their constitutional and political leader. Thus, in addition to the paternal, historic and spiritual bonds which bind the Eritrean and Ethiopian people together, has been added the approval of the world to their claim to be firmly and irrevocably associated with Ethiopia, the Motherland.

CHAPTER 32

Emperor's State Visits

An important, interesting, as well as meaningful aside of the twenty-five years of His Imperial Majesty's reign is his recent international State visits which started at the begining of the summer and ended at the beginning of the winter last year.

The tour which began with the invitation of President Eisenhower to visit the United States of America was undertaken in two parts. Leaving Addis Ababa on Wednesday morning, May 19th, 1954 at 6.30, His Majesty the Emperor visited the United States, Canada and Mexico in the Americas, flew by chartered plane to Nice, France, whence, on the invitation of Marshal Tito, he visited Yugoslavia, then the kingdom of Greece in Europe, returning to Addis Ababa by plane on Tuesday August 3rd. The second wave of the Emperor's international journey for a series of State visits began when he left his capital on Tuesday morning, October 5th, at 10.45 by plane on the invitation of Her Majesty Queen Elizabeth II to visit the United Kingdom. During this second part of the Imperial tour the Emperor visited, outside Great Britain, France, West Germany, Sweden, Norway, Denmark, Switzerland and Holland, and unofficially Austria.

The entourage of the Emperor during his North American visits included: His Imperial Highness Prince Sahle Selassie; H.H. Princess Sebla Desta; H.E. Brigadier-General Abye Abebe, Minister of War; H.E. Tsahafa Taezaz Wolde Guorguis Wolde Yohannes, Minister of Pen and Justice; H.E. Ato Aklilou Habtewold, Minister of Foreign Affairs; H.E. Ato Tafarra Work, His Imperial Majesty's Private Secretary; H.E. Bitwoded Jacques Zervos, Private physician of His Imperial Majesty; H.E. Colonel Makonnen Deneke A.D.C.; Lij Endalkatchew Makonnen, Director General in the Ministry of Foreign Affairs and Chief of Protocol; and Mr. John Spencer, Senior Adviser in the Ministry of Foreign Affairs.

The entourage to the United Kingdom and European Continent State visits included: His Imperial Highness Makonnen Haile Selassie, Duke of Harar; H.E. Tsahafa Taezaz Wolde Guorguis Wolde Yohannes, Minister of Pen and Justice; H.E. Dejazmach Mesfin Sileshi, Lord Chamberlain at the Palace; H.E. Ato Tafarra Work, Private Secretary to His Majesty the Emperor; H.E. Colonel Makonnen Deneke, A.D.C.; and Lij Endalkatchew Makonnen, Director General in the Ministry of Foreign Affairs and Chief of Protocol.

The acclaim with which the Emperor was received from the friendly peoples and the many expressions of appreciation and mutual comprehension shown by his distinguished hosts were a deserving tribute to

410

His Imperial Majesty and a source of great pride and satisfaction to the Ethiopian people.

In these days of personal diplomacy the visits have had the salutary effect not only of bringing the Emperor of Ethiopia into touch with the heads of these friendly states: they brought Ethiopia and the Ethiopians closer to their peoples as well. For Haile Selassie I it has been a personal triumph, for the visits recalled his stand in the 1930's on the then emergent principle of collective security which he has lived to see become a cornerstone of the foreign policy of these nations. Never was the fact highlighted more than when on June 1st, the Emperor addressed the United Nations (successor of the League of Nations) in these more than significant words:

The League of Nations failed basically because of its inability to prevent aggression against my country. But neither the depth of that failure nor the intervening catastrophes could dull the perception of the need and the search for peace through collective security. So it is that here in the United Nations we have dedicated ourselves anew to these high and indeed essential ideals, essential if the world is to continue on the path of peace.

It is a matter of pride and of encouragement that even at the moment when Haile Selassie I pronounced the words above on June 1st, 1954, the principle was being effectively upheld on the Korean peninsula. It is gratifying even more that Ethiopia, which in 1936 was the victim of agression, stands proudly today among the nations taking an active and decisive part in upholding concretely the principle of collective security, by shedding the blood of her sons to defend the integrity of Korea and uphold the dignity of the United Nations.

Undoubtedly there were other aspects of His Imperial Majesty's international tour. As Regent of the realm, His Majesty the Emperor, in 1924, had visited Europe and the Middle East. He was in voluntary exile in the United Kingdom from 1936 to 1940; at the Bitter Lakes, in 1942, he met President Roosevelt and Sir Winston Churchill. All these visits were, in some measure, reflected in the policy of the Imperial Ethiopian Government under Haile Selassie I. In all of these missions the Emperor was in the service of his country. Not only did these visits consolidate mutual comprehension and understanding between Ethiopia and other nations; they were instrumental in strengthening the Emperor's ideas in building a more progressive Ethiopia. The same barometer could be applied to the extensive international tour undertaken by His Majesty the Emperor at the invitations of Heads of States and Governments.

It is certainly not accidental that the Emperor's visits in these countries included certain centres, the activities of which have direct bearing on important phases of the life and interests of his country. Visits to renowned institutions of learning coincide with the Emperor's ever-present desire to see that education in his realm be as wide-spread and of as high a level possible.

Industrial development has high priority here; hydro-electric plants, stockyard and meat packing and other industries were seen. Ethiopia's economy is basically agricultural. Farms, Agricultural Colleges and such like activities were of great interest. At the University at Minnesota Agricultural Campus, the Emperor gave an address on the rôle of agriculture in Ethiopia.

Interest in Health Institutions abroad was directly related to the Emperor's interest in the public health services of his country, through which he has always joined forces in the fight against diseases in the Empire. And there could be no question of the fact that His Majesty the Emperor in his public utterances during these visits, in his press conferences and in conferring with public figures, spoke without hesitation, in the interest of Ethiopia and her new position in the comity of nations. Speaking at a luncheon in his honour His Imperial Majesty told one thousand of Chicago's business, civic and Government leaders:

Unlimited opportunities exist (in Ethiopia) *for American capital and pioneering spirit in the development of the coffee industry, meat packing and shipping, tannery and shoe industries, tobacco and sugar.*

American business has the added protection not only of a recent Commercial Treaty, but what is equally important an American dollar based currency in Ethiopia. You can therefore freely bring back the profits of your investments.

At the Mansion House in London, when His Majesty the Emperor replied to the toast in his honour by the Lord Mayor of London he said:

This close community of interests finds reflection in the exceptional importance which Britain holds in the commercial affairs and business of Ethiopia. Not only does the British Empire retain by far the largest share of the ever-growing commerce of Ethiopia, but British firms themselves conduct the bulk of the trade and commerce even with other countries. This factor is not without significance, since during the years following the close of the last war, Ethiopia's economy had developed beyond all expectation. The currency in circulation has more than quadrupled. The assets of our national bank have increased 2,000 per cent. Our foreign trade has quadrupled, as have our holdings of foreign exchange. Ethiopia is already enjoying an unparalleled area of prosperity, and in this development, British capital and enterprises will be called upon to play an ever-more important rôle, thus responding to a long cherished hope on my part.

His Imperial Majesty's tour in the United States was particularly significant and covered thousands of miles. It began with an enthusiastic reception in Washington, D. C., the nation's capital, on May 26th. After a three-day stay in Washington as the guest of President and Mrs. Eisenhower, during which the Emperor was introduced to United States' Government leaders, the seven-week visit covering aspects of the nation's industrial, educational, agricultural, cultural and scenic life began.

The high spots of the Emperor's three-day stay in Washington were: an address to the Joint Houses of Congress, an official dinner given in the Emperor's honour by the President and Mrs. Eisenhower; an appearance on television; a tour of national shrines and memorials; and the presentation of an honorary degree to His Imperial Majesty by Howard University, one of America's foremost Negro Universities.

412

Emperor with President and Mrs Eisenhower at the White House

The Emperor's reception in the capital was a grand, cordial and spontaneous tribute to him. The people and officialdom gave him a warm and befitting welcome, which was at every turn accepted by His Imperial Majesty with deep appreciation. He spent the first night in Washington

413

at the White House as guest of the President and Mrs. Eisenhower. On the 28th of May His Majesty the Emperor made the major speech of his American tour to a joint meeting of the two Houses of Congress. The entire diplomatic corps, the President's Cabinet and the judges of United States Supreme Court were also present. The galleries were full to capacity with the press and enthusiastic visitors, eager to see and hear the Emperor when he said:

I count it a privilege to address what is one of the greatest parliaments in the world today — where the forces that make great one of the most powerful of nations have been and are being brought to bear and where issues of world-wide importance have been decided.

The extent of that power and influence and the rapidity with which you have reached such a summit of importance for the rest of the world are unparalleled in world history and begger all conceivable comparisons. Two hunderd years ago today, as I am speaking, General George Washington won the battle of Fort Necessity, a victory in the gradual forging together of the United States.

What a phenomenal progress has been made in that interval of two hundred years, an interval which — you may pardon me as representative of one of the most ancient nations in the world — is surely but a surprisingly short passage of time.

So great are your power and wealth that the budget of a single American city often equals that of an entire nation.

As in the case of other countries, you gave us lend-lease assistance during the war and, at present, both mutual security and technical assistance. Yet, so vast are your power and resources that even after deducting all expenses of the Federal Government, you have met the costs of this assistance in one-quarter of an hour — fifteen minutes — of your annual production.

Of what interest is it to you then, you may well ask, that I, the head of what must be for you a small and remote country, should appear before you in the midst of your deliberations? I do not take it upon myself to point out why Ethiopia is important to the United States — that you can best judge for yourselves, but, rather, to explain to you with brevity, the circumstances which make Ethiopia a significant factor in world politics. Since so much of world politics is, today, influenced by the decisions which you, Members of Congress, reach, here in these halls, it is, perhaps, not unimportant that I set out these considerations for you.

A moment ago, I remarked that, for you, Ethiopia must appear to be a small and remote country. Both of these terms are purely relative. In fact, so far as size is concerned, Ethiopia has exactly the area and population of your entire Pacific Far-West consisting of the states of California, Oregon, Washington and also Idaho. We are remote, perhaps, only in the sense that we enjoy a secure position on the high plateau of East Africa protected by the Red Sea and our mountain fastnesses. However, by the numerous air lines that link us with the rest of the world, it is possible to arrive in Washington from Addis Ababa in less than two days.

414

By one of those strange parallels of history, Ethiopia and a certain well-known country of the Far East who both enjoy highly defensible and strategic positions in their respective areas of the world, both, for similar reasons, simultaneously, at the beginning of the seventeenth century came out of their period of isolation. As in the case of the other country, that isolation came to an end in the latter half of the nineteenth century, with this difference that, upon abandoning her policy of isolation, she was immediately called upon to defend, against tremendous odds, her thous-and-years-old independence. Indeed so bitter has been this struggle against foreign aggrandizement that were it not for our persistence and for the enormous social, economic and material advance Ethiopia has made in the interval, and particularly since the last war, Ethiopia might very well have returned to her policy of isolation.

In consequence, in many respects, and particularly since the last world war, Ethiopia has become a new frontier of widely expanding opportunities, notwithstanding the tremendous setback which we suffered in the unprovoked invasion of our country nineteen years ago, and the long years of unaided struggle against an infinitely stronger enemy. The last seven years have seen the quadrupling of our foreign trade, currency and foreign exchange holdings. Holdings of American dollars have increased ten times over. The Ethiopian dollar has become the only U.S. dollar-based currency in the Middle East today. The assets of our national bank of issue have increased one thousand per cent. Blessed with what is per-haps the most fertile soil in Africa, well-watered, and with a wide variety of climates ranging from the temperate on the plateau, to the tropical in the valleys, Ethiopia can grow, throughout the year, crops, normally raised only in widely separated areas of the earth's surface.

Since the war, Ethiopia has become the granary of the Middle East, as well as the only exporter of meat, cereals and vegetables. Whereas at the end of the war, every educational facility had been destroyed, today, schools are springing up throughout the land, the enrollment has quad-rupled and, as in the pioneer days in the United States, and indeed, I presume, as in the lives of many of the distinguished members of Con-gress here present, school-children, in their zeal for education, take all sorts of work in order to earn money to purchase text books and to pur-sue their education.

Finally, through the return in 1952 of its historic ports on the Red Sea and of the long-lost territory of Eritrea, Ethiopia has not only regained access to the sea, but has been one of the few states in the post-war world to have regained lost territory pursuant to post-war treaties and in application of peaceful methods.

We have thus become a land of expanding opportunities where the Ame-rican pioneering spirit, ingenuity and technical abilities have been and will continue to be welcomed.

A thousand year old history of struggles to defend the territorial integ-rity of our country, the long fight for liberation two decades ago and the recent campaign in Korea have given our army an esprit de corps and a fighting spirit that, I believe, can stand, without misgiving, for com-

415

parison. Today, our fighting forces are among the largest and best trained in the Middle East.

Unlike many other countries, Ethiopia has long been a nation of small, rather than of large land-owners. Moreover, a profoundly democratic tradition has assured in the past, as it assures today, the rise to the highest posts of responsibility in the government, of men of the humblest of origins.

It is but natural, therefore, that a state which has existed for three thousand years, which has regained its independence by the blood of its patriots, which commands the allegiance and loyalty of even its most lowly subjects, and which enjoys an unusually sound economy, should have a regime of marked stability in that area of the world where stability is so frequently absent today.

Such is the state of Ethiopia today about which I am speaking. It is against this background that I wish to talk to you of Ethiopia as a factor in world politics. Her geographic location is of great significance, with her long shore line and its archipelago of hundreds of islands, Ethiopia occupies a unique position on the most constricted but important of strategic line of communications in the world, that which passes through the Red Sea. She also lies on the other most strategic line of communication in the world, namely, the world band of telecommunications which, because of natural phenomena, circles the world at the Equator.

However, in yet a perhaps broader sense is Ethiopia's geographical position of significance. Through her location on the shores of the Red Sea and in the horn of East Africa, Ethiopia has profound historical ties with the rest of the Middle East as well as with Africa. In this respect she stands in a completely unique position. Her culture and social structure were founded in the mingling of her original culture and civilisation with Hamitic and Semitic migrations into Africa from the Arabian peninsula, and, in fact, today, our language Amharic, is a member of that large family of Hamitic and Semitic tongues and, therefore, intimately related to Hebrew and Arabic. Indeed, at one time Ethiopia extended to both sides of the Red Sea as well as north to Upper Egypt.

On the other hand, three thousand years of history make of Ethiopia a profoundly African state in all that term implies. In the United Nations, she has been to the forefront in the defence of Africa's racial, economic and social interests.

Finally, both culturally and geographically, Ethiopia serves to a unique degree as the link between the Middle East and Africa. Situated in the Horn of Africa, and along the shores of the Red Sea, with the desert area of Africa to the north and west, it is but natural that Ethiopia should be the filter known as "he who maintains order between the Christians and the Moslems." A profound comprehension of and sympathy with the other states of the Middle East naturally inspires Ethiopian national policies.

Thus, our social and political outlook and orientation became important not only in terms of Middle Eastern and African but also, in terms of world politics — and this leads me to point to a factor which I consider

416

His Majesty the Emperor rides in state coach with Queen Elizabeth to Buckingham Palace

to be of unique significance. We have a profound orientation towards the west. One consideration alone, although there are others, would suffice to explain this result. The two Americas and the continent of Europe together constitute exactly one-third of the land masses of the world. It is in this one-third that are concentrated the peoples of the Christian Faith. With but rare exceptions Christianity does not extend beyond the confines of the Mediterranean. Here, I find it significant that, in point of fact, in this remaining two-thirds of the earth's surface, Ethiopia is the state having the largest Christian population and is by far the largest Christian state in the Middle East. In fact, Ethiopia is unique among the nations of the world in that it is, today, the one remaining Christian state that can trace her history unbroken as a Christian polity from the days when the Roman empire itself was still a vigorous reality.

The strength of the Christian tradition has been of vital significance in our national history, and as a force for the unification of the Empire of Ethiopia. It is this force which gives us, among the other countries of the Middle East, a profound orientation toward the West. We read the same Bible. We speak a common spiritual language.

It is this heritage of ideals and principles that has excluded from our conscious, indeed, from our unconscious processes, the possibility of compromising with those principles which we hold sacred. We have sought to remain faithful to the principle of respect for the rights of others, and the right of each people to an independent existence. We, like you, are profoundly opposed to the un-Christian use of force and are, as you, attached to a concept of the pacific settlement of disputes.

Our lone struggle before the outbreak of the last world catastrophe as, indeed, our recent participation in the combined efforts and the glorious comradeship in arms in Korea have marked us, like you, in giving more than lip service to these ideals. It is your deep comprehension of our ideals and struggles in which it has been my privilege to lead, at times not without heartbreak, my beloved people, and our common comradeship in arms that have laid a very sure and lasting basis for friendship between a great and a small country.

Last year, we concluded with you a new treaty of friendship, commerce and navigation designed to assure to American business enterprise expanded opportunities in Ethiopia. Our dollar-based currency is also there to assure the ready return to the United States of the profits of their investments. We have entrusted to American enterprises the development of our civil aviation which has surpassed all expectations. To American enterprise we have confided the exploitation of our oil resources as well as of our gold deposits. Although my country is 8,000 miles removed from the eastern seaboard of the United States, United States exports to Ethiopia have, notwithstanding this heavy handicap, pushed forward to the forefront in Ethiopia.

Conversely, the United States stands in first rank of countries to whom we export. Ethiopia has, from the province of Kaffa, given the world the name and product of coffee. The coffee which you drink attains its unique and pleasant American flavor in part, at least, through the added

418

His Imperial Majesty welcomed by Edouard Herriot
an old friend on visit to Lyon, France

mixture of Ethiopian coffee. American shoes are made, in part at least,
from Ethiopian goat-skins which are principally exported to the United
States.

On the other hand, you have given us valuable support, not only in lend-
lease assistance during the war, and today through mutual security and
technical assistance agreements, but you have also powerfully aided us
in obtaining rectification of long-standing injustices. If, today, the brother
territory of Eritrea stands finally united under the Crown and if Ethiopia
has regained her shore-line on the Red Sea it has been due, in no small

419

measure to the contribution of the United States of America. I am happy to take this occasion to express to you, the Congress which has approved this assistance, the sincere and lasting appreciation of my people.

This collaboration with the West and with the United States in particular has taken yet broader forms. There is our military collaboration based on the Mutual Security program. If we leave out the Atlantic group, Ethiopia has been the only state of the Middle East to follow the example of the United States in sending forces to Korea for the defense of collective security.

In so doing, Ethiopia has been inspired by a vision which is broader than her preoccupation with regional policies or advantages. Nearly two decades ago, I personally assumed before history the responsibility of placing the fate of my beloved people on the issue of collective security, for surely at that time and for the first time in world history, that issue was posed in all its clarity. My searchings of conscience convinced me of the rightness of my course and if, after untold sufferings and, indeed, unaided resistance at the time of aggression, we now see the final vindication of that principle in our joint action in Korea. I can only be thankful that God gave me strength to persist in our faith until the moment of its recent glorious vindication.

We do not view this principle as an extenuation for failing to defend one's homeland to the last drop of one's blood, and, indeed our own struggles during the last two decades bear testimony to our conviction that in matters of collective security as of Providence, "God helps him who helps himself."

However, we feel that nowhere can the call for aid against aggression be refused by any state large or small. It is either a universal principle or it is no principle at all. It cannot admit of regional application or be regional responsibility. That is why we, like you, have sent troops half-way around the world to Korea. We must face that responsibility for its application wherever it may arise in these troubled hours of world history. Faithful to the sacred memory of her patriots who fell in Ethiopia and in Korea in defence of that principle, Ethiopia cannot do otherwise.

The world has ceaselessly sought for and has striven to apply some system for assuring the peace of the world. Many solutions have been proposed and many have failed. Today the system which we have advocated and with which the name of Ethiopia is inseparably associated, after her sacrifices of two decades ago, and her recent sacrifices with the United States and others in Korea, finally demonstrated its worth. However, no system, not even that of collective security, can succeed unless there is not only a firm determination to apply it universally both in space and time, but also whatever be the cost. Having succesfully applied the system of collective security in Korea, we must now, wherever in the world the peace is threatened, pursue its application more resolutely than ever and with courageous acceptance of its burdens. We have the sacred duty to our children to spare them the sacrifices which we have known. I call upon the world for determination fearlessly to apply and to accept as you and as we have accepted them — the sacrifices of collective security.

420

It is here that our common Christian heritage unites two peoples across the globe in a community of details and endeavour. Ethiopia seeks only to affirm and broaden that co-operation between peace loving nations.

Later in the day His Majesty the Emperor appeared on a television programme, "Youth Wants to Know," which was seen all over the United States. On this programme he met a group of typical American secondary school students who questioned him about Ethiopia and his opinions on world affairs. The students in this television programme are chosen on the basis of their scholarship and evidence of civic responsibility. Several young Ethiopian students from the Washington area were present.

Another high point of his Washington visit was the awarding of an Honorary Doctor of Laws Degree to His Imperial Majesty by Howard University. For the colourful ceremony, more than 4,000 students, professors, officials of government and education and honoured guests assembled.

As he presented the degree to His Imperial Majesty, President Mordecai Johnson of the University said: "You have never looked back with vindictiveness; but, in keeping with the great and ancient Christian tradition from which you are descended, and with the simplicity of life and singleness of mind which becomes a Christian monarch, you have worked to restore the life of the people from the devastation made by war and occupation."

In reply, the Emperor said to the students: *You are continuing that tradition* (Africa's contribution to progress and culture) *in expanding the new frontiers of thought and science here in these halls of Howard University through the intelligence and efforts of peoples of African origin.*

His Imperial Majesty and his party visited the great National Cathedral in Washington in which various Christian faiths have built and maintained chapels. In the early 1920's as Regent, Ras Tafari Makonnen, had presented this Cathedral with a gold cross; as Emperor, His Imperial Majesty took the opprtunity of making a second gift of a gold and silver censer.

At a state dinner given by His Imperial Majesty at the Ethiopian Embassy in honour of President and Mrs. Eisenhower, the Emperor presented official Ethiopian decorations to President Eisenhower; Admiral Radford, Chairman of the Joint Chiefs of Staff; Mr. Harold Stassen, head of the Foreign Operations Administration; President Mordecai Johnson of Howard University; Mr. Henry Byroade, Assistant Secretary of State for the Near East and Africa; and the U.S. Ambassador to Ethiopia, Dr. Joseph Simonson.

Dr. Simonson received the decoration of the Grand Gordon of the Order of the Star of Ethiopia.

During the visit of His Imperial Majesty to Washington, the U.S. Library of Congress opened a special exhibit honouring his presence in the nation's capital. The exhibit consisted of books, official documents, photographs of Ethiopia's historic buildings and monuments, its educational centers and highlights of its recent past. The exhibit, the first of its kind in the United States, was keynoted by the Emperor's words spoken before the Council of the League of Nations on May 12, 1937: *Apart from the Kingdom of the Lord, there is not on this earth any nation superior to any other.*

The exhibit showed the sacred character of Ethiopian literature as expressed in its liturgies, service-books, lives of saints and Bible commentaries. There were pictures of the visit of His Imperial Majesty to the formal opening of the U.S. Information Service Reading Room in Addis Ababa on December 3, 1949.

In Washington, His Imperial Majesty had his first large press conferences and his first taste of the relentless curiosity of the American newsmen. He was asked questions ranging from his oponion on the war in Indochina to what he liked to eat for breakfast. While in Washington, His Imperial Majesty made an address in which he praised the American press for reporting so exhaustively and objectively. *This objectivity is important,* the Emperor said, *because all other nations must have a clear concept of America's problems and attitudes.*

At a state dinner given in the White House in honour of His Majesty the Emperor, President Eisenhower paid him tribute as a truly great man. The President expressed his feeling in offering a toast to His Imperial Majesty. He said:

"I think it is safe to say that never has any company here gathered been honoured by the presence as their guest of honour of an idividual more noted for his fierce defence of freedom and for his courage in defending the independence of his people.

"I read once, that no individual can really be known to have greatness until he has been tested in adversity. By this test, our guest of honour has established new standards in the world. In five years of adversity, with his country overrun but never conquered, he never lost for one single second his dignity, he never lost his faith in himself, in his people and in his God."

Thanking the President, Emperor Haile Selassie I expressed appreciation for the American aid in assisting Ethiopia's progressive development. The Emperor asserted, *it is characteristic of that extraordinary flexibility of understanding and felicity of spirit with which you, as a nation, have been endowed, and of the trust and confidence which you inspire in the minds of others.*

The Emperor after completing the first stage of his official visit in the nation's capital left to continue his tour in the eastern part of the United States. New York and Boston, two of America's major Atlantic coastal cities, were next visited. Before reaching New York His Majesty made a brief stop-over at Princeton University, one of the nation's oldest, founded in 1746. Visiting the famous University library, he saw some ancient Ethiopian manuscripts on display. Among these were one of the Four Gospels written during the reign of King John in 1650, part of the Gospel of St. Luke written in Ge'ez in the sixteenth century and a seventeenth century book of the saints. There was also a letter written by the Emperor Menelik II in 1900.

422

Emperor with King Paul of Greece on a Greek battleship

The next morning, May 30th, His Imperial Majesty began his second week in the United States by attending early morning worship at the Hellenic Cathedral of the Holy Trinity, the Greek Orthodox Church. Archbishop Michael of the Greek Orthodox Church of North and South America chanted the liturgy while the Emperor occupied a place especially arranged for him at the front of the church. After the service, His Imperial Majesty presented a gold cross to the Archbishop for the Cathedral.

423

The same day, the Imperial Party visited Harlem, a section of New York populated by many Americans of African descent among the other nationalities who live there. His reception there was one of the most enthusiastic he received in the east. The occasion was the Emperor's visit to the Abyssinian Baptist Church, built in 1808 by American citizens of African descent. Thousands of persons cheered His Imperial Majesty as he drove to the church, and hundreds of Ethiopian flags were waved in each city block.

The service was led by the Honourable Dr. A. Clayton Powell Jr., a minister, who is also a Representative of the U.S. Congress. He described His Imperial Majesty as one who had meant much to Americans of African descent because of his leadership in demonstrating the key rôle that developing nations of the continent could play in world history. As the Emperor left the church, he saw that all of the windows in the area, as well as the streets, were filled with enthusiastically waving people. The colours of Ethiopia could be found in the hats and clothes of many of the people.

That same morning, His Imperial Majesty drove to Hyde Park, New York, to visit the Tomb of the late President Franklin Delano Roosevelt and to have lunch with Mrs. Roosevelt. His Imperial Majesty laid a floral wreath on the Tomb of the late President and then said to Mrs. Roosevelt:

As you know, Mrs. Roosevelt, it is a little more than 10 years ago since your husband asked me to come to Hyde Park. I thanked him then and I thank you now. I knew the statesman, the incomparable leader of not only his own but also of so many nations. I feel today, Mrs. Roosevelt, I know more of the man. I shall not even try to express my admiration and my respect for President Roosevelt, and I even hesitate to express my regard for your own great services to humanity and mankind.

Mrs. Roosevelt thanked His Imperial Majesty and congratulated him for leading his nation to such a respected place in the family of nations. She then escorted the Emperor through the mansion, showing him the rooms where President Roosevelt had made many of the decisions that influenced history. In the library, His Imperial Majesty saw the gold globe of the world he had given President Roosevelt and a picture of their meeting aboard a warship in the Red Sea during World War Two. His Imperial Majesty was the last sovereign of any nation to see the late President before his death. The Emperor then signed the guest book and looked over many of the official documents which are reserved for research scholars.

Perhaps the most important part of His Imperial Majesty's visit to New York took place when, on June 1st, he visited the United Nations Headquarters, almost eighteen years after his dramatic appeal to the League of Nations for collective action against Fascist aggression in 1936.

The Emperor was greeted by Secretary-General Dag Hammarskjold and other UN officials. The UN Secretary-General said the Emperor "stands in the perspective of the history of our time as a symbolic landmark, a

424

Marshal Tito welcomes His Majesty the Emperor to Yugoslavia

prophetic figure on the path of man's struggle to achieve international
peace and security through concerted international action."
Hammarskjold also commended the Emperor and people of Ethiopia for
the response to the UN resolution which set up the UN command to
resist aggression in Korea.
His Imperial Majesty and the Secretary-General entered the huge 40

story building and visited the auditorium of the 60-nation General Assembly where Ethiopia's representative H.E. Ambassador Zaude Gabre Heywot, meets with other representatives. The party was led through the halls of the Educational, Scientific and Cultural Organisation, the UN Trusteeship Council and the Security Council. Within the halls of this new structure of the new Organisation, His Imperial Majesty made a speech contrasting his experience in the League of Nations with the new hope brought by the United Nations.

The seven-weeks tour took His Majesty the Emperor to various parts of the United States. After visiting Boston where occasion was taken to visit important centres and to commune with the people, His Imperial Majesty and his entourage left for Ottawa, the capital of the Canadian dominion, where he was also invited to make a State visit.

At a luncheon in his honour at Boston, His Majesty said that the people of other nations *are often impressed rather with the material strength of the United States. Here in Boston we have the opportunity of visiting what is undoubtedly the cultural capital of the United States. We have been tremendously impressed with the wealth of learning amassed around the city of Boston in institutions of unparalleled influence.*

After several busy days in Canada His Imperial Majesty re-crossed the Canadian-American border and re-entered the United States at Detroit, Michigan, to continue his tour of America's Middle West. Containing America's richest farming land where enormous crops of wheat, corn and other grain are produced each year, it is an area famed for its production of dairy products — milk, cheese and butter — and meat packing houses. The Emperor showed particular interest in his tour through America's Middle West.

His Imperial Majesty continued his trans-continental tour of the United States of America by flying over a thousand miles from Minneapolis, Minnesota to Spokane in the state of Washington. America's Far West contains several of the states which were among the last to be admitted to the Union and, therefore, the memories of the adventurous times of explorers and pioneers are still fresh in the minds of its oldest inhabitants. The states of America's West Coast — Washington, Oregon and California — are rich in natural resources. Magnificent forests stretch for hundreds of miles, many of them preserved from destruction as national parks. High-grade ores are abundant in these states and the other states of the Rocky Mountain chain. The fishing industry is carried on off the coast in the Pacific Ocean and one fish in particular, the salmon, has made that industry on the West Coast one of the most lucrative in the world. The scenery of the Rocky Mountains and the Pacific Ocean is awe-inspiring and thousands of campers and sightsee-ers travel there each year to enjoy the beauties of nature.

At Spokane, Washington, the Emperor made a tour of the Grand Coulee Dam, the largest dam in the world. Started in 1933, the project first produced power in 1941. Irrigation is also an important part of the project, and about 100,000 acres of semi-arid land are already under irrigation. One of the primary reasons for the Emperor's visit to this area was

426

to view the multi-purpose hydro-electric project, because Ethiopia has the potential of a large scale water power development. The Emperor expressed pleasure at seeing the dam and added that the project had inspired him to hope that one might be undertaken in Ethiopia some day. During His Majesty's tour of the Pacific coastal states he saw the Boeing airplane plant; visited the United States Army's Seattle Port of embarkation; he visited Fort Miley Veterans' Hospital and spoke to American soldiers wounded in Korea, passing slowly through the wards and at each bed wishing the soldiers *good luck*.

Arriving at San Francisco, the Emperor was greeted by the Mayor who presented him with a crystal goblet "to toast the peace" and a gavel made of California's famed red wood. There was an official welcome by the Governor of California, at which ceremony, in his acceptance speech, the Emperor paid tribute to the American flag — *a flag honoured and known throughout the world.* He compared Ethiopia to California in agriculture and climate and added, *Minerals like those found in California, such as oil and gold, are to be had in Ethiopia, and it is our hope to be able to utilise American knowledge and technicians in making sure that these will be fully explored.* The World Affairs Council of Northern California held a banquet in His Majesty the Emperor's honour at the Press Union League Club where a bust of himself was unveiled—the work of a noted California sculptor who served in Eritrea with the United States Army during World War II.

From San Francisco, the Imperial Party travelled by automobile to Yosemite National Park for a needed one-day vacation. The spectacular mountain region of Yosemite lies between San Francisco and Los Angeles and is on the western slope of the Sierra Nevada Mountains. The park has 752,744 acres of mountains and forests, many lakes, a chain of mountain peaks averaging 10,000 feet or more and five great waterfalls, The Valley itself is a U-shaped trough seven miles long with an average width of a mile.

This is an extremely beautiful place, declared the Emperor as he arrived at his hotel. *It reminds me of wooded regions in the southern part of my country although this, of course, is much more spectacular.* The Imperial Party took a tour of the Valley with park rangers who protect the park's natural features, especially against fire. They visited the Mariposa Grove of 28 giant Sequoia trees which are 10 feet or more in diameter at breast height, these trees are estimated to be thousands of years old.

Many other interesting places were visited, among them Los Angeles. The Emperor toured the movie studios, had luncheon with one thousand persons, a sight-seeing drive through the movie-land homes of Beverly Hills and Belair, inspections of Long Beach Harbour and a look at Southern California's newest oil refinery.

His Imperial Majesty travelled at the head of a block-long caravan of automobiles escorted by a squad of police motorcycle officers. At City Hall, troops from Fort MacArthur formed a smart colour guard on either side of the steps. A second colour guard of the American Legion, America's largest veterans' organisation, stood at the entrance and the Los

Angeles police band struck up the national anthem of Ethiopia as the Emperor was escorted to the platform. The steps and streets were crowded with 3,000 spectators during the welcoming ceremony.

His Imperial Majesty then toured 20th Century Fox Film Studios where he was shown a 19th century set and met some of the actors. He was introduced to an actor outfitted for the rôle of Napoleon, and so it was Emperor meets Emperor. After a look through a Cinemascope Camera, the Emperor made a motor tour of the movie lot, passing quickly through New England fishing villages, Egyptian temples and old southern plantation homes. His Imperial Majesty saw the equipment, the actors, the directors and the sets, all of which together create the American film industry.

In his busy tour of the Pacific Coastal States, His Imperial Majesty had more time for relaxation and for seeing some of the magnificent scenery of that area. Since much of his tour was made by automobile, he had more opportunity to see typical American towns and homes and to catch something of the pulsebeat of American life. Having travelled through the East, the North and the West, His Imperial Majesty could now realize the great size of the United States and the variety among its peoples and its ideas.

His Imperial Majesty stopped briefly in the South-West and deep South. His first visit was made to Stillwater, Oklahoma, the site of the Oklahoma Agricultural and Mechanical College. The ties between Oklahoma A. & M. and Ethiopia are very strong, because personnel from Stillwater are there to organise an Agricultural College. The Jimma Agricultural Technical School, in operation now for over two years, is staffed entirely by teachers recruited from Oklahoma A. & M. The Imperial Agricultural College at Harar now in its last construction stage, will also be staffed by instructors from Stillwater. The operation of both of these schools is a joint project of the Ethiopian and American Governments, the latter working through its Foreign Operations Administration.

His Imperial Majesty, was accepted with great anticipation and excitement, as he stepped from his Trans-World Airlines Constellation. He was greeted by Dr. Luther Brannon, on leave from Oklahoma A. & M. as President of the Imperial Agricultural College of Ethiopia; Dr. Joseph Simonson, United States Ambassador to Ethiopia; Dr. Oliver Willham, President of Oklahoma A. & M.; the Lieutenant-Governor of the State of Oklahoma; and the Mayor of Stillwater.

In front of television and still cameras His Imperial Majesty paid tribute to Oklahoma Agricultural and Mechanical College and its late President, Dr. Henry J. Bennett, who was responsible for that College sponsoring institutions in Ethiopia.

Asked what America could do to help Ethiopia, the Emperor said: *Send us the technicians to aid us in developing our agriculture for the benefit of all people as this great college has done.* The Emperor added he was impressed by the high degree of industrial work in America and its high living standards. He said he would tell his subjects of the warm welcome he had received and that he hoped one day to return to America.

428

His Imperial Majesty guest of Queen Juliana of the Netherlands and Prince Bernhard

Receiving the plaudits of Americans, North, South, East and West, having been given honorary degrees, having bestowed on institutions tokens of Ethiopia's friendship, and decorated distinguished personages with high Ethiopian Orders, His Imperial Majesty concluded his official tour through the United States. Close to the end of the journey he took occasion to answer the invitation extended to him by the President of Mexico, Ruiz Cortines, where many parties were given in his honour and many historic sites visited.

His Majesty's official welcome in the city of New York on June 2nd was the highlight of the fanfare and enthusiasm of his seven-weeks' journey in the three Northern American countries.

His Imperial Majesty received the official welcome of New York City, accorded only to national heroes and outstanding leaders from abroad. The official welcome took the form of a parade up Broadway, lined with high skyscrapers. An estimated 1,000,000 people watched from windows, parks and streets as an open auto carrying His Imperial Majesty led a parade that started at the harbour front. Tons of torn paper, streamers and stock-market tickertape showered down from the tall buildings as the parade passed. The Emperor alternately waved and lifted his cap to acknowledge the applause of the welcoming crowd. Church bells pealed as the Emperor's party passed, while clergymen in full vestments emerged and stood on church steps.

At City Court House, the Emperor was greeted by Robert Wagner, Mayor of New York, who presented him with a scroll reading:

"Our people have a long and profound admiration for you and your gallant country. We have been impressed with your gentleness, your culture, your passion for progress and your character as a great leader of a magnificent and ancient nation."

His Imperial Majesty said that he hoped that more visitors from the commercial and cultural center of New York would visit Ethiopia. He presented the Mayor with two joined elephant tusks, a red and gold shield and two silver-tipped spears.

In addition to his already exhausting schedule, His Imperial Majesty was honoured at luncheons by the Mayor of New York and John D. Rockefeller III, son of one of America's leading industrialists. He was given a dinner by the Secretary-General of the United Nations, Dag Hammarskjold, and shook hands with 1,000 New Yorkers at an official reception.

To add to his collection of honorary degrees, His Imperial Majesty was awarded an Honorary Doctor of Laws Degree by Columbia University, where the Emperor's two grandsons, Merid and Samson, are students. In accepting the degree, His Imperial Majesty said:

Throughout my long reign, I have always been preoccupied with the importance of the educational development of my nation. More of our resources have gone into education than into any other social or governmental activity. We have solicited and are accepting technical assistance from abroad, and in particular from the United States, in this all-important function because history has shown not only that in the letters is to

430

be found the truth, but also that no country can operate in the world without a corps of professionally educated élite of its own nationals.

As in Washington, His Imperial Majesty met the press who deluged him with questions on every topic imaginable. On the subject of Communism, the Emperor was asked what was the amount of penetration of the ideology in Africa. In reply, he said he had no accurate information\ on the situation in other parts of the continent, but pointed out there *was no effective Communist influence in Ethiopia*.

Emperor visits Great Britain

His Imperial Majesty's State visit to the United Kingdom on the invitation of Her Majesty Queen Elizabeth II is of particular interest. The trip to Britain, and especially to Bath, was to the Emperor nostalgic in character. It was there, among the British people that he dwelt in the over four years of his exile. The recollection of such warm sentiments linger when protocol, pomp and circumstances have long been forgotten. In addition, the relation between the two countries, despite the foibles of diplomacy and self-interest with which it has been punctuated for many years, has been mutually the most beneficial among that of Ethiopia's immediate neighbours. It could never be forgotten that it was the British ally who aided in bringing about the happy climax to the five-year fascist occupation, a near-tragedy in the life of this country. Ethiopia's liberation was won by the equal shedding of the blood of British and Commonwealth heroes who contributed selflessly to the common cause. It is in this spirit that the Emperor's visit to the United Kingdom must be viewed.

Leaving Addis Ababa by an EAL Convair plane on October 5th, last year, His Majesty the Emperor stopped over at Wadi Halfa. The Emperor was flown from there to Malta on a 4-engined Argonaut airliner of the BOAC, specially equipped for Royal travellers and previously used by Queen Elizabeth II.

On arrival at Malta on October 6th, His Imperial Majesty was met by the Governor, the Archbishop, the Prime Minister of Malta and the Commander in Chief of the British Mediterranean Fleet, Lord Mountbatten. The occasion was marked by the ceremonial and pageantry for which Malta is renowned.

During His stay in Malta the Emperor was the guest of His Excellency the Governor, who, on the night of the arrival of His Imperial Majesty, held a dinner party in his honour, which was attended by the most important personages of the Island. The next day a large reception was given by the Governor in the State drawing room at Valletta Palace where local dignitaries were presented to His Imperial Majesty and the Duke of Harar. The same night the combined massed bands of the British Forces stationed in Malta played the Retreat in the gardens of Valletta Palace, the residence of the Governor, and Lord and Lady Mountbatten entertained His Imperial Majesty, the Duke of Harar and their suite at a banquet at Admiralty House, the residence of the Com-

431

mander in Chief of the Mediterranean fleet. In this way Lord and Lady Mountbatten were able partly to repay the generous hospitality which they had received from His Imperial Majesty when they visited Ethiopia 12 months previously.

On October 8th His Imperial Majesty embarked in the cruiser H.M.S. "Gambia," which, flying His Imperial Majesty's personal standard and escorted by the Frigate H.M.S. "Surprise," left Great Harbour to the strains of the Ethiopian National Anthem, accompanied by a thundering Royal Salute of 21 guns. Shortly after leaving harbour, jet aircraft of the Fleet Air Arm and the Royal Australian Air Force flew past in formation, and His Imperial Majesty, on board H.M.S. "Gambia", was escorted by helicopters of the Fleet Air Arm. During the next 3 hours His Imperial Majesty witnessed an impressive display of manoeuvres and exercises carried out in his honour by the Mediterranean Fleet, which was under the personal command of Admiral Lord Mountbatten. The Fleet included 4 destroyers of the Royal Pakistan Navy. The manoeuvres included a demonstration of the firing of 6 inch shells from the big guns of the cruisers "Glasgow" and "Bermuda" and a dummy torpedo attack on "Gambia" by destroyers, which also demonstrated the use of anti-submarine depth charges, and there were diving demonstrations by 3 submarines. Jet aircraft landed and took off from the aircraft carrier "Centaur." At the conclusion, some very complicated formation manoeuvres were executed by the whole Fleet, which finished with their steaming past His Imperial Majesty at full speed with their ships' companies cheering and their bands playing the Ethiopian National Anthem. Afterwards the Governor of Malta and Admiral Lord Mountbatten came aboard "Gambia" and took their leave of His Imperial Majesty, who congratulated Lord Mountbatten on the impressive way in which the manoeuvres of his Fleet had been conducted. "Gambia" then proceeded towards Gibraltar with H.M. Destroyers "Constant" and "Charity" as escort.

On October 10th, H.M.S. "Gambia" passed through the Straits of Gibraltar and His Imperial Majesty received a telegramme of greetings and good wishes from the Acting Governor of this great rock fortress at the entrance of the Mediterranean Sea, known in the time of the ancient Greeks as one of the "Pillars of Hercules." His Imperial Majesty replied to the Governor's telegram with a message expressing *Our sincere wishes for the prosperity of Gibraltar.* Later that day when H.M.S. "Gambia" was by now in the high swell of the open Atlantic, he was met by H.M.S. "Triumph" and "St. Kitts," which steamed past at speed accompanied by a Royal salute of 21 guns. "Triumph" then closed in on "Gambia" and His Imperial Majesty's grandson, Lij Iskandar Desta, who is serving as a junior officer in training with the Royal Navy, was rowed over to "Gambia" in a small boat for a brief meeting with his grandfather, the Emperor. This was a unique and historic meeting at sea. In a message to the Captain of H.M.S. "Triumph," who was the Prince's Commanding Officer, His Imperial Majesty expressed the hope that his grandson would *prove himself worthy of his training in the great tradition of the British Navy.* On the morning of October 14th, "Gambia" entered British waters and

432

Emperor visiting Kinderdijk Shipbuilding works before launching of Ethiopian tugboats bought in the Netherlands

steamed into Portsmouth harbour to the accompaniment of a Royal Salute of 21 guns and full Naval honours from the assembled ships at this great British Naval base, which were "dressed overall" with their ship's companies drawn up on deck in full ceremonial order. His Royal Highness the Duke of Gloucester, uncle of Queen Elizabeth, went on board "Gambia" to greet His Imperial Majesty and his suite and conducted the Emperor to his special train which, after His Imperial Majesty had inspected the Naval guard of honour, left for London.

When His Imperial Majesty's special train drew into Victoria Station on

433

the afternoon of October 14th and His Majesty stepped out on the platform, Her Majesty Queen Elisabeth II, accompanied by her husband, the Duke of Edinburgh, moved forward smilingly to greet him and the Duke of Harar. His Imperial Majesty was dressed in the blue and gold uniform of Field Marshal. The other members of the British Royal Family, H.M. Queen Elizabeth the Queen Mother, H.R.H. Princess Margaret, sister of the Queen, the Princess Royal and the Duchess of Gloucester (the Queen's aunts) also greeted the Emperor. The Queen then presented to His Imperial Majesty the group of the highest personages of the Realm who were waiting on the platform. This included the Prime Minister, Sir Winston Churchill, Sir Anthony Eden, then Foreign Secretary, the Lord Mayor and Sheriffs of London and the Chiefs of Staff of the Royal Navy, the Army and the Royal Air Force. Mr. D. L. Busk, H.M. Ambassador at Addis Ababa and the Commissioner of Police for London together with the Mayor of the City of Westminster were also presented. The scene was a dazzling one with the full dress uniforms against a background of a bank of flowers the whole length of the platform and the crossed national colours of Ethiopia and Great Britain. Outside the Station was drawn up a royal guard of honour of 100 men of the Grenadier Guards dressed in brilliant red uniforms and black bearskin headdresses. The band played in salute the Ethiopian National Anthem, followed by "God Save the Queen." The Guard Commander reported to the Emperor in Amharic (learnt specially for the occasion) that the guard was ready for his inspection, and the Queen invited him to do so. With quiet dignity His Imperial Majesty walked between the lines of troops drawn up in their impressive ceremonial order.

The Queen and the Duke of Edinburgh then rode with their guests in an open carriage in a triumphant procession through the London streets escorted by a Sovereign's Escort of the Queen's Household Cavalry on their magnificent horses with their brilliant scarlet or dark blue cloacks, flowing plumes and highly polished steel breast plates gleaming in the October sunshine. The streets were lined with the red uniforms of troops of the Queen's Brigade of Guards, behind whom were massed throngs of people cheering lustily as only a London crowd can cheer. The procession of carriages with their cavalry escort turned into the Mall, the great processional avenue of London, which leads to the Queen's residence. This famous street was decorated the whole way with the flags of Ethiopia and Great Britain.

At the moment when the Queen welcomed the Emperor at Victoria Station Royal Salutes were fired in Hyde Park by the King's Troop, Royal Horse Artillery, and at the Tower of London by the 1st Regiment, Honourable Artillery Company.

After the Emperor and the Duke of Harar had been conducted to their quarters in Buckingham Palace, the Queen's residence, they later left for Westminster Abbey to lay a wreath on the grave of the unknown warrior, and later took tea with Queen Elizabeth the Queen Mother at Clarence House, her residence in St. James. Afterwards at St. James' Palace His Majesty received addresses from the Chairman of the Lon-

*King Haakon of Norway and the Royal family with
the Emperor and the Duke of Harar*

don County Council (the body which governs the Great City of London).

The same evening the Queen gave a State Banquet in honour of her Imperial guests. Before the banquet began she invested the Emperor with the Order of the Garter, the highest British distinction which can be awarded. (The Garter is one of the oldest Orders of Chivalry in the world, having been founded over 600 years ago by the Queen's great forbear, King Edward III, and its membership is limited to 24 living persons). The banquet took place in the great ballroom of Buckingham Palace in the light of six enormous chandeliers. The several hundred guests, who included all the members of the British Royal Family, the Emperor's suite and a distinguished gathering of statesmen and diplomatists, dined off the Queen's gold plate which is only brought out on great ceremonial occasions. The Queen made a speech proposing the health of the Emperor, who replied in English.

In proposing the health of His Imperial Majesty at the banquet in Buckingham Palace the Queen said:

"We greet you as the Sovereign of an ancient Christian State which has many links with our own Church and with other Christian Churches of the world.

"We greet you also as the Sovereign of the country which was the first to regain its freedom during the last war. Under Your Majesty's inspiring leadership, the Ethiopian people have made truly remarkable progress in the years that have followed the war.

"I am very proud of the part that my country played in the liberation of Ethiopia, together with your own patriot forces. In those war-time days close bonds of friendship were forged between our two countries and between the men of our armies who fought together side by side. It is my sincere wish, as I know it is your Majesty's, that this friendship should be preserved and strengthened in the days of peace.

"Your Majesty is no stranger to this country. When your own land was invaded you came here and I would like to think that in England you will always feel at home.

"My husband and I greatly regret that we are not able to welcome Her Imperial Majesty, the Empress. I hope that Her Majesty may soon be restored to complete health and that she may be able to visit us again on some future occasion.

"I welcome Your Majesty's son, His Royal Highness the Duke of Harar, who also knows this country well and whom we are delighted to see here again.

"I am so glad that Your Majesty will remain here for a short time after your state visit is over. You will then have some opportunity of travelling about the country and seeing various aspects of our national life. I know that you will receive a great welcome wherever you go. My people will be anxious to pay tribute to a Sovereign who has brought freedom to his country in time of war and prosperity and enlightenment in time of peace.

"Your Imperial Majesty, in the spirit of friendship and of those common ideals under which we thrive and prosper, I raise my glass to drink to your health, to that of the Empress, and to the prosperity and happiness of the Ethiopian people."

The Emperor replied:

Your Majesty, I have been deeply touched by Your Majesty's kind and gracious words of welcome and by the very generous sentiments which you have expressed in my behalf. Although I have returned to this beautiful land only a few hours ago, Your Majesty has made me feel almost as if I had never departed, already 14 years ago.

For it is not, Your Majesty, my first visit here. I can well remember that 30 years ago this year, it was none other than Your Majesty's revered father, then the Duke of York and later George VI himself, who officially received me at my arrival in this nation's capital. I am ever mindful of his gracious welcome, so fully in keeping with the character of that beloved monarch.

Since that event, thirty years ago, my recollections have been throughout the ensuing years, nourished in the memories of the hospitality of Your Royal Family and of the friendship and affection of the British people during the long years of bitter and enforced absence from our homeland. The friendship of the Royal House and of the British people alone sustained me and my people in our lonely struggles.

436

Such friendship and loyalty have earned our imperishable gratitude and friendship. Your support and the loyalty of the British people whose sons fell at the side of our sons on the soil of our homeland in defence of the just cause and for the liberation of our country make today, the preservation and the strengthening of that friendship and affection a sacred trust.

Her Imperial Majesty the Empress is very sorry that she has been unable to make this visit owing to the state of her health, and she has asked me to convey to Your Majesty her sincere regrets.

I raise my glass in a toast to Her Majesty the Queen, His Royal Highness the Duke of Edinburgh and to the prosperity and happiness of the British people.

Outside, the City of London wore a festival appearance. The flags and decorations in the Mall, and all the principal churches and public buildings, were floodlit to celebrate the arrival of the Queen's Royal Guest. Every London newspaper, except the communist press, featured prominently His Imperial Majesty and his achievements, and most had large and numerous photographs of the Emperor and of the ceremonies during his visit.

Wearing the blue ribbon of the Garter on his Field Marshal's uniform, His Imperial Majesty accompanied by the Duke of Harar, drove in the morning of October 15th from Buckingham Palace to the Guildhall of the City of London. They drove through cheering crowds in an open carriage with a Sovereign's Escort of the Household Cavalry, passing St. Paul's Cathedral, which still bears at its east end the scars of the German bombardment of London in 1940 when Britain stood alone in resistance to the aggressor powers. In Guildhall, the Emperor, having received an address of welcome from the Lord Mayor, presented to him a pair of elephant tusks, a shield and a pair of hunting spears as a gift to the Corporation of the City of London. The scene of action was then changed to the Mansion House, the official residence of the Lord Mayor, where he entertained the Emperor and the Duke of Harar as his guests at a large luncheon party which was attended by the most distinguished figures in the financial and commercial life of the City of London. The City of London, of which the Lord Mayor is the ceremonial head, has ever since Roman days, nearly 2,000 years ago, been an important trade centre and is now the biggest city in the world. The "City of London" proper is a small area between St. Paul's Cathedral and London Bridge and covers only about 4 square kilometres, but within this small area is located one of the world's greatest centres of banking, insurance, finance and commerce.

The evening of October 15th was a brilliant occasion in the history of the Ethiopian Embassy in London, marking as it did the first visit of the Queen and the Duke of Edinburgh, who were entertained to dinner by His Imperial Majesty. A large crowd gathered on the pavement near the Embassy, which is situated in a fashionable quarter overlooking the tree-studded open spaces of Hyde Park of Kensington Gardens. They saw the distinguished company arrive, which included Sir Winston

Churchill, Sir Anthony Eden and a number of distinguished statesmen and diplomats as well as the members of the British Royal Family. Finally the Queen, wearing the Chain of the Seal of Solomon which the Emperor had bestowed on her, arrived, accompanied by the Duke of Edinburgh. They paused to admire the green, scarlet and white livery of the Emperor's principal servants, who had travelled from the Imperial Palace at Addis Ababa specially for this dinner party. In the course of the dinner tedj from the Imperial cellars at Addis Ababa was served. It was a great occasion, but was nevertheless characterised by an atmosphere which was more that of a family dinner party.

On the morning of October 16th the Emperor drove to the Twickenham Technical College where he spent some time in the Electrical Engineering Laboratory inspecting electronic devices and then drove on to Windsor Castle, which he was shown over before lunching there with the Queen and Duke of Edinburgh. His Excellency Mr. D. L. Busk, British Ambassador at Addis Abeba was present.

Windsor Castle is the historic home of the Sovereigns of England and has been a Royal Castle since King William the Conqueror first built the great central round tower nearly 900 years ago. The buildings of the Castle are set up on a high hill dominating the flat country all around the Great Park and the placid river Thames flows just below its ramparts. Within the precincts of the Castle is the Chapel of St. George, patron saint of England as of Ethiopia, the Chapel of the Knights of the Garter. His Imperial Majesty as a Knight of the Order has a stall in the Chapel over which his banner bearing his personal arms will be hung when it has been completed by expert craftsmen.

On leaving Windsor Castle the Emperor's State visit as guest of the Queen ended and he was from now a guest of Her Majesty's Government.

During the afternoon of October 16th His Imperial Majesty visited Eton College, perhaps the most famous of English Schools, which was founded by King Henry VI over 500 years ago. He was conducted around by the Headmaster and saw the boys at work and at play. That same evening he held a reception at the Ethiopian Embassy in London for all the Ethiopian students who are pursuing studies in Britain.

The Emperor drove down from London to Bath during Sunday October 17th and was welcomed by Mrs. Rosalie Sawyer, the housekeeper of his villa "Fairfield," who had been hard at work getting the house ready for His Imperial Majesty. The Emperor found everything just as he left it in 1940 to return to his Empire which he had so tragically left in 1936. It was at villa "Fairfield" that Their Imperial Majesties the Emperor and Empress and their family spent most of their four years of exile. The Emperor's house is located in a delightful situation among the green hills above the ancient grey stone city of Bath, which has a history dating back to the days when Britain was a province of the Roman Empire and Bath began its career as a fashionable watering place around the health-giving mineral springs.

The people of Bath, to whom His Imperial Majesty is a well-remembered

438

King Gustav Adolf of Sweden and the Royal family together with His Majesty the Emperor

and well-loved figure, gave him a rousing reception next day when he drove to the city centre to receive the freedom of the city from the Mayor, who in welcoming the Emperor, made a moving speech. Afterwards His Imperial Majesty with the Duke of Harar and their suite were entertained to lunch at the Guildhall which stands opposite the ancient Abbey Church; on this site the first King of all England, Edgar, was crowned in the year 973 A.D. nearly 1,000 years ago. Afterwards the Emperor visited a number of local Institutions including the Children's Ortheopedic Hospital, to which he presented a cheque for £ 500 Sterling. That evening the Emperor gave a reception at his home to the civic dignitaries of the City of Bath together with many personal friends who had been his neighbours when he lived there as a private citizen during his days of exile. Earlier in the day he had presented to the City a pair of elephant tusks similar to those which he had presented to the Corporation of the City of London.

At the end of the day it was announced that His Imperial Majesty was so moved by his welcome in Bath that he had decided never to dispose of his house there, but that he would keep it as a permanent link with the many friends which he had made in and around the City.

On the morning of October 19th the Emperor and the Duke of Harar drove to Bristol to visit the branch of the British Legion. The British Legion is a Society of men and women who have served in the British Armed Forces. During his exile the Emperor became an honorary member of the branch at Bristol and later its Patron and for his visit the standard bearers of the Legion formed a guard of honour. The Emperor afterwards presented a cheque for £ 200 to the branch for its charitable work among disabled ex-service men and their families.

Later in the morning the Emperor and the Duke of Harar visited Bristol Aeroplane Company's works at Filton, just outside Bristol where they were received by the Board of Directors. They saw a helicopter demonstration and inspected the giant "Britannia" airliner, which is powered by four turbo-jet engines of the latest design and which recently flew from London to Johannesburg in the record flying time of just over 17 hours with only one stop, at Khartoum. The "Britannia," which will come into service on the world's airlines in the near future, is expected to revolutionise air transport. The Bristol Aeroplane Company started making aeroplanes in 1910 and is today one of the most progressive in the world.

His Imperial Majesty with the Duke of Harar drove by quiet country lanes through the green English countryside to Oxford where he was the guest of the Vice Chancellor of the University who is also the Warden of New College. The College was founded in 1440 and the college buildings surrounding a quiet stone quadrangle form an unspoilt group of 15th century English architecture. The Emperor attended the evening service in the College Chapel and later dinea at the High Table in the College Hall with the Warden and Fellows (Professors) and in the presence of the students of the College. His Excellency Mr. Busk, the British Ambassador in Ethiopia, and Mr. C. O. I. Ramsden, the former First Secretary at the British Embassy in Addis Ababa, who are both graduates of New

440

College, also dined at the High Table. Distinguished members of the teaching body of the University were present as the guests of the College. The next day the Emperor lunched at New College and then, accompanied by Earl Halifax, Chancellor of the University and former British Foreign Secretary, walked in procession with the University dignitaries to the Sheldonian Theatre to receive the degree of Doctor of Civil Law. The Emperor was wearing the scarlet and pink robes of his degree. The Sheldonian Theatre was filled with senior members of the University wearing coloured robes of their various degrees and all rose to their feet as the National Anthem of Ethiopia was played on the entrance of the Emperor. The Chancellor pronounced in Latin the grant to the Emperor of the degree in a short speech in praise of His Imperial Majesty's descent from King Solomon, his personality and his achievements for his country, notably in the sphere of education. After the ceremony the procession returned to New College. His Imperial Majesty had, when he was Ras Tafari and Regent of Ethiopia, been similarly honoured by Cambridge University. He is thus an Honorary Doctor of both of the ancient Universities of England, which have an unbroken history in the promotion of sound learning which dates back for over 700 years.

On October 21 the Emperor visited the R.A.F. Station at Duxford, where he was received by the Parliamentary Under-Secretary for Air, Mr. George War M.P., and reviewed an R.A.F. guard of honour which had given him a royal salute to the accompaniment of the Ethiopian National Anthem. His Imperial Majesty inspected the aircrews and aircraft on the ground, took lunch with the Officers of the Station in their mess and was shown the operations room and the working of the control tower. He then witnessed an impressive display of flying which began by one of the latest Hunter jet fighters breaking the sound barrier with a loud double bang at a speed of 705 m.p.h. (1125 k.p.h.). After the Hunter had demonstrated its amazing capacity for climbing and manoeuverability it landed and 24 Meteor jet fighters then took off in rapid succession, and flying in very close formation carried out acrobatics. After their demonstration a number of Canberra jet-engined bombers showed their paces to His Imperial Majesty. After the display the Emperor and his party returned by road to London where a reception was held in the evening for a large number of guests, among whom were senior representatives of British firms that have supplied their goods and services to Ethiopia.

The next day His Imperial Majesty lunched with the Prime Minister, Sir Winston Churchill, at No. 10 Downing Street. After luncheon he visited the London Headquarters of the British and Foreign Bible Society where he was presented with a handsomely bound book containing the text of the Bible in both Amharic and English. He was shown a display of religious books and documents connected with Ethiopia which included some early editions of the Ethiopic scriptures and in particular a manuscript of the Gospels which was written in the fourth century and was discovered in Ethiopia in 1921.

He then visited the Houses of Parliament to be received by members of the House of Lords and the House of Commons. The Emperor was conducted in procession by the Lord Chancellor and the Speaker of the House of Commons.

The same evening His Imperial Majesty appeared in person on British television screens so that his presence was witnessed by the fire-sides of several million British families. His Imperial Majesty told them that his visit to England had given him an opportunity to thank the British people in person for their kindness and sympathy during his self-imposed exile and for their contribution in the liberation of Ethiopia. He was certain that his visit would strengthen good relations between England and Ethiopia.

To finish off a very busy day His Imperial Majesty was entertained to a formal dinner at Lambeth Palace by the Archbishop of Canterbury. Other guests included some of the highest personages in Church and State.

On October 23rd His Imperial Majesty spent a quiet day in London, which included some shopping, and spent the following Sunday, October 24th, in Bath.

On Monday October 25th, the Emperor and the Duke of Harar drove from Bath to Sandhurst where they visited the Royal Military Academy, an institution which trains young men to be regular officers, not only in the British Army but in the Armies of the Commonwealth and other friendly countries. His Imperial Majesty was greeted by a guard of honour which included two Ethiopian Officer Cadets, Ameda Aberra and Dereje Haile Mariam. The Emperor was wearing his full-dress uniform of a Field Marshall and witnessed an impressive parade by the cadets wearing their dark blue uniforms with white equipment. His Imperial Majesty took the salute at the parade in which over 500 cadets took part. One of the cadets on parade was the Duke of Kent, first cousin to Her Majesty the Queen.

That evening His Imperial Majesty and the Duke of Harar attended a reception given by the Anglo-Ethiopian Society in Londonderry House in London. This was a brilliant occasion at this historic house in the course of which the Anglo-Ethiopian Society, which is the principal permanent organ in Great Britain of Anglo-Ethiopian friendship and is rapidly expanding, presented to His Imperial Majesty a splendid album, bound in red leather, containing congratulations to His Imperial Majesty on the occasion of his return to his country in 1941. The Society had long waited for a suitable occasion on which to present it.

The Emperor and the Duke of Harar visited the laboratories of Hunting Air Surveys at Elstree in Hertfordshire on October 26th, where he inspected the latest scientific equipment used for carrying out aerial surveys of land which can even show the geological structure beneath the earth's surface. Some of the officials of the company explained to him how a survey of the agricultural and mineral potential of a country is carried out. The Emperor's visit was filmed by the B.B.C. and was shown on British television screens.

In the afternoon the Emperor received visitors at his Embassy in London and was the guest of honour at a reception given by Mrs. Richard Selig-

His Majesty the Emperor and His Highness the Duke of Harar with King Frederick of Denmark and the Royal family

443

man and Mrs. Corbett Ashby at Lincoln House on Wimbledon Common, on the outskirts of London, where a distinguished company included members of the diplomatic corps in London.

In the evening he dined with Sir Anthony Eden who was at that time Foreign Secretary, at his residence in Carlton Gardens. Among those present were Ministers in the British Government, the Permanent Under-Secretary of State at the Foreign Office, the Governor-General of the Sudan and the Queen's Ambassador to Addis Ababa.

October 27th was the last day of the Emperor's visit. He spent the morning in London and in the afternoon listened to a debate in the House of Commons on the subject of national defence and its cost to the British people. He had early been received at the House by the Speaker.

He took tea with the British group of the Inter-Parliamentary Union in the members' dining room.

The same evening His Imperial Majesty left for France by the Dover-Dunkirk train ferry. The Emperor was travelling in a special coach and was seen off by the Duke of Gloucester, who was representing the Queen at the Station. During the night which the Emperor spent on the train his coach was carried across the sea from England to France on one of the ships specially designed for carrying railway trains.

On leaving England the Emperor sent the following message to the Queen:

On leaving the friendly soil of England I desire to express to Your Majesty my deep and abiding appreciation for the warmth and splendour of the welcome and the hospitality which Your Majesty has shown me and of which I have been the object throughout my visit to England. The countless manifestations of friendship and the spontaneity of the welcome with which the public has greeted me throughout my travels have greatly touched me. I am hopeful that my visit may have served to give yet greater breadth and strength to our traditional friendship.

The Queen replied:

"I thank you very warmly for your message. Your visit to the United Kingdom with your son, the Duke of Harar, has afforded very real pleasure to my husband and myself and to the members of our family. You have seen how delighted the citizens of London were to greet you once again, and I can assure you that their feelings were shared by the whole country. I am glad to know that Your Imperial Majesty will take home with you pleasant memories of your welcome here, which has so clearly confirmed the abiding friendship which exists between Ethiopia and Great Britain."

The series of State visits took His Majesty the Emperor to three North American countries; the United States, Canada and Mexico; to the United Kingdom and ten European countries: Yougoslavia, Greece, France, West Germany, Sweden, Norway, Denmark, Switzerland, Holland and Austria. In them all, both Government and people were cordial and rousing in their reception of and acclaim for His Imperial Majesty. To detail each visit would be a long, if not monotonous report; His Majesty the Emperor's speeches to the people upon his return, reproduced

444

hereunder, explains the situation more vividly than any description that could be attempted. After returning from the first foreign tour, in a message to his people, broadcast from the Imperial Palace, he said:

After long journeys totalling more than 40,000 kilometers, we are, at last back with our beloved people.

We proceeded on a visit to the United States of America at the invitation of President Eisenhower and the reception which we received fully justified our pre-conceptions of American friendship and hospitality.

We have formed the highest regard for the friendship with the President of that Great Power. He is a leader of wide and penetrating vision whose unparalleled record as the Commander-in-Chief who led to victory the forces of the Allies during the last war, has served only to strengthen his devotion to the cause of maintenance of world peace.

As for the American people, it is difficult to convey to you the full measure of the frank and open-hearted friendship of the great masses of the people and admiration for Ethiopia—a country far away which practically none of them had seen. Everywhere we were greeted by cheering thousands massed along the roadsides. Everywhere the press greeted us with sincerest expressions of friendship. Everywhere we encountered expressions of admiration for Ethiopia's long and brave struggle against aggression. The United States of America was one of the few nations of the world that refused to recognise the regime of aggression in our homeland.

Ethiopia has never forgotten and never will forget that act of friendship. Nor indeed, has the American people, two decades later, forgotten our bravery or our contribution to the cause of collective security. Let no one say that public opinion has a short memory or indifference to events in far off lands. We say to you that you have in the great American nation, with whom we fought in Korea for the same cause for which we took up the challenge eighteen years ago, a devoted and sincere friend and ally.

During our visit to the United States, we were able to discuss many questions of importance and, as is natural between friends, success attended these discussions.

We feel that our visit to the United States has served to explain Ethiopia to the American people and to strengthen the great friendship existing between our two countries. The nurturing of that friendship should call forth the united and enthusiastic efforts of our beloved people.

During the course of our visit to America, it was our great pleasure to have visited two other steadfast friends of Ethiopia in the New World— Canada and Mexico. During the difficult post-war years, Canada proved herself to be an outstanding and devoted friend of Ethiopia. We had many difficult questions concerning post-war settlements and, in particular, concerning the reparation of injustices to our brothers in Eritrea. In the settlement of all these problems, Canada has proved herself to be a devoted friend. Our visit to Canada testified to our friendship and it was marked by reciprocal and moving expressions of the friendship of the people of Canada for Ethiopia.

445

Like the United States of America, Mexico, was one of the few great nations of the world to refuse to recognise the regime of aggression in Ethiopia. Mexico has a great liberal tradition which has constantly impelled her to the support of liberty and justice throughout the world. Everywhere we went in Mexico, we were met by tumultuous expressions of friendship by the people everywhere. We were deeply sensible of the spontaneity and warmth of their welcome. A large public square in the capital of Mexico has been named the Plaza Ethiopia in honour of our visit and we personally unveiled the commemoration monument.

We shall shortly name a Square in our capital a symbol of that friendship between our two countries.

Upon the completion of our visit of America, we journeyed to Yugoslavia at the invitation of its illustrious leader, Marshal Tito. It is difficult to describe in words the tremendous national welcome accorded us everywhere by the people of that great and powerful nation; from the massed thousands along each street of Belgrade and in the great factories and centres of industries, to the inhabitants of the smallest hamlets and the farmer in the field. At every moment of our sojourn in Yugoslavia we lived in an atmosphere of the most complete friendship and understanding. During the course of our visit, we were able to discuss problems of great and mutual interest, and we met with complete understanding and agreement. Since the close of the last war, Ethiopia and Yugoslavia have collaborated closely in the international as well as cultural and economic fields and our visit and discussions have served greatly to strengthen and broaden that collaboration.

Yugoslavia is a great and powerful nation whose tremendous energies are impelling her forward, under enlightened leadership, to an even more brilliant future. Ethiopia cherishes her friendship with Yugoslavia and her great people.

It is, perhaps, unnecessary to emphasize the historic friendship which, for over one thousand years, had existed between Ethiopia and Greece. That friendship is today, translated into terms of common ideals, common struggle and common endeavours. During the past two decades, we have both fought against agression, not only in our homelands, but also in Korea. We are both fervently devoted to the causes of justice and collective security. In the field of international affairs, and in particular, at the United Nations, we enjoy a fruitful collaboration.

Our visit to Greece at the invitation of His Majesty the King of the Hellenes, was in keeping with the close sympathies which exist between our two peoples and a cultural agreement signed in Athens during our visit, testifies to that friendship.

Our journeys abroad, though long, have served to enhance the high standing and reputation of Ethiopia and her people. The enthusiastic receptions which we received, not only from the governments but also from the masses of the peoples everywhere, we take as addressed not only to ourself but to our beloved people and to Ethiopia. These many and moving manifestations of friendship and admiration stand as an en-

446

His Majesty the Emperor continues His Tour

447

couragement to us all to live and work to the best of our abilities for the homeland, Ethiopia.

Similarly upon returning to his capital from the extended travels in Europe the Emperor in a similar broadcast, had this to say:

It is two months since we left our capital to visit Europe at the invitations of friendly nations. Although you were kept informed through the news from time to time of the honour and cordial welcome extended to us in every country which we visited, it is our wish to inform you today of our sentiments and observations of our trip.

Although the time at our disposal — only two months — was short, we were able to visit nine friendly nations; which in order of our visit are — England, France, the Netherlands, Germany, Sweden, Norway Denmark, Switzerland and Austria. We passed through the Island of Malta on our way to England where we were happily received by His Excellency the Governor of Malta and Lord Admiral Mountbatten, Commander-in-Chief Mediterranean Fleet. The warm welcome extended us, the respect and spirit of friendship evinced on our behalf during the visits to these friendly nations have moved us greatly.

When we arrived in the United Kingdom, we did not consider ourselves strangers to the country and people, particularly because we had spent there the five years of self-imposed exile. The felicitations showered on us in their traditional fashion, by this people who comforted us during the dark days, upon seeing us after fourteen years, were immeasurable; and we recall as well, with great pleasure, the deep friendliness and kindliness shown us by Her Majesty Queen Elizabeth, the Duke of Edinburgh and the Royal Family which contributed so much to make our stay in the United Kingdom enjoyable.

During our visit in the United Kingdom an Agreement has been concluded and other comprehensive understandings entered into, designed to further the mutual relationship between the two countries. It is gratifying to note that this spirit of mutual comprehension has always existed between both countries.

While we were in France negotiations designed to strengthen the existing good-neighbour relations and to advance mutual co-operation between our countries have started; there is reason to believe that these negotiations will reach a satisfactory conclusion. The warm reception given us in France and the hospitality of the people shall always be remembered. The President and Madame Coty are very respectable and charming hosts.

We retain a vivid picture of the friendly and warm-hearted welcome given us by the Government and peoples of the Netherlands, Germany, Sweden, Norway, Denmark, Switzerland and Austria.

Their Majesties the King and Queen of Sweden and their charming daughter, now the Queen of Denmark, who visited our country in 1935, still have a very pleasant recollection of their stay in Ethiopia. Their Majesties placed their palaces at our disposal and asked us to make ourselves as at home. Their hospitality and kindness on the occasion of our visit to Stockholm and Copenhagen will remain unforgettable.

Our acquaintance and friendship with His Majesty King Haakon go

448

back to those days of our common exile in the United Kingdom — an exile which sprang from the common fate of our two countries. These days of mutual distress have now passed, and having met again under the more agreeable circumstances of peace, their recollections added greatly to the conviviality of our visit to Norway.

In general, our visits to these friendly countries have contributed greatly to make known to the world the progress made by Ethiopia, and to explain her new position. These visits, apart from increasing mutual understanding and strengthening the spirit of friendship, have been found conducive to the possible development of industrial and commercial projects and undertakings beneficial to both parties concerned. We are confident that the outcome will be of advantage to Ethiopia. In the course of our visits to the Scandinavian countries, conversations were entered into concerning the need of technical personnel for our services; the recruiting of a number of suitable technicians is now being negotiated.

Our recent visits to friendly nations is nothing more than another important addition to our constant efforts to see that Ethiopia attain a higher degree of progress, about the fruits of which we are confident.

We deem it appropriate to tell you briefly, in person, about our visit to Europe, so that you should realise that this is not a matter to remain as a mere item of news, but one which must find expression in action.

During our visit to Europe, we had the occasion to see and to speak to our students whom we sent to the various countries of Europe for study. It is gratifying to note that the supreme effort made on our part to prepare as many Ethiopians as possible for higher education and modern techniques has not been made in vain, to enable them to preserve the independence and integrity of Ethiopia which has been passed on to us by our ancestors through untold sacrifices.

The countries we visited are far advanced in education and modern technology; but except in technicians and experts, Ethiopia is not inferior in natural resources to other countries.

We must remember the fact that Ethiopia is for Ethiopians, and that since the right course we have followed so far, in fostering wide-spread education, in providing measures for protecting the health of our people and in raising the general standard of the nation, is yielding promising results, it is the duty of every one to contribute his share towards the greater achievement of this sacred task.

You know the usefulness of work by reference to your livelihood. As a result, the fruits of labour of the Ethiopian people are reflected in the favourable balance of the country's exports and imports.

The reception and honour rendered to us during our visit to the various friendly nations must be considered not only as rendered to ourselves, but also as an honour rendered to Ethiopia and her people.

We are happy to be back in our beloved country and to find ourselves in the midst of our beloved people after our visit to these friendly nations, and we are deeply touched by the affectionate and warm welcome of our people.

On both occasions upon His Imperial Majesty's return to Addis Ababa,

449

he was welcomed back home in a manner most befitting by his government and people. At the Addis Ababa airport Members of the Imperial Family, Princes, dignitaries, all the members of the Ethiopian Cabinet, heads and staff of the various diplomatic missions, foreign advisers, business and civil representatives, senior military officers, distinguished residents of the city and thousands of people provided an atmosphere brilliant with tokens and souvenirs of welcome.

Along the Imperial route triumphal arches were erected, artistically decorated, bearing words of welcome for His Imperial Majesty whose absence was keenly felt. The official welcome on behalf of the citizens was made by the Mayor of Addis Ababa in a tribune erected on the airport in which he mentioned the significance to Ethiopia of His Majesty the Emperor's foreign visits.

A 21-gun salute greeted the Emperor's arrival at the airport on both occasions. Simultaneously the arrival was also heralded in the traditional Ethiopian style by the beating of a drum at the Old Palace. After inspecting the Guard of Honour, picked men of the Imperial Army and Air Force, His Imperial Majesty drove to the Trinity Cathedral for a brief moment of prayer. Thereafter, with the other members of the Imperial Family, the Emperor went to the Old Palace for the official welcome of the Government and a champagne toast. The toast was offered by H.E. the Prime Minister, who in a speech referred to His Majesty's rôle in bringing Ethiopia into beneficial contact with the peace-loving nations of the world. His Imperial Majesty's State visits provided the opportunity of contact with heads of states and statesmen of friendly powers and an exchange of views on matters touching upon the relation between Ethiopia and their respective countries. Particularly significant as well, the visits had a great impact on the international position of Ethiopia, since they helped to renew and stimulate greater world interest in Ethiopian affairs.

450

CHAPTER 33

Conclusion

The title of this chapter—Conclusion—seems ironical in a book of this nature. If, as hinted before, the Haile Selassie I era, the Silver Jubilee of which we celebrate this year, is an "unfinished symphony," a conclusion seems odd. Then again, we are dealing with a "new faith" which, now that it has taken root, as the preceding pages have attempted to explain, places us at this Silver Jubilee, too close to the scene, both in space and time, to arrive at any thorough judgment of its outcome. Ethiopia as a polity has been led on the road of a new experience by a stimulus, the potency of which we can only attempt to inconclusively analyse in these brief concluding pages.

What has the Haile Selassie I era meant to Ethiopia and the Ethiopians in terms of constructive change? The reader might have formed some estimate as he read through the preceding pages. It seems however necessary at this stage to tie together some of the important factors so as to aid his judgement further. In the first place, and comparatively, Ethiopia of 1955 marks a stage of all-round development quite distinct to the embryonic and rather nebulous foundation which existed after the death of Menelik in 1913. This essential difference is characterised particularly by the moral and material progress and also by the present political structure of the Empire.

The earmarks of a living and dynamic polity rests invariably on the response—psychological and civic of the subjects (citizens) to active community responsibility. The make-up of the provinces and subdistricts of Ethiopia, their formerly separatist history and traditions, partially also their tribalism, despite Menelik's successful campaign for unity, did not then produce a political unity in the strict sense. While it laid the foundations for a centralised political entity, neither the time nor the circumstances had permitted it to gain the cohesion necessary to this end. Some of the elements which bind a political entity together—communications, transport facilities and the elaboration of a system of law and administration which could command the respect and allegiance of the majority of Ethiopians in the vast Empire wrought by Menelik's daring, were too rudimentary to be effective. In fact, central authority which Menelik's unification was designed to establish was put into effect by Haile Selassie I.

"The territory of Ethiopia, in its entirety, is, from one end to the other, subject to the Government of His Majesty the Emperor.

"All the natives of Ethiopia, subjects of the Empire, form together the Ethiopian Nation.

"The Imperial Government assures the union of the territory, of the nation and of the law of Ethiopia," state the first two paragraphs of the 1931 Constitution.

451

In this, the great experiment came when this 1931 Constitution was introduced by His Imperial Majesty. A Parliament and responsible ministers were innovations never before known in the history of the country. By these two instruments in the modern political evolution of Ethiopia, the path was open not only for Ethiopians to learn the functions and principles of modern government but also for the growth and extension of these institutions.

A brief commentary on the Ethiopian Constitution will disclose that it is an instrument which emanated under the rarest of circumstances. "The constitution of Sparta," according to Dr. William Archibald Dunning, in his book, *The History of Political Theories,* "sprung from the social basis of the state. The influence which the Sparta constitution exerted in Greek thought was due primarily to the fact that the Spartans was a marked-off class in the population, than to the organisation through which this class performed its political functions." The constitution of Athens, though distinctly different from that of Sparta had as well a historical background based first on the distinction between slaves and freedmen, and secondly, on the division of the latter into nobles and commons. The British constitution, a thing of growth, was progressively fashioned by the desire of the people to reduce the arbitrary power of the monarchy and to vest political power in the hands of the people through their parliament. One of the main documents in the early evolution of the British constitution—the Magna Charta—was agreed to by King John at Runnymede as an alternative of civil war against him by the feudal barons. The United States Constitution came about as the result of a separation of the colonies from Britain through a revolution and the desire of the founding fathers to set up a government with controlled powers. All these fundamental laws grew out of specific social, political and legal conditions.

But how did the Ethiopian Constitution come about? Historically without parallel, His Majesty the Emperor gave the Constitution *"unasked for and of Our own free will."* The *raison d'être* of this grant could hardly be explained on the basis of the political history of the country; it could not be imputed to the exertions of any class of the Ethiopian society; nor has there been any agitation which it was designed to appease. Its religious and ethical basis could be attributed to the Emperor himself, as could be gathered from the two first paragraphs of the Decree which accompanied the 1931 document:

We, Haile Selassie I, Emperor of Ethiopia, having been called to the Empire by the Grace of God and by the unanimous voice of the people, and having received the Crown and the Throne legitimately by anointment according to law, are convinced that there is no better way of manifesting the gratitude which We owe to Our Creator, Who has chosen Us and granted Us His confidence, than to render Ourselves worthy of it by making every effort so that he who comes after Us may be invested with this confidence and may work in conformity with the laws according to the principle established.

Having in view the prosperity of the country, We have decided to draw up a Constitution which safeguards such prosperity based on the laws and We have the hope that this Constitution will be a source of well-being for Ethio-

pia, that it will contribute to the maintenance of Our Government and to the happiness and prosperity of Our well beloved people, and that it will give satisfaction to all. Having expressed and made clear Our Will, We have decided to grant this Constitution.

On the basis of available references, this was a revolutionary move on the part of the Emperor which brought Ethiopia, by one fell swoop, in line with contemporary political thought. That the Constitution consists of a restatement of generally accepted principles of constitutional monarchy as known in the United Kingdom and in the Scandinavian countries indicates that His Imperial Majesty had studied and made himself familiar with comparative constitutional history and thought, with this significant difference: The 1931 Constitution created a new field for the exercise of social and political activity by the Ethiopian people; the people in these countries created slowly and sometimes imperceptibly their constitutions.

This quarter century of practical experience with the Constitution has made it part of the nation's history; has shaped the country's political character; and has become the sheet-anchor of the material conditions of the people. Like the Renaissance, or new birth of the European spirit which sent Christian sailors across the oceans on voyages of discovery, so this new spirit of the 1931 Constitution brought the horizon of achievement within the grasp of all Ethiopians—aristocrat, intellectual, trader and peasant. And for clear evidence of this fact, the social and political register includes today men of noble as well as those of ordinary birth and lineage. The protection and punishment of the Law and the pail of justice are vouchsafed on equal terms to all regardless of former condition. Education, the universally accepted instrument of ordered civilised progress is open to all without distinction. The rights belonging to the nation (people) and its (their) duties have been recognised and defined in Chapter III of the Constitution.

By the act of granting the Constitution the stream of centuries of customs and traditions was arrested and deflected into a hitherto unheard of channel, where the monarch voluntarily limits his own power. Thus the long annals of rule by Imperial prerogative yielded to one by constitutional law, a transition which has been fraught with turmoil and bloodshed in many lands.

What has the 1931 Constitution meant to Ethiopia and the Ethiopians? First, the document defines in unequivocal terms the relation of the people to the monarchy, a relationship which was before not clearly known except through contact with the Imperial prerogatives. The decision then as to what was lawful and what was unlawful rested with the ruler's own positive decision. Ethiopians now know that the fundamental basis of their government, headed by His Majesty the Emperor, is *for increasing the well-being of Our people and aiding their progress on the road to happiness and the civilisation attained by independent and civilised nations.* They know also that they are assured an honoured place in the participation of their governance with their enlightened Emperor, and that the status, *perpetual and immutable,* is guaranteed by the laws springing from the Constitution. The Ethiopian people regardless of tribe, class or previous condition were brought to know their rights and the duties and obligations attendant thereto. That these rights are protected by law and that redress lies in the Courts of Justice. Unlike before, the Haile Selassie I era, characterised by this new and explicit integration of the subjects with the State, has released a new energy among the people. It has opened the door for present and future participation in the ordering of their own well-being.

The legal and constitutional certitude which was brought into being in this era has provided the most agreeable climate for national growth ever experienced in modern times in Ethiopia. Through the security and ordered life which has emanated from a rule of law, moral confidence has grown so that the merchant trades, the farmer ploughs, the student studies and the economic and social structure continues to be built up.

The central authority has moved from its fragmentary character up till 1923, to a position today when it commands the obedience of all the subjects in the far removed areas of the Empire. Nothing has done so much to strengthen this authority and to make the people conscious of what is taking place than the Ethiopian parliament. Parliamentarians, following the advice of His Majesty the Emperor, during their annual vacation, explain as much as is possible to their provinces. The possibility of making themselves eligible for nomination to the Chamber of Deputies has had the effect of broadening the élite in each locality. Suitable aspirants for the Chamber must stand on their record as "good men and true." And Article 32 of the Constitution provides: "Temporarily, and until the people are in a position to elect them themselves, the members of the Chamber of Deputies shall be chosen by the nobility and local chiefs." The proposed constitutional changes then will not be operating in a vacuum; these years have aroused the civic conscience of the people to look forward to more liberal participation in their legislature.

The greater number among those who have been called to the high office of responsible ministers of the Crown are men of lowly birth, nominated to their distinguished posts by His Majesty the Emperor because of their loyalty, experience and ability. The impetus which such opportunities have brought to the young men of this generation could hardly go unnoticed. Vice Ministers have been chosen—several of them—from among young men educated and trained during these 25 years. So also the Directors General and lesser administrative officials—all wielding authority commensurate with their stations.

The Ethiopian farmer, comprising the largest number of the nation's labour force, has been able through the tax and currency reforms, health services and aids provided by the Imperial Ethiopian Government to increase his yields. The stimulation of exports has provided an incentive to produce more and varied crops as a means of securing greater farm income. Farm acreage, especially in coffee and pulses, has more than tripled within the past ten years and many experimental crops are being tried in wide areas. This stepped-up farm production lies at the root of the enormous rise in the volume and value of Ethiopia's exports—80% of which is agricultural, raw or semi-processed items. The increase of imports, especially consumer goods, owes its rise to the fact that the Ethiopian farmer is continuously demanding and purchasing them. Through the internal stability which has been guaranteed by the Government has this economic expansion been made possible.

Ethiopians, traditionally known to have looked upon trade as the province of aliens, have become more and more conscious of the necessity to enter into the commercial field. Local investment in commercial and industrial enterprises has increased considerably with a sharp rise in recent years. It is found that the country's international trade, thanks to the ever-expanding contacts secured by the Imperial Ethiopian Government with many friendly nations, has been extended to a level undreamt of in the 1930's. From the adroit foreign policy initiated by His Imperial Majesty Ethiopians are progressively being benefitted by sharing in the cultural and technological store of friendly nations. Through fellowships and scholarships springing from international co-operation, the number of trained Ethiopians in several vital fields keep increasing. Within the past five years this policy has been accelerated and is momentarily opening the way for the robust self-help on which His Imperial Majesty lays great dependence in the programme of the nation's full evolution.

The present generation of Ethiopians, because of this forward-looking policy, planned and executed within the past twenty-five years, is finding it easier to appreciate what lies behind modern progress. Through the schools and other institutions they are learning the newer ways ushered in by the Haile Selassie I era. Unlike 1941 when His Majesty the Emperor, upon the restoration, found it difficult to find qualified hands to fill administrative positions, an élite of trained men and women is available in many fields. Besides those already trained, over 500 scholars are now studying abroad to add to this number. Nor should it be forgotten that while extensive plans are on foot to develop an all-round and complete educational system, elementary, secondary, vocational, technical and college students continue to graduate from Ethiopian institutions each year. As discussed in chapter 16, a ten-year plan for the further expansion of the nation's educational system has been adopted. It may yet be that when historians begin to appraise the efficacy of the Haile Selassie I era, His Imperial Majesty's drive for the education of his people may be treated as a basic and fundamental factor in spreading the "new faith."

The health of the people today has improved considerably. While much remains to be done in this massive task of fighting against disease, more Ethiopians today are conscious of the importance of seeking modern medical care and of avoiding diseases by observing the simple rule of health. In this field the pupils of the schools, scattered in all parts of the Empire, have been holding high up the torch of health against the superstition of their parents concerning disease and ill-health. Nurses are being trained in increasing numbers, the Medical College and Public Health Training Centre at Gondar is getting ready public health officers, sanitary inspectors, community nurses and other auxiliary personnel needed for rural health centres. Fifteen medical students are among those studying abroad, some in their third and fourth years and one has already graduated from a Medical School in the United Kingdom.

The increase of the national wealth has been phenomenal. Simultaneously, the standard of living of the people generally has risen and continues to rise. The increased volume and value of Ethiopian exports, in recent years have shown visible effects on the standard of living of the producers, who are enjoying a far greater purchasing power, particularly among the producers in the coffee areas. This development has given rise to a greater demand for consumer goods, the distribution of which, among the rural population, has been greatly aided by the programme of road and highway construction undertaken by the Imperial Highway Authority. Specific measures have been taken to increase consumer demand in order to further improve the standard of living and at the same time to prevent too great an accumulation of excess purchasing power. Increased savings, as reported by the State Bank of Ethiopia and encouraged by education, and revised taxation levels have been used to avoid an inflationary trend.

The Empire presents a closer unit, economically, socially and politically bound together by the extensive and well-maintained road system and through the air connections of the Ethiopian Air Lines. Inter-provincial community is now rendered facile and friends and neighbours, businessmen and others interested in the economic development of the country can move freely from one part to another. Cultural ideas flow through these channels, and the central administration has been made more effective. The lives and habits of people of what was considered remote areas of the Empire are more amenable to the change of modernisation which, in turn, strengthens the national spirit. Through the ports of Massawa and Assab which were brought back through the federation of Eritrea to the Motherland, Ethiopia has regained her free contact with the outside world as in the days of "Bhar Negash."

By and large the Haile Selassie I era has brought much tangible benefits to Ethiopia and the Ethiopian people. It secured their independence in the days of mortal peril from 1935 to 1941. It restored a polity in which the majority of the people now live in peace and enjoy a fair measure of prosperity. It saved the national honour by bringing autonomy to the Instituted Church. It has made Ethiopia a respected member of the world community of nations and provided an extended horizon for Ethiopian nationals to rise from stage to stage on the ladder of culture and enlightenment. Through His Majesty the Emperor Haile Selassie I the ancient African kingdom has experienced a Renaissance, the reverberation of which is sure to reach into the regions of space and time and encompass many succeeding generations. If a tribute was necessary, could there be a greater and more befitting one to His Imperial Majesty Haile Selassie I on this Silver Jubilee of his reign?

APPENDIX

I

CONSTITUTION OF THE EMPIRE OF ETHIOPIA
1931

Decree

We, Haile Selassie I, Emperor of Ethiopia, having been called to the Empire by the Grace of God and by the unanimous voice of the people, and having received the Crown and the Throne legitimately by anointment according to law, are convinced that there is no better way of manifesting the gratitude which We owe to Our Creator, Who has chosen Us and granted Us His confidence, than to render Ourselves worthy of it by making every effort so that he who comes after Us may be invested with this confidence and may work in conformity with the laws according to the principles established.

Having in view the prosperity of the country, We have decided to draw up a Constitution which safeguards such prosperity based on the laws and We have the hope that this Constitution will be a source of well-being for Ethiopia, that it will contribute to the maintenance of Our Government and to the happiness and prosperity of Our well beloved people, and that it will give satisfaction to all. Having expressed and made clear Our Will, We have accordingly decided to grant this Constitution.

The Constitution which is to serve as the basis, in the future, for the maintenance of the Ethiopian Government and of the laws which are based on it, and the means of applying such laws once resolved on, will itself set forth the necessity of the measures suitable for ensuring its maintenance in order that this Constitution of Our State may remain perpetual and immutable.

Since our accession to the Imperial Throne of Ethiopia, having received from the hands of God a high mission for the accomplishment of His destinies, We consider that it is Our duty to decree and enforce all the measures necessary for the maintenance of Our Government, for increasing the well-being of Our People and aiding their progress on the road to happiness and the civilisation attained by independent and cultured nations.

We consider that the way to achieve this aim lies in the elaboration of the present Constitution, which will facilitate Government action whilst assuring the happiness of the people who will, in addition, derive from it an honour which will not fail to be reflected on future generations and will permit the Empire to enjoy the inestimable benefits of peace and security.

Animated by this noble desire, and in order to enable Our State and our people to obtain a high place in History, We have, after Our elevation to the Imperial Throne, and in the second year of Our Reign, in the Year of Grace 1923 (A.D. 1931), unasked and of Our own free will, decreed the present State Constitution.

CONSTITUTION OF ETHIOPIA

established in the Reign of

His Majesty Haile Selassie I

CHAPTER I

The Ethiopian Empire and the Succession to the Throne

Art. 1.   The territory of Ethiopia, in its entirety, is, from one end to the other, subject to the Government of His Majesty the Emperor.
All the natives of Ethiopia, subjects of the Empire, form together the Ethiopian Nation.

Art. 2.   The Imperial Government assures the union of the territory, of the nation and of the law of Ethiopia.

Art. 3.   The Law determines that the Imperial dignity shall remain perpetually attached to the line of His Majesty Haile Selassie I, descendant of King Sahle Selassie, whose line descends without interruption from the dynasty of Menelik I, son of King Solomon of Jerusalem and of the Queen of Ethiopia, known as the Queen of Sheba.

Art. 4.   The Throne and the Crown of the Empire shall be transmitted to the descendants of the Emperor according to the Law of the Imperial House.

Art. 5.   By virtue of His Imperial Blood, as well as by the anointing which He has received, the person of the Emperor is sacred, His dignity is inviolable and His power indisputable. Consequently, He is entitled to all the honours due to Him in accordance with tradition and the present Constitution. The Law decree that anyone so bold as to injure the Majesty of the Emperor will be punished.

CHAPTER II

The Power and Prerogatives of the Emperor

Art. 6.   In the Ethiopian Empire supreme power rests in the hands of the Emperor. He ensures the exercise thereof in conformity with the established law.

Art. 7.   The Emperor of Ethiopia will institute the Chamber of the Senate (Yaheg Mawossena Meker-Beth) and the Chamber of Deputies (Yaheg Mamria Meker-Beth). The laws prepared by these Chambers become executory by his promulgation.

Art. 8.   It is the Emperor's right to convene the deliberative Chambers and to declare the opening and the close of their sessions. He may also order their convocation before or after the usual time.

He may dissolve the Chamber of Deputies.

Art. 9.　When the Chambers are not sitting, the Emperor has the right, in case of necessity, in order to maintain order and avert public dangers, to promulgate decrees taking the place of laws. The Law determines that these decrees shall in due course be presented to the Chambers at their first subsequent meeting, and that they shall be abrogated for the future if the Chambers do not approve them.

Art. 10.　The Emperor shall give the necessary orders to ensure the execution of the laws in force, according to the letter and the spirit thereof, and for the maintenance of public order and the development of the prosperity of the nation.

Art. 11.　The Emperor shall lay down the organisation and the regulations of all administrative departments.

It is his right also to appoint and dismiss the officers of the Army, as well as civil officials, and to decide as to their respective charges and salaries.

Art. 12.　The right of declaring war and of concluding peace is legally reserved to the Emperor.

Art. 13.　It is the Emperor's right to determine the armed forces necessary to the Empire, both in time of peace and in time of war.

Art. 14.　The Emperor has legally the right to negotiate and to sign all kinds of treaties.

Art. 15.　The Emperor has the right to confer the title of Prince and other honorific titles, to establish personal estates ("reste-guelt") and to institute new Orders.

Art. 16.　The Emperor has the right to grant pardon, to commute penalties and to reinstate.

Art. 17.　If the Emperor is incapable, either owing to age or sickness, of dealing with the affairs of Government, a Regent of the Empire may be appointed, pursuant to the Law of the Imperial House, in order to exercise the supreme power on the Emperor's behalf.

CHAPTER III

The Rights recognised by the Emperor
as belonging to the Nation, and the
Duties incumbent on the Nation

Art. 18.　The Law specifies the conditions required for the status of Ethiopian subjects.

Art. 19.　All Ethiopian subjects, provided that they comply with the conditions laid down by law and the decrees promulgated by H.M. the Emperor, may be appointed officers of the Army or civil officials, or to any other posts or offices in the service of the State.

Art. 20.　All those who belong to the Ethiopian Army owe absolute loyalty and obedience to the Emperor, in conformity with the provisions of the law.

Art. 21.   The nation is bound to pay legal taxes.

Art. 22.   Within the limits provided by law, Ethiopian subjects have the right to pass freely from one place to another.

Art. 23.   No Ethiopian subject may be arrested, sentenced or imprisoned except in pursuance of the law.

Art. 24.   No Ethiopian subject may, against his will, be deprived of the right to have his case tried by the legally established Court.

Art. 25.   Except in the cases provided by law, no domiciliary searches may be made.

Art. 26.   Except in the cases provided by law, no one shall have the right to violate the secrecy of the correspondence of Ethiopian subjects.

Art. 27.   Except in cases of public utility determined by law, no one shall be entitled to deprive an Ethiopian subject of the movable or landed property which he holds.

Art. 28.   All Ethiopian subjects have the right to present petitions to the Government in legal form.

Art. 29.   The provisions of the present Chamber shall in no way limit the measures which the Emperor, by virtue of his supreme power, may take in the event of war or of public misfortunes menacing the interests of the nation.

CHAPTER IV

The Deliberative Chambers of the Empire

Art. 30.   The Deliberative Chambers of the Empire are the following: a) the First: Chamber of the Senate ("Yaheg Mawossena Meker-Beth"). b) the Second: Chamber of Deputies ("Yaheg Mamria Meker-Beth").

Art. 31.   The members of the Senate shall be appointed by His Majesty the Emperor from among the Nobility (Mekuanent) who have for a long time served his Empire as Princes or Ministers, Judges or high military officers.

Art. 32.   Temporarily, and until the people are in a position to elect them themselves, the members of the Chamber of Deputies shall be chosen by the Nobility (Mekuanent) and the local Chiefs (Shumoch).

Art. 33.   A person who has been appointed member of the Senate may not, during the same parliamentary session become a member of the Chamber of Deputies, and a person who has been chosen as a member of the Chamber of Deputies may not during the same parliamentary session become a member of the Senate.

Art. 34.   No law may be put into force without having been discussed by the Chambers and having obtained the confirmation of the Emperor.

Art. 35.   The members of the Chamber of Deputies shall be legally bound to receive and deliberate on the proposals transmitted to them by the Ministers of the respective Departments. However, when the Deputies

460

have an idea which could be useful to the Empire or to the nation, the law reserves to them the right to communicate it to the Emperor through their President, and the Chamber shall deliberate on the subject if the Emperor consents thereto.

Art. 36.   Each of the two Chambers shall have the right to express separately to His Majesty the Emperor its opinion on a legislative question or on any other matter whatsoever. If the Emperor does not accept its opinion, it may not, however, revert to the question during the same parliamentary session.

Art. 37.   The two Chambers shall be convened annually and shall sit for 8 months. If necessary, the Emperor may cause them to sit longer.

Art. 38.   The Chambers shall be convened in extraordinary session, according to requirements. In this case, it is for the Emperor to fix the duration of their session.

Art. 39.   The opening and closing, and the duration of sessions and recesses shall be fixed identically in respect of the two Chambers. If the Chamber of Deputies is dissolved, the Senate shall adjourn its session until later.

Art. 40.   If the Emperor has made use of his right to dissolve the Chamber of Deputies entirely, he shall arrange for a new Chamber to be assembled within four months.

Art. 41.   Neither of the two Chambers shall commence its deliberations or undertake a debate or a vote without two-thirds of its members being present.

Art. 42.   If during the deliberations of the Chambers the votes are equally divided, the opinion of the group to which the President of the Chamber shall have adhered shall prevail.

Art. 43.   The President of the Chamber shall state in advance whether the question forming the subject-matter of the deliberations is public or secret in character.

If, after a matter has been declared secret, a member brings it to the knowledge of the public by speeches, by the Press, by writings or by any other means, he shall be punished in conformity with the Penal Law.

Art. 44.   The Emperor shall draw up, in the form of a law, the standing orders of the Senate and of the Chamber of Deputies.

Art. 45.   Except in cases of crime, judgment of which cannot be deferred, no member of the Chamber of Deputies may be prosecuted at law during the period of a parliamentary session.

Art. 46.   If after deliberating an important matter, the two Chambers come to different decisions, the Emperor, having received written statements of their respective opinions, shall examine the reasons for their disagreement. After having come to a conclusion on the matter, he shall seek a compromise capable of bringing them to a final agreement, by selecting what he considers best in the two resolutions.

In the event of its being impossible to reconcile the opinions of the two Chambers, the Emperor legally has the right either to select and promulgate the opinion of one, or to defer the question.

Art. 47.   The Chambers may not summon Ministers to their meetings even if they feel the need therefor, without having first obtained the consent of the Emperor. Ministers, on their part, may not attend meetings of the Chambers and take part in their deliberations without having obtained the consent of His Majesty.

CHAPTER V

The Ministers of the Empire

Art. 48.   Ministers shall submit in writing to His Majesty the Emperor their opinions regarding the affairs of their respective Departments; they are responsible for such opinions. Laws and decrees and all other acts emanating from the Emperor in the affairs of the Empire shall bear the Imperial signature; subsequently the Keeper of the Seals (Tsafiteezaz) shall notify them under his signature to the appropriate Minister.

Art. 49.   When the Emperor asks the opinion of his Ministers on an important governmental matter, they shall deliberate together in accordance with the regulations before submitting their opinion to him.

CHAPTER VI

Jurisdiction

Art. 50.   Judges, sitting regularly, shall administer justice in conformity with the laws, in the name of His Majesty the Emperor. The organisation of the Courts shall be regulated by law.

Art. 51.   The Judges shall be selected from among men having experience of judicial affairs.

Art. 52.   Judges shall sit in public. In cases which might affect public order or prejudice good morals, the hearing may, according to law, be held *in camera.*

Art. 53.   The jurisdiction of each Court shall be fixed by law.

Art. 54.   Special Courts shall judge all suits relating to administrative affairs, which are withdrawn from the jurisdiction of the other Courts.

CHAPTER VII

The Budget of the Imperial Government

Art. 55.   The law determines that the receipts of the Government Treasury, of whatever nature they may be, shall only be expended in conformity with the annual budget fixing the sums placed at the disposal of each Ministry. The annual budget shall be framed on the basis proposed by the Minister of Finance during the deliberations of the Chamber of Deputies and of the Senate, whose resolutions shall be submitted for the approval of His Majesty the Emperor.

Done at Addis Ababa, on the 9 Hamlie in the Year of Grace 1923 (16th July, 1931).

AGREEMENT AND MILITARY CONVENTION BETWEEN THE U.K. AND ETHIOPIA

Addis Ababa, January 31st, 1942

Whereas His Majesty the Emperor of Ethiopia, Conquering Lion of the Tribe of Judah, Elect of God (hereinafter referred to as His Majesty the Emperor), wishes to put on record His gratitude and that of His people for the overwhelming and generous aid He has received from the Forces of His Majesty The King of Great Britain, Ireland and the British Dominions beyond the Seas, Emperor of India (hereinafter referred to as His Majesty The King), which has enabled Him and His people to recover their national territory; and

Whereas His Majesty the Emperor, true to His coronation pledges not to surrender His sovereignty or the independence of His people, but conscious of the needs of His country, has intimated to the Government of the United Kingdom of Great Britain and Northern Ireland (hereinafter referred to as the Government of the United Kingdom) that He is eager to receive advice and financial assistance in the difficult task of reconstruction and reform; and

Whereas the Government of the United Kingdom recognise that Ethiopia is now a free and independent State and His Majesty the Emperor, Haile Selassie I, is its lawful Ruler, and, the reconquest of Ethiopia being now complete, wish to help His Majesty the Emperor to re-establish His Government and to assist in providing for the immediate needs of the country:

Now, therefore, His Majesty the Emperor of Ethiopia in person, and Major-General Sir Philip Euen Mitchell, Knight Commander of the Most Distinguished Order of Saint Michael and Saint George, upon whom has been conferred the decoration of the Military Cross, Chief Political Officer Commanding-in-Chief, East Africa, being duly authorised for this purpose by the Government of the United Kingdom,

Have agreed as follows:

Article I.

Diplomatic relations between the United Kingdom and Ethiopia shall be re-established and conducted through a British Minister Plenipotentiary accredited to His Majesty the Emperor and an Ethiopian Minister Plenipotentiary accredited to His Majesty the King, who shall be appointed as soon as possible after the entry into force of this Agreement. His Majesty the Emperor agrees that the Diplomatic Representative of His Majesty the King shall take precedence over any foreign Representative accredited to His Imperial Majesty.

463

Article II.

(a)   His Majesty the Emperor having requested the Government of the United Kingdom to assist him in obtaining the services of British subjects (1) as advisers to himself and his administration; (2) as Commissioner of Police, Police officers and inspectors; and (3) as judges and magistrates, the Government of the United Kingdom will use their best endeavours to assist His Majesty the Emperor in this matter. The number of such British subjects, their salaries, privileges, duties and powers, and the appointments they are to fill, shall be the subject of separate agreements between the Contracting Parties.

(b)   His Majesty the Emperor agrees not to appoint advisers additional to those referred to in paragraph (a) above except after consultation with the Government of the United Kingdom.

Article III.

Subject to the provisions of the Military Convention concluded this day, and of Article VII of this Agreement, the jurisdiction and administration exercised by British military tribunals and authorities shall terminate as soon as they can be replaced by effective Ethiopian civilian administration and jurisdiction, which His Majesty the Emperor will set up as soon as possible. Nevertheless, British military tribunals shall finish any cases then pending before them. The Ethiopian authorities will recognise and, where necessary, enforce decisions previously given by British military tribunals.

Article IV.

(a)   His Majesty the Emperor, having intimated to the Government of the United Kingdom that he will require financial aid in order to re-establish his administration, the Government of the United Kingdom will grant to His Majesty the sum of Pounds Sterling one million five hundred thousand during the first year and Pounds Sterling one million during the second year of the currency of this Agreement. If this Agreement remains in force for a third year, the Government of the United Kingdom agree to pay to His Majesty the Emperor the sum of Pounds Sterling five hundred thousand in respect of such third year, and if for a fourth year, then the sum of Pounds Sterling two hundred and fifty thousand shall be paid in respect of that year. Payments will be made in quarterly instalments in advance.

(b)   His Majesty the Emperor agrees for his part that this grant shall absolve the Government of the United Kingdom from any payments in respect of the use of immovable property of the Ethiopian State which may be required by the British forces in Ethiopia during the war.

(c)   His Majesty the Emperor agrees that there shall be the closest co-operation between the Ethiopian authorities and his British Advisers, to be appointed in accordance with Article II (a), regarding public expenditure.

(d)   In order to facilitate the absorption into Ethiopian economy of the

464

funds to be provided under paragraph (a) above, and to promote the early resumption of trade between Ethiopia and the surrounding territories, His Majesty the Emperor agrees that in all matters relating to currency in Ethiopia the Government of the United Kingdom shall be consulted and that arrangements concerning it shall be made only with the concurrence of that Government.

Article V.

(a) Jurisdiction over foreigners shall be exercised by the Ethiopian Courts constituted according to the draft Statute attached hereto as an Annexe, which His Majesty the Emperor will promulgate forthwith and will maintain in force during the continuance of this Agreement, except in so far as it may require amendment in any manner agreed upon by the parties to this Agreement.
(b) Any foreigner who is a party to any proceedings, civil or criminal, within the jurisdiction of a Regional Communal or Provincial Court, may elect to have the case transferred without additional fee or charge to the High Court for trial. Provisions to this effect shall be included in the Rules of Court.
(c) In the hearing by the High Court of any matter to which a foreigner is a party at least one of the British Judges mentioned in Article II (a) shall sit as a member of the Court.
(d) His Majesty the Emperor agrees to direct that foreigners shall be incarcerated only in prisons approved for the purpose by the Commissioner of Police appointed in accordance with Article II (a).

Article VI.

(a) His Majesty the Emperor agrees to enact laws against trading with the enemy in terms proposed to him by the Government of the United Kingdom.
(b) His Majesty the Emperor accepts full responsibility for seeing that private enemy property is dealt with in accordance with international law. His Majesty agrees to consult with the British Diplomatic Representative as to the measures to be taken to this end.

Article VII.

His Majesty the Emperor agrees:
(a) That all prisoners of war shall be handed over to the custody of the British Military Authorities, who will evacuate them from Ethiopia as soon as possible, and
(b) That he will enact such legislation as may be required to enable the General Officer Commanding-in-Chief the British forces in East Africa and officers acting under his authority to exercise such temporary local powers as may be necessary for the administration, control and evacuation of Italian civilians in Ethiopia.

Article VIII.

The Government of the United Kingdom will use their best endeavours:
(a) To secure the return of Ethiopians in Italian hands, and
(b) To secure the return of artistic works, religious property and the like removed to Italy and belonging to His Majesty the Emperor, the Ethiopian State, or local or religious bodies.

Article IX.

In areas in which the General Officer Commanding-in-Chief the British forces in East Africa may find it necessary to conduct military operations against the common enemy in future, His Majesty the Emperor will, at the request of the said General Officer Commanding-in-Chief, declare a state of Emergency and will confer on the General Officer Commanding-in-Chief the powers resulting from such declaration. Any legislation necessary to secure these powers will be promulgated by His Majesty the Emperor. The Ethiopian Government and local authorities will give such aid and concurrence to the General Officer Commanding-in-Chief as may be needed.

Article X.

His Majesty the Emperor agrees not to conduct any external military operation which, in the opinion of the General Officer Commanding-in-Chief the British forces in East Africa, is contrary to the joint interests of Ethiopia and the United Kingdom.

Article XI.

(a) His Majesty the Emperor will accord freedom of passage to, in and over Ethiopia to duly registered British civil aircraft, provided that such regulations governing air navigation as may be in force in Ethiopia are observed.
(b) His Majesty the Emperor will permit a British Air Transport organisation or organisations, to be designated by the Government of the United Kingdom, to operate regular Air Services to, in and over Ethiopia for the carriage of passengers, mails and freight. For this purpose the said organisations shall be permitted to use such aerodromes, ground equipment and facilities as are available, and to provide such other aerodromes, ground equipment and facilities as may be necessary.
(c) His Majesty the Emperor will not permit foreign aircraft other than British to fly to, in or over Ethiopa without the concurrence of the Government of the United Kingdom.

Article XII.

The present Agreement shall enter in force as from this day's date. It shall remain in force until replaced by a Treaty for which his Majesty the Emperor may wish to make proposals. If it is not so replaced within two years

466

from this date, it may thereafter be terminated at any time by either Party giving three month's notice to the other to this effect.

In witness whereof the undersigned have signed the present Agreement and affixed thereto their seals.

Done this thirty-first day of January 1942 in the English and Amharic languages, both of which shall be equally authoritative except in case of doubt, when the English text shall prevail.

(L. S.)   HAILE SELASSIE I.   (L. S.)   P. E. MITCHELL.

ANGLO-ETHIOPIAN AGREEMENT 1944

His Imperial Majesty the Emperor of Ethiopia, Conquering Lion of the Tribe of Judah, Elect of God (hereinafter referred to as His Imperial Majesty the Emperor) and His Majesty the King of Great Britain, Ireland and British Dominions beyond the Seas, Emperor of India (hereinafter referred to as His Majesty the King).

Whereas, on the 31st January, 1942, an Agreement and a Military Convention were signed at Addis Ababa between His Majesty the Emperor and the Government of His Majesty the King in the United Kingdom of Great Britain and Northern Ireland, with the provision that they should remain in force until replaced by a treaty for which His Imperial Majesty the Emperor might wish to make proposals;

Considering that circumstances have changed since the said Agreement and Convention were concluded, but that while the war continues it is not opportune to negotiate a permanent treaty;

Desiring, as members of the United Nations, to render mutual assistance to the cause of the United Nations and to conclude a new temporary Agreement for the regulation of their mutual relations;

Have accordingly appointed as their plenipotentiaries:—His Imperial Majesty the Emperor: His Excellency, Bitwoded Makonnen Endalkachau, The Prime Minister.

His Majesty the King: For the United Kingdom of Great Britain and Northern Ireland: The Right Honourable, Earl De La Warr, a Member of the Privy Council.

who, having exchanged their full powers, found to be in due and proper form, have agreed as follows:

Article I.

The Agreement and the Military Convention concluded on the 31st January, 1942, are superseded by the present Agreement.

Article II.

Diplomatic relations between the High Contracting Parties shall be conducted through an Ethiopian Minister Plenipotentiary in London accredited to His Majesty the King and a British Minister Plenipotentiary in Addis Ababa accredited to His Imperial Majesty the Emperor.

Article III.

1. The Imperial Ethiopian Government will retain or appoint British or other foreign persons of experience and special qualifications to be advisers or officers of their administration and judges as they find necessary.

468

2. The Government of the United Kingdom will assist The Imperial Ethiopian Government in finding suitable persons of British nationality whom they may desire to appoint.

Article IV.

1. Jurisdiction over British subjects, British Protected Persons and British Companies shall be exercised by the Ethiopian Courts constituted according to the Statute for the Administration of Justice issued by His Imperial Majesty the Emperor in 1942 and the Rules of Court issued in 1943, provided (a) that in Article 4 of Section III of the Statute there shall be substituted for "judges of proven judicial experience in other lands" and (b) that, in the hearing by the High Court of any matter, all persons shall have the right to demand that one of the judges sitting shall have had judicial experience in other lands.
2. British subjects and British Protected Persons shall be incarcerated only in prisons which are approved by an officer who has had experience in modern prison administration.

Article V.

1. The Government of the United Kingdom will (a) relinquish the control and management of the section of the Franco-Ethiopian Railway which lies in Ethiopian territory within three months of receiving from the Imperial Ethiopian Government a formal assurance that satisfactory arrangements have been made for its continued efficient operation, and (b) transfer the control and management of the section of the Railway referred to in (a) above to the organisation specified in the formal assurance.
2. The Imperial Ethiopian Government recognise that the maintenance of the Railway in efficient operation is an essential part of the war effort, and also agree that any traffic for which priority is in future requested by the Middle East Supply Centre or by the British Military Authorities will receive that priority.
3. The Imperial Ethiopian Government, in making arrangements for the operation and management of the Railway, undertake that these arrangements will not be such as to prejudice the legal rights of the Franco-Ethiopian Railway Company.
4. The Government of the United Kingdom will also, before the conclusion of the period specified in paragraph 1 above withdraw from the cantonment of Diredawa and the area north-west of the Railway formerly included in the area defined in paragraph 1 of the Schedule to the Anglo-Ethiopian Military Convention, 1942.

Article VI.

1. The Government of the United Kingdom will make available to the Imperial Ethiopian Government a military mission which shall be a unit

of the military forces of His Majesty the King under the command of the Head of the Mission. It shall be called "The British Military Mission to Ethiopia."

2. The status and privileges of the members of the military mission will be governed by the terms of the annexure to the present Article.

3. The Head of the Mission shall be responsible to the Minister of War of the Imperial Ethiopian Government for the organisation, training and administration of the Ethiopian Army.

4. The policy governing such organisation, training and administration shall be laid down by the Minister of War of the Imperial Ethiopian Government in consultation with the Head of the Mission. The Minister shall have the right to satisfy himself that the policy so laid down is being executed.

5. The Minister of War of the Imperial Ethiopian Government, and the Head of the British Military Mission to Ethiopia shall agree as to the general disposition and movement of the members of the mission, as well as the strength of the mission.

6. The British Military Mission shall be withdrawn during the currency of this agreement if, after consultation between the High Contracting Parties, either of them so desires and gives notice to the other to this effect. If any such notice is given the Mission shall be withdrawn three months after the date of receipt of notice.

Article VII.

In order as an Ally to contribute to the effective prosecution of the war, and without prejudice to their underlying sovereignty, the Imperial Ethiopian Government hereby agree that, for the duration of this Agreement, the territories designated as the Reserved Area and the Ogaden, as set forth in the attached schedule, shall be under British Military Administration.

Article VIII.

All installations, constructions, works or enterprises already constructed in whole or in part by virtue of the provisions of Articles 8 (c) and 9 (b) of the Military Convention of 31st January, 1942 in the areas referred to in Article V (4) shall from date of withdrawal provided for in that paragraph belong in full title to the Imperial Ethiopian Government.

Article IX.

1. The Government of the United Kingdom will accord to civil aircraft duly registered in Ethiopia freedom of passage to, in and over territories under their jurisdiction or authority provided that the regulations governing air navigation in force within these territories are observed. Similarly the Imperial Ethiopian Government will accord to civil aircraft duly registered in any of the territories under the sovereignty, suzerainty, pro-

tection or authority of His Majesty the King freedom of passage to, in and over Ethiopia, provided that the Ethiopian regulations governing air navigation in force are observed.

2.　The Imperial Ethiopian Government will permit a British Air Transport organisation or organisations, to be designated by the Government of the United Kingdom, to operate regular air services to, in and over Ethiopia for the carriage of passengers, mails and freight provided that such regulations governing air navigation as may be in force in Ethiopia are observed. For this purpose the Imperial Ethiopian Government will secure, as far as possible, the constant maintenance of and provide guards for, adequate landing grounds in Ethiopian territory. They will consult with the Government of the United Kingdom with regard to the construction of additional landing grounds or the extension of existing landing grounds, as experience may show to be necessary. The said organisation shall be permitted to use such landing grounds, together with ground equipment and facilities, and to provide such further facilities as may be required.

3.　If the obligations of either High Contracting Party under paragraph 1 or 2 of this Article should be in conflict with his obligations under a future general international agreement or convention relating to civil aviation, the provisions of these paragraphs shall be deemed to be modified so far as is necessary to avoid such conflict.

4.　The Imperial Ethiopian Government will accord freedom of navigation in and over Ethiopia to the Air Forces of His Majesty the King as well as to Allied Air Forces, and will, as far as possible, secure the constant maintenance of adequate landing grounds in Ethiopian territory. They will consult with the Government of the United Kingdom for the construction of additional landing grounds, or the extension of existing landing grounds, as the latter Government may request. The Imperial Ethiopian Government will give all necessary orders for the passage of the personnel of the British Air Forces, aircraft and stores to and from the said landing grounds

Article X.

The High Contracting Parties, on receipt of proof that any enemy aliens or ex-enemy aliens are dangerous to the security of Ethiopia or of any of the adjoining territories under the sovereignty or jurisdiction of His Majesty the King, undertake to collaborate in arrangements for their internment or expulsion.

Article XI.

The High Contracting Parties undertake to carry out all reasonable steps to search for, apprehend and hand over any member of the British or Ethiopian forces who is claimed as a deserter or absentee without leave, upon request made in writing by the competent military authorities of the forces from which he has deserted or absented himself, and transmitted through the diplomatic channel.

Article XII.

The present Agreement shall enter into force as from today's date.

Article XIII.

The present Agreement shall remain in force until replaced by a treaty between the two High Contracting Parties: provided, however, that, at any time after the expiry of two years from the coming into force of this Agreement, either of the High Contracting Parties may give notice to the other of his desire to terminate it. If such notice is given the Agreement shall terminate three months after the date on which this notice is given.

In witness whereof the undersigned have subscribed their signatures to the present Agreement and thereunto affixed their seals.

Done at Addis Ababa, this 19th day of December, 1944, in duplicate in the English and Amharic languages, both of which shall be equally authoritative, except in case of doubt when the English text shall prevail.

(sgd) MAKONNEN ENDALKACHAU.   (sgd) DE LA WARR.
           Prime Minister.

Addis Ababa, December 19th, 1944.

IV

UNITED NATIONS RESOLUTION

Whereas by paragraph 3 of Annexe XI to the Treaty of Peace with Italy, 1947, the Powers concerned have agreed to accept the recommendation of the General Assembly on the disposal of the former Italian colonies in Africa and to take appropriate measures for giving effect to it.

Whereas by paragraph 2 of the aforesaid Annexe XI such disposal is to be made in the light of the wishes and welfare of the inhabitants and the interests of peace and security, taking into consideration the views of interested Governments.

Now therefore,

The General Assembly, in the light of the reports of the United Nations Commission for Eritrea and of the Interim Committee, and taking into consideration:

(a)   The wishes and welfare of the inhabitants of Eritrea, including the views of the various racial, religious and political groups of the provinces of the territory and the capacity of the people for self government;

(b)   The interests of peace and security in East Africa;

(c)   The rights and claims of Ethiopia based on geographical, historical, ethic or economic reasons, including in particular Ethiopia's legitimate need for adequate access to the sea;

taking into account: the importance of assuring the continuing collaboration of the foreign communities in the economic development of Eritrea.

recognising: that the disposal of Eritrea should be based on its close political and economic association with Ethiopia, and,

desiring: that this association assure to the inhabitants of Eritrea the fullest respect and safeguards for their institutions, traditions, religions and languages, as well as the widest possible measure of self-government, while at the same time respecting the constitution, institutions, traditions and the international status and identity of the Empire of Ethiopia,

A.—recommends that:

1.   Eritrea shall constitute an autonomous unit federated with Ethiopia under the sovereignty of the Ethiopian Crown.

2.   The Eritrean Government shall possess legislative, executive and judicial powers in the field of domestic affairs.

3.   The jurisdiction of the federal government shall extend to the following matters: defence, foreign affairs, currency and finance, foreign and interstate commerce and external and interstate communications, including ports. The federal government shall have the power to maintain the integrity of the Federation, and shall have the right to impose uniform

473

taxes throughout the Federation to meet the expenses of federal functions and services, it being understood that the assessment and the collection of such taxes in Eritrea are to be delegated to the Eritrean government, and provided that Eritrea shall bear only its just and equitable share of these expenses. The jurisdiction of the Eritrean government shall extend to all matters not vested in the federal government, including the power to maintain the internal police, to levy taxes to meet the expenses of domestic functions and services, and to adopt its own budget.

4.   The area of the Federation shall constitute a single area for customs purposes, and there shall be no barriers to the free movement of goods and persons within the area. Customs duties on goods entering or leaving the Federation which have their final destination or origin in Eritrea shall be assigned to Eritrea.

5.   An Imperial Federal Council composed of equal numbers of Ethiopian and Eritrean representatives shall meet at least once a year and shall advise upon the common affairs of the Federation referred to in paragraph 3 above. The citizens of Eritrea shall participate in the executive and judicial branches, and shall be represented in the legislative branch, of the federal government, in accordance with law and in the proportion that the population of Eritrea bears to the population of the Federation.

6.   A single nationality shall prevail throughout the Federation:

(a)   All inhabitants of Eritrea, except persons possessing foreign nationality, shall be nationals of the Federation;

(b)   All inhabitants born in Eritrea and having at least one indigenous parent or grandparent shall also be national of the Federation. Such persons, if in possession of a foreign nationality, shall, within six months of the coming into force of the Eritrean constitution, be free to opt to renounce the nationality of the Federation and retain such foreign nationality. In the event that they do not so opt, they shall thereupon lose such foreign nationality.

(c)   The qualifications of persons acquiring the nationality of the Federation under sub-paragraphs (a) and (b) above for exercising their rights as citizens of Eritrea shall be determined by the constitution and laws of Eritrea.

(d)   All persons possessing foreign nationality who have resided in Eritrea for ten years prior to the date of the adoption of the present resolution shall have the right, without further requirements of residence, to apply for the nationality of the Federation and shall be permitted to reside in and engage in peaceful and lawful pursuits in Eritrea;

The rights and interests of foreign nationals resident in Eritrea shall be guaranteed in accordance with the provisions of paragraph 7.

7.   The federal government, as well as Eritrea, shall ensure to residents in Eritrea without distinction of nationality, race, sex, language or religion, the enjoyment of human rights and fundamental liberties, including the following:

(a)   The right to equality before the law. No discrimination shall be made against foreign enterprises in existence in Eritrea engaged in industrial, commercial, agricultural, artisan, educational or charitable activities, nor

474

against banking institutions and insurance companies operating in Eritrea;

(b) The right to life, liberty and security of person;

(c) The right to own and dispose of property. No one shall be deprived of property, including contractual rights, without due process of law and without payment of just and effective compensation;

(d) The right to freedom of opinion and expression and the right of adopting and practising any creed or religion;

(e) The right to education;

(f) The right to freedom of peaceful assembly and association;

(g) The right to inviolability of correspondence and domicile, subject to requirements of the law;

(h) The right to exercise any profession subject to the requirements of the law;

(i) No one shall be subject to arrest or detention without an order of a competent authority, except in case of flagrant and serious violation of the law in force. No one shall be deported except in accordance with the law;

(j) The right to a fair and equitable trial, the right of petition to the Emperor and the right of appeal to the Emperor for commutation of death sentences;

(k) Retro-activity of penal law shall be excluded;

The respect for the rights and freedoms of others and the requirements of public order and the general welfare alone will justify any limitations to the above rights.

8. Paragraphs 1 to 7 inclusive of the present resolution shall constitute the Federal Act which shall be submitted to the Emperor of Ethiopia for ratification.

9. There shall be a transition period which shall not extend beyond the 15th September 1952, during which the Eritrean government will be organised and the Eritrean Constitution prepared and put into effect.

10. There shall be a United Nations Commissioner in Eritrea appointed by the General Assembly. The Commissioner will be assisted by experts appointed by the Secretary-General of the United Nations.

11. During the transition period, the present Administering Authority shall continue to conduct the affairs of Eritrea. It shall, in consultation with the United Nations Commissioner, prepare as rapidly as possible the organisation of an Eritrean administration, induct Eritreans into all levels of the administration, and make arrangements for and convoke a representative assembly of Eritreans chosen by the people. It may, in agreement with the Commissioner, negotiate on behalf of the Eritreans a temporary customs union with Ethiopia to be put into effect as soon as practicable.

12. The United Nations Commissioner shall, in consultation with the Administering Authority, the Government of Ethiopia, and the inhabitants of Eritrea, prepare a draft of the Eritrean Constitution to be submitted to the Eritrean Assembly in its consideration of the Constitution. The Constitution of Eritrea shall be based on the principles of democratic government, shall include the guarantee contained in paragraph 7 of the Federal

Act, shall be consistent with the provisions adopting and ratifying the Federal Act on behalf of the people of Eritrea.

13.   The Federal Act and the Constitution of Eritrea shall enter into effect following ratification of the Federal Act by the Emperor of Ethiopia, and following approval by the Commissioner, adoption by the Eritrean Assembly and ratification by the Emperor of Ethiopia of the Eritrean Constitution.

14.   Arrangements shall be made by the Government of the United Kingdom of Great Britain and Northern Ireland as the Administering Authority for the transfer of power to the appropriate authorities. The transfer of power shall take place as soon as the Eritrean Constitution and the Federal Act enter into effect, in accordance with the provisions of paragraph 13 above.

15.   The United Nations Commissioner shall maintain his headquarters in Eritrea until the transfer of power has been completed, and shall make appropriate reports to the General Assembly of the United Nations concerning the discharge of his functions. The Commissioner may consult with the Interim Committee of the General Assembly with respect to the discharge of his function in the light of developments and within the terms of the present resolution. When the transfer of authority has been completed, he shall so report to the General Assembly and submit to it the text of the Eritrean Constitution.

B. — authorises the Secretary-General in accordance with established practice:

1.   To arrange for the payment of an appropriate remuneration to the United Nations Commissioner;

2.   To provide the United Nations Commissioner with such experts, staff and facilities as the Secretary-General may consider necessary to carry out the terms of the present resolution.

The General Assembly, to assist it in making the appointment of the United Nations Commissioner in Eritrea,

decides that a Committee composed of the President of the General Assembly, two of the Vice-Presidents (Australia and Venezuela), the Chairman of the Fourth Committee shall nominate a candidate or, if no agreement can be reached, two or three canditates for the post of United Nations Commissioner in Eritrea.

V

SPEECH BY HIS MAJESTY THE EMPEROR AT THE TIME

OF SIGNING THE RATIFICATION OF THE

CONSTITUTION FOR ERITREA

By Our Act of Ratification of the Constitution for Eritrea We have today completed an historic phase in the life of the people of Ethiopia and Eritrea.

We have just borne witness to the historic principle of self-determination of peoples, so often belied in these troubled times. Two years ago the United Nations recognised the life-long aspirations of the brothers of Ethiopia and Eritrea for their reunion by recommending rejoining under a federation. In order to make certain that their recommendation should, in final analysis be, not a solution imposed by them, but should, rather, be a solution freely made and adopted by the peoples in question, it was specifically prescribed, on the one hand, that the Constitution should contain provisions adopting and ratifying the federation settlement on behalf of the people of Eritrea. On the other hand, and to that same end, it was prescribed that the Constitution should be ratified by Ourselves. This present Act of Ratification has the significance of constituting the solution of federation, not as an imposed solution, but as one based upon and achieved through the expressed consent of the peoples concerned.

On this historic occasion, We desire to express to the Chief Administrator of Eritrea and to his collaborators in the British Administration Our appreciation of the competence and excellence of manner in which they fulfilled the responsibilities of providing for the election, the convening and the work of the Eritrean Assembly. Also We particularly desire, on this solemn occasion, to bear testimony to the high order of statesmanship, the perseverance, and the faith of the United Nations Commissioner, the author of the Constitution, through whose intelligence, skill and vision, this document which We have now ratified has been made possible. It is a matter of especial satisfaction to Us and We are sure, to the United Nations also, that the distinguished Commissioner is a representative from a friendly land of the New World and that the Latin American genius has been manifested and fructified in the document before Us. We have noted with great satisfaction the highly competent, courteous and dignified manner in which the Constituent Assembly accomplished its task. It has merited the approbation and approval of all. We desire finally, and, in particular, to compliment its young and distinguished President and its Vice President for the high tone and seriousness of purpose which they constantly imparted to the discussions and for their indisputable competence and qualities of leadership.

We invoke the blessing of Almighty God upon this historic instrument and upon the future of Our Eritrean subjects for whom this Constitution and the Federation now chart the course.

VI

SPEECH BY HIS MAJESTY THE EMPEROR AT THE TIME
OF SIGNING THE FEDERAL ACT

When, seven years ago, today, We issued Our first statement on the Eritrean question, the exigencies of world politics excluded participation of all but the largest States, the war leaders, Ethiopia was thus not represented at the all-important first conference, nor indeed, was her voice directly heard until much later. Although political considerations at the beginning stilled the voice of Ethiopia, the just claims of the brothers of Eritrea and Ethiopia were not to be denied. During the five ensuing years, We personally despatched our representatives to no less than eleven international conferences in defence of the interests and aspirations of the brothers of Ethiopia and Eritrea. We directed Our Minister of Foreign Affairs to undertake personally many missions in order to present the claims of justice on Our behalf.

The long years of struggle through many international conferences indicate the extent to which attempts were made to postpone, if at all possible, reaching the basic and ineluctable solution which has now been attained. Already at the Paris Conference, wide-spread and eloquent support was expressed in favour of the Union of the brothers of the two territories. However, at that time, it was openly admitted that considerations, alien to the wishes, interests and welfare of the peoples of Ethiopia and Eritrea required that the settlement of their fate be postponed until solutions could be reached on other territories. The distinguished representative of that great and friendly country, India, stated at that conference: "There is a tendency I notice, to look on the people of these territories as chattels who may be subjects of political deals."

Two years later, in 1948, not only did the four great Powers declare their inability to reach a solution for Eritrea because of alien political considerations, but a further postponement intervened at the United Nations for the same reason. No less than ten commissions were established in order ostensibly to study the question, without, however, shedding any new light on the matter. In the following year 1949, although the United Nations Assembly, by an overwhelming majority fully endorsed the rejoining of Ethiopia and Eritrea, again political considerations completely separate from those concerning the wishes, interests and welfare of the people involved defeated the solution. Similarly, for a second time, in 1949, an additional delay took place with the establishment of yet a second international commission of investigation, the results of which were to confirm the finding of the previous commission. It was, therefore, only in 1950, five years after the opening of the question, that the United Nations made their recommendation to the people of Ethiopia and Eritrea for their rejoining each other through federation.

Throughout the entire period, We as Sovereign and Head of the Empire of Ethiopia, have stood firmly on principles and have resolutely rejected offers for bargaining contrary to the sacred principle of the self-determination of peoples. We have firmly stood on the principle that alone the wishes, interests, peace and security of the peoples in question may be taken into consideration and that all political bargainings must be firmly rejected. Conformably to that policy, We were among the very first publicly to proclaim Our attachment to that principle for Libya in expressing Our conviction that its people devoutly desired independence. We have, at all times, supported every resolution and every amendment to every resolution tending toward that end. Our position as regards the freedom of Somaliland is unique amongst the members of the United Nations, since We have been the sole country consistently to vote for that solution. As regards Eritrea, Our three-thousand-year history and Our own knowledge of Our subjects in Eritrea have, at all times, supported Us in Our conviction as to the justice of the claims made on their behalf.

It was, therefore, with deep satisfaction that We noted confirmation of Our conviction, in the reports of the two Commissions of Investigation of the four Great Powers, confirming the overwhelming desire on the part of the inhabitants of Eritrea for union under federation with Ethiopia. Today, they have achieved, as Our Representative at the United Nations stated on 30th September, 1949, not only independence from foreign domination but also independence in the sense of rejoining their homeland. Not only has the Resolution of the United Nations been expressed in the form of a recommendation to the peoples involved for their acceptance or rejection, not only have the inhabitants of Eritrea fully endorsed the solution of union under federation with Ethiopia, but also We, by Our action of today, have endorsed it on behalf of Ethiopia. The solution is, therefore one of self-determination by the peoples themselves concerned. Its worth and validity have sprung from the mutual consent of the peoples involved.

Moreover, self-determination is being achieved in yet another sense. Not only will the Eritreans constitute and participate in their local government, but they, Christians and Moslems alike, will receive the fruits of self-determination and freedom through the fullest participation in all branches and levels of the Imperial Ethiopian Government. Indeed, today, and for many years passed, Eritreans have participated in significant proportions throughout the branches of our Government, a situation which is without precedent. It is in this sense that a state of Latin-America, the Republic of Cuba, declared already three years ago, that even outright union of Eritrea with Ethiopia would not constitute annexation.

International responsibilities, likewise, are not lost to view, since Eritrea lies on the most important trade route of the world. Through federation, Ethiopia, for so many years cut off from the coast, will now resume her position on the Red Sea. She will meet her international responsibilities

480

with a sober consciousness of the necessity for the enlarged Empire of Ethiopia to contribute to the furtherance of the ideal and principle of collective security embodied in the Charter of the United Nations. Ethiopia cannot but reassert her unalterable attachment to that principle which will, as in the past, inform and guide her policies, as indeed, it must shape and direct the conduct of all states having suffered, as she has in its defence.

BIBLIOGRAPHY

Bagehot, Walter: *The English Constitution*. Oxford University Press, Amen House E.C. 4, London.

Berhanu Dinqué: *From Walwal to Maichew*. Tensai Ze Gubai Printing Press, 1949, Addis Ababa.

Burns, Emile: *Ethiopia and Italy*. International Publishers, New York.

Comyn-Platt, Sir Thomas: *The Abyssinian Storm*. Jarrolds Publisher London Ltd., 34 Paternoster Row, E.C. 4, London.

Dunning, William Archibald: *History of Political Theories*.

Eade, Charles: Winston S. Churchill's *Onwards to Victory*. Cassell & Co. Ltd., London.

Eade, Charles: Winston S. Churchill's *the Unrelenting Struggle*. Cassell & Co. Ltd., London.

Fuller, Major-General J. F. C.: *The First of the League Wars*. Eyre & Spottiswoode, London.

His Majesty's Stationery Office 1942: *The Abyssinian Campaigns*. L.T.A.

Marein, N.: *The Ethiopean Empire-Federation and Laws*, Rotterdam, Royal Netherlands Print & Lythographic Co., 1955.

Mathew Herbert: *Eyewitness in Abyssinia*. Martin Secker & Warburg Ltd., 22 Essex Street Strand, London.

Mathew, David: *Ethiopia*. Eyre & Spottiswoode, London.

Mehteme Selassie Wolde Maskal (Balambras): *Zekre Negar*. Liberty Printing Press, 1949, Addis Ababa.

Mitchell, Sir Philip: *African Afterthoughts*. Hutchinson & Co. (Publishers) Ltd., Stratford Place, London.

Mosley, Leonard: *Gideon Goes to War*, Arthur Barker Ltd., London, 1955.

Muggeridge, Malcolm: *Ciano's Diplomatic Papers*. Odhams Press Ltd., Long Acre, Lond

Newman, Major E. W. Polson: *Ethiopian Realities.* George Allen & Unwin Ltd., Museumon. St., London.

Newman, Major E. W., Polson: *The New Abyssinia*. Rich & Cowan, Ltd., 37 Bedford Square, W.C. 1, London.

Pankhurst, E. Sylvia and Richard K. P.: *Ethiopia and Eritrea*. Lalibela House, 3, Charteris Road, Woodford Green, Essex, England.

Perham, Margery: *The Government of Ethiopia*. Faber and Faber Ltd., 24 Russell Square, London.

Playne, Beatrice: *St. George for Ethiopia*. Constable and Co. Ltd., 10-12 Orange Street W.C. 2, London.

Rennell of Rodd, Lord, K. B. E., C.B.E.: *British Military Administration in Africa* 1941-'47 The Campfield Press, St. Albans, London.

Rey, Charles F., F.R.G.S.: *Unconquered Abyssinia*. Seeley, Service & Co. Ltd., 196 Shafyesbury Avenue, London.

Salvemini, Gaetano: *Prelude to World War II*. Victor Gollancs Ltd., London.

Sandford, Christine: *Ethiopia Under Haile Selassie*, J. M. Dent & Sons Ltd., Aldine House Bedford St., London.

Steer, G. L.: *Caesar in Abyssinia*. Hodder & Stoughton, Ltd., St. Paul's House, Warwick Square, E.C. 4, London.

Steer, G. L.: *Sealed and Delivered*. Hodder & Stoughton Ltd., London.

Talbot, D. A.: *Contemporary Ethiopia*. Philosophical Library, New York.

Tekle Tsadik Mekuria: *History of Ethiopia*. 4th Edition, Artistic Printing Press, 1953. Addis. Ababa.

Templewood, Viscount: *Nine Troubled Years*. Collins, St. James' Place, London.

Trimingham, J. Spencer: *Islam in Ethiopia*. Geoffrey Cumberlege, Oxford University Press, Amen House, London E.C. 4.

Waugh, Evelyn: *When the Going was Good*. Penguin Books, Harmondsworth, Middlesex, England.

Weech, W. N., M.A.: *History of the World*. Odhams Press Ltd., Long Acre, London, W.C. 2.

Zervos, Adrien: *L'Empire d'Ethiopie*.

Ziff, William B.: *The Gentlemen Talk of Peace*. The Macmillan Company, New York.

NEWSPAPERS AND PERIODICALS

Newspapers

Ethiopian Press and Information Department pub.: Addis Ababa, Ethiopia.
1. *The Ethiopian Herald.*
2. *Sandek Alamachin.*
3. *Addis Zemen.*
4. *L'Ethiopie d'Aujourd'hui.*

New Times and Ethiopian News: Woodford Green, Essex, England.

Periodicals

Ethiopian Commercial, Industrial and Agricultural Journal: Addis Ababa.
Ethiopian Review: Addis Ababa.
Ministry of Education Yearbook: 1949–'53, Berhanena Selam Press, Addis Ababa.
Economic Conditions and Market Trends: Statistical Office, State Bank of Ethiopia, Addis Ababa.
Negarit Gazeta: (Ethiopian Government Official Gazette), Berhanena Selam Press, Addis Ababa.
Quarterly Bulletin: Ministry of Commerce and Industry, Addis Ababa, Berhanena Selam Press.

INDEX

Weatherall, General, 104
Wedgwood, Colonel, 113
Wellington Koo, 78
Wheat, 173
White, Colonel, 365
Wilson, General, 301
Wingate, Colonel, later General 82, 88, 89, 92, 93, 101, 104, 106, 110, 270
Women's Welfare Organisation, 344 ff
Wool, 171, 175, 176
Workmen's Compensation, 165
World War II, 80 ff, 97, 209, 314

Yared Gabra-Mika'el, 329

Yemen, 21
Yilma Deressa, 325, 337
Y.M.C.A., 336, 338 ff
Yohannes, 9, 10, 17

Zafrulla Khan, Sir, 375
Zalleka Birru, 92
Zara Yakob, 353
Zaude Gabre Heywot, 426
Zauditu, Empress, 9, 20, 24, 26, 312
Zeeland, M. van, 55, 56
Zervos, Adrien, 285
Ziff, Mr William B., 52, 53

ERRATA

PAGE	PARAGRAPH	LINE	TO READ
1	last	5th	should *like*
8		4th	*humanitarianism*
8		5th	*public* acts
15	2nd	5th	*egress*
15	3rd	last	*neighbours*
20	4th	1st	*accelerated*
22	6th	5th	*his* former
23	5th	1st	*sombre* as
37	last	3rd	His *Majesty*
43	2nd	11th	the *League*
45	5th	8th	only *remained*
57	5th	3rd	to *scatter*
59		3rd	their *nationals*
62	5th	5th	*aggressor*
72	3rd	3rd	*aggressor*
79	8th	2nd	*aggressor*
80	4th	2nd	moral *strength*
80	4th	4th	*successfully*
81		5th	have *been*
89	5th	4th	*campaign*
97	1st	4th	*Ethiopia's*
105	Footnote reference No. 5		G. L. Steer, *op. cit.*
121		4th	*independence*
131		1st	His *Imperial*
136	4th	5th	the *Queen*
141	3rd	8th	in *short*
148		last	5,000 *KW*
149	2nd	6th	brief *period*
161	last	1st	*against*
170	2nd	16th	*agricultural*
176	3rd	6th	new *varieties*
182	1st	12th	provide *schools*
184	1st	13th	*to* Addis Ababa
188	2nd	5th	the *schools*
192	1st	2nd	20 *to* 30
199	4th	6th	*school system*
201	2nd	16th	It *had* the semblance
212	3rd	2nd	*Banca* di Roma
219	3rd	10th	*in* world markets
223		last	*As a corollary*
232	2nd	5th	granted *by* the Bank
297		13th	*spare* tools
328	2nd	8th	is *foretold*
330	2nd	5th	*Grammar*
335		5th	most *beneficent*
374	2nd 3rd and 4th		League *representative*
374	3rd	4th	Ato *Aklilou*
376	3rd	6th	*make* it clear
402	8th	6th	*school* which
420	5th	9th	*successfully*
421	5th	5th	*opportunity*
422	2nd	1st—2nd	*conference*
428	5th	3rd	Henry G. Bennett

NOTE

Inconsistencies in the spelling of Ethiopian words in the text of the book are due to the fact that as yet there is no standard system of transliteration of Amharic into the English language.